CONSOLIDATED GOLD FIELDS IN AUSTRALIA

THE RISE AND DECLINE OF A BRITISH
MINING HOUSE, 1926–1998

CONSOLIDATED GOLD FIELDS IN AUSTRALIA

THE RISE AND DECLINE OF A BRITISH
MINING HOUSE, 1926–1998

ROBERT PORTER

PRESS

Published by ANU Press
The Australian National University
Acton ACT 2601, Australia
Email: anupress@anu.edu.au

Available to download for free at press.anu.edu.au

ISBN (print): 9781760463496
ISBN (online): 9781760463502

WorldCat (print): 1149151564
WorldCat (online): 1149151633

DOI: 10.22459/CGFA.2020

This title is published under a Creative Commons Attribution-NonCommercial-NoDerivatives 4.0 International (CC BY-NC-ND 4.0).

The full licence terms are available at creativecommons.org/licenses/by-nc-nd/4.0/legalcode

Cover design and layout by ANU Press.

Cover photograph John Agnew (left) at a mining operation managed by Bewick Moreing, Western Australia. Source: Herbert Hoover Presidential Library.

This edition © 2020 ANU Press

CONTENTS

List of Figures, Tables, Charts and Boxes vii
Preface xiii
Acknowledgements. xv
Notes and Abbreviations xvii

Part One: Context—Consolidated Gold Fields
1. The Consolidated Gold Fields of South Africa 5
2. New Horizons for a British Mining House. 15

Part Two: Early Investments in Australia
3. Western Australian Gold 25
4. Broader Associations 57
5. Lake George and New Guinea 71

Part Three: A New Force in Australian Mining 1960–1966
6. A New Approach to Australia. 97
7. New Men and a New Model 107
8. A Range of Investments 115

Part Four: Expansion, Consolidation and Restructuring 1966–1981
9. Move to an Australian Shareholding. 151
10. Expansion and Consolidation 1966–1976 155
11. Acquisition and Diversification 191
12. Portfolio Challenges. 197
13. Portfolio Review 1975–1981 219

Part Five: A Majority Australian Owned Mining Company 1981–1989

14. Formation of a Diversified Mining Company 243
15. The Initial Years 253
16. New Interests and Diversification 287
17. The Challenges of the Parent 305

Part Six: The Final Decade 1990–1998

18. Hanson on the Register 329
19. Tumultuous Years 1990–1994 343
20. Final Years 373
21. The End of an Era 391

Afterword: Reflections of Consolidated Gold Fields in Australia. . . . 399

Appendix 1. Technical Terms 413
Appendix 2. Chairmen and Managing Directors 417
Appendix 3. Biographical Information of Key Individuals 419
Appendix 4. Performance of CGFA and RGC Investments 429
Appendix 5. Mineral Sands Performance, 1977–1997 437
Appendix 6. Renison Performance, 1977–1997 441
Appendix 7. Mount Lyell Performance, 1977–1995 445
Appendix 8. Performance of Gold and Other Interests 449
Bibliography 453
Index 463

LIST OF FIGURES, TABLES, CHARTS AND BOXES

Figures

Figure 1. Cecil Rhodes, the founder of The Consolidated Gold Fields of South Africa, along with Charles Rudd 6

Figure 2. The Consolidated Gold Fields of South Africa head office, 49 Moorgate, London 12

Figure 3. Herbert Hoover (second from left) and John Agnew (right) in Western Australia while working for Bewick Moreing 26

Figure 4. John Agnew (left) at a mining operation of Bewick Moreing . . 26

Figure 5. John Agnew (third from left) while on a mine inspection for Bewick Moreing, Western Australia 27

Figure 6. Map of mining leases of the Golden Mile, Kalgoorlie 31

Figure 7. Western Australian Minister for Railways laying the first track of the Meekatharra to Wiluna railway line, 1929. 40

Figure 8. Wiluna gold mine, 1927 41

Figure 9. Panorama of Wiluna mine site, 1930................. 41

Figure 10. Wiluna gold mine poppet head and engine room 42

Figure 11. Pouring first gold, Wiluna, 1935.................... 43

Figure 12. Wiluna gold mine, 1935 43

Figure 13. Aerial view of Wiluna gold mining operation 47

Figure 14. View of Lake View Consols in 1928, renamed Lake View and Star... 50

Figure 15. Associated Tailings, part of the properties controlled by Lake View and Star................................. 51

Figure 16. Aerial view of Lake View and Star facilities 51

Figures 17 and 18. Father and son engineers: John A Agnew
and Dolph Agnew 59

Figure 19. Lake George mining and processing operations,
Captains Flat, New South Wales 81

Figure 20. Final shift at time of closure of Lake George mine, 1962 . . . 82

Figure 21. Alluvial gold mining, Edie Creek, Morobe district,
Territory of New Guinea 88

Figure 22. Location for mining operations undertaken by New Guinea
Goldfields at the junction of Bulolo River and Koranga Creek,
Morobe district, Territory of New Guinea 88

Figure 23. Junker aircraft used for transportation of equipment
into Morobe district, Territory of New Guinea. 89

Figure 24. Bulolo gold dredge, number 3, Morobe district,
Territory of New Guinea 89

Figure 25. Sir George Steven Harvie-Watt 99

Figure 26. Brian Massy-Greene 103

Figure 27. Beach dredge mining conducted by Associated Minerals
Consolidated along the New South Wales coast 118

Figure 28. Titania dredge used on North Stradbroke Island,
Queensland 119

Figure 29. Construction of the railway line from Mount Goldsworthy
mine site to Port Hedland, 1966 126

Figure 30. Iron ore train crossing De Grey River 126

Figure 31. First iron ore shipment from Port Hedland in 1966,
showing crushing facility at Finucane Island. 127

Figure 32. Ship loading, Finucane Island 127

Figure 33. *Harvey S Mudd* at Finucane Island, 1966. 128

Figure 34. Aerial view of Mount Goldsworthy, Pilbara,
Western Australia, 1974. 129

Figure 35. Mount Lyell Mining and Railway Company copper
mining operation, Queenstown, 1963 141

LIST OF FIGURES, TABLES, CHARTS AND BOXES

Figure 36. Renison tin mining operation near Zeehan, west coast
of Tasmania 144

Figure 37. Gold Fields House (right), opened in 1966 153

Figures 38 and 39. Western Titanium's operations, Capel,
south-west, Western Australia. 184

Figure 40. Bart Ryan, managing director of Consolidated Gold
Fields Australia, 1976–1980. 203

Figure 41. Sidney Segal, executive and subsequently chairman
of Consolidated Gold Fields Australia from 1976 to 1980,
then deputy chairman and director until 1982. 204

Figure 42. London Board of Directors of Consolidated Gold
Fields, 1977 228

Figure 43. Max Roberts, executive chairman and then chairman
of Renison Goldfields Consolidated from 1980 to 1994 236

Figure 44. Campbell Anderson, managing director from 1985
and chief executive officer of Renison Goldfields Consolidated
from 1986 to 1993. 254

Figure 45. Mark Bethwaite, appointed deputy managing director
in 1987 and managing director and chief executive officer from
1995 to 1998. 255

Figure 46. Mount Lyell operations, Queenstown, 1984 259

Figure 47. Cross-section of Renison mining operation 262

Figures 48 and 49. Underground mining operations, Renison 262

Figure 50. Mount Lyell cross-section showing mining through
various series of ore bodies to the 50 series 269

Figure 51. Alternative operating strategies for Mount Lyell under
consideration as part of 1984/85 budgetary planning. 270

Figure 52. Site of Porgera gold mine, Enga Province,
Papua New Guinea 290

Figure 53. Rudolph Agnew, chief executive officer of Consolidated
Gold Fields 306

Figure 54. Mark Bethwaite, Tony Cotton and Max Roberts, 1993 . . . 341

Tables

Table 1. Renison Goldfields Consolidated group and divisional financial performance, 1990–1998. 347

Table 2. Mineral sands performance, 1990–1994 357

Table 3. Renison performance, 1990–1997 360

Table 4. Performance of Consolidated Gold Fields Australia investments, 1962–1966 429

Table 5a. Consolidated Gold Fields Australia financial performance, 1967–1973 430

Table 5b. Consolidated Gold Fields Australia financial performance, 1974–1980 430

Table 6. Renison Goldfields Consolidated financial performance, 1981–1989 432

Table 7. Renison Goldfields Consolidated financial performance, 1990–1998 434

Table 8a. Mineral sands performance, 1977–1983 437

Table 8b. Mineral sands performance, 1984–1990 438

Table 8c. Mineral sands performance, 1991–1997 438

Table 9a. Renison performance, 1977–1983. 441

Table 9b. Renison performance, 1984–1990 442

Table 9c. Renison performance, 1991–1997. 443

Table 10a. Mount Lyell performance, 1977–1982 445

Table 10b. Mount Lyell performance, 1983–1989 446

Table 10c. Mount Lyell performance, 1990–1995 446

Table 11. Renison Goldfields Consolidated: Gold interests— Pine Creek (Northern Territory), 1986–1995. 450

Table 12. Renison Goldfields Consolidated: Gold interests— Lucky Draw (New South Wales), 1988–1992 450

Table 13. Renison Goldfields Consolidated: Gold interests— Porgera (Papua New Guinea), 1990–1994 451

Table 14. Renison Goldfields Consolidated: Gold interests—
  NGG Holdings (Papua New Guinea), 1981–1991 451
Table 15. Koba Tin, 1988–1997............................. 452

Charts

Chart 1. Associated Minerals Consolidated pre-tax earnings,
  1962–1997 120
Chart 2. Mount Lyell Mining and Railway Company pre-tax
  earnings, 1962–1995................................ 142
Chart 3. Renison pre-tax earnings, 1966–1997 145
Chart 4. Consolidated Gold Fields Australia financial performance,
  1962–1980 221
Chart 5. Renison Goldfields Consolidated net profit/loss,
  1981–1998 248
Chart 6. Renison Goldfields Consolidated returns on shareholders'
  funds and assets, 1981–1998 248
Chart 7. Renison Goldfields Consolidated group profit
  and principal divisional results, 1981–1990 258
Chart 8. Mount Lyell contribution to Consolidated Gold Fields
  Australia and Renison Goldfields Consolidated group results,
  1977–1995 366
Chart 9. Mineral sands earnings and price trends, 1977–1997..... 379
Chart 10. Renison earnings and tin price trend, 1977–1997 386
Chart 11. Renison Goldfields Consolidated share price
  performance, July 1981 to November 1998 393
Chart 12. Divisional contribution to Renison Goldfields
  Consolidated results, 1981–1998, principal assets 431
Chart 13. Asset and investment contribution to Renison
  Goldfields Consolidated results, 1981–1998 432
Chart 14. Gold interests and contribution to Renison Goldfields
  Consolidated results, 1982–1998....................... 449

Boxes

Box 1. Consolidated Gold Fields Group—United Kingdom
to Australia. 3
Box 2. Key events 1926–1956 23
Box 3. Key events 1959–1966 95
Box 4. Key events 1966–1981 149
Box 5. Key events 1981–1989 241
Box 6. Key events 1990–1998 325

PREFACE

The Consolidated Gold Fields of South Africa was a major British mining house founded by Cecil Rhodes and Charles Rudd in 1892. Diversifying from its South African gold interests, the company invested widely outside South Africa during the following century. This included investments in the Western Australian gold sector from the 1920s and exploration and mining activities elsewhere in Australia and the Territory of New Guinea. In the 1960s, the by then renamed Consolidated Gold Fields, along with Rio Tinto Zinc Corporation and Anglo American, were the three dominant mining houses internationally, and Consolidated Gold Fields and Anglo American were the principal participants in global gold production. In Australia, Consolidated Gold Fields Australia (CGFA) along with Conzinc Riotinto Australia were two new British-sponsored diversified mining companies.

CGFA had ambitious plans and the financial backing from London to establish itself as one of the main mining companies in Australia. It attempted to do so with investments in the historic Mount Lyell Mining and Railway Company and its copper mining and smelting operations at Queenstown in Tasmania, along with an interest in the Renison tin operation, also on the west coast of Tasmania. Mount Goldsworthy Mining Associates was formed as one of the first groups to develop iron ore deposits in the Pilbara of Western Australia, while on the east coast of Australia a major interest in mineral sands was established by the acquisition of mineral sands producer Associated Minerals Consolidated. While the London-based Consolidated Gold Fields ceased to exist in 1989, taken over and dismembered by renowned corporate raider Hanson Plc, its Australian subsidiary, Renison Goldfields Consolidated (RGC), continued for another nine years as a diversified mining group before it suffered its own corporate demise, facilitated by Hanson.

Like other mining companies no longer in existence—North Broken Hill, Western Mining Corporation, Peko-Wallsend, Mount Isa Mines—CGFA and RGC were important participants in Australia's post–World War II mining sector.

This book is a history of a once-great British mining-finance house and its investments in Australia. It chronicles the main stages of the evolution of Consolidated Gold Fields in Australia, reviews the main elements in its portfolio, and examines some of the factors that impeded achievement of the ambitions of its founders and management in Australia. In doing so, it supplements three commissioned histories of the Gold Fields group, although this is the first to look in detail at the group's Australian activities. The Gold Fields group in Australia had a rich and broad history; its ultimate fate did not demonstrate its potential as an Australian mining company.

ACKNOWLEDGEMENTS

Numerous people and institutions contributed to the preparation of this book. Consolidated Gold Fields Australia (CGFA) and Renison Goldfields Consolidated (RGC) business records, held by Iluka Resources, have been an invaluable source of information. The University of Melbourne Archives and the Butlin Archives at The Australian National University, Canberra, both hold excellent collections of company and industry information that have been drawn upon. The latter includes the records of the Lake George mine in New South Wales. I have also consulted a comprehensive collection of business records, mainly related to The Mount Lyell Mining and Railway Company, part of the National Archives of Australia collection held at the State Library of Tasmania in Hobart. A range of information held at the National Library of Australia, Canberra, has formed part of the research. The National Archives of Australia, Canberra and Melbourne offices, provided access to documentary records and photographs. The state libraries of Victoria, Western Australia and South Australia house collections that have been consulted. The Herbert Hoover Presidential Library in Iowa, United States, provided copies of documents, including correspondence between John Agnew and his former mining engineering colleague, Herbert Hoover, as well as photographs, enabling the research to be enlightened by primary material from this source. I am grateful to the various individuals who have willingly assisted me at each of these institutions, including Sophie Garrett and staff of the University of Melbourne Archives and Craig Wright, supervisory archivist, at the Herbert Hoover Presidential Library.

I have had the good fortune to speak with former employees of CGFA and RGC, as well as individuals who worked for the parent company, Consolidated Gold Fields in London. These include former directors, managing directors and executives, as well as those directly involved in the conduct of various mining operations, exploration, marketing and environmental management. In particular, I would like to thank Tony

Hemingway, general counsel of CGFA and RGC between 1970 and 1990. Tony read draft chapters and provided me with his recollection of key events in the history of CGFA and RGC. Ted Wiles, as a young University of Cambridge graduate, was involved with Consolidated Gold Fields in London and in Australia in the early 1960s. I have drawn upon his excellent recollections of Consolidated Gold Fields's initial investments in the country. Others I have spoken with worked in allied industries or organisations and had an involvement with the companies referred to in this book. Dr David Moore read drafts and provided his valuable technical expertise on iron ore and mineral sands. Gillespie Robertson, involved with Utah, also provided valuable assistance. Former RGC executives, including but not limited to, Mike Ayre, Denis Brooks, Keith Faulkner, Roger Shakesby, Colin Cannard, Bryan Ellis, George Lloyd, Paul Benson, Bart Ryan, Campbell Anderson, Peter Robinson, Ron Goodman, Colin Patterson and Dick Patterson, were generous with their time and recollections. A number commented upon drafts, shared their own records and pointed out shortcomings in my interpretations. For information related to the Agnew family history, I am grateful to Delia Buchan and Hugh Agnew. Richard Knight, a former mining executive and researcher on the history of Mount Lyell, read drafts, provided generous access to his voluminous mining history and shared his personal knowledge. Dr Sandra Close and Jim Pollock, mining industry participants and historical enthusiasts, have been a source of feedback, while Mel Davies, honorary research fellow at the University of Western Australia, has shown an interest in this work and shared drafts of his work on Claude Albo de Bernales. Other individuals who assisted in various ways include Sir Rudolph Agnew, Mark Bethwaite, Ronnie Beevor, Graham Campbell, Michael Gleeson-White, Neil Goodwill, Rob Hudson, Jonathan Loraine, Malcolm Macpherson, Bruce McQuitty, Derek Miller, Norman Mills, John Mitchell, Don Morley, Stephen Mudge, Joe Pringle, Ray Roberts, Peter Robinson, Bart Ryan, Nick Ryan, Richard Scallan, Andrew Segal, Jillian Segal, Dr Malcolm Southwood and Dr Peter Woodford. I would like to acknowledge the professional assistance of my editor, Tracy Harwood, as well as ANU Press personnel, notably Emily Tinker.

Finally, my heartfelt appreciation to Aliya for her encouragement and support in the task of researching and writing this book.

NOTES AND ABBREVIATIONS

Notes

Measurements, distances and currencies in this book use both the imperial and decimal systems. Where comparisons are made between periods, a conversion to the most recent measure is used.

Acres to hectares	1 acre = 0.4 hectares
Australian pounds (£) to dollars ($)	£1 converted to $2 at the introduction of decimal currency in 1966
Feet to metres	1 foot = 0.3018 metres
Miles to kilometres	1 mile = 1.6 kilometres
Tons to tonnes	1 ton = 1.016 tonnes

Currency referred to in the text, whether pounds (£) or dollars ($), is Australian unless otherwise stated or where the context makes it evident that British pounds sterling (GB£) is being referred to.

Abbreviations

AMC	Associated Minerals Consolidated Ltd
CGF	Consolidated Gold Fields Ltd
CGFA	Consolidated Gold Fields (Australia) Pty Ltd (1960–1966); Consolidated Gold Fields Australia Ltd (1966–1981)
CMI	Commonwealth Mining Investments (Australia) Ltd
CRA	Conzinc Riotinto Australia Ltd
CRL	Consolidated Rutile Ltd

FIRB	Foreign Investment Review Board
GFADC	Gold Fields Australian Development Company Ltd
MGMA	Mount Goldsworthy Mining Associates Pty Ltd
NCGFA	New Consolidated Gold Fields (Australasia) Pty Ltd (This company is different from New Consolidated Gold Fields, the overseas arm of The Consolidated Gold Fields of South Africa.)
RGC	Renison Goldfields Consolidated Ltd
SREP	synthetic rutile enhanced process

A list of some of the technical terms used is provided in Appendix 1.

PART ONE:
CONTEXT—CONSOLIDATED GOLD FIELDS

PART ONE

Box 1. Consolidated Gold Fields Group—United Kingdom to Australia

The Gold Fields of South Africa, Limited 1887–1892	Registered 9 February 1887 and listed on the London Stock Exchange
	Charles Rudd and Cecil Rhodes joint managing directors; also directors of the De Beers Mining Company
The Consolidated Gold Fields of South Africa, Limited 1892–1960	Formed 2 August 1892 by amalgamation with three other South African companies
	Listed on the London Stock Exchange
New Consolidated Gold Fields Limited	Established 8 August 1919; subsidiary of The Consolidated Gold Fields of South Africa to oversee investments outside South Africa
Australian and New Guinea investments—from 1926	Wiluna Gold Corporation, which owned Wiluna Gold Mines
	Lake View and Star
	Lake George Mining Corporation, which owned Lake George Mines
	Shareholdings in Gold Mines of Australia, Gold Exploration and Finance Company of Australia, Western Mining Corporation, Bulolo Gold Dredging (through The Gold Fields American Development Company), New Guinea Goldfields, Mining Corporation (Australia)
Gold Fields Australian Development Company Limited	Incorporated 5 November 1932, listed on London Stock Exchange
	Interests in Moonlight Wiluna Mine, Mount Ida Mine, Porphyry (1939) Gold Mine
New Consolidated Gold Fields (Australasia) Pty Limited	Registered 22 August 1956, 100 per cent owned by The Consolidated Gold Fields of South Africa
Consolidated Gold Fields Limited 1960–1989	United Kingdom company; name changed to remove reference to South Africa
Consolidated Gold Fields (Australia) Pty Limited	Registered November 1960; all shares taken up by Gold Fields Mining & Industrial (renamed from The Gold Fields American Development Company, a wholly owned subsidiary of the London parent, formed in 1959 with responsibility for investments in Britain, Australia, Canada and the United States)
Consolidated Gold Fields Australia Limited	Registered 26 September 1966 with 22.7 per cent of its shares initially issued to Australian investors; remainder held by London parent

Renison Goldfields Consolidated Limited	Established 24 July 1981 with initial 51 per cent Australian ownership; remainder held by Consolidated Gold Fields. Hanson Plc acquired a 44 per cent shareholding in 1989, following acquisition of Consolidated Gold Fields. Name changed to RGC Limited in 1998. Delisted 17 November 1998 following merger, by scheme of arrangement, with Westralian Sands. Merged entity initially Westralian Sands; name changed to Iluka Resources in 1999

1

THE CONSOLIDATED GOLD FIELDS OF SOUTH AFRICA

A company formed by the young, avowed British imperialist Cecil John Rhodes and his business partner Charles Dunell Rudd, with interests in the diamond mines of the Kimberley and gold mining in the Witwatersrand, became one of the foremost British mining-finance companies in the twentieth century. Emanating from South Africa, the company that Rhodes and Rudd founded, The Gold Fields of South Africa, was registered in London in 1887. In 1892, through aggregation with three other South African mining companies, it became The Consolidated Gold Fields of South Africa, listed on the London Stock Exchange. Apart from its South African and broader international interests, the company, through subsequent forms, associated companies and direct investments, played an influential role in Australia's mining history. It played a major role in the revitalisation of the Western Australian gold industry in the 1930s and the recommencement of mining operations at an important lead and zinc mine in New South Wales; it also made investments in gold mining in New Guinea and a financial and technical contribution to the formation of Western Mining Corporation in association with members of the Collins House Group of companies.

Figure 1. Cecil Rhodes, the founder of The Consolidated Gold Fields of South Africa, along with Charles Rudd. The Sydney offices of Consolidated Gold Fields Australia had a room named after Rhodes, featuring Rhodes's portrait.

Source: National Portrait Gallery Picture Library, London.

1. THE CONSOLIDATED GOLD FIELDS OF SOUTH AFRICA

From 1960, a fully owned subsidiary bearing the name Consolidated Gold Fields (Australia) invested widely and provided great promise that it would stand among the major mining companies in Australia. It existed for just short of four decades and made a major contribution to the development of various facets of Australia's mining sector. It held and facilitated a broad spread of Australian investments, including the Mount Lyell Mining and Railway Company; the Renison tin mining operation; the first iron ore production from the Pilbara, Western Australia; and a dominant position in the Australian mineral sands sector on the east and then on the west coast of the country. In the 1990s, an offshoot of the Gold Fields group—Renison Goldfields Consolidated—was one of the last manifestations of the once-great British mining house formed by Rhodes and Rudd.

...

Gold Fields owed its formation to the entrepreneurial and imperial motivations of its founders.[1] The company derived from the diamond riches of the Kimberley district of South Africa, which led to the formation of De Beers Consolidated Mines in 1888, with Rhodes as founding chairman. De Beers controlled 90 per cent of world diamond production at the time of Rhodes's death in 1902. Cecil Rhodes's reputation was as a promoter and defender of British imperialism. His career and legacy are marked by controversy, with his business interests inextricably intertwined with his political ambitions to establish a growing British-dominated presence across southern and central Africa.

Rhodes and Rudd met in the Kimberley district of the British-controlled Cape Province in the early 1870s and became business partners from 1873. Rudd gained his early education at Harrow School before attending the University of Cambridge, although he did not complete his degree. A notable athlete and cricketer, in 1865 at the age of 21 he journeyed to South Africa.[2] In 1871, he travelled to the Kimberley diggings, unsuccessfully working a diamond claim and then working in his brother's business. Rhodes, nine years Rudd's junior at 17, travelled in 1871 for health reasons from his home in Hertfordshire to the British colony of Natal.[3] While Rhodes was working his brother's diamond claim, the

---
1   Given the various company offshoots of The Consolidated Gold Fields of South Africa, the term Gold Fields will be used on occasions for ease of description.
2   Stearn, 'Rudd, Charles Dunell (1844–1916)'.
3   Marks and Trapido, 'Rhodes, Cecil John (1853–1902)'.

two men met. Interspersed with Rhodes spending time studying at Oriel College at the University of Oxford, the pair acquired multiple diamond mining claims as well as undertaking other ventures, including the supply of pumps for mining operations.

In 1880 Rhodes and Rudd formed De Beers Mining Company that, in 1888 through amalgamation with other diamond mining companies, became De Beers Consolidated Mines. In 1886 both men travelled to the Witwatersrand region near Johannesburg after the discovery of gold. Here they purchased land, not aware of the geological details of what was a massive gold-bearing deposit, some evident near the surface but most buried at depth. Rudd travelled to London to establish the grandly named The Gold Fields of South Africa, Limited. The new company was registered on 9 February 1887 and listed on the London Stock Exchange—one of 10 South African mining companies listed that year—to finance the acquisition of further gold mining company shares and farming land for their planned new gold mining enterprise.[4] Rudd's brother was appointed the first chairman. The early days showed little promise and the company's investments, meant to be directed to gold mining, were made mainly in further diamond mining interests. The investment of Gold Fields of South Africa in diamonds, as opposed to gold, had the unexpected benefit of partially protecting the company from the collapse of the gold price in 1890. Despite this, 1891 was a year of 'unrelieved gloom' with low profits and no dividend payment, influenced by both the low gold price as well as a slump in the value of diamond shares.[5]

The discovery of gold in the Transvaal led to Rudd being dispatched to negotiate a concession in 1888 for access to mining rights in the territory of Matabeleland as part of Rhodes's desire to turn the territory into a British Protectorate. Despite establishing a holding, the existence of competing claimants complicated the situation. Negotiations led to the formation of a company that in turn passed on its rights to the British South Africa Company, for which a Royal Charter was secured in 1889 and a block of shares allocated to shareholders of Gold Fields of South Africa.

---

4   Macnab, *Gold Their Touchstone*, p. 17.
5   Consolidated Gold Fields of South Africa, *The Gold Fields 1887–1937*, p. 32.

The fortunes of Rhodes and Rudd's company were to change when, at the urging of two close associates, they gained the confidence that deep-level mining on the 'Rand' was technically possible and a potentially profitable form of investment. The individuals were Alfred Beit, a diamond mining financier and entrepreneur who assisted Rhodes in the amalgamation of diamond claims and companies to form De Beers Mining, and Percy Tarbutt, a mining engineer. Tarbutt was described as one of the first engineers 'to realize the value of deep-level mines'.[6] As was the case with later Gold Fields' investments, including in Australia, the advancement of technology enabled the lower grade ore of the Rand to be processed through the application of cyanide. To facilitate the investment in deeper horizons, the interests of three other companies were combined to form Consolidated Gold Fields of South Africa on 2 August 1892 with initial capital of GB£1,250,000.[7] Gold Fields acquired other companies on the Rand, establishing a commanding position. In 1895, Consolidated Gold Fields of South Africa reported a 'colossal profit' of over GB£2 million, described by the chairman 'as larger than any realised by any limited liability company in the City of London'.[8] The company also had an unrealised profit of GB£9 million on the book value of its investments.[9]

In 1895 Rhodes had served four years as prime minister of the Cape Colony, quite apart from pursuing his multifaceted business interests. In what proved a fateful misstep in his career, armed men under the control of a Rhodes's associate, Dr Leander Starr Jameson, entered the Transvaal to support British migrant workers in a planned insurrection against the Transvaal government.[10] Rhodes's brother and other associates were enlisted in the venture while arms and munitions were imported by the company under the guise of mining equipment. The attempt was an ignominious failure. Four of the co-conspirators, including Rhodes's brother, were captured and sentenced to death; a fate only avoided by the payment of a GB£25,000 fine. Jameson was handed to the British authorities and served a prison sentence.[11] The failure of the raid and

---

6 Auerbach, 'Albert Beit—South Africa's Financial Genius', p. 33; ICE Publishing, 'Obituary: Percy Frederick Tarbutt', pp. 380–381.
7 The three companies involved in the amalgamation to form The Consolidated Gold Fields of South Africa were African Estate's Agency, African Gold Investment Company and The South African Gold and Trust Agency (Macnab, *Gold Their Touchstone*, p. 31).
8 Consolidated Gold Fields of South Africa, *The Gold Fields 1887–1937*, p. 59.
9 Johnson, *Gold Fields: A Centenary Portrait*, pp. 28 and 35.
10 Butler, 'Cecil Rhodes', p. 262.
11 Macnab, *Gold Their Touchstone*, pp. 61–64.

involvement of a public company in a political undertaking led to Rhodes and Rudd stepping down from their jointly held roles of managing directors of Consolidated Gold Fields of South Africa. With this their roles in the direction of the company diminished. Despite his reputation being badly tarnished in England, in 1899 Rhodes was awarded an honorary doctorate at his beloved University of Oxford only after Lord Kitchener, also due to receive a doctorate, threatened to withdraw if the protestations of Oxford dons against Rhodes were upheld.[12] By 1902, Rhodes had died and Rudd had retired as a director of the company.

Three deep mines remained the cornerstone of Gold Fields' South African gold production. The mines were Simmer and Jack, Robinson Deep and Sub Nigel, referred to respectively as Faith, Hope and Charity. From the early part of the twentieth century the direction of the company began to change under new directors and management, with the role of engineers and technical personnel coming to the fore. From 1909 the company diversified its investments, acquiring interests in the United States, including in light and power companies, alluvial gold mining and oil. In 1911, Gold Fields American Development Company was formed as was the Gold Fields Rhodesian Development Company, absorbing the previously established Consolidated Exploration and Development (Rhodesia) Company. Interests expanded to include a potash and borax plant in the United States and West African gold mining.

The original company memorandum and articles of association introduced legal uncertainty about the company expanding beyond mineral investments and possibly outside South Africa. In 1919, New Consolidated Gold Fields was registered. This entity, with the same directors as Consolidated Gold Fields of South Africa, oversaw the geographical diversification of the group and its willingness to invest in minerals other than gold. By the 1920s, this included interests in activities as diverse as cellulose and chemicals, as well as building and engineering companies. The company developed interests in gold, platinum and copper mines in Colombia and other parts of South America, and oil leases in Texas and Oklahoma. In 1919, New Consolidated Gold Fields took a shareholding in National Mining Corporation, which comprised a consortium of British mining companies formed to explore for and develop new mining ventures. Companies with shareholdings in National

---

12   Maylam, *The Cult of Rhodes*, p. 116.

Mining Corporation included Camp Bird, Oroville Dredging and Mexican Corporation. The first two of these companies were influential in later investments by Gold Fields in Australia and in New Guinea, while Mexican Corporation provided mining engineering expertise to the Australian investments.

John A Agnew, a mining engineer to become influential in Gold Fields' investments in Australia and New Guinea, was a director of National Mining Corporation. In 1922 he joined the boards of New Consolidated Gold Fields and Consolidated Gold Fields of South Africa. Robert Annan, a mining engineer and later managing director and chairman, joined in 1930, while in Johannesburg, Guy Carleton Jones, discoverer of the West Wits line, began with the company. As one writer observed: 'The age of the amiable amateurs, the aristocrats and cricketers was fading; the era of the chairman-engineer was beginning'.[13]

South African gold and the massive deep gold reserves of the Witwatersrand were the basis for the company's development. Gold Fields became one of the most profitable mining-finance houses of the late nineteenth century and expanded its presence internationally in the next. In 1929, Gold Fields moved its head office from 8 Old Jewry in the City of London to 49 Moorgate, the centre for administrative and share registry services, country and commodity analysis, and provision of technical services for the group's investments. It resided there for the next 56 years, while the group's international presence expanded through offices in New York, Bulawayo and Kalgoorlie, with investments spreading to over 25 companies internationally.[14]

Gold Fields' business model was one of facilitating investments in a range of mining companies, dealing in their shares and providing centralised administrative and technical resources. It was a model that survived for an extended period, replaced in the 1960s when separate but affiliated corporate entities were established in various countries, including Australia. As part of its international expansion, Gold Fields made investments in both Australia and New Guinea from the mid-1920s through to the late 1930s, before a hiatus in activity brought about by World War II.

---

13 Macnab, *Gold Their Touchstone*, p. 120.
14 Consolidated Gold Fields of South Africa, *The Gold Fields 1887–1937*, p. 116; Cartwright, *Gold Paved the Way*, p. 138.

Figure 2. The Consolidated Gold Fields of South Africa head office, 49 Moorgate, London.
Source: Reproduced from Consolidated Gold Fields of South Africa, *The Gold Fields 1887–1937*.

Gold Fields' interest in Australia would be rekindled in the 1960s, under another wave of geographical and business expansion. While still heavily reliant on South African gold, Gold Fields adopted an approach in the 1950s and 1960s of diversifying away from these interests. The rationale for this diversification was multifaceted. It was a means of reducing the association with an increasingly internationally isolated apartheid regime and it provided opportunities for investments in minerals other than gold and, to an extent, businesses outside minerals, including manufacturing. It also represented a defensive measure against the possible threat of takeover from rival gold producers in Africa, notably Anglo American and General Mining.

One of the countries selected for this diversification was Australia. While not unfamiliar with Australia as a mining province, having invested in several major mining companies from the 1920s, and being involved with some of the country's most influential mining men in evaluating a range of opportunities over the following decade, the company's approach to establishing a business presence was of a different nature and magnitude in the 1960s. Consolidated Gold Fields (Australia) Pty Limited was established in 1960. It invested widely. The basis was laid for the establishment of an Australian company that had the potential, given the financial, technical and managerial support from London, to become one of the major mining companies in Australia.

2
NEW HORIZONS FOR A BRITISH MINING HOUSE

The Consolidated Gold Fields of South Africa undertook an expansive international investment program in the early part of the twentieth century. New Consolidated Gold Fields was formed in August 1919, with a capital of GB£4.5 million, equal to the capital of The Consolidated Gold Fields of South Africa. This was now a dedicated company for international expansion outside the company's origins and primary source of gold production in South Africa. It supplemented the activities of The Gold Fields American Development Company, formed in 1911 to manage the American interests of the group and that had also pursued investments in gold mines in West Africa, as well as establishing a portfolio of investments in other countries.

Not least of the countries assessed as attractive by New Consolidated Gold Fields was Australia. Here a combination of factors served to assist the company establish business interests, mainly in Western Australian gold mining and, in so doing, contribute to the regeneration of gold mining activities in this state from the late 1920s.

Gold Fields' initial investments in Australia were aided by two sets of factors. First, Australian mining companies continued to establish listings on the London Stock Exchange as a source of deeper financing than could be obtained in Australia. Gold Fields had relationships with all of the main stockbrokers in the City of London that had a knowledge of mining investment opportunities in Australia. The most noteworthy of these were Lionel Robinson & Clark, with its association with WS (William Sydney) Robinson. Robinson was a founding member of the Collins House Group of companies, an informal confederation of Australian businessmen with investments in mining, processing and allied areas. Another London stockbroker was Govett, Sons and Co. and its principal, Francis Algernon Govett.[1] The London broking firms and their associates were influential in introducing Gold Fields to a range of potential mining investments in Australia. Yet another key connection for Gold Fields was Claude Albo de Bernales, a Western Australian entrepreneur active in promoting mining interests in London. He was instrumental in introducing Gold Fields to its first major gold investment in Western Australia, at Wiluna.

The second factor was the existence of individuals with engineering and mining backgrounds who had first-hand experience of mining operations, typically in the Western Australian goldfields. In this regard, two individuals, a father and son, were influential in charting the course of Gold Fields' activities in Australia: John A Agnew and Rudolph (Dolph) J Agnew. John Agnew became a director of Consolidated Gold Fields of South Africa and New Consolidated Gold Fields, serving as their chairman, while Dolph served in operational roles at a number of Western Australian gold mines and on the London board of directors of several group companies.

Gold Fields pursued investments in the 1920s and early 1930s in various Western Australian gold mining ventures, a lead and zinc mine in New South Wales, and two gold mining ventures in New Guinea. In 1930 the company also joined a group of companies established at the initiative of WS Robinson to evaluate mining opportunities throughout Australia. Three companies were established: Gold Mines of Australia, Gold Exploration and Finance Company of Australia Limited, and Western Mining Corporation. Gold Fields held major shareholdings in all three and played an influential role in their early development. For Gold Fields, this provided access to multiple mining opportunities, experienced and well-connected mining men in Australia and a dedicated financing arm. While the association offered much, it ultimately did not provide Gold Fields with the basis to establish the broad business base it sought in Australia. Gold Fields was reluctant to continue to be involved in companies in which South African competitors also had shareholdings,

---

1   Kelly, 'FA Govett, Chairman and Managing Director'; Appleyard and Schedvin, *Australian Financiers: Biographical Essays*, pp. 237–239. The City of London was a major source of funding for Australian mining projects from 1895 to 1899, as well as a source of mining engineering skills, including from the firm Bewick, Moreing & Co (Harvey and Press, 'The City and International Mining', pp. 105 and 114).

2. NEW HORIZONS FOR A BRITISH MINING HOUSE

or to support the evaluation and pursuit of joint mining ventures in Western Australia—a state where it had a presence and where it believed its interests were better served if pursued alone.[2]

Gold Fields established its own investment vehicle for its Australian ventures. In 1932, Gold Fields Australian Development Company was listed on the London Stock Exchange as a holding company for its investments and as a platform for identifying further opportunities in both gold and base metals. A number of investments were made, most notably an extension of the Wiluna gold mining operations, through an involvement in the Moonlight Wiluna mine and associated deposits.

The opportunities evaluated in Australia over a 30-year period from the mid-1920s were extensive and indicated a commitment to establishing a broad-ranging business presence in Australia. The success of the investments varied. Involvement in the Lake View and Star gold mine in the Golden Mile of Kalgoorlie was fabulously successful and the initial investment in the Wiluna gold mine in east Coolgardie provided the company with a shorter, although lucrative source of dividends. Holdings in the Yellowdine and Mount Ida gold mines in Western Australia were profitable, although for shorter periods. The Lake George mine at Captains Flat in New South Wales had a period of profitability in the 1950s but by the second half of that decade it was nearing the end of its economic life. Investments in New Guinea gold mining had mixed outcomes. A range of other investments, including extensions to the original Wiluna deposit, were less successful and losses accumulated. Interests in gold mining in Victoria and the evaluation of an extension of mineralisation on tenements near Mount Isa Mines in Queensland were of marginal value.

As such, there proved relatively little to provide the basis for the group's longer-term involvement in Australia. With the decline of its gold mining interests and limited success in identifying replacement investment opportunities, New Consolidated Gold Fields (Australasia) was established in 1956 and capitalised with A£1 million to undertake exploration and project development activities. This was to little avail. It was not until an international expansion program in the late 1950s, overseen by Sir George Steven Harvie-Watt, the chief executive and deputy

---

2   Gold Fields Ltd, 'Company Profile, Information, Business Description, History, Background Information on Gold Fields Ltd', www.referenceforbusiness.com/history2/74/Gold-Fields-Ltd.html.

chairman of Consolidated Gold Fields of South Africa, that a wider spread of investments in Australia was orchestrated. What followed was the establishment and growth of Gold Fields' presence in Australia in three main phases.

In the period 1960 to 1966 an ambitious and largely successful program of investments occurred under Consolidated Gold Fields (Australia) (CGFA), a wholly owned subsidiary of the British parent.

CGFA established a presence in iron ore, mineral sands, coal, copper, lead, zinc and tin. Its investments spread to minerals processing, manufacturing and agricultural interests, as well as property development. In doing so, CGFA gained ownership of companies that in aggregate were the largest mineral sands producers globally. In securing iron ore tenements in Western Australia, it participated in the first development of iron ore deposits in the Pilbara. It conducted an expansive Australian and international exploration program. The company was also an acquirer of other companies.

Gold Fields' evolution in Australia—the 1960 establishment of a wholly owned subsidiary, the 1966 listing on the Australian stock exchanges and the 1981 'naturalisation' process to become a majority Australian-owned company—promised a great deal. In the late 1980s, despite prior missteps and portfolio challenges, the company's ambitions remained as expansive as they were 30 years earlier. The goal was to establish itself within the top four resource companies in Australia by the late 1990s. However, the challenge of maturing ore bodies, investments in mines that struggled financially under low prices, a lack of material exploration success and the takeover of its parent company in 1989 led to truncation and an ultimate inability to fulfil these ambitions.

In an ironic twist of fate, in the late 1980s Consolidated Gold Fields in London was subject to a long-drawn-out, acrimonious but ultimately unsuccessful takeover attempt by Minorco, a company owned by arch rival Anglo American and its subsidiary, De Beers Mining. While successful in fending off this attempt, Consolidated Gold Fields succumbed to a follow-up takeover offer by renowned corporate raider and asset stripper Hanson Plc. This occurred in 1989 and with it the era of this major British mining-finance house, with its array of international interests, came to an end. The Australian offshoot, Renison Goldfields Consolidated (RGC), existed until 1998, with Hanson its major shareholder.[3]

Repeated attempts to find a buyer or buyers for the Hanson stake were unsuccessful. RGC was not able to reassert its independence as a diversified Australian minerals company. After a period of challenging market conditions and management change at the highest echelons of the company, the desire and opportunity by Hanson to exit its long-held and unsatisfactory shareholding became manifest. In 1998 Hanson was approached by the chief executive officer of the Western Australian–based mineral sands company, Westralian Sands. A merger took place between the smaller Westralian Sands and RGC. There was little in the new entity that reflected the asset base—with the exception of mineral sands—or business approach and cultural attributes of the former Gold Fields presence in Australia.

As with other notable companies of the pre– and post–World War II Australian mining landscape, RGC was folded into another company and its heritage as a separate listed company, in this case with connections extending back to the late nineteenth century, came to an end.

The ambitions of CGFA and RGC were expansive. Much was achieved, although periods of poor financial performance punctuated the 38-year history of the companies in Australia. The company contributed much to the Australian minerals sector. However, it fell short of its potential.

---

3   Renison Goldfields Consolidated, established in 1981, was majority Australian owned. It incorporated the name of what was viewed as its principal and highest-quality asset, Renison, which operated a tin mine in Tasmania. The reference to Gold Fields was retained, although with the adaptation of the original and longstanding use of the two words by their amalgamation into one. In 1998 the company name was shortened to RGC Limited.

PART TWO: EARLY INVESTMENTS IN AUSTRALIA

Box 2. Key events 1926–1956

Year	Event
1926	Wiluna Gold Corporation London established, which, in turn, owns Wiluna Gold Mines
1928	The Consolidated Gold Fields of South Africa acquires interest in Lake View and Star
1929	John Agnew appointed chairman of Lake View and Star Corporation, London Golden Horseshoe acquired by Lake View and Star Lake George Metal Corporation incorporated to take over Camp Bird interests at the Lake George mine, Captains Flat, New South Wales
1932	Gold Fields Australian Development Company listed on London Stock Exchange
1933	New treatment plant capable of treating 50,000 tons of ore per month becomes operational at Lake View and Star
1934	John Agnew appointed chairman of Wiluna Gold Corporation Moonlight Wiluna Gold Mine listed on London Stock Exchange Gold Fields Australian Development Company acquires options over Moonlight Wiluna, Starlight Gold Mine and Horseshoe Wiluna Gold Mine Lake View and Star acquires Associated Gold Mines leases and tailings
1935	Moonlight Wiluna ore treatment commences
1936	Production commences at Bulletin ore body, north of Wiluna Wiluna plant enlarged to treat Moonlight Wiluna ore Dewatering commences at Happy Jack ore body, north of Wiluna Lake View and Star treatment plant for Associated Gold Mines tailings completed Smelter operations at Wiluna commence for treatment of Moonlight Wiluna ore
1937	Lake View and Star agreement to purchase North Kalgurli tailings dumps Lake George Mining Corporation takes over assets of Lake George Metal Corporation (placed into liquidation); mining operations begin at Lake George Mine Smelter operations at Wiluna restricted; operation ceases in 1939
1938	Lake View and Star purchases leases from Imperial Gold Mine leases
1939	Death of John Agnew

1940	Gold Fields Australian Development Company acquires option over leases held by Mount Ida Gold Mine
	Lake View South Extension acquired
1943	Horseshoe Wiluna Gold Mine placed into voluntary liquidation
1945	Moonlight Wiluna Mine closes
1947	Mining at Wiluna (Happy Jack underground) ceases; tailings re-treatment continues to 1948
1951	Wiluna Mines Ltd placed into liquidation
1953	Wiluna mine closes
1956	New Consolidated Gold Fields (Australasia) registered with authorised capital of A£1 million to 'carry out exploration, the development and bringing into production of mining properties and investing in existing mining operations'

3
WESTERN AUSTRALIAN GOLD

Gold Fields' investments in Australia were aided by the presence in the country of experienced mining engineers. Prominent among these was John Agnew, who was appointed a director of The Consolidated Gold Fields of South Africa in 1922 and served as chairman from 1933 to 1939. Agnew was instrumental in several investments by Gold Fields in the Western Australian gold mining sector from the mid-1920s. His son, Rudolph, or Dolph as he was commonly known, also played an important role in the oversight of gold mining interests in Western Australia.

John Agnew was described as having a 'technical brilliance in engineering and a flair for finance' and was viewed at the time of his death as a 'dominant figure in the goldmining industry'.[1] New Zealand born, Agnew studied at the Thames School of Mines, initially working as a mine manager at the Victoria Gold Mining Company in the Thames gold fields.[2] In 1898 Herbert Hoover, the young American mining engineer later to become president of the United States, appointed Agnew, then aged 26, to Bewick, Moreing and Company (Bewick Moreing). The British mining engineering consultancy had had a presence in Western Australia since 1893 and in the first decade of the twentieth century managed 20 mines in Western Australia, accounting for nearly three-quarters of the gold produced in the state.[3]

---

1 *The Times*, 'Obituary: Mr John A Agnew', 4 August 1939.
2 New Zealand Government, 'The Goldfields of New Zealand'.
3 Hartley, 'Bewick Moreing in Western Australian Gold Mining', p. 1.

Figure 3. Herbert Hoover (second from left) and John Agnew (right) in Western Australia while working for Bewick Moreing.
Source: Herbert Hoover Presidential Library.

Figure 4. John Agnew (left) at a mining operation of Bewick Moreing.
Source: Herbert Hoover Presidential Library.

Figure 5. John Agnew (third from left) while on a mine inspection for Bewick Moreing, Western Australia.
Source: Herbert Hoover Presidential Library.

Agnew came to Australia to take charge of the underground mining operations of the Sons of Gwalia gold mine, from 1898, the first of several mines at which he worked for Bewick Moreing. The others included the Golden Age Mine at Wiluna, and the Lake View and Star mine and the Lancefield gold mine near Laverton.[4] In 1899 he accompanied Hoover to China to evaluate mining opportunities as part of Hoover's role as engineer in charge of the newly established Chinese Department of Mines. Mrs Hoover accompanied her husband and at one stage was installed in a settlement for foreigners near Tientsin, which was surrounded by members of the Boxer Rebellion. The settlement came under prolonged bombardment from the Chinese Army and the Hoovers and Agnew were fortunate not to lose their lives.[5] Agnew developed a high regard for both of the Hoovers. He viewed Mrs Hoover as 'the finest woman he had ever known'.[6] He and Hoover developed a close professional and personal relationship. They maintained a correspondence after Hoover had left the employ of Bewick Moreing in 1908 and established his own consultancy in London. Agnew was to say that Herbert Hoover had given him the chance to make his career while, at his death, it was recorded that Hoover's name was the last one Agnew mentioned.[7]

---

4   Cumming and Hartley, *Westralian Founders of Twentieth Century Mining*, pp. 2–4; Nash, *The Life of Herbert Hoover*, p. 303. See also Gibbney and Smith, *A Biographical Register*, p. 7.
5   Herbert Hoover Presidential Library (HHPL), Post Presidential Individual File, Agnew, John A, Correspondence: 1933, 1937, 1939.
6   Letter from Miss EA Rolfe to Mr H Hoover, 7 August 1939, in ibid.
7   ibid.

In 1906, Agnew was appointed Western Australian manager of Bewick Moreing, located at Kalgoorlie, and in 1912 he became general manager. He travelled widely within the state, providing management and technical oversight for the operations that came under the firm's control and evaluating new mining investments. In 1912 WJ Loring, who managed the firm's overall interests from Melbourne, wrote to the London office. The correspondence referred to Agnew and noted that he had been running the firm's Western Australian business for a number of years and during that time had done a great deal of hard work with the consequence that he was 'completely run down in health'.[8] The letter went on to state: 'A month ago he was stricken down by pneumonia, and I am told by his Medical Adviser that if it had been double pneumonia, he would have had a very bad time in getting right again'.[9] The view was he required an extended holiday, and Agnew himself was keen to travel to England. Reflecting the fact that the relationship between Bewick Moreing and Hoover was strained by legal claims following Hoover's departure from the firm, the correspondence remarked upon a letter of June 1912 from Hoover to Agnew. The contents had been communicated to Loring by Agnew's private secretary, who had been dismissed a little time previously by Agnew. Loring wrote:

> In my opinion, while there may be some reason to suspect a bit of collusion between a certain gentleman in London and J.A.A. [John A Agnew] I do not for one moment think there is any reason for us to take any drastic stand in the matter.[10]

Agnew denied any knowledge of the letter, and Loring himself wrote:

> You can quite understand the high regard which Agnew had had for H.C.H. [Herbert C Hoover] ... At the same time this regard has been so great that, more likely, the man on this side has been misled to some extent, especially during the time that certain troubles were going on in London.[11]

---

8   Letter from WJ Loring, Moreing Chambers, Kalgoorlie to Messrs Bewick, Moreing and Co., London, 30 April 1912, p. 4, in Bewick, Moreing & Co, State Library of Western Australia (SLWA), MN2530, 6736A.
9   ibid.
10 ibid.
11 ibid. See also letter from John A Agnew to Herbert Hoover, 3 July 1911, HHPL, Pre-Commerce Subject File, Mining Correspondence, Agnew, John A, 1905–1914.

A later note recorded:

> In 1912 Mr. Agnew began to cause the firm a great deal of trouble in Western Australia. He stated, like Mr. Hoover, that he was very ill, and that he could not continue to carry on the business, he became very irritable, and did the firm considerable harm … However, as the firm knew him to be a very able man, and not suspecting any treachery, they did their best to persuade him to remain.[12]

Agnew had become disenchanted with his employer, based on the level of direction from London and his lack of confidence in Loring's management and technical abilities. After withdrawing an earlier letter of resignation, Agnew resigned in 1912.[13]

After leaving Bewick Moreing, Agnew was employed by Hoover, working from his London office, 1 London Wall Building, the registered office of many of the companies that Hoover had assisted with the formation of, or in which Hoover held an investment. Agnew served on technical committees and as a director of a number of these companies. The interrelationships and cross shareholdings of numerous companies, many formed by Hoover and with the involvement of others influential in the London and international mining and finance scene, were extraordinary. When Hoover made the move from company promoter and mining engineer to wartime services and oversight of the provision of food aid to Belgium, Agnew took over the management of many of Hoover's business interests. Agnew's close relationship with Hoover as one of his chief lieutenants gave him a breadth of connections, mining company involvement and knowledge of investment opportunities that proved invaluable in subsequent investments by Gold Fields in Australia.[14] For Agnew, his reputation for commercial acumen, technical competence and first-hand mining and processing involvement was broadened by associations with leading mining men in the United Kingdom, United States, Australia and other countries. It was his time in London, shaped in no small way by the influence of and opportunities provided by Hoover, that offered him a wider canvas to develop his knowledge, experience and associations.

---

12   Bewick, Moreing & Co, SLWA, MN2530, 6736A.
13   ibid.
14   Agnew declared in 1928 that 'Hoover was the greatest man he had ever known and the ideal for honest, straightforward business conduct' and with a 'kindliness of heart' (Nash, *The Life of Herbert Hoover*, pp. 572–573).

Through his professional standing and directorships on a range of companies, including those in which Gold Fields also retained an interest—including National Mining Corporation, Burma Corporation, Oroville Dredging and Camp Bird—Agnew was appointed a director of Consolidated Gold Fields of South Africa and New Consolidated Gold Fields in 1922. In 1933, he became the fifth chairman of Gold Fields, the first mining engineer to be appointed to this role. He held this position until his death in 1939. He brought his wide-ranging technical expertise, the experience he had acquired in observing Hoover's ruthless efficiency applied to Bewick Moreing–controlled mining operations in Western Australia, his knowledge of technologies for processing complex ores, and his extensive contacts with finance men in the City of London. In addition, he drew upon a deep pool of professional mining engineers—many American—for the identification and pursuit of investments in gold and base metals mining in Australia. Agnew's experience meant that he was pivotal in Gold Fields' early involvement in Australia, and in doing so made a major contribution to revitalising the Western Australian gold mining sector in the 1920s and 1930s.

...

Hoover was a close associate of Francis Govett, the City of London stockbroker and partner in Govett, Sons and Co. Govett, in turn, through an investment by one of his companies in the establishment of Zinc Corporation, became closely connected with WS Robinson and WL Baillieu, key figures in the development of a number of the Barrier mines in New South Wales that spawned the range of industrial and manufacturing interests known as the Collins House Group of companies. Hoover first met Govett when travelling on the same vessel to Fremantle in 1901. Govett was on his way to inspect the Lake View Consols gold mine in Western Australia. English-based investor James Whitaker Wright controlled the mine through his London and Globe Finance Corporation. Following his conviction for fraud, Wright lost control of Lake View Consols.[15] Govett acquired an interest in the company and in 1902 was elected chairman, a role he fulfilled until 1917. When Govett met Hoover on the way to Fremantle he subsequently employed Bewick Moreing, and Hoover in his capacity at the firm, to manage the mine.[16]

---

15 Blainey, *The Rush that Never Ended*, p. 204; Koenig, 'Herbert Hoover—Australian Mining Entrepreneur'.
16 Yule, *William Lawrence Baillieu*, p. 127.

3. WESTERN AUSTRALIAN GOLD

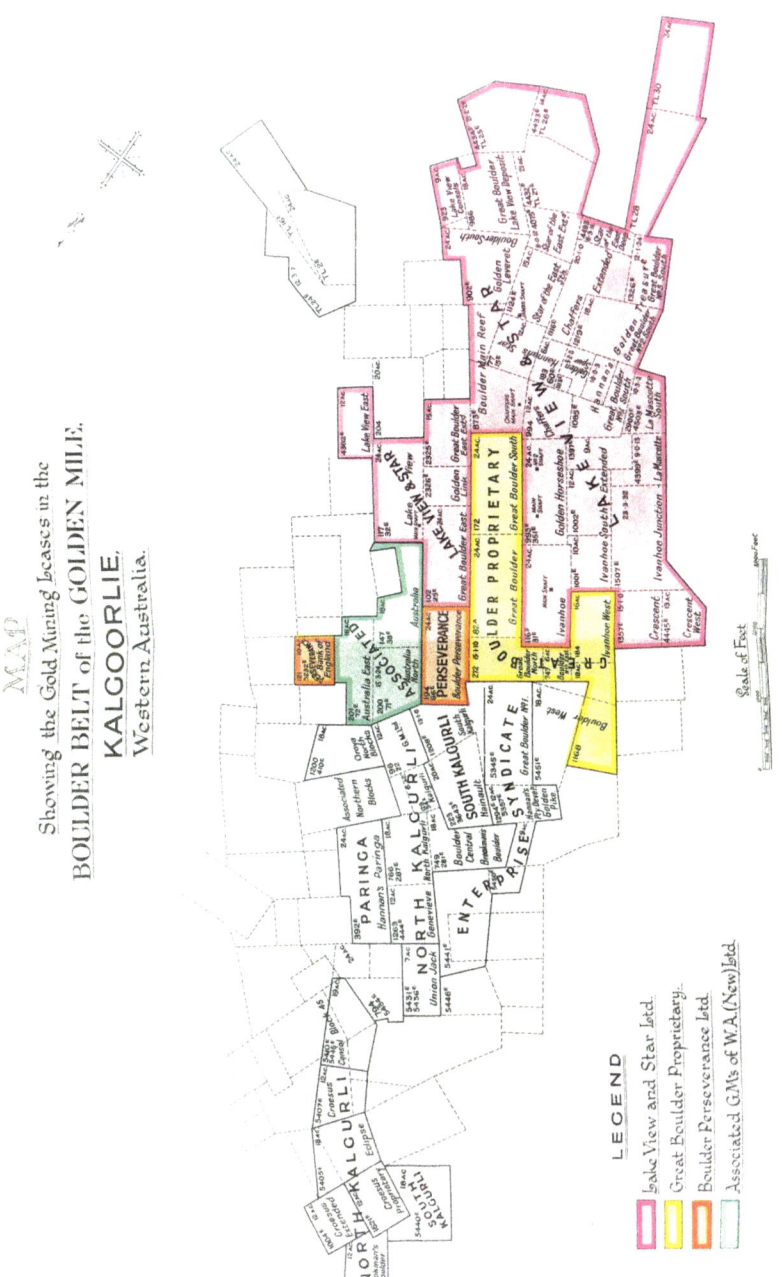

Figure 6. Map of mining leases of the Golden Mile, Kalgoorlie. Lake View and Star represented one of the largest single mining areas.

Source: University of Melbourne Archives (UMA).

Lake View and Star, to be a principal investment of Gold Fields in Australia from the second half of the 1920s, was registered in London in 1910 to acquire the properties and assets of Lake View Consols and Hannan's Star Consolidated. Described at the time as 'one of those meteoric mines, whose occasional flashes dazzle, but whose re-appearance, like the comet is a matter of conjecture', it was uncertain whether what had been 'a wonderful mine' had a life in front of it.[17] Govett served as the initial chairman of Lake View and Star and Hoover was a director during 1911 and 1912. Agnew worked on the mine's initial redevelopment and was described by Govett as 'the chief at Kalgoorlie' and a man 'universally respected'.[18] In 1929 Agnew would assume the chairmanship when it was determined by the directors that Lake View and Star required a chairman 'who had an intimate knowledge of Kalgoorlie and of the mines themselves'.[19]

Agnew also gained the opportunity for involvement in a series of companies that had been sponsored by Hoover. One, Lake View & Oroya Exploration, had been formed by the amalgamation of Oroya Exploration Company and Lake View Consols in 1911.[20] Its registered offices were 1 London Wall Building. Govett served as the chairman and joint managing director with Hoover. Agnew later joined the board as a director. Lake View & Oroya Exploration had a number of investments, including Babilonia Gold Mines in Mexico, The Yuanami Mine in Western Australia, Burma Corporation, the Bawdwin Syndicate mine in Burma, and Lake View and Star. Agnew served on the technical committees of these companies. The bankruptcy of the bankers for the mining companies Camp Bird and Santa Gertrudis led these companies to come under the control of Hoover, who was appointed chairman of both in 1914. Agnew also served on the technical committees of these

---

17 Clark, 'Australian Mining and Metallurgy', p. 65.
18 *The Financial Times*, 14 June 1912.
19 *The Financial Times*, 31 December 1929.
20 O'Brien, *Hoover's Millions*, pp. 164 and 195.

two companies. Camp Bird would play a key role in the investment in the Lake George lead and zinc mine at Captains Flat, New South Wales, to be controlled by Gold Fields.[21]

By 1914 Hoover was the director of 18 mining and financing companies, many of which had cross shareholdings and the involvement of former colleagues and associates. Agnew had become one of Hoover's closest and most trusted associates. He took a central role in managing Hoover's business affairs when Hoover was appointed president of the Commission of Relief in Belgium and moved to Washington. Hoover transferred a number of directorships and engineering consulting responsibilities to his trusted associate and nominated Agnew as the person to take responsibility for dealing with his household effects in London.[22] In July 1914 Hoover formalised the arrangements, writing to Agnew:

> You are to give your entire time and service to the conduct of my business; to undertake such professional work as I may direct, to act as Director or Engineer or Member of Technical Committee of such corporations as I may procure your appointment to … I agree to give you a participation on the ground-floor in any mining business which I may take up.[23]

Agnew succeeded Hoover on a number of company boards, including becoming chairman of Burma Corporation where he had previously acted as Hoover's alternate. Burma Corporation owned a mining operation in Burma that was experimenting with the means to process its complex ore. Zinc Corporation, of which Govett was chairman, had by 1917 taken a one-third interest in Burma Corporation, in part to provide Zinc Corporation with access to this developing technology.[24]

---

21   Camp Bird Limited was incorporated in London in 1900 to acquire the Camp Bird mine, a gold mine in the Mount Sneffels mining district, County Ouray, Colorado. Herbert Hoover was enlisted as chairman in 1914 to restore the financial position of the company. Mining at Camp Bird was temporarily suspended in 1916 and the company carried on a mining-finance business with interests in Santa Gertrudis gold and silver mines, Mexican Corporation, Lake George Mines, Talbot Alluvials and Gold Fields Australian Development Company (from 1932). After having its registered offices at 1 London Wall, Camp Bird's offices were later recorded as 49 Moorgate, London, the offices of Consolidated Gold Fields of South Africa and New Consolidated Gold Fields (London Metropolitan Archives, 'Camp Bird Ltd'; *The Economist*, 8 August 1903. See also *Mining and Scientific Press*, vol. 21, 1920; *The Mining Magazine*, vol. 26, 1922; Stewart, *Thomas F Walsh: Progressive Businessman*).
22   Whyte, *Hoover: An Extraordinary Life*, pp. 130 and 207–208.
23   Letter from Herbert Hoover to JA Agnew, 1 London Wall Buildings, 16 July 1914, arrangement dated 1 July 1914, HHPL, Pre-Commerce Subject File, Mining Correspondence, Agnew, John A 1905–1914.
24   *The Times*, 26 June 1917. See also Kelly, 'FA Govett, Chairman and Managing Director'.

Agnew was a director of Oroville Dredging, later to be associated with New Consolidated Gold Fields' involvement in New Guinea. Agnew was also involved in The South American Copper Syndicate and as chairman of Mount Elliot, which had interests in low-grade copper porphyry ore deposits near Cloncurry in Queensland. A number of these interests, including Mount Elliot, were associated with interests also held by New Consolidated Gold Fields before Agnew became a director of this company.[25]

In 1919, National Mining Corporation was established with capital of GB£3 million. The company was formed by several leading United Kingdom mining houses to organise British capital for mining and metallurgical processing ventures internationally. The founders included New Consolidated Gold Fields, Mexican Corporation, Chemical and Metallurgical Corporation (founded by Richard Tilden Smith, a co-founder with Hoover and director of Burma Corporation), Union Corporation, and The Imperial and Foreign Group. Govett became a director. The registered office for National Mining Corporation was Hoover's London office. The chairman of the new company, FW Baker, was chairman of Camp Bird and Santa Gertrudis and had been involved in the promotion of gold mines, including in Western Australia during the 1890s. He was later influential in the investment in the Lake George mine in New South Wales.[26] He was also a former student and lecturer at the Thames School of Mines, attended by John Agnew.[27] Thomas Baker, general manager of the Fresnillo Mine of Mexican Corporation and later general manager of the Comstock Lode in Nevada, would become managing director of Lake George Mines when it was majority owned by New Consolidated Gold Fields.

Agnew became an initial director of National Mining Corporation and was on the company's technical committee to examine a range of investment opportunities, particularly in base metals. National Mining Corporation acquired an interest in Burma Corporation and helped raise capital by underwriting a share issue in 1920, as well as investing in other companies, including Camp Bird and Santa Gertrudis. Chemical

---

25   *The Financial Times*, 26 October 1928. By the following year it had been determined it was not possible to carry on work on the series of mines in the Cloncurry field (*The Financial Times*, 6 December 1929).
26   Kynaston, *The City of London*, p. 187.
27   FW Baker obtained his BSc with first-class honours in 1899 after winning a scholarship from the Thames School of Mines. It is likely he was a contemporary of Agnew as a student (New Zealand Government, 'The Goldfields of New Zealand').

and Metallurgical Corporation, a shareholder, was formed in 1919 for the purpose of undertaking work on the recovery of lead, silver and zinc from complex sulphide ores, which led to the trialling of the Elmore acid-brine process, using ore from Burma, through a plant at Newcastle in England.[28] Consolidated Gold Fields of South Africa was the major shareholder in National Mining Corporation as well as Chemical and Metallurgical Corporation and, through them, came to hold an interest in the Lake George mine.

Agnew developed an association with Govett through Hoover. In turn, Govett and Hoover had relations with influential individuals, both in Australia and in London associated with the Collins House Group, including brothers Lionel and WS Robinson, and WL Baillieu. Lionel was an expert in Australian mining shares and had established the firm of Lionel Robinson & Clark, initially in Adelaide before relocating to London in 1899.[29] His partner, William Clark, had a reputation as a leading dealer in gold mining shares in London.[30]

It is hard to think of anyone better placed than Agnew to identify and pursue multiple opportunities available for Gold Fields when it turned its attention to international diversification, including Australia. Through his associations, Gold Fields had an insight into the mineral deposits and mines in both Western Australia and other parts of Australia, and the basis for establishing broader business relationships. These included individuals who were influential in the formation of a number of companies, including Gold Mines of Australia, Western Mining Corporation and Gold Exploration and Finance Company of Australia. Agnew worked closely with these companies and Gold Fields in turn established a major shareholding in each. Through his experience in Western Australia, and the association with Govett, he was able to advance Gold Fields' interests in Lake View and Star while through the companies Hoover's interests had spawned, he was able to pursue other opportunities, including the Lake George mine. Mining investment opportunities in New Guinea were also pursued. Agnew also developed a relationship with Australian mining promoter Claude Albo de Bernales, who presented opportunities for investment in the Wiluna and Moonlight Wiluna gold mines in Western Australia.

---

28 *The Mining Magazine*, vol. XXVI, no. 6, December 1922, p. 384. The Elmore process was adopted by Zinc Corporation for the Broken Hill ores to replace the Potter process.
29 Blainey, *If I Remember Rightly*, p. 28.
30 Yule, *William Lawrence Baillieu*, p. 126.

...

Western Australia experienced rapid development of its gold mining sector between 1895 and 1899, aided by the listing of Australian gold mining companies on the London Stock Exchange and the provision of British capital. The advent of the cyaniding process was a major technological development in the ability to treat sulphide ores and made a major contribution to the establishment of numerous mines in Western Australia.[31] Gold production reached its peak by 1903 and then more than halved during the period of World War II and into the 1920s. In 1926 the volume of gold produced was less than a quarter of that in 1903, although Western Australia still represented over two-thirds of the total value of gold produced in Australia.[32] The effects of manpower and equipment shortages brought about by the war years, exhaustion of the alluvial fields and poorer recoveries led to a lack of investment, a slowing of activity and a reduction in employment in the Western Australian goldfields.

While the alluvial fields at Edie Creek in the Mandated Territory of New Guinea were creating something of their own gold rush and was an area in which Gold Fields became involved, prospects for the Australian gold industry appeared bleak. As a mining industry advocate wrote in 1927:

> At present nothing is talked about in industrial circles save wool, wheat, butter and product on the run, the farm or the orchard. To the bucolic mind as well as the man in the factory the welfare of the mining industry, particularly the gold section of it, is a matter of profound indifference. It might as well be dead as far as they are concerned.[33]

Through the provision of capital, technical capabilities and the adoption of modern mining methods, Gold Fields played a pivotal role in the resurgence of gold mining in the state, particularly the mining of sulphide ores.[34] The British mining house became involved in the two largest-producing goldfields in Western Australia in the 1920s and 1930s: Wiluna,

---

31 See Prider, *Mining in Western Australia*; Close, *The Great Gold Renaissance*, pp. 3–7.
32 Gold output in Western Australia peaked at around 2.1 million ounces in 1903 and was at 450,000 ounces in 1925, to decline in the next two years (Government of Western Australia, *Report of the Department of Mines for the Year 1927*, pp. 3–4).
33 Editorial, *Chemical Engineering and Mining Review*, 5 February 1927, p. 167.
34 As Close states in her book on the various gold booms in Australia, the lift in gold output in the 1930s was appreciable but from a low base. She describes it as a 'mini-boom rather than a true boom' (Close, *The Great Gold Renaissance*, pp. 6 and 171). Close also states that in 1924 an exemption from income tax for gold mining came into force as part of efforts to stimulate investment in that sector.

and Lake View and Star. Gold Fields' first investment in Australia was in the Wiluna Gold Mine, which held leases at Wiluna, 525 kilometres north of Kalgoorlie and 940 kilometres north-east of Perth. Wiluna, located on the edge of the Western Desert and at the start of the Canning Stock Route, is an arid area of sandy red earth, minimal rainfall and long, oppressively hot summers. After the discovery of gold in the 1890s it had burgeoned from a small, isolated settlement of several hundred people to a population of over 9,000 by the 1930s. The investment from London was made through Wiluna Gold Corporation, listed on the London Stock Exchange in 1926. Gold Fields' involvement in Wiluna was directly facilitated by Claude Albo de Bernales. Described as superbly elegant, impressive, articulate and a consummate salesman, de Bernales cultivated links with financiers, especially in London, for his numerous mining ventures in Western Australia.[35] According to the noted historian of Australia's early gold mining, Geoffrey Blainey:

> With his monocle he seemed to look right through London investors. For years they failed to see through him. In London, as the price of gold rose, he floated new gold companies. A tall pied-piper, he led a procession of investors into the land of his imagination.[36]

While de Bernales would later be 'scorned in England' with the Stock Exchange of London delisting his companies and Scotland Yard investigating his activities, his securing of British financing was influential in opening up gold mines considered marginal.[37] According to a 1949 report into the affairs of his companies, it was alleged that de Bernales bought out mines that had not been in operation for years, 'spent nothing on exploring and developing the mines … collated information regarding the properties … invariably holding out the mines as good ventures … even though engineers could not make even superficial examinations'.[38] In the case of the investments introduced by de Bernales to Gold Fields, they were largely financially successful, aided by the metallurgical and mining knowledge of Agnew and his colleagues.

---

35 Davies, 'Claude Albo de Bernales', p. 186. See also Bolton, *A Fine Country to Starve In*, p. 86.
36 Blainey, *The Golden Mile*, p. 134.
37 Blainey, *The Rush that Never Ended*, pp. 312–313. See also Laurence, 'de Bernales, Claude Albo (1876–1963)'; MK Quartermaine and E McGowan, 'A historical account of the development of mining in Western Australia', in Prider, *Mining in Western Australia*, p. 15.
38 *The Courier-Mail*, 13 November 1949.

The original mining at Wiluna had created two enormous open cut pits from which oxidised ore had been extracted for over 20 years into the first decade of the twentieth century. While the oxidised ore had been largely exhausted, there remained large quantities of ores compounded with sulphides. It was recognised that Wiluna possessed one of the largest resources of low-grade sulphide ores in the state. However, the ore body was characterised as 'where isolation greatly compounded formidable problems with metallurgical chemistry'.[39] Extraction of the ore was complicated by the presence of pyrite and arsenopyrite (iron arsenic sulphide) that typically required a process of grinding, roasting, cyaniding and heating to high temperatures.[40] In 1911 a revival of sorts took place by the adoption of a roasting process to recover gold from the difficult-to-treat sulphide ores. This was not effective in terms of the level of gold recovery and the area was again abandoned. The challenges related not only to the effective means for recovery of gold from the sulphide ores, but also the isolation of Wiluna, located 160 kilometres from the nearest railway connection. The depletion of local wood supplies within a 20-kilometre radius, exhausted by earlier mining activity, also acted as an impediment to shaft mining at depth.

In 1924, after de Bernales and his syndicate had gained control of the leases, attention was directed to the best means to treat the complex ores. De Bernales raised funds to undertake large-scale research into the means to extract the low concentrations of gold, and a complex multi-stage form of processing was developed. An electrostatic precipitation plant was constructed with an experimental unit erected in 1924. The lack of success with this process led to the adoption of the flotation process that had been used successfully in New South Wales at the Barrier mines near Broken Hill.[41] It was evident that a railway connection was necessary for the provision of material, equipment and power requirements if the planned operation was to be profitable.

Agnew had a familiarity with the deposits of the area. From 1902 to 1904 he had managed the Golden Age Consolidated Mine, which, while a separate ore body, adjoined the Wiluna property. In 1909, while working for Bewick Moreing, an option was taken over the group of deposits, known as Bulletin, located on the east lode of Wiluna. While a shaft

---

39 Colebatch, *Claude de Bernales: The Magnificent Miner*, p. 50.
40 ibid., p. 52.
41 Institute of Mining & Metallurgy, 'General Description of The Wiluna Mines Limited', pp. 2–3.

was sunk to 250 feet and a gold-bearing lode observed, the refractory nature of the ore meant that no further work was undertaken, while the nearby Happy Jack deposit was also developed, to a depth of 90 feet. As Agnew recalled in 1928, it was largely 'on account of the difficulty then apprehended in the treatment of this ore that the company was prompted to abandon the option on the Bulletin group'.[42]

Gold Fields held initial reservations about investing in the Western Australian gold industry. This hesitancy was associated with concerns regarding the combative labour situation, as well as an awareness of various scandals associated with the promotion of speculative or bogus mining ventures in the state. These reservations were overcome through the urging of 'influential associates' who had identified ore bodies of 'great size … persistence and length and reasonably high average value' as well as undertakings obtained by these same associates from the Western Australian Government to commit to build a railway line from Meekatharra to the site of the Wiluna mine, a distance of 175 kilometres.[43] Gold Fields' own evaluation provided it with confidence to take an initial, 'quite modest' stake, viewing the potential of the Wiluna deposit and its northern extensions, as well as other mineralisation in the area, as sufficient to justify its investment. Its confidence was reinforced by the state mining engineer's report of 1927 to the Western Australian Government that determined that 'the Wiluna Mines Ltd's proposition has now been well proved'. The lodes were assessed as long and wide, with 'no visible geological reason why they should not continue to like depths as the Kalgoorlie lodes, and have a similar life of not less than, say, 25 years'.[44] This in turn provided sufficient encouragement for the government to consider a rail connection.

---

42 'Wiluna Gold Corporation', *The Financial Times*, 27 April 1928, Butlin Archives, The Australian National University (ANU), 67/71.
43 The Consolidated Gold Fields of South Africa Limited, 'Report of the Proceedings at the Ordinary General Meeting, 2nd December 1926', University of Melbourne Archives (UMA), Stock Exchange of Melbourne, 1968.0018, Box 67.
44 A Montgomery, 'Report on the Request of the Wiluna Gold Mines, Limited, for Railway Connection of Wiluna with the State Railway System', in Government of Western Australia, *Report of the Department of Mines for the Year 1928*, p. 81.

Figure 7. Western Australian Minister for Railways laying the first track of the Meekatharra to Wiluna railway line, 1929.
Source: SLWA, 2680B, vol. 170.

Wiluna Gold Corporation was the first of de Bernales's major gold company flotations in London. The London Stock Exchange listing was associated with Consolidated Gold Fields of South Africa shortly after taking a major shareholding and Agnew becoming a director. The Wiluna Gold Corporation initially had Sir Frederic Hamilton as its chairman, an associate of de Bernales, until 1934 when Agnew was appointed chairman, a role he retained until his death in 1939.[45] The *Kalgoorlie Miner* recorded the initial investment of Gold Fields, describing it as 'the powerful company operating in South Africa' with its interest in Wiluna associated with the activities of Agnew who had 'for years [been] professionally associated with mining enterprises in Western Australia'.[46]

---

45 Wiluna Gold Mines sought a listing on the Australian stock exchanges in 1930, with a listing on the Adelaide exchange in 1931, followed in 1933 by Brisbane, Sydney and Melbourne. Operations at Wiluna ceased in 1953 (Robinson, William Sydney, UMA, 101/70, Box 4; Wiluna Gold Mines Ltd and Wiluna Gold Corporation Ltd, UMA, Stock Exchange of Melbourne, 1968.0018, Box 353).
46 *Kalgoorlie Miner*, 19 March 1926.

Figure 8. Wiluna gold mine, 1927.
Source: SLWA, BA 2127/2.

Figure 9. Panorama of Wiluna mine site, 1930.
Source: SLWA, BA 144-1/4.

Representations had been made to the Western Australian Government by the de Bernales group seeking the commitment to construct a railway from Meekatharra if work were undertaken on the testing and development of the ore bodies at depth. The commitment of A£250,000 to install modern equipment was made. Mining initially occurred from a western and eastern lode, with a new eastern gold-bearing lode also encountered. The ore at Wiluna required a complex method of processing and extensive experimental work was undertaken to enhance the process.[47] At Wiluna and later at Gold Fields' other main gold mining interest in Western

---

47   Technical investigations by Gold Fields Australian Development Company, owner of the Moonlight Wiluna Gold Mines, were also undertaken in the 1930s on the semi-oxidised ores of this field with the intention of allowing the treatment of these ores to take place along with the sulphide ores at the Wiluna Gold Mines' plant (The Mines Department of WA, 'Report on the Treatment of Semi-Oxidised Ore', p. 1).

Australia, Lake View and Star, oil flotation was employed after crushing to separate the gold, followed by a process of roasting and cyaniding. Wiluna commenced operation of a flotation pilot plant in 1927, which provided initial success with high gold recoveries from the ore in the southern part of the Wiluna deposits, an area encompassing over 790 acres.

Confidence was high that recoveries up to 90 per cent could occur but results proved to be variable and determination of the most appropriate form of flotation remained an area of intense technical review and experimentation involving Agnew and his colleagues. These included the American mining engineer HE (Herbert) Vail, a former Bewick Moreing employee and later involved with Lake View and Star, a mine that had to tackle similar, although not as severe, recovery issues. In November 1927, Vail wrote: 'We are doing better with Lake View & Star and the Wiluna Mines continue to respond handsomely. Once the property is in full swing it will have an important bearing on the affairs of Western Australia'.[48]

Figure 10. Wiluna gold mine poppet head and engine room.
Source: SLWA, B4712611.

---

48   Letter from HE Vail to FL Thomas, 23 November 1927, Butlin Archives, ANU, 67/71.

Figure 11. Pouring first gold, Wiluna, 1935.
Source: SLWA, B/3/16.

Figure 12. Wiluna gold mine, 1935.
Source: SLWA, 7:2951 B/3114.

The development of the mining operations in which Gold Fields had an interest displayed a large degree of technical cooperation. In this regard, Agnew was pivotal, focused on ensuring the best talent was secured through the development, mining, operational and treatment stages. TM (Tom) Owen, the operations manager of Lake George, was seconded to help with the work undertaken at Wiluna on flotation and gold recovery, while in turn Owen had an interest in this technology for its potential to assist with the recovery of sulphur from the pyritic ores at Lake George. The work proceeded over several years. In 1932 Agnew wrote to Owen:

> We are not only dealing with a difficult ore but at the same time we are doing a good deal of pioneer work in the way of applying flotation methods to a straight gold ore and it is obvious that a great deal depends upon our being able to secure experience in work of this character outside the ordinary routine of the gold metallurgist.[49]

Over the period from 1927 to 1930 work at Wiluna focused on sinking a new main shaft and preparations for underground mining from the two main lodes. Development work on the mine shafts and plant construction began in 1929. A new power plant was constructed, a steel head frame erected and electric winders installed while facilities for the complex process to treat the sulphide ore were established. In 1929 the extension of the railway from Meekatharra to Wiluna was substantially complete, while a 'comprehensive housing scheme' was put in place to 'attract and hold labour'.[50] By 1931 most of the plant and machinery had been installed. According to one observer of the operations at Wiluna: 'The plant is easily the best laid out and best equipped gold mining unit in Australia'.[51] Production began in 1931. As was observed at the time, 'if Kalgoorlie ore is refractory, Wiluna is super refractory'.[52] This, along with even greater challenges associated with processing the Moonlight Wiluna ore, which was introduced to the Wiluna facilities from 1935, created ongoing production challenges. Leases to the north were considered prospective and were drilled with two deposits, Bulletin and Happy Jack, planned to be tied back to the Wiluna facilities in the coming years. The milling capacity of the mine was increased by the construction of a new plant with a capacity of 40,000 tons per month.

---

49 Letter from JA Agnew to TM Owen, 27 January 1932, p. 2, Butlin Archives, ANU, 67/71.
50 'Wiluna Gold Corporation, Ltd, Mr John A Agnew's Review of the Year's Work', *The Financial News*, 26 September 1929, UMA, Stock Exchange of Melbourne, 1968.0018, Box 353.
51 *Chemical Engineering and Mining Review*, 5 January 1931, p. 139.
52 *Chemical Engineering and Mining Review*, 8 February 1937, p. 201.

In 1931, an engineer from Gold Fields American Development Corporation, CO Lindberg, was sent to Western Australia to evaluate several gold opportunities as well as to investigate the processing challenges and implications for ore reserves at Wiluna. His investigation, undertaken in conjunction with Owen, involved an 'exhaustive investigation' into the treatment problems at the Wiluna mine.[53] His 1931 report determined that, while 'no cause for alarm', it was unlikely that sufficient ore could be recovered to provide any more than 25,000 tons of the 40,000 tons of capacity of the milling plant.[54] Furthermore, ore yields at depth were determined to be lower than expected. At the company's general meeting in London the following year, the chairman reported that the corresponding 30 per cent reduction in reserves was a 'distinctly disappointing' outcome.[55]

Despite this initial setback, by 1932 the mine could be characterised as 'remarkable', with an 'entirely new lode of a grade well above the previous mine average' having been identified.[56] Evaluation of the Bulletin lease led to a new mineralised ore zone, which enabled reserves to be increased, while ore recoveries to the milling plant had improved, allowing 43,000 tons a month to be treated in 1934. Funds for the development of the Wiluna deposits had been exhausted by 1930 and the Western Australian and Commonwealth governments advanced loan funds of A£300,000 to complete the construction of the plant, with the funds repaid by 1934. In the same year Wiluna provided the London corporation with a dividend of GB£430,279 with a balance of accumulated profits of over GB£718,000, after extinguishing accumulated debt.[57] For Gold Fields, Wiluna was an excellent investment. In the first four and a half years of production, gold to the value of A£3.5 million was extracted with some of the most modern mining methods aiding recoveries and unit costs. According to one writer, the application of modern, large-scale mining techniques, such as those employed at Wiluna and Lake View and Star, enabled the handling of large quantities of low-grade ore and 'opened up a new phase of Western Australian mining, as nothing equal to it had ever been seen in the State before'.[58]

---

53   *Chemical Engineering and Mining Review*, 9 October 1931, p. 3.
54   *Chemical Engineering and Mining Review*, 5 December 1931, p. 85.
55   *Chemical Engineering and Mining Review*, 5 March 1932, p. 222.
56   *The Age*, 26 July 1932.
57   Wiluna Gold Corporation, Limited, 'Directors' Report and Statement of Accounts for the Year Ended 31st March, 1933', UMA, Stock Exchange of Melbourne, 1968.0018, Box 353.
58   Snooks, *Depression and Recovery in Western Australia*, p. 66.

CONSOLIDATED GOLD FIELDS IN AUSTRALIA

In combination with Lake View and Star, Gold Fields had established an involvement in the two largest gold-producing fields in Western Australia. In the 1934 financial year Lake View and Star produced over A£1.2 million worth of gold and Wiluna over A£1 million. Profitability was impressive, with Wiluna generating a profit of GB£615,283 and Lake View and Star, GB£573,097.[59] The share price performance of its investments on the London Stock Exchange was equally impressive:

> Wiluna Gold Corporation ... enjoyed very handsome rises, from a low of 19/- in 1929. By 1931, reflecting shortages and fears of the mine's future, the shares were down to 8/3 but it was only a temporary drop and those that bought them did well. Three years later Wiluna shares climbed to more than ten times that ... It became WA's biggest goldfield after Kalgoorlie.[60]

The fortuitous circumstances for Gold Fields' initial investments in Australia were associated with Dolph Agnew arriving back in Western Australia in 1932, after spending time working in various mines in Western Australia and then in Yugoslavia and northern Italy.[61] In Western Australia, Dolph became general manager of Gold Fields Australian Development Company (GFADC) and took charge of the Wiluna mine and evaluation of the nearby Moonlight Wiluna leases, as well as other mining opportunities. GFADC was designed to act as a vehicle for investments in a range of Western Australian gold mines, and an office was established in Kalgoorlie. Principally, though, it was formed to take a shareholding in the Moonlight Wiluna, Starlight and Horseshoe Wiluna gold mines, and 13 leases at the northern end of the leases already held by Wiluna Gold Mines. The options over Moonlight, Starlight and Horseshoe Wiluna were exercised for A£100,000 and three companies were established with combined issued capital of A£500,000.[62] The leases had been owned by either Commonwealth and Mining Finance Limited or Australian Machinery and Investment Company, both companies under the control of de Bernales. Hamilton and de Bernales served as initial directors of GFADC.

---

59 *Chemical Engineering and Mining Review*, 8 February 1935, p. 168.
60 Colebatch, *Claude de Bernales: The Magnificent Miner*, p. 53.
61 See Appendix 3 for a biographical profile of Dolph Agnew.
62 *The Financial Times*, 20 February 1935. GFADC drew a wide net over potential investment opportunities, taking options over a range of mining operations in Western Australia. In 1934, these included the Gladiator Gold Mine, Laverton district; Pericles Gold Mine, Mount Monger district; Black Range Gold Mines, near Sandstone; and Lochinvar Gold Mine, Broad Arrow District, Kalgoorlie-Boulder Shire (*Sunday Times*, 15 April 1934). Horseshoe Wiluna Gold Mine was wound up in August 1943.

Figure 13. Aerial view of Wiluna gold mining operation.
Source: SLWA, 545813/79.

In 1935 Wiluna began treating ore from the Moonlight mine to the north. Processing of the Moonlight ore introduced greater complexities; the ore was later described by Charles Prior, the former general manager of Wiluna, as one of the most difficult to treat ores in Australia.[63] The arsenopyritic component of the ore led to various technical evaluations of the best means of treatment. The decision was made in October 1936 to adopt a smelting process to remove arsenic, followed by sintering the gold with lead.[64] The process entailed the acquisition of two lead deposits at Northampton.[65] According to a later review of the Moonlight Wiluna ore: 'Never before had a gold ore containing such large amounts of arsenic and antimony sulfides been treated on a large scale'.[66]

---

63   *Chemical Engineering and Mining Review*, 8 February 1937, p. 201. Prior was appointed managing director of Wiluna Ltd in 1935 and was a consulting engineer to GFADC (Cumming and Hartley, *Westralian Founders of Twentieth Century Mining*, p. 133).
64   ibid.
65   The mines were Grand Junction and Wheal May near Northampton, Western Australia.
66   *Chemical Engineering and Mining Review*, 10 July 1952, p. 385.

In 1936, dewatering was undertaken of the Happy Jack leases, located less than a mile north of the Wiluna main shaft, prior to production commencing. According to an industry publication in 1936:

> Wiluna must be ranked as second only to Kalgoorlie's Golden Mile among Australia's goldfields. Recent developments on the main Wiluna leases and on the Happy Jack and Bulletin leases to the north, coupled with favourable results on the Moonlight mine of Gold Fields Australian Development ... have proved large tonnages, and have indicated the probable existence of great extensions.[67]

However, by 1938, challenges associated with the Wiluna deposit had become apparent. A limited reserve life meant that extensive diamond drilling had begun. In addition, while smelting continued intermittently, it introduced technical challenges and higher operating costs. Smelting operations were eventually suspended in March 1938. Speaking at the 1938 annual general meeting of the company, John Agnew observed:

> While results at depth in the main mine were not good, development in the Bulletin and Happy Jack sections gave every promise of furnishing very substantial tonnages of good grade ore ... believing that, if the corner had not yet been turned, it was clearly in sight.[68]

Despite this, mining conditions for both the Wiluna and Moonlight Wiluna deposits deteriorated, while the challenges associated with the war years, including shortages of manpower, created further difficulties. The London corporation reported a loss in 1939 to be repeated in subsequent years. The consulting engineer for Wiluna Gold Corporation reported in 1940 that the Wiluna deposits had a remaining life of two-and-a-half years, with 'no alternative but to cut expenditure to the minimum and concentrate on salving the existing reserves at the greatest possible profit'.[69] By 1940 the Bulletin lode was being treated as a 'salvage proposition'. In 1941 the Moonlight Wiluna mine was displaying a decline in reserves and grade at depth, while exploration activities conveyed 'little prospect of any new ore being discovered'.[70]

---

67 *Chemical Engineering and Mining Review*, 8 August 1936, p. 397.
68 *Chemical Engineering and Mining Review*, 10 February 1939, p. 228.
69 *Chemical Engineering and Mining Review*, 10 January 1940, p. 165.
70 *Chemical Engineering and Mining Review*, 11 March 1940, p. 250 and 10 January 1941, p. 121.

During part of the war years, the Wiluna mine continued to operate only by obtaining a subsidy from the Western Australian and Commonwealth governments, defined as it was as a protected industry due to the production of antimony, used in the manufacture of bullets and shell casings and for which permission to export had been granted.[71] The low-grade ore characteristics of Wiluna made the subsidy essential to maintain a higher rate of production as, unlike other mines, there was not an opportunity to scale back production in any material manner.[72] Planning for operations after the war, in light of the serious contraction in reserves, led to the consideration of the need to acquire additional properties. Options were secured over other deposits, including Mount Charlotte and Porphyry (1939), viewed as necessary replacement sources of ore.[73]

In 1945 Moonlight Wiluna was closed and in 1947 underground mining operations ceased on the Happy Jack leases. Wiluna mining ceased in 1948 after producing more than A£12 million worth of gold over its 15 years of operation, with activities restricted to the processing of residual tailings.[74] By 1949, Wiluna had returned to a small profit solely related to the recovery of tailings. It was a lean period for the London holding company and its major shareholder, with no dividends received for an extended time. Despite the earlier than expected decline in the ore bodies, Wiluna still proved to be one of the largest and most profitable gold mines in Western Australia.[75]

...

---

71   *West Australian Mining and Commercial Review*, vol. 9, no. 6, August 1944, p. 21 and vol. 10, no. 1, March 1945, p. 15. By 1945 it was recognised that the mine was nearing the end of its economic life.

72   Wiluna Gold Corporation, Limited, 'Directors' Report and Statement of Accounts for the Year Ended 31st March, 1945', UMA, Stock Exchange of Melbourne, 1968.0018, Box 353.

73   *West Australian Mining and Commercial Review*, vol. 11, no. 1, March 1946.

74   *West Australian Mining and Commercial Review*, vol. 11, no. 10, December 1946, p. 26; Topperwien, *The History of Wiluna*, chapter 3 and pp. 2–6 for a description of the gold mining activities. See also Heydon, *Wiluna: Edge of the Desert*.

75   In notes prepared by WS Robinson on Western Australian gold mines, Wiluna was described as one of the largest gold mines in Western Australia, producing 1,334,705 fine ounces of gold between 1927 and 1953. The Wiluna district overall produced 1,810,000 fine ounces (Gold Mines of Kalgoorlie, Robinson, William Sydney, UMA, 101/70, Box 4, File 78).

Figure 14. View of Lake View Consols in 1928, renamed Lake View and Star.
Source: SLWA, 1913/1/53.

In 1928, through the influence of Agnew, Gold Fields acquired an interest in Lake View and Star, located in the Boulder end of the Kalgoorlie gold fields. In 1929, Agnew became chairman of Lake View and Star and by 1931 Consolidated Gold Fields was the largest investor while also providing technical assistance and loan funds for the mine's expansion. The mining operation was transformed under Agnew's influence. He drew heavily upon the capabilities of Herbert Vail.[76] Given the sharing of technical expertise at Gold Fields' controlled mines, similar techniques, such as the initial use of oil flotation, were applied across operations. Agnew also recruited another American mining engineer, Joseph Thorn, as manager of Lake View and Star.[77] Thorn became general manager in 1929 and remained in the role for 20 years until 1950, with a record of impressive achievement at the operation that, according to Blainey 'created a virtually new mining enterprise' at Lake View and Star.[78] He was succeeded by Dolph Agnew, who was also a director of the company, from 1951 until his death in 1960.

---

76   *The Daily News*, Perth, 28 July 1934. Vail also provided consulting engineering services to the Wiluna mine.
77   *Kalgoorlie Miner*, 13 May 1950.
78   Blainey, *The Golden Mile*, p. 130.

3. WESTERN AUSTRALIAN GOLD

Figure 15. Associated Tailings, part of the properties controlled by Lake View and Star.
Source: Lake View and Star company publication, UMA.

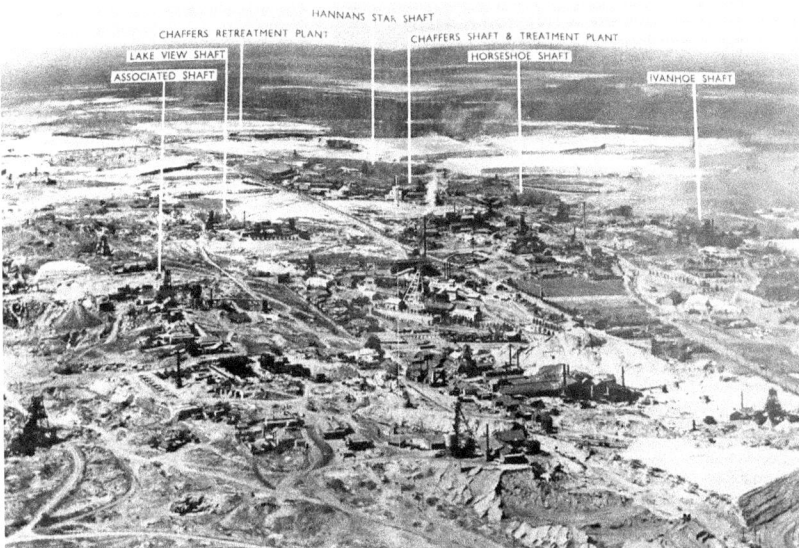

Figure 16. Aerial view of Lake View and Star facilities.
Source: Lake View and Star company publication, UMA.

51

The improvement in the fortunes of Lake View and Star was achieved by a combination of acquiring nearby mines and leases, deeper workings, the implementation of modern mining methods and investment in new equipment, as well as the processing of tailings. In this regard, the commitment of additional capital and technical expertise facilitated the revitalisation of a mine that was viewed to have seen its best days. After the successful trialling of oil flotation at Wiluna, in 1930 Lake View and Star installed the first flotation plant in the state on a production scale to enhance the recovery of gold. The flotation capacity was expanded over the next two years from 5,000 tons per month to 20,000 tons, and then further increased. The mine developed by repeated expansions, which made it possible to extend operations into new ground, as well as through continual technical advancements, including the decision to construct a central treatment plant and to standardise operations. The application of modern techniques for drilling, establishment of the mine's own power source, the transportation of ore by electric locomotives, the installation of electric shaft winders and the use of modern processing techniques were all part of the measures adopted.[79] In turn, these led Lake View and Star to be one of the most modern and efficient operations in Western Australia.

Agnew's and Thorn's efforts were such that in 1932 Lake View and Star was producing at 10 times the 1924 level. In 1930, it was the largest gold-producing operation in the state. In that year it was reported:

> Owing to larger profits earned and to the additional receipts from Australian [currency] exchange and increased price of gold, this Company has been able to pay off its current indebtedness and has financed all its special development, mine preparation and new plant expenditure, in addition to which its liquid reserves have materially increased.[80]

According to a 1934 report on gold mining in Australia, of the operating mines on the Golden Mile, Lake View and Star was considered 'by far the greatest and best equipped'.[81] It by then comprised 37 gold mining leases and six tailings blocks, over an area of 626 acres. In 1935, a series of mine amalgamations occurred, and The Associated Mine was acquired.

---

79 Snooks, *Depression and Recovery in Western Australia*, p. 65.
80 The Consolidated Gold Fields of South Africa, Limited, 'Report of the Directors and Statement of Accounts, 30th June 1932', p. 16, UMA, Stock Exchange of Melbourne, 1968.0018, Box 67.
81 H Byron Moore, Day & Journeaux, *Gold Mines of Australia and New Guinea: Leading Companies*, p. 39.

In 1939, the year of John Agnew's death, Lake View and Star generated a profit of GB£526,459, a record for the company. Dividend payments were at 50 per cent of the profit generated.[82] The aggregation of leases over the years meant that the mine comprised a series of operations, including the Golden Horseshoe, Ivanhoe, Chaffers, Great Boulder Main Reef, Hannan's Star, Lake View Consols, and Associated Group of leases.[83] By 1947, Lake View and Star comprised an area of over 970 acres, with 42 gold mining leases and 22 tailings areas. To 1960 Lake View and Star produced over 5.5 million ounces of gold and paid dividends for 34 years, the last 28 of which to 1960 were consecutive.[84] At its 50th anniversary in 1960, Lake View and Star was the largest gold producer in Western Australia and Gold Fields' most successful investment in Australia, with a shareholding it retained until 1970.[85]

...

Consolidated Gold Fields established a commanding position in the Western Australian gold mining sector due to its investment in Lake View and Star and Wiluna. Lake View and Star was the major gold producer while, according to one report in the 1930s, the development of Wiluna and the technical advances applied were 'responsible in no mean measure for holding the fading hope and creating a new interest in Australian mining'.[86] The period represented resurgent years for gold production in Western Australia from the depths of the decline after the 1890s boom. The gold price in Australia increased from 89 shillings (A£4/9 shillings) an ounce in 1930 to over 195 shillings (A£9/15 shillings) in 1939, to more than 209 shillings (A£10/9 shillings) in the early 1940s, aided by the depreciation of the Australian, British and United States currencies, particularly in the early 1930s.[87] In 1937, Lake View and Star recorded a profit of GB£478,414, while Wiluna recorded a profit of GB£159,512.[88]

---

82 'Lake View and Star, Limited', *The Mining World*, 16 December 1939, UMA, Stock Exchange of Melbourne, 1968.0018, Box 151.
83 Westralia (Western Australia), *1948 Story of the Goldfields*, p. 19; Snooks, *Depression and Recovery in Western Australia*, p. 64.
84 Anon, *Fifty Historical Years, 1910–1960*, p. 16.
85 ibid.
86 H Byron Moore, Day & Journeaux, *Gold Mines of Australia and New Guinea: Leading Companies*, p. 68.
87 Depreciation of the Australian currency in January 1931; British pound in September 1931 and United States currency in April 1933 (Snooks, *Depression and Recovery in Western Australia*, p. 67).
88 *Chemical Engineering and Mining Review*, 8 January 1937, p. 175 and 8 February 1937, p. 215. The profit in 1936 for Wiluna Gold Mines Ltd, the Australian entity, was A£439,894.

Lake View and Star paid total dividends of over GB£1.7 million to 1938, eclipsing returns from the next most productive mine, Sons of Gwalia.[89] The mine also generated annual profits at the end of the 1930s exceeding GB£500,000.

The company had established an exceptional and highly remunerative position, even if the expansions beyond Wiluna and Lake View and Star in the 1940s and 1950s were less successful. In this outcome, John Agnew's role was of central importance. Described by a contemporary as a 'man of vision [with a] remarkable knowledge of mining',[90] he was recorded in the silver jubilee history of Lake View and Star mine in 1960 as:

> A well-known mining engineer who had spent many years on the Kalgoorlie gold field, was a Director of The Consolidated Gold Fields of South Africa, Limited and acting on his advice, the operating subsidiary of this powerful finance house, New Consolidated Gold Fields Limited, offered to provide capital for the development of the Chaffers lease. In the same year well directed driving in the Chaffers area had confirmed the extension of two rich lodes which had previously been worked … and a sum of £150,000 was … raised in equal parts by the Shareholders and by New Consolidated Gold Fields Limited, the latter acquiring options over a further 100,000 shares which were exercised in 1933.[91]

In 1939, Agnew died in California after contracting pneumonia while visiting mining properties. He was 67 years of age. His funeral service in London was attended by dozens of former colleagues and friends, including de Bernales, Sir Frederic Hamilton, representatives of Zinc Corporation and the Agent-General in London for Western Australia. Tributes were paid of him, including by former president Herbert Hoover.[92] At the time of his death Agnew was chairman of Consolidated Gold Fields of South Africa and 12 other companies, and a director of 13 more. His obituary in *The Times* recorded that Agnew had been awarded

---

89 Government of Western Australia, *Report of the Department of Mines for the Year Ended 1938*, pp. 34 and 18.
90 *The West Australian*, 5 August 1939. This comment was made by JF Thorn, who was then general manager of Lake View and Star.
91 Anon, *Fifty Historical Years, 1910–1960*, p. 5. Agnew was also described as far-seeing, courageous and a man who 'saw the possibilities for Western Australian mining' (Uren, *Glint of Gold*, p. 264).
92 *The Financial Times*, 4 August 1939.

a gold medal of the Institute of Mining and Metallurgy in recognition of services in the 'development of mineral resources of the Empire, and to the mining industry'.[93]

Consolidated Gold Fields gained an involvement in two of the main gold mining operations in Western Australia. Its presence as a major participant in Australian gold mining had been established through its own expertise, first-hand knowledge of mining conditions in the state and by an ability to draw upon a depth of mining engineering and metallurgical skills through personnel known to Agnew. In the case of Lake View and Star, it was an interest held by Gold Fields in London until 1966, when Consolidated Gold Fields Australia gained administrative control when its residence as a listed company was transferred from London to Australia. From the sound base established in Western Australian gold mining, Gold Fields' interests expanded, both in Western Australia as well as to other parts of Australia and to New Guinea.

---

93 *The Times*, 4 August 1939.

4

BROADER ASSOCIATIONS

In 1930 Gold Mines of Australia Limited was established in London at the initiative of WS Robinson in conjunction with his brother's stockbroking firm, Lionel Robinson, Clark & Co. The syndicate that formed the company included The Zinc Corporation and Imperial Smelting Corporation, with New Consolidated Gold Fields having a major interest, along with an associated company, Camp Bird.[1] Gold Mines of Australia was designed to undertake large-scale exploration for gold and facilitate potential mine developments in Australia. It was one of the principal companies, along with Gold Exploration and Finance Company of Australia, that pursued multiple investments in mining ventures across Australia and which led to the formation of Western Mining Corporation. New Consolidated Gold Fields was a key participant in the early years, not only as a financier but also in taking a role in reviewing mining prospects. As such, it was ideally placed to take advantage of broader associations in Australia for the pursuit of its mining interests in the country.

Lindesay Clark, who in 1931 became manager of Gold Mines of Australia and technical managing director of Western Mining Corporation at its formation in 1933, recalled that, in its first two years, Gold Mines of Australia considered over 200 proposals for mining ventures.[2] John Agnew and CO Lindberg, a mining engineer and head of The Gold Fields American Development Company, reviewed a number of these

---

1 Gold Mines of Australia Limited, 'List of Shareholdings as at 25 October 1932' and 'List of Shareholdings as at 17 January 1943', University of Melbourne Archives (UMA), Stock Exchange of Melbourne, 1968.0018, Box 99. The initial shareholding was dominated by companies controlled by Consolidated Gold Fields of South Africa, with New Consolidated Gold Fields having a 60 per cent shareholding (Clark, *Built on Gold: Recollections of Western Mining*, p. 3).
2 Ralph, 'Clark, Sir Gordon Colvin Lindesay (1896–1986)'.

prospects. Gold Mines of Australia's initial interests included options related to the Mount Coolon Gold Mine in Queensland, in which Gold Fields was entitled to a one-third interest; Mount Triton Gold Mine, Western Australia; and evaluation of gold opportunities associated with the Berry Leads alluvial system near Ballarat in Victoria. To accommodate the spread of potential activities, a new company, Western Mining Corporation, was incorporated in London in 1933. WS Robinson was again influential in garnering both technical and financial resources, with the shareholding in London including New Consolidated Gold Fields, its associate Camp Bird, and two South African gold mining companies, The Central Mining and Investment Corporation Limited and Union Corporation Limited. North Broken Hill and Broken Hill South were the major Australian shareholders.

The intention was for Gold Mines of Australia to manage all interests in eastern Australia, while Western Mining Corporation would manage Western Australian interests. Agnew was on the London Advisory Committee of Western Mining Corporation. He stepped down due to pressures of work in 1935 and Robert Annan took his place. Western Mining Corporation's early areas of focus included gold properties at Norseman, Mount Magnet, Southern Cross and Kalgoorlie. By 1935 the company was acting as general manager for Gold Mines of Kalgoorlie, Triton Gold Mines, Central Norseman Gold Corporation and Central Yellowdine Gold Mine.[3] To manage the financing of the two companies, Gold Exploration and Finance Company of Australia was incorporated on 21 June 1934, which in turn had a controlling interest in Western Mining Corporation. New Consolidated Gold Fields had an initial 22 per cent shareholding in this company, with both Agnew and Annan serving as directors. Agnew assumed the chairmanship of the board at Gold Exploration and Finance Company's fourth board meeting, on 15 August 1934. His son, Dolph, attended at least one board meeting as his alternate.[4]

3   Western Mining Corporation, 'Balance Sheet at 31st March, 1934 and Reports for the Period Ended 31st March 1934', UMA, Stock Exchange of Melbourne, 1968.0018, Box 343.
4   'Minutes of Fourth Meeting of the Board of Directors of Gold Exploration and Finance Company of Australia Limited, 15 August 1934'; 'Minutes of Eighth Meeting of the Board of Directors of Gold Exploration and Finance Company of Australia Limited, 8 November 1934', UMA, Western Mining Corporation, 2012.0015, Unit 215.

4. BROADER ASSOCIATIONS

Figures 17 and 18. Father and son engineers: John A Agnew, chairman of The Consolidated Gold Fields of South Africa and influential in the company's early investments in Western Australia and New Guinea, and Dolph Agnew, chairman of Gold Fields Australian Development Company.
Source: Image of John Agnew reproduced from Consolidated Gold Fields of South Africa, The Gold Fields 1887–1937.
Source: Image of Dolph Agnew courtesy of Delia Buchan.

Annan also served as a director, as well as being on the board of Gold Mines of Kalgoorlie, a company that was floated by Gold Exploration and Finance Company in October 1934.[5] Apart from its controlling interest in Western Mining Corporation (94 per cent) and Gold Mines of Kalgoorlie, Gold Exploration and Finance Company had shareholdings in a range of other mines while Agnew was on the board.[6] The association with Gold Fields was of importance to the future plans of this Collins House–sponsored group of companies. Colin Fraser, the chairman of Western Mining Corporation, in his address to the 1934 annual general meeting, referred to the assistance provided 'particularly by our friends connected

---

5   Gold Mines of Australia and Gold Mines of Kalgoorlie, National Library of Australia, MS 10353—Western Mining Corporation Online History Collection/Series 4/Subseries 4.02/Items 4.02.038 and 4.02.039. It is noteworthy that in a Western Mining Corporation publication, both John Agnew and Robert Annan are listed, given their roles as directors of Consolidated Gold Fields of South Africa on Western Mining Corporation–related companies (Ralph, *Biographical Sketches of Some Former WMC People*).
6   These included the Champagne Syndicate, Costerfield Gold-Antimony mine, Victoria Deep Leads, Nell Gwynne (BML) Mine, Bendigo Mine, Triton Gold Mine and Western Gold Mine (Gold Exploration and Finance Company of Australia Limited, 'Reports and Statements of Accounts for the Period 23rd July 1934 (the date of incorporation) to 31st March, 1935', UMA, Stock Exchange of Melbourne, 1968.0018, Box 98; see also 'Minutes of Meetings of Directors of Gold Exploration and Finance Company of Australia', UMA, Western Mining Corporation 2012.0015, Unit 215).

with the management of Lake View and Star and Wiluna, the Goldfields Australian Development Co'.[7] In the case of Gold Mines of Kalgoorlie, Lake View and Star provided exploration and technical resources, while a mill on the company's Associated leases was made available for use by Gold Mines of Kalgoorlie for treating oxidised and semi-oxidised ores. Ore bodies close to those of Gold Mines of Kalgoorlie also presented the opportunity for joint development by the various interests.[8]

Gold Fields had established itself in an extraordinary position in relation to a number of companies that had the capability to identify mining prospects across Australia. Its connections, both in London and Australia, were second to none. It had established relations with the foremost mining and businessmen in Australia, with Sir Colin Fraser and Sir Walter Massy-Greene serving as the Australian advisory committee of Gold Exploration and Finance Company.[9] This company, according to Clark, was applying two main methods to Australian gold exploration: aerial photographic surveys and a focus on the evaluation of Precambrian geology.[10] Even here, Gold Fields was influential, with Annan and Agnew suggesting the introduction of aerial photographic surveys across the eastern goldfields of Western Australia. This was a technique that New Consolidated Gold Fields had used successfully in its geological evaluation of the Witwatersrand area of South Africa in the early 1930s.[11] Agnew remained an advocate of aerial surveys of mineral depositions throughout his career. While these surveys in Western Australia identified little in terms of mineralisation, the combination of companies remained active in pursuing various mining projects.

While the loose confederation of shared interests and cross shareholdings was a hallmark of the cooperative business approach of the Collins House Group, the model did not prove suitable for Gold Fields. Blainey noted in his research that the big mines of Kalgoorlie were typically directed from

---

7   Western Mining Corporation Limited, 'Report of Proceedings at First Annual Ordinary General Meeting of Shareholders, held on Thursday, the 30th Day of August, 1934', UMA, Stock Exchange of Melbourne, 1968.0018, Box 343.
8   Gold Mines of Kalgoorlie Limited, 'Reports and Statements of Accounts for the Period 29th October 1934 (date of incorporation) to 31st March 1935', UMA, Stock Exchange of Melbourne, 1968.0018, Box 100.
9   Kennett, 'Fraser, Sir Colin (1875–1944)'; Lloyd, 'Massy-Greene, Sir Walter (1874–1952)'.
10 For a description of the aerial photographic process, which was conducted over an 11-month period using two De Havilland twin-engine aircraft as well as ground geological survey vehicles, see Hernan, *Forgotten Flyer*, pp. 113–125.
11 *West Australian Mining and Commercial Review*, vol. 7, no. 1, 1942, p. 23.

London while the big Broken Hill mines were directed from Melbourne.[12] This may have been one reason why this confederation of interests did not survive. Gold Fields' motivations and those of other shareholders soon began to diverge. The divergence was hastened by the presence of the other South African mining houses. As early as 1934, consideration was given at board level to inviting Johannesburg Consolidated Investment Company to participate in the affairs of the companies. Central Mining and Investment Corporation, the largest gold producer in South Africa, and Union Corporation, were introduced to the consortium by Robinson when he sought to expand the focus of Gold Mines of Australia from eastern Australia to Western Australia. All of these South African groups had interests and operations in areas where Gold Fields operated in South Africa.

Agnew, through his knowledge and that of his mining colleagues in Western Australia, believed that Gold Fields had the best insights into the mineral potential of the state. There was little appetite to share this knowledge with South African competitors nor to do so in a company that had been established to progress interests outside Western Australia. Clark believed Gold Fields' motivation was to confine Gold Mines of Australia's exploration activities to eastern Australia and have the affairs of the company managed from London by Gold Fields itself. Such an approach was consistent with the Gold Fields model and capabilities and would have been viewed as an appropriate arrangement to facilitate the expansion of the interests of the British mining group. That it was not readily agreed to and with calls on capital associated with shareholdings across three companies, the London Gold Fields' board became concerned with how its interests—as opposed to those of competing mining companies in South Africa—were being advanced. In this regard, while Clark believed that 'New Consolidated [Gold Fields] accepted the inclusion of the other partners in Australian exploration', he questioned 'whether they were keen to do so'.[13] When Gold Mines of Australia acquired options for leases at the Norseman field, Western Australia, this was endorsed by Agnew, although on Lindberg's ruling it was rejected. According to Clark:

---

12   Blainey, *The Rise of Broken Hill*, p. 83.
13   Clark, *Built on Gold: Recollections of Western Mining*, p. 23. Clark also addressed this period in an oral interview, National Library of Australia, G Lindesay Clark interview by Alan Hodgart, tape 2, side 2, session 4.

> The ... rejection was to have very serious consequences for the group. It resulted, for a time, in losing all connection with the Norseman field ... New Consolidated, through their interest in Lake View and Star Ltd who operated the largest gold mine in Western Australia, presumably wished to preserve this field of exploration for themselves and not bring it into the general pool. Exclusion from Western Australia was not acceptable to W.S. [Robinson] nor, I imagine, to the other South African partners ... New Consolidated's pressure to keep them from the most extensive area of Precambrian rocks known in the country, and therefore the area with the most potential for major mines, was scarcely a proposition the other partners could accept and a split was ... inevitable.[14]

The divergence of interests was intensified when Gold Fields established its own exploration and investment vehicle, Gold Fields Australian Development Company (GFADC), in 1932, even though this company initially had key members of the WS Robinson group of companies as directors. While this company was focused in large part on the opportunities introduced by Claude Albo de Bernales for the extension of the original Wiluna mine, Gold Fields also had an interest in advancing its own wider exploration and gold mining aspirations in Western Australia and elsewhere in Australia. When Robinson obtained an option on the Occidental Syndicate, which became Triton Gold Mines in the Cue Shire of Western Australia, the conflicting aims of the various groups were brought into sharp relief. New Consolidated Gold Fields gradually severed its relations with the Australian group and its shareholdings in the three companies over the period to 1936. In early 1935 Agnew had resigned as a director of Gold Exploration and Finance Company, 'owing to an ever increasing pressure of business'.[15] He was replaced by Annan as a director. The respect in which Agnew was held was manifest by the warm 'acknowledgement of the Board's indebtedness to Mr. Agnew for the valuable counsel which he had always made so readily available', while Agnew volunteered his continuing 'advice and opinions ... at the disposal of the Directors on any matter'.[16] Annan resigned as a director a year later in February 1936, at which time the involvement of South African mining groups included Central Mining and Investment Corporation, Union Corporation Ltd and Anglo American Corporation of South Africa.

---

14 Clark, *Built on Gold: Recollections of Western Mining*, pp. 23–24.
15 'Minutes of Eleventh Meeting of the Board of Directors of Gold Exploration and Finance Company of Australia Limited, 6 February 1945', UMA, Western Mining Corporation, 2012.0015, Unit 215.
16 ibid.

4. BROADER ASSOCIATIONS

For Clark, the withdrawal of Gold Fields had serious consequences:

> It meant the loss to the Group of the valuable Associated Lease at Kalgoorlie, and that funds for the Bendigo venture were not available from one of the possible major contributors. In the original negotiations for amalgamation to form the Champagne Syndicate it was proposed that the Associated Lease, then the property of Lake View and Star, could be transferred for consideration to the new Kalgoorlie venture … When Gold Mines of Kalgoorlie was formed from the Champagne Syndicate in 1934, New Consolidated withdrew from this proposal and addition of the Associated Lease was refused. This was a great blow to the whole scheme since this lease was by far the most accessible and attractive of the proposed GMK [Gold Mines of Kalgoorlie] titles.[17]

The severing of relations with the expansive mining and secondary processing interests of the Collins House Group of companies may well have also truncated opportunities for New Consolidated Gold Fields, particularly outside Western Australia.

…

GFADC was incorporated and listed on the London Stock Exchange in 1932 with nominal capital of GB£500,000 and GB£285,000 initially issued. Agnew served as the first chairman. Reflecting the then cooperative arrangements with the WS Robinson companies, Lionel Robinson was a director, with Clive Baillieu, a director of Zinc Corporation, as his alternate. GFADC was majority owned by New Consolidated Gold Fields, with Camp Bird as well as Transvaal Agency, in which Frederic Hamilton had an involvement, also having shareholdings.[18] GFADC was

---

17 Clark, *Built on Gold: Recollections of Western Mining*, p. 24. Katzenellenbogen discusses the role of South African mining interests in the Western Australian gold sector. In relation to Consolidated Gold Fields of South Africa, he observed its importance as a source of funding to Gold Mines of Australia and Western Mining Corporation, writing 'it is clear that Consgold's position not only in London, but in American financial circles as well, placed them in a dominant position and severely restricted the possibilities of Robinson to work without them' (Katzenellenbogen, 'Southern African Mining Interests in Australia' pp. 127–128).
18 New Consolidated Gold Fields had taken up a debenture issue by Camp Bird and part of the terms of this arrangement was an agreement to provide Camp Bird with the opportunity to take up 10 per cent of any new business interest by New Consolidated Gold Fields (*The Times*, 15 December 1932). Agnew was responsible for introducing this association, as well as that with Oroville Dredging (to play a role in the New Guinea interests) to Consolidated Gold Fields. Oroville Dredging had been formed in 1909 by FW Baker, who was also involved in the formation of Camp Bird, to acquire the share capital of an American company operating dredges in California and to acquire properties in Colombia (Cartwright, *Gold Paved the Way*, p. 126; *The Mining Magazine*, vol. XXVII, no. 1, July 1922, p. 63).

designed to act as a vehicle for investments in a range of Western Australian gold mines. Principally, though, it was formed to take a shareholding in Moonlight Wiluna Gold Mines, Starlight Gold Mines and Horseshoe Wiluna Gold Mines, comprising leases at the northern end of the field held by Wiluna Gold Mines. Dolph Agnew took charge of the Wiluna mine and the evaluation of the nearby Moonlight Wiluna leases, as well as other mining opportunities following the establishment of GFADC.

The initial focus was on development of the Moonlight Wiluna mine. In 1937, the entire capital of GFADC was called up to take an investment in Yellowdine Investments, which in turn owned 93 per cent of the de Bernales's Yellowdine Gold Development gold mine, near Mount Palmer, west of Kalgoorlie.[19] In 1938, an interest was acquired in the Kintore Mine at Kunanalling, while options over other deposits in the Coolgardie area, including Spargo's Reward Gold Mine (1935), and Comet gold mine, near Marble Bar, were acquired. The option over the Spargo leases at Coolgardie was terminated in 1937 as an expected extension to the ore body could not be identified.[20]

While Lake View and Star, Wiluna and GFADC operated as separate entities, they had common directors, cross shareholdings and developed joint interests in other gold mining prospects. One observer in 1937 remarked on the 'labyrinth of interlocking interests' when referring to the Yellowdine mine, while Moonlight Wiluna had an interest in the Mount Ida Gold Mine and operated this mine, as well as a one-third interest in Porphyry (1939) Gold Mine.[21] Interests were also held in some of these mines by Wiluna and Lake View and Star.[22]

---

19 *Western Argus*, 28 May 1935; *The Advertiser*, 25 September 1935; *Sunday Times*, 19 July 1938; *Sunday Times*, 9 June 1940. According to the July 1938 *Sunday Times* article, a de Bernales's associated company, Commonwealth Mining and Finance, held a 46 per cent interest in the Yellowdine mine.
20 Spargo's Reward Gold Mine (1935) No Liability, 'Reports and Statement of Accounts, for the Period 8th April 1936, to 30th June 1937 and Notice of Annual General Meeting', UMA, Stock Exchange of Melbourne, 1968.0018, Box 259. Again, in 1948 the company tried to grant an option to London mining interests to purchase the mine. This could not be executed due to the 'adverse conditions generally affecting goldmining in Australia'. By this stage the 'finances of the company [were] in a very precarious position' and unless there was a substantial rise in the price of gold 'it may be necessary to consider liquidation of the company'. The company was removed from the official list in 1953, unable to pay its listing fee for that year. It subsequently disposed of its mining equipment (Spargo's Reward Gold Mine (1935) No Liability, *The Annual Report of Directors, for the Period Ended 30th June, 1948*, p. 1, UMA, Stock Exchange of Melbourne, 1968.0018, Box 259).
21 *The Sydney Morning Herald*, 31 July 1937.
22 Wiluna Gold Corporation, Limited, 'Directors' Report and Statement of Accounts for the Year Ended 31st March, 1949', UMA, Stock Exchange of Melbourne, 1968.0018, Box 353.

The decline in the contribution from Wiluna and the short mine life of Moonlight Wiluna led to the consideration of acquiring new mining properties. The chairman of GFADC observed at the 1940 annual general meeting that 'the search for other properties was being prosecuted vigorously' with the most promising being Mount Ida, over which an option had been taken in 1940.[23] Wiluna, in conjunction with GFADC, also held an option to acquire the Mount Charlotte (Kalgoorlie) Gold Mines. The original two-year option was struck in 1941, which allowed Wiluna to take possession of the Mount Charlotte and Hannan's Hill mines and undertake evaluative work. The outbreak of World War II led the option to be extended, while mining operations at Mount Charlotte were suspended. By 1947, Wiluna recommenced work on evaluation of the mine and extended its option to the end of 1950.

...

In the period after World War II, the environment for gold mining in Western Australia remained influenced by shortages of labour, rising costs and a fixed gold price, all of which created operational and financial impediments for existing mines and curtailed new investment. Limited Commonwealth Government funding aided some of the larger mines, but support was not available for smaller, more marginal mines. For Gold Fields, Lake View and Star continued to operate profitably as the 'premier mine' in the state but at Wiluna, and in the case of GFADC, there was the challenge of declining ore bodies and the need to replace these with new operations.[24] In the latter part of 1947, the re-treatment of accumulated residues from Moonlight Wiluna and Wiluna commenced.

In 1948, Dolph Agnew, while in London, was appointed chairman of GFADC, while also serving as a director of Lake View and Star. He returned to Australia in February 1949 and also assumed the general management role of Mount Ida Gold Mine, which began operations in 1951. While it contributed financially, it had a low level of gold production and small reserves. In 1950, Agnew succeeded Joseph Thorn as general manager of Lake View and Star. He served as vice-president and president of the Chamber of Mines of Western Australia in Perth and Kalgoorlie, and as president of the Australasian Institute of Mining and Metallurgy. He was influential in establishing the Gold Producers' Association and

---

23 *Chemical Engineering and Mining Review*, 10 July 1940, p. 389.
24 Government of Western Australia, *Report of the Department of Mines for the Year 1948*, p. 17.

the establishment of the Kalgoorlie and Boulder Mines Medical Fund and welfare scheme.[25] Agnew became an advocate for Gold Fields' interests in Australia and, more broadly, the development of the mining sector in Western Australia. His entreaties to both the Commonwealth Government and state government urged them to do more for the gold sector as it struggled, particularly in the late 1940s as it emerged from the exigencies of the war.[26]

In the 1948 financial year, Wiluna Gold Corporation recorded another loss, while GFADC had accumulated losses that continued through the 1950s, despite generating modest profits in some years. In 1948 Lake George Mines in Australia was converted to a public company, but also experienced the immediate post-war challenges of labour supply, shortage of materials and increasing costs. Development work occurred at Mount Charlotte during 1947 with the shaft enlarged and construction of infrastructure. However, by 1948 the results of the development program were considered disappointing and further expenditure on surface equipment was curtailed.[27] The option lapsed in 1948, as the mine was assessed as 'unworkable' due to the low grade of ore.[28] A one-third interest in Porphyry (1939) Gold Mine was exercised in 1947 but owing to shortages of labour and scarcity of supplies only a limited amount of work was carried out. In November 1947 underground work was suspended in order to concentrate on the erection of an additional plant. During the 1950s the operation was retained on a care and maintenance basis.

GFADC retained its interest in Moonlight Wiluna and Mount Ida and undertook evaluation of other opportunities, which extended to tin mining in Malaya, but it failed to replenish its portfolio with any material new business interests.[29] Mount Ida remained the only operating mining

---

25   *West Australian Mining and Commercial Review*, vol. 8, no. 1, March 1943, p.14 and vol. 10, no. 9, November 1945.
26   Gold Fields Australian Development Company Limited, 'Report of the Proceedings at the Sixteenth Annual General Meeting of the Company Held at Winchester House, London, E.C., 2 on Wednesday, 10th August, 1949', UMA, Stock Exchange of Melbourne, 1968.0018, Box 99.
27   *Chemical Engineering and Mining Review*, 10 December 1948, p. 193.
28   Mount Charlotte (Kalgoorlie) Gold Mines Limited, 'To the Members, 1st December 1941' and 'Report of Directors and Statement of Accounts at 31st August, 1948', UMA, Stock Exchange of Melbourne, 1968.0018, Box 181; Gold Fields Australian Development Company Limited, 'Report to the Directors and Accounts for the Year Ended 31st December 1948', UMA, Stock Exchange of Melbourne, 1968.0018, Box 99. In 1955 Mount Charlotte was sold to the Champagne Syndicate, a subsidiary of Western Mining Corporation (Mount Ida Gold Mines Limited, 'Progress Report for the Period to May 31st, 1938', UMA, Stock Exchange of Melbourne, 1968.0018, Box 184).
29   *Chemical Engineering and Mining Review*, 10 May 1949, p. 304.

venture for GFADC. Expansion activities were undertaken, with the relocation of equipment from the Moonlight Wiluna mine. The mine exploited the richer Timoni leases and operated through the 1950s, generating modest profits, sufficient to extinguish the accumulated losses of GFADC.[30] In 1956, the results of underground development work at Mount Ida were deemed disappointing with 'little or no prospect of the mine extending beyond present known limits' and, as such, dependent on drawing down the existing limited reserves.[31] It continued in operation until 1960. Only Lake View and Star remained a profitable mining operation for Gold Fields, retaining its position as the largest gold producer in Western Australia.

In 1956, New Consolidated Gold Fields (Australasia) (NCGFA) was formed, with authorised capital of A£1 million with the purpose to undertake exploration activities in Australia, bring projects into production and invest in existing properties.[32] This was at the time that Mount Ida's reserves were expected to be soon depleted. This entity was in turn fully owned by New Consolidated Gold Fields, the company set up in 1919 to oversee the group's interests outside South Africa. Frank R Beggs was appointed manager and pursued a limited number of ventures, all unsuccessful.[33] In the period immediately prior to 1960, the prospects for NCGFA were not bright. In 1958 Beggs had identified exploration prospects at Broken Hill and at Mount Isa. A Gold Fields American Development Company representative visited Australia to review each of these. The Mount Isa prospect was further evaluated; it turned out to be an unsuccessful investment and the Broken Hill opportunity also did not amount to anything.

---

30 *Kalgoorlie News*, 21 September 1949; *The West Australian*, 8 July 1954.
31 *Chemical Engineering and Mining Review*, 11 June 1956, p. 291.
32 'Press Announcement Being Released in London on the 9th August 1956', UMA, Stock Exchange of Melbourne, 1968.0018, Box 206. In 1960, Gold Fields American Development Company, a subsidiary of New Consolidated Gold Fields, initially held the Australian interests before it changed its name to Gold Fields Mining & Industrial Limited on 5 September 1960. Gold Fields Mining & Industrial's two Australian subsidiaries included Gold Fields Australian Development Company Limited (65.5 per cent), incorporated on 5 November 1932, which in turn owned the entire share capital of Moonlight Wiluna Gold Mines (Australia), incorporated on 12 October 1931 and that operated the Mount Ida Gold Mine, comprising 11 gold mining leases; and New Consolidated Gold Fields (Australasia) Pty Limited, incorporated 22 August 1956. The Australian-listed companies in which share investments were held were Mining Corporation (Aust) No Liability, Lake George Mining Corporation Limited, and Lake View and Star Limited. Gold Fields Mining & Industrial subscribed A£1,750,000 or GB£1,400,000 in Commonwealth Mining Investments (representing a 54 per cent interest) and on 29 September 1960 purchased 5,000 North Broken Hill shares (Gold Fields Mining & Industrial Limited, 16 September 1960, Renison Goldfields Consolidated Archives (RGCA), Box 12300).
33 See Appendix 3 for a biographical profile of Frank Beggs.

NCGFA invested in Mining Corporation (Australia), listed in 1955, as a way of expanding its exploration interests, in this case for base metals, cobalt and uranium. Two of the initial directors of Mining Corporation were Tom Owen and Ken Craig, individuals who would play a role in the affairs of Consolidated Gold Fields Australia (CGFA) after 1960. Owen was well known to Gold Fields through his involvement with Lake George, serving as operations manager and then chairman. He became an initial director of CGFA while Craig was one of the founders and an initial director of Western Titanium, a company that CGFA acquired in 1969.

In June 1956 the shareholders of Mining Corporation were advised by circular that a drill hole had passed through dolomitic country mineralised with copper. The managing director of the company considered the strike 'so important' to the company that he left for the field 'to examine the position'.[34] Two months later, shareholders of the company were advised that 'offers have been received from important overseas mining groups for a substantial interest in the Company'.[35] By 1957, NCGFA and Pan-American Ventures, a Canadian company, had acquired 47 per cent of the shares of Mining Corporation and appointed two directors, one of whom was Beggs. The company was testing possible southern lateral extensions to the Mount Isa Mine's deposit and conducting other exploration activities, exploring for cobalt, as well as for uranium in Queensland. The new shareholders called an extraordinary general meeting in April 1959 for the purpose of replacing two of the original directors. The non–Gold Fields and Pan-American directors wrote to shareholders expressing concern that 'technical and administrative control' may be assumed by 'two overseas companies' and, in doing so, derail the work being undertaken on the 'brilliant concept on which all our work on Mt Isa is based'.[36]

Beggs conveyed in a letter to a colleague that at 'Mount Isa we have plugged along, watching our cash being thrown down the drain until, finally ... [we] made an agreement ... [to] jointly take control'.[37] The other directors

---

34 Mining Corporation (Australia) No Liability, 'Circular to Shareholders, 18th June 1956', UMA, Stock Exchange of Melbourne, 1968.0018, Box 174.
35 'Memo for the Press, Note for Insertion as an Advertisement, 14th August 1956', UMA, Stock Exchange of Melbourne, 1968.0018, Box 174.
36 Mining Corporation (Australia) No Liability, 'Incorporated in May 1955' and 'To The Shareholders, Mining Corporation (Aust.) No Liability, 3rd April 1959', UMA, JB Were and Son, 2000.0017, Box 666.
37 Letter from Frank R Beggs to Robert T Playter c/- The Gold Fields American Development Company (New York), 27 April 1959, RGCA, 1430, Box 12300.

had planned to issue themselves with sufficient shares to attempt to retain control of the company. Beggs had foreseen this possibility and obtained a Supreme Court injunction to prevent this. His recollection was that:

> We attended a Board Meeting and the opposition were terribly cocky and brought on their motion to issue these shares with broad grins spread all over their faces. Immediately they moved the motion we served the injunctions and I have never seen so many smug grins be so quickly wiped off so many faces. But the extraordinary reaction was that we became the world's biggest … because we had anticipated that they would do just that.[38]

The change in board composition occurred. Beggs assumed the chairmanship with the addition of another director, mining engineer Keith Addison Cameron, who would be highly influential in the events of CGFA, including as an initial director of the company in 1960.[39] It was decided to drill two additional holes, with NCGFA advancing the funds. The results were disappointing, and Beggs advised in 1960 that any additional exploration expenditure 'would be of a speculative' nature and not in shareholders' best interests.[40] Other exploration prospects for Gold Fields in Australia in the late 1950s had also been unproductive. As Beggs wrote forlornly to a colleague in New York:

> We are still chasing madly around the country looking at 'mountains of tin' and 'mountains of lead' and 'huge deposits' of just about every kind of mineral there is, and it never ceases to amaze me how these 'huge deposits' shrink to a 6in [6 inch] leader when they are examined. I have never quite been able to make up my mind as to whether the prospectors really think they have a 'mountain' or whether they just build it up in the hope of finding a sucker.[41]

In 1962, SL (Sidney) Segal, the finance director of CGFA, was appointed chairman of Mining Corporation in place of Beggs. Shareholders' funds had been exhausted and loans of A£28,000 had been incurred,

---

38 ibid., emphasis in original.
39 See Appendix 3 for a biographical profile of Keith Cameron.
40 Beggs called upon Professor KC Dunham of Durham University to report on the company's geological prospects. Durham was later used by CGFA in other capacities, including technical advice on the Mount Goldsworthy iron ore area for Gerald Mortimer (Mining Corporation (Australia) No Liability, *Annual Report for the Year Ended 30th June, 1960*, UMA, JB Were and Son, 2000.0017, Box 666).
41 Letter from Frank R Beggs to Robert F Playter c/- The Gold Fields American Development Company (New York), 27 April 1959, p. 3, RGCA, 1430, Box 12300.

predominantly from CGFA. Segal advised shareholders that a company that had been granted an option to acquire Mining Corporation's Mount Isa leases had been released from its option. The leases were subsequently sold to Mount Isa Mines in exchange for shares. Even with the sale of these shares, the company's liabilities could not be extinguished and Segal advised shareholders that the company had 'come to the end of the road' and was placed into voluntary administration.[42]

The mining interests of Gold Fields in Australia were in decline. By 1960, Mount Ida had ceased, Lake George was near the end of its economic life and Lake View and Star, aided by the withdrawal of the British tax on foreign entities, continued to contribute dividends to the London parent through to 1970. Dolph Agnew died in July 1960. NCGFA was also not successful. As a consequence, Gold Fields in Australia was unable to recruit experienced mining men to join its ranks and provide a technical base to identify, develop and manage mining ventures.[43]

---

42   Mining Corporation (Australia) No Liability, *Annual Report for the Year Ended 30th June, 1962*, UMA, JB Were and Son, 2000.0017, Box 666.
43   An appointment of note made in 1957 was research engineer DF (Douglas) Ainge, formerly of Burma Mining Corporation.

5

LAKE GEORGE AND NEW GUINEA

Through the activities of companies associated with The Consolidated Gold Fields of South Africa, including a number in which John Agnew was involved flowing from his association with Herbert Hoover, participation was secured in a lead–zinc mine in New South Wales. The Lake George mine was located at Captains Flat, 45 kilometres south-east of Canberra in the Australian Capital Territory and 35 kilometres from the town of Bungendore in New South Wales, from where a railway connection was established in 1939. The deposit was first worked for gold from 1882, with the oxidised ore discovered to be underlain by copper-bearing ore. In 1885 blast furnace treatment was introduced and the deposit was worked by two companies until they amalgamated in 1894 as Lake George United Mining and Smelting Company, reconstructed in 1896 as Lake George Mines.[1] Mining was undertaken for copper, lead, silver and gold from 1889 to 1899 when the mine was closed.

The redevelopment of Lake George in the 1920s and 1930s was the result of the interaction of a number of the companies established in London, some with connections to Hoover and several in which Agnew played a direct role. The mine came to the attention of a group of London mining engineers and financing companies. It was recognised as a large sulphide deposit of lead and zinc, with a high proportion of pyrite suitable for the production of sulphuric acid and, in turn, superphosphate. Within Australia, Lake George was viewed as the largest-known lead and zinc

---

1   *Chemical Engineering and Mining Review*, 5 February 1927, p. 179.

deposit apart from those at Broken Hill.[2] The interest came at a time when the United Kingdom Government, after its experiences in World War I, felt a need to assemble technical and financial interests to promote and have access to large base-metals deposits. The challenge of processing complex ores was being tackled at a variety of deposits, not least in Australia, with advances in flotation techniques providing greater confidence that sulphide deposits at depth could be brought into production and be profitable.

In 1925, a London organisation, National Metal & Chemical Bank, which had been formed in 1918 by an Australian-born banker, Richard Tilden Smith, entered into a contract with Australian mining engineer Leslie Vickery Waterhouse to report upon the mining properties at Lake George. National Metal & Chemical Bank had an interest in acquiring an involvement in iron ore, coal and non-ferrous metal opportunities, with a specific interest in sulphuric acid and the potential to manufacture superphosphate.[3] Tilden Smith had an association with Hoover and his investments, including The Burma Corporation, where he was a joint shareholder and director.

The work undertaken by Waterhouse at the abandoned Lake George mine involved dewatering and removing blockages in shafts as well as repairing and replacing equipment. The expenditure was overseen by a local representative, Sir Robert McCheyne Anderson, the grandfather of a future managing director of Renison Goldfields Consolidated in the second half of the 1980s.[4] National Metal & Chemical Bank granted an option to another London-based company, National Mining Corporation, to undertake further development work. National Mining Corporation had been established in 1919 as a consortium of United Kingdom mining houses to overcome perceived deficiencies in coordinating capital for the development of base-metal and other mines. The corporation invested broadly in companies, including those that had been associated with Hoover and Agnew, such as Burma Corporation, Santa Gertrudis, Camp Bird and Mexican Corporation. Each of these companies had interests in mining operations that could benefit from the advancement of technology to treat complex ores. On the National Mining Corporation

---

2   *The Times*, 26 January 1938.
3   *The Times*, 16 July 1918.
4   Campbell McCheyne Anderson, who was managing director and chief executive officer of Renison Goldfields Consolidated, 1985–1993.

board Agnew served as both a director and member of the technical committee, responsible for examining the many operations considered for investment. Burma Corporation, an associated company, was involved in the development of a small experimental plant in England to test the complex ores of the Burma mining operation. Zinc Corporation, of which Govett was chairman, had an involvement in this work for its Broken Hill mine and was a major shareholder in Burma Corporation.

Mining at Lake George recommenced in 1926 when National Mining Corporation took up a sublease from National Metal & Chemical Bank. According to Tilden Smith, writing from London, National Mining Corporation was described as a 'very powerful' company, taking over development of the mine from August 1926, with this company also having an association with Camp Bird.[5] A diamond drilling campaign opened up new drives and extended existing ones. An experienced mining engineer, FL Thomas, was sent to the mine on behalf of National Mining Corporation to continue development work, as well as evaluate the reserves of the deposit. In 1926 samples of the sulphide ores containing, lead, zinc, copper and small amounts of silver and gold were sent to England for evaluation. The complex and lower-grade nature of the ore and the depressed state of the metals market led Tilden Smith to observe in 1927 that 'it is absolutely impossible to induce anybody to install a Plant upon the Lake George Leases under conditions anything like so favourable as the sub-lease which I am in a position to secure from the National Mining Corporation Ltd'.[6]

Camp Bird also retained an option on a sublease that it exercised in 1927. As such, both National Mining Corporation and Camp Bird were committed to advancing the technical evaluation of the Lake George ore body. In 1927 the New South Wales chief inspector of mines was invited to report upon the mine's potential, as a precursor to the London investors seeking New South Wales Government support for a railway connection between Bungendore and the mine site.[7] In 1929, a cooperative business arrangement occurred between Camp Bird and New Consolidated Gold Fields, with Gold Fields gaining representation, through Agnew, on the Camp Bird board. Agnew had been associated with Camp Bird as early as

---

5 Letter from R Tilden Smith to Sir Robert McC Anderson, 29 July 1926, Butlin Archives, The Australian National University (ANU), Box 67, Folder 2.
6 Letter from R Tilden Smith, Adelaide House, London to Sir Robert McC Anderson, 5 October 1927, Butlin Archives, ANU, Box 67, Folder 2.
7 *Chemical Engineering and Mining Review*, 5 February 1927, p. 179.

1914 when Hoover, who was chairman, appointed him to the technical committee of the company.[8] In turn, New Consolidated Gold Fields offered Camp Bird the opportunity to become involved in any ventures it identified.[9] The offices of Camp Bird and its interests in Santa Gertrudis, Mexican Corporation, the London committee of the Fresnillo Company and Lake George Metal Corporation were registered at Gold Fields' offices at 49 Moorgate. By this stage Camp Bird held a 75 per cent interest in Lake George Metal Corporation.

A report on the operation observed that the development at Lake George envisaged a plant at the mine that would represent 'the most modern structure in the southern hemisphere', while Thomas's drilling and development efforts had resulted in 3,000 to 4,000 feet of drives being opened, with the potential that reserves could exceed 1 million tons of lead, zinc, copper and silver, with iron as sulphide ore planned to be used for the manufacture of superphosphate. The attraction of the Lake George mine was its large ore reserves of lead and zinc, with the zinc content being of a high quality. It was considered second only to that of Mount Isa in terms of its lead content, while the high pyritic content of the deposit was viewed as a major source of sulphur production, capable of being made into sulphuric acid for the production of superphosphate and with sufficient feedstock for a superphosphate production level to exceed the entire consumption in New South Wales.[10] Metallurgical research work continued in England. The major drawback to the commencement of operations, apart from market conditions, was that unless a railway connection was built the cost of transport would be prohibitive.[11]

---

8   Nash, *The Life of Herbert Hoover*, p. 567.
9   Camp Bird invested broadly and held interests in Santa Gertrudis, Chemical and Metallurgical Corporation, Durango Timber Corporation, Lena Goldfields Notes, Mexican Corporation, Fresnillo Company, Talbot Alluvials, Gold Fields Australian Development Company, as well as Lake George (Chemical Engineering and Mining Review, *Mining Handbook of Australia, 1939*, p. 106; *The Times*, 4 September 1929, 15 November 1912, 21 December 1926).
10 *Chemical Engineering and Mining Review*, 5 May 1928, p. 230; *The Australian*, 14 January 1939. *The Argus* in 1897 in a special report compared the Lake George deposit with that of Mount Lyell near Queenstown in Tasmania, with both viewed as 'immense deposits of mixed metals'. In relation to Lake George, the report noted: 'it is safe to say that few mines have such immense reserves of ore, fewer still have the lode so well opened up', with the view that 'the venture is certain to be a success, its probabilities are very great, and its possibilities stupendous' (*The Argus*, 20 July 1897, p. 7).
11 *Chemical Engineering and Mining Review*, 5 April 1928.

Through Agnew's network of contacts and the companies associated with National Mining Corporation, a range of specialist personnel were deployed to Lake George to evaluate the deposit and the complex process required for the separation of metals from the pyritic ores. Hugh Rose, a mining engineer associated with Santa Gertrudis, as well as Thomas Childery Baker, travelled to Captains Flat for the planning of mining and milling activities, including overseeing the construction of a pilot plant.[12] Baker, an American who was associated with Mexican Corporation, which operated a mine that had to contend with similar issues related to the treatment of sulphide ores, was responsible for the mine's commencement. He became managing director and chairman of the local company.[13]

Sibley B McCluskey, a metallurgical engineer who had consulted to Fresnillo, yet another company in which Gold Fields had a shareholding, was also sent to Lake George while Tom Owen, who had worked on flotation techniques at the Broken Hill mines, was appointed mine manager. Under Owen's supervision, experimental work on the processing of the sulphide ore was undertaken.[14] Arnold Harris, the mill superintendent at Wiluna, was responsible for ordering the flotation plant at Lake George, while a fellow American, Herbert C Wilkins, who had worked as underground manager at Wiluna, became underground mine superintendent. Yet another American, Charles Prior, the general manager of Wiluna, assisted in the introduction of battery-powered locomotives for underground ore transportation. It was a formidable array of technical experience for the development of what was a complex ore body. The operation of the pilot plant provided 'highly satisfactory recovery of lead and zinc'.[15] According to one contemporary observer, the mine's plant would involve expenditure of £400,000 and was expected to be 'the last word in mining and milling'.[16]

---

12 *Chemical Engineering and Mining Review*, 5 November 1929, p. 42.
13 The Consolidated Gold Fields of South Africa Limited, 'Report of the Directors and Statement of Accounts, 30th June 1926', University of Melbourne Archives (UMA), Stock Exchange of Melbourne, 1968.0018, Box 67.
14 Reynolds, 'Lake George Mines', p. 342. See also State Library of New South Wales, Captains Flat (Lake George) Mine Records, Accession Code 9607575.
15 *The Sydney Morning Herald*, 26 January 1931.
16 *Chemical Engineering and Mining Review*, 5 May 1928, p. 230.

By 1929 the estimate of ore reserves had increased to be in excess of 2 million tons with the main lode in a channel of 5,000 feet in length and with three main ore shoots expected to 'show persistence in depth both in tenor and width'.[17] Lake George Metal Corporation was incorporated in 1929 and had as its registered office that of New Consolidated Gold Fields at 49 Moorgate, London. Robert Annan, later to be chairman of Gold Fields, was one of the directors. The shareholders included New Consolidated Gold Fields and The Gold Fields American Development Company. In 1931 Lake George Metal Corporation had the assets of Lake George Mining transferred to the London corporation, with a value of A£748,499 placed on the assets and equipment of Lake George.[18]

Owen, as the manager of Lake George Mines, was well known to Agnew for his technical expertise. Owen worked assiduously during the period from 1924 through to the early 1930s on the metallurgical challenges associated with the Lake George ore body, with separation issues to the forefront. In this regard, he called on the technical expertise not only of his own colleagues within the Gold Fields group but also that of Sir Herbert William Gepp. Gepp, at the time working as a public servant in the Prime Minister's Department, was a noted mining metallurgist with a long career with the Collins House Group companies, including as general manager of Electrolytic Zinc Company of Australasia.[19] The services of the Council for Scientific and Industrial Research were also used to examine the complex ore body of Lake George.[20]

Market conditions, based on the prevailing price of lead and zinc, meant that the mine remained closed during the early 1930s, with experimental work, including a pilot plant, focusing on the recovery of the pyritic concentrate. Owen made approaches to Broken Hill Associated Smelters regarding the purchase of lead concentrate from Lake George. The oversupply of material from its own mines at Broken Hill meant there was not a ready market for Lake George lead concentrate.[21] In this context, Gold Fields in London was not prepared to fund the

---

17 'Santa Gertrudis Co, Ltd', *The Mining World*, 12 December 1931; Camp Bird, Limited, 'Directors' Report and Statement of Accounts to 30th June 1928', Butlin Archives, ANU, 67/12.
18 Letter from SC Leaman, Secretary of Lake George Metal Corporation to the Secretary of Lake George Mines Ltd, 15 January 1931, Butlin Archives, ANU, 67, 205–210.
19 Kennedy, 'Gepp, Sir Herbert William (Bert) (1877–1954)'.
20 Letter from G Lightfoot, Secretary, Council for Scientific and Industrial Research to HW Gepp, Development Branch, Prime Minister's Department, 19 August 1930, National Archives of Australia (NAA), A786,064/7.
21 Letter from Colin Fraser to TM Owen, 26 February 1932, Butlin Archives, ANU, 67/171.

start of mining operations. Owen was drawn into assisting New Consolidated Gold Fields with its other mining ventures in Australia in the early 1930s, particularly at Wiluna, where he spent an extended period undertaking detailed technical analysis of the treatment plant, in particular the appropriate flotation process for the refractory ores, while work also continued on the recovery of elemental sulphur from pyrite, which comprised 32 per cent of the Lake George ore.[22] For a period, Owen also assisted Oroville Dredging with its aerial survey work in New Guinea, reflecting the interconnections of the companies and personnel in which Gold Fields had interests.[23] Work in assisting the other group companies in Australia also included the Lake George metallurgist, Sibley McCluskey. He spent time at Wiluna assisting the mine manager, Herbert Vail, in the design of the flotation section of the Wiluna mine, as well as that at Lake View and Star.[24] This experience proved invaluable in the flotation experimentation conducted at Lake George.

In 1934, FW Baker, chairman of the London company, visited New South Wales to discuss matters relating to the resumption of mining operations, including holding discussions with the New South Wales Government about a railway connection between the mine and Bungendore.[25] In 1937, Lake George Mining Corporation was formed, taking over the shares of Lake George Metal Corporation, which had been placed into liquidation. Discussions occurred with the New South Wales Government for the construction of a railway link. The New South Wales Government agreed to support the construction of the railway line and in return Lake George Mining Corporation agreed to spend A£600,000 on equipping the property, storage and loading facilities at Port Kembla, and construction of a transmission line and loading facilities at Bungendore.[26] In 1937, with higher metal prices, steps were taken to begin mining operations and contracts were placed for mining equipment.

---

22   *Chemical Engineering and Mining Review*, 8 June 1936, pp. 320–321.
23   *Chemical Engineering and Mining Review*, 8 May 1935, p. 287.
24   Letter from HE Vail to L Thomas Esq, Lake George Mine, 10 September 1929, Butlin Archives, ANU 67/12; Mainwaring, *Riches Beneath the Flat*, pp. 19, 21, 24.
25   Lake George Mining Corporation Limited, 'Report for the Directors, 31st December, 1934', Butlin Archives, ANU, 67/12. Baker was also the chairman of Camp Bird and Santa Gertrudis.
26   *Chemical Engineering and Mining Review*, 15 December 1937, p. 91.

Mining operations commenced in 1937 and milling in January 1939. A£676,000 had been invested in plant and equipment to enable the mine to open, with electrical power generated by a transmission line from the Burrinjuck hydro-electric scheme, shafts sunk and commencement of construction of housing in the nearby township of Captains Flat. The operation gained from the input of Harris, who had worked as a superintendent of the Wiluna gold mine, while the extensive technical resources of various arms of the Gold Fields group had been drawn upon. New Consolidated Gold Fields provided the technical support of its mechanical engineering department. Gold Fields American Development Company assisted, including for the purchase of mining and processing equipment, while Consolidated Gold Fields of South Africa provided input in relation to drilling and reserve evaluation.[27]

Mining was conducted at Lake George during its economic life from 1937 to 1962. The treatment plant incorporated crushing, grinding and flotation, utilising four separate sections for copper, lead, zinc and pyrite. Concentrate was sent by rail to Port Kembla from Bungendore. The mine produced zinc and lead, with smaller quantities of copper, silver and gold, and sulphur from the pyritic ores. In the 1950s the workforce stood at over 500 employees and the company had established housing to attract employees, including 180 homes as well as quarters for single men. The Captains Flat township, located in the valley below the mine, experienced a resurgence with the mine's recommencement. The company supported sporting and cultural activities, and purchased the local theatre and later redeveloped it, installing one of the first cinemascope screens outside Sydney. The township had other facilities including a bank, post office, hospital, police station and courthouse.

After the long gestation before operations began, the mine experienced numerous problems in its initial years. During its first two years the operation was adversely affected by an extended strike at a smelting customer in the United States, the scarcity of shipping and higher freight and insurance costs. In the year to 30 June 1940 an operating loss of GB£72,523 was recorded, with a smaller loss the following year. The first

---

27   The Lake George archival material held at the Butlin Archives, ANU, contains a voluminous collection of technical correspondence from 1938 to 1961 reflecting the breadth and extent of the technical assistance provided by member companies of the Gold Fields group.

annual profit was recorded in 1942.²⁸ As the company's operational issues were being addressed it was faced 'with a new set of problems … beyond its control'—not least the onset of World War II.²⁹

The war imposed challenges related mainly to the availability of labour and the cost of obtaining shipping and war insurance, as well as the limited market for lead concentrate, for which the United States was the only available market. Zinc concentrate, which was being supplied to the British Ministry of Supply, went into oversupply. Requests for higher prices or a premium for zinc concentrate were made but to no avail. Representations were made to both the New South Wales and Commonwealth governments, the latter for relief on lead prices or the potential payment of a lead bonus. These were not forthcoming and the mine was in 'imminent danger of closing down', leading to representations by the New South Wales Branch of the Australian Workers' Union to the prime minister to protect the 'valuable State assets now threatened by extinction'.³⁰ The New South Wales Government provided temporary relief on the cost of hydro-electric power, as well on rail freight charges from October 1940 to June 1942.

The wartime circumstances imposed numerous challenges on the mine and its management. Thomas Baker, as managing director, was active in not only canvassing financial assistance but in multiple requests for mining equipment, financial support to build cottages to attract married men, as well as suitable boots and clothing to deal with the acid nature of the mine water.³¹ Equipment supplies were secured that allowed a copper production unit to commence in early 1942, enabling the copper in lead being sent to the United States to be extracted at the mine.

---

28   Lake George earned a profit of GB£4,000 for the 1942 financial year, the first in the history of the company, associated with an increase in copper recovery and a doubling of pyrite production when a new market was found for about half of the pyrite production (*Chemical Engineering and Mining Review*, 10 June 1943, p. 265; *West Australian Mining and Commercial Review*, vol. 7, no. 5, July 1942, p. 20; 'Lake George Lead Concentrate and Relation to Dollar Exchange and Petrol Purchases', NAA, A461, S373/1/2, p. 90).
29   Letter from the managing director, Lake George Mines Limited to PC Spender, Commonwealth treasurer, 22 July 1940, NAA, A461, S373/1/2.
30   Colonial Treasurer, New South Wales, Sydney, 8 June 1942, Lake George Mines, NAA, A461, S373/1/2; letter from AWU New South Wales Branch to the Prime Minister, 27 August 1930, NAA, A461, S373/1/2.
31   NAA, A1146, N6/4 Part 1.

In 1942, a 'calamity with the tailings dam' necessitated an urgent request to the Commonwealth Government for piping to supply fresh water to the mine and the townsite.³² The support sought of the Commonwealth Government extended to representations to the State Department of the United States to assist Mrs Baker, who had travelled to California before the outbreak of the war, to return to New South Wales to be with her husband. The concern by a Commonwealth Government official with responsibility for the oversight of minerals production was that Baker was 'becoming restive', with a fear that 'his services so important to production will be lost either through break-down or his return to U.S.A'.³³ His possible departure could be averted if arrangements were made for his wife to rejoin him.

The financial assistance from the New South Wales Government was able to be suspended one month earlier than planned. In 1946 an operating profit of GB£38,567 was generated, accumulated losses written-off and the repayment of a loan of GB£726,777 made to the London corporation.³⁴ The mining and processing operations, however, continued to experience challenging conditions after World War II, including increased costs and labour issues. Apart from a 40 per cent increase in rail freight charges in 1947 and other increases, wages rose sharply, while labour turnover and industrial disruption were endemic. In 1948, the average number of men on the payroll was 403 but only an average of 346 attended work at any one time during the year. Turnover of workers was 147 per cent, with the effect that about 'a quarter of the mine employees … leave before they have time to become familiar with or skilled in any operation'.³⁵ Wages had increased an average of 10 to 18 per cent and if the lead bonus was included, by 36 to 44 per cent; a level nearly three-quarters higher in 1948 than in 1939.

The mine's performance also suffered from the vagaries of metal prices and, at times, a fractious industrial relations situation. Industrial disputes and strikes were frequent. In 1942, 250 workers went on strike when water was not available in the change rooms. In that year the company recorded a loss. In August 1947 'a go-slow policy' was followed by strike action in 1948 for an increase in the lead bonus.

---

32 Telegram, 13 July 1942, NAA, A1146, N6/4, Part 1.
33 Letter from Secretary, Department of Supply and Shipping to Secretary, Department of External Affairs Canberra, 2/12/1942, NAA, A1146, N6/4, Part 1.
34 *The Times*, 14 November 1947.
35 *Chemical Engineering and Mining Review*, 10 May 1949, p. 305.

Figure 19. Lake George mining and processing operations, Captains Flat, New South Wales.
Source: NAA, A1200, L39590.

In the following financial year, only 67 days of production were recorded with a strike that ended in May 1949 after an initial 'go-slow' approach in September 1948, followed by a national coal strike that caused a further suspension of operations. Despite being on strike, most of the workers still attended the Captains Flat hotel for the general manager's Christmas drinks.[36] A loss that year was only averted by a considerable amount of concentrate at the mine that was able to be processed.[37]

---

36 Pryke, Van Straaten and Walker, *Boom to Bust—And Back Again*, pp. 48–49.
37 *Chemical Engineering and Mining Review*, 10 July 1950, pp. 410–411.

Figure 20. Final shift at time of closure of Lake George mine, 1962.
Source: Captains Flat Community Association.

In 1954 and 1955 a lock-out occurred, operations were suspended and 300 workers stood down from June 1954 to February 1955. Mine management had to contend with an internecine conflict between two unions—the Miners' Federation and the Australian Workers' Union. As information on signage at what are now the remnants of the mine site infrastructure conveys, separate change room facilities were provided to the different unions. In the 1956 financial year, mine operations were suspended yet again, resulting in a loss for the year, following industrial stoppages relating to the company's right to deepen the shaft by using outside contractors.[38] In 1958, following further industrial disputation, Tom Owen, by then Australian chairman of Lake George Mines, advised the London-based chairman of Lake George Mining Corporation: 'If the men's representatives were deliberately trying to force us to close the Mine you would expect them to adopt the tactics they are following'.[39]

---

38 *Chemical Engineering and Mining Review*, 10 July 1956, p. 325.
39 Letter from TM Owen to Hon RMP Preston, Chairman, Lake George Mining Corporation Ltd, 9 September, 1958, Butlin Archives, ANU, 80, 9.

Despite recording profits in the late 1940s and early 1950s, by the late 1950s the challenges of a maturing ore body and weaker prices had become apparent.[40] A world-wide slump in metal prices, including zinc and copper, and increasing operating costs resulted in a loss in 1958. In the same year, it was viewed that Captains Flat was 'threatened with extinction' due to the decision of the United States Government to restrict imports of lead and zinc.[41]

The major hope for the mine's continuation was the identification of additional ore through deeper exploration drilling, conducted to a depth of 3,000 feet. In 1960 the board of directors was informed that the exploration program at both surface and underground had 'failed to disclose any economic extensions to existing ore bodies or to reveal any new deposits'.[42] In 1960, Owen wrote to the London-based chairman of the company in relation to various matters in the event that the mine and company had to be closed or liquidated, given that the operation had nearly exhausted the availability of profitable ore. Owen raised several challenges facing the company in terms of its continued, if limited operation. These included the risks to continuing mining operations due to the 'unpredictable industrial risk' and, in particular, 'the supply and behaviour of the employees, particularly of the A.W.U. [Australian Workers' Union] men whose membership at Captain's Flat continues as a solid core of admitted Communists'.[43] The risk of pollution to the Molonglo River was highlighted; it was not uncommon for the large tailings dumps containing pyrite to break their banks and spill into the river. The company was also facing claims for damages from local landholders associated with the adverse effects of mining activity on agricultural land in the vicinity of the mine.[44] Owen wrote, in a near exasperated tone:

---

40 Operating profits in British pounds sterling for the London Corporation were: 1948, £291,799; 1949, £324,843; 1950, £498,813; 1951, £892,290; 1952, £1,084,350 (*Chemical Engineering and Mining Review*, 11 February 1952, p. 188).
41 *Chemical Engineering and Mining Review*, 15 November 1958, p. 65.
42 Lake George Mines Pty Ltd, 14 September 1960, Board of Directors, p. 4, Butlin Archives, ANU, 80, 9.
43 Letter from TM Owen to Hon RMP Preston, Chairman, Lake George Mining Corporation Ltd, 27 February 1960, p. 2, Butlin Archives, ANU, 80, 10. Preston had been appointed a director of Consolidated Gold Fields of South Africa in 1946.
44 ibid., p. 3.

> The position facing the future of Lake George being so serious, it would be a great relief to me—and I feel to all of us—if it were possible for you to visit us here in the near future to familiarise yourself with the more important problems and thus assist us in dealing with them.[45]

The approach of the London board was to accept the reality of the mine's closure, allow production to decline while seeking to avoid antagonising the unions and reach a settlement with landowners before the company went into liquidation. The London chairman raised the question of whether the company could take advantage of the location and infrastructure at Captains Flat for the establishment of some other industry. He wrote to Owen:

> The Board in London feel that this matter should be attacked now, and that you should let it be widely known that you are effectively engaging in looking for some industry to take the place of the Mine, and thus incidentally counter the propaganda of the Communists.[46]

In a handwritten addendum to his letter to Owen, the chairman added: 'We all do indeed sympathise with you … in your troubles and anxieties, and regret that there is so little we can do to help'.[47] In effect, closure was the accepted outcome with efforts directed to ensuring the maximum level of funds be returned to London shareholders. A capital return of two shillings per share occurred and a A£300,000 interest-free loan was remitted to Lake George Mining Corporation in December 1962.[48] In March 1962 the mine closed. During the period 1939 to 1962 it had milled over 4 million tons of ore and produced 143,600 tons of copper, 234,600 tons of lead, 386,560 tons of zinc, 346,340 tons of pyrite, 90,057 ounces of gold and 4,963,440 ounces of silver.[49] The mine's equipment was sold, raising A£400,000 in 1963 and in 1964 the London company was placed into voluntary liquidation.

…

Concurrent with its investments in Australian gold companies, Gold Fields pursued gold interests in the Territory of New Guinea, where Australian civil administration had been established through a League of Nations trusteeship in 1921 after the cessation of German occupation.

---

45 ibid., p. 7.
46 Letter from Dick Preston to Tom M Owen, 14 March 1980, p. 2, Butlin Archives, ANU, 80, 10.
47 ibid.
48 Lake George Mines Pty Limited, 'Meeting 14th Day of December 1960', Butlin Archives, ANU, 80, 10.
49 Reynolds, 'Lake George Mines', p. 345.

5. LAKE GEORGE AND NEW GUINEA

Prospecting and minor gold mining activity had been undertaken by Australians in New Guinea since the early 1920s.[50] In Morobe district on the north coast of the country the topography is noted for its rugged and mountainous terrain, with a number of valleys including the Wau and Bulolo. The Edie, Koranga and Wau Creeks flow into the Bulolo River, which courses down a wide gorge. The alluvial gold deposits in Morobe district near the Bulolo River had come to the attention of Cecil John Levien, a district officer with the Australian administration.[51] After resigning from colonial administration, Levien and colleagues established a company, Guinea Gold No Liability, which was listed on the Adelaide stock exchange in 1926. It established a small alluvial plant that recovered 'rich gold including specimens nuggets [sic] of coarse gold' through ground-sluicing operations.[52] The major issue facing this small-scale mining operation was access to the site, which, while only 48 kilometres from the coast, required an eight-day trek to the coast due to the difficult terrain. The company purchased two planes to transport food, merchandise and passengers. The company's chief pilot, Flight Lieutenant Mustar, was given the responsibility to procure larger, all-metal aircraft, capable of transporting heavier equipment to site.[53] The company transferred its aviation activities to a separate company, which would form the basis of the New Guinea national carrier, as well as the foundation of air travel in Papua and New Guinea.

Despite the potential of the area, the financial situation of Guinea Gold, the scale of the investment to develop the area and initial disappointment with the resource potential, led the directors to withdraw from future activities, a decision that was only negated by soliciting assistance from other sources. In 1928, the mining engineer who had responsibility for establishing Mount Isa Mines, William Henry Corbould, travelled to New Guinea on behalf of Leslie Urquhart, then chairman of Mount Isa Mines.[54] Urquhart had an interest in fostering the development of alluvial deposits in New Guinea. Corbould took options over leases and water rights in the upper Bulolo and Edie Creek areas. The Elleyou Goldfields

---

50 The discovery and development of the Morobe goldfields is told in Rhys, *High Lights and Flights in New Guinea*, p. 183. For other accounts of gold mining in Morobe district, see Nelson, *Black, White and Gold*; Idriess, *Gold-Dust and Ashes*; Lett, *Papuan Gold*.
51 Healy, 'Levien, Cecil John (1874–1932)'.
52 Guinea Gold No Liability, 'The Shareholders of Guinea Gold No Liability 7th November 1927', UMA, Stock Exchange of Melbourne, 1968.0018, Box 119.
53 Langmore, 'Mustar, Ernest Andrew (1893–1971)'.
54 Blainey, *The Rush that Never Ended*, pp. 326 and 329; see also Kennedy, 'Corbould, William Henry (1866–1949)'.

Corporation was formed in 1928 to undertake further evaluation in New Guinea.[55] This included a survey for a potential railway to transport the gold recovered to the coast. Given the rugged terrain, this was not practicable and aircraft transportation formed the basis of the development of the area. Urquhart maintained a positive assessment of the gold potential of the area, observing in 1929:

> Since the opening of the Rand, no goldfield exhibiting the potentialities of New Guinea has been discovered, and if the present work in ore development in depth is attended with that success already attained in our work on the numerous valuable gold veins so far found, we shall be fully justified in claiming that in New Guinea we have, under the British flag, a new goldfield of the greatest importance.[56]

Meanwhile in 1928, Placer Development, a British Columbia company, sent a mining engineer and his assistant to New Guinea to evaluate the lower Bulolo leases of Guinea Gold. Consolidated Gold Fields of South Africa had a connection with alluvial gold mining that began when it took interests in the Oroville and Yuba gold-dredging companies in California as early as 1909, and then a prospecting partnership with Placer Development in the 1920s.[57] Placer's evaluation determined the existence of payable gold leases that extended into areas held by Guinea Gold. Some of the Guinea Gold leases were sold to Placer for £50,000, while a new Canadian incorporated company, Bulolo Gold Dredging, was formed in 1930 to work the leases. Consolidated Gold Fields of South Africa and Gold Fields American Development Company subscribed to 200,000 of 467,000 shares available of the total 800,000 shares for the company and thereby contributed a large part of the capital necessary for development work to begin. In addition, the companies acquired 10,000 of 30,000 Placer shares, and held an option over the remaining 20,000 shares, which would become available 12 months after the start of dredging operations.[58] As such, Gold Fields, established a major position in this part of the Bulolo fields.[59] Placer, in turn, held a 22 per cent in Bulolo Gold Dredging.

---

55 *The Times*, 10 December 1928 and Kennedy, *Mining Tsar*, pp. 257 and 258.
56 *The Times*, 13 November 1929.
57 Consolidated Gold Fields of South Africa, *The Gold Fields 1887–1937*, p. 97.
58 Placer Development Limited, 'Bulolo Gold Dredging Limited Flotation, 29/4/30', UMA, Stock Exchange of Melbourne, 1968.0018, Box 256; Guinea Gold No Liability, 'Notice to Shareholders, 13th August 1930', UMA, Stock Exchange of Melbourne, 1968.0018, Box 119; see also Consolidated Gold Fields of South Africa, *The Gold Fields 1887–1937*, pp. 113–114.
59 In 1954, Consolidated Gold Fields of South Africa disposed of its interest in Oroville Dredging and Bulolo Gold Dredging (*The Times*, 10 November 1954).

Urquhart's company had also secured options over leases from Guinea Gold, including those on the upper Bulolo and Edie Creek, through a consideration of shares in a company it established in London for the purpose of conducting sluicing and reefing operations in New Guinea.[60] In 1929, the London-based company, Elleyou Development Corporation, exercised its option and established a new company, New Guinea Goldfields, listed on the Sydney stock exchange, with some of its shares distributed to shareholders of Guinea Gold. This enabled the various interests in the Edie Creek area to be amalgamated. Gold Fields also established a shareholding in this company. The original prospecting company, Guinea Gold, continued to exist, although its main interest was in shareholdings in New Guinea Goldfields and Bulolo Gold Dredging.[61]

Dredging was adopted to mine the alluvial deposits of the Bulolo River, downstream from Wau. Transporting dredging equipment to the remote and mountainous location was challenging. In 1931, the commercial airlift of mining equipment began with the first two of eight 2,000-ton dredges, as well as all other mining equipment, transported to site. Two Junker 31 aircraft flew from Lae on their maiden flight in April 1931, 'glistening in the sun like a huge dragon-fly'.[62] The aircraft subsequently carried in thousands of tons of machinery, all of which had to be custom made to fit inside the aircraft. In 1932, Placer issued additional shares to fund its operations. Oroville Dredging Company acquired 55,000 of the 65,000 shares. Oroville Dredging was considered one of the world's most successful gold-dredging companies and was involved with Placer in gold-dredging activities in Colombia.[63] Consolidated Gold Fields of South Africa had a substantial interest in Oroville Dredging and, as such, gained a further involvement in the Bulolo fields, both as a shareholder in Placer and provider of technical assistance.

---

60 Guinea Gold No Liability, 11 July 1928, UMA, Stock Exchange of Melbourne, 1968.0018, Box 119.
61 State Library of South Australia, BRD65/1/1, Guinea Gold No Liability and PRG 429 Lapthorne, WPA.
62 Rhys, *High Lights and Flights in New Guinea*, pp. 186–187.
63 Placer Development Limited, 'Bulolo Gold Dredging Limited, Memorandum to Shareholders, February 29th, 1932', p. 1, UMA, Stock Exchange of Melbourne, 1968.0018, Box 49.

Figure 21. Alluvial gold mining, Edie Creek, Morobe district, Territory of New Guinea.
Source: NAA, A6510, 2310.

Figure 22. Location for mining operations undertaken by New Guinea Goldfields at the junction of Bulolo River and Koranga Creek, Morobe district, Territory of New Guinea.
Source: NAA, A6510, 2306.

Figure 23. Junker aircraft used for transportation of equipment into Morobe district, Territory of New Guinea.
Source: NAA, A6510, 760544.

Figure 24. Bulolo gold dredge, number 3, Morobe district, Territory of New Guinea.
Source: SLSA, B71530.

Bulolo was referred to as the 'most profitable alluvial gold-mining operation ever undertaken'.[64] From 1932 to 1940, 1,027,263 ounces (32 tons) of gold and 456,921 ounces (14 tons) of silver were recovered.[65] Operations ceased in January 1942 as a result of Japanese bombing attacks that destroyed three of the company's aircraft at the Bulolo aerodrome as well as workshops and storehouses, while the Australian administration's 'scorched earth' policy led to the rendering of other equipment, including dredges, inoperable. Production recommenced after the war and Bulolo was eventually amalgamated into Placer Development in 1966, after dredging operations had ceased in 1965. Sluicing operations continued.

New Guinea Goldfields developed its deposits using an alluvial mining approach as well as shaft mining of reefs at depth. A mill was constructed at Edie Creek in 1935 to support the workings, with a workforce of over 130 expatriate employees and more than 1,000 indigenous employees.[66] In 1933, a profit of A£215,186 was recorded and an initial dividend paid. Compared with the experience of Bulolo Dredging, New Guinea Goldfields' performance was modest and it struggled financially. By 1936 the richer sections of the alluvial fields had been exhausted and by 1941 the underground mining activities were loss-making, with remnant alluvial mining and tribute mining contributing to a modest profit.[67] In June 1937, Julius Kruttschnitt was appointed chairman. Kruttschnitt was at the time both chairman and general manager of Mount Isa Mines. He later played a role as chairman of Commonwealth Mining Investments (Australia), the first investment made by Consolidated Gold Fields (Australia) after it was formed in 1960.

As such, Gold Fields established a presence in gold mining activities in New Guinea through a shareholding in two of the main companies involved in Morobe district. The involvement in Papua and New Guinea was reconsidered in the 1960s and again in the early 1980s when Renison Goldfields Consolidated acquired New Guinea Goldfields in conjunction with its London parent, while a further association with Placer Pacific led to the development of the major Porgera gold deposit in the country in 1990.

---

64 Cartwright, *Gold Paved the Way*, p. 206; see also Waterhouse, *Not a Poor Man's Field*.
65 Bulolo Gold Dredging, Limited, 'Report and Statement of Accounts for the Year Ended 31st May, 1940', UMA, Stock Exchange of Melbourne, 1968.0018, Box 48.
66 UMA, Stock Exchange of Melbourne, 1968.0018, Box 209; Hore-Lacy, *Broken Hill to Mount Isa*, pp. 212–213.
67 *Chemical Engineering and Mining Review*, 9 March 1936, p. 205 and 10 January 1942, p. 163.

Despite the expansive approach that the Gold Fields group had taken in Australia and its territorial possession in New Guinea, in the late 1950s the Australian interests of the British group were restricted to Lake View and Star and Mount Ida. Gold Fields Australian Development Company, despite its promise, failed to provide a base for Gold Fields' ongoing involvement in Australia. It continued to exist, in name only, until December 1967 when, after evaluation of its base-metal exploration opportunities, the company was liquidated.[68] However, the attraction of Australia as a location for mining investment remained: a new chapter in the evolution of Gold Fields' interests in Australia was about to begin.

---

68   *The Times*, 6 December 1967.

PART THREE:
A NEW FORCE IN AUSTRALIAN MINING 1960–1966

Box 3. Key events 1959–1966

1959	Gold Fields Mining & Industrial Ltd, a subsidiary of The Consolidated Gold Fields of South Africa, is formed to oversee activities for Britain, Australia, Canada and New Zealand
1960	Consolidated Gold Fields (Australia) Pty Ltd (CGFA) formed, 7 November Directors: - Sir George Steven Harvie-Watt, Bart, TD, QC - Gilbert Potier - Frank Beggs - Keith Cameron - Tom Owen Share issuance by Commonwealth Mining Investments (Australia) to CGFA, which acquires an initial 54 per cent interest
1961	Acquisition of majority shareholding in Associated Minerals Consolidated Alumasc takeover offer for Lawrenson Holdings Purchase of shares in Wyong Minerals
1962	Lake George mine ceases operation, London corporation placed into liquidation Exploration joint venture—New Consolidated Gold Fields (Australasia) and Cyprus Mines Corporation Joint venture for development of iron ore deposits with Cyprus and Utah Construction & Mining Co.—to become known as Mount Goldsworthy Mining Associates Wyong Minerals becomes a subsidiary of CGFA Heads of agreement, Mines and Quarry Development for incorporation of Blue Metal Products (CGFA resigns as general manager, November 1962) Agreement to purchase Zodiac Syndicate shares in Eastern Titanium Corporation CGFA appointed general manager of Commonwealth Mining Investments (Australia)
1963	Eclipse Mining—cancellation of secretarial and accounting services provided since 1962 CGFA appointed general manager of Wyong Minerals Consolidated Gold Fields of South Africa acquires 90 per cent of shares in Tennant, Sons and Company Limited of London. Tennant is used as marketing vehicle by CGFA

1964	Majority shareholding acquired in The Mount Lyell Mining and Railway Company
	51 per cent shareholding acquired in Zip Holdings, New Zealand
	Stock units in Bellambi Coal Company acquired from McIlwraith McEacharn
1965	CGFA underwriting of share issuances by Renison; provision of loan facilities of up to A£1 million with an option to subscribe for 400,000 shares by 31 December 1968
	Mount Lyell refinery closed after 37 years
	Signing of leases for Mount Goldsworthy iron ore tenements, Western Australia
1966	First shipment of Mount Goldsworthy iron ore
	Conversion to a public company, registered as a foreign company, 26 September
	Main investments: <ul><li>Commonwealth Mining Investments (Australia) 60%</li><li>The Mount Lyell Mining and Railway Company 56%</li><li>Renison 42%</li><li>Zip Holdings 51%</li><li>Associated Minerals Consolidated 62%</li><li>Bellambi Coal 67%</li><li>New Consolidated Goldfields (Australasia) 100%</li><li>Lake View and Star 16%</li><li>Mount Goldsworthy Mining Associates 33%</li></ul>

6

A NEW APPROACH TO AUSTRALIA

In 1951 Sir George Harvie-Watt became managing director of The Consolidated Gold Fields of South Africa and in 1954 was appointed deputy chairman, assuming the role of chief executive officer in that year. In 1960 he became both chairman and chief executive officer. He remained as chairman until 1968. According to AP Cartwright, who wrote one of three histories of Consolidated Gold Fields, Harvie-Watt's appointment to the board was in keeping with the approach to appoint at least one director 'from the world of affairs outside the circle of specialists in mining and mining-finance'.[1] In fact, at his death in 1989, Harvie-Watt was described as belonging to that 'dwindling band of men whose careers straddled the law, the army, politics and business'.[2] In Harvie-Watt, the London board gained a man of great experience and energy: a trained barrister, member of parliament, commissioned Territorial Army officer and commander of the 31st Battalion of the Royal Engineers (later commander of the 6th Anti-Aircraft Brigade). He served as aide-de-camp to King George VI and as Sir Winston Churchill's parliamentary private secretary during World War II, from 1941 to 1945. Churchill, in offering him this wartime role reportedly said: 'What I am offering you is not a job

---

1 Cartwright, *Gold Paved the Way*, p. 233.
2 *The Times*, 26 December 1989.

down in the engine room. I am asking you to serve on the bridge'.³ In the role he managed Churchill's relationships with members of the House of Commons, acting as his 'eyes and ears in the Commons', engaging with foreign delegations and providing Churchill with 'candid assessments', including on the views of colleagues and proceedings within parliament.⁴

Harvie-Watt was steeled in the experiences of politics and the competing challenges of a coalition government during the exigencies of wartime Britain. He recalled his decision to join Consolidated Gold Fields as a full-time director in 1951 as the 'greatest business and personal decision' he ever made.⁵ He initially served as a director while still a member of the House of Commons. Harvie-Watt's experience of mining was limited; his only involvement was as a director of the gold mining company Globe & Phoenix Gold Mining Company and its Phoenix Prince mine in Rhodesia. Instead, Harvie-Watt studied the history of Consolidated Gold Fields and came to his own conclusions about the direction it should be taking. According to Cartwright, Harvie-Watt 'had a capacity for hard work … a wide knowledge of affairs and the ability to make up his mind quickly'. Further:

> He studied the affairs of the company as thoroughly as he had been accustomed to study his brief … The time came when the company's business occupied most of his working day and many of his evenings … Harvie-Watt, surveying the affairs of Gold Fields, made up his mind that the company was relying too much on its old traditions and that it, too, would have to change its methods and adapt itself to the post-war world. He thought … that it needed a more broadly-based investment programme in countries with stable governments.⁶

---

3   Harvie-Watt, *Most of My Life*, p. 3. An obituary of Harvie-Watt stated: 'Churchill would give Harvie-Watt one of his legendary cigars on occasion—and in return PPS [parliamentary private secretary] would have to take the brunt of his tirades and frustration, either at the course of the war or his treatment in the House of Commons' (*The Times*, 26 December 1989).
4   Roberts, *Churchill: Walking with Destiny*, pp. 668 and 741.
5   Harvie-Watt, *Most of My Life*, p. 208.
6   Cartwright, *Gold Paved the Way*, p. 245.

Figure 25. Sir George Steven Harvie-Watt, chairman and chief executive officer, Consolidated Gold Fields, responsible for overseeing a major investment program in Australia from 1960 and for the formation of Consolidated Gold Fields (Australia) Pty Ltd.
Source: George Lipman, *Sydney Morning Herald*, Nine Publishing.

Harvie-Watt realised that the company was at a crossroad. He decided that its investments in some of the 'unsafe parts of Africa' should be reduced; he viewed the company as too reliant on gold and too dependent upon a few mines in South Africa for its production. He changed the name of the company from The Consolidated Gold Fields of South Africa to Consolidated Gold Fields, to reduce the perceived reliance upon one geography. His view of the Gold Fields portfolio structure was that he 'wanted a carousel where all the horses were not down at the same time', reflecting a desire that the company did not have 'all of its interests in one commodity'.[7] In this regard, investments in a range of industries, some outside mining, were viewed as appropriate. Harvie-Watt had a familiarity with Australia through his parliamentary responsibilities. He had visited Australia in 1950 en route to a Commonwealth parliamentary conference in New Zealand. During that visit, he travelled to the Lake View and

---

7   Harvie-Watt, *Most of My Life*, p. 240.

Star mine in Western Australia. He recalled in later life that this visit 'stirred my imagination as to what Gold Fields might do in this land of opportunity'.[8]

Several changes in company structure and funding arrangements provided the basis for an ambitious program of expansion in the 1960s, of which Australia was a key focus and an area of great success. In 1959 a restructuring occurred with the existing dual London company structure of Gold Fields of South Africa and New Consolidated Gold Fields abolished and the subsidiary company absorbed. South African interests were managed by Gold Fields of South Africa, with its head office in Johannesburg. A London-registered company, Gold Fields Mining & Industrial, assumed responsibilities for all other international activities, including in Australia. In September 1960, Gold Fields Mining & Industrial issued GB£5 million worth of debenture stock to fund its international expansion and in November of that year Consolidated Gold Fields (Australia) Pty Limited (CGFA) was formed to provide the basis for the group's expansion in Australia.

...

Despite the dearth of opportunities that had been generated in Australia to that time, the company's representative in Australia, Frank Beggs, expressed his concern that the new approach under Harvie-Watt entailed less of an emphasis on exploration and more on the acquisition of interests in other businesses. Beggs had visited London in October 1960 and wrote that he had 'heard about the new policy which is being doped out' and again expressed his concern that it would be 'wrong to give up on exploration'.[9] However, Beggs could offer little promise that exploration efforts would turn up anything of significance, with his comment to his American colleague that 'we are still pushing on with Mt Isa with the Mining Corporation area but up to date it doesn't look at all hopeful'.[10]

By this stage, Gold Fields in London was orchestrating a wider program of investments in Australia. On 7 November 1960, the appointment of directors to CGFA occurred. Harvie-Watt, Beggs, Gilbert Potier, Keith Cameron and Tom Owen became the initial directors. Board meetings

---

8   ibid.
9   Letter from Frank R Beggs to Robt F Playter, 4 January 1960, Renison Goldfields Consolidated Archives (RGCA), 1430, Box 12300.
10   ibid.

6. A NEW APPROACH TO AUSTRALIA

were held at 15 O'Connell Street in Sydney before office accommodation was leased and meetings held at the AMP building on Circular Quay from May 1962. By November 1960 Gold Fields in Australia had undertaken its first investment: Commonwealth Mining Investments (Australia).

Beggs, writing to his American colleague while surveying the scene, and with little apparent realisation of the magnitude of the changes about to unfold, recorded:

> Other than this Commonwealth Mining business we have had very little excitement out here. We are still examining a large number of prospects and still being disappointed, but we have to keep on in the hope that somewhere, someday, we will turn up a worthwhile ore-body.[11]

Yet Gold Fields representatives from London were active in the country. Investments in Australia were assessed from Gold Fields' head office at 49 Moorgate, London. Gerald Mortimer, a senior Gold Fields manager and mining engineer, examined mineral sands opportunities in New South Wales, which also involved visiting steel works in the United Kingdom to evaluate the advantages of zircon in foundry applications, as well as surveying European demand for mineral sands.[12] In 1963 Potier visited and met with the Western Australian Government in relation to the company's involvement in Mount Goldsworthy, while other representatives were in Australia, considering a range of investments, including oil exploration and production.[13]

The process of expansion in Australia was multifaceted and proceeded apace. By the mid-1960s, Consolidated Gold Fields had established a broad business foundation in Australia. The initial investment of the new Australian offshoot of Consolidated Gold Fields was a listed mining investment company, Commonwealth Mining Investments. Investments were made in copper, through the company's shareholding in The Mount Lyell Mining and Railway Company, Australia's oldest operating copper mine. Through this investment, subsequent control was achieved of Renison and the rich Tasmanian tin resources that proved valuable to CGFA and influenced its strategic considerations into the 1980s. A major

---

11 Letter from Frank R Beggs to Robt F Playter, 9 November 1960, RGCA, 1430, Box 12300.
12 'Note for File, Visit to North British Steel Foundry Limited, Bathgate, Scotland', 4 February 1963, RGCA, Box 12300.
13 Letter from Peter Wallis to SL Segal, 15 May 1962, RGCA, Box 12300.

presence was established in iron ore through a founding involvement in, and development of, the Mount Goldsworthy iron ore deposits in the Pilbara of Western Australia in association with Cyprus Mining Corporation and Utah Construction & Mining. In doing so, a British–American venture would be responsible for the first shipment of iron ore from the Pilbara in 1966.

CGFA, through separate investments in two east coast mineral sands producers, to be later supplemented by the acquisition and control of a west coast mineral sands producer, Western Titanium, established a dominant position in a mineral new to the group. While, under the aegis of New Consolidated Gold Fields (Australasia), exploration had been conducted with Utah on the Blackwater coal deposits in Queensland, an involvement in coal was gained by the acquisition of a majority interest in The Bellambi Coal Company, located near Port Kembla in New South Wales. Manufacturing interests were also established, with an investment in a New Zealand manufacturing company, Zip Holdings. The 1962 takeover of an Australian manufacturing company, RH Lawrenson, by a Consolidated Gold Fields–owned United Kingdom company, Alumasc Holdings, broadened the Australian entity's involvement in manufacturing when the renamed Lawrenson Alumasc Holdings, with manufacturing facilities at Lidcombe in New South Wales, became a subsidiary of CGFA.

The newly established CGFA relied initially on Harvie-Watt, his deputy chairman Potier, fellow director JD (Donald) McCall, as well as Mortimer for its expansion plans. Potier, an accountant by training, had served in the No. 210 Squadron in the Royal Air Force during World War II and been awarded a Distinguished Flying Cross with a bar. He flew Catalina flying boats and Liberators and amassed over 1,050 hours of operational flying time. 'A medium built man ... [with a] brisk, precise approach ... [he] built up an enviable reputation as a clever and astute businessman.'[14] He had lived in Australia and was supportive of and actively involved in the company's expansion. Analytical and investment resources were provided from London, with a young University of Cambridge–educated graduate, Edward (Ted) Wiles, relocating to Australia to assist Mortimer and others with the group's expansion before being made a permanent employee of CGFA.

---

14   *The Times*, 23 January 1968. Potier was appointed chairman and chief executive of Consolidated Gold Fields to succeed Sir George Harvie-Watt in January 1968. He died at the age of 53 on 11 January 1969.

Figure 26. Brian Massy-Greene, appointed general manager of Consolidated Gold Fields (Australia) and managing director in 1962, speaking at the opening of the Mount Goldsworthy iron ore project in 1966.
Source: State Library of Western Australia (SLWA), Aerial Surveys Australia, BA 1475, 268349PD.

Local managerial resources were also strengthened. A 'man of calibre' was considered necessary to run the new Australian operation and John Brian Massy-Greene, son of Sir Walter Massy-Greene, a former federal minister and senator for New South Wales, was appointed general manager effective 14 May 1962. As a businessman, Massy-Greene was general manager at Austral Bronze, a subsidiary company of Metal Manufactures, which had been established by the Collins House Group and listed in 1916 for the production of copper wire. His father had been a director from 1933 to 1952 as well as known to Consolidated Gold Fields through its earlier investments in Australia. Daniel McVey, to be appointed a director of CGFA, was Metal Manufactures' long-serving managing director from

1949 to 1962.[15] Shareholders in Metal Manufactures included Mount Lyell Mining and Railway Company, a company in which CGFA would acquire a majority interest in 1964.[16] The appointment of Massy-Greene was to begin a process of selecting men for senior managerial and directorial positions, well versed in business and with a standing in the community, although often with little direct mining experience.

In a letter to Beggs dated 25 June 1962, following the offer of his appointment by Potier, Massy-Greene wrote:

> I understand that it is the intention of The Consolidated Gold Fields of South Africa Limited to maintain an enduring policy of investment in Australia and that there are no foreseeable circumstances which would cause the substantial withdrawal or disposal of their principal interests in this country.
>
> Mr Potier advised me that it is the policy of the London Board that the main interests of Gold Fields situated outside England should be managed by citizens of the respective countries concerned. In this regard, he said that, irrespective of such substantial growth as may occur in Australia, it would not be the policy at a later date to make an appointment from London to take charge of the Company's interests here.
>
> In the ordinary course of events I could anticipate that in due course I would succeed to the senior executive appointment in the Australian company.[17]

Massy-Greene did rise in the company and made a substantial contribution to its growth in Australia. He was appointed managing director in October 1962. Beggs left the company, departing with an offer to purchase the company's Daimler car.[18] A newspaper article described Massy-Greene as an 'old school tie' man. When interviewed about his role at CGFA, he said there were three company ties: 'one for the South African companies, one for the British companies and one for directors'.[19] He became chairman in September 1966 when Harvie-Watt retired, to allow an Australian to

---

15 See Appendix 3 for a biographical profile of Brian Massy-Greene.
16 Ellis, *Metal Manufactures Limited*, pp. 26 and 36.
17 Consolidated Gold Fields (Australia) Pty Limited, 'Minutes of Meeting of Directors', 8 October 1962, RGCA, Box 12264.
18 Beggs was paid A£20,000 on retirement and offered to purchase the company's Daimler for A£3,000 (Consolidated Gold Fields (Australia) Pty Limited, 'Minutes of Meeting of Directors', 26 October 1962, RGCA, Box 12264).
19 *The Australian*, 10 April 1965.

head the new publicly listed company as both chairman and managing director. Massy-Greene retained the dual roles until he was requested to step down as managing director at the behest of the London board in 1976. Sidney Segal, a South African–born lawyer and stockbroker, and formerly joint managing director of a company acquired by Consolidated Gold Fields of South Africa, New Union Goldfields, relocated to Australia in 1960 and was a highly influential senior finance executive and later director and long-serving chairman.[20] Over the years that followed, board representation was strengthened to include notable Australian businessmen, including Sir Ian Potter and John Darling.

The portents for the future of the company in Australia were favourable. Speaking in 1987, Rudolph Agnew, the grandson of John Agnew, the man who was influential in the establishment of Consolidated Gold Fields' gold investments in Australia, referred to the 'brilliantly carried out' growth by acquisition in Australia that by the mid-1960s had established CGFA 'as a major force in the Australian mining industry'.[21] The nature of that acquisition strategy and its inherent fragility will now be reviewed.

20 See Appendix 3 for a biographical profile of Sidney Segal.
21 Johnson, *Gold Fields: A Centenary Portrait*, p. 159.

7
NEW MEN AND A NEW MODEL

Sir George Harvie-Watt and his deputy, Gilbert Potier, with the involvement of other directors, were instrumental in establishing the basis for Consolidated Gold Fields' expansion into Australia. In this task they were ably assisted by Gerald Mortimer, a senior London-based manager, trained as a mining engineer and having held operational roles in South Africa. He later became deputy chairman and managing director. These early efforts were later supplemented by Brian Massy-Greene and his management team in Australia.

Consolidated Gold Fields (Australia) (CGFA) established a mining-finance house model, with direct investments in a range of listed companies. With one exception, there was no direct involvement in the establishment and operation of new or existing mining operations. The exception was iron ore production in the Pilbara, in Western Australia, where Mortimer was responsible for securing London board support for what was a major investment in a large, new mineral development province in the 1960s. In this case, there was an involvement by two other companies: Cyprus Mines Corporation and Utah Construction & Mining. The presence of CGFA local management experienced in the operation of mining ventures was limited and did not develop in any meaningful sense until the 1970s. It was not until 1981, when Renison Goldfields Consolidated was created, that the company for the first time had direct ownership and operation of the main parts of its portfolio and with it a need to deploy both technical and managerial capabilities, in addition to finance, for the establishment and operation of mining and other ventures.

The approach to acquiring a majority shareholding in a company, as opposed to outright ownership, reflected the deliberate choice made by CGFA in establishing its position in Australia. As Sidney Segal observed in 1966:

> This was the initiation of a technique new to Australia whereby an outside company did not seek to acquire all the shares of a company and so preserved its Australian flavour, and fostered a partnership element between the original Australian investor and the new arrival.[1]

This approach was instrumental in allowing the British company to establish a presence in a range of minerals sectors, including iron ore, mineral sands, copper, tin and coal, as well as diversifying into manufacturing, property development and agricultural interests. The business model reflected the circumstances of the company: its local management presence was limited, while in the burgeoning minerals development environment of the 1960s the establishment of shareholdings, as opposed to direct control of operational mines, was an effective way to gain a foothold in the Australian mining industry. An investment in two manufacturing ventures reflected a propensity for diversification prevalent at the time, as well as a desire to reduce exposure to gold across the Gold Fields group and an attempt to dampen the cyclicality of its mineral investments.

Despite the initial inherent advantages of the CGFA business model, shortcomings and constraints became evident in the late 1960s and early 1970s. Then a combination of the decline in the financial contribution of some key investments, notably iron ore, and the inability to control the cash flows of its other investments, led to a fundamental reconsideration of the business model. It also led to management change at CGFA, with Massy-Greene replaced in 1976 as managing director at the initiative of the London shareholder. Bartholomew C (Bart) Ryan, an experienced Australian mining engineer, was appointed managing director in Australia.[2] He brought both a greater degree of mining and operational experience than his predecessor and, from his posting in London as a director, an appreciation of the capital deployment and dividend considerations of Gold Fields in the context of its wider geographical business interests. Aided by Segal, who assumed the chairmanship, these two individuals and the other directors, which by the early 1970s included Sir Ian Potter,

---

1 'Notes on Redraft of Chapters XXV and XXVI of "History of Gold Fields"', 2 March 1966, Renison Goldfields Consolidated Archives (RGCA), Box 1091.
2 See Appendix 3 for a biographical profile of Bart Ryan.

7. NEW MEN AND A NEW MODEL

John Darling and Sir Daniel McVey, had developed a new business model and structure for the company.[3] This process resulted in the divestment of the company's position in iron ore in 1976, consideration to the sale of its mineral sands interests—or at least some form of rationalisation of the company's Australian position in this sector—and the questioning of the efficacy of the diversified business structure.

Fundamental portfolio alternatives were considered, not least the divestment of all if not most investments, with the retention only of Renison. The inability to implement such a radical portfolio restructuring was due in large part to market constraints. Instead, CGFA emerged from the 1970s with a modification of its portfolio, including a number of the investments made in the 1960s, and with greater disciplines imposed on subsidiaries, yet with the same basic diversified portfolio structure intact. The change to the business structure to address the inherent inefficiencies that emerged from the 1960s quasi-mining-finance house model resulted in a move to a divisional structure, where the underlying businesses became wholly owned by the Australian holding company. The implementation of this 'naturalisation' process was overseen by a newly appointed chairman in 1980, MJ (Max) Roberts, although much of the foundation work had commenced earlier.

...

The initial investment made by CGFA was in a stock exchange–listed company, Commonwealth Mining Investments (Australia) (CMI), established in 1955. When Harvie-Watt visited Australia in January and February 1960, he had requested Frank Beggs to draw up a list of companies he thought might benefit from an investment or injection of funds. Harvie-Watt recalled sitting in his shirt sleeves with Beggs in his hotel suite in Sydney:

---

3   Sir Ian Potter, a Melbourne stockbroker, company adviser and philanthropist, established the firm Ian Potter & Co. In 1970, Potter was a director of over 12 Australian companies, including Boral, McIlwraith McEacharn and Email. John Darling was a businessman and company director of Alcoa of Australia; Austran; British Petroleum; Commonwealth Mining Investments; Monsanto Australia; Sims Consolidated; and Schroder, Darling and Company Holdings. Sir Daniel McVey served as director-general of Posts and Telegraphs from December 1939 and director of War Organization of Industry from November 1941. From February 1944 he held the post of director-general of Civil Aviation. He resigned from the public service in 1946 to enter private industry and served as chairman and managing director of Standard Telephones & Cables (Australia), managing director of Metal Manufactures and Austral Bronze Co. and held managerial and directorial roles at Dunlop Rubber Australia, as well as directorships of Amalgamated Wireless (Australasia), Bellambi Coal Company and McIlwraith McEacharn.

> It was gruelling hot with no air conditioning. He [Beggs] kept on showing me details of very large companies and I said we must aim our sights a lot lower ... I picked up papers relating to a much smaller company ... It was the dossier of Commonwealth Mining. It was just the right size and what I had been thinking of all along. I asked him if he knew the people involved.[4]

The company that attracted Harvie-Watt, and which was reviewed in detail in London, held a spread of investments in most of the main mining companies in Australia at the time. It mirrored, in some respects, the earlier model of Gold Fields investing in Australia with an association with financiers, entrepreneurs and mining men.

CMI was established, in part, due to the absence in Australia in the 1950s of mining-finance companies that, in other countries, were viewed as playing 'a vital part in the development of the mining industry of those countries'.[5] Its charter was to invest in selected mining companies, assist with new flotations, underwrite share issues and advance loan funds. Charles Ord of the stockbroking firm Ord & Minnett played a key role in the establishment of the company. Ord encouraged a number of leading mining professionals to join the board. Its initial investments included Broken Hill South, North Broken Hill, Mount Isa Mines, Mount Morgan and Gold Mines of Kalgoorlie, as well as a holding in companies that were or would form part of the CGFA portfolio: Lake View and Star, Mount Lyell Mining and Railway Company, and Western Titanium.

Harvie-Watt observed a depth of mining experience within CMI, as well as existing professional connections. Julius Kruttschnitt, the chairman, had been general manager and chairman of Mount Isa Mines and also a director and chairman for over 30 years of New Guinea Goldfields, the company in which Consolidated Gold Fields had invested.[6] Keith Cameron, the managing director, had worked for the WS Robinson–sponsored Gold Mines of Australia, a company within the Collins House Group of mining companies. He had worked at Mount Lyell Mining and Railway Company, as well as being a director of New Consolidated Goldfields' more recent investment in Mining Corporation (Australia). He had also worked at North Broken Hill and was managing director of Mount Morgan. Another director, AHP Moline, had been chairman

---

4 Harvie-Watt, *Most of My Life*, p. 251.
5 Commonwealth Mining Investments (Australia) Limited, 'Prospectus', University of Melbourne Archives (UMA), Stock Exchange of Melbourne, 1968.0018, Box 65.
6 Hopper and Lynch, 'Kruttschnitt, Julius (1885–1974)'.

of Mount Kathleen Uranium, as well as general manager of Mount Lyell Mining and Railway Company.[7] Added to these attributes, CMI had sponsored the listing in its own right of a number of companies, including two mineral sands companies—Wyong Minerals and Western Titanium. Harvie-Watt and Mortimer were both attracted to mineral sands as a sector for investment and CMI had a foothold in a number of companies operating on both the east and west coast of the country.

CMI became, in effect, the 'eyes and ears' for Consolidated Gold Fields in Australia in its early days.[8] It also became the progenitor of CGFA's broad involvement in mineral sands, as well as the identification of other companies, such as Mount Lyell and Renison, that became key parts of the portfolio. It led to the identification of companies, including King Island Scheelite and North Broken Hill, that were viewed as appropriate investment opportunities.

The Consolidated Goldfields of South Africa made a proposal through its directors Gilbert Potier and Donald McCall to subscribe for an issue of 3.5 million stock units in CMI in July 1960. The board of CMI considered the proposal and it was declined. Cameron, as managing director, visited London and met the directors of Gold Fields. At his request, the proposal was reconsidered. Yet again the arrangement was declined by his fellow directors. On 4 August 1960 the matter was considered a third time by the CMI board at the behest of Cameron. This time, 'after lengthy discussion it was resolved that the offer be accepted in principle'.[9]

At the first board meeting of CGFA on 9 November 1960, the application for 3.5 million shares in CMI was authorised. CGFA acquired a 54 per cent shareholding and additional shares were purchased the following year. Four CGFA directors were nominated to the board of CMI.[10] In turn, Cameron became a director of New Consolidated Gold Fields (Australasia) and an inaugural director of CGFA in 1960, as well as being employed as a technical officer of the company.

---

7   Moline was general manager of Mount Lyell for four years, 1944–1948 ('Historical Notes of AHP Moline (1877–1965) (Written circa 1961/1962)', State Library of Victoria, MS 10883).
8   I am indebted to Ted Wiles for his recollections of this period.
9   Commonwealth Mining Investments (Australia) Limited, 'Board Minutes', 21 July 1960, 4 August 1960, 10 November 1960, UMA, Commonwealth Mining Investments (Australia) Limited Board Minute Books, 1955–1979, 2012.0202.
10   The initial directors were Harvie-Watt, Potier, Beggs and Gabriel Selmar Reichenbach (Consolidated Gold Fields (Australia) Pty Limited, 'Minutes of Meeting of Directors of Consolidated Gold Fields (Australia) Pty Limited', 13 January 1961, p. 8, RGCA, Box 12264).

The advantage to CMI was that the issuance of shares improved the capital structure of the company and established a relationship with a major mining house with net assets of GBP£46 million. In Australia it provided an association that enabled it to continue to invest, as well as be able to participate in exploration prospecting activities through its association with New Consolidated Gold Fields (Australasia), quite apart from the benefits of 'access to world-wide resources: financial, technical and marketing' provided by Consolidated Gold Fields.[11] CMI was viewed as a mining-finance company with a well-spread portfolio of mining investments in Australia. Significantly, the offshoot of the British mining and finance house, with deep roots in South Africa, had gained a controlling position in an Australian entity that had an involvement in a mineral sector it had known virtually nothing about—mineral sands—as well as an ability to assess a range of other mining investment opportunities in the country.

At Potier's suggestion, A£1 million of the investment in the company was held overseas to enable investment in international mining companies. Consolidated Gold Fields and CMI were able to come to an arrangement with the Commonwealth Treasury whereby they could overcome the investment restrictions then in place, enabling CMI to establish a portfolio that included a spread of both international and Australian investments.[12] In this manner, the company drew upon the expertise of Consolidated Gold Fields' London investment department to broaden its portfolio of investments, both geographically and with the inclusion of industrial companies.

In 1962, Cameron proposed a series of arrangements to his board. CGFA was appointed as investment manager to CMI and the company ceased to incur direct expenditure for prospects or new projects. Instead, this expenditure was incurred by CGFA; the staffing of CMI was also provided by personnel from the company. As such, the company became responsible for the investment portfolio of CMI. CGFA generated a management fee and gained a perspective of investment opportunities across the minerals sector in Australia. Douglas Ainge, an employee of CGFA, became investment manager. Ted Wiles was appointed assistant

---

11 Commonwealth Mining Investments (Australia) Limited, 'Circular to Shareholders', 26 September 1960, UMA, Stock Exchange of Melbourne, 1968.0018, Box 65.
12 By June 1961, the portfolio had a spread of Australian-listed and overseas-listed mining companies, including Anaconda Company, Cyprus Mines Corporation, Kennecott Copper Corporation, Phelps Dodge Corporation and Falconbridge Nickel.

investment manager and head of the valuation department, reporting to Ainge. On the CMI management committee were Massy-Greene, Ainge, Wiles and Michael Gleeson-White (a director and also partner of Ord & Minnett, and later chief executive officer of Schroders Australia). The committee met monthly to provide investment recommendations to the CMI board. CMI occupied offices at Gold Fields House from 1966.

The most notable activity undertaken by CMI that directly influenced the portfolio of CGFA was its involvement in mineral sands. CMI sponsored the share market listing of Wyong Minerals in 1959 with Cameron serving as initial chairman. The predecessor company, Wyong Alluvial, held leases adjacent to Lake Munmorah in New South Wales, which it proposed to develop in the new company through a dredge-mining operation. A shareholding in another east-coast mineral sands producer, Eastern Titanium Corporation, was established, as well as arrangements with two other mineral sands producers for the supply of rutile.

CGFA gained its main involvement in mineral sands through acquiring shares in another east-coast producer, Associated Minerals Consolidated, while also having a shareholding in Wyong Minerals. In 1967, CGFA facilitated a merger of Associated Minerals Consolidated and Wyong Minerals as the first stage of an expanded presence in the mineral sands industry in Australia. It later acquired another CMI-sponsored mineral sands company—Western Titanium—and in so doing established itself as the largest Australian and global producer of rutile, ilmenite and zircon, with mineral sands becoming a major part of its overall portfolio of investments.

Over a seven-year period after CGFA acquired its majority holding in CMI to 30 June 1968, the book value of CMI's investments rose from A$5,692,000 to A$10,971,000 and annual dividends increased from five cents to 11 cents a share. CMI proved to be a successful investment on a number of fronts, although one that created potential conflicts of interests for directors given the broadening of CGFA's own portfolio to include investments in companies in which CMI had also invested. CGFA maintained an investment in CMI until 1978, when its 60.17 per cent interest was sold to National Mutual Life Corporation. With the foundation investment in CMI in 1960, CGFA moved to broaden its business presence in Australia.

8

A RANGE OF INVESTMENTS

In reviewing the Commonwealth Mining Investments (Australia) (CMI) portfolio, Gerald Mortimer became interested in mineral sands and, in particular, rutile and zircon mining activities being undertaken along the beaches of New South Wales and Queensland. His interest was drawn to an investment in Wyong Minerals that was undertaking dredging operations near Lake Munmorah in New South Wales. CMI had a shareholding in Wyong Minerals and had advanced loans to the value of A£170,000 on the surety of shares in the company. The shares were trading below their par value. According to Ted Wiles, who assisted Mortimer with his analysis of investment opportunities in Australia:

> With [Wyong two shillings and sixpence] shares selling at 9d [ninepence] and rutile/zircon in the doldrums it did not look very hopeful but piqued Gerry's interest and was the germ of the subsequent much larger move into the mineral sands industry as demand for the commodity improved.[1]

CMI also sponsored the listing of Western Titanium, which had acquired mineral sands tenements in the south-west of Western Australia and established mineral sands mining, concentrating and processing operations near the rural township of Capel. CMI had also established an investment in Associated Minerals Consolidated (AMC) in 1957. Within its portfolio in 1960, mineral sands represented 9 per cent of all investments: 11 per cent in 1964 and 19 per cent by 1966.

---

1   Ted Wiles, personal communication, 17 January 2018.

In March 1962, Consolidated Gold Fields (Australia) (CGFA) through its own investments and that of CMI had secured a 75 per cent indirect interest in Wyong Minerals. In 1963, the Wyong Minerals' loans were converted to shares and the placement was allocated to CGFA. In that year, CGFA took over the role as general manager of Wyong Minerals. Through CMI and its own direct investments, Gold Fields could see clear advantages in taking a controlling position in the Australian mineral sands sector. It had the ability to acquire a position in the established east-coast industry, as well as to gain a foothold in the emerging industry in Western Australia. Demand for rutile for the manufacture of titanium metal as well as its direct use for welding rod coatings was viewed as favourable. EI du Pont de Nemours and other United States' pigment manufacturers were seeking supplies of chloride feedstocks for the new chloride process of titanium dioxide pigment manufacture. These feedstocks included both rutile and weathered ilmenites, essential for the emerging chloride pigment process that was replacing the traditional reliance on lead-based pigments in paint. Mortimer advised his London-based directors that consolidation and efficiencies in the industry would aid Australia's market position as an international supplier, as well as the business position of CGFA. This prognosis played out as CGFA established itself as the major global producer in mineral sands.

Mortimer's interest in mineral sands reinforced the favourable impression that George Harvie-Watt had of the industry during his visits to Australia. In 1961, after a review of the mineral sands industry and its participants, a majority shareholding was established in AMC. In a letter to the AMC managing director and founder, Joseph Pinter, Frank Beggs wrote that CGFA wished Pinter to remain as managing director, stating: 'It is the policy of Gold Fields to leave management in the hands of the individual Boards of subsidiaries, and I confirm that it would be our intention to follow the policy in the case of Associated'.[2]

Pinter, an enterprising Hungarian émigré, travelled to Australia with his wife Gerda, arriving in Melbourne in May 1935.[3] Pinter had an association with a company from which he obtained a licence to manufacture welding machines and welding rods in Australia. He established a workshop, initially in North Melbourne and later in Carlton. After the fall of France during World War II, Pinter's British supplier could no longer supply

---

2   Letter from Frank Beggs to J Pinter, 6 September 1961, Renison Goldfields Consolidated Archives (RGCA), Box 40938.
3   Based on notes related to Joseph Pinter prepared by IW Morley, author of *Black Sands: A History of the Mineral Sand Mining Industry in Eastern Australia*. See also Routh, 'Pinter, Joseph (1912–1981)'; Associated Minerals Consolidated Limited, 'Annual Report and Notice of Meeting 1977', pp. 8–9; and interview of Pinter in *The Australian*, 6 December 1969.

rutile for welding rods. Instead, Pinter was advised that the material was available from the beach sands on the coast of northern New South Wales. He obtained concentrate from a company operating at Byron Bay. Given this was a mixed concentrate, containing rutile and ilmenite, a means had to be found to separate the rutile. Pinter determined that separation could occur by electromagnetic methods and developed his own separation equipment. A separator was designed and built with whatever materials he could obtain during the constraints of wartime Australia. Through Pinter's separation process, ilmenite, the dominant magnetic fraction, was removed from the concentrate. The concentrate also contained zircon. Pinter designed an electrostatic separator to separate the zircon from rutile.

Quantities of rutile, the highest-grade titanium material, became available for the first time in Australia. The product was shipped to England under special wartime arrangements. Southport, Queensland, where the concentrate was sourced, became the centre of Pinter's operations. Pinter came to an arrangement with a newly formed company, Southport Minerals, and another group, British Minerals, to form Associated Minerals, in which Pinter held a 50 per cent interest. The company acquired titles to mineral deposits near Broadbeach and around Southport as well as on Moreton Island. Pinter upgraded the processing facilities at Southport, installing his own designed electrostatic and electromagnetic separators. The company was publicly listed in 1953 as Associated Minerals Consolidated. Pinter, as managing director, remained in this position as the company evolved under the ownership of CGFA until he retired in 1977.

AMC's activities involved pegging tenements along the coastline of New South Wales, purchasing leases from other operators and acquiring operating companies. Rutile was initially mainly used for welding rod coatings and, to a lesser extent, for the production of titanium metal. Zircon mainly had foundry and refractory applications. AMC's early years were buoyant. Production and sales grew rapidly and with them profitability. While increased rutile output and lower demand caused a decline in the price of rutile, with some merchants and producers forced to sell at 'distressed prices', and failing to survive, it had little impact on the upward trajectory for AMC. According to its chairman, WE Hopkins, 1957 was 'most important in the development of our activities in the Southport-Cudgen area'.[4] By 1959, AMC's rutile sales constituted 19 per cent of Australia's rutile sales, while the company was responsible for 22 per cent of the country's zircon sales.

---

4   Associated Minerals Consolidated Limited, 'Directors' Report to be Presented at the Fifth Annual General Meeting, to be held Tuesday, 17th December 1957', University of Melbourne Archives (UMA), JB Were and Son, 2000.0017, Unit 611.

Figure 27. Beach dredge mining conducted by Associated Minerals Consolidated along the New South Wales coast.
Source: NAA, A1200, 191695.

In 1961 CGFA made a bid for 50 per cent of AMC's shares. The offer, supported by the board of AMC, enabled CGFA to acquire a 58 per cent interest in the company. With its new shareholder's support, AMC moved to acquire a number of other east-coast mineral sands producers. As the 1966 prospectus for the listing of CGFA stated, the company 'in this manner, contributed to the stabilization of what had been a depressed industry, and in the process, built itself into the largest producer of zircon and rutile in the world'.[5] In 1962 CGFA made an offer for 50 per cent of the shares in Wyong Minerals other than those held by CMI. Wyong Minerals became its subsidiary. This and the AMC acquisition were well timed; the rutile price increased by 50 per cent during 1962, associated with chloride pigment producers seeking greater quantities of this material.

---

5   Consolidated Gold Fields Australia Limited, 'Prospectus', 18 October 1966, p. 3, UMA, 1974.0092, Box 857.

Figure 28. Titania dredge used on North Stradbroke Island, Queensland.
Source: NAA Mineral Sands Mining/5.

In the early 1960s, Australia produced 90 per cent of the world's rutile and approximately 60 per cent of its zircon. In terms of the overall minerals sector in Australia, rutile and zircon exports generated approximately A£11 million, relative to total mineral exports, including pig iron and gold of A£109 million and over A£130 million if thermal coal and coking coal were included. As such, while a relatively small sector, CGFA felt confident it had established a position of market influence, as well as further diversifying its minerals investment base.

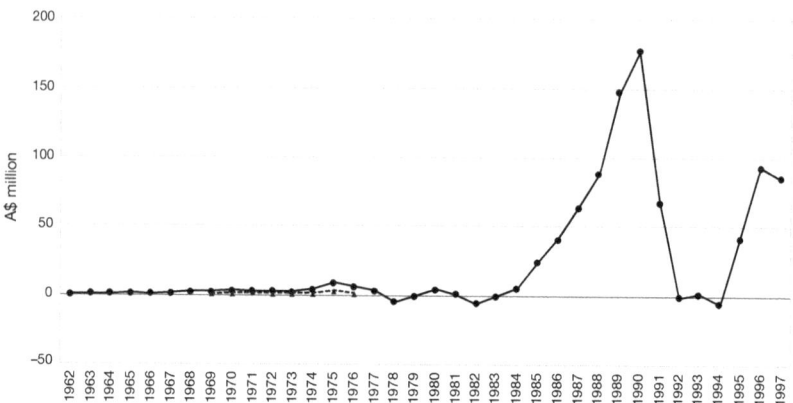

Chart 1. Associated Minerals Consolidated pre-tax earnings, 1962–1997.
Sources: Consolidated Gold Fields Australia Limited, 'Prospectus', 18 October 1966; CGFA and RGC annual reports, 1967 to 1997.

This chart shows the financial performance of CGFA's investment in AMC and subsequent division, AMC Minerals Sands. The years 1969 to 1976 include the contribution from an investment in Western Australian mineral sands producer, Western Titanium. AMC and Western Titanium merged in 1976. The chart reflects the low but relatively stable financial performance until the mid-1980s, when demand for chloride feedstocks, including rutile and synthetic rutile, as well as the demand for zircon, saw a marked appreciation in the financial contribution of mineral sands. In the context of a declining contribution from Renison and the challenges of Mount Lyell, CGFA and RGC developed a preponderant reliance on mineral sands, not reduced until the commencement of production from the Porgera gold operation in the early 1990s.

The initial investments in both CMI and AMC were successful for CGFA, with their combined profits up more than 40 per cent in the 1964 financial year to a new record of A£600,000.[6] Mineral sands became the major part of the portfolio, expanded by the later acquisition of Western Titanium and its merger with AMC. There followed an expansive program of exploration both in Australia and overseas, acquisition of other companies and technological developments, most notably the development of a technology for the beneficiation of ilmenite to a higher-grade titanium dioxide product, to be referred to as synthetic rutile.[7] Mineral sands remained the core part of the portfolio and differentiated the company from its other diversified peers; it would ultimately be a key factor in the aggregation of the successor company—Renison Goldfields Consolidated (RGC)—with another, smaller mineral sands company in the late 1990s.

---

6   *The Times*, 2 December 1964.
7   Typically, a 54 per cent titanium dioxide ilmenite was upgraded to a synthetic rutile product containing around 90 per cent titanium dioxide.

Iron ore—the founding of a new industry

Through New Consolidated Gold Fields (Australasia), exploration prospects for a range of minerals had been evaluated. These included a consideration of bauxite deposits at Gove Peninsula in eastern Arnhem Land, the potential development of an iron ore deposit at Frances Creek, both in the Northern Territory, and a joint venture with Utah Construction & Mining for coal deposits in the Bowen Basin, Queensland. Wider geographical opportunities were also considered with a Consolidated Gold Fields London representative reviewing the Ok Tedi gold and copper mineralisation in Papua New Guinea. Gove and Ok Tedi were discarded as too large as financial undertakings and while drilling occurred at Frances Creek, the resource size was not considered sufficient to commit to further evaluation.[8]

The work of prospectors, notably Lang Hancock and Peter Wright, had identified extensive high-grade iron ore deposits in the Pilbara region of Western Australia, while the Western Australian Bureau of Mines, through its studies at Mount Goldsworthy, provided access to geological information of the potential of this area. New Consolidated Gold Fields (Australasia) conducted a joint exploration program with Cyprus Mines Corporation, a United States' company based in Los Angeles, which included an investigation of iron ore tenements in the Pilbara. Mortimer identified iron ore as one of the main mineral investment opportunities for the newly established Australian company.

Prior to 1960, opportunities to develop this mineral were impeded by the Commonwealth Government's restrictions on the export of iron ore, imposed in 1938. In December 1960, the embargo on iron ore exports was relaxed. This provided the impetus for CGFA to establish a presence in Australia's iron ore sector and with it make a contribution to the establishment of infrastructure that formed a basis of a major industry. It did so in the context of activities by Conzinc Rio Tinto's recently formed Australian subsidiary, Conzinc Riotinto Australia (CRA), in establishing its own major iron ore presence, as well as efforts by other companies near Robe River, Western Australia.

---

8   Ted Wiles, personal communication, 17 January 2018.

In 1961, the Western Australian Government called for tenders to develop iron ore areas of Western Australia, including at Mount Goldsworthy. According to a Consolidated Gold Fields executive:

> We were attracted by this proposition, but the size of the probable capital investment and our own inexperience in this field of open cast mining and bulk transportation of iron ore led us to decide to work in partnership with Cyprus Mines Corporation of Los Angeles and Utah Construction & Mining Co. of San Francisco.[9]

CGFA joined with Cyprus and Utah to spread the risk and capital associated with a large and complex venture. Cyprus and Utah had a joint involvement in a Peruvian iron ore operation and through it established a marketing arm, Marcona, in which they held a combined majority interest. Marcona would be used for the initial marketing of iron ore from Mount Goldsworthy.[10] Utah also brought a mining and construction capability, which proved crucial for the mine and infrastructure development. This included deepening of the entrance channel to Port Hedland, the harbour selected for the shipment of iron ore.

The Western Australian Government tender for the development of Mount Goldsworthy called for proposals for the production and export of up to 15 million tons of iron ore, out of an estimated 30 million tons of reserves. The restriction reflected the requirement to preserve half of the high-quality deposits for potential domestic Australian use.

---

9   DES Barton, 'The Mount Goldsworthy Project', in Consolidated Gold Fields Limited, 'Speeches Given at the Group Conference Held at Gleneagles Hotel, Scotland on 2–9 July, 1964', p. 165.
10   Marcona was owned 46.75 per cent by Cyprus and 42.25 per cent by Utah. The remaining equity interest was held by the founder and chief executive of this entity, Charles W Robinson. I am grateful to Dr David Moore for his input to this section. Moore was recruited by Bart Ryan in London as administration manager for Goldsworthy Mining Limited, where he worked from 1970 to mid-1976. Moore advised the author that the establishment of a dual corporate structure of Mount Goldsworthy Mining Associates and Mount Goldsworthy Pty Ltd was influenced by a requirement of the US participants to avail themselves of a depletion allowance available under the US taxation system, which required them to hold title to the ore. The taxation deductions available in Australia for expenditure to build infrastructure, such as townships for example, could be obtained only by the employing entity. To address this, Goldsworthy Mining was contracted at a fee, initially 10 per cent of cash operating costs (later reduced to 5 per cent), to manage the assets of the employing entity. Goldsworthy Mining was able to secure debt finance in Australia and enter into various non-mining leases, including that for the seabed for Port Hedland Harbour (David Moore, personal communication, 27 August 2018 and 6 September 2018). RIJ Agnew, grandson of John Agnew and later chief executive and chairman of Consolidated Gold Fields Limited, was seconded to Goldsworthy Mining as an administrative superintendent during the construction period for the Mount Goldsworthy project (RIJ Agnew, 'Mount Goldsworthy Iron Ore', *Mining Magazine*, December 1966, vol. 115, no. 6).

The tender required the construction of a loading berth and ancillary harbour facilities at a port to be selected and provision of transport facilities by road or rail between the site and the harbour. If transportation was by rail, it needed to be capable of transporting 1 million tons per annum, with all rolling stock and other infrastructure supplied. Township facilities were also required to be built at Goldsworthy and at Finucane Island, opposite Port Hedland, the site of the port-loading facilities. Each tenderer was required to submit the level of royalty per ton they were prepared to pay. In January 1962, a joint venture, Mount Goldsworthy Mining Associates (MGMA) was established.

Six companies tendered for the right to develop the Mount Goldsworthy deposits; the MGMA joint venture was successful in winning the tender. In February 1962, an agreement was signed with the Western Australian Government for the development of 15 million tons of iron ore at an estimated capital expenditure of A£12 million and a commitment to pay a royalty on lump ore at the rate of 7.5 per cent.[11] Three potential port locations were considered: Cape Keraudren, Port Hedland and Depuch Island. With the initial possibility that exports could be limited to 1 million tons, Port Hedland was ruled out due to the extent of dredging required, with preliminary studies suggesting that Depuch Island may be suitable for the port site. This site, located south of Port Hedland and 110 kilometres from the mining site, was also initially favoured by the Western Australian Government.

In June 1963 the Commonwealth Government liberalised export conditions for iron ore, removing completely the export embargo. That month an export licence was granted covering 64 million tons at a rate of 4 million tons per annum.[12] The higher rate of production improved the economics of the project, but entailed a considerably larger level of capital expenditure, to over A£20 million. With the larger level of export tonnage granted, Port Hedland came back into contention as the most appropriate port on a cost and engineering basis.

---

11   The revenue was net of free-on-board for lump iron ore and 3.75 per cent for fines.
12   Mount Goldsworthy Mining Associates, 'Technical Proposals for the Development of the Mount Goldsworthy Iron Ore Deposits and Port Hedland Harbour', February 1964, p. 1.

The joint venture had three-and-a-half years to complete its evaluation and construction activities, with the final award of a mining licence dependent upon securing suitable sales contracts. In 1963, the feasibility study was underway, with engineers and geologists engaged in drilling and underground tunnelling. CGFA played a key role in feasibility study planning and also in geological and metallurgical evaluation of the deposits, while engineering work was conducted by Utah. The exploration program involved surface geological mapping, surface sampling, diamond drilling, construction of adits and vertical percussion drilling. The evaluation by MGMA determined 'large reserves of high quality iron ore' as well as supplementary deposits that could be developed.[13] The drilling identified approximately 52 million tons of ore from the two initial ore bodies expected to be developed, although ore reserves of at least 190 million tons were identified on the tenements retained by the joint venture.[14]

In 1964 *The Iron Ore (Mount Goldsworthy) Agreement Act* was proclaimed authorising mining activity. The companies were also able to secure access to additional lease areas. Whereas the original agreement covered an area of 25 square kilometres, the new agreement provided an additional 19 'reserves' near to and west of Mount Goldsworthy, known as Area B, encompassing 400 square kilometres and another area, known as Area C, of 1,000 square kilometres to the south.[15] According to one writer, the level of detailed evaluation undertaken of the joint venture 'emboldened them to seek to export the whole of the 64,000,000 tons of the deposit at a rate of 4,000,000 tons per annum' rather than the initial tender for up to 15 million tons.[16] The joint venture developed the Mount Goldsworthy deposit, known as Area A, and then moved to additional deposits at Shay Gap, Kennedy Gap and Sunrise Hill. Production began at 1.5 million tons and planned to exceed 10 million tons per annum. The leases for Mining Areas A, B and C were granted on 5 October 1964 and development commenced.

---

13   *The Times*, 14 December 1962.
14   DES Barton, 'The Mount Goldsworthy Project', in Consolidated Gold Fields Limited, 'Speeches Given at the Group Conference Held at Gleneagles Hotel, Scotland on 2–9 July, 1964', p. 167.
15   *The Times*, 16 October 1964.
16   Lee, *Iron Country: Unlocking the Pilbara*, pp. 33–34.

Port facilities were built on Finucane Island, adjacent to Port Hedland, and an extensive dredging program was conducted by Utah over 26 months, deepening a 7-kilometre channel and creating a turning circle for vessels of up to 60,000 tons capacity. The construction contract for other infrastructure, which included diesel power generation at the mine and port, as well as facilities for crushing, railway, ship loading, water supply and telecommunications, and all buildings for employees and the plant and workshops, was executed in June 1965.[17] A 110-kilometre railway line was constructed from Finucane Island to Goldsworthy. At Goldsworthy, a location without any existing infrastructure, a township had to be created in the barren red soil, with housing, recreational and sport facilities established and sewerage, water and power services for what became a population of over 800 people. Likewise, housing facilities were required on Finucane Island, with more than 60 houses constructed, as well as an apartment block for single employees. A causeway was built to connect Finucane Island to the mainland while the island became the site for ore crushing, stockpiling of ore and loading onto ships. In February 1965 MGMA, through its marketing arm, CIA San Juan SA, a subsidiary of Marcona, signed contracts with Japanese steel mills for the export of 16.5 million tons, beginning with the export of 1.5 million tons of ore in 1966 and then 2.5 million tons in each of the years from 1967 to 1972.[18] The price struck for the first 2.75 million tons was at a rate higher than the subsequent volume contracted, with no escalation allowable in prices for cost increases over the duration of the contract.[19]

---

17   Material Contract No. 5 and Material Contract No. 6, in Mount Lyell Mining and Railway, Co, Consolidated Goldfields 1964–1966 Contracts, UMA, 1974.0067.
18   CIA San Juan marketed and shipped iron ore for its parent company, Marcona Mining Company (Peru). The initial contracts were for 100 millimetre × 6 millimetre ore, considered to be an unusual product, which could include 20 per cent fines. This was later replaced by 30 millimetre × 6 millimetre ore and fines (David Moore, personal communication, 6 September 2018).
19   Raggatt, *Mountains of Ore*, p. 121.

Figure 29. Construction of the railway line from Mount Goldsworthy mine site to Port Hedland, 1966.
Source: NAA, A1200, L54823.

Figure 30. Iron ore train crossing De Grey River.
Source: NAA, A1200, L77644.

Figure 31. First iron ore shipment from Port Hedland in 1966, showing crushing facility at Finucane Island.
Source: NAA, A1200, L55248.

Figure 32. Ship loading, Finucane Island.
Source: NAA, A1200, L55411.

Figure 33. *Harvey S Mudd* **at Finucane Island, 1966.**
Source: NAA, A1200, L55410.

The initial contracts were estimated to generate US$150 million for the joint venture.[20] Financing for CGFA was by means of an arrangement whereby Gold Fields Mining & Industrial advanced loan funds of A£14 million, unsecured and interest free, with A£9 million deemed to have been repaid by allotting Gold Fields Mining & Industrial pre-paid shares in CGFA.[21] In June 1966, the first shipment of Mount Goldsworthy iron ore of 20,000 tons was dispatched; an outcome achieved in a remarkably short period for such a major development and despite cyclonic weather washing away part of the railway in the weeks before the initial transportation of the iron ore. By 1967 CGFA had committed A$13 million to the project, with an obligation for a further minimum payment of A$9.5 million.[22]

---

20 Goldsworthy Mining Pty Limited, UMA, Australian United Corporation, 1980.0088, Box 49.
21 Material Contract No. 10, UMA, 1974.0067.
22 This and other sections in the chapter make reference to both Australian pounds and Australian dollars. This reflects the conversion from imperial to decimal currency, which occurred on 14 February 1966.

Figure 34. Aerial view of Mount Goldsworthy, Pilbara, Western Australia, 1974.
Source: NAA, A6180, 3/7/74/7.

The development of the first commercial iron ore production in the Pilbara by a British–American consortium was a massive undertaking and an impressive achievement for the newly established company in Australia, particularly given it was active on a number of fronts. Mount Goldsworthy represented the first direct operational venture in Australia for CGFA. Mortimer was instrumental in its development, facilitating the investment from London and spearheading the feasibility study work, as well as working to secure the enabling legislation for the project. He was viewed as the 'father' of Mount Goldsworthy for his efforts and, along with Paul Allen of Cyprus, was highly influential in the development and early management of this major Australian mining project.[23] Mortimer

---

23   Cartwright, *Gold Paved the Way*, p. 290.

became the first general manager of the project, seconded from London. Described by one contemporary as 'taciturn but effective', in Harvie-Watt's assessment he was a 'tower of strength to Gold Fields'.[24] Mortimer went on to become chief executive officer and deputy chairman of Consolidated Gold Fields.

The Mount Goldsworthy joint venture was one of four groups that developed iron ore projects in the first half of the 1960s. The others were Hamersley Iron, a CRA and Kaiser Steel joint venture; Mt Newman Iron Ore Company, comprising BHP, CSR and AMAX; and Robe River, involving Cleveland Cliffs. In early 1965, apart from MGMA, two other major contracts for the supply of iron ore from the Pilbara to Japanese steel mills were signed, including 100 million tons from Mt Newman Iron Ore and 65.5 million tons from Hamersley Iron Ore. The Japanese steel mills used the period of contracting negotiations to apply pressure to their existing suppliers, out of India and Malaysia, as well as play the new Australian producers off against each other.

In this environment, consideration was given by MGMA to merging with another iron ore company, while Utah was willing to contemplate the Mount Goldsworthy joint venture facilitating Australian public participation in the project. The consideration by Utah was motivated in part by borrowing restrictions upon the non-Australian listed participants and a preference by some lenders to have equity as collateral. The level of investment for the Mount Goldsworthy development by CGFA, associated with other expenditure in Australia, meant that its British parent also envisaged the need to issue shares in CGFA to Australian investors as part of its funding considerations. While such considerations were not acted upon at the time of first production, they were factors—in an environment of increased resource nationalisation in the 1970s—to lead Mount Isa Mines to be invited to take an equity position in the Mount Goldsworthy project.

By December 1964, Consolidated Gold Fields had committed GBP£7 million to its investments in Australia and by 1966 this had increased to GBP£12 million. Despite five years of record profits by the British company, a pause in its earnings growth occurred in the 1966 financial year, caused by a loss from its American zinc interests, as well as

---

24 Harvie-Watt, *Most of My Life*, p. 252.

restrictions on investments from the United Kingdom. In the light of its funding obligations, particularly for Mount Goldsworthy, a partial listing of the Australian subsidiary became a necessity. This occurred in 1966.

Australian iron ore production peaked in the early 1970s, affected by the circumstances of the Japanese steel industry where capacity was reduced in the face of falling international demand. In negotiations with the Japanese steel mills it proved extremely difficult to achieve price increases. The financial consequences of lower demand and flat prices were compounded by increasing costs, the problems in attracting workers and endemic industrial disputation. These factors led CGFA to re-evaluate its continued involvement in the iron ore industry. The need to commit substantial funds for the next mine development, Area C; other capital requirements of the group; and the weak financial performance of its wider portfolio in the early 1970s led to the decision to sell its interest in the company's single largest investment in Australia to that time. Both CGFA and Cyprus exited their involvement in the Mount Goldsworthy joint venture in 1976.

Manufacturing interests

Diversification from minerals formed part of the investment decision-making of CGFA in the first half of 1960s. The company established a direct shareholding in two manufacturing companies and also participated in smaller direct investments related to industrial companies. Consolidated Gold Fields in London held a majority shareholding in Alumasc, a United Kingdom die-casting business that was a major producer of aluminium casting. An attraction of this business was its involvement in the manufacture of aluminium beer kegs. In December 1961, Alumasc made a takeover offer for the Australian company RH Lawrenson Holdings. The acquisition occurred and the company, renamed Lawrenson Alumasc Holdings, became a subsidiary of CGFA. The business, based at Lidcombe in New South Wales, undertook both metal and plastic die-casting. At a Consolidated Gold Fields management conference in Scotland in 1964, Brian Massy-Greene, in reviewing the investments of the new Australian entity, referred to the history of Alumasc since it had been acquired as not a 'very happy one', although the manufacture of beer kegs was expected to 'find an interesting place in Australian industry'.[25] At the 1965 annual general meeting for Lawrenson Alumasc Holdings, two years after CGFA had invested in the business, and in the context of a reported loss, Massy-Greene observed: 'The die-casting industry is one which continues to be faced with fierce competition and low profit margins on its products'.[26] In 1969, CGFA acquired Consolidated Gold Fields' shares in Alumasc Limited in the United Kingdom and from June of that year Lawrenson Alumasc Holdings was owned 56.5 per cent by CGFA. Lawrenson Alumasc Holdings was retained in the portfolio, with additional investments in acquiring associated business, until sold to Borg Warner (Australia) and James N Kirby in January 1978.

In April 1964, Massy-Greene reported to the Australian board of directors on negotiations being conducted in New Zealand for the acquisition of a 51 per cent interest in the manufacturing company Zip Holdings. Massy-Greene, with his background at the Metal Manufactures group, had a familiarity with the Zip Holdings business. It produced a range of domestic products, including water heaters, irons and electric jugs. Part of the attraction of this company was that, in New Zealand, number plates for vehicles were replaced each year associated with vehicle registration renewal. After a review by the London board, CGFA was given approval to proceed with the acquisition, for just over A£1 million. In July 1964 the company became a subsidiary of CGFA. The initial years saw an improvement in the profitability of the company.[27] However, competitive pressures and increased costs adversely affected the financial performance of Zip Holdings and, as with Alumasc, the shareholding was sold, in 1976 at a profit on the sale of shares of A$358,000.

---

25   JB Massy-Greene, 'Gold Fields in Australia', in Consolidated Gold Fields Limited, 'Speeches Given at the Group Conference Held at Gleneagles Hotel, Scotland on 2–9 July, 1964', p. 156.
26   The loss was A£47,326 (Lawrenson Alumasc Holdings Ltd, 'Address by Chairman to the Shareholders of Lawrenson Alumasc Holdings Limited at the Fifteenth Ordinary General Meeting of the Company, 21st September 1965', UMA, Stock Exchange of Melbourne, 1968.0018, Box 733).
27   Profit after tax in 1964 was just over A$500,000 and A$492,000 in 1965. Profit after tax in 1962 was A$144,000 and A$165,000 in 1963 (Consolidated Gold Fields Australia Limited, 'Prospectus', 18 October 1966, UMA, 1974.0092, Box 857).

Bellambi Coal

Sir Ian Potter, the Melbourne-based stockbroker and businessman, had an influence upon two CGFA investments in 1964: The Bellambi Coal Company and The Mount Lyell Mining and Railway Company. Bellambi Coal was incorporated as a listed company in 1923 following the liquidation of a previous company of the same name, established in 1888. The company conducted coking coal operations on the south coast of New South Wales with an operation at South Bulli Colliery, near Port Kembla.

The major coal-producing province on the south coast of New South Wales had over 10 coal exporters. Bellambi was the fourth-largest Australian colliery and the attraction to CGFA was that it offered 'enormous reserves' and was well placed to take advantage of the growing export market with Japan.[28] The increase in Japanese steel manufacturing activity in the late 1950s and early 1960s led to an increased demand for Australian coal. Bellambi had entered the export trade for coal during 1962 and, as with other producers, took advantage of the burgeoning demand for coking coal by the Japanese steel industry. While CGFA had undertaken joint exploration with Utah in the Bowen Basin, Queensland—to become the major coal production province of Australia—it had not taken this association forward. An involvement, through Bellambi Coal, represented an attractive opportunity for CGFA to broaden its business presence in Australia.

Potter was chairman of McIlwraith McEacharn, a company that provided stevedoring and shipping services to Bellambi Coal and had a shareholding in the company. Following discussions in London with Consolidated Gold Fields directors, Potter forwarded a letter to Massy-Greene in May 1964 offering to sell stock units it held in Bellambi Coal to CGFA. The offer was conditional upon CGFA 'acquiring control but not full ownership' of the company.[29] The purchase of stock units at a cost of A£238,952 occurred in 1964. CGFA had also acquired Bellambi shares through the stock market, representing 17.5 per cent of the issued

---

28 JB Massy-Greene, 'Gold Fields in Australia', in Consolidated Gold Fields Limited, 'Speeches Given at the Group Conference Held at Gleneagles Hotel, Scotland on 2–9 July, 1964', p. 154.
29 Letter from Sir Ian Potter, Chairman, McIlwraith McEacharn Limited to JB Massy-Greene, 8 May 1964; Consolidated Gold Fields (Australia) Pty Ltd, 'Minutes of Meeting of Directors (Australia) Pty Ltd', 15 April 1964, RGCA, Box 12264.

capital of the company. This provided the basis for CGFA to make a formal offer to other Bellambi shareholders. The company's directors supported the offer, viewing it as a basis 'to greatly facilitate the provision of finance necessary for the immediate and long-term development' of the Bellambi operation, including expanding domestic coal sales and those to export markets, as well as extending coke production.[30] Massy-Greene was appointed chairman and in 1964 CGFA owned 65.6 per cent of the company.

After CGFA acquired its holding, a production expansion program was committed to, entailing expenditure of A£1.9 million in 1965 for the installation of mechanised long-wall excavation equipment, extensions to the coal preparation plant and other infrastructure. In the same year, an arrangement was secured with Japanese steel mills and other customers for the supply of 1.25 million tons of coal for three years from March 1967. The adoption of new mining techniques, including the use of long-wall mining equipment, and access to new reserves, were seen as the means to increase production and greatly improve operating efficiencies at the mine. The initial years for CGFA were favourable, with the first annual general meeting of Bellambi Coal under CGFA ownership reporting a profit increase of A£49,263 to A£120,442 and a return on capital of 21.5 per cent. However, as with other investments, Bellambi Coal had a variable performance during CGFA's ownership, influenced by a range of factors including frequent labour stoppages and disruptions, the imposition of levies and financial charges, as well as impediments in dealing with the New South Wales Government in gaining approvals for access to new deposits. During the 1970s, issues with equipment reliability, the adverse effect on coal demand associated with the downturn in the Japanese steel industry, industrial disputes and a Commonwealth Government coal export levy created serious operational and financial issues for Bellambi Coal. CGFA decided, in the face of such factors, to sell its 64 per cent shareholding in 1980.[31]

---

30   'Offer by Consolidated Gold Fields (Australia) Pty Ltd to Acquire Stock in the Issued Capital of The Bellambi Coal Company Limited 1964', UMA, Stock Exchange of Melbourne, 1968.0018, Box 33.
31   The sale occurred to a Shell Company of Australia subsidiary, Austen & Butta, and McIlwraith McEacharn. Proceeds were A$19.1 million, representing a capital profit of A$16 million on the investment (Consolidated Gold Fields Australia Ltd, 'Chairman's Address, Annual General Meeting 15th October, 1980', UMA, Stock Exchange of Melbourne, 1987.0138, Box 70).

Copper—The Mount Lyell Mining and Railway Company

What was considered a fundamental investment for the new mining group in Australian was the gaining of a controlling interest in the historic Mount Lyell copper mining, milling and smelting operation at Queenstown in the north-west of Tasmania in 1964. With this investment, CGFA also gained an indirect interest in the Renison tin operation near Zeehan, 40 kilometres away. As it transpired, Renison formed a key business interest for the group. Both remained major components of the CGFA and RGC portfolios until the second half of the 1990s.

Mount Lyell was initially worked for gold with copper mineralisation discovered in 1893, the year of the formation of Mount Lyell Mining and Railway Company. Mining first occurred at the Iron Blow ore body until the 1920s by both underground and open cut mining methods. By the 1930s, mining had shifted to lower-grade deposits at Mount Lyell, suitable for open cut mining, which continued through to 1972 when replaced by underground mining. Power was obtained from a hydro-electric power station at Lake Margaret. Smelting had been undertaken at Queenstown since 1896. The valleys of Queenstown were often blanketed in a yellow, acrid fog from the billowing smoke stacks of smelters used to treat the pyritic ore. The nearby hills were denuded, first for timber used in shafts and then by the effects of the sulphurous air and acid-forming rain. Smelting and refining operations ceased in 1969 under the control of CGFA.[32] Subsequently, the Mount Lyell operation was confined to the milling and the sale of blister copper and later copper concentrates, sent by rail to Burnie.

In 1958, the chairman of Mount Lyell, Sir Walter Bassett, became concerned that the company may be under takeover threat from Rio Tinto. He wrote to the general manager, HM Murray, opening his confidential letter: 'This is an appeal for immediate and urgent action'. He continued:

---

32   Over this period 656,402 tons of blister copper was produced containing 650,618 tons of fine copper, 16,408,630 ounces of silver and 646,632 ounces of gold (*Annual Report 1 August 1970*, p. 9 in Mount Lyell Mining and Railway Company Limited, Operating Reports 1970, National Archives of Australia, Tasmania (NAAT), Series NS3924, Items 533-540).

> I am certain that we are going to be faced soon with an offer of 'collaboration' by Rio Tinto, whose only idea of collaboration is that of the tiger's complete swallowing. They are wealthy and ambitious and can be utterly unscrupulous. I suspect, too, that they are vindictive because we refused to accept their terms for joint exploration in the north-west and because they now think that we have beaten them to it at Renison.[33]

Bassett had been approached by the group chairman of Rio Tinto for a luncheon in London, a request that Ian Potter, a stockbroker to Rio Tinto, had urged Bassett to accept. Bassett was willing to accommodate a meeting, but saw no need to dine with Rio Tinto's chairman. At the meeting, he was offered financing from Rio Tinto to enable Mount Lyell to increase its production. Bassett respectfully listened, bemused as to why Mount Lyell should accept such an offer even if it accorded with its plans. Basset was later approached by the secretary of Rio Tinto to make arrangements for the Rio Tinto chairman and a number of senior technical personnel to visit the Mount Lyell operation. Again, Bassett felt it would be inappropriate to refuse such a request. However, his suspicions regarding Rio Tinto's motivations were all but confirmed when he enquired of Rio Tinto why such a 'top-brass party' was interested in travelling to Queenstown. Bassett recorded that Rio Tinto's managing director hesitated and then said: 'Well, all I can tell you is that we are not going all that way for the benefit of our health'.[34] Believing a takeover may be imminent, Bassett advised Murray:

> If this is Rio's plan, as it might quite well be, and it could happen almost overnight, our only chance ... is to persuade the market to appreciate our shares as quickly as possible in order to, if possible, make the take-over price prohibitive ... There is apparently nothing else we can do at this stage, and in time, such as splitting the company into two component parts, or writing up our assets and issuing bonus shares.
>
> And now I come to the immediate task ... Will you please look into this for, say, a 50% increase and alternatively for a 100% increase in output, mainly, if not all, from the open cut.[35]

---

33   'Personal and Confidential to Hugh Murray, Penghana, Queenstown, 25 October 1958', NAAT, NS1711/1/770.
34   ibid.
35   ibid.

Murray's response to Bassett was to propose developing an underground mining operation at Prince Lyell, rather than expanding the open cut. In his view, this would facilitate access to the extensive deeper reserves and be more profitable than expanding existing operations.[36] Bassett's concerns with Mount Lyell's vulnerability to be taken over, in the context of Rio Tinto's apparent intentions, were confirmed when another company made an approach to acquire Mount Lyell. This set in train a series of events that ultimately enabled CGFA to acquire a majority shareholding in Mount Lyell. This outcome was facilitated by Boral, a company introduced to the Mount Lyell board of directors by Potter to protect it from an unwelcome takeover offer by Bolivian tin interests.

In 1961, Mount Lyell Mining and Railway Company was reconstructed into two companies. One was an investment company, Mount Lyell Investments, which had holdings in Metal Manufactures, Email, Imperial Chemical Industries of Australia and New Zealand, and Cuming Smith, as well as fertiliser interests through a number of companies.[37] After the reconstruction, the other company, The Mount Lyell Mining and Railway Company, retained its existing mining assets and a shareholding in Renison which it had acquired in 1958, as well as a shareholding in Imperial Chemical Industries of Australia and New Zealand.[38] Consolidated Gold Fields' valuation area in London had decided that Mount Lyell Investments was an appropriate entity for its Australian subsidiary to consider, both for diversification purposes and because of its cash position. In November 1962, CGFA contemplated a merger with Mount Lyell Investments in the form of a reverse takeover.[39] In February 1963, CGFA representatives met the directors of Mount Lyell Investments in Melbourne. The proposal for a merger was 'not well received' and did not progress.[40] While CGFA continued to buy shares in Mount Lyell Investments, by July 1963 Mount Lyell Investments had been acquired by another company.

---

36   Letter from HM Murray, general manager, to WE Bassett, chairman of directors, 30 October 1958, NAAT, NS 1711/1/770.
37   These companies were Commonwealth Fertilisers and Chemicals, Mount Lyell Fertilisers, Australian Fertilizers and Wallaroo-Mount Lyell Fertilisers.
38   The Mount Lyell Mining and Railway Company Limited, 'Circular to Shareholders: Reconstruction of the Company', 29 November 1961, UMA, Stock Exchange of Melbourne, 1968.0018, Box 190.
39   Cartwright, *Gold Paved the Way*, p. 296.
40   *The Times*, 14 December 1962 and 2 December 1964.

CGFA recognised that Mount Lyell Mining and Railway Company, in its own right, provided an appropriate investment opportunity. A major attraction was the potential for expansion of production by accessing the deeper ore body below the existing open cut mine. Drilling at Mount Lyell had identified the potential of an estimated 40–50 million tons of ore at 1 per cent copper. In addition, Mount Lyell's shareholding in Renison was an attraction. A drilling program at Renison in the early 1960s provided encouragement of additional, deeper reserves in the existing Federal ore body, as well as a new ore body, the Bassett Lode in a footwall of Federal ore body.[41] Consolidated Gold Fields in London was aware of the potential of the Renison mine and had established a direct shareholding in Renison. As such, the British and Australian arms of Gold Fields both understood that Mount Lyell and its interest in Renison offered a meaningful opportunity to establish a position in base metals.

In 1963, Mount Lyell Mining and Railway Company came under a foreign takeover threat. After previous overtures had been rebuffed, Patino Mining Corporation, a Quebec-based tin company, in association with British Tin Investment and Consolidated Tin Smelters, made a formal offer to acquire not less than 30 per cent and not more than 60 per cent of Mount Lyell's shares. The motivation was to acquire the 50 per cent shareholding that Mount Lyell held in Renison. The offer for Mount Lyell and, as such, its shareholding in Renison occurred in the same year that Bitumen and Oil Refineries (Australia) Limited (Boral) had acquired control of Mount Lyell Investments.[42] Potter was influential in the arrangements involved in Boral gaining control of Mount Lyell, acting in his role as a *'de facto* corporate planner for Boral, locating suitable acquisitions, carrying out negotiations with the target companies and delivering them to Boral at a good price'.[43]

---

41   Mount Lyell, Confidential Paper, UMA, Stock Exchange of Melbourne, 1968.0018, Box 190; Raggatt, *Mountains of Ore*, pp. 379–380.
42   Boral was incorporated in March 1946 as Bitumen and Oil Refineries (Australia) Limited and changed its name to Boral Limited in November 1963.
43   Yule, *Ian Potter: Financier and Philanthropist*, p. 11.

Bassett, as he had been in the case with Rio Tinto's unwelcome advances, had little interest in considering let alone accommodating the approach by Patino. According to Bassett, Patino's technical review of Mount Lyell's operations was both 'clandestine and <u>most perfunctory</u>'; in his view, Patino had 'no conception of the nature and magnitude of the difficulties still to face the mine'.[44] For Bassett, 'such apparent carelessness' in its investment consideration of Mount Lyell could be explained only by Patino having no real concerns if the Mount Lyell operation failed, with its prime motivation to gain access to the Renison deposits.[45] Discussions were held with the Commonwealth treasurer to persuade the government that the offer was not in the 'best interests of Australia', nor the company.[46]

The Patino takeover offer was rejected emphatically by the directors of Mount Lyell. In November 1963, Boral advised that it intended to make a counter offer to purchase not less than 30 per cent and not more than 50 per cent of the shares in Mount Lyell. The Boral offer, under the direction of its managing director, Elton Griffin, was readily accepted by the directors of Mount Lyell as in the interests of shareholders, as well as national interest.[47] The acquisition occurred, with the 1964 Boral annual report observing that it was 'Boral's first venture into the Australian Metalliferous Mining industry'.[48]

It was unlikely that Boral had a long-term intention of committing to a business investment in Mount Lyell and Renison. By April 1964, Boral had become aware of the level of capital expenditure required for both the operation and development of the Mount Lyell ore bodies. In a letter to Bassett on 8 April 1964, Griffin expressed concerns with the five-year capital expenditure plans of Mount Lyell, seeking an independent review of the longer-term mining outlook.[49] In May, Griffin approached CGFA with the suggestion that it take over the direction of the technical management of Mount Lyell. Potter, given his recent engagement with

---

44 Mount Lyell, Confidential Paper, UMA, Stock Exchange of Melbourne, 1968.0018, Box 190. Underscoring in original.
45 ibid.
46 'Confidential. Discussion—Sir Walter Bassett with Treasurer, 31/10/63', p. 2, UMA, The Mount Lyell Mining and Railway Co, 1974.0067, Box Patino Offer.
47 The Mount Lyell Mining and Railway Company Limited, 'Circular to Shareholders: Take-Over Offers', 3 December 1963, p. 2, UMA, Stock Exchange of Melbourne, 1968.0018, Box 190.
48 Boral Limited, *18th Annual Report—Year ended June 30, 1964*, p. 10, UMA, Stock Exchange of Melbourne, 1968.0018, Box 39.
49 Letter from Elton Griffin to Walter Bassett, 8 April 1964, UMA, The Mount Lyell Mining and Railway Co, 1974.0067, Box Boral Offer.

CGFA and its London directors in relation to Bellambi Coal, identified the opportunity to offer some or all of the Boral shareholding to the newly established mining company seeking to broaden its Australian mining interests. Gold Fields in London had also decided to increase its stake in Mount Lyell 'either by bidding for a portion of the outside shareholdings and/or acquiring part of Boral's holding'.[50]

On 3 June 1964, CGFA was granted approval to send a technical team to Queenstown to undertake a detailed inspection and valuation exercise. The team comprised a range of Gold Fields technical personnel, drawn from the group's London, South African and American operations, headed by Mortimer.[51] CGFA sought a firm option from Boral on the shares it was being offered, exercisable at the completion of the evaluation. Boral declined, instead giving CGFA the option to acquire 4 million shares at six shillings and sixpence eligible within 48 hours, or else negotiate both the quantity of shares and the price at the end of the valuation period, expected to be in a month. While the latter approach was favoured by CGFA, London directed that settlement occur on 4 June. This duly occurred.

Boral offered a further 198,886 shares at six shillings and sixpence, which gave CGFA a 29.74 per cent shareholding. By the end of the year, Boral was aware of the level of capital expenditure required for underground mining activities to access deeper reserves, as well as for the expansion of mining and milling operations at Renison. Griffin and Massy-Greene met on 7 December 1964. The meeting discussed the level of funds required for the exploration and development of underground reserves at Mount Lyell, estimated at A£6.8 million with a potential further A£2 million if a new refinery was constructed. Griffin wrote to Massy-Greene the following day: 'The information now at our disposal, indicating the large sums of money that will be required to fully develop Mt. Lyell has caused us to review our whole position with particular reference to our ability to

---

50   Segal, 'Notes on Redraft of Chapter XXV and XXVI of "History of Goldfields"', 2 March 1966, p. 4, RGCA, Box 1091.
51   The Mount Lyell Mining & Railway Coy Ltd, 'Memorandum for Sir Walter Bassett. From Secretary, Party to Visit Queenstown from Tuesday 16th June 1964', NAAT, NS1711/1/770.

contribute our proportion of the contemplated amount'.[52] Boral offered CGFA its remaining shareholding of 4,840,112 shares at 11 shillings and sixpence. Sidney Segal recalled that:

> Although the price was on the steep side, it was decided on 7th December to accept, making Mount Lyell a subsidiary of C.G.F. (A). with Lyell holding 49.9% of Renison, and Gold Fields [London] a small direct holding, Renison also became a subsidiary.[53]

The purchase price for these shares was A£2,783,066, the single largest share investment CGFA had made in Australia.

Figure 35. Mount Lyell Mining and Railway Company copper mining operation, Queenstown, 1963.
Source: NAA, A1200, L43495.

---

52 Material Contract No. 2, Correspondence between ER Griffin, general manager of Boral Limited and BH Massy-Greene, 8th December 1964, UMA, Mount Lyell Mining and Railway Co, 1974.0067, Box Consolidated Goldfields 1964–1966 Contracts.
53 Segal, 'Notes on Redraft of Chapter XXV and XXVI of "History of Goldfields"', 2 March 1966, p. 5, RGCA, Box 1091.

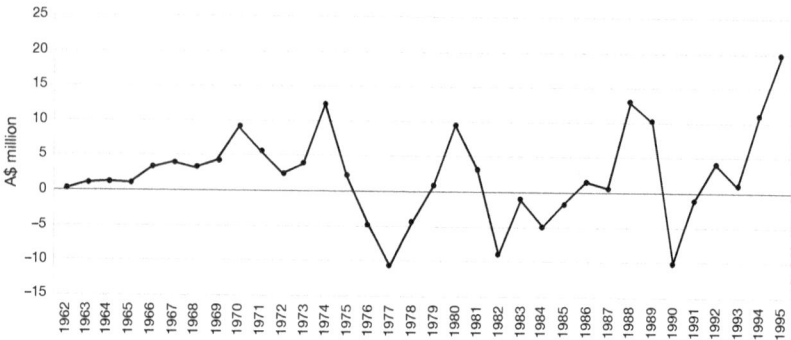

Chart 2. Mount Lyell Mining and Railway Company pre-tax earnings, 1962–1995.
Source: Consolidated Gold Fields Australia Limited, 'Prospectus', 18 October 1966; CGFA and RGC annual reports, 1967 to 1995.

This chart shows the historical performance of Mount Lyell Mining and Railway Company within CGFA and subsequently as part of the Copper Division of RGC. Mount Lyell was the largest single investment in the portfolio in the 1960s. It offered the British group an interest in base metals, and an associated holding in the Renison tin operation. In the 1960s and early 1970s, Mount Lyell provided a strong earnings contribution. Subsequent performance was erratic with multiple loss-making years and severe challenges in terms of the continued operation of the mine, upon which the township of Queenstown was largely dependent. The operation closed at the end of 1994.

With the acquisition, CGFA acquired control of the Mount Lyell copper mine, as well as an interest in the 'jewel in the crown', Renison. In doing so, CGFA had established what was expected to be a long-life base-metal arm within its expanding Australian portfolio of mineral and manufacturing interests. However, CGFA's due diligence of the Mount Lyell operation had been limited at what was a crucial stage of its evolution. Large amounts of capital would be committed to transferring mining from the Prince Lyell open cut mine to underground mining. CGFA was largely content to retain existing Mount Lyell management for this exercise, with only a limited attempt to apply its own technical review to the approach being adopted for underground mining. This approach was modelled on that adopted at Mount Isa Mines, despite the different nature and grade characteristics of the two ore bodies. Operational challenges and consequential poor financial returns from CGFA's investment in Mount Lyell can be ascribed, in part, to the company not applying a greater level of management and technical oversight at the early stages of its involvement. The failure to do so reflected both a paucity of technical resources within CGFA during its initial years, as well as a tendency not to wish to intervene in the management affairs of its investments.

In 1964, Massy-Greene and Mortimer became directors of Mount Lyell, with Brian W Andrew, the company's technical director, and Segal joining the board the following year. In October 1965, Bart Ryan, a mining engineer and later London director and managing director of CGFA, commenced at Renison as general manager.

With the acquisition of Mount Lyell, CGFA had gained a shareholding in a historic mining operation upon which the township of Queenstown and local region in the north-west of Tasmania depended for the major part of their employment, housing and other services. In 1969, more than 1,600 workers were employed by Mount Lyell. Turnover of the workforce was high. In the prior year, 618 men out of 1,555 had left the operation, reflecting both high employment levels in the wider economy, as well as the challenges of attracting and retaining married employees due to the shortage of suitable accommodation in Queenstown.[54] The close relationship between the mining operation, the local population and the regional economy would have implications in future years as to the manner in which CGFA and RGC viewed the retention of their investment during periods of challenging market, operational and financial conditions.

The initial years of Mount Lyell as a subsidiary of CGFA were favourable. In 1966, a net profit of A$2.3 million was recorded, compared with A$840,000 in 1964, aided by a higher copper price. In 1967, the profit increased to A$2.7 million, the second of two years of record profits. As encouraging were exploration results in the Mount Lyell–Tharsis area and Prince Lyell ore bodies, which were testing the downward extension to depths of 2,500 feet below the open cut operation, which had extended to a depth of 1,250 feet. Drilling results indicated that additional copper-bearing ore of up to 45 million tons, containing 1 per cent copper, was obtainable.[55] The prize was major.

The board of Mount Lyell approved the Prince Lyell feasibility study in July 1968. This led to the excavation of an ore shaft for the development of ore bodies below the West Lyell open cut, principally Prince Lyell, as well as the development of other ore bodies including Crown Three, Cape Horn and Twelve West. Associated works included underground crushing

---

54   *1968 Annual Report*, p. 4, in Mount Lyell Mining and Railway Company Limited, Operating Reports 1968, NAAT, Series NS3924, Items 533–540.
55   The Mount Lyell Mining & Railway Company Limited, 'Directors' Report and Accounts and Chairman's Statement', 1964 and also 1965, 1966 and 1967, UMA, Stock Exchange of Melbourne, 1968.0018, Box 190.

facilities and new underground locomotives and rolling stock for ore haulage. Additional accommodation for the workforce was also planned. The smelter was closed and concentrate shipped to the main Japanese customer, with pyrite production to be used in a new acid plant to be developed in association with EZ Industries at Burnie.[56]

Renison—the jewel in the crown

Alluvial tin had been discovered in the Renison Bell area of Tasmania in 1890 and the first concentrating mill built in 1907. The recovery from tin-bearing gossans was exhausted by 1922. Renison Associated Tin Mines was formed with production recommencing in 1936 utilising flotation technology to recover tin sulphides. In 1958, Mount Lyell acquired a substantial interest in the company and in 1960 Renison Limited was registered to acquire the shares in Renison Associated Tin Mines.[57]

Figure 36. Renison tin mining operation near Zeehan, west coast of Tasmania.
Source: NAA, A1200, 16173841.

---

56 *Annual Report, 1st August 1968*, p. 13, in Mount Lyell Mining and Railway Company Limited, Operating Reports 1968, NAAT, Series NS3924, Items 533–540.
57 Renison Limited, *Annual Report, 1978*, p. 3 and *Annual Report, 1974*, p. 7.

8. A RANGE OF INVESTMENTS

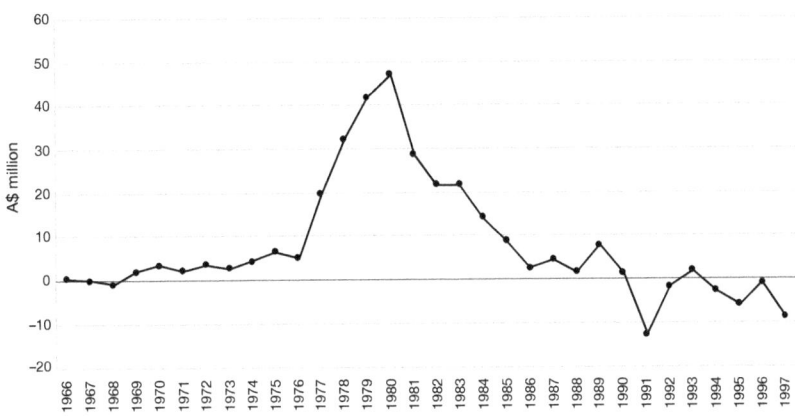

Chart 3. Renison pre-tax earnings, 1966–1997.
Source: Consolidated Gold Fields Australia Limited, 'Prospectus', 18 October 1966; CGFA and RGC annual reports, 1967 to 1997.

This chart shows the performance of Renison within the CGFA and RGC portfolios. Renison was a key investment for the British mining group, with an interest acquired through its holding in Mount Lyell Mining and Railway Company, before majority ownership was obtained. The steady returns in the late 1960s and early 1970s were followed by a marked improvement in financial performance in the late 1970s and Renison's spectacular contribution through the first half of the 1980s. The subsequent decline through the second half of the 1980s and 1990s led to a decision to sell the operation, which occurred in 1998.

With CGFA's acquisition of the majority stake in Mount Lyell in 1965, the company acquired an indirect interest in Renison. CGFA was involved in plans for the development of the mineral potential of Renison. The Renison board decided in 1965 to raise A£4 million for a major expansion program involving underground mining at the Federal ore body, as well as a new underground mine for the recently delineated Bassett ore body. The plans entailed diesel-powered underground mining and a new treatment plant capable of initial production of 350,000 tonnes of ore per year. Consolidated Gold Fields advanced loan funds of A£1 million in exchange for the ability to apply for up to 400,000 Renison shares within a three-year period.[58] CGFA would exercise this option. Renison became a major financial contributor to CGFA over the next two decades and so pivotal within the portfolio that consideration was given in the 1970s to the 'Renison scheme', a plan entailing the

---

58 Renison Limited, 'Circular to Shareholders: Major Expansion Scheme', 9 April 1965 and Material Contract No. 3, UMA, Mount Lyell Mining and Railway Co, 1974.0067, Box Consolidated Goldfields 1964–1966 Contracts.

divestment of all assets in the portfolio, with the exception of a majority position in Renison. While this was not to eventuate, Renison was a key part of the portfolio in the late 1970s and first half of the 1980s.

...

With its wide-ranging Australian investments, CGFA had established an impressive presence as a diversified minerals company, with a major position in iron ore, mineral sands, copper and tin, a listed mining investment company and fledgling manufacturing interests. It continued to expand in the second half of the 1960s, using the model of majority controlled, direct investments, with the introduction of direct Australian shareholding in 1966. The London parent retained majority share ownership, a presence on the board of directors and considerable influence upon decision-making for the deployment of funds. The commencement of the group's investments in Australia in 1960 provided great promise that Consolidated Gold Fields, through its local subsidiary, would stand among the major mining companies in Australia.

PART FOUR:
EXPANSION, CONSOLIDATION AND RESTRUCTURING 1966–1981

Box 4. Key events 1966–1981

1966	Lake View and Star (London Stock Exchange listed) granted Australian residency status
	Associated Minerals Consolidated acquisition of Titanium and Zirconium Industries
	Commissioning of Renison tin mine and mill
1967	First full year of production from the Federal lode, Renison
	Gold Fields Australian Development Company liquidated
1968	Mount Lyell expansion plan commenced
1969	Majority shareholding in Western Titanium acquired by Consolidated Gold Fields Australia
	Mount Lyell smelter and refinery closed
	North-West Acid formed as a 50/50 per cent partnership between Mount Lyell and EZ Industries, to produce sulphuric acid from pyrite from both companies. Sulphuric acid plant constructed at Burnie, Tasmania
	Controlling interest in Lawrenson Holdings acquired
1970	View Star formed as joint exploration vehicle between Lake View and Star and Consolidated Gold Fields Australia
	Production commenced, North-West Acid
1971	Poseidon takeover of Lake View and Star
	Acquisition of OT Lempriere and Company, smelter, refiner and alloy manufacturer
	Acquisition of 51 per cent interest in Ferro Alloys Tasmania and formation of Kemerton
	Lease signed with Hanwright for involvement in McCamey's Monster
1972	Board approval for construction of 30,000 tons ilmenite beneficiation plant
	Gunpowder copper project, Queensland, commenced production (70 per cent interest)
	Mount Lyell: open cut mining ceased at West Lyell, replaced by Prince Lyell and 'A' Lens ore bodies; mining of 10 Series stopes commenced (1972–1976)
	Lion Properties established for residential property development activities
1973	Privy Council refuses leave to appeal against a ruling that allows Western Titanium to proceed with development of Adamson syndicate leases at Eneabba, Western Australia
	Colinas established as wholly owned subsidiary for agricultural pursuits, New South Wales
	Lion Properties Settlement Shores residential development

1974	Eneabba mineral sands development approved
	Commissioning of ilmenite beneficiation plant
1976	Sir Brian Massy-Greene steps down as managing director; retires as chairman later in year
	Bart Ryan appointed managing director; Sid Segal appointed chairman
	Decision to sell one-third interest in Mount Goldsworthy Mining Associates to Consolidated Gold Fields and Mount Isa Mines
	Sale of Pancontinental Mining shareholding generated $3.75 million
	Merger of Associated Minerals Consolidated and Western Titanium, completed 1977
1977	Prince Lyell Extended Plan implemented after approved by Mount Lyell directors in December 1976
	Mining of 20 series stopes at Mount Lyell (1977–1982)
	Sale of Commonwealth Mining Investments (Australia)
	Gunpowder copper project suspended and placed on care and maintenance
1978	Lawrenson Alumasc Holdings sold
1979	Consolidated Gold Fields Australia (CGFA) acquired Jennings Industries' tenements and plant at Eneabba
	Bellambi Coal sale completed
	CGFA entered Porgera joint venture, Papua New Guinea
	CGFA interest in North-West Acid assigned to EZ Industries after accumulated losses
1980	Associated Minerals Consolidated acquisition of Titanium Enterprises, Green Cove Springs, Florida
	Max Roberts appointed executive chairman
	Bart Ryan retires as managing director; remains a director until 1982
	Sid Segal retires as chairman, remains a director until 31 December 1982
1981	Renison Goldfields Consolidated Ltd established 24 July 1981; the largest amalgamation of companies in Australian history to that time
	New Guinea Gold Fields acquired; 50 per cent offered to Consolidated Gold Fields. Renamed NGG Holdings
	Commissioning at Eneabba commenced
	Mount Lyell 30 series mining (1981–1986)

9

MOVE TO AN AUSTRALIAN SHAREHOLDING

While visiting Sydney in 1960, a London Consolidated Gold Fields director, Donald McCall, asked his driver to stop the company Daimler near the Sydney Harbour Bridge. McCall got out of the car and remarked of the view back to Circular Quay, 'this is the dress circle, we must build an office here'.[1] This duly occurred. Consolidated Gold Fields (Australia) (CGFA) accepted a proposal by a consortium of architects in December 1963 for the design and construction of a suitable corporate office building, located at the opposite end of Circular Quay to where meetings in the AMP building were held. The company's presence and ambitions in Australia were symbolised by the opening in 1966, with Sir George Harvie-Watt in attendance, of Gold Fields House which stood impressively on Circular Quay at 1 Alfred Street with expansive views of Sydney Harbour. Sidney Segal played a major role in the planning of the company's landmark building and oversaw the establishment of its art collection, which included works by Russell Drysdale, Arthur Boyd, Sidney Nolan and Jon Percival. Annual general meetings were held in the Rhodes Room, with a portrait of the great man reminding those present of the company's origins. A company annual report over a decade later proudly described Gold Fields House as 'one of the most prestigious buildings in Sydney', while the symbolic importance of this corporate presence was conveyed by Brian Massy-Greene

---

1   I am appreciative to Michael Gleeson-White, a former director of Commonwealth Mining Investments, for this insight (Gleeson-White, personal communication, 6 October 2017). Gold Fields House was designed by architects Mainline-Dillingham-Haunstrup and was one of the first multistorey buildings to be constructed in Sydney. The architects commissioned artist White to capture various stages of the construction of the building, while photographs of its progress were common (White, *The Gold Fields House Story*).

to a meeting of Consolidated Gold Fields' executives in Scotland in 1964, when he stated: 'if we ever wanted to put ourselves on the map quickly, this is certainly one of the ways of doing it'.[2] It was a fitting year for this new corporate presence to be established.

A board meeting of CGFA on 31 August 1966 gave consideration to a planned extraordinary general meeting of shareholders, to be held on 12 September 1966 to convert CGFA to a public company. This was approved and, in October 1966, CGFA issued 5 million ordinary shares at A$2.50, raising A$12.5 million and providing 22.7 per cent of the total issued capital of the company, now styled Consolidated Gold Fields Australia Ltd to Australian shareholders. The high expectations for this new British–Australian mining house were reflected in the offer for shares being oversubscribed; after the offer formally opened at 10 am on 18 October, it closed one minute later, and the company experienced 'phenomenal turnover' in its first month of trading on the Australian share market.[3] Part of the funds raised by the listing were used to reduce indebtedness to Gold Fields Mining & Industrial and the remainder applied to the Mount Goldsworthy project, where the company had an obligation to commit a further A$9.5 million. The value of its investment in Mount Goldsworthy plus the market value of its various share investments totalled A$28.4 million. In 1966, CGFA recorded a net profit after tax of A$2.9 million; profit increased the following year to A$4.1 million, mainly due to the increased contribution from Mount Goldsworthy and Mount Lyell.

Harvie-Watt retired as chairman to allow Massy-Greene to assume the dual roles of chairman and managing director of the Australian subsidiary. Since the original directors, who included Keith Cameron and Tom Owen, there were additions to the board, including Segal as an executive director, JM Burnett, GM Niall and Sir Daniel McVey.[4]

---

2   Consolidated Gold Fields Australia Limited, *13th Annual Report, 1979*, p. 4; JB Massy-Greene, 'Gold Fields in Australia', in Consolidated Gold Fields Limited, 'Speeches Given at the Group Conference Held at Gleneagles Hotel, Scotland on 2–9 July, 1964', p. 154.
3   Consolidated Gold Fields Australia Limited, 'October 18th 1966, News Release'; The Sydney Stock Exchange Limited, 20 February 1967, UMA, Stock Exchange of Melbourne, 1987.0138, Box 70, L. Folders, Secretary (Companies).
4   JM Burnett was the chairman of Commonwealth Mining Investments, as well as managing director of EMI (Australia) Ltd. Gerald Mansfield Niall was a solicitor, barrister at the Middle Temple Inn and partner of Blake & Riggall, chairman of National Mutual Life Association of Australasia and company director of Mount Lyell Mining and Railway Company, Volvo Australia, LM Ericsson, Elder Smith Goldsborough Mort, Reed Consolidated Industries, Elders Finance and Investments, and ANZ Banking Group. Sir Daniel McVey's experience is conveyed in Chapter 7, footnote 3 ('Gold Fields Appoints Three New Directors', 15 December 1966, UMA, Stock Exchange of Melbourne, 1987.0138, Box 70).

Figure 37. Gold Fields House (right), opened in 1966.
Source: 'The Gold Fields Group, Australian Edition', UMA, 1968.0018, Box 67.

Consolidated Gold Fields had contributed capital of A$24.5 million to CGFA since its establishment in 1960, with the market value of its investments increasing to A$45.6 million.[5] The Australian subsidiary company represented 18 per cent of Gold Fields' total profit and 18 per cent of group assets worldwide. Apart from the investments and shareholding already referred to, CGFA also maintained direct investments in lead, zinc, silver and copper through shareholdings in EZ Industries, Mount Morgan Mines, Mount Isa Mines, New Broken Hill Consolidated and North Broken Hill North, and the industrial shares of Broken Hill Proprietary and Imperial Chemical Industries.

A solid foundation for the company's growth in Australia had been established in a period of six years, encompassing a broad suite of minerals and investments in manufacturing, and a majority interest in Commonwealth Mining Investments. The capabilities of the board and management had been expanded and an Australian shareholding introduced. The prospects for the company were favourable. Further growth in the portfolio occurred but with challenges imposed by economic and market conditions, as well as by inherent deficiencies in the business based on a model of direct, majority shareholdings in most of its investments.

---

5   'The Gold Fields Group, Australian Edition', p. 11, UMA, 1968.0018, Box 67.

10

EXPANSION AND CONSOLIDATION 1966–1976

The first 10 years of the existence of Consolidated Gold Fields Australia (CGFA) from 1966 were marked by a combination of factors that saw the evolution of the portfolio that had been established in the early 1960s. These included the consolidation and expansion of key parts of the portfolio. In the case of Associated Minerals Consolidated (AMC) and the company's involvement in mineral sands, the aggregation of this company and Wyong Minerals occurred, while the acquisition of a majority shareholding in Western Titanium—a Western Australian–based mineral sands producer—and further consolidation of smaller mineral sands companies were features of the period. The basis was also laid for the combination of AMC and Western Titanium, such that CGFA's mineral sands interests were conducted through one subsidiary from 1977. This consolidated the company's dominant position in mineral sands in Australia and on an international basis. The company's expansion into a new major mineral sands province—Eneabba in Western Australia—was a major achievement and, with this, the acquisition of one of the two other producers in the province. Technological developments led by Western Titanium resulted in the development of a process to upgrade ilmenite to a higher-grade titanium dioxide product, referred to as synthetic rutile.

In the case of Mount Lyell, Renison and Bellambi, further mine development and expansion plans were implemented that increased production. For the Mount Goldsworthy project, sales contracts were increased and with these annual production levels, through a move to new deposits, as well as exploration drilling that delineated a major new iron ore province. Acquisition opportunities were pursued, designed to add new businesses to the portfolio. An acquisition attempt was made for the tungsten producer King Island Scheelite, while a project to evaluate the potential acquisition of or merger with North Broken Hill was also undertaken. Neither eventuated, although smaller acquisitions were made, including an involvement in a Queensland copper project, Gunpowder, north of Mount Isa, which commenced production in 1972.

Diversification remained a part of the business strategy. Alumasc Holdings, majority owned by the London parent, became a subsidiary of CGFA after the acquisition of an Australian manufacturing company, Lawrenson Holdings. This added to the existing manufacturing involvement through the shareholding of Zip Holdings in New Zealand. Forays into property development occurred and agricultural and pastoral activities in New South Wales were undertaken through the establishment of a company, Colinas. Direct share investments in other mining companies continued, through subsidiary Circular Quay Holdings, which included Pancontinental Mining, North Broken Hill, Poseidon, Mount Isa Mines and a Western Australian mineral sands company, Westralian Sands. All can be considered investments in companies that represented potential acquisition opportunities. Pancontinental Mining was a key share investment for CGFA during the 1970s and again in the 1980s and would lead to a takeover in 1995 as part of a plan to separate the gold assets of Renison Goldfields Consolidated (RGC) and Pancontinental into a separately listed company.

Exploration remained a prime area of activity, as it did through the history of Gold Fields in Australia. It included consideration of nickel opportunities as well as a joint exploration arrangement with Lake View and Star. Oil interests were pursued, and although these did not amount to anything during this period, an investment in oil and gas was reconsidered in 1981. An agreement was concluded between Mount Lyell and Getty Oil Development Company in 1976 relating to exploration tenements in north-west Tasmania. This unincorporated joint venture ended by 1981, although with a subsequent association with Little River Goldfields in what became the Henty gold project.

The early years of the new, partially Australian-owned company were favourable, with improvement in the financial performance of investments and a strengthening financial profile in most years through to 1970.

10. EXPANSION AND CONSOLIDATION 1966–1976

In 1967, the pre-tax operating profit of the investments made by CGFA was $9.3 million, which grew to $27.6 million in 1970. In 1970 Mount Lyell contributed a profit before tax of $9.1 million and Mount Goldsworthy $6.2 million. Renison, as the world's largest producer of tin concentrate, generated $3.5 million and AMC $3.1 million, while Western Titanium contributed $1.4 million.[1] Given CGFA had a majority, but not outright control of most of its investments, this translated into an increase in attributable profit to CGFA shareholders from $4.1 million to $12.3 million over the period (see Appendix 4). CGFA and, in turn, its major shareholder, Consolidated Gold Fields, relied upon the dividends that flowed from its investments. In this regard, annual dividends over the period increased from $1.4 million to $4 million. The main parts of the portfolio remained copper, tin, iron ore and mineral sands, with manufacturing, share investments—direct and through Commonwealth Mining Investments (CMI)—and a smaller, residual holding in gold production through Lake View and Star.

Having invested $30 million in establishing its position in Australia, the company was well placed to capitalise on existing assets by expansions and rationalisation, while also focused on capturing new business opportunities. The promising start to the new company was such that Sir George Harvie-Watt in his review of the 1968 year as group chairman stated 'Consolidated Gold Fields Australia has established itself as a major force in the mineral industry'.[2] The success of the Australian subsidiary was measured in the context that CGFA's profits and market value were in 1968 larger than that of the entire Gold Fields group 10 years previously.

However, by the early 1970s, the performance of individual businesses, most notably Mount Goldsworthy, Gunpowder copper and Mount Lyell, as well as mineral sands, created financial challenges. Weaker export markets, increasing costs and, in the case of several parts of the business, protracted industrial disputes, contributed to weaker cash flows and earnings. The profile from 1970 until 1977 was one of a marked erosion in the financial performance of the business, due to prevailing global economic conditions and a decline in commodity prices, in some

---

1   Consolidated Gold Fields Australia, *Fifth Annual Report 1971 and Notice of Meeting*. The interests held by CGFA in 1971 were AMC, 61 per cent; Bellambi Coal, 67 per cent; Commonwealth Mining Investments, 60 per cent; Lawrenson Alumasc Holdings, 50 per cent; Mount Lyell Mining and Railway Company, 56 per cent; North-West Acid, 28 per cent; Renison 48 per cent; Western Titanium 81 per cent; Zip Holdings, 51 per cent. A one-third interest in the Mount Goldsworthy joint venture was also held.
2   Consolidated Gold Fields Limited, 'Chairman's Review 1968, Sir George Harvie-Watt'.

cases magnified by the quality and operational performance of some operations.³ With a high level of capital expenditure, returns were not adequate and there was pressure on the liquidity and funding position of the company.

For the major London shareholder, the financial performance and prospects of its Australian subsidiary became of increasing concern. This led to various strategic options being canvassed by management and directors. A number of such considerations went to the heart of whether a diversified business model should be retained, or at least one where the major shareholder had little control over the cash flow, capital expenditure or ability to gain operational synergies across its various investments. The concept of 'divisionalisation' was considered, in effect the precursor to the 'Australianisation' process that occurred in 1981 when CGFA acquired outright control of its main subsidiary companies. In the meantime, cash flow pressures led to portfolio divestments, the most notable of which was CGFA's holding in the Mount Goldsworthy joint venture. Other investments were either ceased or, as in the case of the manufacturing businesses, put up for sale and sold between 1976 and 1978. Colinas and its agricultural activities and Bellambi Coal were considered for sale and a process commenced for each. It was a tumultuous time for the company, reflected in a developing lack of confidence by the London parent in Brian Massy-Greene in his role as managing director.

Mount Lyell—the onset of challenges

At the Mount Lyell operation at Queenstown in the second half of the 1960s, an extensive drilling program led to a 150 per cent increase in reserves and with this a major expansion project was planned, designed to increase copper output from 15,000 to 25,000 tons per annum. It was determined that additional ore of up to 45 million tons containing 1 per cent copper was obtainable in the Mount Lyell–Tharsis and Prince Lyell ore bodies.⁴ Exploration was designed to test the downward extension

---

3   Attributable profit to Consolidated Gold Fields Australia shareholders declined from $12.3 million in 1970 to $2.8 million in 1976, before a loss of $11.1 million in 1977, including extraordinary items. The financial performance in the first half of the 1970s was in the context of shareholder funds doubling from 1967 to 1977.
4   The Mount Lyell Mining & Railway Company Limited, 'Directors' Report and Accounts and Chairman's Statement', 1964 and also the reports for 1965, 1966 and 1967, University of Melbourne Archives (UMA), Stock Exchange of Melbourne, 1968.0018, Unit 190.

10. EXPANSION AND CONSOLIDATION 1966–1976

of the ore bodies to depths of at least 2,500 feet, more than double the depth of the ore body that had been accessed by the open cut mine. In 1967 Mount Lyell sent a study team overseas to examine the possibility of developing the ore body under the open pit. Consideration was also given to the construction of a smelter, either at Port Kembla or in Europe. Given the existing constraints upon housing an expanded workforce, Queenstown as a likely option for a new smelter was precluded from consideration. Mount Lyell management also had a desire to move away from the reliance on a contract with Electrolytic Refining and Smelting Company for the treatment of blister copper to an arrangement where concentrate could be sold to Japan with the benefit of a guaranteed floor price. Agreement was reached with Mitsubishi Metal Mining Company to purchase all of Mount Lyell's copper concentrate above the contractual obligation to Electrolytic Refining and Smelting. With this agreement and Commonwealth Government approval for the export of copper concentrate to Japan, the construction of a smelter, which had in any case been assessed as not economically viable, was no longer necessary.

Favourable copper prices contributed to an improved performance and in 1967 the profit earned by Mount Lyell was the highest in 74 years. By 1968, detailed studies determined the means to mine the Prince Lyell ore body by underground mining methods, progressively replacing reliance on the open pit, which was expected to be exhausted by 1972. Development of the upper levels of the Prince Lyell ore body began in 1968. This was the precursor to the mining of a series of progressively deeper stopes, from the 10 series through to the 60 series, until the mine closed in 1994. The initial capital expenditure estimate for mining the underground ore body was $21 million, although within a year this increased to $35 million. Funding this expenditure occurred through a combination of bank debt, for which Mount Lyell's shareholding in Renison was part security, as well as an equity issue. CGFA itself undertook a rights issue in 1969 raising $8.6 million, part of which repaid loans to Gold Fields Mining & Industrial and part of which was used to strengthen the cash resources of the group for further investments, including that planned at Mount Lyell.

Pyrite as a by-product from Mount Lyell led to the decision to construct a sulphuric acid plant at Burnie, in partnership with EZ Industries, with the company North-West Acid formed in 1970. This proved to be a spectacularly unsuccessful investment, with innumerable commissioning issues, followed by a range of ongoing technical problems and production outages that meant that the operation did not meet its production capacity in any year. External factors, such as the sulphur price, removal of Tariff Board bounties and importation of superphosphate into Australia, impeded North-West Acid gaining improved prices. Losses were recorded in most years, with write-offs in carrying values and accumulated losses. In 1978, the main customer—ICI—advised that it did not wish to extend its contract beyond 30 June 1980. By this stage, with poor operational and financial performance, serious industrial disputation, the replacement of the operation's general manager and an inability of Mount Lyell to sell its interest, it was determined that production would cease.[5]

By 1972 mining from the underground section of the Prince Lyell ore body was contributing over 40 per cent of copper production. The West Lyell open cut ore body closed in September of that year. Copper prices between mid-1967 and 1971 were generally favourable. Profit for Mount Lyell peaked at $9.1 million in 1970, aided by the devaluation of the Australian dollar, compared to $890,000 in 1965, the year CGFA acquired a majority shareholding. Three leaner years followed, with large copper inventories, held by the London Metals Exchange and by customers in Japan, overshadowing the market and depressing prices. Mount Lyell's customer, Mitsubishi, sought a 25 per cent reduction in its contractual tonnages in 1971, although this was not agreed to. Concerted efforts were made to reduce costs, including by a reduction in the workforce. By 1974 market conditions had recovered temporarily, with record prices and copper sales leading to an operating profit of $12.4 million. Copper prices peaked in April 1974 but then declined precipitously. With a world recession, copper demand contracted sharply at a time when increased supply had been incentivised by earlier higher prices. These factors, the operation's relatively high cost structure, as well as the major capital expenditure program implemented during 1968, eroded Mount Lyell's cash flow and created a serious financial situation. By 1975 Mount Lyell was facing severe financial challenges.

---

5   Copies of agenda papers for board meetings of North-West Acid Pty Ltd, 3 December 1969 – 15 December 1979, National Archives of Australia, Tasmania (NAAT), NS3244/1–5. I am grateful to Richard Knight who reviewed the chemical characteristics of the pyrite feedstocks from Mount Lyell and EZ Industries and suggested the respective chemical characteristics may have worked against their effective blending, with the EZ Industries' pyrite, from Roseberry, despite being slightly higher in sulphur, containing 'dirty elements', especially lead, zinc and arsenic (Richard Knight, personal communication, 6 February 2019).

In 1974, the Mount Lyell directors had investigated the means to separate the mining and investment activities of the company, including its shareholding in Renison. This action was in response to a forecast estimated cash deficit for the 1976 financial year of $16 million. Two methods were considered to address the financial circumstances: the extension of the company's loan facilities or the sale of the company's 44.5 per cent holding of Renison shares. The initial decision was to retain the Renison shares as they were viewed as a valuable long-term asset, not to be disposed of to resolve what was considered 'a short-term liquidity problem'.[6] Bank cash facilities of $5 million were increased to $10 million with consideration of putting in place additional facilities of $16 million. CGFA's requirement of the Mount Lyell directors for providing guarantees for part of these bank facilities was the development of a five-year plan for the operation. Various options were considered, including a commitment of essential capital expenditure only, placing the mine on care and maintenance, continuation of the development of the shaft or closing the mine.

The financial circumstances of Mount Lyell deteriorated, with a looming cash deficit of $24 million. Gold Fields' commodities division in London further reduced its forecast copper price. If the forecast were to eventuate, Mount Lyell's overdraft requirements would climb to $28 million in the second half of 1977, with little likelihood of additional bank financing becoming available nor CGFA being prepared to advance further funds.[7] The serious financial situation was compounded by the mine's reduced output and lower grades, while production was also lost as a result of two fatal accidents in 1975. Meetings were held with the Commonwealth Government, where the company conveyed its inability to meet a tax instalment payment of $225,000. The results of financial analysis tabled at a meeting with officers of the Department of Minerals and Energy made clear that Mount Lyell 'was rapidly going into a financial situation from which it may not recover'.[8]

---

6   The Mount Lyell Mining and Railway Company Limited, 'Minutes of Meeting of Directors', 26 June 1975, p. 3, NAAT, NS3924/1/57, Items 90–102.
7   The Mount Lyell Mining and Railway Company Limited, 'Minutes of Meeting of Directors', 10 December 1975, p. 1, NAAT, NS3924/1/57, Items 103–115.
8   The Mount Lyell Mining and Railway Company Limited, 'Minutes of Meeting of Directors', 18 December 1975, p. 3, NAAT, NS3924/1/57, Items 103–115.

Refinancing options were reconsidered by the Mount Lyell board, with a particular interest by the CGFA-appointed directors. Given the critical liquidity situation, it was considered appropriate to now sell Mount Lyell's shareholding in Renison. This decision was of major significance to CGFA. Mount Lyell's shareholding in Renison had been 'loosely pledged' to the company's bank as security against its loans and, as such, could be called upon by the banks for repayment of the outstanding loans.[9] A forfeiture of the Renison shareholding would be a calamitous outcome for CGFA, since a major motivation for investing in Mount Lyell was the indirect interest it provided in Renison. Consolidated Gold Fields in London had become concerned with the fate of a major investment of its Australian subsidiary, not least because it also held a direct interest in Renison. Bart Ryan, the group's deputy chairman and deputy managing director, was dispatched from London to attend Mount Lyell board meetings. TF Lanz, an executive director of CGFA and a former general manager of Mount Lyell, as well as the general manager, DPC Sawyer, were summoned to London to provide detailed technical and financial information on the position and prospects of Mount Lyell.

In 1975, the decline in the copper price led to a loss from mining and processing operations, only offset by the company forward-selling a major part of its copper production at higher prices. A profit for the year of $2.2 million was recorded.[10] Despite the temporary financial reprieve, the concerns of the CGFA board and that of the London directors were growing. The June 1975 board minutes recorded: 'The Chairman noted that the company was in serious trouble and is incurring a heavy loss on present copper prices. The current cash deficiency is running at the rate of some $1.5 million per month'.[11] Later in the year, operational options were again canvassed. These included closure of the mine, cessation of all capital expenditure and mining out of existing reserves over an 18-month period, as well as ceasing mining but continuing with the capital expenditure program.[12]

---

9   Mount Lyell Copper Mine, 'Submission from Dept. of National Resources, Senate Select Committee', 26 November 1976, Renison Goldfields Consolidated Archives (RGCA), Box 746.
10   The loss from mining operations was $8.3 million, with a profit from forward selling copper of $8.5 million. Three years of losses followed and a barely break-even result in 1979 (The Mount Lyell Mining and Railway Company Limited, *Annual Report 1975 and Notice of Meeting*, p. 3).
11   Consolidated Gold Fields Australia Limited, 'Minutes of Meeting of Directors', 25 June 1975, p. 2, RGCA, Box 12246, RGC 11588.
12   Consolidated Gold Fields Australia Limited, 'Minutes of Meeting of Directors', 26 November 1975, p. 2 and 'Minutes of Meeting of Directors', 17 December 1975, pp. 4–5, RGCA, Box 12246, RGC 11588.

A restriction of $500,000 on capital expenditure was imposed by CGFA on the Mount Lyell board and management. The sale of the Renison shares, as well as a Mount Lyell's holding of ICI shares, proceeded, an action that was viewed externally to the company as a 'desperate bid to allow … [it] to survive'. As Massy-Greene explained: 'The question we have had to face is how we should try to keep the company going for the time being'.[13] Upon the sale of Mount Lyell's shareholding in Renison, CGFA acquired its entitlement, as well as the shortfall in uptake by other shareholders. Given its 56 per cent holding in Mount Lyell and its 31 per cent direct holding in Renison, CGFA held an effective 46 per cent shareholding in Renison. This increased after the Renison shares sale process; an outcome that was criticised by some within the Commonwealth Government as a deliberate means of enabling CGFA, as an overseas company, to gain greater control of Renison.

For the CGFA board, the parlous situation for Mount Lyell was compounded, in a portfolio sense, by the 'very depressing' iron ore outlook; Bellambi Coal suffering serious industrial disputes and a loss for the year; and the necessity to accelerate plans to double copper production from the Gunpowder project in Queensland to attempt to improve the operational efficiency and financial performance of this recently acquired but poorly performing operation.[14] Consideration was given to the sale of Bellambi Coal as well as other assets. However, the sale of CGFA's investments, at a time of depressed mineral markets, in itself created a conundrum, recognised by Donald McCall, the London chairman. The situation available to the group was to sell income-generating assets, which were needed, or attempt to sell assets that were generating losses and, therefore, not readily saleable.[15] The situation facing CGFA's portfolio would provoke a fundamental reassessment of the nature and structure of the Australian company's holdings.

By early 1976, the board of Mount Lyell believed that it had no option but to cease production unless government financial assistance was forthcoming. In effect, the increased reliance on underground mining sustained production levels, although with increased unit operating costs, in an environment of adverse exchange rates and rampant cost inflation.

---

13   *The Age*, 17 February 1976.
14   Consolidated Gold Fields Australia Limited, 'Minutes of Meeting of Directors', 26 November 1975, p. 3, 17 December 1975, p. 5 and 27 August 1975, p. 3, RGCA, Box 12246, RGC 11588.
15   Consolidated Gold Fields Australia Limited, 'Minutes of Meeting of Directors', 26 February 1976, RGCA, Box 12246, RGC 11588.

As such, the financial performance of the operation remained highly sensitive to the copper price. The capital expenditure program of $32 million for the Prince Lyell shaft subsequently increased to $45 million by 1976, in part reflecting adverse inflationary effects with inflation at over 13 per cent. It was estimated that an additional $11 million was required for completion of the number one shaft and underground crushing station. By October 1976, the price of copper fell further in world markets, adversely affected by the depreciation of the pound sterling. In the context of this rapidly deteriorating financial situation, revised copper price forecasts from London determined that the trigger price at which the contingency plan to close the mine would be activated was close to being reached.[16] Instead, it was decided to continue copper production but postpone the remaining capital expenditure and retrench 38 employees and have another 25 employees take early retirement.

During 1976, Charles Copeman, an executive of CGFA, was appointed chairman of Mount Lyell, taking over from Massy-Greene. He recalled in later life that his directions from London were to close the Mount Lyell operation. Instead, a modified mining plan that reduced the estimated economic life of the operation from 12 to six years was implemented. The work on this plan was already in train, under the initiative of Sawyer, the Mount Lyell general manager. Sawyer, tall, tough and direct, had been general manager of Renison and was moved to Mount Lyell. He was viewed as not having existing allegiances to management and the workforce at Queenstown and, as such, capable of implementing radical changes. The Prince Lyell Plan entailed a 40 per cent reduction in the workforce through the retrenchment of 450 employees. The milling operation was reduced from seven days to five days per week. It was expected that the plan would enable Mount Lyell 'to remain solvent on a cash basis', although not profitable.[17] Ryan held the view at the time that the ultimate closure of the mine remained a possibility, although devaluation of the Australian dollar in November 1976 provided some respite for the operation. As part of the evaluation of operating settings for Mount Lyell, management was also pursuing the sale of its interest in North-West Acid. This operation had been suffering both production and

---

16   'Submission to the Senate Select Committee to Inquire into Mount Lyell Mining Operations', 18 November 1976, pp. 2–3, NAAT, NS3357/1/185.
17   The Mount Lyell Mining and Railway Company Limited, 'Minutes of Meeting of Directors', 28 October 1976, p. 3, NAAT, NS3924/1/57, Items 128–137.

demand offtake issues, as well as the adverse effects of low sulphur prices. Approaches to ICI for it to purchase the Mount Lyell share elicited a lack of interest.

The seriousness of the situation facing Mount Lyell and the social and economic consequences of a reduction in employment levels in Queenstown and the surrounding townships led to the appointment of a Senate Select Committee. The committee began hearings in November 1976. Multiple submissions were received, including one from Professor Geoffrey Blainey of the University of Melbourne, author of the seminal work on the history of Mount Lyell. His submission encapsulated the core of the concern by government and trade unions: that the planned reduction in workforce could 'inflict on the local residents, and indirectly on the whole Tasmanian economy, a financial loss that would far outweigh the subsidies required to sustain the mine in the near future'.[18] Following the Senate Select Committee hearings, the Commonwealth Government was asked to consider the introduction of a subsidy to support the Australian copper mining industry, a request referred to the Industries Assistance Commission. Subsidies to Mount Lyell were forthcoming. The operators of Emu Bay Railway were approached to achieve a reduction in freight rates, while Mitsubishi was asked to reduce its smelting charges; a request it was initially reluctant to accommodate while Mount Lyell was receiving government subsidies.

The company decided to extend the Mount Lyell Plan by continuing to mine in what was referred to as the 'A' lens and at Cape Horn and Prince Lyell, but defer the remaining capital expenditure for the installation of underground crushing facilities and new locomotives for the deepening of the Prince Lyell shaft. This revision to the plan became known as the Prince Lyell Extended Plan. It was approved by the Mount Lyell board in December 1976, in the context of a half-year loss of $5.7 million. The new plan entailed a reduction in ore production from 2.2 million tons to 1.5 million tons, the introduction of a five-day working week, centralisation of mining activities and rationalisation of surface engineering activities, and reduction of the workforce from 1,100 to

---

18   Blainey, *The Peaks of Lyell*. Blainey's submission contained within Australian Senate, 'Report of the Senate Select Committee on Mount Lyell Mining Operations', 3 December 1976, p. 13, NAAT, NS3357/1/186.

720 workers.[19] A range of other initiatives were taken to reduce costs, while the Tasmanian Government was approached for the purchase of the company's interest in the Lake Margaret power station.

In effect, the Prince Lyell Extended Plan was a 'holding operation', designed to reduce the levels of operating loss and conserve cash while retaining the option of moving to the deeper ore horizons at Prince Lyell in the future.[20] Not for the last time, the Mount Lyell workforce displayed a high level of cooperation and support for management initiatives. As the Senate Select Committee report stated:

> The close identification with and involvement of the people of Queenstown in all aspects of community life coupled with the unique relationship with the Company and the community, industrially, socially and culturally, has induced a community spirit and understanding not readily found elsewhere.[21]

The acting general manager, RM (Dick) Patterson, advised employees in 1977 that their efforts had resulted in a 25 per cent reduction in operating costs, an improvement in the grade of ore recovered and a 12 per cent reduction in the cash break-even level. Mount Lyell was held within the RGC portfolio until 1994, the year after Mount Lyell celebrated a centenary of operation, when, as part of the company's copper division, a decision was made to close the operation.

Renison—a key part of the portfolio

Renison's performance in the CGFA portfolio was, in many respects, the inverse of that of Mount Lyell. Initial poor performance, with an improvement in mining and operations, meant that Renison not only moved from being an indirect holding through the Mount Lyell shareholding to a direct subsidiary of CGFA, but also the asset viewed

---

19 Mount Lyell board minutes indicate that 100 employees left voluntarily and 46 were retrenched (The Mount Lyell Mining and Railway Company Limited, 'Minutes of Meeting of Directors', 23 December 1976, p. 2, and 27 January 1977, NAAT, NS3924/1/57, Items 128–137).
20 The statement to employees was provided associated with the interim results for the 1977 financial year that showed a loss of $3.4 million (NAAT, NS 3924/1/57, Items 147–157).
21 Australian Senate, 'Report of the Senate Select Committee on Mount Lyell Mining Operations', 3 December 1976, p. 13, NAAT, NS3357/1/186.

as of the highest quality in the portfolio by the mid-1970s. The 1976 decision, borne of necessity, to sell Mount Lyell's shareholding in Renison enabled CGFA to increase its shareholding to 51.09 per cent.[22]

In 1963, Renison's available ore reserves increased 30 per cent to 4 million tons as a result of drilling and development work. In the following year plans were advanced to increase throughput by mining at depth in the Federal ore body and by increasing processing capacity by the construction of a new mill. The plans involved a two-phase expansion: an immediate increase in ore treatment capacity to 200 tons per day and a scheme to move to 1,000 tons per day within two years, with the potential for additional expansion. At an original estimate of $8 million, the plans included additional housing for workers at Zeehan, along with the facilities at the mine site. Funding of the development occurred by a rights issue undertaken by Renison as well as a $2 million loan advanced by CGFA, in return for later exercising an option to acquire 400,000 Renison shares. Those responsible for the planning and construction of the mill had experience with lead–zinc processing in Broken Hill, although not a tin operation. The commissioning of the mill operations occurred in December 1966. Initially, the fine cassiterite tin oxide, with its association with massive sulphide mineralisation, from the Federal-Bassett fault structure posed technical challenges for milling. The ore was hard, with the fine cassiterite crystals making separation of the tin difficult. Initially, recoveries were as low as 30 to 40 per cent, with operational challenges necessitating the need to develop a skilled workforce able to manage the complexities of ore feed and mill settings. Technical problems in commissioning the new treatment plant and higher depreciation levels for the old plant meant that after an investment of $9.5 million, the company generated a meagre $40,000 profit in the 1967 financial year. In 1968, the first full year of production from the Federal lode, low recoveries contributed to a loss of $910,000, with no dividend payment.

The blending of the Federal-Bassett ore with a carbonate ore zone helped improve recoveries. Furthermore, considerable experimental work was undertaken on flotation of cassiterite from tin ores. The metallurgical team at Renison was supported by experts from Mitsubishi and the Freiberg Institute of Berlin, as well as by technical input from the Gold Fields group in Australia, the United Kingdom and South Africa. Mitsubishi, Renison's

---

22 Consolidated Gold Fields Australia Limited, *Tenth Annual Report 1976 and Notice of Meeting*, p. 6.

principal customer, had undertaken research on tin flotation to maximise the recovery of tin from its own complex base-metal mine, Akenobe in Japan. Experimental work using Renison ore occurred in Japan and a pilot plant was constructed at Zeehan.[23] Mitsubishi provided the reagent used at Renison. By 1969, the metallurgical issues encountered had been addressed through blending of the ore and installation of additional gravity separation equipment, while the trials for recovery of tin by the new flotation process proved encouraging. Tin in concentrate production doubled with a study in progress to increase ore treatment from 400,000 to 1 million tons per annum. By 1970, Renison had established itself as Australia's largest tin producer. The loss of the previous year was converted into an operating profit, with annual profits before tax climbing from $3.5 million in 1970 to over $19 million in 1977, before rising to $47 million in 1980.[24]

While other parts of the portfolio struggled financially in the mid-1970s, Renison represented the one shining light and, in 1977, was among the top twenty most profitable Australian companies.[25] This was despite constraints on production associated with restrictions by the International Tin Council that, in 1975, imposed an 18 per cent reduction in Australian tin exports, at the stage when domestic consumption had declined.[26] Renison represented an impressive, high-quality investment. It would centre in considerations by the CGFA board as to how the portfolio may be restructured, with one consideration being the divestment of all other investments while retaining a majority interest in Renison.

Mount Goldsworthy—growing disenchantment

CGFA's one-third holding in the Mount Goldsworthy joint venture was the initial centrepiece of the company's portfolio in Australia. In 1967, Ryan had been appointed general manager of Goldsworthy Mining, the operating company for the Mount Goldsworthy joint venture. His appointment was noteworthy in the context of later events; he became a director and deputy chairman of Consolidated Gold Fields in the United

---

23 Goodman and O'Keefe, 'Tin ore treatment at Renison Limited'.
24 The after-tax result for 1980 was $21.4 million. See Appendix 4.
25 Bambrick, *Australian Minerals and Energy Policy*, p. 8.
26 Consolidated Gold Fields Australia Limited, 'Minutes of Meeting of Directors', 25 June 1975, p. 2, RGCA, Box 12246, RGC 11588.

10. EXPANSION AND CONSOLIDATION 1966–1976

Kingdom and from 1976 managing director of CGFA. He would also be one of the key individuals responsible for CGFA's decision, and that of the London parent, to divest the holding in the Mount Goldsworthy joint venture.

In 1966 first production commenced, with Mount Goldsworthy's profit of $1.1 million in that year representing over a quarter of the group's total. Sales volumes grew progressively, with the one millionth ton of iron ore shipped in January 1967. In June of that year an agreement was reached with a consortium of Japanese steel mills to supply a further 3.25 million tons of iron ore fines in addition to the 16.5 million tons of lump ore already contracted. Trial shipments were underway to European customers, with plans to expand annual production by the development of additional deposits to the north-east at Shay Gap and Kennedy Gap. In June 1968 the Mount Goldsworthy joint venture concluded an additional sales contract for 10 million tons of iron ore to Japanese steel mills over 10 years beginning in October 1969.[27] By 1969, expansion plans were being progressed to increase Mount Goldsworthy production to 8 million tons per annum, with ore sourced from Mount Goldsworthy, Shay Gap and Kennedy Gap.

As part of Harvie-Watt's chairman's address to the 1968 Consolidated Gold Fields group annual general meeting in London, he referred to the 'outstanding item of interest' in Australia as the 'continuing progress … at Mount Goldsworthy'.[28] By the early 1970s contracts were in place for 60 million tons of lump and fine. CGFA's share of profit in 1970 increased to $7.1 million of which $6.2 million was incorporated into CGFA group accounts. By 1971 the move to the new deposit at Shay Gap was underway, enabling the increase of production to 8 million tons per annum from 6.8 million tons.

Mount Goldsworthy Mining Associates undertook an evaluation of another iron ore deposit on its tenements, Mining Area C. In 1970, an exploration program was undertaken of this temporary reserve, encompassing an area of 1,100 square kilometres. Exploration identified a major resource, estimated at over 700 million tons of high-grade Marra

---

27   The two contracts included one for 10 million tons over 10 years, made up of lump ore and fines and another for just over 1 million tons of fines for a five-year period (*The Canberra Times*, 15 October 1968).
28   Consolidated Gold Fields Limited, 'Chairman's Review 1968, Sir George Harvie-Watt'.

Mamba ore, an ore that had not to that stage been produced in Western Australia. The joint venture partners proceeded with a preliminary feasibility study, which was completed in 1973.

The interest in iron ore in Western Australia was also associated with CGFA, Cyprus Mines Corporation and Utah Construction & Mining Co. acquiring an option in 1970 to take an interest in a joint venture to evaluate the potential development of temporary reserves controlled by Hancock Prospecting and Wright Prospecting (Hanwright). These included deposits known as McCamey's Monster and the Western Ridge iron ore deposits. By 1972, with Mining Area C as a potential deposit to be developed, the CGFA board recognised that it had, in effect, a conflict of interest between its consideration of Mining Area C and that for the development of McCamey's Monster. This led to a consideration for the extension of the period of withdrawal from the McCamey joint venture to allow evaluation of the Mining Area C deposits to continue. As it transpired, the McCamey's deposit was acquired by BHP and developed in 1993 as the Jimblebar deposit.

From 1972, CGFA's future involvement in iron ore came under intense scrutiny. The factors that caused a decline in the attraction of the sector for CGFA were multifaceted. They included a severe downturn in the Japanese steel industry, the adverse impact on shipments associated with a prolonged Japanese seaman's strike, the devaluation of the United States dollar and further revaluation of the Australian dollar, as well as increasing operating costs and an increased level of industrial disputes at the mining operations. A serious decline in sales levels and profitability occurred, at a time when the mining expansion at Shay Gap, for which a new township had been constructed, was underway and when a decision for a major capital commitment for Mining Area C was imminent.[29] In 1973, associated with reduced sales and higher operating costs, accumulated profits from Mount Goldsworthy Mining Associates were drawn upon to allow a $4.3 million reported profit for CGFA: lower than the previous year's $5.7 million. The effects of the constraints upon the Japanese steel industry became apparent, with increased operating costs and a 'constant escalation in salaries and wages' for Mount Goldsworthy

---

29   The development of the township of Shay Gap, 60 kilometres from Goldsworthy, involved a radical concept in housing styles. The architect, Lawrence Howroyd, designed houses in clusters with central air conditioning facilities, cables buried underground and traffic banned from the central parts of the township. As Howroyd explained, his design sought to 'remove the wide and frightening horizon' (Film Australia, *Living Way Out*, 1977, wanowandthen.com/Shay-Gap.html).

adversely affecting the operation.³⁰ In 1974, the devaluation of the United States dollar and lost production due to industrial disputes meant that the financial contribution of Mount Goldsworthy was $236,000—an uninspiring outcome at the peak stage of capital commitment and with the necessity for further large sums to be expended if production was to be increased through the development of Mining Area C.

In 1975, the financial contribution had improved, due to higher shipments, higher prices negotiated in 1974 with Japanese customers and a devaluation of the Australian dollar. However, these benefits were largely offset by a further escalation of costs, a higher waste-to-ore ratio at the mines—particularly at Mount Goldsworthy—as well as poor equipment performance reliability, due in part to the difficulty of recruiting and retaining skilled operational and maintenance personnel. A financial contribution to CGFA of $1.3 million was recorded. Worse was yet to come. The escalation of costs in 1976 by over 26 per cent, along with reduced shipments, resulted in a loss for CGFA from Mount Goldsworthy of $2.3 million. This loss was partially mitigated by a further drawdown on reserves, with a loss of just under $2 million recorded.³¹ By this stage CGFA's disenchantment with iron ore was almost complete.

Massy-Greene advised the president of the Nippon Steel Company of the challenges facing Mount Goldsworthy at a meeting in Melbourne in 1974 prior to the commencement of the annual price negotiation. He recorded:

> I spoke of Goldsworthy's present and future position emphasising that the increasing reduction in profitability of our iron ore undertaking is a matter of great concern to the joint venture companies and their shareholders. I emphasised that the financial return on our investment was inadequate and I made some general observations about the need for a considerably better return on the investment so as to ensure the availability of capital for the development of existing and new mines and laid particular stress on the need for better prices to justify the development of new areas.³²

---

30 Consolidated Gold Fields Australia Limited, *Sixth Annual Report 1972 and Notice of Meeting*, p. 2.
31 For the 1976 financial year, the year that the sale of Mount Goldsworthy occurred, the loss incurred by Consolidated Gold Fields Australia was a further $2 million (Consolidated Gold Fields Australia Limited, *Eleventh Annual Report 1977 and Notice of Meeting*, p. 6).
32 Telex Massy-Greene, 3 July 1974, RGCA, 6616, Box 12612.

The response from the customer representative was not encouraging. As Massy-Greene recorded, it related to 'the usual treatment of how badly the steel industry faired in recent times' and its lack of profitability.³³

Pricing and contractual arrangements required the involvement of the Commonwealth Government, a matter that consumed considerable management and board time. The Australian iron industry participants were under direction from Canberra that any pricing arrangement had to be submitted to the Department of Minerals and Energy. Reflecting the often-varying approaches of the industry participants to pricing outcomes, one of the Mount Goldsworthy joint venture partners observed to Massy-Greene:

> In all of this we find it ironic, but nonetheless gratifying that Australian producer solidarity stems in large measure from pressures by the Whitlam Government and especially from its chief bere [sic] noir, F. X. Connor. However distasteful the pressures and interference, they seem a welcome contrast to those early days when Hamersley and Mt. Newman were dying to see who could make the greatest price concessions.³⁴

Price negotiations with the Japanese steel mills proceeded over July and August 1974. Mount Goldsworthy sought a 35 per cent increase in line with that sought by Hamersley. These efforts were undercut by Mt Newman which sought a 25 per cent increase and then a 7.5 per cent increase the following year.³⁵ The 'brevity' of a crucial meeting of the marketing representatives for Mount Goldsworthy with the head of the delegation for the Japanese steel mills was viewed as an 'unwillingness [by the Japanese steel mills] to discuss further any proposal for a 35PCT [35 per cent] increase, or equivalent US DLR [dollar] flat rate', with the objective to secure Mount Goldsworthy's agreement to the Mt Newman agreement for use 'as a lever against Hamersley'.³⁶

A Utah representative expressed his lack of satisfaction with the negotiating abilities of Marcona on behalf of the Mount Goldsworthy joint venture:

---

33   ibid.
34   Telex Allen, Cyprus for Massy-Greene, 3 June 1974, RGCA, 6616, Box 12612.
35   Telex Kober, 10 July 1974, RGCA, 6616, Box 12612.
36   Telex S Iki Vice President, Marcona for Allen/Massy-Greene/Wallace, 17 July 1974, RGCA, 6616, Box 12612.

> The negotiating effort … must be one of the most ineffectual on record, ultimately consisting of 'me too' reactions to agreements reached by others. We believe this was a totally inappropriate and unnecessary posture for Goldsworthy to assume … Unfortunately, Mr. Connor may have been correct when he called us hillbillies.[37]

CGFA shared Utah's disquiet and was instrumental in having Marcona replaced as the marketing arm for Mount Goldsworthy.

A meeting followed of all the iron ore producers with Lennox Hewitt, Secretary of the Department of Minerals and Energy, and the minister, Rex Connor. Both were underwhelmed by the then agreed 20 per cent price increase. Hewitt indicated he was expecting a 25 per cent increase and a further 7.5 per cent for other contractual arrangements under review, while Connor emphasised the importance of iron ore as a source of export income and made his expectation clear that a 30 per cent increase should be sought, advising the participants to 'go back to the mills as soon as possible to achieve this'.[38]

Consideration of the development of the Mining Area C deposit was in the context that the Mount Goldsworthy joint venture believed it would not be able to fulfil its contractual requirements from the Goldsworthy, Shay Gap and Sunrise Hill deposits without the further development of other deposits, such as Nimingarra and Kennedy Gap. Development of the much larger Mining Area C deposit was viewed as a more efficient approach than developing multiple, smaller areas. As such, the progressive development of Mining Area C was envisaged from mid-1978 through to 1981. Mining Area C's entry to the market was dependent, however, on global demand for steel that, given the state of the Japanese steel industry, was near impossible to forecast. Complicating the situation further was the likely commencement of new iron ore production from the Ivory Coast and Brazil. Despite technical presentations to the Japanese steel mills in 1973 and the supply of lump iron ore samples, the Japanese customers suspended consideration of Mining Area C and other deposits due to their inability to forecast future demand in the face of uncertainty for steel demand.[39] By October 1974 an updated Mining Area C feasibility study had been completed. While the financial returns were acceptable it was the view of the joint venture that if development were to proceed

---

37 Telex Wallace for Kober, 24 July 1974, RGCA, 6616, Box 12612.
38 Telex for Allen/Massy-Greene/Wallace/Bilhorn, August 1974, RGCA, 6616, Box 12612.
39 Telex Kober to Allen/Massy-Greene/Wallace, 10 September1974, RGCA, 6616, Box 12612.

it would have to occur quickly; to defer a decision would make the project economics vulnerable to an escalation of costs, estimated to be at least 10 per cent annually.

In 1975, an internal review by CGFA of the Mining Area C project took place. The deposits then being mined—Mount Goldsworthy, Shay Gap and Sunrise Hill—were expected to be exhausted by 1979. The smaller deposits were considered to not justify investment. As such, it was concluded:

> Any long term future of Goldsworthy therefore, is seen to attach to the reserves of Mining Area 'C' (MAC) and the effort has been directed at the development of the MAC Marra Mamba reserves. These amount to some 700 M.T. [million tons] of 'geological' reserves in the whole of Area 'C', with an approximate 280 M.T. of 'mineable' reserves.[40]

Mount Isa Mines had been invited to take equity in the Mount Goldsworthy project, in order to increase total Australian participation. A concept considered by CGFA, although not pursued, was that once Mount Isa Mines entered the joint venture, CGFA's 25 per cent interest in Mount Goldsworthy could be transferred to a public company and listed on the Australian stock exchange. The new entity was contemplated to include a shareholding by the Japanese steel mills to reinforce their commitment to the development of Mining Area C.[41]

CGFA's consideration of its options for continued involvement in Mount Goldsworthy was made in the context of the financial performance and growth prospects of the overall CGFA portfolio. These included the likely need for major investment in mineral sands, with the Eneabba project in Western Australia undergoing detailed examination during 1974. High interest rates and associated issues with funding projects weighed heavily on board deliberations. Directors remained concerned and unconvinced about the merit of continued involvement in iron ore. In 1974, the views of the managing director and chairman of CGFA were summarised as follows:

---

[40] Consolidated Gold Fields Australia Limited, '"MAC" Project Review', p. 1, RGCA, 9286, Box 12301.
[41] ibid., p. 67.

> The incremental effect on annual profit of C.G.F.A. is minimal despite the increased capital requirements ... [with] large developments and cash requirements ... required in future to open up not only the smaller reserves in the north but Mining Area 'C' to the south. [He] summarized the position by stating that the decision must now be made as to whether C.G.F.A. continues to develop its interests along with its co-venturers in the expansion of iron ore operations or just allows its present operations to continue at some 8,000,000 tonnes per annum and face up to future requirements as and when they come along.[42]

CGFA's perspectives were also influenced by the 'chaotic' industrial situation associated with the iron ore operations, with a view of the CGFA board that the joint venture should 'stand firm ... against industrial blackmail' by the unions.[43] A CGFA director also lamented the 'Government's failure, after more than 10 months in office, to enunciate its resources policy in clear terms'.[44] The deteriorating financial performance in the 1970s meant that an increase in export prices became an imperative. In 1975, a joint venture delegation to Japan sought a 39 per cent increase in iron ore prices, at a meeting with the steel-producing customers. A report following the visit conveyed that the 'Japanese were very depressed and were adopting the position that there was no prospect whatsoever of any price increase at the present time'.[45] This, the likely need for further Australian participation in the ownership of Mount Goldsworthy, as well as the straitened cash position of CGFA, weighed upon board deliberations. A decision on the company's commitment to Mining Area C was required by 1976. The orientation of the board was not to be involved in the Mining Area C development, given the level of capital expenditure and the limited likelihood of securing a contractual offtake from customers at materially higher prices than those prevailing. As will be conveyed in the next chapter, the future of Mount Goldsworthy in the CGFA portfolio was a matter of intense consideration during 1976.

---

42   Consolidated Gold Fields Australia Limited, 'Minutes of Meeting of Directors', 23 January 1974, p. 4, RGCA, Box 12264.
43   Consolidated Gold Fields Australia Limited, 'Minutes of Meeting of Directors', 24 April 1974, p. 3, RGCA, Box 12264.
44   Consolidated Gold Fields Australia Limited, *Seventh Annual Report 1973 and Notice of Meeting*, p. 5.
45   Consolidated Gold Fields Australia Limited, 'Minutes of Meeting of Directors', 28 January 1976, p. 9, RGCA, Box 12246, RGC 11588.

Bellambi—mixed fortunes

The investment in Bellambi Coal offered mixed fortunes for CGFA. As with iron ore, industrial disputes, as well as a burdensome regulatory environment in terms of duties and other financial imposts, added to the complexities of the business. After a 1965 arrangement with the Japanese steel mills and other customers for the supply of 1.25 million tons for three years, by 1969 arrangements were in place for the delivery of 6.3 million tons over a five-year period to 1974. Arrangements for a further 7.5 million tons were subsequently secured. The contracts delivered revenues of $150 million. This was sufficiently attractive for an expansion program to open up a further seam at South Bulli and install two additional long-wall mining units.[46]

In 1967, technical issues with the implementation of a long-wall unit led to production outages that resulted in the Japanese customers deferring the commencement of the new contract for a year; a level of accommodation that was a feature of the relationship by Bellambi's main Japanese customers, notwithstanding frequent production disruptions. Despite geological and ongoing technical challenges, the long-wall unit contributed to higher production and a second continuous long-wall miner was in operation by January 1969. In that year a new sales contract with Japanese customers was finalised with a higher selling price agreed.[47] In 1970, production output was adversely affected by industrial unrest in the Illawarra region arising from union demands for a shorter working week. Despite the prior year investments, Bellambi suffered a major decline in profits in 1970. Profits halved from 1969 as a result of a combination of difficult mining conditions, a delay in obtaining replacement parts for one of the long-wall mining units and the idling of mining operations for 10 days due to strike action.[48] In 1970 Corrimal Coke was purchased, expanding Bellambi's existing coke facilities. While this contributed to a 150 per cent increase in coke sales in 1971, it was a relatively minor part of overall revenues.

---

46   Consolidated Gold Fields Australia Limited, *Third Annual Report 1969 and Notice of Meeting*, p. 19.
47   The Bellambi Coal Company Limited, *81st Annual Report and Notice of Meeting, Year Ended June 30, 1969*, p. 4.
48   The Bellambi Coal Company Limited, *82nd Annual Report and Notice of Meeting, Year Ended June 30, 1970*, p. 3.

In the early 1970s, the recession in the Japanese steel industry reduced steel production levels, a factor also evident in the performance of CGFA's involvement in the supply of iron ore through the Mount Goldsworthy joint venture. The global context also included an emerging currency crisis with the United States' decision to cancel the direct international convertibility of the United States dollar to gold, and its implications for the devaluation of this currency. Massy-Greene expressed little concern in relation to the implications for Bellambi and, in terms of the performances from 1971 to 1973, his view was justified. He believed the reduction in steel production would not have an effect on coking coal sales unless there was a reduction in pig iron production. Furthermore, the contracts with Japanese customers were expressed in sterling with the opportunity for 'additional corrective measures for both buyer and seller in the event of a revaluation or devaluation of the currency'.[49] The Japanese buyers proved to be reliable consumers of coal, although as Japanese stocks of imported coal increased from already high levels as steel capacity reduced, additional markets for Bellambi coal were sought, including in Europe, as well as the establishment of contracts in Taiwan, South Korea and China.

Industrial disputes continued to be a feature of the New South Wales coal fields. Production from one of the company's coal-washing production facilities, Federal Coke Works, was suspended in November 1971 while shipments of coal were adversely affected by the All-Japan shipping strike. Notwithstanding these factors, the 1971 net profit after tax was $320,952, a record for the company. Despite this, the Bellambi board was concerned that the company's investment and increase in its workforce by 18 per cent had delivered only a 2 per cent production increase. Massy-Greene, chairman of Bellambi, warned that the 'unit cost of production had increased at an "alarming rate" in the context of broader challenges brought about by a world currency crisis and recession in the Japanese economy'.[50]

The environment was also one of continuing challenging geological conditions and equipment reliability issues. The operation was also affected by industry-wide union actions, including the progressive reduction in working hours from 40 to 35 and agitation for increased wages.

---

49   The Bellambi Coal Company Limited, 'Address by Chairman: JB Massy-Greene', in '83rd Annual Meeting', 24 September 1971, p. 2.
50   The Bellambi Coal Company Limited, *83rd Annual Report and Notice of Meeting, Year Ended June 30, 1971*, p. 4; The Bellambi Coal Company Limited, 'Address by Chairman: JB Massy-Greene', in '83rd Annual Meeting', 24 September 1971, pp. 1–2.

Associated with increased regulatory requirements, there was a need to commit additional capital expenditure to comply with pollution measures related to the company's coking coal facilities. Notwithstanding these factors, the company's investment in mechanised long-wall equipment and an expansion of the workforce resulted in coal production increasing by 22 per cent in 1972 and a further 14 per cent in 1973. Profitability in both years increased to over $400,000.[51]

Bellambi's favourable financial performance came to a jarring holt in the 1974 financial year. The company recorded its first loss in 50 years, despite the 1973 financial year performance being the second highest on record. While a dividend continued to be paid, the reasons for the financial decline were conveyed starkly:

> The predominant cause of the loss was industrial action taken by the company's employees as part of a nationwide campaign by all the mining unions. This expressed itself in the form of strikes, bans and other disruptions to production, all designed to force the company to comply with the Union's demands for higher wages and other benefits.[52]

Over 100 days were lost at the coke works and 20 days at the colliery operations. Coal production for the full year declined by 19 per cent, and coal sales were 16 per cent lower. A retrospective element in two employment awards meant that $355,000 in additional costs were incurred. The loss after tax for the year was $639,796.[53] The only saving grace was securing a further contract for an additional 6 million tonnes of coal to be supplied over five years and a substantial increase in price that, in the view of the company, 'more appropriately related to contract export prices charged by other countries after adjustment ... for quality differentials'.[54] Largely as a result of the renegotiated sales price, Bellambi returned to profit in 1975, with a record net operating profit of $1.2 million, achieved despite lower coal sales. In June 1975 the company warned of a 'dramatic worsening of the industrial situation'.[55] As a consequence of industrial

---

51   The Bellambi Coal Company Limited, *84th Annual Report and Notice of Meeting, Year Ended June 30, 1972*, p. 4; The Bellambi Coal Company Limited, *85th Annual Report and Notice of Meeting, Year Ended June 30, 1973*, p. 6.
52   The Bellambi Coal Company Limited, *86th Annual Report and Notice of Meeting, Year Ended June 30, 1974*, p. 8.
53   ibid., pp. 8 and 9.
54   The Bellambi Coal Company Limited, *87th Annual Report and Notice of Meeting, Year Ended June 30, 1975*, p. 6.
55   ibid.

action, the company was unable to conduct parts of its mining operation in an efficient manner, and notices of termination of employment were issued to 899 employees in August 1975.

Charles Copeman was appointed chairman of Bellambi in 1975. In the context of his later role as managing director at Peko-Wallsend in reforming what were considered disruptive work practices and in improving the productivity of that company's Pilbara iron ore operations, the industrial challenges he tackled at Bellambi were influential in informing his subsequent management approach.[56] He expressed the company's concerns in public forums, highlighting a myriad of government imposts and constraints, as well as identifying an industrial relations environment antithetical to company profitability. Not least, Copeman expressed his concerns with the Commonwealth Labor Government, observing:

> The consequences of the intervention by the Minister for Minerals and Energy of the Australian Government, The Hon. R.F.X Connor, in the negotiations between the company and its Japanese steel mill customers. By creating the precedent for direct Government intervention, the future basis for negotiations between the commercial parties must now be uncertain.[57]

The 1975 Commonwealth budget included the introduction of a coal export duty of $6 per tonne, with undertakings sought from coal companies that they would not seek to recover this duty on pain of export approvals being refused. Requirements to comply with the *New South Wales Clean Air Act*, for which the company had spent over $1.2 million, and the uncertainty associated with the outcome of a New South Wales Government commission of enquiry into whether mining would be permitted in the vicinity of stored waters, added to the concerns held by directors of CGFA about the investment in Bellambi.[58] The company's financial reporting typically began by detailing the level of operating income generated and then the amount paid to various levels of governments through duties, income tax, coal royalty, payroll tax and levies. These payments often constituted 80 per cent of operating expenses.

---

56 Michael Copeman, 'Vale Charles Copeman, Hero of Robe River', Quadrant Online, 11 July 2013, quadrant.org.au/opinion/qed/2013/07/vale-charles-copeman/.
57 The Bellambi Coal Company Limited, *87th Annual Report and Notice of Meeting, Year Ended June 30, 1975*, p. 7.
58 ibid.

In 1976, Bellambi achieved a markedly increased price for its coal sales, reflecting the renegotiation of prices to international levels. The following year marked the high point of CGFA's financial involvement in Bellambi, with a net profit in the 1977 financial year of $5 million, compared to $1.3 million in 1976 and $220,000 in 1964, the first year of CGFA's involvement. Coal sales exceeded 940,000 tonnes compared with 580,000 tonnes the previous year, while new contracts were signed with Chinese and Taiwanese customers.[59] Two years later in 1979, despite coal production reaching 1.1 million tonnes, an operating loss of $367,000 was recorded. Industrial disputes at Port Kembla during March and April 1979 meant that all deliveries to customers ceased and the company again sought approval to stand down employees. Payments to governments in the year exceeded the company's total operating revenues, with an additional impost—a recently introduced transport coordination levy—adding to the existing charges, along with demurrage costs incurred associated with port congestion and industrial disputation at Port Kembla.

Further issues relating to government policy settings created uncertainty. The New South Wales Government asked Bellambi to cease road transport of coal to Port Kembla and instead use rail transport. For the operation this entailed an additional $11 million in expenditure and higher freight charges. Copeman wrote to the New South Wales deputy premier:

> It has been with the greatest concern that I have put to you and your ministerial colleagues recently the financial position of this company. The effect of one setback after another has not only put the company into a loss, but it has created a situation in which no investor could be expected to be willing to commit further vitally-needed capital funds to maintain the company's production capacity, without a clear prospect of the company being able to return to strong profitability … The destruction of investor confidence has had a very serious effect, not only on financial matters, but much more importantly in my view, on the morale of the Bellambi work force.[60]

---

59   The Bellambi Coal Company Limited, *89th Annual Report and Notice of Meeting, Year Ended June 30, 1977*, p. 4.
60   Letter from Charles Copeman, chairman, Bellambi Coal Company Limited to The Hon LJ Ferguson, 14 August 1979, pp. 1–2.

Furthermore, the company was no closer to gaining clarification as to whether approvals would be forthcoming from the state government for mining in areas for which applications had been lodged. The situation was close to calamitous. As Copeman stated at the 1979 Bellambi Coal annual general meeting:

> This most disappointing result illustrates the way in which a fundamentally profitable trading enterprise can be rendered unprofitable by events beyond the influence of the Company. I refer of course to the need to meet government imposts which take no account of the financial conditions of the enterprise, and to the crippling industrial actions … at Port Kembla.[61]

The prospects were bleak, not least because from April 1979 the company was forced to accept a reduction in its selling price for the next two years, with no ability to achieve any price escalation to match cost increases.[62]

CGFA, as its major shareholder, had contributed to Bellambi achieving higher levels of production and increased profitability in large measure through a major investment in the adoption of mechanised mining. As Copeman conveyed in 1978: 'As a technical achievement it [mechanised long-wall mining] has been of the highest order of merit, and without it [the] Company would have been financially moribund'.[63] In the first half of the 1970s, in the context of the circumstances confronting CGFA with problems related to Mount Lyell, Gunpowder and Mount Goldsworthy, consideration was given to the sale of Bellambi. This had come to the fore with the poor 1975 result, although the decision was forestalled by the ability of Bellambi to improve its performance. However, by 1978, fundamental challenges were evident relating to CGFA's ongoing investment in Bellambi, associated with gaining access to new deposits to extend mining operations and maintain production. Such outcomes were dependent on the New South Wales Government granting approvals, an outcome in which the directors had little confidence.

After an extended period during which the company had increased production, improved production efficiencies and diversified markets, the prospects, as Copeman conveyed, were for a 'period of severe cost

---

61 The Bellambi Coal Company Limited, 'Address by Chairman: Mr AC Copeman', in '91st Annual Meeting', 25 September 1979, p. 1.
62 ibid., p. 2.
63 The Bellambi Coal Company Limited, 'Address by Chairman: Mr AC Copeman', in '90th Annual Meeting', 26 September 1978, p. 3.

price squeeze, exacerbated by shipping difficulties … which … have left their mark in the form of increased charges and the risk of loss of buyer confidence'.[64] The investment in Bellambi Coal was retained until 1979, when sold. Bellambi was to be a forerunner to another, more protracted planned entry into New South Wales coal; this time in association with Dalgety in the Hunter Valley.

Mineral Sands—multiple strands

CGFA's mineral sands portfolio had two main components. One was the east-coast operations centred upon the activities of Associated Minerals Consolidated (AMC) and the other the Western Australian operations based upon the activities of Western Titanium. A majority shareholding interest in Western Titanium was established in 1969. AMC, under the direction of its managing director, Joseph Pinter, embarked on a process of expansion and acquisition of other mineral sands producers along the coast of northern New South Wales and into Queensland, including dredge-mining activities, initially on South Stradbroke Island and then on North Stradbroke Island. The main products were rutile and zircon. The east-coast ilmenites had a high chrome content and, as such, had limited commercial application. Rutile was used in an array of applications, including for the manufacture of titanium metal and for welding, although the main use was as a feedstock for the manufacture of pigment used in the production of paint. Zircon was used in refractory applications, including the lining of blast furnaces used in steel making, as well as in ceramic manufacture and a range of more specialised uses.

The major trend influencing the industry was the advent of pigment production using the chloride process. While largely initiated by the United States pigment producer, Du Pont, other pigment producers had or were seeking to adopt the chloride process. On the west coast of Australia, Western Titanium had based its initial business, in the late 1950s and early 1960s, on the supply of sulphate ilmenite that, with its low chrome content, was an ideal feedstock for the then dominant sulphate pigment production industry. The advent of chloride pigment production created a potential issue in terms of the ability of the Western Australian producers, of which Western Titanium and Westralian Oil (to become

---

64 ibid., p. 5.

Westralian Sands in 1968) were the largest, to supply this emerging sector. More generally, there was also the issue of the continued availability of sufficient rutile, or an alternative product, to meet the increasing demands of chloride pigment producers. The mineral sands producers in Western Australia had access to only limited amounts of rutile in the assemblage of ore bodies. The solution was to seek to beneficiate or upgrade ilmenite to a product with a higher titanium dioxide content that could be used for chloride pigment production. In this regard, Western Titanium was the pioneer in undertaking research and small-scale experimentation to upgrade ilmenite.

AMC had taken an active role in the first half of the 1960s in acquiring smaller mineral sands producers and had established a dominant position as an Australian producer of rutile and zircon. Its operations, typically dredge mining on the forefront of beaches, were conducted at numerous locations in New South Wales. The process of acquiring other producers continued, albeit on a lower scale, in the second half of the 1960s. In 1967, the decision was made to merge AMC with Wyong Minerals, the latter company with dredge-mining operations at Lake Munmorah in New South Wales.[65]

AMC expanded its operations on South Stradbroke Island with the construction of a large dredge and associated concentrating plant, which were commissioned in 1968. The operation maintained the company's position 'as the largest single producer of rutile and zircon sand in Australia, and for that matter the world'.[66] In 1969, AMC acquired all of the issued capital of TAZI, a company majority owned by Rio Tinto that was undertaking mining of rutile and zircon on North Stradbroke Island.[67] This acquisition was associated with a loan advanced by CGFA. The acquisition provided AMC with access to ore reserves and mining equipment on North Stradbroke Island, supplementing its position on South Stradbroke Island. Expansions occurred elsewhere along the east coast and AMC continued to flourish.

---

65   The leases were adjacent to Lake Munmorah, an area of 760 acres tested by Wyong Alluvials. Wyong Alluvials also held 67.5 per cent of the issued capital of Eastern Titanium Corporation and an interest in the proceeds from the agreement between that company and Coffs Harbor Rutile NL.
66   Associated Minerals Consolidated Limited, 'Chairman's Address Presented to Shareholders at the Sixteenth General Meeting of the Company', 12 September 1968, p. 1, UMA, AW Muddyman Collection, 1995.0041, Unit 96.
67   Associated Minerals Consolidated Limited, 'Notice to Stock Exchange', 20 March 1969, UMA, JB Were and Son, 2000.0017, Unit 611.

Figures 38 and 39. Western Titanium's operations, Capel, south-west, Western Australia.

Sources: NAA, A1200, L92729, and Iluka Resources archives.

10. EXPANSION AND CONSOLIDATION 1966–1976

In 1969, CGFA acquired an interest in Western Titanium. CGFA had already considered the acquisition of Western Titanium's neighbour, Westralian Sands, in the south-west of Western Australia, and held a sufficient shareholding in this company to have an employee of CGFA appointed as a director to its board. However, Western Titanium was viewed as a more suitable means to pursue the implementation of ilmenite upgrading technology. By 1969, the situation for CGFA in terms of acquiring a controlling interest in Western Titanium had 'become quite critical' in the context of the apparent success of its beneficiation process and an offer made by a United States company for both shares in Western Titanium and a longer-term offtake agreement.[68] Sidney Segal, an executive director of CGFA, held discussions with Consolidated Gold Fields in London and was authorised to match the offer for Western Titanium by the United States company.[69] A CGFA board meeting minute in 1969 recorded:

> In view of the great importance of the upgrading of ilmenite, C.G.F.A. should use every effort, to acquire the Western Titanium process but also ... should be prepared to take up a commanding position in ilmenite, in view of once the fact that the ilmenite upgrading process is proved to be viable and economical, the future economics of rutile production may be limited.[70]

CGFA acquired a 19 per cent shareholding in 1969, with an offer made to acquire a majority position. While initially rejected, a revised offer was accepted by the board of Western Titanium and by November of that year CGFA's shareholding stood at 61 per cent, later to increase to 85 per cent. Western Titanium became a subsidiary of CGFA. Segal was appointed chairman, after commencing as a director in April 1968. His role was transformed into executive chairman, which he retained until 1976. Western Titanium played an instrumental role, not only in the development of ilmenite upgrading technology, but in the establishment of CGFA's position in a major new mining province in Western Australia— Eneabba—where large reserves of ilmenite were ideal for use in DuPont's chloride process plants or for upgrading to synthetic rutile.

---

68 Consolidated Gold Fields of Australia Limited, 'Minutes of Meeting of Directors', 23 July 1969, p. 2, RGCA, Box 12264.
69 ibid.
70 Consolidated Gold Fields of Australia Limited, 'Minutes of Meeting of Directors', 25 June 1969, p. 2, RGCA, Box 12264.

The consequences of the expansionary program in the 1960s meant that AMC was producing 125,000 tons of rutile in 1969, compared with 14,000 tons 10 years previously. Zircon production had increased to 110,000 tons from 11,000 tons over the same period. AMC was the largest producer of rutile and zircon, supplying more than 40 types of mineral sands products to 33 countries. Profit after tax of $1.6 million in 1969 grew to $5 million in 1975, before retreating in the subsequent years until after the merger with Western Titanium.

The governmental focus on mineral sands mining reflected the increasing environmental and regulatory opposition to mining, both in New South Wales and Queensland. It was a trend that grew in intensity and resulted in restrictions upon AMC's activities in the 1970s and cessation of the company's mining operations on most of the east coast, with the exception of North Stradbroke Island, by the 1980s. In October 1968 the New South Wales Government established the Sim Committee to report on mineral sands mining along the coast of New South Wales. It laid out proposals for one-third of the land designated for mining between Tweed Heads and Port Stephens to be preserved with the remaining areas subject to strict conditions for mining. Within 10 years, in October 1977, the New South Wales Cabinet determined that no further approvals for mineral sands mining within the extended Myall Lakes National Park would be approved. Later that year the New South Wales Planning and Environment Commission gazetted direction orders over extensive areas within the vicinity of existing national parks and nature reserves. Similarly, in Queensland, the *Beach Protection Act 1968* presented a direct threat to mining activities on Moreton and Stradbroke Islands.

Mining rehabilitation activities became a more prominent part of the company's reporting and promotional activities, with annual reports, chairman's addresses and other materials making reference to the amount of land rehabilitated and the quality of the work undertaken. Pinter became an advocate for the industry's interests and encouraged a program of progressive rehabilitation of areas affected by mineral sands mining along the New South Wales coast. The result was that large areas were restricted from mining; reserves of both zircon and rutile were sterilised, restricting mining plans in new areas, and also truncating the life of some operations.

10. EXPANSION AND CONSOLIDATION 1966–1976

CGFA's involvement in Western Australia, through Western Titanium, provided a bulwark against the restrictions on its east-coast mineral sands business and an entry into ilmenite upgrading. Western Titanium had undertaken pilot plant work for the upgrading of ilmenite in the early 1960s, which led to a feasibility study for a larger-scale plant. By the end of 1967 the decision was made to construct a 'semi-commercial' plant. The plant, with a capacity of 10,000 tons per annum, was commissioned in Capel in 1968. Despite considerable experimentation and adjustments to plant settings, by 1969 a sufficient tonnage of the new product had been produced to enable customers to trial it in their plants.[71] Customer reports were encouraging and demonstrated that the material could be processed in chloride pigment plants. In the early 1970s various modifications were trialled and the plant was placed on a commercial operating basis from January 1971. In 1974, a larger plant was commissioned with a nominal capacity of 30,000 tons per annum. The development and marketing of an upgraded ilmenite product, referred to as synthetic rutile from 1976, transformed the product offering and financial characteristics of Western Titanium.

By the early 1970s, the original high-grade deposits held by Western Titanium, near Capel, were nearing the end of their economic life. While mining was transferred to a new set of deposits, these were marked by lower heavy-mineral content, as well as an increase in indurated material and a higher clay content. In 1975, mining and production challenges were associated with low-grade ore recovery, exacerbated by a shortage of water. A downturn in the pigment market reduced demand for ilmenite and meant that product had to be stockpiled. The cancellation and deferment of orders was, according to Segal, 'assuming significant proportions'.[72] This, and the demand for higher-grade titanium dioxide feedstocks, such as rutile for the chloride market, led to lower ilmenite production. The mining conditions at Capel also prompted the company to evaluate exploration opportunities in other areas. Eneabba, 196 kilometres north of Perth, would be one of the areas.

---

71 Western Titanium NL, *Annual Report 1970 and Notice of Meeting*, p. 5.
72 Consolidated Gold Fields Australia Limited, 'Minutes of Meeting of Directors', 23 April 1975, p. 2 and 28 May 1975, p. 3, RGCA, Box 12246, RGC 11588.

The early years of the 1970s were challenging for CGFA's mineral sands interests. For AMC, revenues and profitability declined for three successive years to 1973. Lower rutile demand in 1971 and 1972 led to 150 employees in the company being retrenched. Production was lowered and an intensive cost reduction program implemented. The strengthening in the Australian dollar, while favourable in terms of the prices received, caused the company to be concerned at the increasing vulnerability of its products to substitutes or alternative sources of supply, including the planned development by others of Eneabba production in Western Australia, as well as that from Sierra Leone and Richards Bay Minerals in South Africa.[73] Operating conditions in 1974 and 1975 improved, with markets for products strengthening, enabling additional mining plant capacity to be brought into production. Despite the challenges the company was facing, with the undermining of its east-coast business by reserve depletion and government restrictions, profitability in 1975 and 1976 were the highest the company had recorded. While issued equity had increased threefold since the mid-1960s, the return on equity was above 25 per cent.

On the Sunday evening of 22 November 1971, Segal, the chairman of Western Titanium, received a telephone call in Sydney from Peter Nairn, managing director of Western Titanium. Nairn was at Eneabba and had observed a pegging frenzy, much of it conducted by local farmers, for ground considered to be prospective for mineral sands. He advised Segal of the resource potential of the area and the need for Western Titanium, and in effect CGFA, to move quickly to capture some of the opportunity. The following day Segal received a follow-up telex, outlining the potential of the Eneabba district. The telex read:

> Have examined most significant deposit of heavy mineral in Eneabba area ... Area being pegged rapidly by, among others, Allied Minerals, Mining Advisors, Ilmenite Pty Ltd and individuals from local area and Perth. In view of pegging rush consider that WTNL [Western Titanium NL] should tie up part of the area at least by immediate negotiations with claim applicants, and then initiate further prospecting in general area. Can initiate discussions with applications of approximately 8000 acres of mineral bearing ground which has potential of

---

73 Associated Minerals Consolidated Limited, 'Chairman's Address Presented to Shareholders at the Twentieth General Meeting of the Company held on 5th October 1972'; Associated Minerals Consolidated Limited, 'Chairman's Address Presented to Shareholders at the Twenty-first General Meeting of the Company held on 4th October1973', UMA, JB Were and Son, 2000.0017, Unit 611.

Ilmenite 7,000,000 tons
Zircon 6,000,000 tons
Leucoxene 4,000,000 tons
Rutile 2,000,000 tons

> Negotiations extremely sensitive for a number of reasons including reluctance of possible vendors to associate with CGFA. They consider that pressure could be brought to bear to restrict rutile production because of upgrade commitments ... potential of area most impressive ... Interest being shown by other companies is a measure of real potential of the area and this must be considered in relation to future WTNL operations.[74]

Segal was 'determined to go to Perth as soon as possible to investigate the matter on the spot'.[75] There followed a convoluted process whereby Western Titanium struck an arrangement with Jim Adamson, part of a farming syndicate involving himself, Tony Freebairn and Jerry Hayes, that had been involved in pegging tenements at Eneabba. The arrangement with Adamson provided Western Titanium with access to an extensive tenement holding and, with it, the potential to participate in production from a new mineral sands province. However, the arrangement struck with Adamson was contended by Freebairn and Hayes not to be binding. They had also established an arrangement with another company—Allied Minerals—with mining aspirations at Eneabba. There followed a protracted legal dispute, with the position of Freebairn and Hayes, on behalf of Allied Minerals, upheld in the Supreme Court of Western Australia. Western Titanium challenged this ruling in the High Court, with its appeal upheld. This ruling, in turn, was challenged by Allied Minerals in the Privy Council. In 1973 the Privy Council declined to hear Allied Mineral's appeal, endorsing Western Titanium's rights to the tenements. With this, Western Titanium could proceed with the development of its interests at Eneabba.[76]

Throughout the period of the legal dispute, Western Titanium had made overtures to Allied Minerals, whose partner was Du Pont, the United States pigment producer, for a possible merger of interests.[77] This was not to occur at this stage. Instead, Western Titanium proceeded with its own development plans at Eneabba in the early 1970s. This resulted in the first

---

74 Telex for Segal from Nairn, 23 November 1970, RGCA, Box 12612, RGC 6500.
75 Eneabba Statement by SL Segal, 25 May 1971, RGCA, Box 12612, RGC 6500.
76 A review of the establishment of CGFA's position in the Eneabba mineral sands province is available in Porter, *Below the Sands*, pp. 81–95.
77 Consolidated Gold Fields Australia Limited, 'Minutes of Meeting of Directors', 26 September 1973, RGCA, Box 12248, RGC 11576.

commercial production in 1974, although with persistent commissioning problems during a period of severe downturn in mineral sands markets. Meanwhile, two other parties, Jennings Industries and Allied Minerals, had developed their own mineral sands operations at Eneabba.

The establishment of Western Titanium's position at Eneabba, along with the development of synthetic rutile, represented two of the most important developments for the company and of the mineral sands industry in Australia. For CGFA, it enabled the reliance on east-coast deposits and the maturing south-west Western Australian deposits—in the context of the transformation of the production base and product requirements of the main pigment customer base—to be largely supplanted by production from Eneabba. It also established the logic for the merger, or in effect takeover in 1976, at the behest of CGFA, of Western Titanium by AMC.

AMC and Western Titanium operated until 1976 as separate subsidiaries of CGFA. While the geographical separation of their operations provided some differentiation in their activities, the reality was that their product offerings were similar, and often in competition. While Western Titanium was making advances in the process to beneficiate ilmenite, AMC harboured similar ambitions and pursued its own development work. It became apparent that this duality of interests, particularly during periods of poor market conditions and lower prices, was not sustainable.

Following the merger of AMC and Western Titanium, AMC acquired the two other producers at Eneabba, Jennings Industries and Allied Eneabba. In doing so, AMC, or as it had become, RGC Mineral Sands, established itself as the dominant producer of mineral sands in Australia. The company later undertook mining activities in Florida and Virginia. The technical work on ilmenite beneficiation in the south-west of Western Australia, where two kilns had been constructed, provided the foundation for the development of a further two kilns at Geraldton, Western Australia, for which the Eneabba ilmenite was an ideal feed source.

Mineral sands had become the cornerstone of the CGFA portfolio, with the company establishing a prominent position for its products both in Australia and internationally. However, wider portfolio considerations and CGFA's concerns with its high level of indebtedness through the 1970s led to a review of the continued retention of mineral sands within the portfolio. Aggregating CGFA's mineral sands business with other industry participants was considered, as was the complete divestiture of its mineral sands holdings.

11
ACQUISITION AND DIVERSIFICATION

Consolidated Gold Fields Australia (CGFA) pursued acquisition opportunities with the intention to expand its portfolio. However, the availability of businesses that would be financially material to the group, or provide it with mineral diversification, were limited. While several opportunities were evaluated and in one case pursued, a key acquisition and important step in strengthening the group's involvement in mineral sands was the acquisition of Western Titanium in 1969. Outside mineral sands, consideration was given in 1967 to the acquisition of another Australian-listed mining company, through a project named Project Bee.[1] Board minutes in relation to this project recorded:

> The Chairman explained that other acquisitions were undertaken prior to the advent of the mining boom and such opportunities will probably not arise again. He pointed out that the two principal avenues of expansion open to C.G.F.A. were by acquisition and by exploration. As far as acquisition was concerned, a survey had been made of all mining companies which could be considered to be of interest to C.G.F.A. Of all of them the Bee Company appeared to be the logical and best choice at the present time.[2]

---

1   Consolidated Gold Fields Australia Limited, 'Minutes of a Special Meeting of Directors', 14 December 1967, p. 1, Renison Goldfields Consolidated Archives (RGCA), Box 12264.
2   Consolidated Gold Fields Australia Limited, 'Minutes of Meeting of Directors', 19 August 1967, p. 1, RGCA, Box 12264.

The company is likely to have been North Broken Hill, one of the largest participants in the Broken Hill lead–zinc mines.[3] However, it was determined that the ability to acquire a controlling interest in the company would involve 'too large a commitment of the company's resources' and was not pursued.[4] North Broken Hill would be reconsidered in the 1990s as a potential acquisition opportunity.

By August 1968, another acquisition opportunity had been identified: King Island Scheelite (1947). As a basis for the future development of CGFA, few companies had been identified in terms of their potential availability or materiality. King Island Scheelite was 'one of the few'.[5] The company was involved in mining for tungsten on King Island near Tasmania. After two meetings with directors of the company, the board of CGFA was confident that the directors of King Island Scheelite would provide unqualified support for the acquisition. In September 1968, with CGFA having provided details of its offer to King Island Scheelite shareholders, Peko-Wallsend made a competing bid. A revised CGFA offer for 50 per cent control, underwritten by the London parent, was made. By December, a revised offer was forthcoming from Peko-Wallsend. CGFA contemplated a further, higher offer, including its own shares. This bid failed, with Peko-Wallsend gaining control.[6]

In 1971 CGFA, with Mitsubishi Metal Mining (Australia), Kinsho-Mataichi (Australia) and Mitsubishi Development, acquired the Mammoth and Mount Oxide copper deposits, known as the Gunpowder Complex, 120 kilometres north-west of Mount Isa, Queensland, from provisional liquidators and receivers. CGFA's interest was 70 per cent. Initially developed as an open cut mining operation, underground mining of the deposits began in 1972. The first copper concentrate was shipped by the joint venture to Japan in April 1972. Through further development of the Mammoth ore body, as well as production on a nearby ore body, it was planned to nearly double production by increasing concentrator capacity and installing additional grinding mills. By 1975, a loss was recorded and

---

3   Ted Wiles (personal communication, 18 April 2017) recalled that Commonwealth Mining Investments examined a number of companies, including North Broken Hill.
4   Consolidated Gold Fields Australia Limited, 'Minutes of Meeting of Directors', 19 August 1967, p. 1, RGCA, Box 12264.
5   Consolidated Gold Fields Australia Limited, 'Minutes of Meeting of Directors', 19 August 1968, p. 1, RGCA, Box 12264. See also King Island Scheelite Limited, *King Island Scheelite Mine*.
6   Consolidated Gold Fields Australia Limited, 'Minutes of Meeting of Directors', 16 February 1969, p. 2, RGCA, Box 12264.

the following year, despite the achievement of higher levels of production and the entire output being sold to Mitsubishi Metal, another loss was recorded. Despite investment to substantially increase production, the decline in copper prices meant that the financial performance was poor. In September 1977 the mine was placed on care and maintenance and while an acid-leaching program operated for a period in the early 1980s, this activity was suspended in 1982. In 1984 the assets of the operation were sold.[7]

In 1971 CGFA acquired OT Lempriere and Company, an established smelter, refiner and alloy manufacturer. The acquisition was part of a plan for a nonferrous metals processing complex that, in 1971, was also associated with the acquisition of a 51 per cent interest in Ferro Alloys of Tasmania, and the formation of a company, Kemerton. CGFA tendered unsuccessfully for shares in Aberfoyle, as part of the liquidation of interests held by Mineral Securities Australia, and while it also had the opportunity to tender for shares in the mineral sands company Cudgen RZ and its shareholding in CRL, this did not proceed. CGFA's successor company, Renison Goldfields Consolidated (RGC), later acquired both Cudgen RZ and CRL.[8]

Diversification outside minerals remained under consideration. In 1972, the company became involved in real estate and property development through a subsidiary, Lion Properties. This company undertook a canal-fronted real estate development for housing on the shores of the Hastings River at Port Macquarie, New South Wales. CGFA's 50 per cent interest in this development was viewed as 'modest diversification', as was the establishment in 1973 of Colinas, with a landholding of about 3,000 acres in the Macleay Valley and nearby areas of New South Wales for growing

---

7   In September 1977 it was announced that Gunpowder would be placed on a care and maintenance basis. On 30 June 1978, Gunpowder was transferred to Circular Quay Holdings. From this time, with leaching operations, Gunpowder Copper was fully reimbursed by the joint venturers for all costs and as such was not recorded as making either a profit or loss. An agreement was reached with the Japanese joint venture partners whereby Circular Quay Holdings acquired the outstanding 30 per cent held if the project proceeded to a full-scale leaching operation (Consolidated Gold Fields Australia Limited, *12th Annual Report 1978*, pp. 9 and 35; Renison Goldfields Consolidated Limited, *Report on the 1981 Financial Year*, p. 30).
8   CGFA had concerns with the impact on rutile prices, a key product for Cudgen and CRL, associated with the potential supply of upgraded ilmenite. The assessed short-life reserves of Cudgen and the cash position of AMC were factors in the decision by CGFA not to tender (Consolidated Gold Fields Australia Limited, 'Minutes of Meeting of Directors', 28 July 1971, RGCA, Box 12248, RGC 11576).

poplar trees and raising cattle.⁹ The involvement in agricultural activities was considered by the CGFA board as a 'worthwhile diversification' and although profits were not expected to be recorded for some years it was anticipated that returns from this venture would be generated at 'about the time the Goldsworthy northern reserves began to run down'.¹⁰ By 1976, however, management had become concerned at the cash outflow for Colinas, and attempts were made to sell the venture. The company's property diversification, which included a warehousing complex at Lidcombe near Sydney, did not fare much better. In 1976, with weak property market conditions, the further development of what had become known as Settlement Shores at Port Macquarie was restricted to the less expensive lots.

Circular Quay Holdings had been established as a fully owned subsidiary. The intention was for this company to hold direct investments in mining companies, some of which were of acquisition interest to CGFA. In this regard, CGFA drew upon an established Gold Fields' model where an investment portfolio was held in listed companies that did not form part of the group's major ongoing company investments.¹¹ Circular Quay Holdings became the forerunner to the establishment of an investment division in 1984.

Exploration remained a central component of CGFA's approach to attempting to identify new resources and develop production opportunities. A wide range of initiatives were pursued, including a joint venture with Mitsubishi Metal Mining (Australia) in the Norseman area, Western Australia; nickel exploration at Mount Tyndall and North Dundas in Tasmania; a nickel laterite evaluation with Dalgety in New Caledonia; an interest in an oil exploration company, Beaver Exploration; and an exploration presence in the Philippines. A kaolin project in Western Australia was also investigated for an extended period.

An interest in coal in New South Wales was established through an association with Dalgety Australia, which led to a joint venture to evaluate, trial mine and attempt to develop coal resources in the Hunter Valley. In 1968 discussions were initiated with Dalgety & New Zealand

---

9   Consolidated Gold Fields Australia Limited, 'Minutes of Meeting of Directors', 20 December 1972, p. 5, RGCA, Box 12246, RGC 11576.
10 Consolidated Gold Fields Australia Limited, 'Minutes of Meeting of Directors', 26 March 1973, p. 1, RGCA, Box 12248, RGC 11576.
11 Consolidated Gold Fields Limited, London, no date, p. 7 (copy held by the author).

Loan, of which Brian Massy-Greene was a director, with a view to establishing a joint venture to develop a coal prospect at Ravensworth in the upper Hunter Valley of New South Wales. The following year a joint venture agreement was in place, pending New South Wales Government ministerial approvals for the revocation of ministerial reserves. In what was a portent for continuing delays and impediments in advancing this venture, it was observed at the CGFA board meeting in June 1969 that 'the matter was still in progress but was moving slowly'.[12] A separate company, Durham Holdings, was established to acquire the Ravensworth mineral rights on an equal entitlement basis between CGFA and Dalgety. Charles Copeman, the manager of the mining and exploration division, proceeded with plans to consolidate a large area in the upper Hunter Valley for potential coal mining while discussions commenced with the New South Wales Government in relation to the establishment of rail transport, as well as coal loading facilities at Port Stephens. CGFA's and RGC's pursuit of a major coal operation at Glendell consumed considerable management time and expenditure over the next two decades, but to little avail. RGC sold its interest in the Glendell joint venture in January 1992.[13]

The Lake View and Star gold mine in Western Australia was the one interest retained from the period of investment by the London parent in Australia prior to 1960. In 1966 the residence of Lake View and Star was transferred to Australia with CGFA taking over technical and administrative services previously supplied from London.[14] CGFA held a 16 per cent interest. Various attempts were made to broaden the business base of Lake View and Star, including by CGFA and Lake View and Star tendering for rights to prospect for nickel at Lake Rebecca, North Kalgoorlie. An exploration company, View Star, was established. The plan was to list the company on Australian stock exchanges but instead Lake View and Star undertook a rights issue and established an arrangement with CGFA enabling it to take an interest in any of the exploration projects. Profitability of the Lake View and Star mine declined from $560,000 in 1960 to $287,000 in 1968. In 1970 a shortage of labour and a decline in gold price led to

---

12 Consolidated Gold Fields Australia Limited, 'Minutes of Meeting of Directors', 25 June 1969, p. 1, RGCA, Box 12264.
13 RGC sold its interest to the Liddell joint venture.
14 The transfer to Australia had been considered earlier, in the 1940s, to avoid the British excessive profits tax. The London board came to the decision not to take this course of action, due in part to close association with New Consolidated Gold Fields from which Lake View and Star company obtained 'valuable technical and financial assistance' (*West Australian Mining and Commercial Review*, vol. 16, no. 1, March 1951, p. 15).

the rationalisation of mining operations and cessation of further mine development activity. The mine recorded a loss and no dividend was paid. Poseidon NL made an offer to acquire CGFA's shareholding. While the board of CGFA did not view the offer as particularly attractive, its view was that 'the alternative of living with a dying mine appear[ed] to be even less so'.[15] By early 1971, the Poseidon offer was declared unconditional and CGFA's ownership and 45-year involvement with one of Australia's foremost gold mines came to an end.[16]

...

Despite the efforts to grow and diversify the portfolio, the managing director and chairman, Massy-Greene, in writing about the outlook for the 1976 financial year, warned:

> The present indications are that this year will be the most difficult in the history of the Company. Continuing low metal prices, falling demand and escalating costs are having a material adverse effect on the profitability of both the Group and the Company. Export quotas set by the International Tin Council ... together with a drop in local demand have necessitated a cutback of tin concentrates produced at Renison Limited. This will materially affect the results.[17]

What was in train at management and board level was a fundamental review of the composition of the CGFA portfolio, and by the London board, the Australian management structure.

---

15 Consolidated Gold Fields Australia Limited, 'Minutes of Meeting of Directors', 28 October, 1970, p. 2, RGCA, Box 12248, RGC 11576.
16 Lake View and Star, Limited, 'Directors' Report and Statement of Accounts for the Year Ended 30th June, 1970'.
17 Consolidated Gold Fields of Australia Limited, *Ninth Annual Report 1975 and Notice of Meeting*, p. 7.

12

PORTFOLIO CHALLENGES

Mount Lyell's survival in question

Charles Copeman, a senior executive of Consolidated Gold Fields Australia (CGFA), was appointed chairman of Mount Lyell Mining and Railway Company in late 1976. With his responsibilities as chairman of Bellambi Coal, this was one of two demanding directorships he held while an executive director of CGFA. Despite being asked by the London directors to close Mount Lyell, he instead oversaw the continuation of the operation although at a much reduced scale and with an approach to both the Tasmanian and Commonwealth governments for financial assistance.[1] The continuation or otherwise of Mount Lyell was an important economic and social issue for Tasmania. In terms of seeking governmental financial support, CGFA and the board of Mount Lyell were aided by the fact that voting intentions in Tasmania were crucial in Commonwealth electoral outcomes for both of the two major political parties. As such, the continuation of mining operations at Mount Lyell gained a high level of bipartisan support.[2]

---

1   Charles Copeman, interview by John Farquarson, National Library of Australia, session 2.
2   Copeman recorded that the Tasmanian premier asked the Liberal Party opposition leader, Max Bingham, into his office, and that Bingham phoned the prime minister, Malcolm Fraser. Fraser was concerned at the electoral consequences of the potential closure of Mount Lyell. Subsequently, payroll tax exemptions were granted by the Tasmanian Government, while Commonwealth subsidies were also forthcoming. Copeman also recorded that when Fraser met the CGFA managing director and chairman, Massy-Greene, he inquired how much the Australian dollar needed to decline in value to keep Mount Lyell operating (Charles Copeman, interview by John Farquarson, National Library of Australia, session 2).

The report of the Senate Select Committee that investigated the impact of the potential closure of Mount Lyell on the regional economy was followed in 1977 by an Industries Assistance Commission inquiry into whether financial support should be provided to Australian copper producers, most notably Mount Lyell.[3] In briefing notes Copeman prepared for his engagement with the Industries Assistance Commission, it was detailed that since CGFA had acquired its 56 per cent interest in Mount Lyell in 1964 for $11.9 million, there had been capital expenditure of $61 million, with CGFA receiving $10.1 million in dividends of which $3.1 million came from Mount Lyell companies other than mining. As such, the original investment in Mount Lyell, based on the then current share price, had delivered a real rate of return of 0.24 per cent.[4]

It was made clear that closure was likely if governmental assistance was not forthcoming. While not a part of the assistance sought, CGFA also conveyed that its North-West Acid joint venture operation with EZ Industries was also in a parlous financial state.

The Industries Assistance Commission examined the serious repercussions for the township of Queenstown and the regional area if the Mount Lyell operation were to close. Its interim report concluded:

> The community of Queenstown is almost entirely dependent on the Mount Lyell mine and existing adjustment measures appear inadequate to deal with the scale of economic and social stress which would occur there if the mine were to close … The immediate effect of the closing of the mine would be to increase substantially the level of unemployment in Queenstown and Gormanston.[5]

The financial circumstances of Mount Lyell relative to the more favourable operating conditions of Renison highlighted the deficiencies of the CGFA group structure, something that had been under active consideration since 1975. As Copeman conveyed at the inquiry:

---

3   The Senate Select Committee recommended governmental financial assistance for Mount Lyell, given the adverse effects on unemployment in an area with few alternative employment opportunities (Australian Senate, 'Report of Senate Select Committee for Mount Lyell Mining Operations', 3 December 1976, Renison Goldfields Consolidated Archives (RGCA), Box 746).
4   Part of notes prepared for Industries Assistance Commission and request by Mt Lyell for assistance, RGCA, Box 746.
5   'Report of Senate Select Committee for Mount Lyell Mining Operations', 3 December 1976, Renison Goldfields Consolidated Archives (RGCA), Box 746).

The Goldfields group, as I think you understand, is a group of strange structure ... Renison and Lyell are owned roughly 35% to 40% foreign and the rest is owned by Australians ... It puts the group into a situation where it does not just direct that there is a surplus cash in one company and say it should go into this company because that other company is short ... [consequently] the rather poor financial position the company has got into [is] largely as a result of the Mount Lyell problem and one or two other problems in the group.[6]

Copeman went on to state:

I think these are very sobering occasions for all of us when we are dealing with matters of very great personal significance to people who live in this community. I think it is not something any of us are trained for or that any of us have particularly clever answers to, except to say we have spent three years trying to come up with, and in those three years we have come up with, a lot of better answers. We have run out of answers now, and that is why as an ultimate step we have asked for this inquiry.[7]

In 1977, Mount Lyell sought temporary financial assistance from the Commonwealth Government to offset losses and forestall what the company conveyed would otherwise be the necessity to close the operation. In 1978, this became a request for an interest-free loan of $632,000 with a company statement made that if this assistance was not forthcoming it would be viewed 'as an indication of the Government's attitude' and, as a consequence, the company 'would take steps to close the mine'.[8] The loan funds sought were for capital equipment, including trucks to maintain continuity of production. The government's consideration of this request was influenced by the possibility that Mount Lyell may close and, if forced into liquidation, the company may not be in a position to meet severance payments for workers. In addition, the potential impact on employment levels at Electrolytic Refining and Smelting's operations at Port Kembla was a consideration if this operation were not able to be supplied with copper concentrate from Mount Lyell.[9] The first of a series of government financial

---

6   Extract from 'I.A.C. Inquiry re Copper Ores and Concentrates, Tuesday 6th September, 1977', official transcript of proceedings, pp. 632–636, RGCA, Box 746.
7   ibid., p. 636.
8   Cabinet Minute, Canberra, 15 August 1977, Decision No. 3624, National Archives of Australia, Tasmania (NAAT), A12909, 1584; Cabinet Minute, Canberra, 28 February 1978, Decision No. 4726, NAA, A12909, 1937.
9   Cabinet Minute, Canberra, 28 February 1978, Decision No. 4726, NAA, A12909, 1937.

assistance measures were implemented with a $3.3 million Tasmanian Government subsidy, although the government did not accede to an offer to purchase the Lake Margaret power station from the company.

From 1977, the revised operating plan for Mount Lyell—the Prince Lyell Extended Plan—was implemented. The main features of this new plan included an indefinite deferment of further capital works on the new Prince Lyell shaft complex, reduction of ore production from 2.2 million tons to 1.5 million tons per annum, the introduction of a five-day milling week, the centralisation of mining activities to the large lower-cost ore bodies, rationalisation of surface engineering facilities and the reduction of the workforce. The workforce was reduced by the retrenchment of 225 employees, taking the number of employees to 727 from over 1,000 12 months earlier.[10] After achieving reductions in freight charges from Emu Bay Railway, the renegotiation of a three-year agreement with Mitsubishi generated savings of $6 million.[11] Plans were also made for the closure of the loss-making North-West Acid plant, with EZ Industries assuming Mount Lyell's interest in 1979. Despite these activities, Mount Lyell remained loss-making in 1977 and 1978. An increase in the copper price meant an operating profit of $795,000 was recorded in the 1979 financial year and by 1980 the company's profit had increased to $9.5 million, enabling the payment of a dividend for the first time since 1975. Repayment of the subsidies advanced by the Tasmanian Government also commenced in 1980. During the period, mining occurred from the Prince Lyell ore body, with mining advancing through a series of stopes from the 10 series to the 30 series, along with mining from other ore bodies, including Cape Horn and Crown Lyell. Larger underground trucks were purchased to reduce haulage costs as deeper mining occurred, while other initiatives were implemented, such as the replacement of the grinding mills with larger units. Exploration expenditure also increased.

By 1981, Mount Lyell was again adversely affected by low copper prices and unfavourable currency movements. Copeman had resigned as chairman and as an executive of CGFA in 1981. His replacement as chairman of Mount Lyell was LW Skelton, an executive director of CGFA, who observed in August 1981 that there was 'little opportunity for effecting further economies or increasing production to offset escalating

---

10   Industries Assistance Commission, 'Interim Report, Copper Ores and Concentrates', p. 20.
11   The Mount Lyell Mining and Railway Company Limited, 'Minutes of Meeting of Directors', 23 November 1978, p. 4, NAAT, NS 3924, Items 253–261.

costs' and that in the absence of a material improvement in copper prices the financial outlook for Mount Lyell was again parlous.[12] Furthermore, adoption of the earlier Prince Lyell Plan had meant a predominant reliance on a single source of ore for milling. Varying grades of mineralisation obtained from the Prince Lyell ore bodies meant there were impediments to achieving an appropriate quality and mix of ore feed grade to the milling plant. In effect, Mount Lyell was entering yet another period of challenging operating and financial conditions whereby options for the mine's continuation or closure again came under consideration.

Mount Goldsworthy divestment

An internal company study in March 1976 led to a decision to divest CGFA's position in iron ore. The study identified depletion of the iron ore reserves in the northern areas of the Mount Goldsworthy tenements. In turn, it was recognised that the long-term future of the joint venture would be dependent on the development of the reserves in the southern tenements, especially Mining Area C. At a board meeting in January 1976 that considered how CGFA could fund its commitment to Mining Area C, Donald McCall, the London chairman and managing director, stated that the 'whole iron ore position regarding the C.G.F.A. Group needed immediate and careful review'.[13] The principal issue was the likely capital expenditure of at least $550 million and how CGFA would fund its one-third share.

Bart Ryan, who had become managing director in July 1976, and who had earlier direct experience of the Mount Goldsworthy iron ore operation, believed the capital cost could increase to at least $900 million. For him, it was whether this was an appropriate investment, with the 'problem of financing the investment … not insurmountable but formidable'.[14] In fact, based on a 1974 re-examination of the development of Shay Gap on then prevailing costs and prices, it was determined that 'at the present time development of Mining Area "C" does not appear to be a viable proposition'.[15] At a time when the Australian group's investments were

---

12 The Mount Lyell Mining and Railway Company Limited, 'Minutes of Meeting of Directors', 27 August 1981, p. 2, NAAT, NS 3924/1/57, Items, 169–179.
13 Consolidated Gold Fields of Australia Limited, 'Minutes of Meeting of Directors', 28 January 1976, p. 9, RGCA, Box 12246, RGC 11588.
14 Consolidated Gold Fields Australia Limited, 'Minutes of Meeting of Directors', 26 May 1976, p. 9, RGCA, Box 12246, RGC 11588.
15 ibid.

showing poor or variable returns, with the exception of Renison, and where further capital was in all likelihood required for a number of these investments, the issue with a large capital commitment to its iron ore operations was recorded at board level as follows:

> Mr Ryan noted that the investment would not produce a return until the 1980's, yet it would have to be made at a time when we already have committed substantial investments which themselves would not show returns for some years, for example, Gunpowder, Mount Lyell, Western Titanium and Bellambi. Mr Ryan therefore posed the question as to whether it was sensible for Consolidated Gold Fields Australia even to contemplate a massive investment in MAC and expressed the view that there was a strong case for full divestment if a buyer could be found at a sensible price.[16]

A concern expressed was that if CGFA was not able to follow through on the development of Mining Area C, the current operations at Mount Goldsworthy, Shay Gap and Sunrise Hill could be adversely affected before their reserves were exhausted. The likelihood was that part of the workforce would leave these operations before their completion to secure alternative employment, with a difficulty in replacing these workers.

In Sid Segal's view, the London parent was better placed to raise the finance required for the potential development of Mining Area C. He believed that the interest burden of an investment in Mining Area C for CGFA would be 'huge' and in the context of a number of projects and a high level of debt, 'a divestment deal which gives us cash would best serve our interests'.[17] It was recognised that one of the other joint partners, Cyprus Mines Corporation, was financially stretched and had no other Australian interests. While Utah Construction & Mining Co. was in a stronger financial position, its interest in the Bowen Basin coal deposits was expected to consume its attention and financial resources. Ryan indicated his intention to make 'some delicate preliminary soundings' to Utah executives to see whether they may be interested in increasing their stake in Mining Area C.[18] Approaches were also made in 1975 to Melbourne-based mining companies, while CGFA contemplated offering participation of up to 10 per cent to Japanese steelmakers. An agreement was instead reached with Mount Isa Mines in August 1976 for it to acquire a 20 per cent interest in the Mount Goldsworthy joint venture.

---

16   ibid.
17   ibid., p. 11.
18   ibid., p. 10.

Figure 40. Bart Ryan, managing director of Consolidated Gold Fields Australia, 1976–1980.
Source: Alan Purcell, *Sydney Morning Herald*, Nine Publishing.

Figure 41. Sidney Segal, executive and subsequently chairman of Consolidated Gold Fields Australia from 1976 to 1980, then deputy chairman and director until 1982.

Source: Image courtesy of Jillian Segal.

Given that the Mount Goldsworthy joint venture had not been successful in negotiating a contract with the Japanese steel mills for Mining Area C iron ore tonnage, the board came to the decision that involvement in the Mining Area C development 'was not an appropriate investment for Consolidated Gold Fields Australia'.[19] Segal, as the chairman, conveyed a longer-term view of the company's iron ore interest:

> Whilst the present picture for iron ore was bleak with low iron ore prices and an appalling cost structure, the Chairman felt it must be recognised that the Japanese would remain dependent upon Australia indefinitely into the future for a very significant part of their iron ore requirement. He noted that their offtake from Australia was currently in excess of 50% of their requirements and that the Japanese will always need ore. It had always been the Chairman's view that once we got to the point of obtaining a contract for MAC it would be possible to restructure our interests by disposing of part of it to the Australian public … [and] this is still the way to proceed.[20]

Ryan, however, was of the view that the iron ore industry in Western Australia had 'descended into industrial anarchy'. Furthermore, in his view Hamersley Iron Ore had invested 'huge sums … and the return on investment was extremely poor'.[21] He warned that the route proposed by the chairman was a 'possible duplication of the Robe River experience' and was firmly of the view that iron ore was 'unlikely to be a good investment for a very long time'.[22] Ryan recommended complete divestiture. This was the board's decision, with the London parent, Consolidated Gold Fields, indicating it would consider acquiring some part of the interest on divestiture. The sale of a 30 per cent interest of CGFA's one-third holding in Mount Goldsworthy to Mount Isa Mines was agreed and in May 1977 an extraordinary general meeting of shareholders was held to seek approval for the sale of the residual 70 per cent interest to a Consolidated Gold Fields subsidiary, CGF Iron Pty Ltd.

---

19 Consolidated Gold Fields Australia Limited, 'Minutes of Meeting of Directors', 25 August 1976, p. 4, RGCA, Box 12248, RGC 11575.
20 ibid., p. 5.
21 ibid., pp. 5–6.
22 ibid., p. 6.

Segal addressed shareholders to explain the reason for the sale, conceding:

> We have become disenchanted with iron ore. We lost money last year and we are losing money this year ... Even if we had a different view, we saw ourselves as unable to find our share of the funds necessary to open up Mining Area 'C' ... Combined, we would have been exposed to too great a risk and our whole enterprise put at risk if the future iron ore operation failed to perform, in that prices were too low, costs were too high and/or demand proved to be inadequate, and natural disasters befell us.[23]

The payment from Consolidated Gold Fields for its interest was in two parts. An amount of $12.47 million was paid on completion of the transaction to sell CGFA's interest in the Mount Goldsworthy joint venture. The second component was a payment of $19.8 million that would be made when and if production commenced from Mining Area C.

CGFA's involvement in iron ore initially formed one of the major bases of its earnings and cash flow. The divestment was a seminal strategic decision. It was the most profound change in the CGFA portfolio up until that time. It occurred in the context of considerable disquiet by the London parent about the overall financial performance and management of its Australian subsidiary that, in turn, contributed to Massy-Greene's replacement as managing director and his retirement as chairman. Although inconceivable to realise at the time in light of business conditions, but as alluded to by Segal, it may also rank as one of the most profound inhibitions on the longevity of the Gold Fields group in Australia. Nonetheless, part of the Goldsworthy interest was retained by the London parent. There was a later attempt to reacquire this interest by Renison Goldfields Consolidated. However, by this stage, Consolidated Gold Fields had come under takeover threat first from Minorco and then by Hanson. The parent's interest in the Goldsworthy joint venture that, under other circumstances, was likely to be returned to the Australian entity was sold, not to Renison Goldfields Consolidated, but to BHP.

---

23 'Chairman's Speech 1976 Extraordinary Shareholder Meeting on 6th May 1977 for Sale of 70% of its Interest in Mount Goldsworthy JV to CGF Iron Pty Ltd, a Wholly Owned Subsidiary of Consolidated Gold Fields', p. 2, RGCA, Box 12246, RGC 11584.

Portfolio restructure

The sale of CGFA's interest in the Goldsworthy joint venture was associated with a review of the wider portfolio. Bellambi Coal remained on the market, and eventually sold in 1979, after Copeman advised that he was no longer able to recommend further capital expenditure for the operation. Production from the Gunpowder copper project was suspended in September 1977, with CGFA's investment folded into the group company, Circular Quay Holdings. Commonwealth Mining Investments (CMI) was retained in the portfolio and while contributing to CGFA's overall performance, it presented its own challenges. Apart from the board's view that CMI's turnover of some of its investments four times a year was incompatible with CGFA's position as a public company, the other issue was that a decision to dispose of a particular share investment might be 'inimical to the interests of the Group as a whole' and if such shares were offered to CGFA, the issue of 'insider trading' may be encountered.[24] The CGFA board initially considered taking over CMI, although this idea was abandoned. Instead, the sale of CGFA's shareholding to National Mutual occurred in 1977. The CMI board minutes of 22 March 1978 recorded:

> The Chairman stated that before formally closing the Meeting he felt it was appropriate to express his deep personal regret that the long and close relationship between CGFA and CMI had come to an end. During the seventeen years which had elapsed since CMI became a member of the Gold Fields Group, the skilful management exercised by CGFA had enabled the Company to achieve a considerable measure of success during a period of rapidly changing and sometimes extremely difficult market conditions.[25]

Smaller investments in agricultural activities through Colinas were a continuing disappointment and efforts were made to sell this business. The interest in North-West Acid was surrendered in 1979. CGFA had maintained an investment in Pancontinental Mining since the discovery of the Jabiluka uranium deposit, with close to a 15 per cent shareholding and a seat on the Pancontinental board, while also supporting the company's

---

24 Consolidated Gold Fields Australia Limited, 'Minutes of Meeting of Directors', 24 August 1977, p. 13, RGCA, Box 12246, RGC 11590.
25 Commonwealth Mining Investments (Australia) Limited, 'Minutes of Board Meeting', 22 March 1978, University of Melbourne Archives (UMA), Commonwealth Mining Investment (Australia) Limited Board Minute Books, 1955–1979, 2012.0202.

exploration activities. In 1976, as part of the company's rationalisation of assets in the context of straitened financial circumstances, its shareholding in Pancontinental was sold, generating $3.75 million in cash.

Questioning the involvement in mineral sands

Preceding a broader strategic consideration of the role of mineral sands in the CGFA portfolio, the merger of Associated Minerals Consolidated (AMC) and Western Titanium was seen as the first, logical step in rationalising the group's involvement in the mineral sands sector, quite apart from the expected greater efficiencies to be achieved by integrating the two subsidiaries. The merger proceeded in the context of AMC's high level of debt, a dramatic decline in rutile prices in 1972, the collapse of the zircon price—as demand for zircon as a refractory material in Japanese steel plants reduced—and a serious shortfall in production from the recently commissioned Eneabba operation in Western Australia. Furthermore, the two companies faced a potential competitive threat associated with the entry of additional sources of supply from South Africa and Sierra Leone. Overlaying these issues was AMC's declining reserve base as a consequence of the regulatory restrictions on its Australian east-coast operations.

The amalgamation of the two companies reflected deeper concerns regarding the value of retaining mineral sands in the portfolio, given the high level of capital being committed to the industry with inadequate returns generated. The view of one CGFA director was that 'AMC needed Western [Titanium's] reserves and likely future profitability'.[26] As to Western Titanium's prospects, it was the view of another director 'that the company could founder in the next year or so unless the merger takes place, or CGFA were to pour in money'.[27] A 1976 internal CGFA document formalised the plan for AMC's takeover of Western Titanium. The merger was seen to be in the best long-term interests of both companies and as offering greater financial stability for Western Titanium, less risk from adverse mineral sands markets and benefits for AMC in terms of additional reserves and access to Western Titanium's 'strong position in ilmenite upgrading technology'. Other benefits included advantages in

---

26 Consolidated Gold Fields Australia Limited, 'Minutes of Meeting of Directors', 13 December 1976, p. 2, RGCA, Box 12248, RGC 11576.
27 ibid.

marketing, the enhanced potential 'of becoming the largest and lowest cost producer in the growing beneficiated ilmenite area through technological leadership and scale economies', as well as reducing the complexities and capital inefficiencies for CGFA in having two subsidiaries, which on occasions—as was the case with synthetic rutile—pursued competing business interests.[28]

With AMC's growth options severely truncated as a result of environmental opposition to sand mining along parts of the New South Wales coast, as well as Queensland, the use of this company's technical and marketing skills across the broader portfolio of mineral sands opportunities provided by Western Titanium was viewed as the basis for the next phase of the company's evolution. With this, increased interest from the investment community was expected, with an improved ability to raise equity capital.[29] An announcement of the proposed merger was made in September 1976, with the merger ratified at an extraordinary general meeting in October 1976.[30]

After the merger, mineral sands market conditions deteriorated. In 1977 circumstances were parlous, with the industry experiencing a period of uncontrolled competition, such that Copeman observed:

> Mr. Mortimer would probably see similarities in the current position with that which prevailed fifteen or sixteen years ago when CGF had commenced investing in this country in that again there was destructive competition and a need to restore order.[31]

In 1977, the company's annual report noted the 'critical oversupply position', particularly for zircon, and an outlook that is 'not encouraging' without some form of industry 'rationalisation'.[32] Zircon prices dropped from close to US$200 per tonne in 1974 and 1975 to US$80 per tonne between 1978 and 1980, before a partial improvement to above US$100 per tonne in the early 1980s. Underpinned by contracts, the rutile price showed less volatility, although prices still declined in 1978.

---

28 'Summary Proposal for the Merger of Associated Minerals Consolidated Limited and Western Titanium Limited', 15 July 1976, RGCA, Box 12303, RGC 25508.
29 ibid.
30 Consolidated Gold Fields Australia exchanged 4,466,343 direct shares in Western Titanium for 3,509,269 shares in AMC—a ratio of 5.5 AMC shares for every 7 Western Titanium shares.
31 Consolidated Gold Fields Australia Limited, 'Minutes of Meeting of Directors', 26 January 1977, p. 5, RGCA, Box 12248, RGC 11575.
32 Consolidated Gold Fields Australia Limited, *Eleventh Annual Report, 1977 and Notice of Meeting*, p. 6.

Market conditions were described by the company as 'one of destructive competition between Australian producers'. It was noted that 'until the situation improves, the company and the whole industry face a period of uncertainty in an over-supplied world market'.[33]

In 1978, the first full year after the merger, AMC recorded a loss of $4.9 million. The following year a barely break-even result was achieved. No final dividend was paid in 1977 and dividend payments were not made in the following two years. Segal conveyed the 'stark evidence of the depths of the depression in which the mineral sands industry has languished ... [with] conditions in our industry ... undoubtedly the worst in its history'.[34]

Despite the merger of AMC and Western Titanium, the composition of the portfolio and, in particular, the attractiveness of continuing to invest in mineral sands remained under board scrutiny. Apart from market conditions, the mineral sands business encountered multiple challenges. Extensive problems were experienced in the commissioning of the Eneabba deposit in Western Australia. A CGFA report in January 1977 noted the 'performance at Eneabba is of serious concern. The expected upturn in production and quality of product has not been achieved'.[35] A range of issues were identified, including a limitation on plant utilisation levels and throughput, a shortage of clean water, a shortage of separation capacity and the failure to consistently produce on-grade product. A major issue was the quality of the ore body being mined, with regions of 'rubbly laterite' and occasional 'massive lumps' of clay-bound material that caused damage to and blockages of the handling system.[36] Given the contraction of AMC's operations on the east coast and the maturation of Western Titanium's reserves near Capel in Western Australia, Eneabba was a central component of the company's production base. It was viewed as a prime source of rutile and zircon, as well as essential in ensuring the availability of ilmenite for synthetic rutile production.

AMC was confronted with a number of critical decisions, based on its operating experience at Eneabba, which were viewed as affecting both the short-term and long-term prospects of the company. After four years of mining, the high-quality ore on the eastern side of the northern leases

---

33   Associated Minerals Consolidated Limited, *Annual Report and Notice of Meeting 1977*, p. 2.
34   Associated Minerals Consolidated Limited, 'Chairman's Address Annual General Meeting, 29 September 1978'.
35   'Western Titanium—Situation Report 17 January 1977', RGCA, Box 748S.
36   ibid.

had been largely depleted. In 1978, rutile production was 35,000 tonnes. Without remedial action, production was likely to decline to 14,000 tonnes per year in three to four years. The short duration of the Eneabba mine plan created a sense of urgency for a new mining strategy to be implemented. A plan to expand rutile production was developed although the planned higher production would, at best, only compensate for the reduction from the company's east-coast operations.

Furthermore, the advent of a new competitive force, Richards Bay Minerals in South Africa, and an industry structure in Australia in which, in the words of the managing director, 'the players were seeking to cut each other's throats', created an imperative for change in the Australian industry, including some form of rationalisation.[37] Various means to achieve a more efficient structure in the overall mineral sands industry in Australia were considered, including encouraging another major minerals company to build a position in the industry, with CGFA prepared to assist this outcome, if required, by selling its interest in AMC. CGFA approached CRA (Conzinc Riotinto Australia), which had interests in mineral sands in Australia, and Union Corporation, an equity participant in Richards Bay Minerals. The intention was to allow them to acquire AMC or establish a position in the new Eneabba province to facilitate more cooperative marketing arrangements.

The 'deep depression' in the industry, in the directors' view, required a rationalisation of the number of industry participants. The board was initially encouraged by CRA's expected re-entry into mineral sands by the company pursuing arrangements with Allied Eneabba and engaging in discussions with Jennings Industries, the two other mining participants at Eneabba. It was believed this might facilitate a rationalisation of the then uncoordinated development of the Eneabba deposits by three parties. Ryan held discussions with CRA, conveying the benefits of a more consolidated structure of marketing arrangements from its involvement in the industry.[38] He indicated that CGFA 'would not oppose CRA's deals with Allied and A. V. Jennings, nor would it resist CRA's entry to the East

---

37 Consolidated Gold Fields Australia Limited, 'Minutes of Meeting of Directors', 27 July 1977, p. 8, RGCA, Box 12246, RGC 11590.
38 Consolidated Gold Fields Australia Limited, 'Minutes of Meeting of Directors', 28 April 1977, p. 9, RGCA, Box 12248, RGC 11575.

Coast industry'.[39] AMC was itself interested in acquiring Consolidated Rutile Limited on North Stradbroke Island. In the view of the CGFA board:

> If all the proposed deals were to come off, the nett effect would be that CRA and AMC would together control 80% of Australian rutile and zircon production ... the hope existed that the South Africans would be prepared to join in an orderly marketing program.[40]

The financial context of CGFA's support for its mineral sands business interests and the corresponding need for a more orderly marketing environment were recorded in board minutes in August 1977:

> Mr Landrigan [an executive director] emphasized the degree to which C.G.F.A. was already backing its minerals sands producers and the extent to which this assistance is going to have to increase. It was envisaged by the end of December, if C.G.F.A. continued to provide support, its total exposure could be as high as $35 million.[41]

CGFA began buying rutile from AMC to store, allowing the company to buy it back during more favourable market conditions. In 1978, Kerr-McGee, a pigment producer, was offered 55,000 tonnes of rutile and an option to acquire a further 27,000 tonnes. It was offered to Kerr-McGee at a price of $150 per tonne, in conformity with AMC's 'fire sale' strategy, whereby no profit was achieved but the proceeds contributed to improving the cash position of AMC.[42] At the same time, zircon was 'grossly oversupplied'.[43] Segal held discussions regarding rationalisation of the zircon market, although proposed marketing initiatives with another Eneabba producer, Allied Minerals, were not progressed due to concerns by DuPont, its partner, relating to United States antitrust considerations. It was likely that the depressed market conditions for zircon would be

---

39   Consolidated Gold Fields Australia Limited, 'Minutes of Meeting of Directors', 25 May 1977, p. 7, RGCA, Box 12248, RGC 11575.
40   ibid.
41   Consolidated Gold Fields Australia Limited, 'Minutes of Meeting of Directors', 24 August 1977, p. 6, RGCA, Box 12246, RGC 11590. JP Landrigan had joined the company in 1963 and became financial controller before being appointed an executive director in August 1975.
42   Consolidated Gold Fields Australia Limited, 'Minutes of Meeting of Directors', 22 February 1978, p. 2, RGCA, Box 12246, RGC 11590.
43   ibid., p. 8.

12. PORTFOLIO CHALLENGES

exacerbated by production commencing from Richards Bay Minerals. In this context, the chairman said 'it was imperative that A.M.C. take a cold, hard look at its future and plan accordingly'.[44]

In 1977, McKinsey & Company was commissioned to undertake a review of the mineral sands industry and AMC's place within it. AMC's high level of debt remained a key issue. The desire was to have debt reduced sufficiently to allow the recommencement of dividend payments. It was recognised that AMC would likely require an injection of funds, which occurred in 1979 and 1980 through two separate rights issues. In September 1977, the initial findings of the McKinsey report were presented to the CGFA board of directors. Its main conclusion was that Eneabba's potential performance could be substantially better than had been expected and that rutile could be produced at a higher rate. The following month, the board considered the final McKinsey report. The options presented included continuing to operate the business with no major changes, instituting further substantial cutbacks in production with the intent to manage the company for cash, and expanding the business with a view to establishing market leadership and, as such, being in a position to influence mineral sands prices. This option was expected to optimise the benefits for AMC, with 'an essential first step' the acquisition of Allied Minerals. A final option of quitting the business and disposing of the mineral sands assets was also presented.[45]

The board determined that 'AMC be placed on a survival footing' and that merger discussions be initiated with Allied Minerals. Segal believed that a merger would be difficult to achieve and instead proposed an alternative approach that entailed a 'vigorous pursuit of [the] beneficiation route' through an arrangement with Tioxide, one of the major pigment customers. Discussions were held with Tioxide, designed to secure an offtake arrangement for the upgrading of ilmenite to produce synthetic rutile.[46] Tioxide's London board determined in 1977 that its support for an additional beneficiation plant was not warranted in light of the global pigment situation.[47]

---

44 Consolidated Gold Fields Australia Limited, 'Minutes of Meeting of Directors', 27 July 1977, p. 8, RGCA, Box 12246, RGC 11590.
45 Consolidated Gold Fields Australia Limited, 'Minutes of Meeting of Directors', 26 October 1977, pp. 3–4, RGCA, Box 12246, RGC 11590.
46 ibid., p. 5.
47 Consolidated Gold Fields Australia Limited, 'Minutes of Meeting of Directors', 23 November 1977, RGCA, Box 12246, RGC 11590.

In considering the arrangements for industry rationalisation, Ryan held discussions with several parties for a potential 'four-way merger' at Eneabba. Board minutes noted that:

> It appeared the concept would be supported by DuPont, Allied Minerals, and the Western Australian Government, and to some extent by Union Corporation ... but [Union Corporation] was not prepared to see Consolidated Rutile itself merge its operations. It appeared, as a result of McKinsey's work, that unless Richards Bay were prepared to co-operate in market rationalisation the projected Eneabba merger would not correct the zircon market.[48]

McKinsey's option of expanding the business and acquiring Allied Minerals' Eneabba operations was viewed by the CGFA board as something that should be explored. Discussions with Allied Minerals and DuPont were held. It became apparent that 'DuPont's main interest lay in having a stable ilmenite source', rather than continuing as an equity holder in an Australian mineral sands operation.[49] This was the basis for the eventual acquisition of Allied Eneabba as part of CGFA consolidating the production base at Eneabba.

Despite the support of most of the Australian directors, Rudolph Agnew, the Consolidated Gold Fields group chief executive officer and deputy chairman, expressed his opposition to the proposed acquisition:

> Mr Agnew informed the Board that he could not recommend to C.G.F. that it support the proposal or participate therein ... [with] further major investment in the minerals sands industry ... intolerable.[50]

The Australian directors accordingly determined not to pursue the acquisition. As such, this prime component of consolidation in what was becoming the key mineral sands production province in Australia was forestalled, if only temporarily.

---

48 Consolidated Gold Fields Australia Limited, 'Minutes of Meeting of Directors', 28 September 1977, p. 5, RGCA, Box 12246, RGC 11590.
49 Consolidated Gold Fields Australia Limited, 'Minutes of Meeting of Directors', 21 December 1977, p. 4, RGCA, Box 12246, RGC 11590.
50 Consolidated Gold Fields Australia Limited, 'Minutes of Special Meeting of Directors', 10 February 1978, p. 1, RGCA, Box 12246, RGC 11590.

The disposal of AMC remained under consideration. The main factor forestalling a decision to sell was the expectation that a better price may be gained in the future, although the view in the first half of 1978 was that 'this did not appear particularly likely on our present view of the industry'.[51] Ryan, a less-than-enthusiastic supporter of the mineral sands business, pointed out:

> A.M.C. would not be profitable for two years at least and thereafter would provide only a minimal return. It was clear that the only way this picture could change would be for a dominant producer to take control of the industry and change the pricing structure and it had been agreed that this was not a position which CGFA should seek to obtain at this time.[52]

By June 1978, the disposal of its mineral sands businesses appeared impracticable, with other alternatives then under consideration, including CGFA purchasing the minority interests of AMC or reducing its shareholding below 50 per cent and thereby decreasing its obligations in relation to loan guarantees.[53] Whether DuPont would be a buyer of AMC was discussed by directors although rejected as unlikely given DuPont's approach to not typically holding positions in offshore operations due to the antitrust laws of the United States.

The situation, compounded by the likely market obstacles in executing plans to sell other assets in the portfolio to facilitate a potential joint venture with Utah to acquire Renison, led to the board's consideration 'to "batten down" and try to make the group work as it is'.[54] A degree of optimism had also entered the board's thinking on the mineral sands industry. In July 1978, the view was expressed that 'it appeared that AMC would no longer present a grave threat to CGFA'.[55] The Titanium Enterprises' mineral sands operation in Florida had also come to the company's attention, viewed as an opportunity for CGFA to effect a progressive consolidation of the mineral sands industry, in this case by the application of AMC's technology to 'transform' a United States

---

51 Consolidated Gold Fields Australia Limited, 'Minutes of Meeting of Directors', 22 March 1978, p. 11, RGCA, Box 12246, RGC 11590.
52 ibid., p. 10.
53 Consolidated Gold Fields Australia Limited, 'Minutes of Meeting of Directors', 28 June 1978, p. 2, RGCA, Box 12246, RGC 11592.
54 ibid., p. 4.
55 Consolidated Gold Fields Australia Limited, 'Minutes of Meeting of Directors', 26 July 1978, p. 4, RGCA, Box 12246, RGC 11592.

operation.⁵⁶ Segal observed optimistically 'that CGFA had come into the mineral sands industry when it was in gross disarray and this is again the situation in this country'. For him, 'the present time may thus be another good take-off point for growth'.⁵⁷

In early 1979, the findings of another McKinsey study of AMC were received. It proposed a low-risk expansion strategy that would entail AMC taking a lead in the rationalisation of the Eneabba field. In the case of Allied Eneabba (formerly Allied Minerals), this was envisaged through a joint venture or marketing arrangement, with an outright acquisition not seen as appropriate given Allied Eneabba's level of debt. Discussions with Jennings were also proposed. The acquisition of Titanium Enterprises in the United States, which was in progress, was viewed by McKinsey as 'a useful but less attractive stratagem'.⁵⁸

The projected profile of CGFA's mineral sands business by McKinsey was one of moderate growth, highlighting the need to reduce debt, which brought to the fore the need for a rights issue. Discussions with Allied Eneabba and DuPont began in early 1979 regarding a joint venture, while CGFA's view in relation to Jennings Industries was that, while it would like to have Jennings' leases as 'reserves for the future', it was thought it would 'not be prudent to make a bid for [Jennings'] fixed assets except, possibly, for the wharf facilities'.⁵⁹ Ryan realised that a deal to acquire Titanium Enterprises could provide the necessary rationale for AMC to approach shareholders with a rights issue.

At a special meeting of directors on 11 April 1979, the board resolved to support a rights issue, predominantly for the purpose of acquiring the Titanium Enterprise mineral sands operation in Florida, but also to allow the partial repayment of CGFA loans to AMC. A company report presented to the board in the same month on the optimisation of the Eneabba reserves provided encouragement for 'the aggregation of further reserves', with the proposal that CGFA acquire the Jennings leases on

---

56   Consolidated Gold Fields Australia Limited, 'Minutes of Meeting of Directors', 23 August 1978, p. 4, RGCA, Box 12246, RGC 11592. The prospect of the sale of AMC had not been completely abandoned.
57   Consolidated Gold Fields Australia Limited, 'Minutes of Meeting of Directors', 22 November 1978, p. 5, RGCA, Box 12246, RGC 11592.
58   Consolidated Gold Fields Australia Limited, 'Minutes of Meeting of Directors', 24 January 1979, p. 5, RGCA, Box 12246, RGC 11592.
59   Consolidated Gold Fields Australia Limited, 'Minutes of Meeting of Directors', 28 February 1979, p. 13, RGCA, Box 12246, RGC 11592.

behalf of AMC and 'ware-house' them for future use.⁶⁰ By this stage, Jennings had formed its own board subcommittee to progress the sale of its Eneabba operations. On 30 November 1979, Jennings Industries was acquired by CGFA.

...

Considerable efforts were expended to address the operational and market-related challenges of the main investments of the CGFA portfolio during the 1970s. These included a divestiture of some holdings, such as iron ore, and the attempted improvement in the financial prospects of others through cost reduction and production efficiency activities, in the case of Mount Lyell, or aggregation activities, in the case of mineral sands. While progress was made on all of these fronts, the fundamental consideration remained the appropriate structure of CGFA's business model. This matter was addressed in detail from the mid-1970s and would lead to the formation of a new corporate structure in 1981.

---

60   Consolidated Gold Fields Australia Limited, 'Minutes of Meeting of Directors', 26 April 1979, p. 8, RGCA, Box 12272.

13

PORTFOLIO REVIEW 1975–1981

The decade of the 1970s presented a range of external influences, mostly negative, for Consolidated Gold Fields Australia (CGFA) and its main investments. Global economic challenges associated with the first oil shock and the global economic recession that followed between 1973 and 1975 had an adverse impact on the demand for minerals. In Australia, a Commonwealth Labor Government adopted a nationalistic approach to resource ownership. Inflation was rampant, costs increased and interest rates rose. Domestic and market pressures for the Australian group were overlaid by challenges for the British parent, which had a combative shareholder on its register from the early 1980s that would manifest in an acrimonious takeover attempt in the late 1980s. Quite apart from the external pressures, it was evident that the CGFA portfolio had various inherent structural deficiencies.

CGFA's financial position highlighted concerns about the structure of the portfolio, most notably the extent to which CGFA as the majority shareholder in other companies could influence its investments and, in turn, its own cash flow and balance sheet characteristics. The initial model of investing in a range of companies had the advantage of enabling CGFA to establish a rapid presence in Australia by spreading its investments over a number of mining companies and minerals and, in some cases, manufacturing. This spread was thought to provide a degree of protection from a downturn in the commodity price in any one. The lack of total ownership of subsidiaries also enabled CGFA to maintain 'something of an Australian appearance'.[1] Since 1973, however, it had become apparent that this business model had inherent deficiencies. The triggers for a review related, in part, to the decline in the financial contribution from Mount Goldsworthy, compounded by depressed prices for copper, mineral sands and tin that led to budgetary forecasts in 1975 and 1976 for 'zero profit for CGFA for two years and, possibly, no dividend for those years'.[2]

In 1976, earnings declined by 62 per cent to $2.8 million before a $4.2 million loss was recorded in 1977 (see Chart 4). CGFA dividends halved from 12 cents in 1975 to six cents in 1976 and remained at this level in each of the subsequent two years. Mount Goldsworthy, Mount Lyell and Gunpowder were loss-making, while market conditions adversely affected the performance of Associated Minerals Consolidated (AMC) and Western Titanium. The manufacturing investments of Zip Holdings and Lawrenson Alumasc Holdings were not material to the group's earnings or cash flow, while other ventures, in the case of Colinas, Lion Properties and North-West Acid, were financial disappointments. Bellambi, which, like iron ore, had wider issues to contend with and was circumscribed in terms of its access to new deposits and challenged by regulatory and financial burdens, made a useful financial contribution, with the exception of 1975. Renison remained the one solid contributor to CGFA's financial performance, making an operating profit after tax of $4 million in 1975 and $3.3 million in 1976.

The 'declining profit picture' was compounded by other financial constraints, including the limited ability to borrow, an absence of control over the cash flow of subsidiaries and no 'unarguable right' to direct capital expenditure or the dividend policies of the companies in which it was invested.[3] There were inefficiencies in terms of board representation on what were eight operating company boards, two joint ventures and 13 lesser subsidiary companies. The work of directors was onerous and some assumed quasi-managerial roles.

---

1   Consolidated Gold Fields Australia Limited, 'October 1975 Review and Proposal, October 10, 1975', p. 1, Renison Goldfields Consolidated Archives (RGCA), Box 12301, RGC 9287/04.
2   ibid., p. 18.
3   ibid., p. 9.

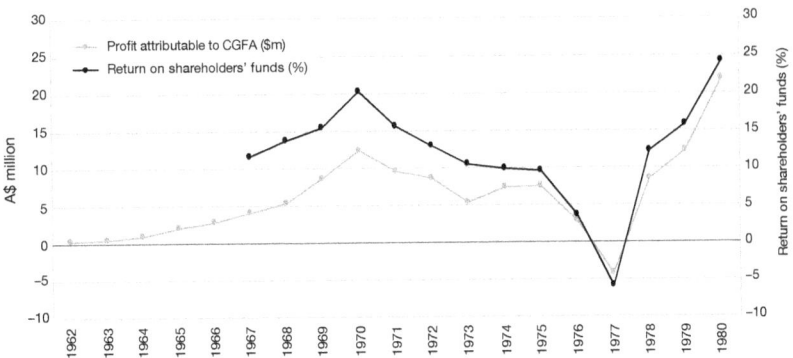

Chart 4. Consolidated Gold Fields Australia financial performance, 1962–1980.

This chart shows attributable profit, after tax and extraordinary items, for CGFA. Return on shareholders' funds is shown for 1967–1980 (data for 1962–1966 was not available). CGFA commenced operations in 1960 and in 1966 gained Australian shareholding. The chart shows the decline in profitability and return on shareholders' funds during the 1970s, before a recovery in the late 1970s. See Appendix 4 for more information.

Sources: Consolidated Gold Fields Australia Limited, 'Prospectus', 1974 (University of Melbourne Archives (UMA), 1974.0092); CGFA annual reports, 1967 to 1980; Renison Goldfields Consolidated, *Report on the 1981 Financial Year*.

Furthermore, while CGFA sought the application of standard procedures within its subsidiary companies, no meaningful benefits were able to be achieved through the adoption of common procurement or contracting procedures. In areas such as marketing, personnel training, specialised engineering, insurance and finance, efficiencies and shared capabilities were also unable to be achieved. CGFA's 68 per cent foreign ownership at a time of increasing resource nationalisation was also emerging as an impediment to the company's ambitions. It created constraints on its expansionary plans, especially in the context of opportunities for joint venture arrangements, diminishing CGFA's level of involvement in new projects and limiting its funding ability. CGFA's borrowing capacity was also limited based on its major assets being shares in partly owned subsidiaries.

Brian Massy-Greene believed that while the group structure 'had served [CGFA] well in the past' there were clear reasons for a review, associated with diminishing returns from iron ore and Gunpowder Copper, the scale of investment required for new projects, and the inability to deploy surplus funds from subsidiaries or to 'adjust dividend flows' or apply 'capital rationing'; quite apart from the attitude of both the Commonwealth and state governments to a majority foreign owned company.[4] The consequence was that CGFA's position to fund projects, either by equity or debt, was 'extremely limited', inhibiting growth opportunities, with an inability to utilise the tax benefits of losses from one subsidiary against profits from another and a limitation on paying dividends to the level expected from overall profits.[5] Conflicts of interest were also evident between the multiple companies, some of which operated in the same industry. This was most markedly the case in mineral sands. CGFA's two main mineral sands investments, AMC and Western Titanium, often acted at cross purposes. An internal CGFA document noted:

> The conflict of interest is seen at its worst ... where the two companies independently vie with one another in the market. Not unexpectedly one attempts to achieve sales at the expense of the other ... The ... situation is worsened by the inhibitions that prevent the free interchange of technical expertise—the optimization of the use of resources, processes and people.[6]

Furthermore, both companies were seeking to develop a technology to beneficiate ilmenite; a process that Western Titanium was more advanced in than AMC.

A 1975 company report determined: 'The nature of the constraints is such that they will intensify rather than recede with time. The conclusion must be that as presently constructed, CGFA's visible potential for further growth is severely restricted'.[7] In the context of these considerations, the position of Mount Lyell was viewed as 'extremely critical', with adverse movements in the copper price necessitating a survival plan—the Prince Lyell Extended Plan—as well as government financial support for the continuation of the operation. For mineral sands, the financial challenges associated with sector cyclicality and debt levels were also apparent.

The capital requirements of parts of the portfolio were also a cause for concern. As early as 1971, with an estimated requirement of $40 million of expenditure over five years, the challenges were serious enough for Massy-Greene to hold a meeting with the prime minister to seek a relaxation of Reserve Bank guidelines for additional borrowing. The company had recently acquired a 70 per cent interest in the Gunpowder mining

---

4　ibid., p. 1.
5　ibid., p. 2.
6　ibid., p. 17.
7　ibid., p. 15.

complex from its liquidators for $6 million. This expenditure, associated with falling metal prices, lower demand and the Australian currency crisis, had placed 'a strain on C.G.F.A.'s funds'.[8] CGFA was required to obtain a standby financial facility of $5 million in 1972 to meet its immediate financing requirements. All of these factors generated a need for fundamental reassessment of the portfolio structure and business model, of which the major issue was holding majority, as opposed to outright control, of subsidiaries.

In 1976, the group profit in the United Kingdom declined by 34 per cent. Of the decline in total revenues by GB£9 million, mining revenues declined by over GB£8 million. The Australian arm of the group was a major contributor to this decline and 'a cause for concern' to the parent to the extent that the Australian company 'being rationalised' was considered warranted.[9]

While CGFA's strategic considerations were informed by a management analysis in 1975 of the inherent inefficiencies of the business model that had evolved from the early 1960s, the potential solutions to such inefficiencies were multifaceted. Underlying a range of considerations was a view of 'divisionalisation': that control of 100 per cent of the cash flow, management and operations of its subsidiaries would be a more effective business model. However, CGFA was not a fully independent entity; the views of its major shareholder were influential and several courses of action proposed in Australia were not supported by the board in London. A proposal from London to increase its share ownership of CGFA entered the consideration at one stage, including a move back to 100 per cent ownership. Furthermore, the challenges facing the parent, not least associated with a combative major shareholder on its register, influenced the dynamics for the Australian company, as it would later, when Hanson acquired Consolidated Gold Fields in the late 1980s.

The proposal raised by an internal review of the CGFA structure was for the main operating subsidiaries of the company to become 100 per cent owned in a new structure, which would in turn result in Consolidated

---

8 Consolidated Gold Fields of Australia Limited, 'Minutes of Meeting of Directors', 22 December 1971, p. 1, RGCA, Box 12248, RGC 11576; Prime Minister's Department, 'Consolidated Gold Fields Australia Limited, Group Finance', 26 February 1972, p. 2, National Archives of Australia, 72/492.
9 Consolidated Gold Fields Limited, *89th Annual Report 1976*, p. 8.

Gold Fields' interest reduced. In correspondence with the chairman of Consolidated Gold Fields in the United Kingdom in 1975, Massy-Greene conveyed the situation as follows:

> The Australian Group has reached a critical decision point in its history ... we see that we are now constrained to such an extent that the future of C.G.F.A. itself is bleak and the prospects for the subsidiaries are at best very slow growth, and at worst, say in the case of Mount Lyell, extinction.[10]

Massy-Greene was 'strongly of the view' that a restructuring remained necessary, with other directors supporting the concept although, according to one, it would first be necessary for CGFA to 'endeavour to get rid of the loss makers in the Group'.[11] According to Massy-Greene:

> The alternative, that is to continue on our present path of being vulnerable and constrained because of our financial weakness, government policy and intra group conflict, could lead to a gradual contraction of the Group with C.G.F.A. itself becoming a rather uninspiring holding company for a generally rather unexciting group of subsidiaries ... I regard the question of the inadequacy of the Group structure and our proposal to overcome the problem as the most important matter to have arisen since your original Australian investment decision.[12]

The Australian management and directors were diligent in their consideration of the options available to the company. A rationalisation of investments occurred: the sale of Mount Goldsworthy, the merger of AMC and Western Titanium, the sale of Mount Lyell's shareholding in Renison, the divestiture of Zip Holdings, the sale of the interest in OT Lempriere and the willingness to pursue the divestment of Colinas and Lawrenson Alumasc Holdings. A sale process for Bellambi Coal took place and the sale of most direct share investments occurred between 1975 and 1976. More fundamental structural changes were contemplated, including whether to retain an interest in mineral sands, while work commenced in 1975 on what was referred to as a 'special project'.

---

10 Consolidated Gold Fields Australia Limited, Correspondence from JB Massy-Greene to JD McCall, Chairman, Consolidated Gold Fields Limited, 22 October 1975, p. 2, RGCA, Box 12301.
11 ibid.
12 ibid.

Despite these measures, the London group's financial challenges and its disquiet at the capital allocation skills of its Australian subsidiary became manifest in a lack of confidence in and subsequent actions to replace Massy-Greene as managing director. What was seen as Massy-Greene's level of independence and desire to support the interests of Australian shareholders, relative to the London parent, did not aid his standing. At an Australian board meeting in March 1976, a Consolidated Gold Fields director, Gerald Mortimer, to become group chief executive from July 1976, was asked to state the position of the London board. The board minutes recorded:

> Mr. Mortimer stated that the critical point had come about a year ago when it became increasingly clear to CGF that CGFA was headed for a severe downturn … Mr. Mortimer stated that the problem as London sees it is, fairly simply stated, that they no longer have confidence in the leadership of the management here in Australia … [with] no alternative but to ask for a change of management.[13]

It was proposed that Bart Ryan, an Australian although then a London director and deputy chairman, take up the role of CGFA's managing director, with Massy-Greene to continue as chairman.[14] As Lord Denman, a Consolidated Gold Fields London director conveyed, the situation was that the loss of confidence in Massy-Greene was 'only [in] the management function of the Chairman' and not in his role as chairman.[15]

Massy-Greene refuted the position taken by the Consolidated Gold Fields London board. The board minutes record that:

> [Massy-Greene] felt very strongly that the management of CGFA must be, and must be seen to be, in the hands of the Australian Board and if there is to be a change in management, the initiative for that has to come from Australia. There is no way in which CGF London can properly take a decision and simply hand it to the CGFA Board as a fait accompli and on a no debate basis.[16]

---

13   Consolidated Gold Fields Australia Limited, 'Minutes of Meeting of Directors', 24 March 1976, pp. 2 and 4, RGCA, Box 12246, RGC 11588.
14   ibid., p. 4.
15   ibid.
16   ibid., p. 5.

A spirited board-level discussion ensued. Each of the other directors of CGFA expressed their concerns with the approach of the London board, as well as the professional slight to their Australian colleague, although one, at least, appreciated the consequences of a lack of confidence in Australian management. Sid Segal expressed the following sentiments, as recorded in the board minutes:

> He agreed with Sir Ian Potter that life in Australia had been very difficult for a considerable period of time and referred to the attitude of the previous Government; the fact that CGFA was a so-called 'foreign company'; the difficult situation in the metal markets overseas and the extraordinary escalation of costs. All in all, it had been a very tough row to hoe. Whilst those are the facts and whilst they are exculpatory, if confidence has been lost, this is a fact of life and one must look for a remedy. Mr. Segal said that he was appalled as a member of the team which had built a company of such high reputation that things should have come to this pass but he expressed the hope that the Board could find some way of overcoming the problem, hopefully under the Chairmanship of Sir Brian.[17]

Massy-Greene's interpretation of events, after listening to the views of his fellow Australian directors, was recorded as follows:

> The Chairman then stated that the London Directors would have seen from the foregoing discussion that the London proposal would not be carried by the CGFA Board if that Board decided to test the matter. If that decision were taken, there would be a very serious situation.[18]

A serious impasse between the two boards of directors was avoided when Massy-Greene stipulated he would relinquish the managing directorship but only if terms acceptable to him were reflected in an amendment to his contract. Terms were agreed. Massy-Greene received a retirement allowance of $400,000, a car with garaging facilities, an office and a private secretary in addition to his ongoing director fees. Given the magnitude of this payment, relative to the salary package of the incoming managing director of $50,000, there were director concerns about whether this arrangement might require notification to the stock exchange.

---

17   ibid., p. 6
18   ibid., p. 7.

The payment, to be referred to as an 'emolument', was paid in part by CGFA and in part by the British parent. *The Bulletin* commented on the 'unusually heavy "golden handshake"', which represented 22 per cent of the total dividend payout of $1.6 million paid by the company in that year.[19]

Ryan was appointed managing director. Initially, it was a strained environment within Gold Fields House. The relationship between Massy-Greene and Ryan had already been tense with Ryan directed by his London colleagues to take a role in reviewing some of the problem investments in the portfolio, including by assuming the directorship of Mount Lyell. At a retirement function for a long-serving executive, Douglas Ainge, tensions came to the surface. With wives of the executive group present, the normal practice was not to commence smoking until after the Royal toast had been made. At the suggestion of one of the wives, who was keen to light a cigarette, Ryan stood up and proposed the Royal toast. Massy-Greene did not stand and was visibly annoyed at what he considered the usurping of his role. Massy-Greene stood, saying that Mr Ryan did not understand it was his role as chairman to propose the toast, which he duly did and then left the function. Massy-Greene had to be coaxed back to the function by his colleagues, with Ryan agreeing to leave.

Massy-Greene did not stand for re-election as a director at the annual general meeting in 1976 and Segal, the long-serving executive and director, and a man described as 'unreserved … with a ready-wit and a quick mind' assumed the role as chairman.[20] Changes in board representation and management also occurred in London. Donald McCall retired as chairman and chief executive officer in London in 1976 and Mortimer assumed the role of group chief executive.

---

19   *The Bulletin*, 6 November 1976.
20   *The Australian*, 5 June 1977.

Figure 42. London Board of Directors of Consolidated Gold Fields, 1977, after a change in management in both London and Australia; Rudolph Agnew third on left, Bart Ryan fifth on left.
Source: Image courtesy of Jillian Segal.

...

There followed a comprehensive review of the strategic options available to the Australian company. A range of portfolio restructuring alternatives were considered, some with the input of external management consultants. These considerations related both to the efficacy of the diversified business model and some of the individual major investments. In relation to the former, while there was no change in the group's philosophical support for a diversified business model, there was at one stage a willingness to contemplate the abandonment of this model, even if only temporarily. The more fundamental issue was how the current portfolio of diversified interests was owned and managed and the utility of the approach in having majority interests, as opposed to outright ownership of subsidiary companies. There were concerns with individual assets—as has been described—the most notable of which were Mount Goldsworthy, Mount Lyell and the company's mineral sands investments, although Gunpowder and Bellambi also had specific issues. The considerations related to the maturity and cost-competitiveness of some investments, the level of capital employed or required to be deployed, the ability of the group to fund this investment, the implications for the balance sheet and the likelihood of generating adequate returns.

One view as to how the portfolio might be restructured included the radical concept known as the 'Renison scheme'. This, in effect, contemplated disposing of all assets except Renison. Board minutes in 1978 described the proposal as follows:

> The concept was being examined of implementing the Renison proposal; selling the Company's interests in Bellambi, AMC, Pancontinental and the poplar project [Colinas], the result of all of which would be that CGFA's assets would comprise [a] 52% direct … interest in Renison, plus about $60 million in cash. This would make CGFA a very attractive vehicle for a merger into an Australian company and would provide a strong base from which to grow.[21]

The approach, undertaken either individually by CGFA or through a merger with Renison—which at one stage was contemplated to involve Utah Mining Australia—was believed to provide the potential to control the cash flow of the best asset in the portfolio. The associated cash proceeds from the sale of other investments were seen as sufficient to allow the company to start over again as a mining company or contemplate a merger with another minerals company in Australia.

In this regard, given prior considerations and the parent's shareholding in the company, North Broken Hill was a prime contender. Michael Beckett, a London executive director who had joined the Australian board, confirmed Consolidated Gold Fields' acceptance in principle to a dilution to 30 to 35 per cent in the parent's interest in any such joint venture. The reverse takeover of Renison was investigated and involved discussions with the Tasmanian Government in terms of stamp duty relief associated with such a transaction. Eventually, the concept of a reverse merger of Renison with CGFA was thought to have a low likelihood of success. In its place, a joint venture with Utah to establish majority ownership in Renison came under consideration. On 9 August 1979 a special meeting of CGFA directors was convened. The original purpose of the meeting was to consider a merger with Utah. While the prospect of this merger had

---

21 Consolidated Gold Fields Australia Limited, 'Minutes of Meeting of Directors', 17 May 1978, p. 10, RGCA, Box 12246, RGC 11590.

receded by the time of the board meeting, the two companies remained in contact in relation to a takeover of Renison. Advice was provided to the board on the likelihood and practicability of this course of action and, based on this advice, the reverse takeover concept was shelved.[22]

Apart from the Renison scheme, there was consideration as to how individual parts of the portfolio may change. Many of the options pursued—the Renison scheme, the merger with Utah, the aggregation of minerals sands interests with other companies, and the divestments of smaller assets and investments—came up against market reality. Contemplated transactions proved impracticable, other parties were not willing to become involved in the CGFA strategy, and investments that were loss-making or had other inherent deficiencies could not readily be sold. In mineral sands, it proved more practicable for CGFA to adopt the role of 'aggregator', as a means to effect greater efficiency in the industry, rather than this role being played by others as CGFA had sought to encourage. Further, as a cyclical business, market conditions improved; this was the case for mineral sands as well as Mount Lyell, which paid its first dividend since 1975 in 1980. In fact, CGFA declined an acquisition offer for Mount Lyell on the basis of 'the fact that Mount Lyell had been in dire straits was no reason to jettison it now when the company had clearly become much more viable'.[23]

With market recovery came a rekindled confidence that a leaner business could now display more attractive financial characteristics. Furthermore, new interests had been secured. While the period from 1976 to 1980 was one of the most quiescent in terms of new investments by CGFA, a one-third interest in the large Porgera gold deposit in Papua New Guinea and the acquisition of a mineral sands dredge-mining operation in Florida provided new sources of cash flow.

The board considered multiple strategic options, which included the acquisition of the minority interests in AMC and in Mount Lyell. Reflecting the multifaceted nature of the board's strategic considerations over the decade, a board paper in July 1979 recommended the abandonment of 'efforts to find a single solution to all the Group's structural problems' and instead pursue a series of individual steps with the expectation

---

22 Consolidated Gold Fields Australia Limited, 'Discussion Draft, Board Papers—September 1979, Review of Group Strategy', p. 4, RGCA, Box 12272.
23 Consolidated Gold Fields Australia Limited, 'Minutes of Meeting of Directors', 22 February 1978, RGCA, Box 12246, RGC 11590.

of a similar outcome.²⁴ The options considered by the board had led to asset divestments, but solutions related to its main investments, including AMC, were no closer to resolution. The acquisition of minority interests now appeared the favoured course of action. A plan for a scheme of arrangement would be progressed that would facilitate a naturalisation process for the subsidiaries of CGFA.²⁵

However, it became apparent that the potential use of CGFA's scrip to acquire minority interests would result in a consequential reduction in the holding of its parent company. This was not viewed favourably by Consolidated Gold Fields in London. At a discussion by the CGFA board in November 1979, the chairman stated that the company had been looking at 'divisionalisation' but that the concept had run up against the parent's 'dilution problem'.²⁶

The views of the London board were communicated without ambiguity. Two London directors, including Rudolph Agnew, submitted a paper to the Australian directors. The content of the paper recognised the constraints imposed by the minority shareholdings on management actions and that advancement of the CGFA business had been 'locked into a circumstance of stalemate'. Furthermore, while it acknowledged there was no 'lack of imaginative efforts … to disentangle this putative structural flaw', the authors of the paper, on behalf of the London board, could not support a dilution of its 70 per cent shareholding.²⁷

Agnew's paper recorded:

> CGF has been reluctant to endorse proposals which would have the effect of reducing its interest … below the present 70 per cent level. This was not because of pig-headed determination to hang onto 'control' for its own sake, but because CGF felt no assurance that CGFA had developed concrete long term plans which would lead to secure, successful and growing business …

---

24 Consolidated Gold Fields Australia Limited, 'Minutes of Meeting of Directors', 26 September 1979, p. 5, RGCA, Box 12272.
25 Consolidated Gold Fields Australia Limited, 'Minutes of Meeting of Directors', 23 April 1980, RGCA, Box 12260, RGC 11517.
26 Consolidated Gold Fields Australia Limited, 'Minutes of Meeting of Directors', 21 November 1979, p. 2, RGCA, Box 12272.
27 Consolidated Gold Fields Australia Limited, 'Mr Agnew and Mr Wood to the Directors, The Shareholding Structure of the CGFA Group' in 'Board Papers—November 1979', p. 1, RGCA, Box 12272.

> While convinced that it is essential to resolve, as soon as possible, the identity crisis which is demoralising CGFA and fragmenting its directors, it is our belief that there is little wrong with CGFA's basic shareholding structure.[28]

Instead, the paper went on to propose that the British shareholding be maintained at 70 per cent, if not increased to 75 per cent. The novel proposal was that if the interests in subsidiaries were reduced to 52 per cent and if the Australian Government would be prepared to consider them 'naturalised' under foreign investment guidelines, then the British parent's ownership would, as a result, not exceed 40 per cent. Under this arrangement: 'should FIRB [Foreign Investment Review Board] … so rule, we could commit that future CGFA operations would be similarly naturalised once the development stage had been passed', and if this was not forthcoming, Agnew suggested that the shareholding could be reduced in subsidiaries to 49 per cent. The exception was Renison, which would be maintained at 52 per cent, to enable all options to be kept open 'on this most important source of earnings and cash flow'.[29]

The proposal created consternation, if not confusion, among the Australian directors. Consideration of the ownership structure of CGFA was occurring at a stage when Consolidated Gold Fields had come under a share ownership threat from the Anglo American–affiliated company, Minorco. Alluding to the challenges that the British company was experiencing with Anglo American as a shareholder and potential acquirer, Segal suspected:

> That there was much more to the proposal than appeared. That would tie in with what C.G.F. was trying to do with its own shareholders whose support it was trying to enlist as the best method of repelling 'the Hun at the gate'.[30]

The legal firm Schroder Darling on behalf of Consolidated Gold Fields, had made a submission to the Foreign Investment Review Board (FIRB) in early 1980 undertaking that CGFA's three main listed subsidiaries—Renison, Mount Lyell and AMC—would be naturalised, or at least owned

---

28 ibid., p. 2.
29 ibid.
30 Consolidated Gold Fields Australia Limited, 'Minutes of Meeting of Directors', 21 November 1979, p. 5, RGCA, Box 12272. Segal was referring to the Minorco shareholding in Consolidated Gold Fields and the uneasy relationship with this Anglo American–owned company.

51 per cent by Australian shareholders within three years.[31] Astonishingly, the approach by Consolidated Gold Fields to the FIRB had not been advised beforehand to the CGFA board. The board on 23 April 1980 recorded the following:

> A very long discussion ensued during which some Directors queried the advisability of C.G.F. moving in the proposed direction and expressed the view that if such a move were to be made a share offer by C.G.F. would probably be easier to recommend than cash. Mr. Beckett [a Consolidated Gold Fields director and group managing director] said that having regard to recent events in London this now seemed to be less likely to be possible but that [Consolidated Gold Fields'] attitude was not fixed and the Board was of the view that this alternative could be explored.[32]

Given the potential for a higher share ownership of CGFA by Consolidated Gold Fields, an independent adviser—Capel Court—was appointed to determine a fair value for the CGFA shares. Within three months it was apparent that Consolidated Gold Fields was now envisaging moving to 100 per cent ownership of CGFA. Again, direct soundings had been taken with the FIRB, much to the chagrin of the Australian directors. While the FIRB appeared willing to entertain the original proposal of 75 per cent ownership of CGFA by Consolidated Gold Fields, its potential move to 100 per cent ownership elicited the view that Australianisation 'was a rare privilege and one which it was inappropriate to confer in this instance'.[33] The directors of CGFA were appraised that if there were to be a move to 100 per cent ownership it was likely that the FIRB would seek CGFA's shareholding in the three main subsidiary companies to be diluted, such that the 'minimum acceptable level of dilution so far as F.I.R.B. was concerned would be such as would ensure that foreign ownership of the subsidiaries did not exceed what it would have been had C.G.F. owned 75% of C.G.F.A'.[34]

The London parent was experiencing considerable disquiet about the direction and possible independence of the Australian directors and management. It rankled London directors that a majority owned

---

31   Consolidated Gold Fields Australia Limited, 'Minutes of Meeting of Directors', 23 April 1980, p. 2, RGCA, Box 12260, RGC 11517.
32   ibid.
33   Consolidated Gold Fields Australia Limited, 'Minutes of Meeting of Directors', 25 June 1980, p. 4, RGCA, Box 12260, RGC 11517.
34   ibid., p. 3.

subsidiary displayed a degree of independence that may not accord with their perspective. Likewise, London was concerned with the performance of some of CGFA's underlying subsidiaries, most notably AMC, which Agnew stressed had to be placed on a 'sound basis' for the future.[35] Also, as Segal intimated, London saw a value in having a higher shareholding in, if not outright ownership of, CGFA to prevent any possibility of Minorco or Anglo American acquiring a significant shareholding in CGFA, thereby frustrating their overall attempt to acquire control of Consolidated Gold Fields.

The cross directorships between CGFA and Consolidated Gold Fields created an interesting situation for some directors. Ryan, as managing director of CGFA, was also a director of the London board. He informed his fellow directors in Australia that he had advised the FIRB that Consolidated Gold Fields would not be prepared to see its interest in the subsidiaries reduced to below 49 per cent. This elicited the response from one of the other CGFA directors that Ryan should make it clear in his dealings with the FIRB that he is 'acting for C.G.F. and not C.G.F.A.' and that he 'had no authority from the C.G.F.A Board on the matter'.[36] Ryan expressed his own view that the British parent should not proceed with its approaches for increased ownership of CGFA. In his view, it ran the risk of a rejection that would damage CGFA's relationships with the Australian Government. The following month Ryan could advise on 'a weakening of London's insistence that it would not wish to see its stake in the Company reduced'.[37]

Agnew planned to travel to Australia to attend a board meeting to discuss the situation with the Australian directors in early 1980. However, events in London intervened. A minority stake had been acquired in Consolidated Gold Fields by various nominee companies of De Beers, part of Harry Oppenheimer's controlled Anglo American group. Then on 12 February 1980 the holding increased a further 15 per cent, bringing Anglo American's total holding in Consolidated Gold Fields to over 25 per cent. Given these events, Agnew's planned discussion with the Australian directors remained in abeyance.

---

35 Letter from RIJ Agnew to SL Segal and BC Ryan, 12 December 1979, RGCA.
36 Consolidated Gold Fields Australia Limited, 'Minutes of Meeting of Directors', 25 June 1980, p. 4, RGCA, Box 12260, RGC 11517.
37 Consolidated Gold Fields Australia Limited, 'Minutes of Meeting of Directors', 23 July 1980, pp. 2–3, RGCA, Box 12260, RGC 11517.

In the context of the share ownership challenges of Consolidated Gold Fields and varying views of the structure and ownership of CGFA's direct investments, a change in the board and management structure of CGFA occurred in 1980. At the meeting of directors in July 1980, Max Roberts was appointed deputy chairman of CGFA at the directive of group chief executive, Agnew. Roberts, an Australian, had turned 60 and reached the statutory retirement age at Burmah Oil in the United Kingdom. He was well known to a number of the Consolidated Gold Fields' directors and was recognised as having overseen a complex process of portfolio reconfiguration at Burmah Oil. He was viewed as the man to oversee the next stage of CGFA's evolution. Roberts's role at CGFA entailed executive responsibilities before his planned move to the role of chairman and interim chief executive.

Ryan had effectively been replaced and he indicated his intention to resign as managing director at the end of the year. Ryan had been a rising star in Gold Fields, serving as general manager of both Renison and Mount Goldsworthy before moving to London to serve as an executive director and joint deputy chairman from December 1972 to May 1976. He and Agnew were contenders for the role of chief executive officer and chairman of Consolidated Gold Fields. While Ryan stepped down as Australian managing director, he remained a director of CGFA until 1982, and was retained as a consultant to Consolidated Gold Fields.[38] Segal also indicated his intention to step down as chairman and did so at the October 1980 board meeting, becoming deputy chairman to allow Roberts to assume the chairmanship.

In December 1980 Roberts reported to his CGFA colleagues on discussions in London where agreement in principle had been achieved to the concept of Australianisation, whereby majority shareholding would be provided to Australian investors. Consolidated Gold Fields' interest would reduce to about 46 per cent. Consolidated Gold Fields expressed its desire to maintain its direct investment in North Broken Hill and Mount Goldsworthy, separate to the new Australian-listed entity. Roberts indicated there was now 'an acceptance by C.G.F. that if Australianisation did not occur, the Australian Group had nowhere to go'.[39]

---

38   At the RGC board meeting of 26 August 1982, it was recorded: 'Mr. Ryan responded by expressing his regret that he was departing from the Company while it was experiencing difficult trading conditions and wished the Company well for the future' (Renison Consolidated Goldfields Limited, 'Minutes of Meeting of Directors', 26 August 1982, p. 12, RGCA, Box 11328, BRD 38).
39   Consolidated Gold Fields Australia Limited, 'Chairman's Address, Annual General Meeting', 17 December, 1980, p. 2, RGCA, Box 12260, RGC 11517.

Figure 43. Max Roberts, executive chairman and then chairman of Renison Goldfields Consolidated from 1980 to 1994.
Source: Quentin Jones, *Sydney Morning Herald*, Nine Publishing.

With Roberts's appointment, the various strands that had been explored during the 1970s in relation to the structure of the group in Australia were drawn together in an approach that saw the formation of four wholly owned operating divisions of a company with majority Australian ownership structure.[40]

The initial plan for the reorganisation of CGFA entailed it becoming a fully owned subsidiary of Renison and that Mount Lyell and AMC would in turn become wholly owned subsidiaries of CGFA.[41] This approach

---

40 In 1981, CGFA was 69.8 per cent owned by Consolidated Gold Fields. In turn, CGFA had an ownership of Renison Limited (53.7 per cent), The Mount Lyell Mining and Railway Company Limited (56.1 per cent) and Associated Minerals Consolidated Limited (63.1 per cent), as well as a range of other direct interests, including the Glendell coal deposit (50 per cent), the Porgera gold deposit (33.3 per cent), the Gunpowder copper project (70 per cent), a 9.9 per cent shareholding in Pancontinental Mining Limited, an 11.11 per cent interest in the McCamey iron ore deposit in Western Australia and an exploration interest in a steaming coal deposit at Eneabba. Consolidated Gold Fields held a 4.8 per cent interest in Renison ('Joint Announcement on the Proposed Merger of Consolidated Golds Fields Australia Limited, Renison Limited, Associated Minerals Consolidated Limited, The Mount Lyell Mining and Railway Company Limited, 10th March 1981 and Scheme of Arrangement between Associated Minerals Consolidated Limited and its Members', UMA, Stock Exchange of Melbourne, 1990.0080, Box 29).
41 The Mount Lyell Mining and Railway Company Limited, 'Minutes of Meeting of Directors', 25 February 1981 and 10 March 1981, National Archives of Australia, Tasmania, NS3924, Items 238–245. The previously listed companies of Mount Lyell, AMC and Renison ceased trading on 24 July 1981.

was changed in March 1980, with the intention to establish a newly incorporated company, Renison Goldfields Consolidated Limited, which would fully own Mount Lyell, Renison, AMC and CGFA. Renison Goldfields Consolidated was duly established on 24 July 1981 as a majority Australian owned, diversified mining company with 100 per cent owned subsidiaries and listed on 27 July. It was a complex process with innumerable challenges. Its formation was through a merger, via scheme of arrangement, of CGFA with its four subsidiaries. It was the largest such merger in Australian corporate history, requiring separate voting by the shareholders of the main investments over the same day. Consolidated Gold Fields retained 49 per cent ownership. The company took its position as one of a number of substantial Australian mining companies listed on the Australian Stock Exchange. In 1980 resource companies constituted 55 per cent of the market capitalisation and 17 of the top 25 companies were mining companies.[42]

The granting of naturalised status meant Renison Goldfields Consolidated became an Australian company in terms of foreign investment guidelines, allowing it to develop new mining ventures in its own right without the need to seek Australian partners. It would also have access to the resources and cash flows of each business to deploy as appropriate for further growth, while efficiencies in borrowing, in taxation arrangements and in operational costs could be achieved. As it transpired, the financial interests of the group had also begun to turn. After dreadful financial performances in 1976 and 1977, a group profit tax of $12.3 million was reported in 1979. In 1980 profit increased by over 77 per cent and was one of the strongest financial years that CGFA had experienced since establishing in Australia. By this stage, however, the nature of the business model had evolved and the asset base had changed. The company entered its third and final phase in Australia, as a majority Australian owned, naturalised company, named Renison Goldfields Consolidated.

---

42 The companies, apart from Renison Goldfields Consolidated, were BHP, CRA, Mount Isa Mines, CSR, Western Mining Corporation, Woodside Petroleum, Comalco, Hamersley Holdings, Bougainville Copper, Santos, Southern Petroleum, North Broken Hill, Central Pacific Minerals, Peko-Wallsend, Utah Mining and Moonie Oil. A decade later, six resource and energy companies were in the top 25 listed companies on the Australian Stock Exchange by market capitalisation.

PART FIVE:
A MAJORITY AUSTRALIAN OWNED MINING COMPANY 1981–1989

Box 5. Key events 1981–1989

1981	Renison Goldfields Consolidated (RGC) established, 24 July
	New Guinea Gold Fields acquired; 50 per cent shareholding offered to Consolidated Gold Fields. Renamed NGG Holdings
	Mount Lyell mining progressed from lower part of 20 series to 30 series (to 1986)
1982	Naturalisation status granted by the Foreign Investment Review Board, 19 May
	Consolidated Gold Fields disposes of its interest in Tennant Trading (Australia) Pty Ltd to RGC
	Glendell coal joint venture with Dalgety Australia Ltd (50 per cent interest) formed
	Gunpowder copper project: limited leaching and cementation operations discontinued
1983	David Elsum appointed managing director (24 October; resigns 28 September 1984)
	Assets of Mount Lyell sold to Renison, with Renison appointed to act as agent for carrying out mining operations of Mount Lyell
1984	Sale of Bow zirconia micro ionising facilities, New Hampshire, to Ferro Corporation
	$16.4 million share placement
	RGC acquires Consolidated Gold Fields' interest in Consolidated Gold Fields/RGC exploration joint venture (formed in 1979)
	NGG Holdings becomes fully owned by RGC
	Investment Division formed with $20 million funding
	Minora Resources listing in which RGC participates
	Mining on Moreton Island restricted by Commonwealth Government decision
	Gunpowder Copper fixed assets sold
1985	North Stradbroke operation sold after depletion of ore reserves; mining by Associated Minerals Consolidated ceases on east coast after 52 years
	Pine Creek gold production, Northern Territory, commences
	Sale of Mount Lyell's interest in the Lake Margaret power station to the Tasmanian Government
	40 series mining Mount Lyell (1985–1990); decision to commit to 50 series and 60 series
	Completion of acquisition of Allied Eneabba tenements and plant at Eneabba
	Campbell Anderson appointed managing director, effective 15 April
	Max Roberts steps down as chief executive officer, 31 December

1986	Campbell Anderson commences as chief executive officer, 1 January
	Construction of new mill and carbon-in-pulp plant at NGG Holdings mine, Wau
	Mount Lyell produces 100 millionth tonne of ore
	Disposal of Gold Fields House head lease to AMP
1987	Commissioning of synthetic rutile plant C at Narngulu, Western Australia
	40 series commissioned, Mount Lyell
	Financial assistance provided by Tasmanian Government to allow extension of ore reserve development to 50 series and 60 series at Mount Lyell; mine closure extended from 1989 to 1994
	Gunpowder Copper project placed on care and maintenance
	Mark Bethwaite joins RGC as deputy managing director
1988	Draft feasibility study for Porgera presented to the Government of Papua New Guinea
	Construction of timber milling and drying facilities at Kempsey (Colinas); viewed as a means to facilitate disposal of this asset
	75 per cent interest in PT Koba Tin, Indonesia, purchased for $51 million
	Lucky Draw gold mine, Burraga, New South Wales commissioned 29 December, expenditure of $19.6 million. Discovered by RGC in 1985
	Dredge mining introduced at Eneabba South deposit
1989	Hanson all-cash takeover offer for Consolidated Gold Fields
	RGC attempts to acquire the Consolidated Gold Fields 70 per cent interest in Mount Goldsworthy joint venture; Hanson sells interest to BHP
	Board approval for acquisition of Dalgety's interest in Glendell Coal joint venture; agreement later reached for payment of $8 million
	RGC enters into joint venture with Costain to tender for New South Wales Electricity Commission coal contract
	50 series mining commences at Mount Lyell
	Eneabba West development approved—capital expenditure estimate of $134 million
	Lucky Draw gold development commences production
	Development approval by Government of Papua New Guinea for Porgera; RGC interest reduced to 30 per cent as government takes a 10 per cent equity in the project

14

FORMATION OF A DIVERSIFIED MINING COMPANY

Renison Goldfields Consolidated Limited (RGC) came into existence as a majority owned Australian mining company on 27 July 1981. Max Roberts was the executive chairman. The company's shareholder base through to 1989 included Consolidated Gold Fields, initially at 49 per cent. The boards of the previous companies were disbanded and the board of the new company included three representatives from its major shareholder, as well as previous non-executive directors of Consolidated Gold Fields Australia (CGFA).[1] Naturalisation status was granted on 19 May 1982. This required at least 51 per cent Australian

---

1   In the 1982 financial year, the company's first full year, RGC had three Consolidated Gold Fields' directors: RIJ Agnew, group chief executive and deputy chairman (and chairman-designate); ME Beckett, executive director; and AP Hichens, managing director-finance. Sidney Segal, former chairman of CGFA, was a director, along with Bart Ryan, the former managing director. Both retired at the end of 1982. The other independent directors were GM Niall, director of CGFA since its flotation in 1966; J Darling, who had joined the board in 1974; ES Owens, former chairman of Associated Minerals Consolidated and director of CGFA since 1977; and K Wood, previously a director of Renison and Mount Lyell. Apart from Roberts, three other executive directors were represented on the board: WP Murphy, formerly chief executive of Tennant Trading; LW Skelton; and BE Wauchope; while AD Hemingway, a member of RGC's executive committee, attended and participated in all board meetings. Hemingway, as general counsel and general manager of corporate affairs, had one of the most extensive levels of involvement in the evolution of CGFA and RGC. At his final board meeting in June 1990, it was recorded: 'The Chairman thanked Mr A. D. Hemingway for his great dedication to RGC and its predecessor, C.G.F.A. Mr Hemingway's wisdom, commitment and advice were of significant benefit to the Group'. A London-based director also expressed the appreciation of Consolidated Gold Fields for Hemingway's assistance, 'particularly during the period of Minorco's bid for CGF' (Renison Goldfields Consolidated Limited, 'Minutes of Meeting of Directors', 28 June 1990, Renison Goldfields Consolidated Archives, Box 11329, BRD 38/04).

shareholding, the majority of the directors to be Australian citizens and an understanding by the Australian board that independence from its principal foreign shareholder would be assured. In the view of the chairman, naturalised status would 'be zealously guarded' and provide the new entity with greater flexibility to pursue its business aspirations.[2] In fact, after Hanson became the major shareholder in 1989, it sought successfully to overturn the naturalised status of RGC in 1993 and appoint its own executive chairman. This would be a matter of considerable board discussion and conflict between the independent directors and Hanson's London chairman and management.

Expectations for the new company and its role in the Australian resources sector were high. Free of the need to seek increased Australian ownership via joint ventures or Foreign Investment Review Board approvals, RGC saw its growth in Australian and in overseas jurisdictions as occurring through exploration, project development, acquisitions and, where appropriate, diversification into other commodities. It also expected to gain the benefits from direct ownership and management of its main businesses. The newly formed RGC initially had three fully owned main subsidiaries—Renison, Mount Lyell and Associated Minerals Consolidated (AMC). These were later formed into separate divisions: tin, with Koba Tin acquired in 1988; copper; mineral sands; and a gold division including New Guinea Goldfields, Pine Creek, Lucky Draw and Porgera from 1990. RGC also reported upon its trading and marketing activities through Tennant Trading, which was acquired from Consolidated Gold Fields in 1982. An investment division was formed in 1984 and from 1993 Narama coal came into operation.[3]

Within the portfolio were remnants of CGFA's portfolio. These included Colinas, the primary production entity with interests in afforestation and cattle grazing near Kempsey, New South Wales. A 70 per cent interest was retained in the Gunpowder joint venture, now held within Circular Quay Holdings, while a 50 per cent interest was maintained with Dalgety Australia in the Glendell joint venture. This Hunter valley coal project represented the main opportunity for the group to re-enter the coal sector after the divestment of Bellambi, although other coal opportunities were considered,

---

2   Renison Goldfields Consolidated Limited, 'Report on the 1981 Financial Year', p. 3. RGC lost its naturalised status in 1993, when Hanson made application to the Foreign Investment Review Board for changes to director and chairman appointment arrangements, which had the effect of nullifying the naturalisation status.
3   The reference in this chapter is to financial years, ending 30 June.

including the acquisition of an interest in the Blair Athol coal deposits in the Bowen Basin, Queensland, and the development of steaming coal resources at Eneabba in Western Australia. Neither eventuated. The project to develop the Glendell leases proved a protracted and frustrating process for the company. In the end, only a proportion of the lease area available to RGC was developed through the Narama operation.

A key component of the envisaged growth of the group was through Gold Fields Exploration, responsible for the exploration activities of the company in Australia and the region. This was an entity in which the London parent had an indirect interest, with funding of exploration activity partially reimbursed by Consolidated Gold Fields. The arrangement was established in 1979 and existed until 1984 when RGC took full responsibility for its exploration activities. A marine aggregate project off the coast of New South Wales was evaluated at the instigation of Consolidated Gold Fields in an association with its subsidiary company ARC Marine. This project planned to undertake dredging of sand and gravel off the coast, including at Broken Bay at the entry of the Hawkesbury River, north of Sydney. The lack of support by regulators for a contentious environmental activity meant that it did not progress.

While the formation of RGC as an Australian mining company presented the opportunity to transform the existing portfolio, its evolution over the next decade and a half was influenced to a large extent by the three main pillars of its asset base: AMC, Renison and Mount Lyell. In 1981, the funds employed were represented as mineral sands 45 per cent, tin 25 per cent, copper 10 per cent, and gold and other investments 20 per cent. In the 1997 financial year, the last year in which the company issued financial accounts, the assets employed were mineral sands 48 per cent; gold 38 per cent; tin 10 per cent; and coal, other base metals and a small copper exposure, 4 per cent.[4]

While RGC held bold aspirations, management and the board of RGC had an appreciation of the inherent constraints of the portfolio. Challenges were evident in the company's first years, most notably through to 1987, associated with poor market conditions and pricing outcomes, particularly for mineral sands and copper, as well as the maturity and

---

4   In the intervening period, Mount Lyell and its copper production contribution had been closed and sold; the asset values at Renison had been reduced while gold assets had increased, reflected by RGC's 55.8 per cent interest in Goldfields Limited (Renison Goldfields Consolidated Limited, *Annual Report 1997*, pp. 27–30 and 57).

operational challenges of Mount Lyell and commissioning issues for the Eneabba mineral sands operation. The characteristics of the portfolio, and the difficulties created by market conditions, dominated the early life of RGC. RGC's financial performance was weak during 1982 to 1984 and, while improving in 1985 and 1986, it was only from 1987 that the financial performance could be considered adequate, with a contribution from new operations. What followed in 1989 and 1990 were two of the company's strongest years in financial terms.[5]

In the early 1980s, Renison was the highest-quality asset in the portfolio. As the world's largest underground tin mine, it had been the major earnings contributor to CGFA in the years leading to RGC's formation. Its contribution continued, although in the first half of the 1980s, the International Tin Council imposed restrictions on tin production, which in turn produced inefficiencies in the unit costs of production and a lower level of tin sales. There followed the collapse of the tin buffer system in 1985 and a decline in the tin price. Operationally, the industrial relations climate at Renison, often fractious, worsened. Renison's financial contribution peaked in 1980 and then steadily declined (see Chart 10, Chapter 8).

Mount Lyell was in its 87th year of operation in 1981. While accessing deeper ore reserves offered the opportunity to extend the life of the operation, low copper prices and the inability to offset this decline with lower costs meant that Mount Lyell was the most problematical asset in the RGC portfolio. In 1981 and 1982, Mount Lyell was viewed as in a crisis situation. Copper prices were the lowest in real terms for four decades, creating a cash deficit that meant that 'the Company's survival ... [was] at risk'.[6] In 1982, the operation was closed temporarily. A long-term planning exercise resulted in the decision to proceed to mining deeper horizons, with work recommencing on the underground crushing and hoisting project, accessing the 30 and 40 series ore bodies and subsequently developing the 50 and 60 series.[7]

---

5   See Appendix 4. RGC recorded successive profit increases from 1983 to 1987. In 1987 a return on shareholders' funds above 20 per cent was achieved and return on assets of 10 per cent. In the 1986 financial year, a new gold mining operation, Pine Creek, made a financial contribution and unlike the previous year there were no extraordinary items recorded in the reported results.
6   The Mount Lyell Mining and Railway Company Limited, 'Minutes of Committee Meeting', 28 May 1982, p. 6, National Archives of Australia, Tasmania (NAAT), NS3924, Items 288–295.
7   The Mount Lyell Mining and Railway Company Limited, 'Long Term Mining Plan, Progress Report–November 1982', NAAT, NS3357/1/105. In 1982, mining from the 30 series was nearing completion with mining of the 40 series planned, supplemented by satellite mining from Cape Horn. Drilling evaluation also occurred for the 50 and 60 series ore bodies, later to be mined.

14. FORMATION OF A DIVERSIFIED MINING COMPANY

The AMC mineral sands assets were, by 1981, based at Capel and the newly acquired province of Eneabba in the north of Western Australia, along with a dredging operation at Green Cove Springs, Florida. The east coast operations had predominantly been closed, while RGC's mining and processing operations on North Stradbroke Island ceased in 1985. Prospects for mining leases on Moreton Island remained but, due to environmental opposition to mineral sands mining on Fraser Island, the likelihood of this occurring remained slight. The opportunity was extinguished by Commonwealth Government restrictions on issuing export licences for mineral sands mining. The company was also operating two synthetic rutile kilns, developed as a result of the technical advances by Western Titanium. Production capacity was expanded by the construction of a third kiln, as well as the development of a new form of synthetic rutile in an attempt to resolve the issue of high levels of radiation in some of the Eneabba ilmenites. Mineral sands exploration success stands out as a high point of RGC's exploration activities, with new provinces identified in the United States and in the Murray Basin of Victoria. While mineral sands remained a core part of the portfolio, it created frequent challenges in terms of financial performance. Mineral sands enjoyed periods of strong financial performance, but also extended periods of low returns.

In 1989, a fundamental change in the shareholder base of RGC occurred when Hanson Plc acquired Consolidated Gold Fields in the United Kingdom. Its motivations were in part opportunistic but also motivated by a desire to gain control of the Amey Roadstone business within the Consolidated Gold Fields' portfolio. The acquisition followed an unsuccessful takeover attempt by Minorco, an Anglo American affiliated company, which RGC management was active in assisting its parent to defend against.

With Hanson gaining control of Consolidated Gold Fields in the second half of 1989, it became the largest shareholder of RGC; with this a new dynamic emerged for the RGC board and management. Hanson's shareholding was associated with an initial year of strong RGC financial performance in 1990, followed by four poor years, including two that were loss-making, before a recovery in reported profits in 1995 and 1996, and then a loss in 1997, in large part due to the effects of asset write-downs associated with prior year investments (see Charts 5 and 6). Hanson's shareholding, board and subsequent management representation had a major influence on the fate of RGC as an independent, diversified mining company in Australia.

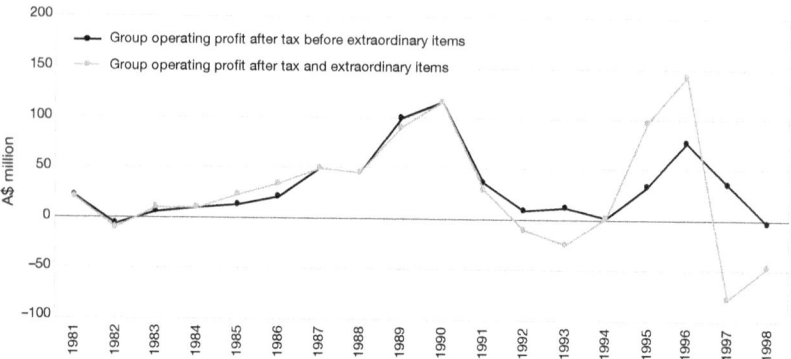

Chart 5. Renison Goldfields Consolidated net profit/loss, 1981–1998.

This chart shows RGC's profitability from 1981 to 1998. Extraordinary items influenced results in a number of years. See Appendix 4 for details of extraordinary items. Average operating profit after tax before extraordinary items was $27.9 million. Average operating profit after tax and extraordinary items was $31.0 million.

Sources: RGC annual reports, 1990 to 1997. 1998 data for period to 30 June is derived from 'Information Memorandum in Relation to a Recommended Merger by Scheme of Arrangement between RGC Limited and Westralian Sands', pp. 34 and 56–57. Financial information for this year includes RGC's interest in Goldfields.

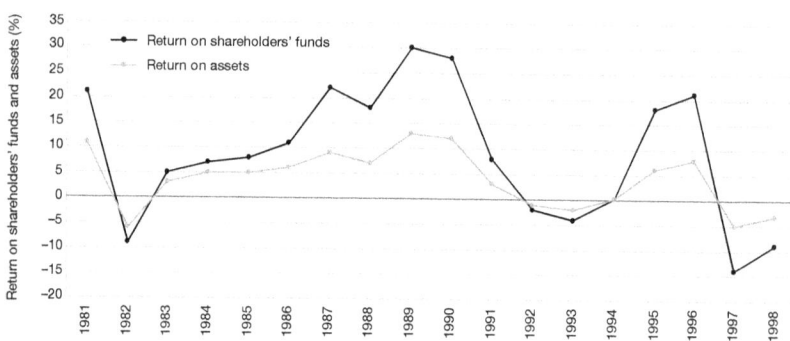

Chart 6. Renison Goldfields Consolidated returns on shareholders' funds and assets, 1981–1998.

This chart shows RGC's returns on shareholders' funds and assets, after extraordinary items, over the period 1981 to 1998. Average return on shareholders' funds was 8.9 per cent and return on assets averaged 3.9 per cent over this 18-year period.

Sources: RGC annual reports, 1990 to 1997, and 'Information Memorandum in Relation to a Recommended Merger by Scheme of Arrangement between RGC Limited and Westralian Sands', pp. 34 and 56–57.

...

RGC's approach to the management and growth of its portfolio had a number of consistent elements. Exploration remained a cornerstone. RGC maintained a well-resourced and technically competent exploration team, which in the mid-1980s included 50 geoscientists. Part of the exploration team was located in Canberra so as to be close to national geophysical data, with offices also in Darwin, Perth and the Philippines. Exploration expenditure increased every year from 1981, with the exception of 1991 and 1992, when under straitened financial circumstances and the scrutiny of the new major shareholder, budgets were trimmed. Even so, Hanson was prepared to support a large increase in exploration expenditure in its final two years of its shareholding in RGC.[8]

Exploration occurred in Australia, Papua New Guinea, the Philippines, the United States, Europe, and other jurisdictions. A ranking or prioritisation of minerals was adopted, with efforts directed to both the extension of the resource and reserve base of existing operations, which included Renison, Mount Lyell and Eneabba, as well as seeking new mineral provinces and deposits. RGC's exploration activities led to the development of two smaller Australian gold mines, as well as mineral sands deposits in the United States, and the opening up of the Murray Basin mineral sands province in Australia. Through its support for the listing of oil and gas exploration company, Minora Resources, RGC had an indirect involvement in exploration activities in the energy field.[9] Project development activities were undertaken, which included the Pine Creek, Lucky Draw and Henty gold mines, the Eneabba West development, Old Hickory, the expansion of the Koba Tin operation, as well as a contribution to the determination of the form of ore processing adopted at Porgera.

Acquisition activity formed an important element of the company's approach. Several company acquisitions were considered. In mineral sands, RGC undertook the final aggregation of the Eneabba deposits by the acquisition of DuPont's stake in Allied Eneabba in 1985, following the prior acquisition of the Jennings Industries assets, gaining overall control of this major mineral sands province. In 1996, the acquisition of Cudgen RZ provided RGC with control of Consolidated Rutile Limited and its mining activities on North Stradbroke Island, as well

---

8   Exploration expenditure in 1996 and 1997 was $43.3 million and $50.5 million, respectively. In the previous five years it had averaged $21.8 million.
9   Minora merged with Discovery Petroleum NL in 1994 with RGC retaining an interest.

as its 50 per cent interest in the Sierra Rutile mineral sands operation in Sierra Leone, then not in production due to a civil war. Numerous other mineral sands acquisition opportunities were considered, although not progressed or not successful. The company's tin production base was expanded by the takeover in 1988 of the CSR and Boral interests in an Indonesian tin mining company, PT Koba Tin. Acquisitions to establish a presence in new commodities included a review of the Blair Athol coal deposits in the Bowen Basin, Queensland, with an approach made to ARCO Coal Australia. Consideration was given to acquiring the Cerro Corona gold and copper deposit in Peru, while other company acquisition opportunities evaluated, although not advanced, included North Broken Hill and Mount Isa Mines.

The establishment of an investment division occurred in 1984, viewed as a way to generate trading profits on share investments, as well as establish strategic holdings as a potential precursor to acquisition or merger activity. Tennant Trading acted as a source of revenue generation through commodity trading and marketing with, at one stage, over 65 per cent of its revenue generated from non-RGC derived businesses.

Corporate restructuring initiatives were considered. The most notable was the establishment in 1995 of a separate gold company, Goldfields Limited, to house RGC's gold interests and mount a takeover of Pancontinental Mining to acquire its gold assets, with the non-gold assets either acquired by RGC or sold. This transaction was finalised in 1996, although RGC was not successful in obtaining sufficient shareholder support to proceed to compulsory acquisition of all of the shares in Pancontinental Mining, an impediment it also encountered with the Cudgen RZ acquisition. A proposal by RGC in the late 1980s to acquire the 70 per cent interest in Mount Goldsworthy held by Consolidated Gold Fields was not successful when Hanson, as the new owner of Consolidated Gold Fields, sold the interest to BHP.

Hanson, as the major shareholder from 1989 to 1998, had little commitment to a diversified mining company model and minimal experience of mining. As an industrial conglomerate it typically held a much shorter time horizon for a return on capital from its investments than that employed by the RGC board and management. Disquiet by Hanson at the financial performance of RGC and the structure of the portfolio was evident from an early stage of its shareholding. While RGC management and Hanson investigated various means by which the Hanson shareholding could be sold to other parties, none eventuated until 1998. While Hanson can be considered to have exercised patience with its investment in RGC over nine years, this patience reached its limit, in part influenced by a patchy record of financial returns from its coincident investment in RGC, lack of confidence in the corporate management of the business and the emergence of yet another period of weak market conditions—particularly for mineral sands—requiring, in effect, a large capital requirement to replenish a portfolio of maturing assets. In addition, changes within the broader Hanson portfolio made the retention of a shareholding in an Australian diversified mining company even less logical.

In late 1992 and again in 1993, Hanson approached the Foreign Investment Review Board, without prior notification to the RGC board. The approaches reflected the malaise in the relationship between Hanson and the non-Hanson RGC directors and senior management. Hanson, in effect, sought the ability to appoint its own executive chairman, purportedly as a basis for growing its interests in Australia and the Pacific Rim region, but essentially to exert more management and financial control. For the non-Hanson RGC directors, it was seen as a covert attempt to take over the company without the payment of a premium and proceed with the further dismemberment of the RGC diversified portfolio. Hanson's overtures, despite vigorous opposition from RGC's chairman and managing director, resulted in overturning the naturalised status of RGC, in management change and, in turn, a Hanson-appointed candidate selected as deputy chairman, to become chairman within a year. Further management change followed and, in 1998, the Hanson-appointed chairman assumed dual executive and chairmanship responsibilities.

The instability within RGC played into the hands of the managing director of Westralian Sands, Malcolm Macpherson. He made an approach to Hanson in London in 1998 and proposed a combination of the two companies. By July 1998 there was a merger implementation agreement and in December of that year RGC held its final board meeting at Gold Fields House, Circular Quay, Sydney. Six RGC directors resigned and six Westralian Sands directors were appointed to the new entity that initially took the name Westralian Sands.[10] Macpherson became the managing

---

10   The name was changed to Iluka Resources in 1999.

director of the new merged entity. Only one former RGC executive was represented on the executive of the new company. The corporate head office of RGC in Sydney was closed and most of the corporate staff dismissed. Hanson shortly thereafter exited its shareholding.

Westralian Sands exerted management and board control, and undertook the almost complete rationalisation of the RGC non-mineral sands assets.[11] As such, RGC ceased to exist either in name or in terms of the continuity of a diversified mining portfolio. A company with a pedigree, through Consolidated Gold Fields, stretching back over 100 years and with a direct involvement in Australia for over 70 years, including 38 years as an Australian diversified mining company, had reached the end of its existence. It was an underwhelming conclusion for a company with such a proud heritage in the global mining industry.

The following chapters will describe the main elements of the management of the RGC portfolio from 1981 to 1989; the events leading to the takeover of Consolidated Gold Fields by Hanson, and the final years of RGC's existence before its merger with Westralian Sands in 1998.

---

11 The exceptions were Narama coal and the Mining Area C royalty entitlement, which did not contribute financially until 2003, after the formation of Iluka Resources, when BHP began production from Area C.

15

THE INITIAL YEARS

Max Roberts commenced with Renison Goldfields Consolidated (RGC) in 1981 in the role of executive chairman. After an external search for a managing director and chief executive officer, in October 1983 David Elsum was appointed managing director. Elsum was the founding managing director of Capel Court investment bank, the adviser retained by the board of Consolidated Gold Fields Australia (CGFA) in 1980 when seeking an external valuation of its shares in the event that Consolidated Gold Fields increased its shareholding. Elsum's tenure was short-lived. By September of the following year he had left the company. The RGC announcement associated with his departure stated that 'his transition to mining [from finance] had proved more difficult than expected'.[1] Media reports indicated that he found mining a 'little slow', a surprising observation to say the least in light of the multiple challenges confronting RGC, including for its two key assets, Renison and Mount Lyell. Roberts resumed the role of executive chairman.

In April 1985 Campbell McCheyne Anderson's appointment as a director and managing director was announced. Anderson assumed the role of chief executive officer from January 1986. Roberts knew Anderson from their time working together at Burmah Oil and had been associated with him professionally and personally since 1971 both in the United States and United Kingdom. The two forged and maintained a close and productive working relationship. Both were strong individuals, with an irreverent sense of humour and strong intellect, and worked to build RGC into one of the major mining companies in the country.[2]

---

1   *The Sydney Morning Herald*, 2 April 1985 and 10 January 1985. Roberts said he was 'after someone with the knowledge and intelligence to look after the company' (Greenwood, 'Renison's Rocky Revival', p. 18).
2   See Appendix 3 for biographical profiles of Max Roberts and Campbell Anderson.

Figure 44. Campbell Anderson, managing director from 1985 and chief executive officer of Renison Goldfields Consolidated from 1986 to 1993.

Source: RGC company image held by author.

Figure 45. Mark Bethwaite, appointed deputy managing director in 1987 and managing director and chief executive officer from 1995 to 1998.
Source: RGC company image held by author.

Another key senior management appointment was FM (Mark) Bethwaite, a former Olympic sailor and managing director of North Broken Hill who joined the company in the newly created position of deputy managing director in February 1987.[3] On the announcement of Bethwaite's appointment, it was indicated that he would be responsible for new business development, the group's investment division, and head office technical and computing functions.[4] In effect, he operated in the role of chief operating officer, taking a close involvement in the oversight of mineral sands, Renison and Mount Lyell. The arrangement worked well, freeing up Anderson to consider broader strategic options, including acquisitions as well as direct engagement in extensive political negotiations, as occurred for Mount Lyell and Porgera. A disciplined and highly competitive man, Bethwaite succeeded Anderson as managing director in September 1993 and remained in this role until January 1998. Subsequent to his departure, the Hanson-appointed chairman, Tony Cotton, became executive chairman.

During the first half of the decade, market and operating conditions for RGC were challenging. From 1982 to 1985 RGC generated a return on assets of less than 3.5 per cent and return on shareholder funds of less than 5 per cent. The company recorded a loss of $10 million in its first full year.[5] By 1984, the expectations for the new publicly listed and majority Australian owned RGC had not been fulfilled. One business commentator wrote that RGC had been 'heralded as Australia's next big mining house in 1981' but had failed to live up to expectations and had, in fact, been 'something of a dog' in terms of share price performance in its first year of existence.[6] In the three subsequent years profits increased from $10 million to $23 million in 1985, although the 1985 result was aided by $10 million in financial support from the Tasmanian Government, as well as other forms of assistance, provided to Mount Lyell. It was an inauspicious beginning for the new mining company. The period 1985 to 1990 saw a recovery in the company's financial performance, with five

---

3   See Appendix 3 for a biographical profile of Mark Bethwaite.
4   RGC News Release, 'Appointment of Mr Mark Bethwaite as Deputy Managing Director', 16 February 1987 (copy held by the author).
5   The loss after tax of $10.2 million included pre-tax extraordinary items of $3.3 million, which included the write-down in the value of government and semi-government bonds (Renison Goldfields Consolidated Limited, *Annual Report 1982*).
6   Greenwood, 'Renison's Rocky Revival', p. 16.

consecutive years of profit growth, primarily aided by a marked recovery in the performance of the mineral sands business. The company recorded two outstanding years financially in 1989 and 1990 (see Chart 7).

In the period 1986 to 1990, the return on assets averaged 9.4 per cent and return on shareholders' funds averaged 21.8 per cent. The company's share price performed strongly before the 1987 share market crash, with RGC's standing in the investment market at its height. A series of stockbroker reports remarked favourably on the attributes of the company and its portfolio management capabilities. A London-based broking analyst in 1987 described RGC as 'one of the leanest, fittest and most profitable of the Aussie resource majors' with mineral sands 'one of the most profitable segments of the whole mining industry ... RGC is very much the dominant force in the minerals sands market'.[7] Another lauded the company as 'a diverse, cost effective producer which protects it from many of the cycles in commodity prices'. As the largest producer of mineral sands this was expected to make it a 'market maker rather than taker'.[8] RGC's balance sheet strength, interest cover and market capitalisation of over $1.1 billion made the company highly marketable from an investment market perspective:

> Renison Goldfields Consolidated ... has been one of the most successful mining houses in Australia over the last few years. Basically, RGC has chosen the right mix of commodities for the current cycle. The Company did not get involved in the coal boom in a major way and it concentrated on expanding into mineral sands and gold.[9]

---

7   Kleinwort Gieveson Securities, 'London Investment Research Renison Goldfields Consolidated', 10 July 1987, pp. 1 and 3, Brierley Collection.
8   May Mellor Laing & Cruickshank Ltd, 'Renison Goldfields Consolidated Ltd, June 1987', Brierley Collection.
9   Jardine Fleming, 'Renison Goldfields Consolidated', p. 1, Brierley Collection.

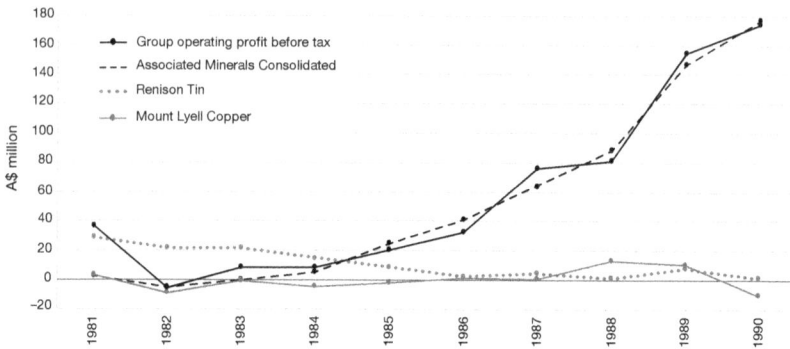

Chart 7. Renison Goldfields Consolidated group profit and principal divisional results, 1981–1990.

The chart displays the earnings contribution of Associated Minerals Consolidated, Renison and Mount Lyell over the period 1981 to 1990, along with the group's pre-tax earnings. The group pre-tax result is closely aligned with the AMC results in most years, as the contribution from Renison and Mount Lyell declined during the decade of the 1980s.

Source: RGC annual reports, 1981 to 1990.

The company during this period, and through to 1993, was under the managing directorship of Anderson. RGC invested broadly, establishing new gold mining operations in Queensland and the Northern Territory while laying the basis for the development of the large Porgera gold mine in Papua New Guinea that began production in 1990. Assets of the company increased by over 165 per cent. The company held bold ambitions. An external management consultant was appointed and, in a 1988 strategy review, the company stated its aim to become the tenth-ranking company in Australia by market capitalisation within five years and to be fourth behind BHP, CRA and Western Mining Corporation in 10 years.[10]

Renison, with its tin mining operations near Zeehan in Tasmania, remained the key asset in the portfolio. It was the one that the company had relied upon for the majority of its operating profit in the previous five years, and was expected to continue to make a major financial contribution.[11] However, the operations of the International Tin Council (ITC) had a major

---

10 Mark Bethwaite, 'RGC Memorandum 20th June 1988, Strategy Review 1988', Renison Goldfields Consolidated Archive (RGCA), Box 5345, RGC 3615.

11 The operating profit of CGFA between 1977 and 1981 was $38.2 million, including losses from operations such as Mount Lyell ($12.3 million). Renison was profitable in each year with a total operating profit of $46.7 million (Renison Goldfields Consolidated Limited, 'Report on the 1981 Financial Year', p. 7).

influence on Renison's performance during the 1980s. Quotas on tin sales imposed by the ITC between 1982 to 1985 hampered production settings for Renison's operation and led to variable and lower financial performance through the decade, before entering the 1990s loss-making.

Mount Lyell recorded cumulative losses from 1982 through to 1985 but then, dependent on government and other financial support, achieved a recovery in financial performance before further losses in the 1990s. Mount Lyell's future remained a prime area of management and board consideration through the 1980s. Mineral sands had four very poor years before a partial recovery in 1985 and then a period of stronger financial performance through to 1990 (see Chart 9, Chapter 20).

...

Figure 46. Mount Lyell operations, Queenstown, 1984.
Source: NAA, A6135, K20/2/2.

In 1981, RGC had acquired New Guinea Goldfields, a company that Gold Fields had invested in during the 1920s and 1930s. Apart from gold mining by alluvial and open cut methods, the acquisition involved an interest in various tyre retailing businesses as well as electricity distribution in Papua New Guinea. However, the main attraction of this acquisition was the exploration potential it was considered to provide in and around the area near Wau, where mining was conducted. Gold Fields exploration staff had visited the area in 1980 and identified compelling similarities to the Porgera deposit with what was viewed as a high likelihood of discovering large bulk, low-grade gold deposits.

Tennant Trading was acquired in 1982 from the ownership of Consolidated Gold Fields and was developed as a marketing vehicle for RGC. Tennant Trading had two main functions: marketing and shipping of ores and concentrates produced by the company and by other mining operations, as well as acting as an agency for the import and export of raw materials. This included metals and concentrates, metallurgical raw materials, industrial minerals and chemicals, as well as futures trading.

Organisationally, a major restructure occurred in 1983: Mount Lyell became the Mount Lyell copper division; a tin, gold and mineral sands division was also established. RGC also acquired the exploration interests held by Consolidated Gold Fields in Gold Fields Exploration, assuming responsibility from the prior arrangement, established in 1979, where funding of exploration expenditure in Australia and the Asia-Pacific region was shared with Consolidated Gold Fields in London. A share placement generated $23 million, allowing the purchase of Consolidated Gold Fields' interest in New Guinea Goldfields, which was renamed New Guinea Gold Holdings. RGC also re-entered the share investment field by the establishment of an investment division in 1984.

Renison—external influences

During the first five years of RGC's existence, Renison remained the major contributor to overall group results, although its performance declined from 1981 and dramatically reduced for the rest of the decade. At the time the world's largest underground tin mine, its competitive position in terms of tin concentrate production was pitched against typically lower-cost, but often lower-grade alluvial mines. For Renison, the mining operation was characterised by a combination of greater fragmentation of the ore body and associated metallurgical challenges and a requirement for deeper mining to access reserves to extend production. In the early 1980s, a more confrontational industrial relations environment developed. In 1980, for example, an estimated $6 million in pre-tax profits was lost due to industrial disputes while in the following year industrial disputes also had an adverse impact on profits.[12] By 1981, after a strike lasting over five weeks, the industrial relations situation was viewed at board level as a 'matter of serious concern'.[13] It did not improve noticeably until sustained efforts were made to improve communication between management and the workforce, following the appointment of MWD (Mike) Ayre as general manager.

Joe Pringle, president of the underground workers for the Australian Workers' Union, personified the tough and often combative industrial relations environment at Renison. Pringle had commenced at Renison in 1965. An old-style unionist, he operated on the basis of a handshake agreement being sufficient but became disenchanted with and antagonistic to the introduction of more formalised industrial relations arrangements. When an industrial relations function was established, he saw this as an additional layer of management reinforcing an increased detachment of those in control from the workforce. These factors, as well as decisions he considered antithetical to the welfare of the workforce—such as mine management evicting the widow and two daughters of a recently killed mine worker from company housing—created an antagonistic attitude to management.[14]

The Australian Workers' Union demonstrated its willingness to act in a belligerent and uncooperative manner. A dispute in late 1984 related to remuneration relativities of one of the 25 designated categories for underground work proceeded to the Australian Conciliation and Arbitration Commission. After exhaustive deliberations that upheld the existing arrangements, the Australian Workers' Union ignored the commission's ruling and reimposed bans.[15] The industrial relations environment, associated with the actions of the ITC—in first imposing sales constraints and then the release from late 1985 of excess global stocks onto the tin market—compounded the challenges facing the operation.

---

12   Consolidated Gold Fields Australia Limited, 'Minutes of Meeting of Directors', 23 April 1980, p. 4, RGCA, Box 12272.
13   Renison Goldfields Consolidated, 'Minutes of Meeting of Directors', 5 November 1981, p. 4, RGCA, Box 11328, BRD 38.
14   Joe Pringle, personal communication, 20 October 2018.
15   National Archives of Australia, Victoria, B206, C6578/1984.

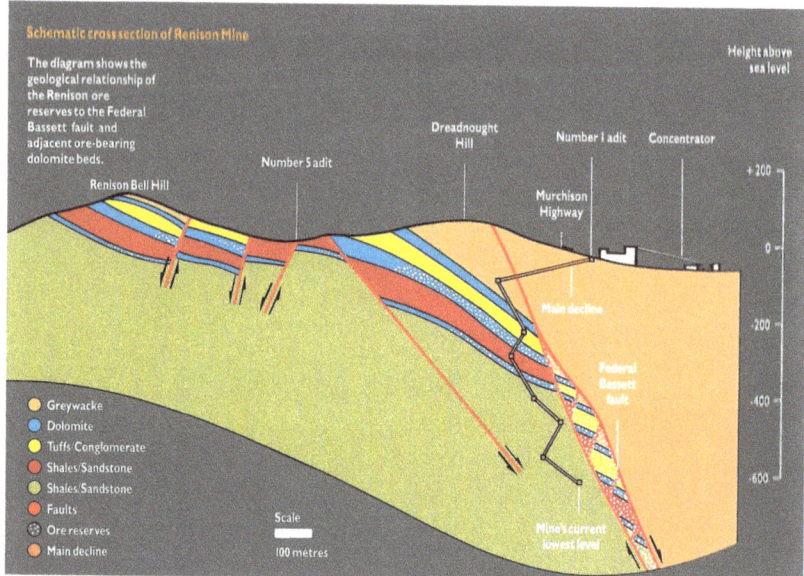

Figure 47. Cross-section of Renison mining operation.
Source: Renison Goldfields Consolidated Limited, *Annual Report 1987*.

Figures 48 and 49. Underground mining operations, Renison.
Sources: NAA, 1200, L59830, L59828.

15. THE INITIAL YEARS

The ITC imposed export restrictions from April 1982. With recessionary conditions affecting the world economy, global tin consumption was at 85 per cent of global production.[16] While initially a 15 per cent restriction, it was subsequently increased to nearly 40 per cent. Australia's position as an ITC member was unique, because as well as being a major exporter of tin it was also a consumer. Through much of the time that ITC restrictions were in place for Australian producers, including Renison, domestic demand remained weak.

Coming after the completion of a program to expand production and increase concentrator capacity in 1981, production now had to be reduced with restrictions on concentrator utilisation levels, as well as the manner in which the mining operation was conducted for much of the period between 1982 and 1986. The lower level of production had an adverse impact on Renison's unit cash costs of production. This led to management actions to address the cost structure of the operation that, in turn, adversely affected the industrial relations environment. The budgetary settings for the 1983 financial year assumed that 15 per cent of mill operating performance could be affected adversely, while navigating a move to a 38-hour week presented the possibility of additional industrial unrest.[17]

During this period, a policy was adopted of not retrenching employees, as a result of Roberts making this commitment while addressing the workforce.[18] Instead, the approach adopted included the introduction of a five-day week and extended periods of operational closure, particularly over Christmas periods, as well as a pay freeze. The approach preserved employment levels but reduced the take-home wages of the workers, which, in turn, created demands for increased wages. Other measures to improve the efficiency of the Renison operation and reduce costs in the context of lower production were necessary. These focused initially on voluntary redundancies, but later involved far-ranging structural changes in the level of the workforce and work practices. Industrial disruption worsened with frequent workplace bans imposed. In August 1983 mill workers refused to undertake mill repairs or maintenance on weekends,

---

16 For a discussion of the International Tin Agreement and the 1985 collapse of the buffer system, see Mallory, 'Conduct Unbecoming: The Collapse of the International Tin Agreement'.
17 Renison Limited, 'Minutes of an Operating Committee Meeting', 31 May 1982, RGCA, Box 12254.
18 John Mitchell, personal communication, 7 November 2018.

while the workforce was operating on a five-day working week. By April 1984, while operating on restricted production settings, Renison's general manager believed that:

> [The] work-force's commitment to the Company had not equated with the Company's efforts to preserve their employment through the no retrenchment policy. Consequently, he considered that the work-force should be informed that the Company was not prepared to continue with a no retrenchment policy.[19]

The industrial relations climate at site was not assisted by frequent emissions of carbon disulphide and the risk to the health of workers. Suspicion existed on both sides. The compensation of one worker affected by emissions led management to observe that the condition of another employee 'deteriorate[d] shortly after ... a worker's compensation payout ... for a similar incidence'.[20] Management was also concerned at what it saw as the union's 'strike now talk later approach' with established grievance mechanisms rarely employed. As a result, inordinate management time was used in dealing with numerous minor grievances, which nonetheless led to stoppages. In 1985, the operation was severely affected by industrial disruption to an extent that it confirmed to the company's board and management the dire circumstance of its 'inability to control the Renison workers'.[21]

Through to 1985, Renison's production settings continued to be restricted by tin export controls, equating to up to 60 per cent of the operation's capacity in some periods. Roberts pointed out at an RGC annual general meeting that countries not bound by the ITC agreement were involved in smuggling tin into the market. In the case of the United States, it was also drawing down from its strategic stockpile. Roberts, exasperated by events, indicated to shareholders that he had 'suggested to the Australian Government, it should either insist on this smuggling being stopped or allow Australian producers to smuggle the same tonnage'.[22] Shortly thereafter, in October 1985, the insolvency of the ITC meant that the buffer stock manager system collapsed with the closure of the two principal tin exchanges, the London Metals Exchange and Kuala

---

19 Renison Limited, 'Minutes of an Operating Committee Meeting', 2 April 1984, RGCA, Box 12254.
20 Renison Limited, 'Minutes of an Operating Committee Meeting', 29 July 1985, RGCA, Box 12254.
21 Renison Goldfields Consolidated Limited, 'Minutes of Meeting of Directors', 29 August 1985, p. 5, RGCA, Box 11328, BRD38/02.
22 Renison Goldfields Consolidated Limited, 'Chairman's Address to the Fifth Annual General Meeting', 25 October 1985, p. 8, RGCA, Box 14284, BRD38/07.

Lumpur Tin Market, and attendant turmoil and volatility in the global tin market. Large quantities of tin were introduced into the market, leading to a marked reduction in the tin price. Relative to the period between 1981 and 1986, the tin price received by Renison declined in Australian dollar terms by 32 per cent or over 50 per cent in real terms in the subsequent four-year period to 1990.

In the context of the crisis in world tin markets and decline in the tin price, Renison's operations in 1986 returned to a 24 hour, seven-day setting in an attempt to improve the unit cost of production. During the latter part of 1986, Renison did not sell tin concentrate into what remained a weak market. Budgetary planning for the 1987 financial year assumed a tin price of only $8,500 in the first half and the potential for an increase to $9,500 in the second half, lower than the cost of production. Placing the operation on a care and maintenance basis remained an option.[23]

In 1986, after production constraints were lifted, Renison moved from its previous practice of selling tin concentrate to smelters to an arrangement where it had the tin concentrate toll-treated, enabling the company to sell tin metal directly. This arrangement was handled by Tennant Trading from 1987. However, sales for the 1986 financial year were 31 per cent lower than the previous year; the average price received declined by 12 per cent and the contribution to group profit by Renison declined by 71 per cent to a historical low. While sales and profitability recovered in 1987, Renison's period as the prime contributor to RGC profitability had ended. Industrial disruption remained an ongoing issue. In 1987, the underground section of the Australian Workers' Union directed all of its members to take leave over Christmas, an action that was rejected by management. This action followed a range of industrial disputes including claims against management that it had been responsible for instigating police searches of some employees' homes.

In March 1988, the general manager of the Tin Division of RGC, John Mitchell, was transferred after a gruelling period in the role. Dick Winby was in the role for a short period before another manager, Mike Ayre, who had been general manager at Mount Lyell, was appointed general manager. Ayre's appointment was designed to make wholesale changes to an operation that was suffering challenges on a number of fronts.[24] With a cost of

---

23   Renison Limited, 'Minutes of an Operating Committee Meeting', 28 April 1986, RGCA, Box 12254.
24   Mike Ayre, personal communication, 30 October 2018.

production higher than the prevailing tin price, the outlook for profitability remained bleak. Industrial disputation and the power of the unions in disrupting management initiatives was endemic, while operationally there were challenges in mining and processing the complex ore body. Seven separate unions operated on site and were emboldened by previous management acquiescence to demands in more favourable periods of financial performance. The lost time injury rate was high with multiple trivial incidences of work-related time off work being taken. The mining activities suffered high dilution rates while mill recoveries were poor.

Despite the efforts of prior management, the company had not been able to arrest the decline in the parlous financial state of the operation. Ayre commenced a major process of organisational and operational restructure, which entailed changes at the management level of the operation, dismissing most of his departmental heads. His attitude, as recalled by one former colleague, was to convey to the management group that they were there 'to help the people in blue overalls do their job'; a sentiment not necessarily universally shared by the management team.[25] Workforce numbers were also required to be reduced. An initial phase, in March 1989, involved seeking voluntary retrenchments; 97 employees elected to take this option. This resulted in a substantial reduction in the workforce such that at June 1990 there were 345 employees compared to 524 in 1981.[26]

The resource life of the operation ranked as one of the greatest challenges. Despite a view prevalent at board and executive level that Renison had almost unlimited resources from which to draw, the reality was that with prevailing tin prices even the reserves level was under question if not able to be produced economically. It was essential for Renison to develop a new mine plan, combined with the implementation of operational efficiencies, to enable reserves to be mined economically. Coincidentally, in 1989 a more rigorous code for the determination and reporting of reserves was introduced in the Australian Stock Exchange listing rules and, under this framework, a comprehensive review of the reserves and resources of Renison was conducted.[27]

---

25 Colin Cannard, personal communication, 25 September 2018.
26 Renison Goldfields Consolidated Limited, *Annual Report & Notice of Meeting 1983*, p. 18; Renison Goldfields Consolidated Limited, *Annual Report 1993*, p. 23.
27 The code was the Joint Ore Reserves or JORC Code: Joint Ore Reserves Committee of the Australasian Institute of Mining and Metallurgy, Australian Institute of Geoscientists and Minerals Council of Australia (JORC), *Australasian Code of Mineral Resources and Ore Reserves (The JORC Code)*, 1999.

The reserve and resource estimation process was complex, given the multitude of ore bodies and need for decisions about realistic, economic cut-off grades. In 1989, prior to the exercise, proved and probable reserves were estimated at 5.5 million tonnes, with a view that there were a further 20 million to 25 million tonnes likely to be available for mining. It was this latter category of less well-defined resources that provided what turned out to be a false confidence of an extended operational base for Renison. After the completion of the reserve and resource estimation process, proved and probable reserves reduced by over 40 per cent. The categorisation of available resources, likely to be developable under then current assumptions, was reduced by half while a large level of the much less likely to be developed resources, forming the backbone of previous estimates of mine life, was removed completely.[28] What had been viewed as a mine life of one to two decades became closer to six years. Ayre and Renison's senior geologist, Colin Cannard, flew to Sydney to explain the outcome to Anderson, the managing director, who was then facing portfolio challenges on a number of fronts.

During 1989 and 1990 greater attention to mine planning and ore body definition reduced the dilution rate, or amount of waste material sent with ore to the mill for processing. A reduction in the rejection rate of ore resulted in a heavy media plant being shut down. In 1989, this resulted in an 8 per cent improvement in mill head grades and achievement of record tin production, while in the following year mill recoveries increased further. The factor not assisting the operation was the continuing weak tin price, which decreased by over 20 per cent between 1989 and 1991. Employee numbers were reduced by a further 20 per cent in 1988 with a further reduction in 1989. Despite weak tin prices, a small profit was recorded in the 1990 financial year, although a loss of $12.7 million was recorded in the following year. The future of Renison, at one stage the largest financial contributor to CGFA and RGC, and the world's largest underground tin mine, was in the balance.

In April 1988, RGC's tin assets were expanded by the acquisition of a 75 per cent interest in Koba Tin, then undertaking mining operations on Bangka Island, Indonesia. The alluvial mining operation was supplemented by the introduction of a dredge and Koba Tin made its first

---

28 Reserves and resources after 1989 are not strictly comparable with pre-1989 figures because of the different methodology. However, 1991 proven reserves were reported as 2.2 million tonnes, compared with 1989 proven reserves of 4.6 million tonnes. See Appendix 6.

contribution to RGC in the 1989 financial year. In that year, Koba tin sales were at a similar level to those of Renison, but its financial contribution was markedly higher.[29] Renison remained in the RGC portfolio until its sale in 1998; Koba Tin continued to operate up to the time of the merger with Westralian Sands, and under the ownership of Iluka Resources until divested in 2002.

Mount Lyell—measures for survival

RGC's copper interests—the Mount Lyell operation in Tasmania and the Gunpowder Copper project in Queensland—posed challenges to the group during the first half of the 1980s. Gunpowder, a conventional mining and milling operation, had ceased in 1977 and the mine placed on a care and maintenance basis. A small-scale leaching operation was conducted, producing quantities of final product that offset part of the idling costs. The Japanese customers were keen for the mine to reopen as a source of copper concentrate. CGFA had given initial consideration to reopening the mine on a non-conventional basis using in situ leaching of the three ore bodies, given its assessment was that a conventional mining project would generate a low rate of return and have a long financial payback period.[30] In 1981 a pre-feasibility study commenced on a leaching project and, a year later with sufficient confidence gained from that study, a definitive feasibility study commenced for an operation using solvent extraction and electro-winning. As this option had an estimated capital expenditure of $26 million, and with the financial performance highly sensitive to the prevailing copper price, the decision was made to suspend leaching and cementation operations and place Gunpowder on care and maintenance.[31] Other parties were approached to buy the operation, with no success. In 1983, RGC's interest in Gunpowder increased to 83.55 per cent through the acquisition of Mitsubishi Development's interest. By November 1984 the disposal of the assets of Gunpowder had occurred.

---

29 Koba Tin had tin sales of 6,435 and 7,000 tonnes in 1989 and 1990, compared with Renison tin sales of 6,933 and 7,001 tonnes, respectively. The combined two-year contribution to RGC's operating profit before tax was $32.5 million for Koba Tin and $9 million for Renison (Renison Goldfields Consolidated Limited, *Annual Report 1993*, p. 23; Renison Goldfields Consolidated Limited, *Annual Report 1997*, p. 65).
30 Consolidated Gold Fields Australia Limited, 'Minutes of Meeting of Directors', 26 March 1980, p. 2, RGCA, Box 12272.
31 Renison Goldfields Consolidated Limited, 'Minutes of Meeting of Directors', 29 July 1982, p. 7, RGCA, Box 11328, BRD38.

15. THE INITIAL YEARS

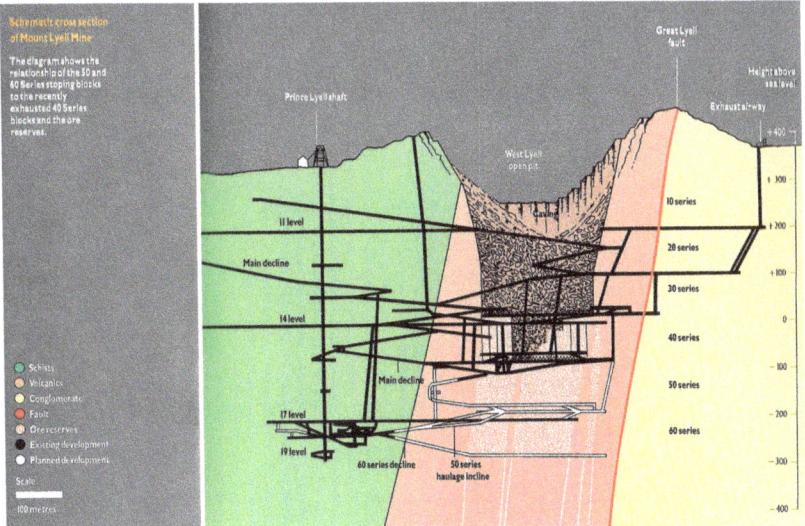

Figure 50. Mount Lyell cross-section showing mining through various series of ore bodies to the 50 series.
Source: Renison Goldfields Consolidated Limited, *Annual Report 1987*.

Since 1976, with cessation of work on the Prince Lyell shaft project, forward planning at the Mount Lyell operation had been on the basis of a three-year rolling life. The adaptation of decline haulage systems allowed ore extraction from the Prince Lyell 20 series, half of the 30 series and an ability to commit to mine the Prince Lyell 40 series. By 1984, the 20 series and a portion of the 30 series had been developed. Selective satellite mining occurred at the Cape Horn and North Lyell areas. This approach had avoided major capital expenditure required for deepening the Prince Lyell shaft while the purchase of modern equipment and technical innovation had reduced operating costs. However, the price of copper continued to decline in real terms, with substantial financial losses incurred. In 1977 an operating loss of $10.7 million before tax was recorded, with a write-down of fixed assets of $16.8 million. Meanwhile, a drilling program had produced encouraging results. The challenge for the future of the mine was whether a commitment to mine ore at deeper levels at Prince Lyell and Western Tharsis could be justified economically.

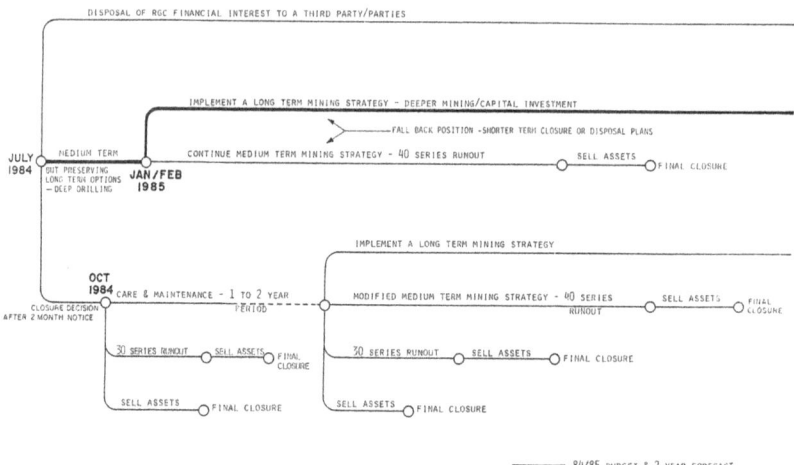

Figure 51. Alternative operating strategies for Mount Lyell under consideration as part of 1984/85 budgetary planning.
Source: Internal RGC document (copy held by the author).

Mount Lyell recorded losses from 1982 to 1985. The company retained a pessimistic view of the copper price outlook, associated with a change in long-term demand for copper due to substitution by other products, increasingly efficient usages of the product and global production capacity in excess of existing demand. Moreover, the scope for further, material cost reductions at Mount Lyell was viewed as limited.[32] In 1982, the board of RGC considered options in relation to the future, including disposal of Mount Lyell, placing the mine on care and maintenance for one to two years, or implementing a long-term mining strategy that would entail the development of the 50 and 60 series. Radical changes in operating arrangements were considered, including the introduction of a four-day paid week along with extended periods of mine closure. With losses running at $1 million per month, closure was viewed as the likely outcome at completion of mining operations from the 30 series, estimated to be in 1985. The board urged management to identify options to attract alternative industries to Queenstown to make use of infrastructure, as a means of offsetting the devastating effects closure would have on the local community. Consideration was given to acquiring an overseas company, with a view to relocating part of its operations to Tasmania.

---

32 Renison Goldfields Consolidated, 'Minutes of Meeting of Directors', 26 August 1981, p. 8, RGCA, Box 11328, BRD38.

During the three financial years 1982 to 1984, Mount Lyell's accumulated losses before tax amounted to $15 million, reversing the profits of the previous three years. In 1984, in view of the financial position and the depressed copper price outlook, contingency planning for closure was updated.

In the same year, a proposal was prepared by an external adviser for the reorganisation of Mount Lyell, as part of a process for exploring divestment options. One option was for the establishment of a listed copper trust in which Mount Lyell would be held, with the Tasmanian Government viewed as a potential unit holder. This approach, if implemented, would avoid the need for RGC to make a direct capital investment to develop the deeper ore horizons, as well as potentially avoid future rehabilitation issues, a factor increasingly to the fore in management and director considerations. It was recognised that the trust proposal would be difficult to implement; a necessary precondition for its establishment included a substantially higher copper price, at a time when long-term demand for copper was viewed as in decline. Furthermore, mine infrastructure was old and incurring increased costs to maintain and the operation was noted for entrenched labour problems.[33] The decision recommended, as a result of a strategic review, was that the mine be closed. It was determined that the financially and socially responsible manner to implement this decision was to adopt a medium-term plan and cease mining at the completion of the 40 series ore body, estimated to be in 1989.[34]

Direct forms of government financial support were considered essential for the mine to continue to operate under this plan. A period of intense engagement with the Tasmanian and Commonwealth governments followed. In 1982 approaches were made to the Tasmanian Government for financial assistance in the form of relief from payroll tax. In addition, approaches were made to Mitsubishi, the buyer of Mount Lyell's copper concentrate, for a reduction in smelting charges.[35] While government assistance and other relief measures were sought, mine closure planning continued. However, planning also considered arrangements for Mount

---

33 'Report Prepared for Renison Goldfields Consolidated Limited on the Mt Lyell Reorganisation', August 1984, RGCA, Box 1091.
34 AG Robertson/RM Patterson to Executive Committee, 'Review of Strategic Options for Mount Lyell Copper Division', 11 September, 1984, National Archives of Australia, Tasmania (NAAT), NS3357/1/187.
35 Renison Goldfields Consolidated Limited, 'Minutes of Meeting of Directors', 29 July 1982, p. 4, RGCA, Box 11328, BRD38.

Lyell to continue with a reconfiguration and reduction in the workforce and the commencement of drilling of the 40 series to allow mining and ore retrieval through an access ramp from the main decline to the surface. Planning was also begun for the Prince Lyell crushing and hoisting project, as the basis for potentially accessing the deeper 50 and 60 series ore bodies.

In March 1984, Roberts and the London chairman and chief executive officer, Rudolph Agnew, met the Tasmanian premier to advise him of the financial state of the operation. They provided details of the historical operation of Mount Lyell since 1970, including the level of profits earned, number of employees and contribution to the Tasmanian economy. In effect, the Tasmanian premier was 'put on notice regarding the extent of RGC's concern about the continuing unprofitability of the Mount Lyell operation'.[36] Approaches were also made to Commonwealth Government ministers outlining the parlous financial state of the operation. Senator Peter Walsh, the Commonwealth minister for resources and energy, visited Queenstown and addressed the workforce. He indicated to assembled workers that there would be no Commonwealth Government assistance for Mount Lyell. He had to be escorted out of the back door of the football club to avoid the ire of the assembled workers.[37]

At a subsequent meeting with the Tasmanian premier in August 1984, which was preceded by a series of strikes at the operation, Roberts advised that the losses being incurred 'were becoming unbearable'.[38] The premier was advised that the only option, if the mine was to remain open beyond the current 30 series, would be if the company achieved a 'guarantee that it would not have to bear any losses past that time'.[39] With financial support from the Tasmanian Government it was envisaged that production could be extended to the exhaustion of the 40 series and potentially provide the opportunity to proceed with the development of deeper zones. The company recognised that the continuation of production, along with a potential recovery in the copper price, were the only factors that may improve the prospects for the sale of the operation.

---

36   Renison Goldfields Consolidated Limited, 'Minutes of Meeting of Directors', 29 March 1984, p. 2, RGCA, Box 11328, BRD38/02.
37   Mike Ayre, personal communication, 21 October 2018.
38   Renison Goldfields Consolidated Limited, 'Minutes of Meeting of Directors', 29 July 1982, p. 4, RGCA, Box 11328, BRD38.
39   Renison Goldfields Consolidated Limited, 'Minutes of Meeting of Directors', 30 August 1984, p. 3 and 25 September 1984, pp. 5–6, RGCA, Box 11328, BRD38/02.

15. THE INITIAL YEARS

At a further meeting with the premier on 17 October 1984, Roberts discussed the copper trust concept through the formation of a new company. It was proposed that this trust be one-third owned by RGC and two-thirds by the Tasmanian Government. The trust would acquire the mining lease and sell all of the equipment to a commercial leasing company, with RGC providing management services at cost.[40] This proposal gained little support from the Tasmanian Government. Later in the month, Roberts followed up in writing, warning of the 'desperate situation' confronting Mount Lyell:

> Despite its remarkable improvement in productivity in recent years, the mine lost $4.8 million in the year to 30th June last and that, at current prices, the losses are accumulating at a rate of $1 million per month … We are thus looking at possible losses in this financial year of $12 million having suffered losses in the three preceding years totalling $14.9 million … further significant cost reductions are not achievable and it is impossible for the RGC Group to continue to absorb losses of the magnitude currently being suffered.[41]

Roberts advised the premier that, despite a formal decision not having been made by the RGC board, he believed there was no option other than to close the mine at the end of either 1985 or 1988. In a form of brinkmanship, he explained:

> At this stage I would like to make one thing quite clear—my Company is not seeking Government assistance at all and is strongly of the opinion that it is in the best interests of all concerned to close the mine at the end of the 30 Series—that is the Short Term Plan … in 1985.[42]

The company's view was that some of the Mount Lyell workforce could be absorbed by the Hydro Electric Commission that was establishing a presence in Queenstown to undertake extensive tunnelling works. Mount Lyell could make available its stock of 250 houses and 50 flats, along with workshops and other facilities. For Roberts, it was a fortuitous opportunity that Mount Lyell's closure plans and those of the Hydro

---

40 Letter from MJ Roberts, Executive Chairman RGC, to Premier of Tasmania, 17 October 1984, RGCA, Box 1091.
41 Letter from MJ Roberts, Executive Chairman RGC, to Premier of Tasmania, 30 October 1984, p. 1, RGCA, Box 1091.
42 ibid., p. 2.

Electric Commission might coincide. RGC had come close to deciding to close the Mount Lyell operation. However, Roberts added in his letter to the Tasmanian premier:

> Notwithstanding ... the above ... should the Tasmanian and/or the Federal Governments believe that the benefits arising from extending operations to 1989 in terms of direct and indirect employment, tax revenues export earnings and State and regional finances, justify the cost of support, then we would be prepared to co-operate with Government/s in the development and implementation of a plan to achieve this.[43]

It was made clear that it was 'absolutely fundamental to the Company's willingness to co-operate' that it be at no cost to the company, 'whether from a cash or profit point of view'.[44] Discussions proceeded on the basis of the Tasmanian Government making available financial assistance to support continued operation. Meanwhile, concessions were negotiated with the Emu Bay Railway, which agreed to a reduction in its haulage charges, while Mitsubishi agreed to a reduction in refining charges.

In 1984 and 1985 further reductions in the workforce were achieved through early retirements, while increased rental charges were applied for employee housing and a decision was made to cease intake into the company's apprenticeship scheme. By February 1985 the retrenchment of 107 employees was completed following voluntary redundancies and the early retirement of over 50 workers. During the years 1983 to 1986, the Mount Lyell workforce had been reduced from over 700 to 525 employees.

The major structural changes in the workforce, achieved by management with cooperation of the workforce, meant that for the 1984 financial year production was the highest since the start of the Prince Lyell Extended Plan and productivity of copper per employee the highest ever achieved.[45] Despite the reduced number of workers, there was an improvement in operational performance, in terms of ore treated and the grade recovered, with a commencement of the development of the next ore deposit, the 40 series ores. Evaluation of the 50 series and 60 series ore bodies also provided encouragement that both contained substantial reserves at

---

43   ibid., p. 5.
44   ibid., p. 6.
45   Mount Lyell Copper Division, 'Minutes of Operating Committee Meeting', 25 July 1984, p. 2, NAAT, NS3924, Items, 347–359.

favourable grades.⁴⁶ Completion of the extension of the main decline of the Prince Lyell shaft to the 50 series ore body, along with completion of the underground crusher, were expected to allow greater efficiencies by enabling ore haulage over shorter distances, while higher copper grades and an increased gold content at depth were also expected to improve the operation's financial performance.⁴⁷ However, with the copper price necessary for a break-even financial outcome being well above the level RGC was budgeting, Mount Lyell was again at the crossroads.⁴⁸

Ayre, the general manager of Mount Lyell, had adopted an approach of 'opening the books', advising the workforce of the financial circumstances of the operation. While there were sporadic industrial disputes, usually influenced by broader union claims, workers and the unions 'put their shoulder to the wheel' and were generally supportive of management's efforts.⁴⁹ A 'self-help' package was agreed with the workforce, which included continuation of a 40-hour week, agreement to cooperate with the company to achieve efficient workplace practices and the centralisation of some functions, a 'no-strike' agreement and the retrenchment in early 1985 of 87 employees in addition to the 37 employees already planned to be retrenched. The Queenstown Council was asked to reduce its rates by 50 per cent. It agreed to a 25 per cent reduction, which saved the company $30,000 for the 1986 financial year, while an increase in house rentals and reduction in heating subsidies for employees, along with other measures, were expected to reduce operating costs by over $9 million.⁵⁰

By December 1984, after a further meeting with the Tasmanian premier, Roberts was able to set out a formal package for agreement, which included the sale of the company's interest in the Lake Margaret Power station to the Hydro Electric Commission for $5 million, an immediate cash payment by the Tasmanian Government of $5 million and government acceptance that Mount Lyell would not be responsible for any rehabilitation other

---

46 Estimated at 5.1 million tonnes for the 50 and 60 series, at a tin grade of 1.77 per cent and 1.95 per cent, respectively (Mount Lyell Copper Division, 'Minutes of Operating Committee Meeting', 24 October 1984, NAAT, NS3924, Items, 347–359).
47 Renison Goldfields Consolidated Limited, 'Minutes of Meeting of Directors', 29 July 1982, p. 4, RGCA, Box 11328, BRD38.
48 In 1984 the break-even cash costs for Mount Lyell were estimated to be $2,200 and $2,580 per tonne for the 1984/85 and 1985/86 financial years, respectively, with a budgeted copper price for 1984/85 of $1,550 per tonne (RGC Memorandum, 2 August 1984, p. 2, RGCA, Box 1091).
49 Mike Ayre, personal communication, 21 October 2018.
50 Mount Lyell Copper Division, 'Minutes of Operating Committee Meeting', 27 November 1985, p. 1, NAAT, NS3924, Items 360–373.

than the removal of plant and surface equipment.⁵¹ Overtures were made by the Tasmanian Government for matching Commonwealth Government assistance. While Prime Minister Bob Hawke did not accede to providing direct financial support, additional Commonwealth funds were provided to the Tasmanian Government with it able to allocate these funds as it saw fit.⁵² Mount Lyell, in effect, had been living on a knife edge in terms of its continuation. One former RGC executive recalled that, when travelling in Queenstown on holiday with his wife, they reached the shopping centre and word had got around that there was a director in town who had come to Queenstown to shut the mine.⁵³

With the devaluation of the Australian dollar, Mount Lyell's cash break-even copper price declined to $1,810 in March 1985, relative to a prevailing copper price of $1,900.⁵⁴ The financial assistance and market conditions strengthened the board's confidence of the prospects for Mount Lyell. In April 1985, when the copper price had increased to $2,300, forward selling of product was considered, leading directors to contemplate an outcome that had previously seemed inconceivable: 'the possibility of Mount Lyell reporting a profit, as against the large losses being projected when assistance from the Tasmanian Government was accepted'.⁵⁵

While continuing to be loss-making in 1985, Mount Lyell returned to moderate profitability in 1986. During 1987, the stabilisation and improvement of the financial performance enabled planning to commence on studies for mining to the 50 series and 60 series, with an intention to produce at a reduced annual throughput but with recovery of higher-grade ore.⁵⁶ These studies noted achievements in improving productivity, as well as a markedly improved geological understanding of the Prince Lyell ore body at depth. In turn, these provided encouragement for the future of the Mount Lyell operation with an internal assessment that, with future planned mining grades, 'Mount Lyell ... cannot be considered a low grade

---

51 Letter from Max Roberts, Executive Chairman, to Premier of Tasmania, 21 December 1984, p. 1, RGCA Box 1091.
52 Letter from RJL Hawke to Premier of Tasmania, 30 January 1985, RGC, Box 1091.
53 Tony Hemingway, personal communication, 4 December 2018.
54 Renison Goldfields Consolidated Limited, 'Minutes of Meeting of Directors', 28 March 1985, p. 4, RGCA, Box 11328, BRD38/02.
55 Renison Goldfields Consolidated Limited, 'Minutes of Meeting of Directors', 24 April 1985, p. 3, RGCA, Box 11328, BRD38/02.
56 Renison Goldfields Consolidated, 'Minutes of Meeting of Directors', 27 November 1987, p. 5 and 29 January 1987, pp. 5–6, RGCA, Box 11329, BRD38/03.

copper mine'.⁵⁷ Extension of the operation would require an estimated $23 million of capital expenditure. The Mount Lyell management, with the endorsement of the RGC board, proceeded to operate the mine to the end of the 40 series, estimated to be at the end of 1989, with confidence to be able to proceed to the development of the 50 and 60 series.⁵⁸

Mount Lyell's future had once again been at a crossroad. Anderson advised his colleagues of the main features of the arrangements for Mount Lyell progressing with 50 and 60 series mining, thereby extending the mining operations by five years to 1994. The approach entailed improved productivity by lifting the cut-off grade and, in so doing, overcoming 'a major stumbling block of previous long term plans, namely high capital expenditures in early years resulting in large cash exposures'.⁵⁹ Anderson advised that 'a possible extension of the life of the Mt. Lyell mine could have attractive upside'. He also warned: 'It certainly has considerable downside'.⁶⁰

The agreement with the Tasmanian Government was formalised in March 1987, referred to as the Prince Lyell 1995 extension. A commitment to maintain employment within stipulated ranges was agreed, although the company would be discharged from these obligations if the copper price fell below defined levels over any continuous six-month period.⁶¹ The company's announcement of the agreement pointed to the benefits of the devaluation of the Australian dollar for mine profitability, while completion of the work on shaft hoisting and the underground crusher facilitated the mining of the new horizons.⁶²

During 1988, delineation drilling of the deeper ore bodies began. A haulage shaft was established from the existing Prince Lyell shaft and an underground crusher installed. Production commenced from the 50 series in 1989. However, a review of mine plans indicated a lower cut-off

---

57   The Mount Lyell Mining and Railway Company Limited, 'The Mount Lyell Extended Plan 1987', p. 2, NAAT, NS3357/1/129.
58   Renison Goldfields Consolidated Limited, 'Minutes of Meeting of Directors', 28 February 1985 and 28 April 1985, RGCA, Box 11328, BRD38/02; Renison Goldfields Consolidated Limited, *Annual Report 1985*, p. 14.
59   Campbell Anderson to Non-Executive Directors, 5 November 1986, p. 2, RGCA, Box 1361.
60   ibid., emphasis in original.
61   Letter from C McC Anderson to Hon Robin T Gray, Premier of Tasmania, 14 March 1987; letter from Premier of Tasmania to Mr C McC Anderson, 16 March 1987, RGCA, Box 1091.
62   'RGC Announcement to the Australian Associated Stock Exchanges and the Press, Extension of Operations at Mt Lyell Copper Mine', 16 March 1987, RGCA, 91/207, Box 1091.

copper grade that, when associated with low ore availability, necessitated attempting to improve the competitive position of Mount Lyell yet again, particularly in the context of the commencement of new, competing international sources of copper production.[63] Closure of Mount Lyell was once more under management and board consideration.

Mineral sands—east to west coast

Mineral sands constituted the largest component of the RGC portfolio. At the time of RGC's formation, Associated Minerals Consolidated (AMC) had 17 mining and processing facilities. These encompassed operations on the east coast of New South Wales; on North Stradbroke Island, Queensland; at Capel and Eneabba, Western Australia; and in the United States at Green Cove Springs in Florida, as well as a zirconia plant in New Hampshire. The company operated two synthetic rutile kilns. Mineral sands leases were held on Moreton Island and exploration activities were conducted on Tiwi Islands, Northern Territory, and on the east coast of the United States.

Mineral sands was initially a drag on the group's performance but rebounded to make a major contribution in the second half of the decade. Operating challenges featured prominently, reflected in declining ore grades, particularly at Eneabba and Capel, and production inefficiencies associated with the commencement of the Florida operation. Increasing costs were a feature of the division. The Eneabba expansion project, designed to address the challenge of lower grades by achieving higher rutile and synthetic rutile production, struggled to achieve targeted output. Production was below projected estimates with a corresponding increase in unit costs. Similarly, the Florida operation was initially producing at approximately half of projected estimates.

There were other issues related to RGC's mineral sands division. Directors had been appraised before RGC's formation in 1981 that, in relation to investment market feedback, there was 'a good deal of unhappiness with regard to A.M.C.', with the 'company having had two rights issues

---

63 Renison Goldfields Consolidated Limited, *Annual Report 1990*, p. 18.

in recent times and then passing its interim dividend'.[64] In 1983, WP Murphy, the executive director of marketing, also advised directors of the decline of AMC's standing in the mineral sands market:

> Mr Murphy commented that AMC, had not, in its recent history, been well-regarded as a supplier in the mineral sands market, and thus, an immediate priority is to regain AMC's previous high standing, thereby increasing its share of the market … [T]he Chairman explained that the fault, which led to the deterioration of AMC's standing, appeared to be with the Management structure existing in AMC over the previous four years.[65]

The company also faced reputational issues related to historical practices in the disposal of mineral sands processing by-products, including monazite. Health concerns related to the disposal of tailings in New South Wales were raised in the state parliament and led to an agreement under which AMC bore some of the cost of cleaning up areas of contamination at Bryon Bay.

The financial challenges facing AMC were evident before RGC's formation in 1981 with concerns about the high level of stock being held by it and other producers, the cancellation of orders for part of the company's synthetic rutile production and the Florida operation encountering operational issues associated with the dredging of indurated material.[66] The outlook for the 1983 financial year was bleak, with $50 million of assets employed and a loss forecast. The board of RGC asked management of AMC to present alternatives for 'returning AMC's operations to profitability'.[67] Roberts advised AMC's management that they would have to operate on internally generated funds in the future. He emphasised to the division that it 'could not continue to be a cash drain on the Group'.[68] Faced with poor financial results, weak markets and 'strongly escalating costs', a reorganisation of the business began in the second half of 1981

---

64 Consolidated Gold Fields Australia Limited, 'Minutes of Meeting of Directors', 22 April 1981, RGCA, Box 12260, RGC 11518.
65 Renison Goldfields Consolidated Limited, 'Minutes of Meeting of Directors', 26 May 1983, p. 8, RGCA, Box 11328, BRD38.
66 Renison Goldfields Consolidated Limited, 'Minutes of Meeting of Directors', 28 August 1982, p. 9, RGCA, Box 11328, BRD38/02.
67 Renison Goldfields Consolidated Limited, 'Minutes of Meeting of Directors', 26 August 1982, p. 6, RGCA, Box 11328, BRD38/02.
68 Renison Goldfields Consolidated Limited, 'Minutes of Meeting of Directors', 28 April 1983, p. 7, RGCA, Box 11328, BRD38.

and continued through to 1983.[69] The reorganisation occurred in the context of a worldwide recession and business conditions that deterred customers from confirming orders. In the case of Eneabba, the situation was compounded in 1982 by Kerr-McGee, a pigment customer, not accepting Eneabba ilmenite due to its high radiation levels and DuPont delaying acceptance of synthetic rutile.[70] The largest synthetic rutile kiln, plant B, was idled in December 1982.

The head office was relocated from the former AMC site at Southport in Queensland to Perth, with a reduction of personnel. Marketing offices in Southport, Sydney, Tokyo and London were closed. Further rationalisation of the Australian east-coast operations took place and the company's zirconia facility in New Hampshire was sold in 1984. In the same year, the company warned that the Commonwealth Government's denial of export permits on Moreton Bay would lead to the closure of the group's east-coast operations at the end of 1985. This subsequently occurred.[71] In 1985, the company advised that it had ceased all mining operations in New South Wales, with poor market conditions compounding the effect of restrictive government actions on the industry. This brought to a close a 52-year involvement by the company on the east coast of Australia.

The program for improvement in operational performance, which included continued investment at Eneabba, Capel and Florida, began to show results. At Eneabba, capital expenditure to expand production, which began in 1981, contributed to a reduction in unit costs of over 20 per cent by 1983. By 1984, production had increased by 25 per cent through various initiatives, including relocation of the mining plant to enable mining of a higher-grade part of the ore body.[72] At Capel, ilmenite production was reduced and new mining and processing methods were introduced, including a bucket-wheel excavator that was relocated from the Jerusalem Creek operation in New South Wales, reducing mining costs by 40 per cent, leading to improved profitability. Synthetic rutile production was also constrained.

---

69 Renison Goldfields Consolidated Limited, *Annual Report 1982*, p. 13.
70 Renison Goldfields Consolidated Limited, 'Minutes of Meeting of Directors', 25 February 1982, p. 2, RGCA, Box 11328, BRD38.
71 Renison Goldfields Consolidated Limited, *Annual Report and Notice of Meeting 1983*, p. 4; Renison Goldfields Consolidated Limited, *Annual Report 1984*.
72 Renison Goldfields Consolidated Limited, *Annual Report 1984*.

In the 1983 financial year, despite a 29 per cent decline in sales tonnages and a 'significant deterioration in rutile and synthetic rutile prices', the completion of capital expenditure programs had led to 'substantial cost reductions' and the 'curtailment of production [had] brought a significant turnaround in results'.[73] After suffering a loss of $5.5 million in 1982, this figure was reduced to a loss of $287,000 in 1983 and in 1984 the company recorded a profit of $5.3 million. The adjustment to the business had been substantial. In the 1984 financial year, AMC's production levels commenced at 60 per cent of capacity, allowing a reduction of product inventory. This and the closure of other industry capacity and an improvement in demand meant that RGC's mineral sands production lifted progressively to 'approximately 90% of capacity at year end'.[74] During the year, synthetic rutile kilns A and B were reactivated. Plans were also put in place for an additional kiln to be located at Narngulu, near Geraldton. Expansionary activities at Eneabba and Green Cove Springs resulted in combined rutile, zircon and synthetic rutile production increasing from 324,000 tonnes in aggregate to 590,000 tonnes over the five-year period from 1985 to 1990. Sales volumes of these products increased by a similar level.

Radioactivity related to elevated levels of uranium and thorium in some of the ilmenite produced at Eneabba posed a potential challenge to product acceptance by customers. The solution was further technical advances that led to a new synthetic rutile product—synthetic rutile enhanced process (SREP)—which typically had a higher titanium dioxide content and uranium and thorium levels within customer specifications. SREP was more expensive to produce and its economic attractiveness as a product proved not to be compelling.

The context for the further development of synthetic rutile included favourable long-term demand forecasts for high-grade titanium dioxide feedstocks, associated with the expected continued adoption of the chloride pigment process in preference to the sulphate pigment process for the production of titanium pigment. In addition, the reduced availability of rutile, given the decline in east-coast operations, was also a factor. The advent of a mineral sands operation in Sierra Leone represented a new source of rutile; however, there were concerns by pigment producers of

---

73 Renison Goldfields Consolidated Limited, *Annual Report and Notice of Meeting 1983*.
74 ibid.

country risk and reliability of supply from this source. These concerns were to be borne out by the violent events associated with rebel incursion into the country in the early 1990s.

In a note to directors, Anderson conveyed the commercial imperative to proceed with a third synthetic rutile kiln:

> If AMC does not offer such supplies it is our judgment that SCM and NL [National Lead] will be obliged to step up their own exploration activities to secure rutile and/or ilmenite resources. If they are successful in locating suitable ilmenite resources … they could be in a position of going into SR manufactures themselves. Given that Westralian Sands SR plant is commissioned satisfactorily and operates to design specification, AMC's hitherto technological monopoly will no longer exist. There is no effective patent protection … The commitment to and timing of Plant C is therefore seen by AMC as a defensive, as well as profitable, investment.[75]

RGC's synthetic rutile developments progressed with the construction of the additional plant—plant C—at Narngulu in 1986. SCM, a major pigment producer, effectively underwrote the development of plant C with an 80,000 tonnes per annum commitment to the synthetic rutile product. Ilmenite feedstock was supplied from Eneabba. In combination with the plants at Capel, RGC's synthetic rutile capacity was planned to increase to 172,500 tonnes per annum. Plant C was commissioned in June 1987, although it did not reach nameplate capacity. The plant was designed to produce a 92.5 per cent titanium dioxide product, referred to as premium synthetic rutile. Contracts for the product provided for price bonuses or penalties for titanium dioxide content either above or below the 92.5 per cent level. The failure to meet this standard, as well as defined chemical specifications, created a situation in which price penalties were incurred. These adversely affected the financial returns generated from RGC's synthetic rutile business. The lower titanium dioxide content and pigment plant operational implications in using a product with finer characteristics unintentionally placed RGC's synthetic rutile product in direct competition with slag and, in particular, the higher-grade slag products that Rio Tinto's Canadian operation planned to produce.

---

75 Campbell Anderson, 'Note to Directors Renison Goldfields Consolidated Limited, AMC—Plant C Project', 13 May 1985. SCM Chemicals was acquired by Hanson Plc in 1986.

In the view of the RGC marketing team, the inconsistency in achieving a premium-grade synthetic rutile and concerns with radiation levels led some customers to the use of slag. In fact, one pigment customer, SCM, advised RGC's marketing personnel in 1994 that 'RGC must have a viable SREP product and that … operations in W.A. must lift their game'.[76]

As in previous periods, the possibility of some form of industry rationalisation was considered. This included a combination of the southwest Western Australian operations of RGC and Westralian Sands. RGC also remained alert to the possibility of acquiring the other producer at Eneabba: Allied Eneabba. Discussions were undertaken with Westralian Sands and Allied Eneabba in regard to the rationalisation of the industry. According to the chairman's feedback to the board in February 1982, Westralian Sands seemed in favour of some form of rationalisation and 'may even be keen to buy us out'.[77] Other means for the rationalisation of the industry remained under consideration and, in April 1982, these included discussions with Western Mining Corporation, which was believed to be examining possible re-entry into the mineral sands sector.

As early as 1974, CGFA was in discussion with DuPont, the major shareholder in Allied Eneabba, in relation to a potential joint venture or joint marketing arrangement at Eneabba. In 1979, CGFA had approached Allied Eneabba and held the view that 'Dupont [sic] had not rejected the idea of rationalising the Eneabba field by means of [a] joint venture with A.M.C.'.[78] AMC was of the view that the acquisition of Allied Eneabba's leases would improve the company's market share and make possible cost savings through the rationalisation of operations. Allied Eneabba was struggling with high debt and after returning to profitability in the first half of 1984, suffered an operating loss. A further loss was recorded in 1985. Operational problems were compounded by mining challenges in parts of the ore body with rubbly material, or 'coffee rock', that Allied Eneabba's mining equipment was not suited to handling.

---

76 RGC Mineral Sands Customer Call Report, 30–31 August 1994, RGCA, Box 9573, File C93 005.
77 Renison Goldfields Consolidated Limited, 'Minutes of Meeting of Directors', 25 February 1982, p. 3, RGCA, Box 11328, BRD38.
78 Consolidated Gold Fields Australia Limited, 'Minutes of Meeting of Directors', 22 June 1979, p. 3, RGCA, Box 12272.

In this context, in 1984, RGC gave further consideration to holding discussions with DuPont to 'ascertain their attitude to a possible acquisition'.[79] Instead, DuPont approached RGC to explore the possibility of it making a takeover bid for Allied Eneabba. DuPont had become increasingly concerned with Allied Eneabba's operational and financial performance and level of debt. According to an RGC document:

> DuPont has doubts about Allied Eneabba's financial viability in the medium to longer term ... [and] saw RGC as having demonstrated financial strength and sand mining expertise to achieve these economies and to guarantee a stable source of supply to all of Allied Eneabba's customers.[80]

RGC made a takeover bid for Allied Eneabba in October 1985. It followed an agreement with DuPont to purchase its 50 per cent interest at a lower price than offered to other shareholders via an amendment to the ilmenite supply contract in place between DuPont and Allied Eneabba. DuPont, at the time, was the only pigment producer able to use Allied Eneabba ilmenite. By February 1986 RGC had acquired control of Allied Eneabba. With the acquisition, RGC became the sole producer in what had become the main mineral sands–producing province in Australia.

As a result of a surge in demand for zircon in refractory usage in Japan and increased usage in tile and sanitary glaze applications, associated with a reduction in supply from the east coast of Australia, the zircon price increased from around $90 per tonne in 1980 to over $550 per tonne in 1990. Sales revenue, which had remained relatively flat over the first half of the 1980s, showed a fourfold increase from 1985 to 1990. Aided by generally robust market conditions, mineral sands remained the most important operating division of RGC. In every year from 1985 to 1990, mineral sands was by far the largest earnings contributor. The negative or low return on assets, which had been a feature of the period to 1984, was reversed in the subsequent years to 1990. In 1990, in what was the peak year of performance for both RGC and mineral sands, mineral sands contributed $176 million pre-tax to a total RGC pre-tax operating profit of $173 million. The only other asset in the RGC portfolio that came close to the contribution of mineral sands was the Porgera gold operation,

---

79 'Arwon Acquisition Proposal', 8 October 1984, RGCA, Box 11932, RGC 11472-02. Arwon was the RGC code word for the Allied Eneabba acquisition.
80 Renison Goldfields Consolidated Limited, 'Takeover of Allied Eneabba Limited' (draft RGC submission to FIRB), p. 8 (copy held by the author).

after it commenced production in 1990 (see Chart 13, Appendix 4). RGC's profit after tax increased from $24 million in 1985 to $116 million in 1990, with the return on shareholders' equity increasing from less than 10 per cent in 1985 to an average above 20 per cent during the next five years. However, in the five years following 1991, a marked reversal in the financial performance of RGC occurred, due in large part to a decline in the financial performance of the mineral sands division.

16

NEW INTERESTS AND DIVERSIFICATION

Exploration remained a key basis for the planned growth of the company. From 1984, Renison Goldfields Consolidated (RGC) reassumed full responsibility for its exploration program from the previous joint funding arrangement with Consolidated Gold Fields. Roger Shakesby was the general manager for exploration, located in the Sydney office of RGC, with exploration offices in Canberra, Queensland and Western Australia. With the appointment of Colin Cannard as general manager of exploration in 1994, the exploration function was relocated to Perth.

Exploration and business prospects evaluated included the Porgera gold deposit in Papua New Guinea in conjunction with join venture partners Placer Pacific and Mount Isa Mines, exploration tenements at Wau in Papua New Guinea, an offshore marine aggregates deposit in New South Wales, the Glendell coal project in the Hunter Valley of New South Wales with Dalgety Australia, gold and base metal exploration in Australia, and a gold prospect in the Philippines. Mineral sands exploration was conducted in Australia and in the United States; RGC discovered major mineral sands resources in the east coast of the United States in the 1980s and in Victoria, Australia in the 1990s. The marine aggregates project involved evaluative work in association with Amey Roadstone Constructions, a company in which the London parent had a major investment. The potential for a public inquiry and the anticipated public concerns associated with this activity eventually led to this project being discontinued. The rights to an interest in a large steaming coal deposit at Eneabba in Western Australia were acquired from private owners in 1980.

Exploration determined sufficient reserves to support the feed for a major power station and while evaluation work was undertaken with the State Electricity Commission, the project did not proceed.

As part of a diversification of the RGC portfolio, the company had had an interest in oil exploration and in 1981 evaluated the means by which entry could be obtained to a potential oil field, from acquiring an existing company, through to farm-in deals. Involvement was achieved, not by direct RGC exploration activity, but by acquiring an interest in an oil and exploration company, Minora Resources, with an initial $5 million investment. RGC funded the company's exploration efforts and in December 1984 Minora was listed, at the time the largest single cash raising by an Australian exploration company. RGC had an initial 16.67 per cent interest and was the largest shareholder. RGC held the interest in Minora, increasing to 33.3 per cent, until 1995 when the company was delisted following a scheme of arrangement with Discovery Petroleum.

From exploration activity, several projects were developed and brought into production from 1985 to 1990. RGC earned a 49 per cent interest in the Pine Creek gold deposit, 220 kilometres south-east of Darwin in the Northern Territory, by a payment to Enterprise Gold Mines of $1.5 million in 1983. A definitive feasibility study was undertaken and RGC increased its equity by a further 11 per cent. The joint venture for the development of Pine Creek was incorporated in 1985 and commissioning of the mine occurred in late 1985. RGC mined Pine Creek from the main, Enterprise Pit, until 1993 as well as other pits until mining ended in late 1994. The Lucky Draw gold project, at Burraga, near Bathurst, New South Wales, was discovered by RGC in 1985. Commissioning began in 1988 and continued until 1991. In Tasmania, exploration undertaken 30 kilometres north of Queenstown since 1968 led to a joint venture between Mount Lyell and Getty Oil in 1976, which was then transformed into a joint venture with Little River Goldfields that would lead to the discovery of the Henty gold deposit. A feasibility study for the Henty project was undertaken in 1991 and 1992 and production from the Henty mine commenced in 1996.[1] In 1988, the Mount Coolon gold project in Queensland was subject to a feasibility study. Ore reserves were not to expectations and deeper drilling was unsuccessful in locating ore with gold grades sufficient to justify progressing with the development.

---

1   RGC (Tasmania) Limited, 'Henty Gold Project, Feasibility Study', 1991, Renison Goldfields Consolidated Archives (RGCA), Box 3536.

At Wau in Papua New Guinea, geological investigation entailed the reinterpretation of mine data, aerial photography of the area, the acquisition of new tenements, and drilling at Wau and on associated leases. RGC also undertook a range of efforts to improve the production output from the Wau gold deposits. In 1983 the Wau mill expansion was commissioned, doubling mill capacity while in 1985 a carbon-in-pulp plant was constructed, later to be upgraded to increase throughput. The plant was designed to increase the recovery of gold and silver from partially oxidised and primary ores, given the reserves of the oxidised ores had been exhausted in 1985 and the original mill closed.[2] The mine displayed a variable operating performance, encountering hard ore and low grades. Drilling on nearby leases discovered mineralisation and expectations were that new deposits would be available. An evaluation of the deposits found that a previous view of a series of lenses was not the case, with the distribution of gold being more variable and, as such, requiring more closely spaced drilling to ensure adequate mine control as to the grade and characteristics of the ore selected for mining. By 1988 the future of Wau, which commenced the calendar year cash-flow negative, was viewed as being dependent on the Kerimenge exploration prospect, 20 kilometres away. As the operation was not achieving its budgetary targets, options for the future of the mine were considered, which included a closure earlier than expected in 1991. In July 1989, the board resolved to close the Wau mine.[3] This was despite the assessed potential of the Kerimenge deposit.

In the Philippines the Nelesbitan gold prospect was drilled and a small project was progressed, with what was assessed as a minimal initial investment. The project was viewed as a way of testing RGC's ability to operate in the Philippines, given the company's exploration efforts had identified what was considered a promising portfolio of potential mineral projects. In May 1988 a contract security force was established, in preparation for construction. Loan funds of $11 million were raised and production began in May 1990 from a small open pit operation. Terrorist activity was prevalent in the vicinity of the mine, with the manager of a nearby mine taken hostage. It was a poorly conceived project, involving a low-grade resource that had not been well delineated, quite apart from the security issues. The operation encountered technical difficulties and shortly after its commencement, given 'questionable profitability and … significant security problems', the mine

---

2   Renison Goldfields Consolidated Limited, *Annual Report 1985*, p. 12.
3   Renison Goldfields Consolidated, 'Minutes of Meeting of Directors', 27 July 1989, p. 4, RGCA, Box 11329, BRD38/04.

was placed on a care and maintenance basis.[4] The company's Philippines business entity, Goldfields Philippines Corporation, was sold in 1994 to Acoje Mining, a Philippines company.

Porgera gold

Figure 52. Site of Porgera gold mine, Enga Province, Papua New Guinea.
Source: Photograph held in the possession of the author.

Porgera was undoubtedly the key element of RGC's exploration, project development and metallurgical test work in the 1980s. Placer and Mount Isa Mines entered into the original joint venture for exploration at Porgera in August 1975. The deposit was located in Enga Province of Papua New Guinea, an area of remote and rugged mountain terrain. Gold had been first reported in the area in 1938 by government officers. In 1964, after the amalgamation of Bulolo Gold Dredging with Placer Development, mapping and shallow drilling was carried out. Mount Isa Mines also

---

4   Renison Goldfields Consolidated, 'Minutes of Meeting of Directors', 23 August 1991, p. 7, RGCA, Box 11329, BRD38/04.

carried out trenching, mapping and channel-sampling activities and conducted a small-scale sluicing operation. The major proportion of the gold occurred in submicroscopic particles associated with pyrite. This meant that conventional direct cyanide leaching resulted in low gold recoveries.

In early 1978, Placer decided it was appropriate to introduce a third company to the joint venture, notably one experienced in gold metallurgy. Experimental work undertaken to that time on the sulphide ore indicated considerable processing complexities, with low attendant gold recovery. In 1979 Consolidated Gold Fields Australia (CGFA) was selected as the project's third participant. The terms agreed were for CGFA to match Placer's expenditure and earn a one-third interest. The arrangement was structured as a two-stage option: prior to December 1978, CGFA would conduct a metallurgical program on samples of the Porgera ore and, subject to these results, had the ability to spend the balance of $1 million on exploration. The outcome was that Placer agreed to sell part of its interest to CGFA, with the three joint venture partners each holding a one-third interest.[5] While in 1981 reserves were seen to be adequate for development, the presence of pyrite was viewed as presenting uncertainties as to the level of ultimate gold recovery. In fact, the overwhelming characteristics of Porgera in the early 1980s were 'formidable engineering and metallurgical problems' quite apart from the high capital expenditure likely to be required for a project in a remote area without, at that stage, an identified source of power generation.[6] RGC personnel played a major role in overcoming the metallurgical problems during the next decade, leading to the phased development of the major gold mine from 1990.

The discovery of a higher-grade mineralisation zone at Porgera occurred in 1983. This, along with a solution to the metallurgical treatment of the ore, were major milestones for the project. The new mineralisation, referred to as zone VII, when initially delineated, contained an estimated 15 million tonnes of ore with a gold content of 6 grams per tonne, compared with the existing reserves of 1 million tonnes at 3.55 grams per tonne. The level of reserves in zone VII subsequently increased. Peter Robinson, later to become an executive director of RGC, was recruited from South Africa

---

5   Letter from EJ Eldridge, Director, Placer Exploration Limited to Assistant Director, Department of National Planning, Papua New Guinea Government, 3 January 1979, RGCA, Box 1091.
6   Renison Goldfields Consolidated Limited, 'Minutes of Meeting of Directors', 16 December 1981, p. 7, RGCA, Box 11328, BRD38.

and played a key role in metallurgical test work. Over a period of three years, work was conducted to determine the means to liberate the gold locked in the pyrite lattice structure. Various approaches included ultra-fine grinding, roasting, bacterial leaching and pressure oxidation to extract the gold particles, followed by cyanidation. In a Sydney suburb, Warman Laboratory undertook work on behalf of RGC, treating the sulphide ore in autoclaves at high temperatures and under pressure. The process was effective in liberating the gold particles. For Robinson, this was a 'Eureka moment' for the project. Pilot test work was subsequently undertaken on pressure oxidation techniques with a bulk ore sample sent to Canada.[7]

By 1986, the completion of an initial adit into zone VII had occurred. Planning proceeded on the basis of the development of an underground mine accessing high-grade ore zones and subsequently an open pit to access the lower-grade bulk reserves. Pressure oxidation was determined as the most appropriate means to process the ore. The discovery of the Hides gas field by BP provided a potential source of energy for the operation of the planned high-pressure oxidation cells. In this context, a 1986 internal report on Porgera stated:

> RGC perceives the Porgera project as providing an excellent opportunity of rare quality for furthering ... [corporate] objectives. Despite the evident difficulties associated with its development Porgera is, in RGC's view, a world class ore body holding promise of high rewards for courageous, entrepreneurial endeavour.[8]

In 1988 the feasibility study for the mine was completed. Subsequent to the study, additional high-grade ore was discovered that required a reconsideration of the development approach. The development plans were submitted to the Government of Papua New Guinea in November 1988. By 1989 the signing of a mining development contract had occurred and a special mining licence granted to allow the joint venture to commence construction. At that stage mine development was scheduled to take three years and three months and involve an expenditure of approximately $1 billion, with development occurring through a phased approach.

---

7   Peter Robinson, personal communication, 6 November 2018; Renison Goldfields Consolidated Limited, 'Chairman's Address to the Fifth Annual General Meeting, 25 October 1985', p. 7, RGCA, Box 14284, BRD38/07.
8   RGC, 'Objectives for Porgera', 4 September, 1986, pp. 1–2, RGCA, Box 1361.

Campbell Anderson described the Porgera project as 'uniquely large and complex in many different areas—metallurgically, logistically, politically, environmentally'.[9] The conditions within Papua New Guinea, from a security and political point of view, created challenges. At the time that the Porgera loan facilities were being negotiated, riot police had been stationed on Bougainville Island, where CRA's mining activities were occurring, with the government considering imposing martial law.

Given the importance of Porgera to the group's production and financial profile, and the relatively short duration and lower contribution from other gold production sources, the RGC board was keen to ensure the expeditious development of the project. In 1987 there was disquiet in relation to Placer's management of the project. The London managing director of Consolidated Gold Fields, Rudolph Agnew, approached the managing director of Placer suggesting that RGC replace Placer as operator. This was not to occur but Placer's project management team was strengthened as a result of RGC's representations. The feasibility study by the joint venture partners was presented to the Government of Papua New Guinea. RGC negotiated with a syndicate of 14 international banks for its financing arrangements, a US$260 million loan facility.

The approach adopted for development entailed initial mining of the high-grade underground mineralisation, with the project to proceed in phases: underground mining followed by a process of surface mining of refractory ore to be processed by the installation of a pressure oxidation circuit. High-grade ore from underground mining was processed in the first circuit for 18 months followed by the second larger circuit. The phased approach allowed the high-grade part of the deposit with refractory gold to be recovered and treated using a concentrator plant. This allowed time for the large autoclaves to be brought onto the site and for the development of the power station with gas from the Hides field.[10] This power source enabled the operation of a more complex pressure oxidation plant to treat the lower-grade ore from open cut mining.[11] In 1989 construction of the first stage of the project began and proceeded well, notwithstanding the remote location of the deposit and the mountainous terrain. Large Russian helicopters were used to fly in much of the heavy equipment, a modern-day version of the use of Junkers when the Bulolo goldfields

---

9   Renison Goldfields Consolidated, Letter from Campbell Anderson, 6 September 1989, RGCA, Box 1361.
10 Renison Goldfields Consolidated Limited, *Annual Report 1988*.
11 Jackson and Banks, *In Search of the Serpent's Skin*, pp. 75–81.

were developed in the 1930s. Commissioning occurred in August 1989 and first gold production from the high-grade zone VII reserves followed. Porgera became the major earnings contributor to RGC over the next five years.

A protracted process of engagement by the joint venture partners with the Government of Papua New Guinea occurred in relation to ownership levels for the project. The government's initial agreement to purchase 10 per cent of the project from the joint venture partners was exercised in 1989 through a subsidiary of the state-controlled Mineral Resources Development. Contentions raised by the Government of Papua New Guinea that it had been misled about the size of the deposit and its production profile resulted in a dispute between the joint venture partners and the government, relating to the level of government ownership, as will be discussed in Chapter 19.

Attempt to re-establish a position in coal

CGFA, with Dalgety Australia, had acquired an interest in the Glendell coal project in the Hunter Valley in 1979. The development of the deposits, which provided RGC with the opportunity to re-enter coal production, had been under active consideration since that time. The Glendell coking coal project had initially planned to commence in March 1983. This timing was repeatedly deferred by a labyrinth of issues. Development did not occur under RGC's ownership, with the rights to the deposit eventually sold in 1992. Impediments encountered related in large part to the New South Wales Government: in the granting of a mining lease, the achievement of clarity on the requirements for front-end payments for infrastructure, and arrangements to gain access to railway and port facilities. The combative union situation also weighed heavily on the project, as did the need to secure contracts before a commitment to ordering major equipment.

In 1980, as part of efforts to advance the project, discussions had been held with Japanese steel companies. These discussions, to obtain a contractual underpinning for sales, included offering the Japanese a 20 per cent interest in the project. Charles Copeman, then involved in Bellambi Coal, was engaged in these negotiations. Expectations were that a mining lease would be granted in early 1981. The RGC board considered a proposal, supported by Max Roberts, that it was necessary to order capital equipment for the project—despite a financial return that would not occur for five years—so as to demonstrate to potential Japanese customers that the prospects of the project proceeding were real. In turn, a contractual underpinning from the Japanese steel mills was necessary for financing. Assurances for the granting of a mining lease were not forthcoming from the state government, with issues related to Dalgety's status as a foreign company and uncertainty as to whether a process of naturalisation for Dalgety would need to occur before or after the granting of a mining lease. RGC was of the view that the naturalisation process could occur after the granting of a mining lease. However, the company was disabused of this notion two years later. An RGC board minute in November 1981 encapsulated the situation RGC faced in relation to the project:

> The inaccessibility of the Premier, his recent statements on coal royalties, the need for clarification on front-end payments [for infrastructure], the union situation, housing, shipping, railway and port facilities all had increased concern about the viability of the project.[12]

By 1982, Roberts had still been unsuccessful in securing a meeting with the premier, although departmental advice he received suggested that the mining lease terms would be 'non negotiable and could be regarded as final'.[13] Agnew, representing the parent company as a director of RGC commented that, in the circumstances, the project 'could only just be regarded as acceptable'. In his view it would not proceed 'if further adverse factors became apparent'.[14] A month later, Roberts, reporting on discussions with the New South Wales Government, indicated that he had conveyed to the government that the 'numerous and heavy imposts' may well have 'killed' the project.[15] The company pressed on but faced further obstacles. A public environmental review process in 1983 generated opposition to the project from a local citizen's action group that was supported by the Newcastle Trades and Labour Council. Although the opposition was unsuccessful in preventing development consent being granted, it further delayed the project.[16]

---

12 Renison Goldfields Consolidated Limited, 'Minutes of Meeting of Directors', 25 November 1981, p. 2, RGCA, Box 11328, BRD38.
13 Renison Goldfields Consolidated Limited, 'Minutes of Meeting of Directors', 25 February 1982, p. 6, RGCA, Box 11328, BRD38.
14 ibid.
15 Renison Goldfields Consolidated Limited, 'Minutes of Meeting of Directors', 24 March 1982, pp. 1–2, RGCA, Box 11328, BRD38.
16 Renison Goldfields Consolidated Limited, 'Minutes of Meeting of Directors', 29 September 1983, p. 10, RGCA, Box 11328, BRD38.

In May 1982, Roberts finally secured his long sought-after meeting with the premier, at which he was advised that the New South Wales Government's financial share from the project would be in the order of $51 million per annum. Roberts advised the premier: 'For the project to proceed, the Company also had to derive an adequate return and to achieve this the cake would need to be redistributed'.[17] One of the RGC directors posited the view that the New South Wales Government was reluctant to grant Glendell a mining licence because of union activity to 'resist the development of new coal mines'.[18] The interminable delays caused Dalgety to seek to sell its shareholding, while RGC considered alternative coal investments, including in the Blair Athol coal deposits in the Bowen Basin, Queensland.

Roberts observed to shareholders at the 1984 annual general meeting that: 'It is a matter of some regret that negotiations with the New South Wales Government have been going on now for 4 years—I would not tolerate a mill of ours grinding so slowly'.[19] With the Glendell development consent to lapse in mid-1986 unless sufficient preliminary work was undertaken, RGC stoically pressed ahead with another governmental meeting, this time with the minister for mineral resources and minister for energy. This meeting, as with others, proved to be 'most unhelpful'.[20] RGC considered buying out Dalgety's interest in Glendell, which subsequently occurred in 1989, as well as in Nardell and the Durham coal compensation scheme. The Narama area of the Glendell leases was owned by a subsidiary of Renison, The Nardell Colliery, a joint venture with Costain Australia. Together RGC and Costain would successfully tender for an Electricity Commission of New South Wales coal supply arrangement and, with this,

---

17 Renison Goldfields Consolidated Limited, 'Minutes of Meeting of Directors', 26 May 1983, p. 2, RGCA, Box 11328, BRD38.
18 Renison Goldfields Consolidated Limited, 'Minutes of Meeting of Directors', 24 November 1983, p. 8, RGCA, Box 11328, BRD38.
19 Renison Goldfields Consolidated Limited, 'Chairman's Address to the Third Annual General Meeting, 20th October 1984', p. 17, RGCA, Box 14284, BRD38/07.
20 Renison Goldfields Consolidated Limited, 'Minutes of Meeting of Directors', 28 February 1985, p. 6, RGCA, Box 11328, BRD38/02. The company received advice in May 1986 that a lease would not be granted until the joint venture with Dalgety was 'Australianised'. This outcome was 'contrary to earlier advice that Australianisation would not be necessary prior to generating a lease' (Renison Goldfields Consolidated Limited, 'Minutes of Meeting of Directors', 29 May 1986, p. 17, RGCA, Box 11328, BRD38/02).

coal production commenced from the Narama joint venture in 1993.[21] The Glendell tenements were not to be developed by RGC despite more than a decade of effort.

Iron ore

In 1985, the Goldsworthy extension project, which entailed the development of the Nimingarra iron ore deposits occurred. This enabled the mining rate to be sustained at 7 million tonnes per annum for another 17 years, with the potential for further expansion to 8.5 million tonnes per annum through planning for the development of Mining Area C.[22] The project also required construction of a beneficiation plant at Finucane Island to process lower-grade ore. The capital required was contributed by Consolidated Gold Fields, which held the interest previously owned by CGFA. In 1987 Consolidated Gold Fields' shareholding in Mount Goldsworthy increased to 70 per cent as a result of committing $90 million for the project. BHP held the remaining 30 per cent. While RGC no longer had any direct involvement in Mount Goldsworthy, it retained an arrangement where it would receive a payment associated with the start of production from Mining Area C. This was later converted into a royalty arrangement, although no financial benefit from this royalty was derived during RGC's period of ownership of the entitlement. Mining Area C would, however, prove to be a highly lucrative and valuable royalty stream, valued in the billions of dollars, after its commencement in 2003, at which time it was held by a successor company to RGC, Iluka Resources.

RGC retained an interest in McCamey Iron Ore Associates. This remained the company's sole exposure to iron ore following the divestiture in Mount Goldsworthy in 1977. In 1985, Mount Isa Mines was looking to dispose of its Australian iron ore interests. The RGC board discussed the potential of increasing the company's interest in McCamey Iron Ore Associates, with the following record:

---

21 Negotiations were also conducted with the New South Wales Government in relation to a royalty entitlement to coal tenements held by RGC and Dalgety, in the name of Freehold Coal, which had been expropriated in January 1982 from the company Durham Holdings Pty Ltd. Coal was also expropriated from the Nardell Colliery that was also jointly owned by Dalgety and RGC.
22 Goldsworthy Mining Limited, 'Board Meeting', 24 November 1986, RGCA, Box 11348.

> Mr. Agnew commented that CGF viewed the Pilbara as having the potential for continued profitable operations and the ability, subject to industrial climate allowing, to be the major iron ore supplier to the Pacific region. Mr. Agnew expressed the view that CGF's iron ore interest, being located in Australia, should eventually be under the RGC corporate structure.[23]

Approval was provided for RGC to increase its interest in the McCamey joint venture, although production did not occur during the period of RGC's ownership.

In 1989, when the Hanson takeover of Consolidated Gold Fields was nearing its conclusion, as will be discussed in Chapter 18, Anderson initiated a process to attempt to have RGC acquire the Consolidated Gold Fields interest in Mount Goldsworthy. RGC undertook an evaluation of Mount Goldsworthy as a precursor to an offer to acquire Consolidated Gold Fields' 70 per cent interest. The board discussion recognised the benefit to RGC if Consolidated Gold Fields was able to acquire BHP's 30 per cent interest in Mount Goldsworthy.[24] It was viewed that this would provide the basis for the control and operation of Mount Goldsworthy to be transferred to RGC and with this the potential to attract other participants and capital by establishing a separately listed Australian iron ore company. In July 1989 the general manager of Goldsworthy Mining, Alfred Kober, attended an RGC board meeting for this purpose at the suggestion of London director Michael Beckett. The board minutes conveyed:

> The Managing Director commented that if RGC was interested in entering the iron ore business this would be the last opportunity and that it should undertake an appraisal of Goldsworthy prior to a decision by Hanson to sell, so that upon a sale decision by Hanson RGC could act quickly.[25]

It was clear that Hanson, which had by this time acquired Consolidated Gold Fields, had no intention of retaining an interest in an iron ore operation in Australia. The Mount Goldsworthy joint venture participants struggled with the Hanson representation in gaining approval for any level

---

23 Renison Goldfields Consolidated Limited, 'Minutes of Meeting of Directors', 28 March 1985, p. 9, RGCA, Box 11328, BRD38/02.
24 Renison Goldfields Consolidated Limited, 'Minutes of Meeting of Directors', 27 August 1987, pp. 12–13, RGCA, Box 11329, BRD38/03.
25 Renison Goldfields Consolidated Limited, 'Minutes of Meeting of Directors', 29 July 1989, p. 1, RGCA, Box 11329, BRD38/04.

of expenditure for the project. Anderson held discussions with Hanson in December 1989 and indicated a willingness to bid $65 million for the Hanson interest in Mount Goldsworthy. The bid was deemed 'not acceptable' and soon after BHP acquired the interest.[26] If the course of events were to have been different, RGC would have established a major involvement in the development of iron ore, including at Mining Area C in the Pilbara.

Diversification and acquisition

Diversification activities included the continued involvement in the New South Wales agricultural venture, Colinas. Throughout the 1980s Colinas failed to provide any meaningful financial contribution or prospect that it would. As in earlier periods, its sale was considered an appropriate option, although the opportunity to achieve this remained limited. Instead, various ventures were pursued, such as the use of poplar wood for match-flint manufacture and milling of the harvested timber, as well as cattle raising. All failed to provide meaningful returns.[27]

In May 1986, RGC surrendered the lease it held for its corporate head office, Gold Fields House, to AMP for a payment of $25.8 million. The proceeds offset an accounting adjustment of $12.2 million representing the excess of the purchase price for Allied Eneabba relative to the assessed value of the assets. This improved RGC's profit performance after tax for the year to $34.6 million, the highest reported profit of RGC since its formation in 1981.[28]

An investment division, established in October 1984, had initial funds of $20 million to invest, for the purposes of trading and for establishing strategic holdings in companies. A motivation was to enhance RGC's investment market knowledge of listed Australian companies and to provide a basis for acquiring interests that may be the precursor to a full acquisition. RGC's investments in Mount Isa Mines and Pancontinental

---

26   Renison Goldfields Consolidated Limited, 'Minutes of Meeting of Directors', 14 December 1989, p. 4, RGCA, Box 11329, BRD38/04. Jerry Ellis, BHP Minerals' executive general manager, and later chairman of BHP, was responsible for the acquisition of the Consolidated Gold Fields' stake from Hanson (Jerry Ellis, personal communication, June 2017).
27   Renison Goldfields Consolidated Limited, 'Minutes of Meeting of Directors', 25 January 1989, p. 10, RGCA, Box 11329, BRD38/04.
28   Renison Goldfields Consolidated Limited, *Annual Report 1986*, p. 32.

Mining fell into that category. In 1987, RGC established Project Almond, the proposed acquisition of North Broken Hill, with $125 million approved for this purpose. An assessment was made of the value of North Broken Hill's mining and smelting operations, updating previous studies of the company. The conclusion was that the acquisition of North Broken Hill's zinc assets could be justified at a premium over the entire company's purchase price. The feasibility of this depended, however, upon the valuation placed by others on North Broken Hill's non-zinc assets and the share market price at which control could be achieved. In the first half of 1987, RGC and North Broken Hill had a similar market capitalisation of approximately $1.1 billion. An acquisition to gain control of the zinc assets was viewed as practicable and would have been assisted by Consolidated Gold Fields in London, given its own shareholding in North Broken Hill.[29] The transaction would have been noteworthy in the Australian mining sector and may have influenced RGC's fate. However, it did not proceed.

A number of other acquisition opportunities were considered. These included a consideration in 1987 to acquiring Placer Pacific, RGC's joint venture partner in the Porgera gold project, as well as a complex strategy for the potential acquisition of Mount Isa Mines. In 1989, $20 million of the $50 million of funds within the investment division were held in shares of this company. Discussions were held by Anderson with the chairman and chief executive officer of Mount Isa Mines, with a view to a possible combination of the two companies, but these discussions did not progress to finality.[30] The acquisition of Westralian Sands was also considered.[31]

---

29 Renison Goldfields Consolidated Limited, 'Project Almond', RGCA, Box 12510.
30 The complex strategy involved RGC acquiring an initial 7 per cent of Mount Isa Mines (MIM) shares, funding this investment by issuing 15 million shares, with Consolidated Gold Fields not taking up its entitlement and diluting to 40.26 per cent in RGC. RGC and Consolidated Gold Fields would then make a joint takeover for MIM; Asarco (that owned 32.4 per cent in MIM) would sell its Consolidated Gold Fields' shareholding with RGC then acquiring 36.7 per cent of MIM from Consolidated Gold Fields in exchange for 73.8 million RGC shares. In the final phase, RGC would sell MIM's cross shareholding in Asarco for $221 million and issue 49.12 million shares to Consolidated Gold Fields, enabling Consolidated Gold Fields' shareholding in RGC to increase back to 48.95 per cent. RGC would then utilise the attendant cash to reduce RGC's debt (untitled paper, RGCA, Box 973).
31 The acquisition was considered at a time when Westralian Sands was owned 61 per cent by two of its major pigment customers.

16. NEW INTERESTS AND DIVERSIFICATION

These considerations demonstrated that RGC, under Anderson's tenure as managing director, saw benefits in aggregation at the mid-tier market capitalisation level of Australian mining companies. Apart from efforts to establish a presence in coking coal through the development of its Glendell coal leases in New South Wales, RGC held discussions with Arco Australia in 1983 relating to its 15.39 per cent interest in the Blair Athol coal project in Queensland. These discussions reflected an interest in establishing a position in coking coal at a time when the uncertainties relating to progress with the Glendell project were evident, even though RGC would have an equity, as opposed to operating position, in any venture with Arco. The board authorised management to proceed with an indicative offer of $25 million to $30 million. Discussions were held with Roderick Carnegie, managing director of CRA, the operator and other joint venture participant. While CRA indicated it was not seeking to increase its interest in the project, it preferred that the Arco interest not be sold to an entity with a foreign shareholding. As such, it left open its option to exercise its pre-emptive rights.[32] The acquisition was not pursued further.

In 1988 alone, RGC considered five further potential acquisition opportunities. The acquisition of Paringa Mining and Exploration Co., in which AGL was a major shareholder, and which in turn had a 45 per cent interest in North Flinders Mines, was one such consideration. While RGC began acquiring shares in North Flinders Mines, the opportunity did not proceed. The potential to acquire another producer of mineral sands, Mineral Deposits, was considered while an evaluation was made of acquiring CSR's minerals division, and through this the Indonesian tin mining operation Koba Tin. The challenge RGC had was that it wished to avoid financing acquisitions and subsequent projects that may have impeded its ability to finance the major Porgera gold project.[33] The indicative acquisition cost of Koba Tin was $40 million; $25 million to $30 million was allocated for Mineral Deposits; and an envisaged $25 million to purchase the Granny Smith gold prospect in the CSR portfolio.

---

32 Renison Goldfields Consolidated Limited, 'Minutes of Meeting of Directors', 27 January 1983, p. 8 and 24 February 1983, p. 4, RGCA, Box 11328, BRD38.
33 Renison Goldfields Consolidated Limited, 'Minutes of Meeting of Directors', 15 February 1988, p. 5; 24 March 1988, p. 4 and 27 April 1988, p. 2, RGCA, Box 11329, BRD38/03.

Mineral Deposits was of interest to RGC following an indication from its major shareholder, BHP, that it was willing to sell a major part of its non-core assets. An RGC board note reviewing the potential acquisition of Mineral Deposits observed:

> Although Mineral Deposits was a high cost producer, acquisition of it would allow AMC to bring into operation this high cost production in periods of supply deficits, thus providing a barrier to entry or expansion by external producers in times of high cost. In addition, Mineral Deposits was a poor marketer, selling its rutile product approximately $30 per tonne below market with a consequential $5.00 per tonne effect on AMC's prices. Acquisition of Mineral Deposits would allow it to achieve a $30.00 increase in prices and AMC a $5.00 increase. Acquisition of Mineral Deposits' engineering business would provide additional insight into other mineral sands producers.[34]

The acquisition did not proceed.

In January 1988, Anderson sought board approval in relation to the acquisition of CSR's minerals division. CSR held a 37.5 per cent interest in Koba Tin in Indonesia, as well as exploration interests in Australia and Indonesia. Boral had an equal interest in Koba Tin. Anderson saw the opportunity to undertake back-to-back acquisitions and gain a controlling ownership of an alluvial tin mining operation on Bemban Island, Indonesia. In May 1988, RGC was successful in its purchase of both the CSR and Boral interests in Koba Tin. An RGC bid for the Granny Smith gold deposit was not successful, with RGC's bid of $45 million falling below a competitive bid of $65 million by Placer Pacific.

By 1988 funds committed to the investment division had increased from $20 million to $50 million. Apart from its role in identifying potential acquisition opportunities, part of the motivation was that the funds in the investment division could be liquidated as required to 'smooth out variances in profit performance' for the group.[35]

---

34   Renison Goldfields Consolidated Limited, 'Minutes of Meeting of Directors', 24 March 1988, p. 7, RGCA, Box 11329, BRD38/03.
35   Renison Goldfields Consolidated Limited, 'Minutes of Meeting of Directors', 29 October 1989, p. 9, RGCA, Box 11329, BRD38/03.

In the nine years since its formation RGC's financial performance had improved markedly, mainly associated with the recovery in mineral sands markets. The Koba Tin acquisition had proven useful as a contributor to group earnings and cash flow and was a partial offset to the decline in contribution from Mount Lyell. A major new gold production source at Porgera was to commence in 1990, with this more than replacing the smaller contributions from the two gold operations in Australia and New Guinea Gold Fields. It would rank as a material contributor to the group's overall performance. The two other major assets in the portfolio, Renison and Mount Lyell, were facing challenges, and their financial contributions were by now minor. Efforts to establish a position in coal and reacquire the Mount Goldsworthy interest were not successful. The market standing of RGC had been enhanced after a challenging first half of the decade. The opportunities appeared favourable for the 1990s. However, a decline in market conditions and a major change in the shareholding structure of RGC was to have an influence, ultimately, on RGC's fate as an independent, diversified mining company.

17

THE CHALLENGES OF THE PARENT

A major influence upon Renison Goldfields Consolidated (RGC) from 1989 through to the cessation in 1998 of its existence as a company was a series of corporate events related to the London parent, Consolidated Gold Fields. During the early 1980s, De Beers Consolidated Mines, a company associated with Anglo American Corporation of South Africa, established a shareholding in Consolidated Gold Fields. This shareholding was subsequently transferred to a company that was controlled by the Oppenheimer family, Mineral and Resources Corporation Limited, or Minorco. Domiciled in Luxembourg, Minorco was the overseas arm of the Anglo American–De Beers group. It claimed to be the largest gold producer in the non-communist world and was jointly owned by De Beers (21 per cent), Anglo American Corporation (39 per cent) and the Oppenheimer family (7 per cent). Anglo American, formed in 1917, had had two chairmen: Sir Ernest Oppenheimer and his son, Harry Oppenheimer. The group had diverse interests in a range of minerals, with a major presence in gold mining in South Africa. Members of the Oppenheimer family were represented on the boards of both companies. It was a contention of Consolidated Gold Fields, in opposing the Minorco bid, that the board of Minorco was 'largely in the pay ... [and] depends for its future prospects upon the bounty of Anglo American and/or Mr. Oppenheimer or his family'.[1]

---

1   Rudolph Agnew, the chairman and chief executive officer of Consolidated Gold Fields stated: 'The Chairman of the company [Minorco], Mr. Olgivie Thompson is in the pay of the family. He is Deputy Chairman of Anglo American. He is Chairman of De Beers as well as Minorco and is Chairman designate, as we understand it, of Anglo American itself' (transcript, Monopolies and Merger Commission, United Kingdom, p. 32, Renison Goldfields Consolidated Archives (RGCA), Box 138).

Figure 53. Rudolph Agnew, chief executive officer of Consolidated Gold Fields, responsible for the spirited defence against the takeover attempt by Minorco that, despite being successful, led to Hanson acquiring Consolidated Gold Fields, London.

Source: Shutterstock/ *The Independent*, October 1988.

17. THE CHALLENGES OF THE PARENT

Consolidated Gold Fields was Anglo American's nearest rival and the second-largest gold producer, mainly through its 49 per cent interest in Gold Fields of South Africa. The Oppenheimer interests, in turn, had an 11 per cent shareholding in Gold Fields of South Africa. Harry Oppenheimer, according to one writer, was concerned that Consolidated Gold Fields' diversification activities might involve a plan to sell its stake in Gold Fields of South Africa. If acquired by a rival South African mining group, General Mining, Anglo American's predominance in gold production would be threatened. 'Thus ... it was the internal politics of South African gold mining industry that came to spark one of the most far reaching and bitter corporate battles ever.'[2]

The De Beers approach to attempt to prevent this outcome was to hold a minority shareholding in Consolidated Gold Fields. This stake was acquired through complex subterfuge using various nominee companies of De Beers. This activity led Consolidated Gold Fields' chairman, Lord Erroll, to warn shareholders at the company's annual general meeting in November 1979 of 'a possible creeping acquisition', while requesting the Department of Trade to investigate the acquisition of the company's shares.[3] There followed the infamous 'dawn raid' on Consolidated Gold Fields' register on 12 February 1980, orchestrated by Anglo American's London broker Rowe and Pitman. The share raid was speculated to be in response to a view that Gencor may have been preparing to make its own takeover attempt of Consolidated Gold Fields and Gold Fields of South Africa.[4] Utilising 30 of their staff on telephones, Rowe and Pitman acquired close to a further 15 per cent of Consolidated Gold Fields shares over the course of 40 minutes. An announcement indicated that it was not the intention of De Beers to move beyond a 29.9 per cent shareholding and that it was not seeking to change the management of Consolidated

---

2   Jamieson, *Goldstrike: The Oppenheimer Empire in Crisis*, pp. 63 and 65.
3   Department of Trade, 'Consolidated Gold Fields Limited, Investigation under Section 172 of the Companies Act 1948', report by Bryan James Welch and Michael Charles Anthony Osborne (inspectors appointed by the Department of Trade), Her Majesty's Stationery Office, London, 1980, p. 1.
4   Gencor was created by the 1980 merger of General Mining and Finance Company and Union Corporation, two companies involved in gold mining in South Africa. Union Corporation owned the original interest in Richards Bay and assisted in the formation of Richards Bay Minerals. Gencor bought Billiton International from Royal Dutch Shell in 1994 and had an interest in Richards Bay Minerals, which Rio Tinto operated.

Gold Fields 'in which it had great confidence'.[5] The Anglo American and De Beers holding was transferred to Minorco, with two Minorco directors appointed to the board of Consolidated Gold Fields, including Rhodes scholar Julian Ogilvie Thompson, chairman of Minorco and De Beers.

Minorco reportedly considered a proposal from an investment adviser for it and British mining group Rio Tinto Zinc to acquire and subsequently break up Consolidated Gold Fields. Thompson raised this proposal with Rudolph Agnew, chairman and group chief executive of Consolidated Gold Fields. According to Bill Jamieson, who wrote on the Minorco saga, Agnew 'was not keen at all' and realised that Consolidated Gold Fields was now vulnerable on a number of fronts.[6]

A proposal for a friendly merger between Minorco and Consolidated Gold Fields was considered and arrangements put in motion. According to Jamieson, the Consolidated Gold Fields board, including Campbell Anderson, the managing director of RGC, considered the proposal. Anderson, who could not attend the meeting in London, presented a letter expressing the views of the Australian subsidiary. Michael Beckett, a Consolidated Gold Fields executive director who also sat on the boards of Gold Fields of South Africa and RGC, tabled Anderson's letter. He described it as 'a powerfully written piece, listing the formidable political problems that an Anglo American-controlled Gold Fields would face both in Australia and in Papua New Guinea. It would vote the company off the international mining map'.[7]

The proposal for a merger was not supported. Subsequently, Consolidated Gold Fields increased the stake it held in Newmont Mining Corporation to 26 per cent, following an agreement with Newmont in October 1981, ratified at a Gold Fields extraordinary general meeting. This holding increased to 49 per cent after renowned corporate raider, T Boone Pickens and his investment group Ivanhoe Partners, attempted a takeover of Newmont in September 1987. Newmont and Consolidated Gold Fields signed a 10-year agreement, with Consolidated Gold Fields agreeing to limit its shareholding to under 50 per cent. Newmont declared a US$33 per share dividend to all stockholders, which assisted

---

5   Department of Trade, 'Consolidated Gold Fields Limited, Investigation under Section 172 of the Companies Act 1948', report by Bryan James Welch and Michael Charles Anthony Osborne (inspectors appointed by the Department of Trade), Her Majesty's Stationery Office, London, 1980, p. 2.
6   Jamieson, *Goldstrike: The Oppenheimer Empire in Crisis*, p. 91.
7   ibid., p. 99.

Consolidated Gold Fields to increase its ownership in Newmont from 26 per cent to 49.7 per cent. Pickens was blocked from proceeding with its takeover of Newmont by a ruling in the Delaware Supreme Court.[8]

At the time, Anglo American Corporation was also believed to be stalking Newmont. By increasing its position, Consolidated Gold Fields thwarted Pickens's takeover attempt. However, this action only served to annoy Anglo American and Minorco. The Newmont dividend was paid in 1987 in the context of the October 1987 share market crash, with the shares of the heavily indebted Consolidated Gold Fields falling sharply. Similar to the situation that would later manifest when Hanson became a major shareholder of RGC, an uneasy relationship existed between Consolidated Gold Fields and Minorco, with the major shareholder viewing:

> The problematic earnings per share performance and the standstill dividend record with an understandable apprehension—it had paid £6.16 a share … by the time of the Newmont investment … that was down to £4.85 … When, if at all, would the Agnew strategy deliver.[9]

Tensions between the two sides were all too evident. In 1985, Consolidated Gold Fields moved its corporate office to 31 Charles II Street, St James Square.[10] The location generated derision within the Anglo American and Minorco camps. The new premises were referred to as 'Versailles' during the acrimonious takeover battle that followed. In 1987, to mark the centenary of Consolidated Gold Fields, two bronzes statues of Cecil Rhodes, the founder of both The Consolidated Gold Fields of South Africa and De Beers Consolidated Mines, were cast. They were exchanged between Anglo American and Consolidated Gold Fields in a temporary gesture of goodwill, given the shared heritage of the two companies. The statues would feature in Hanson's later takeover of Consolidated Gold Fields, which was in large part a consequence of Minorco's unsuccessful takeover effort and shareholding in Consolidated Gold Fields.

---

8   The Pickens and Ivanhoe Partners bid was launched in early September 1987 and by November had been withdrawn (*The New York Times*, 1 September 1987 and 19 November 1987).
9   Jamieson, *Goldstrike: The Oppenheimer Empire in Crisis*, p. 83.
10 The site of the Consolidated Gold Fields offices had been the former residence of the 8th Duke of Norfolk and during World War II had been the Supreme Headquarters of the Allied Expeditionary Powers under Dwight D Eisenhower.

Having been spurned in terms of a merger, Minorco set about making a hostile bid for Consolidated Gold Fields. Minorco made its first bid on 21 September 1988. The £2.9 billion bid lapsed, referred to the Monopolies and Merger Commission and the Takeover Panel for investigation in relation to insider dealing, given the large volumes of Consolidated Gold Fields shares traded in the three days preceding the bid. Senior management, including Anderson, appeared before the United Kingdom Monopolies and Merger Commission. Anderson's arguments focused on the implications of a successful Minorco bid for the mineral sands part of the business in Australia. He highlighted the consequences of further concentration in the mineral sands industry, including the potential sale of RGC shares by Minorco to Rio Tinto Zinc's Australian subsidiary, CRA. According to Anderson, if CRA took 'control of BP minerals', it presented the possibility of CRA also having 'a significant position in the Richards Bay mineral operations in South Africa'.[11] Anderson also conveyed that he had heard 'speculative comment[s]' that Minorco had engaged in discussions with Cooksons, the largest global purchaser of zircon. If RGC's mineral sands assets were to be sold to Cooksons, there would be 'major competitive problems … throughout the world'.[12]

The commission cleared the bid, allowing Minorco to make a renewed £3.2 billion offer of cash and shares. The bid was the largest in British history. The stakes were high; the battle pitted two major companies against each other. Agnew, a former cavalry officer in the King's Royal Irish Hussars, with 'immense charm … [and] a soldier's firmness'—tall, handsome, silver-haired and with a languid air—assembled a formidable response, with active assistance from the company's subsidiaries, including RGC.[13] Consolidated Gold Fields reportedly spent over £30 million on its multifaceted defence efforts, which included retaining United States–based private detectives. Consolidated Gold Fields was advised by the investment bank First Boston and two of its 'Wall Street legends', Bruce Wasserstein and Joe Perella. As if the defence was not sufficiently complex, two 'black nights' appeared on the scene. These were Kohlberg Kravis Roberts, leveraged buyout experts, proposing a management buyout; and Cavenham Forest Industries, established by British businessman Sir James (Jimmy) Goldsmith with the assistance of his lieutenant, Al 'Chainsaw'

---

11   Renison Goldfields Consolidated Limited, Memorandum from C McC Anderson to Executive Directors, 12 January 1989, p. 30, RGCA, Box 17848, RGC 28660.
12   ibid.
13   Macnab, *Gold Their Touchstone*, pp. 303–304; *The Independent*, 7 May 1994.

Dunlap, which had aspirations to acquire Newmont. Jonathan Loraine, a young member of the Consolidated Gold Fields business development group, recalled that it was 'our job … to keep them occupied', while also assisting with the main defence effort.[14]

Agnew mounted an aggressive and wide-ranging defence to what was seen as the opportunistic approach by a trivial and tax-contrived company. The tone was set early when Agnew, in drawing a distinction between owning assets in South Africa and being potentially owned by South African interests, stated: 'You can deny your bastard sons, you can't deny your parents'.[15] Sir Michael Edwardes, former chief executive of British Leyland and a non-executive director of Minorco, was appointed chief executive to lead the Minorco bid. His industrial and management skills in turning around the fortunes of British Leyland and his pugnacious style were seen as appropriate in leading the bid and ultimately taking charge of one of Britain's foremost mining houses. The no-holds-barred contest included a verbal assault by Agnew on the South African–born Edwardes, including 'allusions to his lack of mining ability and his small stature'.[16] Agnew intentionally mispronounced his name, 'Edwardees' and referred to him as the 'pip squeak'. The battle was vitriolic. Agnew stated that he was 'outraged by the bid' and described Minorco as 'totally motivated by secrecy and tax avoidance' and that the company was 'just trying to get their hands on our assets to compensate for the failure of their own policies' and to compensate for its own 'bankrupt' business policy.[17] The defence also centred heavily on the adverse implications of South African de facto control over both the British operations of Consolidated Gold Fields and its American and Australian interests. According to one observer:

> Gold Fields did not go quietly. The company had already been bruised by a stock raid in 1980 that had left Oppenheimer interests with nearly a third of its shares. This time, it was prepared. Marshalling attorneys, political lobbyists, investment analysts and detectives on both sides of the Atlantic, Gold Fields loosed a fusillade of charges against Minorco, ranging from allegations that a frenzy of insider trading in London and Johannesburg had preceded the bid, to speculation that Minorco's corporate cousin,

---

14 Jonathan Loraine, personal communication, 27 March 2017.
15 Jamieson, *Goldstrike: The Oppenheimer Empire in Crisis*, p. 140.
16 *The Independent*, 7 May 1994.
17 *The Times*, 4 October 1988 and 5 October 1998.

De Beers, had sold industrial diamonds to the Nazis in World War II. The evils of South African ownership became Gold Fields' rallying cry.[18]

The Consolidated Gold Fields response branded Minorco as representing 'poor management, poor record and poor prospects', with the potential for 'damaging South African control'.[19]

The Minorco bid was ultimately thwarted based on potential concentration in the gold sector. However, it was also suggested that mineral sands had played a role in Minorco's considerations:

> It is Renison's key role in the supply of mineral sands (it is the world's largest producer, delivering 30% of the west's titanium oxide, 40% of its monazite, and 45% of its zircon) which could have been Minorco's greatest prize. AAC [Anglo American Corporation] has no mineral sands operations worth speaking of (merely a 5% holding in Gencor which owns the vital Richards Bay Minerals deposits dominated by RTZ [Rio Tinto Zinc]). Just after Minorco made its play for ConsGold, a detailed report on the world mineral sands industry, prepared for the Dublin-based company Kenmare, showed that world demand for zircon would outpace supply until 1994, as the strategic mineral found new applications in electrical ceramics (and the world's nuclear industries). Its price was calculated to increase dramatically ... Initially the Monopolies and Mergers Commission (MMC) looked as if it was only going to scrutinise Minorco's play for mineral sands.[20]

Conspiracy-style theories abounded. One suggested that a successful Minorco takeover might provide South Africa with a sufficient share of gold and other strategic minerals, including titanium, to influence supply and inflate prices:

> When applied to strategic metals like titanium, however, Gold Fields' claims seem more compelling. Gencor, the leading Western producer—mining 29 percent of the high-grade feedstock manufacturers require to make titanium metal—is owned and

---

18 *The New York Times*, 19 March 1989.
19 Shareholder circular, 'Consolidated Gold Fields PLC, Share in a Valuable Future, Reject Minorco', March 1989, p. 1 (copy held by the author). A further shareholder circular was sent in April 1989 with details of 'an unprecedented scheme' with a targeted compound earnings growth of 20 per cent over three years and, if not achieved, the distribution of assets with a special preference dividend (Consolidated Gold Fields PLC, 'Value Today—and Value Tomorrow. Stay with Gold Fields', April 1989, pp. 1 and 3) (copy held by the author).
20 Moody, *The Gulliver File: Mines, People and Land*, pp. 98–99.

operated in South Africa. The second-largest source, Renison—extracting 25 percent of the West's feedstock—is an Australian company in which Gold Fields owns a 48 percent interest. The Minorco takeover would place 54 percent of the world's non-Soviet, high-grade titanium in South African hands. Investment analysts familiar with precious metals warn that Gencor and Oppenheimer companies might then collude to control the world market for titanium, as they previously have done with platinum.[21]

RGC's concerns were deep-seated, relating to the fate of its business in light of a successful Minorco bid, whether from the potential disposal of Minorco's shares in RGC—possibly to another major mining company—or Minorco holding a major shareholding position. For RGC, the dangers to the Australian business if Minorco succeeded in its bid were 'enormous'.[22] RGC board minutes in September 1988 noted: 'in discussing RGC's position relative to CGF, it was agreed that RGC should use its best endeavours to assist CGF in rebutting Minorco's bid … and [it] would be disadvantaged if Minorco's bid were to succeed'.[23] Within RGC, a defence committee was formed comprising Anderson, Mark Bethwaite, BE Wauchope (executive director, finance) and AD Hemingway (group general manager, corporate affairs).

The support from the Australian arm was unequivocal and robust. In writing to Agnew, Anderson observed:

> I have absolutely no doubt that this would have a serious adverse effect on the very close relationships that we have been able to build with our customers in the mineral sands industry … This stability would be threatened by any perception of South African control of supply, putting at considerable risk the very large profits which we presently enjoy from our major position in this industry.[24]

---

21 *The New York Times*, 19 March 1989. In reviewing the Minorco bid for Consolidated Gold Fields, the United Kingdom Monopolies and Merger Commission believed that the risk of a merger resulting in 'collusion in the supply of titanium [had] been exaggerated'. It is noted that the largest shareholding in Richards Bay Minerals was held by British Petroleum, which had agreed in principle to sell its shareholding to RTZ, not Gencor. In the view of the commission, Anglo American would have 'no effective influence' through its small shareholding in Gencor (Monopolies and Merger Commission, 'Minorco and Consolidated Gold Fields PLC: A Report on the Merger/Situation', February 1989, p. 61).
22 Consolidated Gold Fields Australia Limited, 'Minutes of Meeting of Directors', 29 September 1988, p. 3, RGCA, Box 11329, BRD38/03.
23 ibid, p. 1.
24 Letter from Campbell Anderson to RIJ Agnew, Chairman, Consolidated Gold Fields PLC, 20 September 1988, RGCA, Box 17848, RGC 28660.

The Minorco bid came at a time when Australian political opposition to the South African regime was intense. As such, there was concern with the possible reaction from trade unions in Australia if RGC was owned or controlled in part by South African interests. An internal RGC note recorded:

> Because of the damage perceived by the RGC Board to the long-term relationships that have been developed with customers in the mineral sand market and the operational difficulties with which the Board recognised the RGC Group could be confronted in its operations in Australia by virtue of any perception that the Group had become South African controlled and the reaction of the Australian trade union movement to that situation, RGC procured its US subsidiary, which operates in the mineral sands industry, to join other CGF interests in the United States in an approach to the President to exercise his powers under the United States Defence Act in relation to the bid.[25]

The significance of both Australian and international opposition to the apartheid regime in South Africa was never far below the surface in the arguments mounted. The implications for control of RGC's gold assets by South African interests, particularly in Papua New Guinea, were a part of RGC's opposition to the Minorco bid. The takeover attempt of the London parent also came at a crucial stage in the development of the Porgera gold project, with the joint venture awaiting the Papua New Guinea Government's response to the feasibility study. It was of concern to the RGC board that the Minorco bid for Consolidated Gold Fields may have been the reason for what was seen as the 'procrastination' of the Papua New Guinea Government in its decision-making process.[26] A Minorco takeover was viewed as a potentially 'catastrophic' outcome by Anderson. His contention to the Monopolies and Merger Commission was that RGC 'would be kicked out of Papua New Guinea' if South African control occurred.[27] Papua New Guinea Prime Minister Rabbie Namaliu publicly declared his opposition, stating:

---

25 Note to Directors Renison Goldfields Consolidated Limited, 22 March 1989, RGCA, Box 17848, RGC 28660.
26 Renison Goldfields Consolidated Limited, 'Minutes of Meeting of Directors', 29 August 1988, p. 7, RGCA, Box 11328, BRD 38/03.
27 Renison Goldfields Consolidated Limited, Memorandum from C McC Anderson to Executive Directors, Monopolies and Mergers Commission, 12 January 1989, p. 28, RGCA, Box 17848, RGC 28660.

> We cannot allow the apartheid regime to benefit from our rich resources … if the takeover goes ahead we shall force RGC to divest its interests in PNG. PNG will not be a party to any racist regime that has for so long suppressed the vast majority of its population.[28]

In a letter to shareholders, RGC's chairman, Max Roberts, conveyed the strained relationship associated with Minorco's share ownership of Consolidated Gold Fields. He wrote that, while there had been attempts at cooperation, 'these attempts have invariably failed because of the manner in which Minorco would seek to exercise its influence and, in particular, because the influence would be perceived to be dictated effectively by the Oppenheimer family in South Africa'.[29] The implications were seen to be 'potentially so adverse' that RGC shareholders were urged to contact their state or federal members of parliament to petition the British Government. Roberts visited Britain, gave media interviews and met with officials of the Office of Fair Trading, having written to its director-general. In relation to the implications of a Minorco takeover on RGC's mineral sands interests, he wrote:

> We are concerned that if this takeover proceeds, the world's mineral sands industry will be dominated by South African companies, which on the basis of press reports we understand are, or can be controlled by the Oppenheimer family. We believe this could be damaging to the mineral sands industry in general and RGC's interests in particular.[30]

Through Anderson's efforts, RGC secured representations by state premiers, including the Tasmanian premier, who wrote to Australian Prime Minister Bob Hawke in October 1988 regarding the viability of Mount Lyell in the event of a Minorco takeover. Hawke met with Margaret Thatcher, the British prime minister, to ensure that there would be no threat to RGC, and Australian Government representations were also made to the United States secretary of state.[31] In September 1989, the Western Australian deputy premier wrote to the agent general in London, expressing the Western Australian Government's interest in RGC's mineral

---

28   Cited within In the Matter of Renison Goldfields Consolidated Limited, Brief to Advise, RGCA, 28661.
29   Minorco Bid for Consolidated Gold Fields Limited, Letter from MJ Roberts, Chairman, 12 October 1988, RGCA, Box 17848, RGC 28660.
30   MJ Roberts to Sir Gordon Borrie QC, Director General of Fair Trading, 12 October 1989, In the Matter of Renison Goldfields Consolidated Limited, Brief to Advise, RGCA, Box 17848, RGC 28660.
31   *The Sydney Morning Herald*, 13 October 1988.

sands operations, as well as the Mount Goldsworthy iron ore project in which Consolidated Gold Fields had an interest in the operating company and a 'similar proportion of the huge iron ore reserves known as Mining Area C'.[32]

A range of actions were considered, reflecting the extent to which RGC was prepared to go to defend its independence from potential Minorco control. Legal advice was sought in relation to the 'powers of the directors of RGC to enter into arrangements on behalf of the company aimed at frustrating the current contested takeover bid'.[33] A proposal developed under the pseudonym 'Fan Club' entailed a plan for 'associates of CGF to buy up to £100 million of CGF shares to prevent Minorco passing [the] 50 per cent level'. It was proposed that RGC invest up to $50 million and that Newmont and Gold Fields of South Africa purchase shares in Consolidated Gold Fields 'very late in the period for which the Minorco offer is open'.[34] Advice made reference to the question of the legality of any attempts to frustrate a bona fide bid and concluded: 'The issue of insider dealing by the directors and the advisers is one which must be viewed with concern, and it is not clear how far it can finally be resolved certainly so far as the advisers are concerned in relation to implementing this proposal'.[35]

Proceedings were commenced in the New South Wales Supreme Court by RGC against Minorco, with Consolidated Gold Fields joined in the proceedings, which contended that Minorco's acquisition of more than 50 per cent of the voting shares of Consolidated Gold Fields would result in a breach of the Companies (Acquisition of Shares) Code in the state.[36] Other plans were more exotic. They included advice from a range of advisers for mechanisms, including a management buyout by RGC staff and senior executives, associated with external institutions. Others included RGC and Newmont forming a 'special purpose joint venture

---

32   Office of the Deputy Premier to Hon Ron Davies, Agent General London, 23 September 1989, In the Matter of Renison Goldfields Consolidated Limited, Brief to Advise, RGCA, Box 17848, RGC 28660.
33   Allen Allen & Hemsley, In the Matter of Renison Goldfields Consolidated, Brief to Advise, RGCA, 28661.
34   Renison Goldfields Consolidated Limited, 'Minutes of Meeting of Directors', 20 April 1989, p. 1, RGCA, Box 11329, BRD38/03.
35   To Mark Bethwaite, 22 March 1989, RGCA, Box 17848, RGC 28660.
36   RGC Announcement to the Stock Exchange and Press, 18 October 1988 (copy held by the author).

company' to bid for Consolidated Gold Fields and establish a 'newco' in the United Kingdom, with assets such as Peabody Coal, Porgera and Gold Fields of South Africa sold to reduce debt.

Another proposal considered an 'alternative equity' approach, which included a variation of an institutional and RGC management buyout, with a demerger of RGC into four separate companies—each separately listed. Yet another proposal was to restructure the shape of the North Broken Hill and Energy Resources of Australia (ERA) share registers to enable Consolidated Gold Fields and RGC to acquire an interest in them and forestall a potential Elders bid for North Broken Hill and ERA. A tie-up with North Broken Hill following its merger with ERA was also considered. A proposal for a reverse takeover by Elders Resources received short shrift from Anderson, who advised the defence committee: 'The proposal had "nowhere to go"! Apart from the fact that the terms suggested … are ludicrous, I don't believe the company's assets have any attraction for us'.[37] Arrangements were planned for the disposal of the Minorco shareholding in RGC if it were to be successful, with a list of possible buyers identified, including Mount Isa Mines, Western Mining Corporation, Pioneer International, North Broken Hill, Queensland Coal Trust Resources, Bell Resources, BHP, Poseidon, Consolidated Press Holdings and Santos, as well as international groups such as DuPont and Iwatani.

Internal RGC efforts were further stimulated by correspondence received in February 1989 advising that Minorco had appointed a company in Australia, Aries Consultants, to dispose of Consolidated Gold Fields' 'passive investment' in RGC if it were successful in its acquisition plans. While RGC was considering potential buyers of a future Minorco stake, other companies were viewing a potential Minorco takeover as a means of gaining access to RGC's assets. Mount Isa Mines built a shareholding during this period and its 4.1 per cent stake, which was held until January 1994, fuelled speculation that it could be a potential acquirer of RGC, particularly as both companies had an interest in the Porgera gold project in Papua New Guinea.[38] Five Australian mining companies were reported to have approached Aries' Australian representative, while Western Mining Corporation and CRA were mooted as potential buyers of RGC's

---

37   Renison Goldfields Consolidated Limited, Memorandum from Campbell McC Anderson to Defence Committee, 31 March 1989, RGCA, Box 17848, RGC 28660.
38   Mount Isa Mines sold its stake in January 1994 at a reported loss on the acquisition price of $12.8 million (*The Weekend Australian*, 8–9 January 1994).

assets.³⁹ Westralian Sands, the other major mineral sands producer in Australia, retained an interest in acquiring or merging its own south-west Western Australian assets with those of Associated Minerals Consolidated. It approached Tioxide, the company's major shareholder and customer, to express an interest in the unfolding situation:

> Re Minorco. Could you ascertain on the grapevine: whether the Renison Goldfields sell-off is a likely outcome of the merger; who may be the purchasers; would likely purchasers be prepared to sell off Associated Minerals Consolidated, which is of interest to WSL [Westralian Sands Limited].⁴⁰

Consolidated Gold Fields' activities in conjunction with those of Newmont were ultimately successful in thwarting Minorco. The Consolidated Gold Fields board had requested United States President Ronald Reagan to block the bid as it may harm the national security interests of the United States. However, legal action in the United States court system restrained Minorco from proceeding with its bid based on a likely breach of antitrust legislation in regard to the reduction of competition in the gold market.

On 16 May 1989, Judge Michael Mukasey of the New York District Court in Lower Manhattan decided that the injunction barring Minorco from taking over Consolidated Gold Fields would not be lifted. This legal action had been pursued by Newmont given that the British Takeover Panel had barred Consolidated Gold Fields from such legal action without a shareholder vote. Minorco conceded defeat and the company was debarred from making another takeover attempt for 12 months. The response from within RGC was ebullient. In a note to RGC directors, Anderson stated that he would not burden them with copies of the 'Magnificent Mukasey's' judgements that had dealt the 'final death blow' to Minorco. He ended his note: 'I suggest we all send him Christmas cards!!'⁴¹

The British media described the outcome in May 1989 as the end of 'an eight year saga of one of the world's stormiest corporate relationships coming to a sulphurous end'.⁴² However, any respite for the Consolidated

---

39 *The Sydney Morning Herald*, 28 April 1989.
40 AC Pearson to Mr David Searles, Tioxide House, London, 2 February 1989, RGCA, File IND021.
41 Renison Goldfields Consolidated Limited, Memorandum from C McC Anderson to RGC Directors, CGF/MINORCO, 17 May 1989, RGCA, Box 01381.
42 *The Sunday Telegraph*, 25 June 1989.

Gold Fields and RGC boards from further corporate distractions was short-lived. Jamieson, in his account of the Minorco saga, wrote: 'On 17 May, the day after Minorco had thrown in the towel … [there was] a report that Lord Hanson was "sniffing around", enquiring about Minorco's stake in Gold Fields'.[43] Edwardes contacted Lord Hanson and arranged a meeting at which he was told something that made him 'catch his breath'—namely that during the course of the Minorco bid, Lord Hanson had been approached by one of Consolidated Gold Fields' advisers to be a potential white knight.[44] Minorco came to an arrangement with Hanson whereby its 29.9 per cent stake, plus the acceptances for a further 24.9 per cent of Consolidated Gold Fields' shares would be available to support a Hanson bid for Consolidated Gold Fields.[45] This arrangement was described by one observer of the events as Minorco's 'cyanide kiss of goodbye'.[46]

On 22 June 1989, Hanson made an all-cash takeover offer for Consolidated Gold Fields, having gained Minorco's 29.9 per cent holding in addition to its own. Edwardes, given the personal and professional bruising he had received, was—not unexpectedly—'delighted to accept Hanson's offer'. Minorco exited the battle to pursue its ambitions—not to be fulfilled—of becoming a major global resources company. One journalist who followed the affair observed: 'Not that Minorco was smarting. Nothing more lifted its spirits now than the vicarious prospect of Hanson taking ConsGold apart: this would be Minorco's revenge—a Hanson bludgeoning. The dismemberment, as they saw it, would be far more ruthless than anything they planned'.[47]

The Hanson offer valued Consolidated Gold Fields at £3.1 billion, which was lower in total than the Minorco cash and scrip bid, although later increased to £3.5 billion. Hanson, a conglomerate, held interests in a range of companies[48] and was described as 'one of the most fearsome corporate predators on either side of the Atlantic'.[49] The initial Hanson bid was

---

43 Jamieson, *Goldstrike: The Oppenheimer Empire in Crisis*, p. 210.
44 ibid., p. 211.
45 Gibson, *Battlefields of Gold*, p. 47.
46 Jamieson, *Goldstrike: The Oppenheimer Empire in Crisis*, p. 213.
47 *The Sunday Telegraph*, 25 June 1989.
48 Hanson then held interests in Imperial Tobacco, Ever Ready Batteries, London Brick, Butterley Brick and Crabtree Electrical. In the United States, its shareholdings included Smith Corona Typewriters, SCM Chemicals, Ground Round Restaurants, Kaiser Cement, Gove Crane, AMES Tools, Jacuzzi Whirlpool Bath and Spa Products, and Faberware Cookware.
49 Moody, *The Gulliver File: Mines, People and Land*, p. 101.

rejected by Consolidated Gold Fields. However, Agnew was reported as saying: 'Unlike Minorco, Hanson is a serious company and any approach to it has to be seriously considered'.[50] Agnew indicated his intention to 'meet Lord Hanson to impress upon him the true worth of Gold Fields'. The engagement between the two major British companies was, according to Agnew, 'perfectly correct and civilised: two great British companies meeting to discuss. It was rather old fashioned, the way things *used* to be done'.[51] Hanson, despite ownership through its American arm of SCM, a company that had pigment production capacity, displayed little interest in mining and exploration. The prime appeal of Consolidated Gold Fields was its Amey Roadstone Construction group, with its major position in road construction materials in the United Kingdom.

On the other side of the world, the RGC board was well aware of the potential implications for the Australian business. As with Minorco, these could entail the dismemberment of the Australian entity or it being auctioned off to one of the large mining groups. Mount Isa Mines remained of concern in this regard, with an internal company note describing the company as 'running around the world approaching an embarrassing number of companies to try and put a deal together' to acquire Hanson's interest in RGC.[52]

In a joint letter from Roberts and Anderson to Lord Hanson, they wrote that the RGC board had considered the implications of a Hanson takeover of Consolidated Gold Fields:

> You will no doubt be aware that the RGC board viewed the proposed takeover of CGF by Minorco as being seriously detrimental to the interests of all the Company's shareholders ... the Board ... recognises that if the Hanson bid for CGF succeeds there will, of necessity, be some changes ... In the absence, at this time, of any indication of your company's plans for CGF's interests in RGC should your bid succeed the Board can only speculate but it believes that a sale by CGF of its interest is a not unlikely event. If that were to occur, the purchasers would almost certainly be

---

50   *The Sunday Telegraph*, 25 June 1989.
51   ibid., emphasis in original.
52   Briefing Note for Conversation, 1 January 1991, RGCA, Box 17848, RGC 28662.

compelled to bid for the remainder of our shares under Australian takeover law and RGC, as presently structured, would likely cease to exist.[53]

It was indicated that a premature decision to dispose of RGC to other shareholders would not be of benefit to shareholders. It was pointed out that with the commencement of the Porgera operation in Papua New Guinea, the 'renascent tin operations in Australia' and strengthening of the mineral sands operations, 'RGC is poised on the verge of a substantial growth period'.[54]

Lord Hanson communicated to Anderson:

> Following our telephone conversation this morning I am writing to confirm that, in the event of a successful takeover of Consolidated Goldfields by Hanson, we would expect an early exchange of views with you and your board. We have no plans to dispose of Consolidated Goldfields' 46% interest in Renison … We are looking forward to a cordial relationship between our two companies in the years ahead, to our mutual benefit.[55]

On 4 July 1989, an increased offer of £3.5 billion was made by Hanson. The Consolidated Gold Fields board accepted the offer. Lord Hanson had a signed letter delivered to the chairman of Consolidated Gold Fields:

> I am sure that the recent Minorco takeover offer has been a source of concern to you. In an effort to resolve this problem to the satisfaction of all concerned, we have today concluded an agreement with Minorco for them to accept an offer from us for all their shareholding, on the condition that Hanson makes a bid for all the outstanding shares in your Company. This we propose to do and I would very much like to discuss this with you. Our own feeling is that your Company and ours would be able to work together very satisfactorily and I hope you will seriously consider recommending our offer to your shareholders?[56]

---

53   RGC Limited, The Lord Hanson from MJ Roberts AM Chairman and C McC Anderson Chief Executive and Managing Director, 3 July 1989, RGCA, Box 17848, RGC 28660.
54   ibid.
55   Hanson by Fax to C McC Anderson Esq from AGL Alexander, 25 July 1989, RGCA, Box 17848, RGC 28660.
56   Letter from Lord Hanson to RIJ Agnew Esq, Chairman, Consolidated Gold Fields PLC, 21 June 1989, RGCA, Box 17848, RGC 28660.

In a move out of keeping with Hanson's usual approach to former management of acquired companies, Agnew was offered and accepted a position on the Hanson board, a position he maintained until June 1991. This meant he also served as a director of RGC. Another former Consolidated Gold Fields director, Beckett, also continued to serve on the RGC board. One former Consolidated Gold Fields employee recalled that if Minorco had been successful with its bid, all employees except Agnew were likely to retain their jobs; with Hanson acquiring Gold Fields, it was the opposite outcome. Coincidentally, Sir George Harvie-Watt, a major influence on the establishment of Consolidated Gold Fields' presence in Australia from 1960, and a former chief executive and chairman of the London group, died in December 1989 just after the takeover by Hanson had been finalised.

A 102-year history of a major South African and British mining and finance house had come to an end. According to one observer: 'It was a bitter end to one of the proudest names on the London Stock Exchange'.[57] The closure and retrenchment of Consolidated Gold Fields' head office personnel and the sale of its interest in Gold Fields of South Africa followed shortly thereafter. The company's vast store of business records was also, lamentably, destroyed.

One contemporary participant recalled that a request was made of Hanson by Minorco to have the other of the two statues of Cecil Rhodes, cast for the centenary celebration of Gold Fields and located in the Consolidated Gold Fields office, provided to them. When Hanson personnel came into the Consolidated Gold Fields London office and dismissed its personnel, the statue had gone, taken for 'safe keeping' by a senior Consolidated Gold Fields employee.[58] Hanson generated £1.1 billion in the first six months associated with the 'rationalisation' of Consolidated Gold Fields' businesses. The ramifications for the shareholding of the Australian business and its existence as a diversified mining company would be profound.[59]

---

57 Jamieson, *Goldstrike: The Oppenheimer Empire in Crisis*, p. 220.
58 Jonathan Loraine, personal communication, 27 March 2017.
59 'Hanson Interim Report 1990', 15 May 1990, p. 2 (copy held by the author).

PART SIX:
THE FINAL DECADE 1990–1998

Box 6. Key events 1990–1998

1990	Porgera Stage 1 commissioned, $425 million total expenditure (RGC equity, 33.3 per cent); first gold bullion poured
	Decision to increase synthetic rutile capacity at Narngulu, Western Australia, by extension of one kiln and construction of a fourth kiln
	Nelesbitan gold mine, Philippines—production commenced May and ceased later in year
	Transition at Mount Lyell to 50 series ore body
	Mining at Wau, Papua New Guinea, ceased with exhaustion of ore
	September 1990—100 years of mining on Renison leases
1991	Porgera—Stage 2 pressure oxidisation circuit of three autoclaves and oxygen plant commissioned
	Lucky Draw gold mine, New South Wales, reached the end of its economic life; accumulated ore stockpile drawn down
	Commissioning of Eneabba West mining operation—$129 million expenditure
	Narngulu synthetic rutile kiln commissioned—$106 million expenditure
	Pine Creek—RGC acquired remaining 40 per cent interest to take holding to 100 per cent
	Renison survival plan—increase in cut-off grade, workforce reduced from 350 to 250
	Trial of Mount Lyell seven-day underground operation commenced
	Approval for exploration shaft for Henty Gold project and development, subject to preconditions, including Little River Goldfields funding commitment
1992	Porgera—completion of Stage 3: expansion of concentrator capacity, underground crushing station and other works
	Tennant Trading sold
	Interest in Glendell Coal sold to Liddell joint venture
	Board approval to proceed with full development of Henty gold mine, $53 million capital of which RGC's interest was $34 million. Little River Goldfields could not fund its share; RGC moved to a 100 per cent interest
	Hanson approached Foreign Investment Review Board in relation to appointment of executive chairman

1993	Narama coal production commenced (RGC, 50 per cent), operated by Peabody Resources
	Porgera interest reduced to 25 per cent
	Campbell Anderson resigned as managing director and chief executive officer
	Mark Bethwaite appointed managing director and chief executive officer
	Tony Cotton appointed deputy chairman
	Porgera Stage 4A expansion completed
	Renison Rendeep development in train
	Henty gold mine opened
1994	Max Roberts retired as chairman after 14 years
	Tony Cotton appointed chairman
	Mining Area C iron ore royalty arrangement concluded
	Trialling of synthetic rutile enhancement process (SREP)
	Pine Creek mine ceased, November
	Mount Lyell closed, December
	Colinas wound up and operations ceased; landholding sold
	Goldfields Philippines Corporation sold
1995	Formation of Goldfields Limited (formerly RGC Pty Ltd)
	Takeover of Pancontinental Mining
	Renison: Rendeep approved—$34 million capital expenditure
	Koba Tin, Indonesia: Bemban dredge project commissioned—$22 million expenditure
	Porgera Stage 4B expansion commissioned
	Koba Tin smelter commissioned
1996	$11.4 million capital expenditure to modify a kiln to commercially produce SREP
	Cudgen RZ takeover, with interest in Consolidated Rutile Limited and Sierra Rutile
	Rendeep commissioning of hoisting shaft allowing access to deeper ore reserves
	Pancontinental Mining takeover completed with non-gold asset acquisition and sale process
	Thalanga acquired 100 per cent; net proceeds from sale of non-gold assets of $81 million
	RGC holds 58.5 per cent in Goldfields Limited
	Old Hickory, Virginia, United States—production commenced; $53 million capital expenditure
	Henty gold mine, Tasmania (held by Goldfields Limited)—production commenced

1997	Heads of agreement for Cerro Corona copper/gold project in Peru
	Acquisition of Reward copper/gold ore body near Thalanga, Queensland
1998	Mark Bethwaite resigns
	Tony Cotton assumes role of executive chairman
	Merger by scheme of arrangement announcement with Westralian Sands, July
	Merger completed with RGC shareholder vote on 11 December
	14 December—final RGC board meeting held; resignation of all RGC directors (except Cotton and Campbell) and appointment of six Westralian Sands directors
	Initial name of merged entity, Westralian Sands, changed to Iluka Resources in 1999

18

HANSON ON THE REGISTER

Hanson gained a 43.5 per cent shareholding in Renison Goldfields Consolidated (RGC) in July 1989 as a result of its acquisition of Consolidated Gold Fields. Shortly after this RGC obtained advice relating to options available to it to re-establish its independence, free of its new major shareholder.[1] These included RGC being the buyer of the Hanson holding or replacing it with a new single shareholder. Another option was the establishment of a 'mining house' structure in which investors could hold direct interests in 'pure' mining operations, with mining infrastructure owned by the multiple mining operations. In this form, RGC could be divided into three companies—mineral sands, tin and gold—with a jointly owned services company. RGC could be allocated shares in all three listed companies. A variety of other options were explored, although none were implemented. Instead, Hanson retained a shareholding in RGC for nearly a decade before exiting its holding through an arrangement with another listed company, Westralian Sands.

---

1   An internal note prepared by the RGC finance director, Bryce Wauchope, contained background information on Hanson for the information of executives and directors. It included the following: Hanson Plc was incorporated in England on 8 November 1959 under the name C Wiles Limited; it became a public company in March 1964. The name Hanson Trust Limited was adopted on 14 November 1969 and changed to Hanson Trust Public Limited Company on 11 November 1981 and changed to Hanson Plc on 3 December 1987. Three United States forays and one in the United Kingdom had occurred: in March 1986, SCM Corporation, manufacturer and seller of chemicals, coatings resins and typewriters; April 1986, Imperial Group Plc, a company engaged in tobacco, brewing and leisure industries; March 1987, Kaiser Cement Corporation, a US cement manufacturer; December 1987, Kiddie Investments, a diversified US-based manufacturing and services company (Renison Goldfields Consolidated Limited, 'Memorandum: C McC Anderson from BE Wauchope, Hanson Plc', Renison Goldfields Consolidated Archives (RGCA), Box 5336).

RGC operated independently, yet with a watchful and often demanding major shareholder that was represented on the board by three directors nominated by Lord Hanson. Christopher Collins, later to become vice-chairman of Hanson and chairman after Lord Hanson retired, had come to live in Australia and was a director of RGC from 1989.[2] He returned to the United Kingdom in May 1991 although had a continuing oversight of RGC's activities through a corporate development role at Hanson. Collins rejoined the RGC board in 1994 and, as chairman of one part of the then demerged Hanson group, played an instrumental role in the merger of Westralian Sands and RGC. When Collins returned to London, Brian Gatfield, who worked with the advisory firm Gatfield Robinson Wareing, replaced him as a director. Rudolph Agnew stepped down as a director of RGC and was replaced by Tony Cotton, a Hanson executive.[3] RC (Richard) Mason was the other of the three Hanson-nominated directors on the board.

Max Roberts and Campbell Anderson had achieved an understanding from Hanson that they had a right to place the Hanson shareholding in the hands of others. Amid the market conditions and poor financial start to the 1990s, attempts were made to place the Hanson shareholding. In advising AGL (Anthony) Alexander, Hanson's chief operating officer, in October 1990, Collins wrote:

> CA [Campbell Anderson] updated the board on his conversation with you, in which you indicated that disposal of the holding was on the back burner in the present climate and that achieving the 90/91 budget was now the chief priority in Hanson minds. He still felt that a long term solution should be sought and he would maintain his efforts in this area.[4]

Late the following year Alexander advised Anderson that Hanson 'remains a willing seller, at an appropriately realistic price'.[5] In fact, Hanson was active in seeking buyers for its stake. RGC's prime consideration in relation to potential acquirers was to ensure an arrangement that minimised the likelihood of a full takeover offer if more than 20 per cent of Hanson's

---

2   See Brummer and Crowe, *Hanson: The Rise and Rise of Britain's Most Buccaneering Businessman*, p. 9.
3   See Appendix 3 for a biographical profile of Tony Cotton.
4   Fax from Christopher Collins to Anthony Alexander, 5 October 1990, 'To: AGLA, From: CDC, 4 October 1990, RGC September Board Meeting and Visit to Tasmania', RGCA, Box 17848, RGC 28661.
5   AGL Alexander letter to C McC Anderson, 4 December 1991, RGCA, Box 17848, RGC 28661.

total shareholding was offered to an individual company. At the June 1991 board meeting, the chairman advised that an investment bank had been briefed in relation to potential acquirers. Alexander advised that while it remained a willing seller, it 'would not accept anything less than $7 per share at the present'.[6] The share price at the time was in the five dollars. RGC's assessment was that the book value of the Hanson shareholding in RGC was approximately $2.60. From RGC's perspective, Hanson's preoccupation with achieving a value higher than where the share price was trading was an impediment to the divestment of its shareholding. The adviser confirmed that a total placement of the Hanson stake would be difficult and would 'certainly demand a deep discount'. Anderson proffered the view that National Mutual—with which RGC had a close association—might agree to acquire part of the Hanson stake.[7]

This did not progress and instead, in 1991 and 1992, plans were put in train to establish a strategic relationship with Sumitomo Corporation, a large conglomerate and one of Japan's leading trading firms with interests in steel, chemicals and other materials. The arrangement envisaged allowing Sumitomo to take a shareholding in RGC, sufficient for it to be the company's largest shareholder. Sumitomo would not acquire more than 20 per cent of RGC and therefore not be obliged to make a full takeover bid for the company. Hanson's remaining 24 per cent shareholding was planned to be distributed to institutional investors. The proposed arrangement with Sumitomo Corporation followed an earlier engagement with Sumitomo Metal Mining in the first half of 1990, which came close to being executed at a contemplated price of $12 for each RGC share. However, this did not proceed associated with the collapse of the Japanese share market.[8] Mark Bethwaite made multiple visits to Japan to pursue the arrangement with Sumitomo. Daiwa Securities was retained as an adviser to engage with Sumitomo, with Anderson informing Daiwa that 'our present largest shareholder … has confirmed … that they would be willing to negotiate the sale of their shareholding in order to facilitate such a strategic partnership'.[9] The progression of the arrangements with

---

6   Notes of Renison Board Meeting Held Thursday, 27 June 1991, p. 2, RGCA, Box 17848, RGC 28661.
7   Facsimile to Mr AR Cotton from Brian PR Gatfield, 'Notes on RGC Board Meeting—Thursday 18 June 1992', 22 June 1992, RGCA, Box 17848, RGC 28661.
8   FMB [Francis Mark Bethwaite], Statement to Hanson Plc, 13 December 1991, RGCA, Box 17848, RGC 28661.
9   Campbell McC Anderson to Daiwa Securities, 21 November 1991, RGCA, Box 17848, RGC 28661.

Sumitomo was influenced by Mount Isa Mines' shareholding in RGC and its longstanding relationship with Sumitomo. When Sumitomo became aware that Mount Isa Mines was contemplating an acquisition of RGC this complicated the situation. It was believed Sumitomo would be reluctant to interrupt a potential offer by Mount Isa Mines and, in fact, may instead work with Mount Isa Mines on a joint bid for RGC.[10]

To expedite progress, Anderson proposed a three-way discussion involving Hanson, RGC and Sumitomo to determine that, if Sumitomo 'could give some reasonable price expectations', Hanson would be willing to put Sumitomo into 'the box seat' and deal exclusively with Sumitomo for a specified period. Anderson realised that unless 'RGC (and therefore effectively Hanson) "could knock MIM [Mount Isa Mines] out of the race" then Sumitomo because of their relationships with MIM were *most unlikely* ... to take this matter any further'.[11] The arrangement with Sumitomo did not proceed. Work was also pursued in relation to the identification of potential North America mining companies with a 'troublesome shareholder', with the concept that RGC would offer to acquire the 'troublesome shareholder' in exchange for assistance in breaking up the Hanson shareholding and establishing a cross shareholding.[12]

Westralian Sands remained an interested observer of the fate of the Hanson shareholding in RGC. Its managing director, Malcolm Macpherson, approached Robert de Crespigny of Normandy Poseidon to determine whether his company might have an interest in acquiring the gold assets of RGC, with Westralian Sands acquiring the mineral sands assets. Macpherson received the feedback from de Crespigny that none of the major mining houses were interested in acquiring RGC due to the 'complexity of the situation' and the 'over-priced nature of the company'.[13] Despite this response, Poseidon's legal adviser had approached the Foreign Investment Review Board (FIRB) seeking approval for a 19.9 per cent bid for RGC, although this also did not proceed.[14] In 1993, Westralian Sands held discussions with Western Mining Corporation to determine

---
10   File Note, 16 December 1991, RGCA, Box 17848, RGC 28661.
11   File Note CMcCA, 23 December 1991, RGCA, Box 17848, RGC 28661. Emphasis in original.
12   ibid.
13   Westralian Sands Limited, File, Phone Conversation with Mr Robert de Crespigny, Normandy Poseidon, MH Macpherson, 13 April 1992, RGCA, File IND021.
14   Note for File, Normandy Poseidon Bid for Renison, HR Dent, Assistant Secretary Foreign Investment Review Board, 15 September 1993, National Archives of Australia (NAA), A9275 F1992/4302 Part 2.

the basis of a potential joint proposal to Hanson to acquire RGC's mineral sands assets in Australia, with a view that Westralian Sands acquire the Capel assets and Western Mining Corporation acquire the assets in the Geraldton region.

In 1992, several other options were considered as part of attempts to free RGC of the Hanson shareholding. A proposal was presented by Anderson to the RGC board in a paper entitled 'Possible Disposal of RGCMS [RGC Mineral Sands] to Hanson Plc'.[15] The paper proposed that Hanson acquire the mineral sands division and at the same time divest its shareholding in RGC. While the board accepted the advantages of facilitating the disposal of Hanson's shareholding, the proposal did not progress. An 'acceptable value' for the RGC mineral sands assets was not considered achievable, while an expansion into the North American gold industry—as was proposed—was not considered 'strategically attractive' and the company's balance sheet was such that retention of existing equity was required, rather than the cancellation of existing shares.[16] In 1993, Hanson also investigated the placement of its shareholding with a range of Australian institutions. An investment bank indicated its willingness to underwrite the placement of the entire share and convertible note holding of Hanson.[17] This provided the opportunity for RGC's shareholding base to be transformed and for Hanson to exit at an attractive share price. As with other proposals, it did not proceed.

As early as May 1991, Roberts had corresponded with Alexander regarding his retirement. The understanding before Hanson had become the major shareholder of RGC was that Anderson would succeed Roberts as chairman, allowing Bethwaite to step into the role of managing director. Alexander expressed Hanson's 'strong view' that the roles of chairman and chief executive should be kept separate and, in the context of Hanson's concerns with the financial performance of RGC, indicated its preference for 'a strong independent Chairman', with reservations expressed 'about Campbell [Anderson] "moving upstairs"'.[18]

---

15 Renison Goldfields Consolidated Limited, 'Minutes of Meeting of Directors', 30 July 1992, p. 4, RGCA, Box 1130, BRD38/05.
16 ibid., p. 5.
17 Renison Goldfields Consolidated Limited, 'Minutes of Meeting of Directors', 27 August 1992, p. 6, RGCA, Box 1130, BRD38/05.
18 AGL Alexander to MJ Roberts, 9 May 1991, RGCA, Box 17848, RGC 28662.

In late 1992 and during 1993 an event occurred that created a near-crisis in the relationship between the independent directors of RGC and Hanson. In December 1992, Hanson, through its Australian legal advisers, approached the FIRB in relation to overturning aspects of the 1981 naturalisation status of the company, with discussion about the position of the chairman and chief executive officer as part of these representations. The approach to the FIRB had been made without the initial knowledge of the independent directors of RGC. The matter was advised to Roberts by the legal firm acting on behalf of Hanson. It was evident that Hanson wished to appoint its own executive chairman and take action in relation to the portfolio composition, potentially retaining only mineral sands and an interest in coal. The chief executive of Hanson, DC Bonham, in his representations to the FIRB, wrote:

> You will obviously be aware that we have been concerned at the direction taken by the company and the reduction in profits and dividends over the last three years ... In view of our inability to play an active role, we looked at ways of disassociating ourselves from RGC. The fact that the market was too weak to allow us to exit would tend to indicate that others have also become disillusioned with RGC's present business prospects. Under the existing circumstances RGC will not receive any additional capital investment through the Hanson Plc group, which itself makes capital raising from other outside sources more difficult ... We would certainly wish to be more active in managing RGC and have a greater say in the selection of its chief operating executives.[19]

The situation was so serious that at a board meeting, Roberts requested Anderson to read the July 1989 press release concerning the acquisition of Consolidated Gold Fields by Hanson and its undertakings at the time. The board minute recorded:

> The Chairman commented that he had no knowledge as to Hanson's reasons for making its application to FIRB. He surmised that its attitude to RGC would reflect Hanson's failure to sell its shareholding in a falling market; its belief that the Company had consistently failed to achieve Budget profitability due to declining metal prices; its view that poor management decisions led to overinvestment in the mineral sands industry, and the Group's decision not to sell its Porgera investment. Hanson may be

---

19   DC Bonham, Chief Executive, Hanson Plc to AM Hinton, The Treasury, 18 March 1993, NAA, A9275 F1992/4302, Part 1.

dissatisfied and [wish] to control the Board and then introduce Hanson management direction. The Board would need to consider the interests of all shareholders in reaching a response to Hanson's application.[20]

The Hanson-appointed directors were unable or unwilling to shed any light on Hanson's motivations, although one noted that 'Hanson was not a passive investor and might be expected to want a more active say if it believed changes to improve shareholder value were required'.[21] The independent directors expressed their concerns as to what some saw as a possible attempt by Hanson to gain management control, and by means of its 40 per cent shareholding, effective control of the company. For independent directors, this would be detrimental to the interests of other shareholders. According to Anderson, Hanson's application would have the effect of cancelling the company's naturalised status, with management control increasing from London, to the detriment of the company's prospects.[22] A contrary view expressed by one of the Hanson-appointed directors was 'that if the public were appraised of Hanson's application he anticipated the share price would respond favourably'.[23] Nonetheless, the determination was that the non-Hanson directors would oppose the Hanson application to the FIRB.

The RGC directors remained resolute in their opposition to Hanson's attempt to overturn the company's naturalised status; seen as a means of acquiring control of the company without paying a premium for such control. The challenges associated with its major shareholder were occurring at a time when Standard & Poor's had downgraded RGC's credit rating from BBB+ to BBB, the Government of Papua New Guinea was seeking to increase its shareholding in the Porgera gold mine and the financial performance of the company continued to deteriorate.

Collins attended a board meeting held in Queenstown, Tasmania, in March 1993. At the board meeting it was agreed that a professional 'head-hunter' be engaged to identify a replacement for Roberts as chairman. It was agreed that Anderson be considered for the role.[24]

---

20 Renison Goldfields Consolidated Limited, 'Minutes of Meeting of Directors', 5 January 1993, p. 2, RGCA, Box 1130, BRD38/05.
21 ibid.
22 ibid., pp. 3–4.
23 ibid., p. 4.
24 Renison Goldfields Consolidated Limited, 'Minutes of Meeting of Directors', 29 March 1993 and 19 April 1993, p. 2, RGCA, Box 1130, BRD38/05.

The following month, further consideration at board level occurred in relation to the Hanson matter. At this meeting, it was revealed that Hanson had made a further application to the FIRB, this time explicitly related to its desire to be able to appoint an executive chairman. Such an outcome would effectively displace the roles provided by Roberts and Anderson and place Bethwaite's position, as deputy managing director, in doubt, as it was planned that he would be next in line to be appointed managing director.

Instead, Lord Hanson offered Roberts the services of a full-time Hanson executive, Tony Cotton, as an executive chairman of RGC. Lord Hanson wrote to Roberts:

> We feel strongly that the only way to tackle RGC's endemic problems is for us to nominate and the board to appoint, an executive chairman with the experience necessary to focus full time, with RGC's executive team, on RGC's problems. The profit decline from over A$100m in 1989/90 to a loss in 1991/92 confirms that Renison has a serious financial problem ... Renison's current malaise means there is a huge task for Tony Cotton and the executive team. I would have thought Mark Bethwaite as managing director and Cotton as executive chairman, would be an excellent combination.[25]

By this stage, there was little trust and minimal goodwill between the two parties. Roberts wrote to Lord Hanson that the future intentions of Hanson with regard to RGC were:

> Insufficiently specific, in regard both to the future direction of the company and to management responsibilities, to allow the Board to make an informed judgement on supporting or opposing your application to be released from the 1991 undertakings ...
>
> Despite extensive involvement with the company for four years, Hanson has explicitly declined ... to provide further details, other than to nominate the specific Hanson employee sought as a full-time Executive Chairman ... Hanson's request is effectively a carte blanche to take operational, investment and financial control.[26]

---

25 Lord Hanson to Max Roberts, 20 April 1993, NAA, A9275 F1992/4302, Part 1.
26 Max Roberts to Lord Hanson, 19 April 1993, NAA, A9275 F1992/4302, Part 1.

The views of the independent RGC directors were presented with civility but concern. One director stated:

> Hanson in its documentation showed a consistent disinclination to be specific regarding its intention for the Company. RGC has repeatedly and consistently stated itself to be a mining and mineral exploration group whereas Hanson's position, at least up until now, had been that it would prefer the Company's dismemberment.[27]

For another, his concerns were summarised as:

> Hanson appeared to have no interest in the mining industry and had quickly disposed of CGF's mining interests, retaining only the ARC Roadstone Division. Hanson was now proposing no definite business plan for the Group, although it was asking the Board to cede control to it … The language presently being used by Hanson was very similar to that used in correspondence to CGF at the time of its takeover by Hanson.[28]

Anderson expressed his views:

> If Hanson nominated the chairman then the chairman should be non-executive but in the absence of written plans concerning their intentions for the Group he [Anderson] would be unable to support such an appointment. A non-executive chairman with 40% shareholding equates to control with there being little difference between an executive or non-executive chairman in this situation unless there are detailed written commitments.[29]

By May 1993, Roberts in representations to the minister for resources made clear his disdain for the nature of Hanson's approach and its intentions:

> Being caught by a falling market, they now wish to take over without a take-over offer … As part of its application to FIRB, Hanson has found it convenient to make a number of statements about its intentions for RGC. Most of these have lacked specific content. In relation to others, Hanson has been unwilling to make a <u>commitment</u> to adhere to them. I also note that Hanson has not disowned a continuing intention to close or sell mines, reduce

---

27 Renison Goldfields Consolidated Limited, 'Minutes of Meeting of Directors', 19 April 1993, p. 3, RGCA, Box 1130, BRD38/05.
28 ibid., p. 4.
29 ibid., p. 6.

exploration expenditure, close the Australian head office etc. Further, in response to a specific request from RGC, Hanson has refused to commit RGC to having a majority of its assets invested in the mining industry, unless independent directors agree to the contrary. At the same time as being unwilling to give any specific commitments to RGC's future participation in the Australian mining industry, Hanson is proposing the appointment of a U.K.-employed Hanson executive, with no previous involvement in the resource industry, as an Executive Chairman of RGC ... In short, Hanson has, over an extended period of time, sought to move RGC in the direction of a liquidation of many of its assets and the abandonment of its role as a major Australian mining house with the capacity and function of discovering and developing this nation's mineral resources.[30]

Anderson, likewise, 'saw it as inconceivable' that Cotton would come to Australia 'to manage a mining company' and that while 'Hanson's correspondence refers to expansion being undertaken as opportunities arise ... it has liquidated all its mining assets'. While he believed Hanson's attitude may change, 'it is unlikely to have changed with regard to mining'.[31] Anderson's proposals to the board were recorded as the following:

> The Managing Director suggested that if the Board was to cede control, i.e. allow Hanson to appoint its nominee as chairman, the Board should—
>
> i. obtain Hanson's clear understanding that on the basis of a Board of 13 members, five would be independent and Hanson would not vote its shares on their re-election. The five would nominate their own replacements and Hanson would neither nominate alternatives nor vote on replacements.
>
> ii. in recognition that it would be unreasonable to prohibit Hanson from moving away from mining, obtain a clear understanding that to undertake fundamental diversification agreement by a majority of the five independent directors would be necessary.
>
> iii. obtain Hanson's approval for a re-capitalisation of the Company prior to the ceding of control to ensure that the independent directors do not need to go cap in hand to the controlling

---

30 The Hon Michael Lee, Minister for Resources and Tourism from MJ Roberts, Chairman RGC, 20 May 1993, NAA, A9275, F1992/4302 Part 1. Emphasis in original.
31 Renison Goldfields Consolidated Limited, 'Minutes of Meeting of Directors', 19 April 1993, p. 3, RGCA, Box 1130, BRD38/05.

shareholder to obtain essential capital. A rights issue at a deep discount, perhaps a 1 for 2 at $2.00, prior to ceding control could provide appropriate re-capitalisation.[32]

For Anderson, in his engagement with the Treasury officials handling this matter, Hanson's philosophy and approach was that of an 'absentee landlord' wishing to maintain tight control from London, while Roberts was convinced that Hanson was not a long-term investor in RGC or Australian resources.[33]

Discussion by directors concurred that, if a takeover was being planned by Hanson, this should not occur without a premium being paid. By August 1993, a resolution—or at least a compromise—to what had been a tense and vexatious situation was determined. It was clear, given Hanson was dissatisfied with the operational management of the company's assets, that its concerns lay with Anderson and Roberts in their management and strategic oversight of the direction of the company.[34] The arrangement determined was that Anderson leave the company, Bethwaite be appointed managing director, Roberts be re-elected and remain as chairman for a further year and Cotton be appointed deputy chairman and assume the chairmanship on Roberts's retirement. The draft announcement circulated at the board meeting stated, in part:

> The company's largest shareholder, Hanson Plc, has indicated that upon Mr. Roberts' retirement they would wish to see the appointment of a Chairman other than from within the company itself … As it is now apparent that Hanson Plc will not endorse the appointment of Mr. Anderson as Chairman, it has been mutually agreed that Mr. Anderson will retire from the company's employment.[35]

---

32 ibid.
33 Note for File, Meeting with Representatives from Renison Goldfields Consolidated (RGC), 18 February 1993 and Submission to Foreign Investment Review Board on Behalf of The Board of Renison Goldfields Consolidated Limited, 20 January 1992, p. 17, NAA, A9275 F1992/4302, Part 1.
34 Lord Hanson had communicated to the federal treasurer in July 1993: 'May I reiterate a statement made by Tony Cotton, one of our directors, to Tony Hinton at the FIRB that "We should emphasise that Hanson respects RGC's operational management. Hanson believes that the mines are well run and does not anticipate having to make a major input in this area"' (The Hon John Dawkins, The Treasurer, from Lord Hanson, 23 July 1993, NAA, A9275 F1992/4302, Part 2).
35 Renison Goldfields Consolidated Limited, 'Minutes of Meeting of Directors', 23 September 1993, p. 10; 'RGC Announcement to the Australian Stock Exchange and the Press', 6 September 1993, RGCA, Box 1130, BRD38/05.

There was discussion among the directors of the appropriate wording to avoid any professional slight to their colleague Anderson. The final release issued stated that Anderson had accepted the position as chief executive officer of North Broken Hill Peko Limited and, as a result, it was mutually agreed that Anderson would retire from the company's employment, effective 25 September 1993. As such, shareholders were spared the details of what had been an acrimonious and highly unsettled period for the company. At Anderson's final board meeting, Roberts conveyed his appreciation for Anderson's contribution and their friendship, commenting that he could not have asked for more of the relationship with his managing director. Anderson shortly thereafter became managing director of North Broken Hill. Hanson's application to the FIRB resulted in RGC losing its naturalised status. Bethwaite was appointed managing director and chief executive officer in what was an unenviable set of circumstances for a new leader of the company.

Roberts retired as a director in February 1994. A board colleague stated that 'Roberts steered RGC over the last 14 years from a group of related but unjoined companies to a unified group in the mineral industry' that 'saw both prosperity and difficult times'.[36] Cotton was appointed chairman on 24 February 1994. His appointment as chairman was publicly described as bringing with it a 'closer collaboration' with RGC's major shareholder, while the support of Hanson, particularly in the financial sense, was 'anticipated for RGC's growth strategy'.[37] The reality was that Hanson wished to exert greater control of RGC, particularly given the recent poor performance of the company and lack of confidence in executive management. A greater alignment of interests was conveyed, publicly at least, with Bethwaite saying to the media: 'Tony's [Cotton's] appointment means that I can get on with running the business rather than looking over my shoulder'.[38] Reflecting this greater Hanson oversight, Collins rejoined the RGC board in 1994 at the directive of Lord Hanson.

---

36 Comments by John Darling (Renison Goldfields Consolidated Limited, 'Minutes of Meeting of Directors', 24 February 1994, p. 7, RGCA, Box 14284, BRD38/08).
37 Renison Goldfields Consolidated Limited, *Annual Report 1994*, p. 2; *The Australian*, 27 December 1993.
38 *The Bulletin*, 16 November 1993, p. 87.

Figure 54. Mark Bethwaite, Tony Cotton and Max Roberts, 1993. Following the departure of Campbell Anderson, Bethwaite was appointed managing director and Tony Cotton, a Hanson executive, deputy chairman. Max Roberts stayed on as chairman for 12 months with Cotton succeeding him as chairman. Cotton assumed the executive chairmanship in 1998 after the departure of Bethwaite.
Source: Kate Callas, *Sydney Morning Herald*.

The evident dissatisfaction of Hanson with its investment in RGC formed the backdrop of RGC's business activities for the remainder of the 1990s. Hanson remained a shareholder of RGC until 1998 and, while generally supportive of management's efforts, its shareholding was premised on the ability to exit at an appropriate stage. This was hardly a favourable basis for the management of a mining company that required major investment over an extended period to rebuild parts of its portfolio that were both mature and technically challenged. The opportunity for Hanson to exit its shareholding arose when arrangements were put in place to initially reduce and subsequently exit its holding through a merger by scheme of arrangement between Westralian Sands and RGC.

19

TUMULTUOUS YEARS 1990–1994

Hanson acquired its controlling interest in Renison Goldfields Consolidated (RGC) in 1989. This year and 1990, its first full year of ownership, were favourable ones for the group. Profit after tax and before extraordinary items in 1989 was $100 million, rising to $116 million in 1990. The company recorded a return on shareholders' funds close to 30 per cent in each year. The two years were the best financially that RGC had recorded since its establishment in 1981. Campbell Anderson awarded employees with a bonus equivalent to one week's salary. It was an encouraging start to Hanson's coincident investment in an Australian company flowing from its acquisition of Consolidated Gold Fields in the United Kingdom. However, global economic conditions deteriorated in 1991 and 1992, with recessionary conditions as well as tumultuous political and military events, including the Gulf War.

The implications of the volatile and uncertain conditions for commodity prices and, as such, RGC's financial performance, were severe. Mineral sands, the largest contributor to group earnings, suffered straitened financial performance over the next five years. In an internal memorandum in 1991, Bryan Ellis, group general manager of marketing, warned of 'formidable hurdles' for mineral sands, including an oversupply of titanium dioxide feedstocks, pressure on the zircon price and RGC's diminishing competitive position in synthetic rutile production.[1]

---

1   Memorandum, Bryan Ellis, AMC Mineral Sands Marketing, 4 June 1991, Renison Goldfields Consolidated Archives (RGCA), Box 3536.

From a financial contribution of $176 million in 1990, earnings more than halved in 1991 and were then either negative or marginally positive for the next three years.

Relative to 1989 and 1990 the average tin price received by RGC declined by over 20 per cent in the following two years; the copper price declined by over 12 per cent and, while mineral sands prices remained reasonably stable in 1991, there were major declines in the prices of rutile and zircon.[2] The adverse impact of lower prices on revenue was compounded by lower sales volumes, including the forfeiture of sales by some customers, particularly for mineral sands. Combined zircon, rutile and synthetic rutile sales in 1991 and 1992 were 40 per cent lower than in the prior two years.

These factors had an adverse effect on the margin and profitability of the individual divisions and RGC as a whole. Porgera gold mine, which commenced production in 1990, was the major earnings contributor to RGC for the next five years. Despite this RGC was profitable—and only marginally so—in two of the next four years. RGC's profit in 1991 reduced by nearly two-thirds compared with 1990, while accumulated losses were recorded through to 1994 (see Table 19.1). The financial circumstances of RGC led to considerable scrutiny and disquiet on the part of Hanson. This included questioning the veracity of the diversified business model and a process of asset divestitures, including the consideration—urged by Hanson—for the sale of either mineral sands or Porgera, as well as the implementation of 'survival plans' at both Renison and Mount Lyell. The market challenges for management were added to by the need to develop Eneabba West as part of the continuation of this operation for the production of ilmenite that, in turn, was necessary to underpin synthetic rutile production. RGC and its joint venture partners had to contend with claims by the Government of Papua New Guinea to increase its interest in the Porgera project from 10 per cent to 30 per cent, with a potential threat of expropriation of part of the interest held by the joint venture partners.

Meanwhile, RGC management was also investigating means by which the Hanson shareholding could be reduced or placed with others. As conveyed in the previous chapter, a major issue arose at board level in 1993 when Hanson applied to the Foreign Investment Review Board, without first advising the independent directors, to overturn RGC's

---

2   Renison Goldfields Consolidated Limited, *Annual Report 1993*, pp. 22–24. The zircon price halved over 1992 and 1993 compared with 1990.

naturalised status. It would be a dramatic period for the company, with only a partial restitution in its financial performance by 1996. At that stage, there had been a change of managing director and a Hanson director appointed chairman.

...

An *Economist* article on Hanson in the possession of an RGC executive had the following section underlined:

> In Hanson, the budget, once agreed, is a contract between business managers and headquarters. Each month's results are picked over in the businesses's board meeting, with a head-office manager present in a non-executive role. Any shortfall must be explained. If headquarters is uneasy with the excuses given, it sends a 'flying squad' of accountants to check it out ... Failure, on the other hand, leads to dismissal.[3]

In another indication that the environment under the new shareholder may be different, the same executive retained and made notations on the following article from the *Financial Times* referring to Lord Hanson and Lord White, the two titular heads of the Hanson empire:

> [The] Hanson-White relationship has two weaknesses which could be even more significant, according to those who have worked closely with them. The first is vanity. Employees are berated for not washing their hair, or for having dandruff on their collars. Lord Hanson's receding hairline is a matter of constant attention. He is fascinated by trichology—a medical study of hair loss. After attending a clinic for hair loss, he hired a trichologist to work on the hair of his directors. 'We were encouraged to go once a fortnight,' says one. 'It was part of Lord Hanson's desire for respectability. We had to look good. I think he's a little insecure.' ... Former colleagues say the second weakness is the company's pursuit of acceptability, recognition and a place in the very corporate establishment White and Hanson have crusaded against.[4]

RGC was to experience elements of this inquisitorial approach, particularly from its deputy finance director, RA (Ross) Chiese—if not a concern with trichology—in its early encounters with Hanson personnel.

---

3   *The Economist*, 25 May 1991.
4   *The Financial Times*, 20–21 July 1981.

In the early 1990s, Hanson's concerns with the financial state of the RGC business related to the high level of debt and exposure to foreign currency movements to the extent that the company could be viewed, in Hanson's perspective, as a 'currency play'.[5] Chiese sought frequent and detailed information on budgetary and other matters from RGC management. He undertook operational visits, including one in 1991. He reported back to Cotton, then an executive of Hanson and later deputy chairman and chairman of RGC. In one set of correspondence, Chiese observed:

> I had a much more satisfactory visit this time and have formed a more favourable view of the managements abilities, although the financial thrust of the company is not as much at the forefront as it would be say in Hanson and undoubtedly the budget has been constructed more as a possible target than an absolute deliverance.[6]

He assessed that Porgera was progressing well and that the Lucky Draw gold mine, closed in August 1991, had been a successful investment. There was much in his assessment that was not favourable. The mineral sands division was viewed as 'a drain on RGC resources ... loses A$27 million after interest in 91/92 and A$13m in 92/93'.[7] Chiese's inquisitorial approach led to a request for attendance at an RGC board meeting. This tested Anderson's patience:

> Your additional request to attend a Board Meeting is clearly something which is out of the ordinary and a request which I, having discussed with the Chairman, must unfortunately decline. Although you are an employee of our largest shareholder, Hanson does already have three appointments to the Board and as far as I am aware these appointments provide a satisfactory communication to Hanson. It never has been in the past, nor do I suggest it should be in the future, appropriate for additional attendees at such meetings ... Might I repeat, yet again, my request that for the sake of good order in the relationship between our two companies you initially direct inquiries of a non routine nature to myself.[8]

---

5   AGL Alexander to C McC Anderson, Treasury Matters, 19 February 1991, RGCA, Box 17848, RGC 28661.
6   To AGLA [AGL Alexander]/ARC [Tony Cotton] from RANC [Ross Chiese], Renison Budget Review 1991/92, p. 4, RGCA, Box 5336.
7   ibid.
8   Telex to RA Chiese, Hanson Plc London from Campbell McC Anderson, 30 October 1990, RGCA, Box 973.

Chiese became an alternate director to Cotton. His approach in this capacity at board meetings was no less terrier-like. He was critical of the separation of the marketing function in Sydney from operations. He peppered management with his observations and questions, which related to a range of matters, including stock levels being in excess of requirements, budgetary settings appearing optimistic, the lack of success of exploration and his view that administrative expenditure needed to be reined in.[9]

Table 1. Renison Goldfields Consolidated group and divisional financial performance, 1990–1998.

$m	1990	1991	1992	1993	1994	1995	1996	1997	1998
Group operating profit/(loss) after tax and extraordinary items	116.0	25.3	–10.1	–24.4	1.8	97.4	142.8	–78.0	–46.1
Divisional contribution to results									
Associated Minerals Consolidated	176.6	67.2	–1.0	1.3	–5.5	41.5	93.3	85.1	69.6
Renison Tin	1.2	–12.7	–1.7	2.0	–2.7	–6.0	–1.0	–8.6	5.4
Mount Lyell Copper	–10.1	–1.2	4.1	1.1	11.0	19.6			
Koba Tin	9.3	2.1	4.9	8.3	2.0	4.4	8.7	10.9	25.4
Porgera Gold		68.6	103.0	59.0	66.5	42.9	37.3	43.7	35.6
Lucky Draw Gold	18.2	5.9	0.7	0.5					
Pine Creek Gold	0.8	–6.7	0.9	–1.8	–3.1	1.6			
Paddington Gold						–0.5	–5.7	–1.0	14.9
NGG Gold	3.5	–3.5							
Henty Gold								–0.4	–2.5
Thalanga Base Metals						–0.7	6.6	2.5	–6.5
Kundana Gold						1.0	20.4	12.0	10.2
Narama Coal				6.5	13.3	12.0	10.6	11.3	10.3
Trading	0.8	0.5	0.5	0.4	0.1	0.4	–0.1		
Investments	4.2	4.0	0.3						

Financial information includes RGC and the gold interests held through RGC's approximate 56 per cent shareholding in Goldfields Limited after 1995. The Paddington, Thalanga and Kundana interests were all acquired as a result of the 1995 acquisition of Pancontinental Mining.

Sources: RGC annual reports, 1991 to 1997; 'Information Memorandum in Relation to a Recommended Merger by Scheme of Arrangement between RGC Limited and Westralian Sands Limited', 1998.

---

9   ibid. Many of the observations were dutifully handled by management, for example, explaining stock levels of concentrate that were in excess of three months of production requirements because some had higher uranium and thorium levels and, as such, needed to be blended.

Chiese expressed concerns as part of the budgetary review process of production problems at Renison, Mount Lyell and Pine Creek, and remarked on the 'very expensive closure' of the Nelesbitan gold mine in the Philippines.[10] In preparations for the 1992 financial year budget, he observed to his Hanson colleagues that 'the cash flow deficit for 1990/91 is projected at A$242m which has increased net debt to A$443m' with a consequent gearing of 'almost 100%' and a 'return on capital employed of about 6%'.[11] Chiese's view was that the budget for the 1992 financial year had 'more downside than upside' and that the share price was 'over-valued'. Further, his assessment was that the Renison operation 'will probably not survive and further reductions may be needed at Mount Lyell'. Accordingly, cash needed 'to be raised from disposals, [with] further reductions in working capital and development expenditure ... required to reduce the gearing'.[12]

The assessment by the new shareholder was conveyed starkly:

> The company itself has got itself into a severe problem in that it is too highly geared, a dropping EPS [earnings per share], ROCE [return on capital employed] at AMC [Associated Minerals Consolidated] is far too low (and likely to be so for the next couple of years) the interest bill is crippling and there is little prospect of higher profits unless gold and mineral sands prices increase. It has therefore nowhere to go at present ... The management do not appear to have 'got the message' regarding cash and cash flow management, whether they understand that the budget is a commitment and not necessarily a target, only time will tell. Without doubt, they made an over-optimistic judgement in its present form, at least AMC is well set for any improvement in its market position.[13]

Christopher Collins wrote to Tony Alexander on this matter, in the context of prevailing RGC debt levels:

> To have a target of reducing net gearing to 110% shows just what a problem the company faces. Until this gearing has been significantly reduced, Renison will be exposed to constant financial blizzards. As far as the strategy of a diversified mining

---

10 To AGLA [AGL Alexander]/ARC [Tony Cotton] from RANC [Ross Chiese], 14 June 1991, RGCA, Box 17848, RGC 28661.
11 ibid., p. 2.
12 ibid.
13 ibid., p. 8, emphasis in original.

house is concerned there is one shareholder who has considerable reservations about the validity of this policy. It certainly does not look too hot at the moment. In light of these views, I do not see why it is a waste of time to appraise the reduction of the business into two main streams. Would you discuss this further with Campbell and Max … We remain unconvinced that enough is being done and we strongly suspect that when all the financial appraisals have been completed (again hopefully well ahead of the next Board Meeting) our views will be proved correct.[14]

The perspectives of the Hanson-appointed directors and those of other directors were often at marked variance. In July 1990, Anderson reported on a discussion with Hanson's chief operating officer, Alexander. The board minutes record that Alexander had emphasised the 'desirability of a steadily increasing profit' from Hanson's investment in RGC. This reflected an industrial company perspective, but one not necessarily relevant to a mining company where demand, commodity price and unit cash costs are all factors that could come into play in influencing the earnings profile.

Anderson, imposing and tall of stature, with an intellectual and verbal felicity to match, exercised great forbearance at times to numerous Hanson questions and observations. In this case, his observations were recorded as follows:

> Although emphasising that in the mining industry, where operations are susceptible to the vagaries of world metal markets, a continually increasing profit was not always achievable, the Managing Director fully accepted the benefits to all shareholders of progressive profit increases and confirmed that all reasonable efforts would be taken during the Budget year to achieve a profit increase.[15]

On another occasion, Anderson was supportive of a management recommendation to secure mining leases in the United States even though they may not come into production for at least 10 years. For Collins as a Hanson director, this proposal was 'difficult', as the expenditure did not comply with Hanson's preferred payback period of four years. Anderson suggested that any payback considerations should also be made

---

14   CD Collins to AGL Alexander, Renison, 1 March 1991, RGCA, Box 17848, RGC 28661.
15   Renison Goldfields Consolidated Limited, 'Minutes of Meeting of Directors', 26 July 1990, p. 16, RGCA, Box 11329, BRD38/04.

on the basis of the implications of increased competition to RGC and the 'effect on mineral sands prices if another group brought these deposits into quick production'.[16] As such, the framework for considering the factors influencing the business and the time frames for investments often diverged between RGC management and its largest shareholder.

More fundamentally, Hanson questioned the efficacy of the diversified business model. There were numerous requests to consider focusing the portfolio to one or two key businesses, which typically entailed, in Hanson's thinking, the retention of mineral sands and the Porgera operation in Papua New Guinea, although country and currency risk associated with the investment in Papua New Guinea was of ongoing concern to Hanson.

Alexander wrote to Max Roberts suggesting a more radical consideration in terms of the company's structure as a means of addressing the financial issues facing RGC:

> We particularly emphasised our great concern about Renison's [RGC's] level of gearing and the clear prospect, on the basis of the figures provided for the next three years, that this gearing is not going to be significantly reduced ... We discussed with Campbell the serious strategic problems that the level of gearing has created and described to him our concern that with the level of borrowings created in recent years, coupled with the rapid downturn in the fortunes of the mineral sands business, Renison is now in a highly constricted situation without the ability to take on new opportunities as they arise. One way to solve this would be to dispose of one or other of the mainstream activities—either Porgera or mineral sands ... We made it clear we would not support a Rights Issue ... The name of the game at Renison for the next three years must be cash flow. The company has got itself into a box from which it will be difficult to emerge without hard decisions. Unless the gearing is rectified we see no potential for really worthwhile growth through the 1990's which must be essential for both the shareholders and for the job satisfaction of the management.[17]

---

16 Renison Goldfields Consolidated Limited, 'Minutes of Meeting of Directors', 26 October 1989, p. 16, RGCA, Box 11329, BRD38/04.
17 By Fax, AGL Alexander to M Roberts, 24 June 1991, RGCA, Box 5336, File 2-4.

A financial adviser was asked to assess the value of RGC's interest in Porgera and the mineral sands operations. In 1991, Cotton expressed his preference for the sale of the Porgera stake. The flotation of RGC's interest in Porgera was proposed with Anderson presenting a report detailing the complexities involved in preparing a prospectus for such an occurrence. Porgera was retained.[18]

Cotton took a more favourable view towards mineral sands, writing: 'On balance we would prefer to keep the mineral sands business as both price and demand are clearly at the bottom of the cycle. We are sure that this company has excellent long term market and growth prospects'.[19] A wider consideration of the RGC portfolio structure was undertaken. The board endorsed the planned divestment of the company's coal assets, including Glendell and Narama, as well as Tennant Trading and the agricultural assets of Colinas, while consideration was also given to the divestment of the Investment Division. Efforts to generate cash were associated with selling shares in all but one of the companies held within its Investment Division in 1991. Tennant Trading was sold in 1992.[20] Renison, a major part of the portfolio, was suffering from low tin prices and operating in accordance with a 'survival plan', while options for the closure of Mount Lyell were being considered.[21] A sale process for Mount Lyell failed to elicit interested parties willing to submit a bid. In October 1991 a share placement occurred of 10 per cent of RGC's issued share capital, raising $85 million. Hanson did not take up its entitlement in this share issue.[22] These actions, and others, enabled RGC to reduce its net debt from $442 million to $332 million and its net debt to equity ratio from 92 per cent to 60 per cent.

Hanson was never comfortable with its investment in RGC, an investment that was not consistent with its usual outright ownership arrangement and ability to scrutinise and control the level of capital expenditure. According to Cotton's later recollection, Hanson would not have expected

---

18 Renison Goldfields Consolidated Limited, 'Minutes of Meeting of Directors', 25 July 1991, p. 3, RGCA, Box 1130, BRD38/05.
19 Facsimile to Max Roberts, Renison, from AR Cotton, 24 July 1991, RGCA, Box 17848, RGC 28661.
20 Renison Goldfields Consolidated Limited, 'Minutes of Meeting of Directors', 28 March 1991, p. 15, RGCA, Box 1130, BRD38/05.
21 Renison Goldfields Consolidated Limited, 'Minutes of Meeting of Directors', 23 May 1991, RGCA, Box 1130, BRD38/05.
22 17.9 million shares were placed with institutional shareholders at $4.80 per share, a 5.5 per cent discount to the prevailing weighted average share price.

to maintain its shareholding in RGC for the length of time it did and, in his view, 'Hanson would have been receptive to offers that gave what was full value'.[23] In fact, Hanson over the years had several opportunities to sell some or all of its shareholding at prices between $4.20 and $9.50, while a potential sale arrangement with Sumitomo would have secured a price above $10.00.[24] 'One particular regular enquirer' was Norm Fussell, the chief executive officer of Mount Isa Mines, a company that held a shareholding in RGC and was seen as a potential acquirer of the company. He was viewed by RGC as 'running around the world approaching an embarrassing number of companies to try and put a deal together'.[25] No offer fulfilled the expectation of full value for Hanson's controlling position. Hanson considered approaching an advisory firm to evaluate the options it had available, including obtaining a new controlling shareholder or pursuing a reconstruction of the company. It also considered approaching the Foreign Investment Review Board to increase its shareholding beyond 44 per cent.

Through the influence of the independent directors, the RGC board saw little merit in restructuring the company into one or two main business streams as proposed by the Hanson directors. Collins described such a concept as 'alien to a diversified mining house'.[26] He advised his colleague in London:

> It was accepted that the Executive's endorsement of the strategy to remain as a diversified mining house was made on philosophical grounds rather than on the basis of a financial case. I suggested that, as proof of the strategy's soundness, a financial appraisal of a head office move to Perth and sell off operations other than AMC and Porgera should be prepared. It was felt that this was so far away from a strategy which the Board could contemplate that it would be a waste of time. Members remembered debating the disposal of mineral sands, which lost $5m in 1982 … RGC regards itself as having a diversified portfolio of cyclical mining interests, which require a long term approach.[27]

---

23 Tony Cotton, personal communication, 6 January 2017.
24 The Hon Michael Lee, Minister for Resources and Tourism, from MJ Roberts, Chairman RGC, 20 May 1993, National Archives of Australia, A9275 F1992/4302 Part 1.
25 RGC Briefing Note, 1 January 1991, RGCA, Box 17848, RGC 28662.
26 Christopher Collins to AGL Alexander, 11 March 1991, RGCA, Box 17848, RGC 28662.
27 To AGLA [AGL Alexander] from CDC [Christopher Collins], 1 March 1991, [re] RGC February Board Meeting, 28 February 1991, p. 4, RGCA, Box 17848, RGC 28662.

The decline in the group's financial performance resulted in a need for additional borrowing facilities, as well as to curtail expenditure. The sale of assets, requested by Hanson, and one of the few options available to generate additional funds, remained under active consideration. At the March 1991 board meeting, directors agreed that the company should attempt to sell its coal and iron ore interests, as well as Mount Lyell. Colinas remained earmarked for sale although with continued difficulty in attracting interested buyers. The sale of the investment portfolio, a part of the business that Hanson was adamant should be sold, was deferred. Collins also proposed the sale of 'peripheral assets' and exploration projects, such as Pine Creek and the Henty gold project.[28] Exploration expenditure was reduced from $19 million to $16 million as part of 1992 budget planning, although one of the Hanson directors sought a 50 per cent reduction and questioned whether the group's head office should be relocated from Sydney to Perth. Hanson directors were of the view that actions to address the level of debt, by deferring capital expenditure and reducing costs, were of paramount importance. Their view was that management efforts did not 'go anywhere deep enough' in the context of challenges associated with the equity position in Porgera and the reduction in RGC's credit rating in 1992.[29]

Notes on a board discussion of the financial outlook for the 1992 financial year recorded:

> The Chairman's request for Directors' views produced a unanimous comment from non-executives that the budget was unacceptable … there were inadequate solutions offered. CmcA [sic, Campbell McC Anderson] rejected the proposition that a 'survival plan', embracing radical change was needed and, commenting upon each material area of the business, gave reasons why it would be very difficult to implement change in the near term without damaging the Company. Directors made it clear that the status quo was not an option and asked that the Managing Director re-address: (1) Asset Sales; (2) Exploration and Development Budgets (3) Administration and Head office (structure and costs).[30]

---

28 Renison Goldfields Consolidated Limited, 'Minutes of Meeting of Directors', 24 January 1991, p. 15, RGCA, Box 1130, BRD38/05.
29 Renison Goldfields Consolidated Limited, 'Minutes of Meeting of Directors', 24 February 1991, p. 13, RGCA, Box 1130, BRD38/05; Christopher Collins to AGL Alexander, 11 March 1991, RGCA, Box 17848, RGC 28662.
30 Renison Goldfields Consolidated Limited, 'Minutes of Meeting of Directors', 18 June 1992, p. 4, RGCA, Box 1130, BRD38/05. The board note also indicated: 'At the Chairman's Committee, read out correspondence and confirmed FMB [Mark Bethwaite] had been told he would become CEO next year'.

It was determined there was a need for '"radical action" ... to ensure the Company's continuity'.[31] At a 1993 board meeting, Chiese commented that Hanson saw the mineral sands operations as the group's 'biggest problem area'.[32] In his view, 'with approximately 800 employees there did not seem to be a single person responsible for the Division'.[33] In the context of financial challenges and the evident anxiety of the Hanson-appointed directors, Anderson cautioned directors to be careful about 'kneejerk responses to a downturn in the cycle' and to avoid what was referred to as 'precipitative short-term action which may jeopardise the long-term future'.[34]

Mineral sands—competition and cyclicality

In 1991, Anderson stated that the mineral sands market was the worst it had been for seven to eight years.[35] The lack of demand for mineral sands products in the early 1990s was followed by a precipitous decline in the zircon price. Even though it was believed to have a floor price of $450 per tonne, it dropped as low as $125 per tonne in early 1992 and was to decline further. Richards Bay Minerals, which became the global leader in titanium slag production, created a competitive threat not only for high-grade titanium dioxide products, but also zircon. The zircon price came under pressure in part due to the approach of Richards Bay Minerals in considering zircon a minor part of its overall revenue stream and, as such, a by-product to its main sources of production. In a situation in which any revenue contribution from zircon could be viewed as an offset to the cost of production of its principal products, this created a pricing dynamic that was not beneficial for RGC, given zircon was a more meaningful part of its revenue profile.

A contemporary participant conveyed that the demand for zircon in the 1980s meant that 'the envelope was pushed to get volume at the expense of quality'. In this regard:

---

31   ibid., pp. 4 and 8.
32   Renison Goldfields Consolidated Limited, 'Minutes of Meeting of Directors', 24 June 1993, p. 3, RGCA, Box 1130, BRD38/05.
33   ibid.
34   ibid.
35   *The Australian*, 26 July 1991.

19. TUMULTUOUS YEARS 1990–1994

> Specifications that were termed as 'typical' were stretched to 'maximum' and on occasions beyond. At the end of the 80s and beginning of the 90s, zircon in particular was in huge demand and some of our biggest and best customers were force fed out of spec material in order to push volume through. When the market started to turn around in … 1991, those customers pushed back and not only refused to buy more, they were demanding rebates on the off grade material they had been given. Producing the volumes of zircon that RGC was producing at that time, it took but a few months of no sales to build up an immense working capital and no constraint on production was initiated.[36]

Higher zircon prices, influenced by an earlier surge in demand in refractory usage in Japan, had caused customers in the steel industry to seek substitutes or reduce the amount of zircon used, with partial substitution in refractory and foundry sands applications. A similar situation became evident for zircon use in tile applications. While the prospects for chloride feedstock demand were more favourable due to the continued growth of chloride pigment production capacity, the nexus between feedstock demand and global economic growth remained influential. As such, in 1991 an 'unexpected sharp decline in the market volumes for titaniferous dioxide feedstock and in market volumes and prices for zircon as a result of world recession and capacity increases' changed the landscape yet again.[37]

In a memorandum to Anderson in August 1991, Mark Bethwaite, as deputy managing director, wrote: '[The] current AMC structure is more appropriate to the strong growth phase of recent years than the operational and expenditure restraint required by current poor mineral sands markets'.[38] The costs in the Perth office were excessive, with too many levels of management and overlap with functions performed in the Sydney office. The challenges associated with Eneabba and synthetic rutile expansion work had caused the numbers in the office to swell. The Perth office was closed and replaced by a smaller divisional office at Geraldton. In a communication to employees, Bethwaite observed: 'I am aware that these changes will not be welcomed by some staff … The mineral sands industry is under extreme pressure and RGC Mineral Sands must meet this challenge'.[39]

---

36   Bryan Ellis, personal communication, 20 April 2017.
37   Renison Goldfields Consolidated Limited, *Annual Report 1991*, p. 1.
38   To C McC Anderson from Mark Bethwaite, RGC Restructuring and Overhead, 19 August 1991, RGCA, Box 1130, BRD38/05.
39   RGC Mineral Sands Limited Announcement, 15 June 1992. On 30 April 1992, AMC changed its name to RGC Mineral Sands.

In 1992 a task force was formed, chaired by Bethwaite, to examine the future of the mineral sands division. Influenced by the marketing actions of Richards Bay Minerals, RGC was required to be 'an aggressive seller [of zircon] ... and prepared to match prices'. The consequence was that zircon prices fell during the year from an already low price of $190 per tonne to $120 per tonne, with the price not appearing to 'have reached its floor'.[40] The task force presented its interim findings in July 1992. These included that RGC should remain in mineral sands, focus on high-grade titanium dioxide feedstocks by retaining existing assets and not invest downstream. A focus on competitiveness was called for, while it was also identified that the issue of high radioactivity in Eneabba ilmenite needed to be addressed.

The Eneabba North mine closed for 12 months, while commissioning of Eneabba West was accelerated, and one synthetic rutile kiln was idled. Development of the Eneabba West deposit began in 1991 on tenements previously owned mainly by Allied Eneabba. Expenditure originally estimated at $55 million subsequently increased to $115 million when ore reserves increased from 143 million to 227 million tonnes. With this, the scope of the project increased to enable higher production of rutile, zircon and ilmenite. The dredge for the operation was constructed in the Netherlands, employing the world's largest underwater bucket-wheel with a floating processing plant. Final expenditure exceeded $135 million.

The operation was plagued by commissioning problems. Harder than expected mining conditions caused high wear rates on equipment, such as the bucket-wheel of the dredge, pumps, and pipelines between the dredge and concentrator. Lower ore grades and lower than expected recoveries, combined with the low level of equipment availability, added to operational and financial challenges. Commissioning issues continued throughout 1991 prior to the dredging operation being shut down to effect necessary equipment modifications. The Eneabba North mine reopened in March 1992 and Eneabba South was shut down. Both processing plants serving the operation were idled for part of 1991. Meanwhile, commissioning of synthetic rutile kiln D was completed by August 1991. The Green Cove Springs operation in Florida continued to operate with continued demand for its products. A definitive feasibility study had commenced following the discovery of the Old Hickory deposit in Virginia, United States, although this was suspended in light of market conditions.

---

40   Renison Goldfields Consolidated Limited, 'Minutes of Meeting of Directors', 26 March 1992, p. 9, RGCA, Box 1130, BRD38/05.

Overall RGC earnings in 1991 were $29 million. Losses were recorded for the next two years before a small profit and subsequent partial recovery (see Table 19.2). In this context, one of the Hanson-appointed directors queried whether the AMC investment was 'too big a part of the Company and making the Company vulnerable to fluctuations in mineral sands price changes'.[41] The concerns with mineral sands were part of wider portfolio issues, with a report prepared in 1991 on the company's capital expenditure profile, cash flow and potential for the sale of 'peripheral assets'.[42] Mineral sands market conditions remained poor, in terms of price and demand, during 1992, although conditions stabilised by 1993, with production increasing and the mineral sands division generating a small profit.

Table 2. Mineral sands performance, 1990–1994.

	1990	1991	1992	1993	1994
Sales revenue ($m)	356.7	236.3	173.4	201.9	208.3
Contribution to group profit ($m)	176.6	67.2	–1.0	1.3	–5.5
Share of group assets ($m)	369.3	514.4	502.2	469.0	445.4
Capital expenditure ($m)	151.8	163.8	17.0	8.3	12.3
Production (tonnes)					
Rutile	113,271	95,002	58,209	81,453	93,492
Synthetic rutile	166,739	123,150	169,041	203,466	161,190
Zircon	310,552	162,607	95,433	190,107	254,093
Ilmenite	740,206	470,457	568,155	722,441	635,970
Sales (tonnes)					
Rutile	106,897	87,896	59,319	87,584	89,670
Synthetic rutile	179,475	118,895	150,855	201,205	171,175
Zircon	263,403	167,293	151,757	188,801	254,771
Ilmenite	389,842	306,201	275,689	277,310	310,505

See Appendix 5 for more detailed information.

Sources: RGC annual reports, 1991 to 1997; 'Information Memorandum in Relation to a Recommended Merger by Scheme of Arrangement between RGC Limited and Westralian Sands Limited', 1998.

After being idled, Eneabba West recommenced in May 1993, following major modifications to the dredge. In the meantime, RGC had over $200 million worth of mineral sands assets that had been idled and

---

41   Renison Goldfields Consolidated Limited, 'Minutes of Meeting of Directors', 25 January 1991, p. 15, RGCA, Box 1130, BRD38/05.
42   ibid.

not generating a return.⁴³ The Eneabba South dredge, concentrator and processing plant, which had not been in operation since early 1992, were decommissioned and the balance sheet carrying values written-down.

In 1994, an internal strategic planning group reviewed future challenges and opportunities for the mineral sands business. The major threats to the business were identified, including the continuation of synthetic rutile production associated with the availability of suitable ilmenite feed—in part related to the 'economic viability of Eneabba West' and the 'sharp reduction' in zircon from Eneabba. The means to address these challenges included investigating the acquisition of an Indian rare earth company in Kerala as a potential source of ilmenite for the kilns at Narngulu. Furthermore, the Old Hickory deposit in Virginia was considered as a smaller-scale, high-grade deposit to offset the expected decline in the high-grade zircon strands in Eneabba.⁴⁴

By 1995, the production output of the mineral sands division exceeded 1 million tonnes for the first time in five years. After three years of poor performance, profitability improved although it was well below the profit levels of the late 1980s. An RGC board paper observed a more optimistic future for mineral sands: 'We have every reason to face the future with confidence'.⁴⁵ Increased United States pigment production and high pigment plant utilisation rates were associated with synchronised world economic growth. Synthetic rutile production was running at full capacity and RGC was able to structure contractual arrangements in Australian dollars, eliminating some of the foreign exchange rate risk. Cessation of the Sierra Rutile mining operations in January 1995 also contributed to market tightness for high-grade feedstocks, while a seven-week strike at Richards Bay Minerals in South Africa added to the disruption to market supply. Titanium dioxide prices increased and new contracts, including a 10-year agreement with pigment customer SCM, were put in place. Revenue from zircon represented over a third of revenues for the mineral sands division of RGC and the company advised in its 1996 annual report that it had the capacity to produce 55 per cent of the world's rutile, 30 per cent of its synthetic rutile and 36 per cent of its zircon.

---

43   Renison Goldfields Consolidated Limited, 'Minutes of Meeting of Directors', 25 February 1993, p. 4, RGCA, Box 1130, BRD38/05.
44   Renison Goldfields Consolidated Limited, 'Minutes of Meeting of Directors', 23 April 1992, p. 19, RGCA, Box 1130, BRD38/05.
45   Renison Goldfields Consolidated Limited, Board Papers, Mineral Sands Market Update, January 1995, RGCA, Box 13609, R40-36G-024.

Renison's challenges

In 1990, tin prices were their lowest in real terms for 30 years. The cost of production was $8,700 compared to the prevailing tin price of around $8,000. Mike Ayre, the general manager of Renison, assembled a team to look at further options for the operation and to improve financial performance (see Table 19.3). His work in this regard was undertaken in conjunction with CD (Colin) Patterson, the mine superintendent and later general manager. Given that there had been two exercises to reduce the size of the workforce it was viewed that the opportunities for 'marginal' improvement had been exhausted and more far-reaching changes were necessary to attempt to put the mine on an even financial keel.[46] The RGC board was appraised of the details of the operating strategy for Renison in January 1991, designed to reduce operating costs to $6,000 per tonne. A comprehensive plan was formulated, the main elements of which were a reduction in employee numbers from 340 to 250; changes to operating conditions and terms of employment, including a planned reduction of employee pay by approximately 20 per cent; reconfiguration of the milling operation; and a ban on overtime.[47] It was expected that these proposals would generate industrial disruption and a two-month stoppage was envisaged as a consequence of progressing with them despite the workforce being 'fully appraised of the parlous state of the mine operation and the significant losses being incurred'.[48] Patterson had engaged with the workers on site and was confident, along with other management, that the company's proposals would be accepted. At the mine site on 27 February 1991, the survival plan proposal was put to a vote of the workforce.[49] From an RGC board perspective, the management of both Renison and Mount Lyell were on notice. In the words of Bethwaite, 'they must achieve their targets or the mines would close'.[50]

---

46   Renison Goldfields Consolidated Limited, 'Minutes of Meeting of Directors', 25 October 1990, p. 11 and 26 November 1990, p. 4, RGCA, Box 1130, BRD38/05.
47   The plan was for a five-day mill operation over 234 days and planned annual tin production of 5,500 tonnes (Renison Goldfields Consolidated Limited, 'Minutes of Meeting of Directors', 17 January 1991, pp. 22–23, RGCA, Box 1130, BRD38/05).
48   ibid., p. 23.
49   Renison Goldfields Consolidated Limited, 'Minutes of Meeting of Directors', 24 January 1991, p. 22, RGCA, Box 1130, BRD38/05.
50   Renison Goldfields Consolidated Limited, 'Minutes of Meeting of Directors', 23 June 1991, p. 3, RGCA, Box 1130, BRD38/05.

Table 3. Renison performance, 1990–1997.

	1990	1991	1992	1993	1994	1995	1996	1997
Sales of tin metal ($m)	66.5	46.8	36.9	62.3	48.3	55.3	65.6	65.1
Contribution to group profit ($m)	1.2	–12.7	–1.7	1.9	–2.7	–6.0	–0.9	–8.6
Share of group assets ($m)	45.4	33.0	32.1	28.6	31.5	44.2	69.9	41.5
Return on assets (%)	2.6	–38.5	–5.3	6.6	–8.6	–13.6	–1.3	–20.7
Capital expenditure ($m)	6.6	5.9	2.5	5.4	7.0	14.9	30.6	11.3
Production								
Ore treated ('000 tonnes)	742	548	534	565	624	650	706	692
Grade (% tin)	1.34	1.23	1.41	1.5	1.5	1.4	1.6	1.7
Tin sales (tonnes)	7,001	6,217	5,114	7,407	6,842	7,164	7,953	8,165
Recovery (%)	78.5	76.2	79.6	80.1	82	78	76	73
Average tin price ($/tonne)	9,269	7,355	7,178	8,414	7,055	7,712	8,273	7,422

See Appendix 6 for more detailed information.

Sources: RGC annual reports, 1991 to 1997; 'Information Memorandum in Relation to a Recommended Merger by Scheme of Arrangement between RGC Limited and Westralian Sands Limited', 1998.

Despite the expected agreement of workers and the Trades and Labor Council to the company's proposal, the mass meeting of workers at site failed to support the company's restructuring proposals. Joe Pringle, an entrenched union figure and representative of the underground workers, directed his members to vote against the proposal. The vote was lost. Bethwaite had travelled to the site for the vote. He spoke with Pringle and said that he would be leaving by car in 20 minutes and unless Pringle changed his view, the mine would be closed. Bethwaite drove off with no change in Pringle's stance.[51] It was a bitter disappointment to Bethwaite, who had been impressed with the attitudes of the union representatives he had met on site earlier in February. In a note to Ayre, who decided it would be best for him to leave Renison at this time and hand over to Patterson, Bethwaite observed that 'the outcome of the mass meeting demonstrates that neither the specific changes nor the attitudes to allow

---

51 Mike Ayre, personal communication, 21 October 2018.

Renison to survive have yet been achieved'.[52] He authorised that the mine be closed and if necessary placed on a care and maintenance basis for up to six months, after which permanent closure would occur.

On 6 March 1991 the workforce was locked out. Patterson received a telephone call from the premier of Tasmania, Mike Field, asking him to attend a meeting in Hobart. At the meeting were representatives of the Trades and Labor Council and other peak unions in Tasmania. After a day-long meeting, the unionists present agreed that support be provided for the company's 27-point plan. Patterson convened a meeting of the reassembled workforce. Pringle was invited onto the dais, shook Patterson's hand and joked that he was being fired. The meeting of workers provided unqualified support for the Renison survival plan, including agreement to a program of voluntary redundancies, with 207 employees electing to accept redundancy arrangements.

Later that month, the company advised that management was working 'towards a viable operating strategy' with a workforce of 250 and employees having accepted, on average, a 23 per cent reduction in earnings with eligibility to participate in a profit-sharing scheme. Accordingly, the board agreed to reopen the operation, which occurred on 2 April 1991.[53] A day later, the underground mining employees were stood down following a decision by the Australian Workers' Union not to supply supervision for mining operations, despite previous written undertakings to do so. This was yet another impediment to the smooth operation of Renison.

At the same time that major operational and organisational change was occurring, expenditure was committed to the identification of potential ore reserves at deeper horizons. What was referred to as the 'Rendeep project' commenced. In the context of reduced reserves and the uneconomic nature of current mining operations, the identification of additional reserves was imperative as a means of extending production at Renison. Rendeep mineralisation had been recognised for some years, with sporadic drilling having occurred to depths of 600–1,200 metres over a length of 2.5 kilometres by 600 metres. The drilling, however, involved a relatively small number of drill holes at wide spacings. Using geostatistical techniques, an estimate of inferred resources was made. However, further

---

52 To MWD Ayre from Mark Bethwaite, 1 March 1991, National Archives of Australia, Tasmania (NAAT), NS3988/1/125.
53 RGC Announcement to the Australian Stock Exchange and the Press, Renison Tin Division, 28 March 1991 (copy held by the author).

exploration drilling was necessary to delineate the mineralisation with sufficient confidence to enable a feasibility study to proceed. Having defined an area of likely mineralisation, drilling occurred from the surface during 1989 and 1992. The drilling was expensive and was undertaken while Renison was generating inadequate returns or losses. The last hole drilled as part of the program encountered an intersection of 40 metres of ore at a grade of 11 per cent tin, in what was referred to as the Blackwood ore body. It became evident there was a significant resource. However, further delineation was required to support the technical data needed for a feasibility study. The North Basset drive was established from the North Basset rise ventilation shaft and used to extend the exploration drilling, enabling the delineation to be completed. By 1994 development work had begun with the aim of accessing an ore reserve of 3.3 million tonnes at a tin grade of 1.96 per cent.[54]

Richard (Dick) Scallan, who had previously run the Eneabba operation in Western Australia, commenced at Renison in 1991 as general manager. He too encountered a militant industrial relations climate, with many of the workers tough and combative. Pringle, who had been a thorn in the side of previous management, had left but still had ongoing influence with the workforce, directing activities from his backyard shed in Zeehan. When Scallan arrived he realised he had to break this situation of mistrust and animosity. Furthermore, he viewed the work environment as terrible, with a high level of work accidents. He adopted symbolic but important changes, such as changing into protective clothing in the same area as the workforce, rather than a separate management change area. He erased the lines in the staff carpark that separated the cars of management from those of the general workforce and emphasised personal safety by insisting that protective clothing, gloves, eye goggles and hearing devices be worn.[55] He also instituted an extensive cultural change program.

In October 1993, the RGC board considered the feasibility study for the development of the Rendeep deposit. Rendeep was believed to have the potential to extend mining operations by 10 to 20 years. Recoveries were expected to be as high as 84 per cent, the level being reported from the existing Renison mining operations. By June 1994, it was resolved by the board that $34 million be committed for the Renison shaft project to

---

54   Colin Cannard, personal communication, 25 September 2018.
55   Dick Scallan, personal communication, 18 May 2018.

access the higher-grade ore in Rendeep.[56] It became clear after production began that estimates of recovery of tin from ore mined had been overly ambitious and were not achieved, undermining the basis for the project and the longevity of Renison in the portfolio.

Mount Lyell—steps to closure

In June 1989, Keith Faulkner commenced as general manager of Mount Lyell Copper Division. In February 1990 a strategic planning team was formed to examine future options in relation to the Mount Lyell operation, designed to improve financial outcomes and provide a plan for the mine's continuation. Under legislative arrangements with the Tasmanian Government, RGC had undertaken to surrender the leases on completion of the 60 series ore body. Faulkner was of the view that copper production could still continue beyond this with the resource 'still the largest, and second most valuable (in terms of "in ground" value) in Tasmania'.[57] An external consultant was retained. The exercise was conducted in the context of a year-to-date loss of Mount Lyell of $4.6 million, compared with an expected budgetary outcome of $12.3 million. By June of that year, the loss had grown to $11 million, compared to the budgeted expectation of a $20.9 million profit. Of the $31.9 million variance, $29 million related to lower prices and $2.1 million to lower volume outcomes.[58]

The loss for Mount Lyell was in the context of a substantial loss for Renison and although AMC was profitable, it was $41 million below its expected budgetary outcome. Bethwaite highlighted the challenge of the financial performance of Mount Lyell entering the 1991 financial year. In an internal memorandum he wrote that the budget estimates for the group were 'critically vulnerable to downturn in the copper price' and that 'it is critical that Mount Lyell contribute positively to an overall Group result which is bearing the full effects of the current recession'[59] (see Chart 8).

---

56 Renison Goldfields Consolidated Limited, 'Minutes of Meeting of Directors', 23 October 1993, RGCA, Box 1130, BRD38/05; Renison Goldfields Consolidated Limited, 'Minutes of Meeting of Directors', 2 June 1994, RGCA, Box 14284, BRD38/08.
57 Memorandum to Mark Bethwaite from Keith Faulkner, Strategic Planning, 3 December 1990, NAAT, NS1711/1/782.
58 Renison Goldfields Consolidated Limited, Board Papers, Mount Lyell Copper Division, March 1990, and Board Papers, July 1990, NAAT, NS3924, Items 459–469.
59 Renison Goldfields Consolidated, Memorandum, 5 April 1991, RGCA, Box 2978.

On 14 June 1991, the gravity of the mine's situation was communicated to the Mount Lyell workforce. A notice entitled 'Our Situation is Critical' was given to the workforce, stating 'we have failed to meet the targets necessary for us to survive in the world copper market ... [and] We are not competitive!'[60]

On 25 June 1991, Faulkner issued a further general notice, entitled 'Three Month Survival Plan. Seven Day Operation'. This communication indicated that the operation had three months to demonstrate it could meet its cost and production targets in the context of a lower copper price and with the mine's operation moving from a five-day to a seven-day operation. The blunt warning Faulkner delivered to the workforce included: 'If we cannot do that we do not have a viable mining operation'.[61] The Mount Lyell workforce demonstrated its commitment to do what it could to help the operation continue and, among other measures, the usual notice period to change working arrangements was dispensed with and the operation moved to a 40-hour week. According to Faulkner, the workforce understood that the mine could still be profitable and its response to the challenge was 'enthusiastic and gratifying'.[62] The challenge posed was met. The company issued a stock exchange release on 26 September advising that the three-month trial had been successful in improving productivity and unit costs. The mine also made the transition from production from the 50 series to the 60 series ore bodies.

Faulkner had commissioned another internal report to identify and evaluate alternative means of operation. However, despite this work and the temporary reprieve, the decision had been taken at a corporate level that Mount Lyell would not continue beyond the mining of the 60 series stopes. The 'mine's invidious cost and competitive position' precluded delineation drilling below the 60 series stopes.[63] In anticipation

---

60   General Notice, Our Situation is Critical, 14 June 1991, NAAT, NS3357/1/138.
61   General Notice, Three Month Survival Plan, Seven Day Operation, 25 June 1991, NAAT, NS3357/1/138.
62   Renison Goldfields Consolidated Limited, Mount Lyell Copper Division, Operating Committee Report, July 1991, NAAT, NS3924, Items 483–495.
63   Email from Mark Bethwaite to KE Faulkner, 7 August 1990, NAAT, NS3357/1/138. This email also directed the cessation of exploration below the 60 series, with approval to recommence to be based on evidence of sustained performance in the 1991 financial year. It was also requested that discussions commence with the Tasmanian Government in relation to early closure. The report prepared for Faulkner and delivered about the same time as Bethwaite's email offered no clear alternatives for the operation of the mine, short of fundamental changes to the mining techniques and structure of the workforce, in themselves impractical given the established labour and employment arrangements (Operational Alternatives for Mount Lyell Copper Division, 20 August 1991, NAAT, NS 3357/1/138).

of a potential sale or closure, in November 1990 a reorganisation had been undertaken that involved dismantling the 1983 Mount Lyell and Renison interrelationship. The change, for accounting and taxation purposes, was designed to place Mount Lyell 'in an optimal state for sale or liquidation'.[64] An external adviser was appointed to prepare sales documents for Mount Lyell. A detailed evaluation was undertaken in 1991 including a consideration of which mining companies could be approached that may have an interest in evaluating and acquiring the operation. It was recognised there were constraints to this approach being successful: the mine had been marginal for many years due to its low grade and had been severely capital constrained. Cyprus Minerals considered the acquisition of Mount Lyell but by the end of 1991 it indicated that it was no longer interested.[65]

In July 1992, the general manager informed the workforce, through a series of meetings at site, that there were no plans to mine the 70 series or any other ore source on the leases held by the company. By 1993 a decision had been made that Mount Lyell would close at the end of 1994 and, on 24 March 1994, a public announcement was made of the scheduled closure on 15 December. Mine production ceased on 8 December 1994 with 171 employees retrenched during the following week. Mount Lyell exhibited a strong operational and financial performance in its last year. Profit and operational cash flow exceeded the budget. Grade, recovery and ore treatment were all favourable and safety performance met expectations. This was a commendable outcome, given this was the final period of operation and employment for most of the workforce, many of whom had been associated with Queenstown and the mine for most of their working lives.

64 Renison Goldfields Consolidated, Memorandum, Mount Lyell/Renison Re-organisation, 29 November 1991, RGCA, Box 297807.
65 Memorandum, Cyprus Minerals—Mt Lyell, 19 December 1991, RGCA, Box 3536.

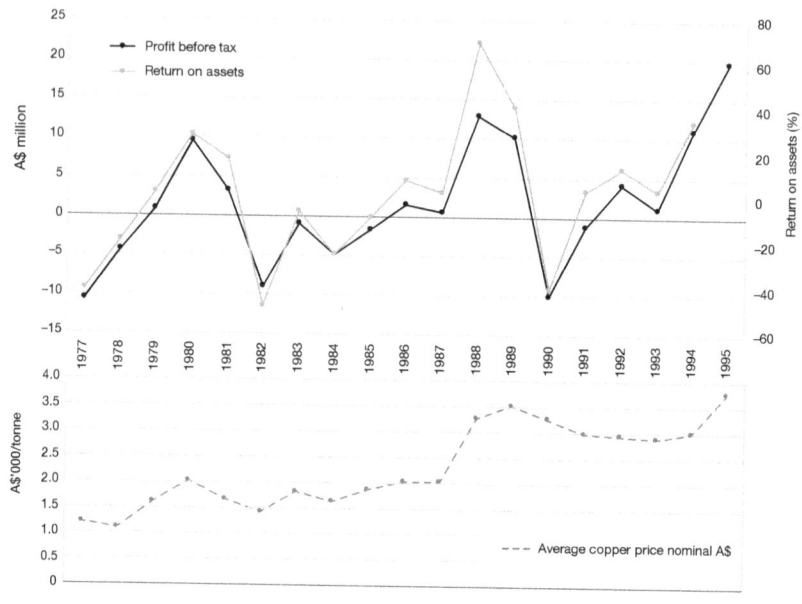

Chart 8. Mount Lyell contribution to Consolidated Gold Fields Australia and Renison Goldfields Consolidated group results, 1977–1995.

This chart shows the historical performance of Mount Lyell from 1977 to its closure at the end of 1994. Mount Lyell displayed a poor earnings profile throughout the period shown with only brief periods of profitability, including the final two years of operation. Annual average return on assets was 2.6 per cent or, excluding the 1994 financial year when assets had been written-down, 0.6 per cent. See Appendix 4 and Appendix 7 for more information.

Sources: RGC annual reports, 1991 to 1997; 'Information Memorandum in Relation to a Recommended Merger by Scheme of Arrangement between RGC Limited and Westralian Sands Limited', 1998.

The Tasmanian Government announced that it had awarded the Mount Lyell leases to Gold Mines of Tasmania, effective 31 December 1994. Mount Lyell, one of Australia's oldest and most historic mining operations and one of Consolidated Gold Fields Australia's key initial investments in establishing in Australia, closed after 101 years of operation. An '"End of Era" Lights Out Ceremony and Community Barbeque' was held on Saturday 17 December at Queenstown attended by the workforce, their families and members of the Queenstown community.[66]

---

66 Renison Goldfields Consolidated Limited, Board Report, Mount Lyell Copper Division, December 1994, NAAT, NS3924, Items 522–532.

Gold and other interests

The RGC portfolio experienced other changes in the first half of the 1990s. The Lucky Draw gold mine, discovered in 1985 and so-named as a result of a ballot draw to award the lease as pegged by two companies on the same day, commenced production in 1988. It performed well and made an impressive, if short, financial contribution, closing in July 1991.

RGC held an interest in the Pine Creek gold deposit, 225 kilometres south-east of Darwin. The mine began production in October 1985 and continued for nine years to the end of 1994. RGC held an initial 49 per cent interest that increased to 100 per cent when its partner, Enterprise Gold Mines, defaulted on its financial commitments in 1991. Mining took place within the Enterprise open cut deposits, followed by mining at a series of satellite deposits, including Czarina, Gandy's Hill, North Gandy's Hill and International, with the latter three deposits acquired during the course of the mining operation. Initial mining progressed well with a doubling of throughput and expansion of milling capacity. By 1993, grades at the Enterprise pit were declining, with mining exhausted earlier than scheduled. Access to the subsequent, smaller deposits with lower grade and lower throughputs; the need to relocate roads, including the Stuart Highway; acquisition costs of landholdings; and expenditure being depreciated over a shorter period adversely affected profitability after two strong initial years.

The Nelesbitan gold mine was viewed as a means of testing RGC's entry into gold mining in the Philippines. The operation was spectacularly unsuccessful. After commencing in May 1990, the operation was suspended six months later in October 1990 due to technical problems and an outlook of 'questionable profitability', as well as a deteriorating security situation in the area where the mine operated.[67] The Wau gold mining operations in Papua New Guinea, acquired as part of the purchase of New Guinea Goldfields in 1981, encountered varying ore grades and ceased operation in September 1990.

---

67   Renison Goldfields Consolidated Limited, 'Minutes of Meeting of Directors', 23 August 1990, p. 7, RGCA, Box 11329, BRD38/04.

RGC had undertaken exploration between Rosebery, the site of Mount Lyell and near Renison in Tasmania. As the fault zone encountered had pyrite and low incidences of gold, the decision had been made to relinquish the ground. Before doing so, Roger Shakesby conducted a review, utilising one of RGC's most experienced geologists, Lindsey Newnham, as well as an international consultant. None of the drill cores had been assayed for gold, only copper. Re-assaying showed high grades of gold over varying widths. This proved to be the birth of the Henty gold project.[68] Further drilling confirmed the discovery of what was referred to as zone 96, a highly mineralised section 350 metres to 500 metres below the surface.

The Henty project progressed to a feasibility study. Approval was granted for project development in 1992, with capital expenditure of $53 million authorised. Given the inability of the joint venture partner, Little River Goldfields, to finance its share of the expenditure, RGC moved to a 100 per cent holding. This process delayed the commitment of the project but also enabled a re-evaluation of the development approach, with a decision to develop horizontally from two levels instead of one. Prior to production commencing, an RGC geologist had identified geological alteration 2 kilometres away from the Henty ore zones to be accessed by the planned development. Drilling to the zone encountered gold-bearing ore. This potential was not exploited by RGC directly but by Goldfields Limited, in which RGC had a 55.8 per cent interest from 1996. With Goldfields acquired by Delta Gold and in turn this combined entity acquired by Placer, the full potential of Henty, a significant gold discovery, was realised by other companies.

Similar to the Narama coal operation, the Koba Tin operation in Indonesia provided a valuable new production and revenue source to the group during the first half of the 1990s, although not sufficiently material to offset the decline in some of the previous mainstays of the portfolio. Additional reserves were identified and a second dredge was acquired to develop the Bemban area of the operation. Koba Tin would be one of the few non-mineral sands assets retained after RGC and Westralian Sands merged in 1998.

Progress on the development of the Glendell coal deposits in the Hunter Valley in New South Wales remained laboriously slow and, as such, stymied the basis for RGC's re-entry into the export coal market. Despite development approval having been granted in May 1983, issues relating

---

68   Roger Shakesby, personal communication, 9 December 2018.

to the foreign ownership status of its partner, Dalgety, continued to impede progress. RGC eventually sold its interest in 1992 after a decade of effort. A joint venture with Costain, also in the Hunter Valley, led to a successful tender to supply steaming coal to a power generation facility in New South Wales. The Narama coal project commenced production in January 1993 and contributed modest profits to RGC.

RGC retained a payment entitlement associated with Area C of the Pilbara iron ore deposits in Western Australia. The entitlement flowed from earlier changes in Consolidated Gold Fields Australia's ownership of its Mount Goldsworthy iron ore interests when, under a 1977 agreement, both RGC and Cyprus were entitled to a one-off payment of $19.8 million on the commencement of production from Mining Area C. RGC believed that an alteration to the financial arrangements might serve to expedite the development of the resource.[69] George Lloyd, RGC's exploration and development group general manager, had responsibility for generating an immediate payment for this future entitlement. Negotiations were conducted with BHP on the basis of substituting the payment when production commenced with a smaller up-front payment and royalty. In lieu of a future payment, a payment of $2.5 million to RGC and a future in-perpetuity royalty entitlement to be paid when production began and exceeded 5 million tonnes, were negotiated. During RGC's existence, Mining Area C did not contribute financially in terms of royalty payments. In the merger documentation with Westralian Sands issued in 1998, Mining Area C warranted scant attention, with an estimated value of $10 million to $14 million ascribed in the independent expert's report.[70] As such, the royalty entitlement that flowed to Westralian Sands and then Iluka was a 'sleeper' in terms of its future valuation and cash flow.

Porgera ownership challenges

The proposed development approach for the Porgera gold mine in Papua New Guinea had been submitted to the Government of Papua New Guinea in November 1988. Phase one of the project was commissioned in September 1990 and the mine was officially opened on 20 October 1990. The project advanced through various stages, with the pressure oxidisation

---

69   Renison Goldfields Consolidated Limited, 'Minutes of Meeting of Directors', 3 February, 1994, p. 9, RGCA, Box 14284, BRD38/08.
70   Information Memorandum in Relation to a Recommended Merger by Scheme of Arrangement between RGC Limited and Westralian Sands Limited, 1998, pp. 179–180 (copy held by the author).

circuit, involving three autoclaves, commissioned in September 1991 to be followed by the expansion of concentrator capacity and following stages that included the installation of a fourth autoclave. Porgera's financial contribution to RGC was pivotal, constituting the main earnings stream in the early 1990s.

In 1992, the president of Placer Dome, a shareholder in Placer Pacific and one of the three joint venture participants in Porgera, received correspondence from a Papua New Guinea Government minister. The correspondence contended that, in light of revenues and the value of production doubling from the original feasibility studies, the government had been misled about the size of the deposit and the potential production profile. The government was now seeking a 30 per cent interest. The contention led to uncertainty about the ownership structure of the joint venture and caused the companies in the joint venture to issue an Australian stock exchange release on 12 November 1992. The release stated that, based on correspondence from John Kaputin, the minister for foreign affairs, the joint venture participants were 'continuing to seek clarification of the Government's position including the question of other options being considered [by the Government]'.[71] Prime Minister Paias Wingti became involved, claiming that the joint venture, at the time of the 1989 negotiations, had made 'outrageous claims' not supported by subsequent events. Placer, Mount Isa Mines and RGC explained both publicly and in direct engagement with government officials and ministers that when the Papua New Guinean Government equity of 10 per cent was exercised in 1989 there was no legislation to support the current claim for 30 per cent government participation ownership, with exploration conducted after 1989 leading to the discovery of a high-grade zone, while metallurgical test work had improved the project's financial returns. The joint venture participants refuted any claims that they had misled the government.

The contention about the level of government ownership, and an often strained behind the scenes engagement with government officials, was taking place when RGC had a $250 million syndicated loan with a Bank of Papua New Guinea guarantee. Given increased concerns regarding Papua New Guinea's credit exposure and the uncertainty about the ownership structure of the Porgera project, the international banks

---

71   Draft Australian Stock Exchange Release, Placer Pacific, 12 November 1992, RGCA, Box 1091.

involved in the loan would not agree to proceed with loan extensions and restructuring. RGC was placed on a negative credit watch in November 1992.

Anderson played a prominent role in the joint venture engagement with the Papua New Guinea Government. He believed that Papua New Guinea's desire to increase its equity in the project was based on two fundamental misunderstandings: that in 1989 the Papua New Guinea Government had the right to acquire equity greater than 10 per cent and that the Porgera joint venture deliberately understated the potential of the Porgera project. Accordingly, he did not wish to see RGC's interest reduced and 'resolutely opposed' the allegations of misleading conduct. His view was that, if the government wished to pursue its own political imperative to increase its equity in the project, the joint venture participants should cooperate and insist that an independent market valuation form the basis of any such negotiations.[72]

It was proposed to the government that it appoint an independent consulting firm to report on their matters of concern. In turn, the joint venture participants made representations to Australian Government ministers, including the Foreign Affairs minister, to seek to persuade the Government of Papua New Guinea to moderate its claims against the companies. A concern, whether well founded or not, was that an intermediary may be offering funds to the Government of Papua New Guinea for increased equity in Porgera, the reopening of the Bougainville mine and the potential refinancing of the government's 22.5 per cent interest in the Kutubu oil project.

In January 1993, the government detailed its concerns about its equity in the Porgera project in writing to the joint venture. These concerns related to the provision by the joint venture of ore reserve and resource information, the increase in gold production, an increase in indirect costs and the financial performance of the Porgera joint venture, relative to the government's initial expectations. In the same month, Julius Chan, the minister for finance and planning, announced a major review of the country's fiscal regime for mining, petroleum and gas. For the Porgera joint venture participants, this raised the question as to whether any legislative or fiscal changes would also relate to the equity position of Porgera. The concern within the joint venture was of 'double jeopardy'

---

72   File Note, Tuesday 1 December 1992, RGCA, Box 1091.

in the form of possible reduced equity in Porgera and higher taxes on the project. Implicit, or at least in the view of the joint venture, was a veiled threat that expropriation legislation may be introduced into the Papua New Guinea Parliament to achieve the government's desired outcome.

While the Papua New Guinea Government had insisted on an additional 20 per cent equity in the Porgera project, agreement was reached in March 1993 for an additional 15 per cent government equity, providing it and the other participants each with a 25 per cent holding. While there was concern about the commercial terms of the offer, there was also a view that the offer may be presented by the government on a 'take it or leave it' basis, with the alternative to accepting the arrangement further negotiation or unilateral government legislative action. Such an outcome was not viewed favourably by the three participating companies for the future of the project. On 13 March 1993, a heads of agreement was signed. Despite the uncertainty and change in equity holding, Porgera represented the most important new asset for RGC and partially compensated for the lower financial contributions from the previous stalwarts of the portfolio—Renison and, to a lesser extent, Mount Lyell.

20
FINAL YEARS

The final years for Renison Goldfields Consolidated (RGC) involved a combination of concerted efforts to grow the business and a number of expansive corporate activities. These were overseen by managing director, Mark Bethwaite, until his departure in 1998. The strategic direction after 1994 was based on several pillars: a consideration to new sources of production in mineral sands, through acquisition arrangements and exploration; a South American focus, initially upon Bolivia but extended to Peru; and a corporate restructuring exercise involving the acquisition of Pancontinental Mining and establishment of a separately listed gold company. RGC continued to face portfolio challenges with mature assets, as well as variable market conditions.

In 1994, after a loss in the previous two years, RGC recorded a barely break-even profit after tax with no dividend paid. While there was a recovery in financial performance after 1994, a market downturn became evident by 1997 that presaged a period with a need to reshape budgetary settings to attempt to achieve further cost reductions, with yet another strategic review as to the configuration of the business. Several investment decisions made by the company were contributory factors in weakening its financial position, generating initial poor returns and subsequent asset write-offs. Acquisition activity when pursued, in the case of Pancontinental Mining and Cudgen RZ and CRL, was impeded by a minority institutional shareholding that prevented RGC gaining outright ownership control. Exploration success occurred on a number of fronts, especially in mineral sands, but the period for such success to be translated into production, revenue or share market value meant that the value was not realised by RGC. Internal and external reviews of the business occurred, culminating in a Boston Consulting Group review.

Management change occurred with Bethwaite leaving the company in early 1998 and Tony Cotton assuming the joint roles of chief executive officer and chairman. In the same year, the managing director of Westralian Sands approached Hanson in London proposing a combination of the two companies. The challenges being experienced by RGC and a difficult budgetary outlook contributed to the decision by Hanson and members of the board to accept the overtures from Westralian Sands.

The largest financial investments by the company in the 1990s, and those with a poor financial outcome, were the decision to dredge mine Eneabba West, the commitment to a fourth kiln in Western Australia and the decision to invest in the Rendeep deposit at Renison. In total, the three investments entailed capital expenditure of around $300 million. Eneabba West suffered protracted commissioning issues and immense difficulties in dredging the rocky and indurated Eneabba West ore body. Mineable reserves were reduced and lower recoveries led to higher operating costs, adversely affecting the profitability of what was one of the largest investments by RGC. The decision to commit to a fourth synthetic rutile kiln, and adoption of the technology to upgrade Eneabba ilmenites to a higher titanium dioxide product, through the synthetic rutile enhanced process (SREP), resulted in lower than expected outputs and product quality issues, along with a higher than initially planned capital expenditure. The decision to develop the deep Renison ore body, Rendeep, proceeded on a basis that, as would become apparent, overestimated recoveries from the ore body. Lower recoveries and an adjustment of likely recoverable reserves meant that the $35 million investment made in 1995 failed to achieve expected outcomes.[1] It was a sobering failure of planning and management and board oversight. A $30 million write-down was made three years later in the 1998 financial year, with a process put in train to sell the Renison operation.

While there was a recovery in market conditions and an improvement in the company's financial performance, the asset base was reliant on two main businesses: mineral sands and the Porgera gold operation. Renison was earmarked for sale. Koba Tin and Narama Coal were the only other assets that made positive contributions, and these were relatively minor. Despite the major commitment to exploration and the acquisitive activities of the group, the ability to establish other, longer-term bases of production and revenue was not achieved.

---

1   Renison Goldfields Consolidated Limited, 'Minutes of Meeting of Directors', 2 June 1994, p. 2, Renison Goldfields Consolidated Archives (RGCA), Box 14284, BRD38/08.

However, the final period of the company's existence saw a number of initiatives seeking to establish new sources of production. The company acquired Cudgen RZ that, in turn, gave RGC control of CRL and its mineral sands operations on North Stradbroke Island in Queensland, as well as an interest in a mineral sands dredge mining operation in Sierra Leone. The progressive development of Porgera occurred, with open cut production commencing in 1993, following the depletion of the underground reserves. A major corporate restructuring led to the takeover of Pancontinental Mining and the establishment of a separately listed company, Goldfields Limited, which retained the gold assets of both RGC and Pancontinental. In turn, RGC acquired some of the Pancontinental non-gold operations and divested others, allowing debt to be reduced materially. An involvement in the privatisation of the Bolivian tin industry was evaluated, although not pursued. A major investment in a Peruvian copper and gold mine was progressed to a stage where RGC was well placed to acquire this operation. However, other events were then unfolding, while the unpreparedness of the major shareholder to commit additional capital when the mainstay of the business—mineral sands—was facing ore body maturity and weak market conditions, meant this opportunity was not pursued. In 1998, a process of evaluation and due diligence resulted in a July 1998 announcement of the intention to merge with Westralian Sands by a scheme of arrangement. By December this was completed.

A mineral sands strategic planning group was formed in 1994 to assess the options and approach for the division. The group identified that the major challenges to the business in the short term related to the successful adoption of the SREP technology, as well as the economic viability of the Eneabba West mine. Medium-term challenges related to an expected reduction in zircon production, as well as the ongoing availability of suitable ilmenite for synthetic rutile.[2] The latter factor had become a more important imperative given the revised, less expansive scope of the Old Hickory project in Virginia. The RGC board approved the development of the Old Hickory deposit for $53 million in 1996. It was the company's first mineral sands operation in six years. The deposit had been first drilled in 1988 as part of wider exploration efforts in Virginia and North Carolina, which identified two other deposits. The deposits were considered to be centrally located to customers in the United States, most notably DuPont. While undertaking initial exploration there had been 'fierce competition

2   ibid., p. 3.

for mineral rights and the need to quickly define the resource areas'.[3] Exploration by rival companies, including by DuPont, meant that RGC's drilling program was accelerated and the work completed was, according to an internal report, less 'systematic than desirable'.[4] The level of ore body delineation had consequences in the commissioning and early stages of production at Old Hickory.

The initially planned dredge mining operation was assessed as not economic. A revised plan for a smaller-scale dry mining approach provided flexibility to access the higher-grade sections of the deposit. It had been assumed that a synthetic rutile plant would be constructed on site, as part of the company's consideration of locating synthetic rutile capacity closer to its end markets. The initial mining and production experience at Virginia was not favourable. Mine production during 1997 was less than forecast, with poor mineral recovery. Rocks caused production interruptions, while the mining unit plant suffered a 'catastrophic failure'.[5] In addition, a major geological fault was discovered in a mining pit. A cost overrun of US$10.5 million was advised to the board in March 1997. While production output increased, issues with product quality persisted.[6] A further feasibility study led to approval for the construction of a second mine and concentrator plant at a nearby deposit to enable blending of ore.

RGC continued to pioneer technology in the development of synthetic rutile. Research initiated in 1989 was designed to develop a process to reduce the uranium and thorium levels in some of the Eneabba ilmenites, which had become an issue for the sale of synthetic rutile to pigment customers. During 1990, it was decided that total annual synthetic rutile capacity be increased to 260,000 tonnes with a $104 million upgrade project. A new plant, plant D, was designed to produce a lower uranium and thorium content synthetic rutile product, called SREP. RGC had an expectation that all of its kilns could be converted to the production of SREP, although this was not to occur. The development of SREP proved to be a protracted process with a multitude of technical challenges. Initial test work was not successful and produced material of variable titanium dioxide content. The delay in providing product to customers created a potential threat of force majeure. At the same time, a competitive threat from Rio Tinto was evident with its Canadian operation evaluating ilmenite ores from India that

---

3   RGC Summary Report, Old Hickory Mine, January 1993, RGCA, Box 3162.
4   RGC Mineral Sands Old Hickory Project, Technical Summary, April 1993, p. 10, RGCA, Box 3162, 626–9.
5   Sale, 'A Fortunate Life: 45 Years in Heavy Minerals', pp. 24–25.
6   ibid.

were low in uranium and thorium and seen as suitable for the production of chloride slag, a competing product to synthetic rutile. Closer to home, Westralian Sands was well advanced in its own synthetic rutile production expansion plans, confident that the quality and consistency of its product would enable it to take market share from RGC.

Trial parcels of SREP were provided to chloride pigment customers for evaluation during 1995. One pigment customer, SCM, received its first shipment for its British plant and fed it into a chlorinator. The bed defluidised, or 'froze'. SCM did not want to use SREP again.[7] Following operational improvements and an expenditure of over $11 million in 1996, plant D was modified with commercial production commencing in 1997. The company produced a record tonnage of synthetic rutile. However, in 1997, the Narngulu synthetic rutile operations, with two kilns operating, including one devoted to SREP, generated a loss. Operational and financial issues persisted with SREP.

The development of SREP was associated with one of Australia's longest running legal disputes. A CRA subsidiary filed a Federal Court application in 1994 seeking an injunction to prevent RGC from making SREP on the grounds of process infringement.[8] Litigation followed with a cross-claim lodged in 1997 by RGC. A royalty was paid to Rio Tinto until the resolution of the legal dispute after RGC ceased to exist.

Marketing challenges for zircon from Eneabba emerged in the 1990s. Prior to Eneabba's development in the 1970s, most of the global supply of zircon was sourced from Australian east-coast mineral sands producers. Supply was plentiful and it was typically of a premium quality, able to fulfil most customer requirements. Initially, on the west coast, the Capel-sourced zircon was of a lesser quality and typically classed as standard grade. In volumetric terms, zircon was also a small component of the production stream from southwest Western Australia. With the progressive development of Eneabba, zircon supply increased. This additional supply was necessary to partially offset the decline from east-coast mining activities. In the early 1980s, the focus of the sale of Eneabba zircon was in foundry applications, with technical work undertaken to persuade foundry operators of the benefits of

---

7 Bryan Ellis, personal communication, 15 May 2017. I am grateful to Bryan Ellis for his review of the sections related to synthetic rutile, SREP development and zircon marketing. The interpretations drawn are mine.
8 *RGC Annual Report 1994*, p. 13.

zircon relative to more traditional foundry sands.[9] A boost in demand for Eneabba zircon came from the Japanese steel industry that turned to Eneabba zircon because of its coarse grain size, suited for refractory applications. At the same time, zircon usage in the Italian ceramics industry increased.

As a result of heightened demand and the reduction of supply, zircon prices increased from around $88 per tonne in 1980 to over $460 per tonne in 1990. The escalating price caused the Japanese steel mills to seek to reduce their reliance on zircon and investigate alternative products. As such, a combination of factors led to a sharp decline in zircon demand and prices in the early 1990s and a consequential serious impact on the contribution of mineral sands to RGC's overall earnings (see Chart 9). In 1991, zircon prices declined to around $320 a tonne and dropped again to half this amount the following year. The market challenges for RGC were heightened by customer concerns with the quality of Eneabba zircon. The coarse grain size from some parts of the deposit and high iron content meant that it was not assessed as a premium product, particularly for ceramic-based applications. Ceramic customers also reduced their purchases of Eneabba zircon. A large build in zircon stocks followed. This had severe financial consequences for the mineral sands business of RGC.

A major portfolio reconfiguration took place in 1995. Pancontinental Mining had been identified as a target for acquisition. It was decided that the group's gold exploration projects be transferred to a wholly owned subsidiary, RGC Pty Limited, with this company converted to a public company—Goldfields Limited.[10] The objective was to consolidate the gold mining interests of RGC and Pancontinental and transfer the non-gold assets of Pancontinental to RGC. The expectation was that a gold listed company would generate a higher equity market premium, while the RGC portfolio would be further diversified by having access to a range of lead, silver and other assets from Pancontinental. Goldfields was the bidding vehicle for Pancontinental Mining, with RGC providing funding for the non-gold component of the portfolio in part through the issuance of RGC convertible notes, convertible into Goldfields shares and with funds to be repaid by the later sale of Pancontinental non-gold assets.[11]

9　Bryan Ellis, personal communication, 29 May 2017.
10　The gold projects and exploration interests transferred to Goldfields Limited were Porgera (Papua New Guinea), Paddington (Kalgoorlie, Western Australia), Kundana (Kalgoorlie), Henty (Tasmania) and Wau exploration (Papua New Guinea). Pancontinental was the owner of the Paddington and Kundana gold projects (RGC, 'Prospectus: Goldfields', 7 April 1995; RGC Ltd, 1 December 1994, p. 4, RGCA, Box 2810).
11　RGC Ltd, 1 December 1994, p. 4, RGCA, Box 2810.

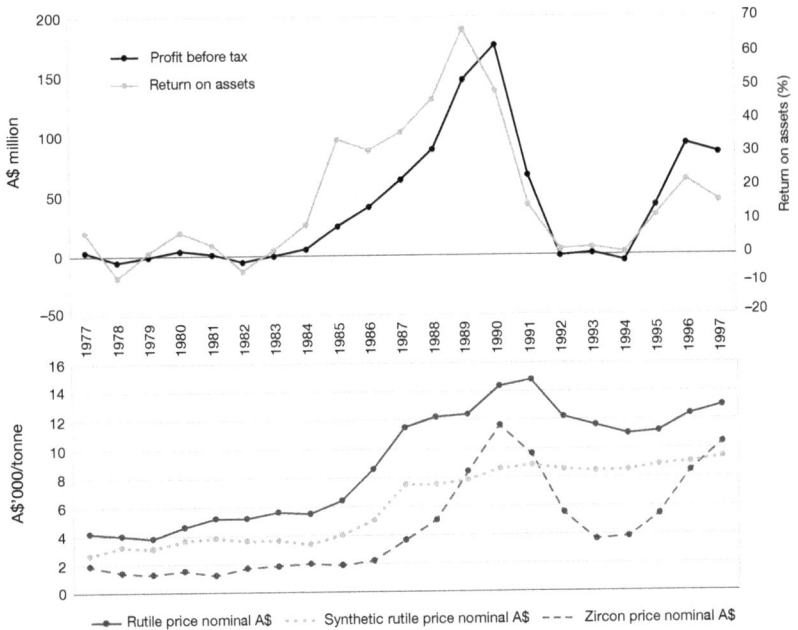

Chart 9. Mineral sands earnings and price trends, 1977–1997.
The chart displays the Associated Minerals Consolidated contribution to Consolidated Gold Fields Australia and RGC earnings, as well as Australian dollar mineral sands prices between 1977 and 1997. After an extended period of poor returns from 1977 until 1985, returns improved from 1985 until 1991 and then declined before a partial recovery in 1996. Data for 1998 was not available. Average return on assets was 15 per cent, aided by several strong earnings years. One third of the years displayed a negative or zero return on assets, reflecting the cyclicality of the performance of the mineral sands part of the portfolio. See Appendix 4 and Appendix 5 for more information.
Sources: Renison Goldfields Consolidated, *Report on the 1981 Financial Year*; RGC annual reports, 1990 to 1997.

RGC had approached Pancontinental in 1994 with a proposal to restructure and merge RGC and Pancontinental through a scheme of arrangement. This approach was rejected. A takeover bid for Pancontinental was launched in February 1995 after RGC had acquired a 14.9 per cent interest. The share and cash bid consumed much of the year. The Pancontinental board and management offered resolute resistance. Pancontinental argued that it had sought to provide shareholders with a balanced portfolio of assets and that its shareholders were now being offered shares in a pure gold company with its predominant asset located in Papua New Guinea, yet with 'no meaningful information about the increased risk of holding shares in such a company'.[12] A cross-claim was

---

12 The Directors, Goldfields Limited, Pancontinental Mining Limited—Part A Statement, 8 March 1995, pp. 1–2, RGCA, Box 2810.

brought in the Federal Court of Australia, claiming that the Goldfields Part A statement was defective in 'numerous critical respects'.[13] It was contended that Goldfields had failed to provide earnings and cash flow forecasts, with Pancontinental having a mining engineer swear an affidavit arguing the inadequacy of financial information presented and refuting the contention that merging Pancontinental's and Goldfields' gold assets would 'automatically attract the premium to which these statements refer and thereby add additional value to the company'.[14] RGC was directed to reissue its takeover documentation to include three-year financial forecasts. Pancontinental's defence also included an attack on RGC's management ability and a threat to float its own gold assets.

The delay led to a revised and higher offer to Pancontinental shareholders. By June 1995, Goldfields had become entitled to 80 per cent of Pancontinental's shares. An Australian investment management institution, QBE Insurance Group, acquired a shareholding of over 10 per cent, preventing RGC from compulsorily acquiring all of Pancontinental's shares. Instead of outright control, RGC gained an 87.7 per cent holding. A change of board occurred, with Cotton assuming the chairmanship of Goldfields Limited and Peter Cassidy becoming the managing director and chief executive officer.[15] A complicated process followed by which Pancontinental's non-gold assets were valued for sale or purchase by RGC. RGC acquired some and tendered unsuccessfully for a number of Pancontinental's non-gold assets. The proceeds from the sale of assets reduced RGC's debt, as well as contributing to RGC's record profit after tax in 1996 of $142 million.[16] Goldfields had a poor start to its corporate existence with its first full year profit of $11.1 million, compared with a prospectus forecast of $25 million to $35 million. The prime Pancontinental asset, Paddington, recorded a loss for the year.[17]

---

13 ibid.
14 Between Pancontinental Mining Limited and Goldfields Limited, Affidavit, p. 10, RGCA, Box 2810.
15 Letter from AR Cotton, Chairman Goldfields to LT MacAlister, Chairman Pancontinental Mining Limited, 16 June 1985, RGCA, Box 2810.
16 These included a 5.56 per cent interest in Central Queensland Coal Associates and Gregory Joint Venture (sold for $240 million in 1996). The operating assets of Pancontinental contributed $16.4 million to RGC's pre-tax earnings in the 1996 financial year. The sale of these interests generated $81 million pre-tax and $66 million after tax and outside equity interests (*RGC Annual Report 1996*, pp. 19 and 39).
17 RGC, 'Prospectus: Goldfields', 7 April 1995; Goldfields Limited, *1996 Annual Report*. Goldfields continued to operate until 2001 when it merged with Delta Gold to form the company AurionGold. In turn Placer Dome acquired AurionGold in November 2002.

Hard on the heels of the Pancontinental transaction, RGC acquired Cudgen RZ and through this an interest in a Queensland-based mineral sands company, CRL. Cudgen RZ Limited had been involved in sand mining in the eastern states since the 1940s. CRL was incorporated in 1963 and listed as a public company in 1965 after which it became predominantly owned by Cudgen RZ. In late 1994, RGC undertook a detailed review of CRL, based on its view that South African controlling shareholder, Gencor, might consider divesting its shareholding. Gencor had a mineral sands division in a joint venture with Rio Tinto Zinc (RTZ) at Richards Bay Minerals. Given that RTZ controlled the processing and marketing of products, Gencor's position was seen to provide it with few synergies or market benefits related to its position in CRL. As such, Gencor was viewed as potentially willing to sell its stake in Cudgen, particularly when it announced that it was purchasing Billiton International Minerals from Shell in 1994, incurring a high level of debt.

RGC's assessment was that CRL in 1994 was trading at a premium to its valuation and had an exposure to substantial political risk associated with its 50 per cent interest in a dredge mining operation in Sierra Leone. However, discussions with Gencor were instigated. In January 1995, mining activities at the Sierra Rutile operation ceased when rebels invaded the mine site. Consequently, CRL's market capitalisation halved. From RGC's perspective, it was clear there was not going to be a short-term resolution to this situation. Nonetheless, it saw a longer-term opportunity and proceeded with the acquisition of Cudgen and, in turn, acquired an interest in CRL and the Sierra Rutile operation.

During 1996, RGC acquired control of Cudgen RZ through the acquisition of Gencor's 19.9 per cent interest followed by an on-market offer for the remainder of the shares. By August 1996, RGC owned 76.7 per cent of Cudgen, with Cudgen controlling 50.1 per cent of CRL. In December 1996, CRL announced a rights issue that RGC partially underwrote and through this acquired a further direct interest in CRL of 4.1 per cent. The Sierra Rutile deposits were ascribed no value in the transaction with the control of this deposit and its potential reactivation seen as an option with future value.

The control of CRL, as well as Sierra Rutile, was seen as useful industry consolidation that may positively influence pricing dynamics. The takeover of Cudgen strengthened RGC's share in both the zircon and chloride titanium dioxide feedstock markets. Its share of the former increased from

30 per cent to 36 per cent and the latter from 23 per cent to 33 per cent. With the recommencement of production from Sierra Rutile, RGC's rutile market share would double from 25 per cent to 50 per cent.[18] As with its takeover of Pancontinental Mining, the same institutional shareholder, QBE Insurance Group, acquired a minority interest. This frustrated RGC from gaining 100 per cent control and being able to integrate CRL into its mineral sands division.

In January 1995 the Sierra Rutile operation was invaded by the Revolutionary United Front, a Liberian rebel force that had entered Sierra Leone in 1994. Most of the workforce was able to escape by vehicles and then by barge to Freetown. One employee was shot and killed and another died in a truck accident while fleeing the site. A number of employees were held hostage and not released until April 1995; one employee died in captivity. Following the attack, a private security company, Lifeguard, a subsidiary of South African Executive Outcomes, provided security for the mine site.[19] Bethwaite visited the site and observed a 'mine looted within an inch of its life.[20] An internal RGC report indicated that a mine recommencement in early 1998 was planned. However, a violent coup d'état in 1997 forced the elected president into exile. All expatriate mining personnel at the site were withdrawn and recommencement plans suspended. Senior RGC management had to expend considerable time in engagement with international lenders, as well as planning for recommencement of mining operations. Despite plans to recommence mining operations, this did not occur during RGC's ownership of Sierra Rutile. The operation's assets were fully written down by the board of CRL, upon which RGC had a majority director representation.[21]

The management of CRL's operation on North Stradbroke Island also involved numerous challenges. CRL's Bayside dredge and concentrator—one of two in operation—was upgraded and a move from one ore body to another was undertaken. This resulted in a six-month break in production at one of the two mines on the island. Due to these activities, production output and sales reduced in 1996 and 1997. The operation encountered numerous environmental issues, including the leakage of diesel into the groundwater. Water management issues were prevalent, with a retaining

---

18 Prudential Bache Securities, RGC Limited (RGC), 14 August 1996, Brierley Collection.
19 Sierra Rutile Limited, *Sierra Rutile: A History*, pp. 106–108.
20 Mark Bethwaite, personal communication, 30 March 2017.
21 *RGC Annual Report 1997*.

wall failing at one deposit resulting in the inundation of a wetlands area, while a levee bank failed at another. RGC's involvement in CRL was short-lived and unsatisfactory financially. In 1996, CRL recorded a profit of $11.7 million. The following year, abnormal items related to the write-down in the value of Sierra Rutile led to a loss of $89 million. A further $33 million in write-downs occurred in 1998, related mainly to the value of loans advanced by CRL to Sierra Rutile. A loss of $14.4 million after tax was reported.

A recovery in the mineral sands market was evident from 1996. In that year RGC recorded a net profit of $142 million, the highest since its formation, although aided by a $66 million after tax contribution from the sale of some of Pancontinental's non-gold assets. Mineral sands constituted 40 per cent of the total assets of the company. With the reduction of direct gold-related revenues, as RGC's interest in Porgera was now held through Goldfields, mineral sands represented the major area of growth for the group.[22]

Exploration remained an area of organisational commitment. One of the exploration objectives for RGC was the discovery of at least two Eneabba class discoveries.[23] The focus in Australia was on the Murray Basin, encompassing large areas of Victoria and New South Wales. The plan was for an ambitious basin-scale level of geological analysis with an initial 80 kilometre traverse planned. Instead, drawing upon the expertise of Peter McGoldrick and geologist Andrew Cook, several exploration targets were identified. Drilling occurred and on the first day three discoveries were made of strand line deposits showing attractive zircon and rutile assemblages. A tenement holding of over 55,000 square kilometres was subsequently secured. A successful exploration program had delineated a major new mineral sands province in Australia. In 1997 a pre-feasibility

---

22 RGC acquired an 87.7 per cent beneficial interest in the Thalanga base metals mine through the Goldfields bid for Pancontinental and after the takeover RGC tendered for and acquired a 100 per cent ownership of Thalanga. RGC acquired a 66 per cent interest in the Mount Windsor Joint Venture, located 50 kilometres east of Thalanga, consisting of the Highway and Reward copper deposits. The development of the Highway project was approved in 1998 for an expenditure of $37.6 million. The gold interests, apart from Porgera, for which RGC had a beneficial interest through its shareholding in Goldfields, included Kundana and Paddington. RGC's Henty gold mine commenced production in June 1996 after board capital expenditure approval of $53 million in July 1992, and subsequent arrangements to acquire the interest held by Little River Goldfields.
23 The overall exploration program (1994–1998) had the following main targets: 5 million ounces of gold; 20 million tonnes of copper, zinc, lead, gold, silver (Rosebery type); 10 million tonnes of zinc, lead, gold (Century type); and 100 million tonnes of porphyry or Proterozoic copper/gold (Colin Cannard, personal communication, 25 September 2018).

study was commenced for the development of one set of deposits, near the Victorian township of Ouyen. Exploration permits were also issued and evaluated in Tamil Nadu, India, while negotiations in relation to the potential development of the Kerala mineral sands project were protracted. Failure to advance suitable arrangements led to RGC walking away. In Sri Lanka, mineralisation was identified leading to RGC undertaking drilling activities. In the United States, exploration resulted in the discovery of mineral sands mineralisation in Georgia, Camden, Tennessee South, North Carolina and Virginia.

Koba Tin in Indonesia expanded through the addition of a dredge at the Bemban deposit, while a smelter was constructed and commissioned in December 1995 to enable direct metal production from the increased output and benefit from lower treatment charges.

In October 1993, the RGC board considered the feasibility study for the development of the Rendeep deposit, with a proposal made for further drilling, although not the approval of the project due to the low tin price. Expectations conveyed to the board were that Rendeep had the potential to extend mining operations by 10 to 20 years, although on the basis of prevailing tin prices in 1993 much of this additional resource potential was deemed uneconomic. By June 1994, the board resolved to commit $34 million for the Renison shaft project to access the higher grades in Rendeep and contribute to expected higher profitability and a longer mine life.[24]

According to the RGC 1994 annual report, drilling of Rendeep delineated a probable reserve of 3.3 million tonnes with a tin grade of 1.96 per cent. This probable reserve estimate represented a more than 100 per cent increase, as well as a material increase in the existing grade of recoverable tin of 1.5 per cent. The experience of producing from Rendeep would be markedly different. Mining from the Rendeep ore body began in 1996. Milling recoveries of tin from ore were expected to be as high as 84 per cent, the level being reported from the existing Renison mining operations. By August 1996, Renison tin recoveries were at the mid-70 per cent level. By November, low tin recovery was better understood in terms of the variability in ore types being processed.

---

24 Renison Goldfields Consolidated Limited, 'Minutes of Meeting of Directors', 23 October 1993, RGCA, Box 1130, BRD38/05; Renison Goldfields Consolidated Limited, 'Minutes of Meeting of Directors', 2 June 1994, RGCA, Box 14284, BRD38/08.

However, this led to some mineralisation, previously categorised as ore, being taken out of the mine plan. As such, the expected uplift in reserves and recovery of higher-grade ore did not occur; within a year of the commencement of Rendeep, the estimated mine life had been reduced from 13 years to nine years. Relative to the position in 1994, probable ore reserves were reduced by 70 per cent by 1997, while proved and probable reserves in total decreased by 46 per cent. Despite a higher tin grade, recoverable tin was lower.

By March 1997, the operation was continuing to suffer recoveries below expectations, which was 'severely impacting on profitability'.[25] Tin prices had declined and the value of the Australian dollar had appreciated. Renison's contribution to group profit declined from $1.9 million in 1993, representing a 7 per cent return on assets, to four years of subsequent losses (see Chart 10). These factors were the forerunners to a write-down in the carrying value of Rendeep of a similar magnitude as the original investment. The decline in the contribution of what was once the 'jewel in the crown' was absolute. This led to a review of the operating strategy for the mine, with further reductions in the workforce and the decision to sell the operation while some value was still capable of being obtained.

In the preparation of the recommendation for the sale, an internal RGC report outlined the financial history of Renison. During the second half of the 1960s and first half of the 1970s, Renison generated satisfactory returns, while the second half of the 1970s and first half of the 1980s was the mine's 'halcyon' period. The third decade, from the mid-1980s to the 1990s, was associated with structural changes in the tin industry. By 1998, Renison had become only one of two underground mining operations in an industry dominated by lower-cost soft rock and alluvial production sources. The conclusion of the review was that Renison—at one time the principal asset of the group—had provided acceptable returns for only a third of its operating life.[26] The operation was sold in 1998.

---

25 Renison Goldfields Consolidated, 'Minutes of Meeting of Directors', 27 March 1997, p. 2, RGCA, Box 14284, BRD38/08.
26 RGC Limited Board Papers, Sale of Renison Tin Mine Assets, August 1998, RGCA, Box 11348.

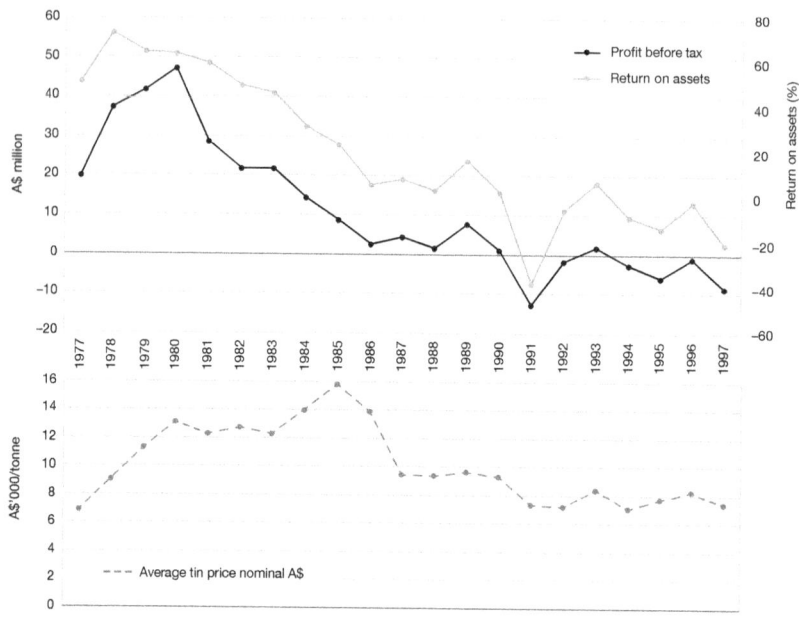

Chart 10. Renison earnings and tin price trend, 1977–1997.

Renison's contribution to group earnings was strongest in the 1970s and early 1980s, before a decline in the mid-1980s, in part related to higher operating costs and reduced ore grade. In 1985, the collapse of the International Tin Council Buffer Stock Manager system resulted in historically low tin prices and a period of low to negative earnings. During the period shown in the chart, Renison's average annual return on assets was 20 per cent with the period 1977 to 1985 displaying a strong contribution with an average return on assets of 60 per cent. From 1986 the average annual return on assets fell to –3.7 per cent. See Appendix 4 and Appendix 6 for more information.

Sources: Renison Goldfields Consolidated, *Report on the 1981 Financial Year*; RGC annual reports, 1990 to 1997.

...

Despite the numerous portfolio challenges and the impediments that had been placed on the group's two main acquisitions, RGC remained expansive in its strategic thinking. The company investigated potential involvement in a recapitalisation process for the Bolivian tin industry.[27] Bolivia was viewed as attractive in terms of mineral prospectivity, including tin, and that in combination with RGC's involvement in Renison and Koba, there was an opportunity to increase the company's share of global tin production. Part of the Bolivian Government's program of privatisation involved the introduction of investors to provide capital

---

27   RGC, EM Vinto Capitalisation Bolivia, Vinto Corporation, March 1997, RGCA, 408-01, Box 4049.

20. FINAL YEARS

for the development of two tin mines and the EM Vinto tin smelter. RGC considered bidding to acquire a half interest in Vinto Corporation. However, the assessed returns were viewed as low while managing the transition of the mines to developed country standards was expected to involve a range of social issues. The risks of operating in the country also became evident when, on two separate occasions, sticks of dynamite were thrown at RGC personnel. The bid did not proceed.

The company also evaluated a silver, lead and zinc investment at the San Cristobal mine in southern Bolivia. In Turkey, the Cerattepe gold and base metals project was progressed through a non-binding offer, while in Peru the company investigated the Cerro Corona copper and gold project. In May 1997, negotiations for Cerro Corona were concluded and by June the offer had been accepted subject to determination of payment terms.[28] In December 1997 the RGC board resolved not to exercise an option to proceed with the acquisition of Cerro Corona, although management was provided with the opportunity to evaluate the acquisition further.

RGC's 1997 financial year results included abnormal items totalling $142 million, associated with write-downs in the carrying value of Renison, Capel, a number of the Pancontinental assets and Sierra Rutile.[29] The company recorded a loss after abnormal items. Planning for the 1998 financial year assessed that cash flow generation and the balance sheet situation were satisfactory, although profitability was not. Operational problems at Renison, which was expected to be loss-making; lower production from the Thalanga base metal operation, acquired from Pancontinental; and a poor market for mineral sands pointed to a weak business outlook. Internal reports indicated that, for a number of operations, including Thalanga, Renison, Capel and Florida, 'the operating strategy is "survival" '.[30] For the Capel mineral sands operation, the decline in demand for sulphate ilmenite and lower ore grades meant that high levels of capital would be required to extend the life of this operation beyond two years. For an asset that had operated for over 40 years, the decline of the market for Capel ilmenite, and a requirement for major additional capital to sustain production, placed 'a question over Capel's

---

28 Renison Goldfields Consolidated Limited, 'Minutes of Meeting of Directors', 29 May 1997, p. 3 and 26 June 1997, RGCA, Box 14284, BRD38/08.
29 The main items on a before-tax basis were Renison $30 million, Thalanga Base Metals $50.1 million, Paddington Gold $26.4 million, Sierra Rutile $25.3 million and Capel $15.0 million (*RGC Annual Report 1997*, p. 38).
30 RGC Budget 1997/98 and Forecasts, RGC Budget 1997/98, RGCA, R40-36G-014, 452-04.

long term mine plan'.[31] The Sierra Rutile operation had been expected to recommence in early 1998. The political situation within the country meant this likelihood was delayed a further 18 months and, in fact, Sierra Rutile did not produce under RGC ownership.

These factors necessitated a further restructuring in mineral sands, with increased provisions for closure and environmental legacy issues, as well as redundancy planning associated with short mine lives, particularly at Capel. The outlook for the Florida dredge operation was 'bleak' without dry or satellite mining, although the company's United States' activities provided some encouragement due to success in regional exploration and the potential to acquire other mineral sands deposits.[32] Nonetheless, even with the inclusion of CRL and Old Hickory in mine plans—the latter about two-thirds complete—these factors were not considered sufficient to offset the deterioration in the ore bodies at Eneabba and Capel.

In fact, Eneabba, described as the division's 'powerhouse, with zircon as a main contributor to the cycle peaks', was viewed as determining the future of the division.[33] The budgetary outlook for Eneabba reflected 'the harsh reality of the orebody deterioration expected in the coming years', with key challenges related to 'zircon grade and recoverability'.[34] Further, the capital expenditure requirements for the mineral sands division were substantial: an estimated $470 million over three years. Detailed proposals for rationalising the Eneabba and Narngulu operations were prepared, and implemented in the latter part of 1998. Eighty people were made redundant, synthetic rutile output was reduced and the Eneabba mineral processing plant was closed.

As such, in 1997 and 1998 RGC was facing challenges on a number of fronts. Apart from the failure of Renison to perform as expected, zircon prices had weakened, with stocks building, presaging another period of poor market conditions. The company was involved in ongoing litigation associated with SREP and major customers were refusing to accept the product. In mid-1997 another legal issue arose when the main customer of Narama coal refused to pay for shipments delivered in June and August of that year, leading to preparations for legal proceedings.

---

31 RGC Mineral Sands Board Report, Divisional Summary, May 1997, RGCA, R40-36G-014, 452-04.
32 ibid., p. 4.
33 RGC Mineral Sands Budget 1998, 27 May 1997, RGCA, R40-36G-014, 452-04.
34 ibid.

Goldfields was struggling with some of its assets: a write-down occurred, with the longevity of the Paddington gold mine in Western Australia reduced when a feasibility study did not support the reserve estimate and its closure was brought forward. Operationally, Porgera was affected by drought and production ceased for a period.

Peter Housden, the finance director, commissioned the Boston Consulting Group to undertake a report on the financial parameters of the company. An informal meeting of board members and the executive committee occurred on 8 November 1997 following receipt of the Boston Consulting Group report. It was apparent that the board, and particularly the Hanson directors, were seeking a broader-ranging strategic review. This was undertaken, although the review was not welcomed by all members of the executive group. Pressure on management was intense and internal dissension at the senior ranks of the company—some long held and some generated under the pressure of widespread portfolio challenges—became evident to directors. Approaches by two members of the executive group to directors over drinks at a Christmas function at the home of Tony Cotton alerted the board to tensions within the Sydney management of the company.

While opportunities in Bolivia, Turkey and Peru were being progressed, the Boston Consulting Group came to the conclusion that mineral sands should be the core focus of the company. In the context of challenges on a number of fronts—financial, technical and operational—and with an increasingly restive major shareholder, Grahame Campbell, a recently appointed director, recalled that the 'major shareholder was applying pressure and it was clear … that a major shakeup was on the cards'.[35] At a board meeting on 6 January 1998, directors were advised that Bethwaite had tendered his resignation. Cotton assumed the role of interim chief executive officer. Campbell recalled that the position of the directors in searching for a new chief executive officer was 'difficult for the board … by Hanson announcing that it wanted to sell its holding'. He also recalled that Vince Gauci, the former chief executive officer of Pancontinental Mining, was identified as a suitable candidate for the role of RGC chief executive officer. However, he had to be advised that his job may

---

35   Campbell, *Clarinets, Pipelines and Unforeseen Places*, p. 493. Peter Mason was a fellow director appointed at the same time as Campbell.

be short-lived as the company might be sold. According to Campbell: 'Vince accepted our advice and went on to lead MIM [Mount Isa Mines] successfully'.[36]

On 26 February 1998, Cotton, as executive chairman, announced that the company was undertaking a comprehensive review of its business, associated with the reduction in profitability ascribed in part to the decline of the profitability of Eneabba, as well as high costs associated with production of the SREP product. A decision was made to close the Capel mine in June 2000. While not mentioned in the public release, funding issues had arisen for CRL, with the company evaluating short-term facilities to cover its working capital requirements. There was also a subordinated debt issue in providing the necessary funds for the move of a dredge to a new ore body. Without this mine move, according to an internal report, 'the value of CRL would be significantly reduced'.[37] The Boston Consulting Group review led to a 'new RGC business plan', which confirmed mineral sands as the company's core business and with plans to concentrate management, financial and technical resources on the assets within this division.[38]

From early 1998, RGC management was also involved in a new activity: the planning for a merger with Westralian Sands. A public announcement was made in July 1998 of an agreed merger by scheme of arrangement between Westralian Sands and RGC. The following months saw this arrangement progressed, finalised and approved by shareholders of RGC before the end of the year.

---

36   ibid., p. 494. Gauci had been offered a senior executive role within RGC or Goldfields at the time of the Goldfields takeover of Pancontinental but did not avail himself of either of these opportunities.
37   Renison Goldfields Consolidated Limited, 'Minutes of Meeting of Directors', 19 January 1998, p. 3 and 26 March 1998, p. 4, RGCA, Box 14284, BRD 38/08.
38   RGC News Release, RGC Implements Comprehensive Business Review, 26 February 1998 (copy held by the author).

21

THE END OF AN ERA

The merger of Westralian Sands and Renison Goldfields Consolidated (RGC) took place in 1998. Prior to this, a director recalled RGC as a fragmented company, without a full-time managing director, acquisitions that had not been appropriately consolidated in part due to at least one blocking shareholder and management of some operations heavily influenced by the centre.[1] The logic for a Hanson exit from its shareholding in RGC was heightened by Hanson's own corporate dynamics and what appeared to be the onset of yet another tough set of market conditions facing the RGC business.

The year 1996 was a watershed in Hanson's shareholding of RGC. In January 1996, Hanson announced its demerger into four separate entities. The sprawling conglomerate model of Hanson was falling out of favour with investors. With company revenues of US$17 billion, it had become harder to identify and make acquisitions material to Hanson's business model and investment market appeal. By October 1996, two parts of the Hanson group had been separated: Millennium Chemicals and Imperial Tobacco. In February 1997, the energy segment of the group demerged as The Energy Group. This left Hanson primarily as a building materials company in which the RGC interest resided. Hanson's focus was on the North American building materials market of aggregates, concrete and sand. This was at odds with holding an Australian diversified resources company. The fit seemed further out of place when Hanson divested several businesses in 1998, primarily to fund acquisitions in the North American market. Although Hanson was prepared to support continued investment

---

1   The director was Grahame Campbell. See Campbell, *Clarinets, Pipelines and Unforeseen Places*.

in 1996 and 1997 in mineral sands, and had been supportive of the RGC takeover of Pancontinental Mining, it drew the line at supporting the investment case for the Cerro Corona deposit in Peru.

If Hanson's corporate dynamic was not a reason for active consideration of divesting its stake in RGC, the 1998 budgetary setting for RGC and the mineral sands division, in particular, put the rationale beyond doubt. RGC had shown a deterioration in profitability from 1996. In the two following years to June 1998, RGC suffered losses of $124 million, with corresponding negative returns on assets and shareholders' funds and an average return of only 4 per cent between 1994 and 1998. Debt levels remained elevated. RGC's share price had declined from above the $6 level in 1996 to below $2 in 1998, and with it the value of Hanson's investment (see Chart 11). The Boston Consulting Group had been engaged to help determine a new strategic direction for the company. In this context, the continued commitment to a diversified mining company with assets that had provided variable performance—with only three years in Hanson's eight years of control showing a return on equity above 10 per cent—was a matter of major investment concern for the British group. As such, a combination with Westralian Sands, when the opportunity arose, was both logical and opportune.

Malcolm Macpherson, the managing director of Westralian Sands, saw an opportunity to aggregate two companies—one, in his estimation, that had successfully grown and developed synthetic rutile capacity and the other in which management was assessed unfavourably in the context of high overheads and mining costs. The fact that RGC's major shareholder's patience had been stretched thin, and the company was without a chief executive officer, provided such an opportunity. The combination of the two companies also made sense in the context of international competition and consolidation of the customer base in mineral sands.

The merger between RGC and Westralian Sands provided a solution to an increasingly unsatisfactory set of operating and financial conditions. It provided access to the management of Westralian Sands that had generated superior total shareholder returns, albeit in a more limited portfolio of assets. For Hanson, the merger provided the means to exit its shareholding and to do so at a healthy premium to the prevailing share price. Hanson exited its shareholding following the merger at $4.25, relative to an assessed fair value of $3.00 per share at the time of the merger announcement and an average share price of $2.30 in the preceding 12 months. The original book cost of Hanson's shareholding was around $2.60.

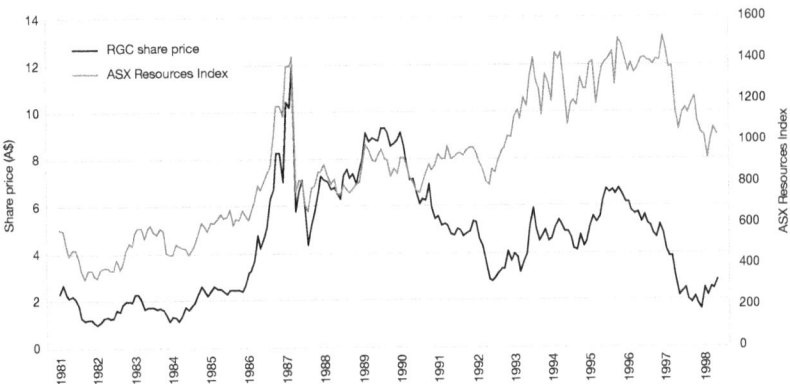

Chart 11. Renison Goldfields Consolidated share price performance, July 1981 to November 1998.

The chart displays RGC's share price performance to 1998, relative to the ASX Resources Index, from the company's naturalisation in 1981. The share price began the period at $2.30 and ended the period at $2.82. This represents a 22 per cent increase (not adjusted for share issuances and not taking account of dividend payments) over an 18-year period, while the Resources Index increased by 79 per cent over the same period. The monthly RGC share price peaked at $12.07 in 1987, prior to the September 1987 share market crash. After the two strong financial years of 1990 and 1991, the RGC share price materially underperformed the broader index. RGC's share price displayed its strongest absolute and relative performance in 1986 and 1987, and from 1988 to 1990. The periods of lower relative performance were from 1991 to 1992 and from mid-1995 to June 1998.

Source: Bloomberg share price data.

Macpherson met Christopher Collins on 20 March 1998 in the Hanson London office.[2] By the end of the meeting, an agreement was reached, confirmed by a handshake. Collins recalled: 'I reacted positively to the idea of a merger with Westralian as a route to exit. I then attended the next RGC board and briefed Tony Cotton on this idea'.[3] The board meeting was held in Sydney on 26 March and Cotton, along with George Lloyd, briefed their advisers. Following the proposal, RGC engaged with Westralian Sands, with due diligence work commencing. In April 1998, RGC executives were informed that merger arrangements were in train and they were offered a bonus of 100 per cent of salary with termination provisions extended from 18 months to two years to secure their involvement during the process.[4]

---

2   Christopher Collins, personal communication, 9 April 2017.
3   Christopher Collins, personal communication, 4 January 2017.
4   RGC Confidentiality Agreements, 3 April 1998, Renison Goldfields Consolidated Archives (RGCA), 462-01.

The Westralian Sands' board provided its support for the merger. The gaps in knowledge required to complete the valuation exercise with sufficient confidence, as well as the risk of a hostile bid from another market participant, led to an arrangement where RGC and Westralian Sands agreed that a merger with an approved determination of respective net present values of the two businesses and the combined businesses would occur through an open due diligence process. This proceeded over the first half of 1998. Regular meetings were held between senior RGC and Westralian Sands management, with one major issue related to the unrealised losses from the RGC foreign exchange hedging. Westralian Sands bought options for $16 million for the 'overhedged RGC position' and with an agreement to an adjustment in the merger terms.[5]

It was to be a merger between two companies of vastly different asset bases and cultures. RGC had net assets of over $1.1 billion and a workforce of 3,374 people. Westralian Sands had net assets of $290 million and a workforce of 431 people. For Westralian Sands, the combination would bring the company a number of benefits. It would provide it with a rutile production stream, as opposed to the limited higher-grade titanium dioxide product suite in its portfolio. It would enable a move away from its predominant sulphate ilmenite production base and provide access to chloride ilmenite from both Eneabba and the United States operations of RGC, which was important to Westralian Sands' ambitions to expand its synthetic rutile production. Furthermore, the combined entity would have materially higher zircon production, six times greater than that of Westralian Sands. The merger would also provide Westralian Sands with new production sources: the potential for production in the United States, access to a new mineral sands province in the Murray Basin across Victoria and New South Wales, production potential in Sri Lanka, as well as the potential for the reactivation of rutile production from CRL's holding in Sierra Rutile. Market and customer factors played a role in the logic for the aggregation, with the concentration of customer ownership then not matched on the producer side.[6] A more diversified portfolio of mineral commodities was not a prime motivation of Westralian Sands; its intent was to remain focused on mineral sands.

---

5   Westralian Sands Limited, 'Minutes of Meeting of Directors of Westralian Sands', 17 December 1988, RGCA, Box 14633, BRD 2/11.
6   Macquarie Equities, Westralian Sands/Renison, 25 August 1998, Brierley Collection.

21. THE END OF AN ERA

Macpherson presented to the directors of RGC in the boardroom of Gold Fields House in Sydney on 25 June 1998. The RGC board met again on 23 July and 24 July. Lloyd delivered the merger presentation. The merger implementation agreement was signed on 24 July and on the same day an announcement to the Australian Stock Exchange was made for a scheme of arrangement in which RGC would become a wholly owned subsidiary of Westralian Sands.[7] The merger would create a combined entity with total assets of $1.2 billion and revenues of $800 million, making it one of the top 10 minerals companies in Australia and the second-largest mineral sands company globally. RGC shareholders would own 62 per cent and Westralian Sands' shareholders would own 38 per cent of the merged entity.[8] RGC's 56 per cent interest in Goldfields was excluded from the merger by the offer to RGC shareholders of one RGC Gold Unsecured Note per RGC share. Post-merger, Hanson would have a 23.8 per cent holding and agreed to a restriction in its voting power to 19.9 per cent in the first six months. Cotton would be the first chairman of the merged company and Macpherson the managing director.

One broking analyst wrote: 'The merger encompasses a solution to the main problems facing RGC over the last six months—lack of leadership, obstacles to a mineral sands focus and an expensive administrative structure'.[9] More fundamentally, it facilitated achievement of Hanson's motivation to exit its shareholding in RGC.

Macpherson presented the benefits of the merger to shareholders. He conveyed that the merger had been initiated by Westralian Sands and the merged company would, essentially, have the same Westralian Sands' management. A limited number of RGC employees would be invited to join the new company's management. The head office would be located in Perth. On an operational basis, growth was to be based out of the United States, with expansion potential in Virginia, Florida and Georgia. Domestically, the intention was to close dredging operations at Eneabba West and close the mineral separation plant at site, as well as close the smaller of the two RGC kilns at Capel. RGC production opportunities in the Murray Basin were likely to be pursued, although the timing was

---

7   Renison Goldfields Consolidated Limited, 'Minutes of Meeting of Directors', 23 July 1998, p. 2 and 24 July 1998, p. 1, RGCA, Box 14284, BRD38/08.
8   Each RGC share was eligible for 0.6556249 Westralian Sands' shares plus an RGC Gold Unsecured Note (Information Memorandum in Relation to a Recommended Merger by Scheme of Arrangement Between RGC Limited and Westralian Sands Limited, 1998).
9   Macquarie Equities, RGC & WSL Merger, 27 July 1998, Brierley Collection.

pushed out in the new company's planning. The Murray Basin projects, considered by RGC to have development potential as early as 2001, would be developed at a later date. RGC's exploration tenements in Sri Lanka were considered to 'be subject to too much sovereign risk to be viable at this point'.[10]

On 11 December, a shareholder vote occurred and the merger was endorsed. The outcome of the merger, despite initial assurances to the contrary, left matters in no doubt that Westralian Sands' management had come out on top. From the RGC side, there was the view that management selection overwhelmingly favoured former Westralian Sands' management, and that experienced RGC personnel were not seriously considered, with few exceptions, for senior roles. Many accepted redundancies.[11]

On 14 December 1998 the RGC board held its final meeting on the 24th floor of Gold Fields House. Overlooking Circular Quay and Sydney Harbour, Gold Fields House was an impressive corporate presence, the building having opened in 1966 as a symbol of the intentions of an expansionary British mining house recently established in Australia, although with an involvement in the country stretching back to 1926. Reminders of the heritage of the company were evident: the portrait of Cecil Rhodes and the Rhodes Room where annual general meetings were held. It was a bitter irony that this company was folded into the smaller Westralian Sands, the directors of which often held their board meetings at the company's premises in rural Capel, a two-hour drive south of Perth. All of the RGC directors with the exception of Cotton and Campbell resigned, and all existing Westralian Sands directors and management gained main positions within the newly established entity.

Before the end of 1998, the Sydney office of RGC at Gold Fields House was closed with the retrenchment of 200 administrative personnel in Sydney and at other locations. A Westralian Sands' executive remembered visiting Gold Fields House and the boardroom following the merger and retrenchment of most RGC staff. The notable artwork collection had gone, some sold by auction and some selected for Westralian Sands.

---

10   ibid.
11   These included Peter Housden, director finance; Peter Robinson, director, operations; Keith Faulkner, managing director, mineral sands; George Lloyd, group general manager, exploration and development; Peter Grigg, general manager, South Capel; Peter Myers, general manager, Eneabba; Alan Breen, general manager, synthetic rutile division; Russell Clarke, general manager, Virginia; Neil Condon, general manager, commercial.

21. THE END OF AN ERA

The stock of wine had been consumed. The fine boardroom table was marked by multiple indentations of women's heels; the post-merger RGC 'celebration' was evidently a raucous affair.

Within a year, Cotton had resigned as chairman and a Westralian Sands' director appointed to the role. The merged company retained the name Westralian Sands before a name change occurred in 1999 to Iluka Resources.

In 1999, the RGC Capel mining and separation plants were closed and mining operations at Eneabba West ceased. Progressively over the next two years, most of the non-mineral sands assets of RGC were divested. The residual interest in Goldfields Limited was sold in the first half of 1999. Thalanga was the first of the former RGC assets to be divested, in September 1999, for $30.7 million. In November of that year Iluka was paid an outstanding amount of $23 million for Renison, following the sale arrangement with Murchison NL effected by RGC in 1998. Koba Tin was the one non-mineral sands asset intended to be retained, given the similarities in mining approach to mineral sands. However, falling tin prices, an unstable political environment in Indonesia and the inability of local authorities to control illegal mining on the company's leases led to a suspension of production followed by withdrawal from the country. The sale of Koba Tin was announced in November 2001 and finalised the following April. Iluka sold its 75 per cent interest to the Malaysia Smelting Corporation Board for US$14 million cash and a US$6 million deferred consideration.

In 2002, Narama remained the only non-mineral sands asset in the Iluka portfolio, apart from the Mining Area C iron ore royalty, yet to make a contribution. The 50 per cent interest in Narama was retained until 2007 when sold. The interests in Sri Lankan exploration tenements were sold in the face of a deteriorating security situation in the country. CRL, partially owned by Iluka, sold its 50 per cent interest in Sierra Rutile in 2001. Iluka's interest in CRL continued until divested in 2009.

There was a logic in the combination of Westralian Sands and RGC. There was a shared recognition, even if not articulated publicly, that the combination could serve to paper over some of the deficiencies of both companies, buy time and create a new, more efficient and forceful business entity. Both companies had inherent weakness and deficiencies in their portfolios and, by definition, in their growth prospects. The logic, however, was more compelling for Westralian Sands. Macpherson played his hand well, given Westralian Sands' limited portfolio of production assets and exploration potential. For RGC, the outcome was, in effect, determined by its major shareholder. Hanson had reached the stage where its continued involvement in an Australian minerals company made little strategic or financial sense. It readily accepted the opportunity to quit its less than satisfactory investment.

A major Australian diversified mining company with its lineage stretching back to 1887 with the formation of The Gold Fields of South Africa, by Rhodes and Rudd, was folded into a smaller company, the operations of which were based predominantly in Western Australia.

AFTERWORD: REFLECTIONS OF CONSOLIDATED GOLD FIELDS IN AUSTRALIA

A financial journalist writing in 1977 made the following observation about Consolidated Gold Fields Australia (CGFA):

> When ... floated to the Australian public a decade ago, aficionados of the business scene saw it as a major competitor to CRA ... Two of the mother country's biggest and most interesting mining groups would cross swords, by proxy, through their Australian offshoots. One would emerge with the title of Australia's major mining house.[1]

On the basis that the opportunities available to both CGFA and Renison Goldfields Consolidated (RGC), relative to CRA, were similar, it is intriguing that the fate of the two companies was so different.

A company with notable historical mining origins and a track record of impressive achievement in Australia—not least ownership of Lake View and Star, Wiluna, control of Renison and Mount Lyell, part owner and developer of Mount Goldsworthy and at one stage the largest global mineral sands producer—was folded into a company with more constrained ambitions and a more limited business focus, both geographically and in terms of its range of mineral products. With the 1998 merger—or, as the architect of the combination referred to it, takeover—there was the demise of a company that had an influential involvement in the Australian mining sector for 72 years and the origins of which, through

---

1   Terry McCrann, 'What Went Wrong at Gold Fields House?', *The National Times*, 14–19 November 1977, p. 64.

The Gold Fields of South Africa, stretched back through a diverse heritage of 112 years.[2] That many associated with CGFA and RGC expressed regret at the outcome is not surprising.

Consolidated Gold Fields' existence in Australia had a number of different facets, related both to the period and nature of its portfolio structure. Initially, from the 1920s, the involvement was directed from London, with investments made predominantly through companies established on the London Stock Exchange. This London-based mining-finance model proved lucrative for the British company. The early investments of Gold Fields in Australia entailed access to gold reserves at Wiluna and Lake View and Star, with a high level of technical expertise applied to the metallurgical and mining challenges. Both were excellent investments. They enabled Gold Fields to establish insights into the opportunities available more broadly in the Australia mining sector through the knowledge and expertise of men with an involvement in the country. John Agnew stands out in this regard. Both Agnew and The Consolidated Gold Fields of South Africa had connections with prominent mining and finance men in London, as well as developing an association with the companies established by WS Robinson, including Gold Exploration and Finance Company, Gold Mines of Australia and Western Mining Corporation.

Through the connections Agnew had with companies associated with Herbert Hoover, Gold Fields gained an involvement in the Lake George lead and zinc mine, while also establishing interests in two gold mining ventures in New Guinea. The decision to form the group's own development vehicle in Australia, through the London listing in 1932 of Gold Fields Australian Development Company, demonstrated an intention to become involved in a wider spread of Australian mining operations. In this regard, the company's activities were aided by the involvement in both managerial and directorial positions by Dolph Agnew.

From the 1940s, the Australian interests of Consolidated Gold Fields were of variable quality and mature. By the 1950s the portfolio was restricted to Lake View and Star, Mount Ida gold mine and Lake George mine. Evolution of the initial interests into a broader-based portfolio of mining assets, with an Australian management and technical capability, was truncated by the fact that exploration and other business-generation activities during the 1940s and 1950s were largely unproductive.

---

2 Malcolm Macpherson, personal communication, 10 February 2017.

An attempt to reinvigorate the Australian portfolio through the establishment of New Consolidated Gold Fields (Australasia) in 1956 was not successful.

For the next phase of the group's development, Gold Fields operated, essentially, according to a mining-finance model. The approach, overseen by Sir George Harvie-Watt in the late 1950s and early 1960s, drew upon experts in London to undertake assessments of industries and companies for potential investment. The major difference to the prior approach was that Gold Fields was prepared to acquire a controlling interest in companies in Australia under a local management and board.

It proved an effective approach. In the midst of a mining boom in Australia, Gold Fields by 1964 had secured interests in a spread of minerals and in several leading Australian mining companies: Mount Lyell Mining and Railway Company, Renison, Bellambi and Associated Minerals Consolidated (AMC), as well as an interest in a major iron ore province. Its attempts at diversification, in manufacturing, were designed to align with Harvie-Watt's desire to ensure that all the 'horses on the carousel' were not down at the same time. By 1966, CGFA contributed 18 per cent of the Consolidated Gold Fields group profits: higher than the United States at 14 per cent. Financing from London and an expanded Australian board representation established a sound base for Consolidated Gold Fields to become an influential participant in the Australian mining sector. These were, in some respects, the halcyon days for Consolidated Gold Fields' Australian presence.

In 1966, Australian shareholding was introduced and with it the opportunity for CGFA to access a financing base beyond that of its London parent. CGFA continued to invest widely. Direct investments were made and exploration pursued, although no new businesses of any scale were developed, at least initially. Further, investments in agriculture and property development were small, outside the realm of the expertise of a mining group and either financially unsuccessful or not material.

Through the 1970s the management and directors of CGFA were often stretched in terms of the demands placed upon them. This was displayed by Charles Copeman's and Bart Ryan's efforts in dealing with industrial relations, governmental and operational challenges, including those at Bellambi Coal, and in seeking governmental financial assistance for the continuation of mining operations at Mount Lyell. Likewise, Sidney Segal was involved with tenement acquisition discussions and legal challenges as executive chairman of Western Titanium.

In large part, however, CGFA acted as an investor in a range of companies, providing an oversight capacity with regard to its mining investments. The composition of the board and, to a lesser extent, senior management, with few having either direct or deep mining operational experience, meant that a financial, rather than a mining perspective, was brought to the consideration of the portfolio structure and management approach. While CGFA was active in seeking to direct aspects of its portfolio, in many areas it was content to allow existing management to run activities. To a large extent, this was the case at Mount Lyell, Renison and AMC, where existing management was retained until the second half of the 1970s. This reflected the limited organisational resources of CGFA as well as a reluctance to intervene in the technical, operational and financial management of its investments, lest this upset the minority shareholders. This impeded a more thorough, wide-ranging and integrated approach to the technical and operational management of the portfolio, as well as delaying the establishment of a deep pool of technical capabilities within CGFA.

More fundamentally, by 1975 the inherent constraints of the Consolidated Gold Fields mining-finance model had become apparent. Holding majority shareholdings as opposed to total control of subsidiaries and their cash flows was identified as a fundamental constraint to the management and development of an integrated portfolio of minerals. This constraint, combined with the maturity and financial performance of some of the main investments, led to CGFA's business model being described within the company as 'a rather uninspiring holding company for a generally rather unexciting group of subsidiaries'.[3]

---

3   Consolidated Gold Fields Australia Limited, Correspondence from JB Massy-Greene to JD McCall, Chairman, Consolidated Gold Fields Limited, 22 October 1975, p. 2, Renison Goldfields Consolidated Archives, Box 12301.

AFTERWORD

According to the historical perspective of the chief executive and chairman of Consolidated Gold Fields, Rudolph Agnew:

> By then [mid-1960s] we had sold thirty per cent to the public ... and had got into a classic business muddle. Management wasn't sure whether to be a growth or an income company, and equally unsure who was its master—the seventy per cent owners in London or the thirty per cent in Australia. Matters were further complicated by the fact that most of the operations were themselves public companies, thus creating yet more conflicts. These conflicts prohibited vital structural changes and the company declined dramatically throughout the 1970s.[4]

Major portfolio configuration was contemplated and elements of this undertaken in the 1970s: the sale of the interest in Mount Goldsworthy, the merger of AMC and Western Titanium, and the divestment of the shareholding in Commonwealth Mining Investments. However, given the financial performance of some of the investments of the Australian company and the increasing dissatisfaction of the major London-based shareholder, a deep-seated review of the nature of the business model took place. This led to the direct ownership of assets and, with this, the opportunity for the application of a greater depth of mining and technical management expertise to operations within the company's control.

The basis was laid for a naturalisation process that occurred in 1981. Despite initial opposition in London to a dilution of Consolidated Gold Fields' shareholding in its Australian subsidiary, the transition to a 'naturalised' Australian company, with fully owned subsidiaries, was implemented. Coincidental with this move to an Australian-controlled business, the company lost two of its most experienced senior mining executives—Ryan and Copeman. Both were knowledgeable about the individual assets of the portfolio and capable of building strong mining teams. In the case of Ryan, his replacement by Max Roberts reflected the strained relationship with Agnew that had emanated from their earlier competition for the managing directorship of Consolidated Gold Fields. Roberts's appointment saw Ryan step down as managing director and leave as a director within two years.

---

4   Quoted in Johnson, *Gold Fields: A Centenary Portrait*, p. 159.

Copeman, with his depth of mining experience, considered himself a contender to run RGC. He was viewed by his colleagues as reliable in a crisis, but for some was an emotionally complex individual. With Roberts's appointment, Copeman recognised that his prospects for further advancement in RGC had come to an end. Copeman went on to a controversial but accomplished executive career in other mining companies.[5]

The managing directors appointed to RGC had no direct mining experience, although Mark Bethwaite had the benefit of running a major mining company in North Broken Hill. Roberts and Campbell Anderson had a background in the oil sector. The boards of CGFA and RGC typically appointed men with little direct mining, metallurgical or engineering experience to lead the companies over their existence. Ryan was the exception in becoming managing director. Few of the operational personnel advanced to corporate executive positions. The composition of the board of directors, impressive in terms of business reputation, reflected an orientation towards men with financial, banking, legal and other professional experience. Little, if any, of the directors' capabilities or experience related to strategy formulation in the mining sector or the identification, development and efficient management of ore bodies.

In effect, the earlier attributes of the mining-finance model, employed when CGFA was established in the 1960s, flowed through to subsequent periods. Two directors, who served during critical periods in the evolution of the company, had 22 years tenure each. One was drawn from merchant banking and the other from law.[6] According to an executive, one was recalled as rarely asking questions at board meetings related to mining matters. He became animated, however, with the grammatical nuances of a stock exchange release. With the exception of Michael Beckett, an experienced mining professional appointed by Consolidated Gold Fields

---

5   Copeman, a mining engineer, joined the company in 1969 and became an executive director in July 1974. In later life, he recorded that Max Roberts 'didn't want me to be around' and he left to join the board of Peko-Wallsend before becoming its chief executive officer in April 1982 (Charles Copeman, interview by John Farquarson, National Library of Australia, session 2).
6   GM Niall, a director from 1966 to 1988 and J Darling from 1974 to 1996. Other directors appointed after 1981 included RM Craig, former chief investment officer of AMP; K Wood formerly of Coopers & Lybrand; VT Christie, the former managing director of the Commonwealth Bank; JA Strong, principal partner at a legal firm and previous chief executive of Australian Airlines (although Strong had been a site manager at Nabalco and executive director of the Australian Mining Council). RCH Mason, appointed a director in 1989, had been general manager of Ampol Ltd, a petroleum refiner and distributor.

who served between 1981 and 1998, none of the independent directors had mining experience. While directors were diligent in seeking to understand the company, its markets and its operations, the strategic direction of the company lacked board representation of those with a deep experience of mining.[7]

According to a former senior RGC operational person, there was a view that corporate management and the board tended to cast their investment net too widely, with an attempt to pick 'winners' within the portfolio. A corollary was that the major assets in the portfolio, such as Renison and Mount Lyell, did not receive sufficient focus at board level in terms of the management of metallurgical, cost, competitive or market considerations. The consequences may have been not to understand the challenges and opportunities of the portfolio, nor to consider some options for assets. These may have included divestment in favourable market conditions, as opposed to when operational and financial performance was in decline, or extended idling with a view to recommencement when market conditions were more favourable.

Operational general manager Mike Ayre observed that the focus on the 'bottom line in good times' and an over-reliance on long-term commodity price forecasts—which inevitably meant that 'every dog has its day'—led to a lack of focus on 'the fundamentals of the day'. In turn, this tended to create a 'firefighting' response when losses became unsupportable, instead of an ongoing approach to the provision of the necessary managerial, technical and financial resources to improve the competitive cost position of operations.[8] Further, a 'middle age bulge' was observed in terms of departmental heads at sites and senior executives in Sydney, which—in his view—stifled enthusiasm, created a loss of young talent and created 'low energy operations'.[9] His observations of the head office included:

---

7   According to one senior executive, two directors that fell into this category were K Wood and RM Craig. An exception to directors appointed that had industry experience was GD Campbell, a consulting engineer, although he was appointed towards the end of RGC's existence, in 1996.
8   These observations were made to Campbell Anderson by Mike Ayre, then general manager of Renison and previously general manager of Mount Lyell. They followed a management a session involving consultants Pappas Carter Evans & Koop that had been retained by the company (letter from MWD Ayre, General Manager, to Campbell Anderson, 15 February 1988, National Archives of Australia, Tasmania, NS1711/1/781).
9   ibid.

> From my viewpoint, R.G.C. will start becoming vigorously competitive when conversations, both in the office and after hours with Sydney personnel are about plans and ideas for growth rather than about rumours and personal misgivings. This will only happen when rumour is replaced by fact and feeling of participation.[10]

Exploration remained a cornerstone of the company's activities. Exploration resulted in new gold mining operations in the 1980s, although these were small and short-lived. Unlike a company such as Western Mining Corporation, exploration did not deliver multiple or material resources. There was a view from some geological staff that RGC did not have the necessary appetite for risk nor the time frames for expenditure to test some geological opportunities. The limited material success in exploration created an impetus for acquisition activity in an attempt to broaden the composition of the portfolio. This included the contemplation of integration with other minerals groups, including North Broken Hill, Paringa Mining, Mount Isa Mines and Cerro Corona. Little eventuated, although Koba Tin was acquired and made a useful financial contribution to the portfolio from the late 1980s.

Efforts to broaden the portfolio into bulk commodities, by establishing a coal business through the Glendell coal project, did not eventuate. Narama was a paler manifestation of what had been envisaged in coal, although it made a useful financial contribution in the final stages of RGC's existence. Forays into oil exploration and production were not material.

The company, despite its commitment to exploration and its willingness to be acquisitive—both of which resulted in new production sources—was not able to generate material new revenue streams as it entered the 1990s. An acquisition of or merger with North Broken Hill or Mount Isa Mines, as had been contemplated, may have facilitated a broadening of the business base and a diversification of cash flows, but did not occur. An acquisition of RGC by another minerals company with an expansive perspective may have also aided such an outcome.

Overall, the fundamental issues within the portfolio remained; the contribution of Renison faded in the second half of the 1980s while Mount Lyell struggled financially for most of that decade. Mineral sands represented the major deployment of assets and was often the overwhelming financial contributor—both positively and adversely—

---

10   ibid.

from 1985. By the 1990s, given the inability to broaden the portfolio to new operations, RGC had become largely reliant on mineral sands. This meant, for a company that considered itself a diversified miner, exposure to a small and inherently volatile commodity sector, vulnerable to shifts in supply and demand, as well as a new competitive dynamic from South Africa. A major part of the revenue base of the business—zircon—experienced more pronounced pricing variability as new entrants viewed zircon as a by-product to their principal product stream. In terms of titanium dioxide products, pigment customers were astute enough to play mineral sands producers off against each other. This context and the maturity of RGC's mineral sands operations, with associated operational, cost and product quality challenges, and need for major capital expenditure, introduced inherent constraints and challenges for the portfolio.

The main opportunity, Porgera, was advanced to a development stage by the early 1990s. With Porgera, the prospects were favourable for a diversification of the company's revenue stream to offset the decline from Mount Lyell and Renison and rebalance away from the dominance of mineral sands. This occurred to some extent, although the economic and market conditions of the early 1990s adversely affected overall performance.

The acquisition of Consolidated Gold Fields by Hanson in 1989 introduced a new dynamic for the RGC board and management: a major shareholder whose orientation to rebuild and manage a diversified mining company did not form part of its business motivation. Hanson was never enamoured with a diversified business model nor were the financial criteria it applied, as an industrial-oriented conglomerate, aligned to those of the management of a resources company. Hanson reinforced a financial perspective to the structure of the portfolio, as opposed to encouraging strategic initiatives that may have assisted RGC in rebuilding its portfolio of mining assets. Hanson's prime focus was on maximising its exit price from its coincidental Australian investment. In this regard, it had opportunities, but its desire to generate a premium to the prevailing share price of RGC meant that opportunities were foregone and its shareholding retained much longer than envisaged.

The 1993 effort by Hanson to install its own executive chairman and unwind the naturalised status of RGC reflected a lack of confidence in RGC corporate management. Its intention to appoint

Tony Cotton—a competent Hanson executive but with no mining knowledge or experience—conveyed an intent for RGC that was not to grow the company unless it facilitated a liquidity event. Strained board relationships were evident and Hanson's activities were viewed by independent directors as an attempt to achieve a de facto change in control, if not ownership. It was the beginning of the end for RGC as an independent Australian diversified mining company.

The situation of a major and often demanding shareholder required a management ability to curb demands and avoid a brutal approach to cost reductions, divestitures and capital constraints that may have more severely truncated growth options. Anderson was a bulwark in this respect, although it cost him his position. There was an often combative relationship between Anderson as managing director and Lord Hanson. Anderson's relationship with Tony Alexander, the chief operating officer of Hanson, was one close to mutual disrespect. Anderson was wont to wear Mickey Mouse ties when meeting with Alexander. Likewise, Roberts had reached a view about Hanson that conveyed a deep suspicion and lack of alignment with what he and his fellow directors saw as the interests of non-Hanson shareholders. These circumstances, and the lack of confidence Hanson held of Anderson's ability to address the financial challenges of RGC, led to the unwinding of the plan for Anderson to assume the chairmanship after Roberts retired. A compromise to the initial Hanson plan to have Cotton as executive chairman was to appoint Bethwaite managing director and Cotton chairman.

Considerable effort was expended to seek alternative holders for the Hanson stake. Inevitably, this distracted senior levels of management from the more fundamental challenges of the portfolio, inhibited broad-ranging strategic considerations of how the portfolio could be recast and contributed to a dynamic at board level that was not conducive to the pursuit of the interests of all shareholders. This corrosive situation existed for most of the 1990s.

Whether removing the Hanson shareholding would have fundamentally changed the future of RGC is conjecture. There is little overt evidence that Hanson impeded the plans of management. The exceptions were not proceeding with the Cerro Corona acquisition in Peru in 1998 and a limitation of exploration expenditure. The ultimate lack of support for

AFTERWORD

Cerro Corona did not reflect opposition to evaluating this opportunity; a heads of agreement had been signed and the investment opportunity featured prominently in a company annual report while Cotton was chairman. However, this was occurring while merger arrangements were in train with Westralian Sands. It made little sense to advance a major investment in South America in this situation.

Under the circumstances, Hanson could, on one level, be considered a patient shareholder for nine years. Support was provided for the Cudgen and CRL acquisition, for the bold and complex Pancontinental Mining takeover and formation of a separate listed gold company, Goldfields. While Hanson's position on the register may not have altered the prospects for RGC as a diversified mining company, it facilitated the aggregation with Westralian Sands. As proposed by Malcolm Macpherson of Westralian Sands, Hanson was willing to take advantage of a means to exit its shareholding. RGC executives and other management had little role to play in the new entity, while most of the RGC non-mineral sands assets were carved out of the portfolio soon after the combination. There was little done by the RGC directors to attempt to alter this outcome, despite RGC being the dominant entity in the merger arrangement.

The Gold Fields' entities and companies in Australia proved themselves to be bold, acquisitive, sophisticated and well-resourced in terms of their capabilities. The companies drew in, and broadened the professional experiences of, many reputable and high-quality mining people, such as John and Rudolph Agnew, Brian Andrew, Keith Cameron, Charles Copeman and Bart Ryan. Others drawn from broader business and finance backgrounds were also influential, including Sid Segal, Brian Massy-Greene, Max Roberts, Campbell Anderson and Mark Bethwaite. Many of the RGC executives and operational management had, or went on to have, creditable careers in mining in Australia and internationally. There was a group of skilled technical, metallurgical, operational, geophysical, geological and environmental management personnel, including those drawn from the graduate program. The company had the technical capability to tackle and implement a range of mining, ore resource and metallurgical opportunities in an exemplary fashion and did so, although with some notable exceptions. It had been at the forefront of technology in terms of flotation, processing, geological interpretation and ilmenite upgrading and contributed to product and market development across a range of mineral products.

A poor financial track record, however, can invite criticisms. There were views that CGFA then RGC, at times, acted and spent outwardly in a manner that did not befit its rank as a mid-tier market capitalisation mining company. Some working at an operational level looked upon some manifestations of the corporate function in Sydney with thinly veiled disdain. Whether examples of hubris or a lack of clear strategic direction played any meaningful part and had adverse consequences in terms of the fundamental performance or prospects of the company, is hard to judge. Some involved with the company suggest they did. Anecdotal examples include the use of the company's Daimler in the early days; the wine collection; construction of an internal staircase in Gold Fields House to expedite access from the executive floor; and private dining rooms with, at one stage, a butler on hand. Directors travelling to Queenstown on the west coast of Tasmania for Mount Lyell board meetings typically flew on chartered aircraft, even during the darkest days of this operation.

For some operational personnel, the granting to executives of what was regarded as highly generous retention and termination arrangements during the merger with Westralian Sands was confirmation that some in the corporate office were more concerned with their own interests than those of the wider workforce. While more egregious examples can be replicated for other companies, they formed some individuals' perspectives of CGFA and RGC. The company's corporate presence on Circular Quay, meant to epitomise its quest for status and success in Australia, possibly became anachronistic: a symbol of its unfulfilled promise.

Despite its ambitions, RGC did not achieve the size, financial performance nor influence of BHP or Rio Tinto. It, along with North Broken Hill, Western Mining Corporation, Peko Wallsend, Mount Isa Mines, Broken Hill South, Normandy and others, was acquired or subsumed in the context of the broader aggregation of mining companies and the expansion of BHP, Rio Tinto and other global mining groups.

There is much in the shape and history of a mining company that is outside its control. The history of CGFA and RGC shows their buffeting, at frequent intervals, by economic and geopolitical forces, with the attendant adverse impact on demand for and the price of products, quite apart from the usual bad luck and missteps that are endemic to companies in the resources sector. In the case of CGFA and RGC, diversification did not provide the protection from all horses on the carousel being down at the same time, to use Harvie-Watt's phrase. For RGC there was also the challenge of change of 'control' from a longer-term and generally supportive and aligned major shareholder in terms of appreciation of the dynamics of the mining sector in Consolidated Gold Fields, to Hanson, a company that had a markedly different business model.

Despite this, the portfolio structure and nature of RGC's assets were the major influences on the company, its performance and its prospects. With the possible exception of Porgera, which was brought to RGC by Placer and would be held within another company from 1996, RGC had an absence of world-class assets in the 1990s. Renison, Mount Lyell and AMC's east-coast mineral sands portfolio had closed or were near the end of their economic lives. In the case of mineral sands, while earlier operations had been replaced by Eneabba and Green Cove Springs, by the mid-1990s these too were maturing or not of a scale to be material to the performance or prospects of the company. New sources of mineral sands production had been identified, particularly in the Murray Basin in Victoria and in the United States, but, with the exception of Old Hickory in Virginia, were some years from development.

In the 1990s opportunities for a wider corporate aggregation were considered but not pursued, with the exception of the Pancontinental acquisition. The Cudgen and CRL acquisitions built on an established market position in mineral sands, providing few benefits in terms of economies of scale or a strengthened market position. The Pancontinental acquisition, planned to enhance the market value of the company's gold assets and diversify its non-gold portfolio, was stymied by a minority shareholder. It also did not deliver a material diversification to the RGC portfolio through the Pancontinental non-gold assets, most of which were not of a high quality. By its nature, the acquisition also led to the largest and most financially remunerative asset, Porgera, being withdrawn from the RGC portfolio, although a residual interest was held through the investment in Goldfields Limited.

Unlike BHP and Rio Tinto, RGC was not able to develop large, bulk commodity or export-oriented businesses—such as iron ore, coal or bauxite—or a large-scale precious metal operation. These may have provided benefits in terms of economies of scale, market position and influence, sharing of technical competence and the ability to extend production through reserve delineation drilling or obtain technology and unit-cost efficiencies. In turn, these may have led to a greater consistency in cash flow generation.

The reality in 1998 was that RGC had a portfolio of declining mineral sands ore bodies, solid but not material overall contributions from Koba Tin and Narama, but little else to generate adequate returns or provide resource and production longevity, portfolio efficiencies, the sharing of technical expertise across the portfolio or market scale. Despite strategic reviews undertaken in the 1980s, solutions to the inherent challenges RGC faced were not found and the outcome of a 1998 review was to focus back upon the company's mineral sands business.

Even in a situation where RGC management may have been able to exert a greater influence in terms of the post-merger management and strategic considerations within Westralian Sands, and bring its wider minerals industry experience to the fore, the aggregation of the two companies did not create a fundamental change in the overall involvement in the minerals sector in Australia. The combined entities' market position in mineral sands was strengthened but did not provide a basis for a wider expansion of the portfolio.

Overlaying the portfolio challenges was a board and management dynamic that had become strained. Given the Hanson shareholding and board presence, towards the end there was a malaise in the culture of the company, an inability to orient it to excel in terms of productivity or efficient reserve recovery, to inject fresh talent or provide career opportunities for professional personnel. There was also a lack of motivation at director level for the next round of strategic and portfolio growth considerations in what was emerging as yet another cycle of declining prices, after a period of seemingly insurmountable portfolio challenges.

After Bethwaite's departure, the absence of a full-time chief executive officer and the difficulty in attracting someone of the necessary calibre to look expansively and afresh at the company's options compounded these issues. Hanson's disenchantment with its investment of nearly a decade had become complete, while the overall Hanson group dynamic made the continued shareholding in an Australian mining company untenable.

With this confluence of factors Renison Goldfields Consolidated and its British–South African mining heritage, established in Australia in the 1920s, came to an end.

APPENDIX 1.
TECHNICAL TERMS

adit	A horizontal opening driven into an ore body from the side of a hill.
alluvial	Fine, unconsolidated minerals from weathered rocks typically formed in a river system.
assemblage	Relative composition of valuable heavy minerals of ilmenite, zircon and rutile in ore (in the case of mineral sands).
beneficiation	A process that improves the value of a mineral or in the case of ilmenite beneficiation (known as the production of synthetic rutile), the leaching of iron at high temperatures to create a product with a higher titanium dioxide content.
carbon-in-pulp	Ore is crushed, ground and dissolved by cyanide solution, with gravity separation used to recover coarse gold while pulped ore is agitated in tanks with granules of activated carbon added to adsorb the gold.
cyanide extraction	Use of sodium cyanide acid to extract gold from ore, often involving precipitation by means of metallic zinc.
deposit	An ore body of defined mineral characteristics considered to have the potential for commercial recovery.
dilution	Contamination of ore-bearing rock with barren rock, thereby affecting the level of recovery of metal.
dredging	Use of large excavators to extract free-flowing ore or sand, such as mineral sands or tin, in a dredge pond.

flotation	A method used to extract low-grade and complex ores, including gold, silver, copper, lead and zinc. Finely ground ore containing minerals is placed in a solution, typically water although pine oil was used in some of the earlier approaches, with the use of a reagent or frothers to separate the minerals and have them adhere to air bubbles, with the minerals skimmed off for drying. Sulphide and non-sulphide minerals are recovered by froth flotation.
grade	The classification of an ore based on estimated level of valuable mineral content.
leaching	Removal of soluble salts or metals from ore by the use of a solvent.
oxidised ore	Part of a mineralised formation that due to action or air and water has been changed wholly or in part into oxides and carbonates.
pyrite	Iron sulphide mineral, often accompanied by gold in mineral deposits. Able to be used in the manufacture of sulphuric acid and in turn superphosphate.
refractory	An ore that is difficult and costly to treat for the recovery of valuable minerals.
reserve	An identified mineral resource that, based on an assessment of a range of qualifying factors or variables and typically including a feasibility study, is considered to be economically recoverable.
resource	Identified mineral occurrence that, subject to a range of qualifying factors, is considered to have some potential for commercial development.
roasting	Heating of sulphide ores to a high temperature in the presence of air.
seam	An underground layer of a mine, for example, a coal seam.
shaft	An extracted column that provides access to an ore zone in a mine, or is used for ventilation or the transportation of ore, equipment or workers.

APPENDIX 1

slag	A smelting process to upgrade ilmenite to a higher titanium dioxide content product, referred to as titanium or sulphate slag.
sluicing	Typically, the use of a sluice box to separate a valuable metal, such as gold or tin, from sand or gravel.
stope	A step-like excavation that is formed as ore is removed from around a mine shaft.
sulphide ore	Fine-grained mineral or chemical compound consisting of sulphur but with no oxygen contained within a rock formation. In the case of gold, it usually occurs in its metallic state and is commonly associated with sulphide minerals such as pyrite, in low concentrations.
tailings	Waste material resulting from the extraction of mineral-containing ore.

Sources: Various sources consulted, although mainly drawn from *Mining Handbook of Australia*, 1936, pp. 21–29 and *Close, The Great Gold Renaissance*, pp. 264–266.

APPENDIX 2. CHAIRMEN AND MANAGING DIRECTORS

Consolidated Gold Fields (Australia) Pty Ltd	
1960–1966	FR (Frank) Beggs, chairman and acting chairman from 1961 (retired 26 October 1962)
	Sir George Steven Harvie-Watt (attended as chairman on occasions)
	JB (Brian) Massy-Greene (appointed a director 8 October 1962; general manager, effective 1 October 1962 and later in October managing director), served as acting chairman on occasions from 1963
Consolidated Gold Fields Australia Limited	
30 September 1966–1976	Sir JB Massy-Greene, chairman and managing director
	BC (Bartholomew) Ryan, managing director, appointed May 1976
	SL (Sidney) Segal, chairman, appointed October 1976
	RIJ (Rudolph) Agnew, appointed to the board on 1 December 1976 to fill vacancy created by Sir Brian Massy-Greene not seeking re-election
1977	Bart Ryan, managing director (to December 1980)
	Sidney Segal, chairman
Renison Goldfields Consolidated Limited	
1981	MJ (Max) Roberts, executive chairman
	Sidney Segal, deputy chairman
1983	DL (David) Elsum, managing director (until September 1984)
1984	Max Roberts, chairman (by the time of the publication of the 1984 annual report, Roberts was again chairman and chief executive)
1985	Max Roberts, chairman
	Campbell McC Anderson, managing director

1986–1993	Max Roberts, chairman
	Campbell Anderson, managing director and chief executive officer
	FM (Mark) Bethwaite, deputy managing director
1994–1998	AR (Tony) Cotton, chairman, appointed February 1994
	Mark Bethwaite, managing director and chief executive officer; appointed 1993, resigned January 1998
	Tony Cotton, executive chairman

Source: Information based on annual reports published for the financial years indicated.

APPENDIX 3. BIOGRAPHICAL INFORMATION OF KEY INDIVIDUALS

John Alexander Agnew, Chairman, The Consolidated Gold Fields of South Africa

John Agnew was born in New Zealand in 1872.[1] After studying at the Thames School of Mines, he worked at the Thames gold fields on the north island of New Zealand. Agnew married Ellen Solan in 1895 and they had three children, including Rudolph John Agnew. In 1898 Herbert Hoover, then a young American mining engineer, appointed Agnew, aged 26, to the British mining engineering firm of Bewick, Moreing and Company (Bewick Moreing). Agnew came to Australia to take charge of the underground mining operations of the Sons of Gwalia gold mine, and the following year accompanied Hoover to China where he had responsibility for developing several new mines. Returning to Western Australia, Agnew managed several other Bewick Moreing–operated mines, including the Golden Age Mine, East Murchison United, Vivien Gold Mine and the Lancefield Gold Mine. Agnew was involved in the management of Bewick Moreing's agency and exploration company, London & Western Australia Exploration Co. and its successor, London, Australian & General Exploration Co.[2]

---

1 Information on the Agnew family history was supplied by Delia Buchan, daughter from the second marriage of Rudolph (Dolph) Agnew and Roma Leigh Stephens, and Hugh Agnew, grandson of Dolph Agnew from his first marriage to Pamela Geraldine Campbell.
2 Cumming and Hartley, *Westralian Founders of Twentieth Century Mining*, pp. 2–3.

In 1906, Agnew was appointed Western Australian assistant general manager of Bewick Moreing, located at Kalgoorlie, and from 1912 general manager. Agnew resigned from Bewick Moreing in 1912 and joined Hoover in London. When Hoover moved from mining engineer and company promoter to oversight of the provision of food aid to Belgium, Agnew took over the management of Hoover's business interests, including holding directorships on a range of companies that required technical input in various countries. According to Sir Rudolph Agnew, John Agnew's grandson and a person who played a major role in Gold Fields as chairman and group chief executive officer in the late 1970s and 1980s, his grandfather persuaded Hoover not to sell his share investments, but allow him to manage them on his behalf, with some later sold at an enhanced profit. Hoover provided Agnew with a part of the profit from the sale of those shares.[3]

In 1922, Agnew was appointed a director of The Consolidated Gold Fields of South Africa. In 1933, he became chairman, the first mining engineer to be appointed to the position.[4] A major part of Agnew's career encompassed the responsibilities as chairman of The Consolidated Gold Fields of South Africa and its major gold mining interests in the Rand and Transvaal, as well as broader international interests. Agnew also played a direct role in the company's investments in Australia, which included establishing a major shareholding in what became the two largest gold producers in Western Australia in the 1930s, Wiluna and Lake View and Star. He was also responsible for Gold Fields making technical and financial contributions to the formation of several Collins House group companies, not least Western Mining Corporation, as well as investments in the Lake George Mine at Captains Flat in New South Wales and gold mining properties in New Guinea.

In 1939, Agnew died in California after contracting pneumonia while visiting mining properties. He was 67 years of age. Herbert Hoover said that the 'British Commonwealth had lost its most eminent mining engineer'.[5] As one contemporary recalled of Agnew: 'He had a wide knowledge of man and things ... a great sobriety and sagacity of judgment, amazing industry, and a sense of probity and a habit of straightforwardness which

---

3   Sir Rudolph Agnew, personal communication, 9 August 2018.
4   Macnab, *Gold Their Touchstone*, p. 120; see also Wilson, *The Professionals: The Institute of Mining and Metallurgy, 1892–1992*, p. 227.
5   *The Financial Times*, 4 August 1939.

commanded the confidence of all whom he came into contact'.[6] Agnew had been awarded a gold medal of the Institute of Mining and Metallurgy in recognition of services in the 'development of mineral resources of the Empire, and to the mining industry'.[7] In Western Australia, the township of Agnew was named after him.

Rudolph John Agnew, Chairman, Gold Fields Australian Development Company

Rudolph Agnew, or Dolph as he was known, was born in Thames, New Zealand on 9 May 1896. He travelled with his parents to Western Australia and was educated at Christian Brothers College, Perth. Dolph then lived in London when his father moved to take up employment with Hoover. He studied mining engineering at the Royal School of Mines.[8] He volunteered for the Artists Rifles, 28th Battalion London, in 1916 while still a student. Dolph arrived in Perth in 1919 and travelled with his wife to Kalgoorlie to take up a position at the Ivanhoe Gold Corporation and later at Great Boulder Perseverance Gold Mining Company. He attended the Kalgoorlie School of Mines to further his mining studies, gaining a Diploma in Mining.

He returned to England in 1925 and became surveyor at the Mill Close lead mine in Derbyshire. In 1928, the family, which now comprised three children, travelled to Yugoslavia where Dolph took up an appointment as assistant manager with Central European Mines in Mezica, a lead–zinc mine located near the border with Austria. He took a position as superintendent of a zinc mine of Societa Anonima Miniera, Cave del Predil, in northern Italy from 1931.[9] Dolph returned to Western Australia via London in 1932 as general manager of Gold Fields Australian Development Company and to take charge of the Wiluna mine and the evaluation of nearby leases, as well as investigate other mining investment opportunities on behalf of Gold Fields. During World War II Dolph served with the Department of Munitions in Victoria. In 1946 he returned again to England to take up duties with the Gold Fields group in London

---

6 'Wiluna Gold Corporation', *The Mining World*, 16 December 1939.
7 *The Times*, 4 August 1939.
8 Royal School of Mines, *Register of Old Students, 1851–1920 and History of the Royal School of Mines*, Royal School of Mines Old Students' Association, 1920, p. 17.
9 Delia Buchan, personal communication. See also Rudolph John Agnew, www.nmrs.org.uk/resources/obituaries-of-members/a/rudolph-john-agnew/ and Cumming and Hartley, *Westralian Founders of Twentieth Century Mining*, p. 3.

before returning to Western Australia in 1950. He was general manager of Lake View and Star from 1950 and a director from 1956. With only brief periods in London, he lived in Western Australia for the remainder of his life as chairman of the London-listed Gold Fields Australian Development Company and Mount Ida Mine.

Dolph proved himself a skilled, practical mining man. He preferred the activities of the mine site to the administrative responsibilities of a company executive or the board room in London. He was an advocate for the development of the mining sector in Western Australia, serving as vice-president and president of the Chamber of Mines of Western Australia in Perth and Kalgoorlie. His services to the mining industry led to him being awarded the Coronation Medal of the Australian Institute of Mining and Metallurgy in 1953. Dolph Agnew died in 1960 at the age of 64 and is buried at the Kalgoorlie Cemetery.

Frank R Beggs, Chairman, Consolidated Gold Fields (Australia)

Frank Beggs was the first Australian representative of New Consolidated Gold Fields (Australasia), established in 1956, and was appointed managing director and chairman of Consolidated Gold Fields (Australia) in 1960, retiring in October 1962. Beggs had been general manager of British Metal Corporation (Australia) before resigning in 1954 to be appointed general manager of Rye Park Scheelite, as well as holding directorships of Uranium Corporation of Australia Pty Ltd, Tungsten Consolidated Ltd and Drilling Corporation of Australia Pty Ltd. In 1955 he was appointed to the board of Pacific Uranium and Oil Syndicate Ltd to fill a casual vacancy.

Keith Addison Cameron, Managing Director, Commonwealth Mining Investments (Australia), Director of Consolidated Gold Fields (Australia)

Keith Cameron was born in 1902 and died in 1967. He was the first managing director of Commonwealth Mining Investments and a director of Consolidated Gold Fields (Australia). Cameron was employed at Mount Lyell Mining and Railway Company, and worked in Canada, Alaska and also Mount Isa Mines. He had a close association with the Collins House group of companies, having been on the manager's staff of Gold Mines of Australia and a director of Gold Mines of Kalgoorlie and Bendigo Mines. He was also managing director of Mount Morgan. John Agnew had contact with Cameron when he was a director of Lake View South, while Dolph Agnew and Cameron were both members of the Kalgoorlie Chamber of Mines. Cameron also had an association with New Consolidated Gold Fields (Australasia) in the 1950s as a director of one of its investments.[10]

John Brian Massy-Greene, Managing Director and Chief Executive Officer, Consolidated Gold Fields Australia

Brian Massy-Greene was born in 1916 and died in 2001. He was educated at Sydney Grammar School, Geelong Grammar School and University of Cambridge. Massy-Greene worked at Metal Manufactures before enlisting and serving as a lieutenant in the Australian Imperial Force, New Guinea. After the war, he joined Austral Bronze, a subsidiary of Metal Manufactures, and was general manager before joining Consolidated Gold Fields (Australia) in 1962. During and after leaving CGFA, Massy-Greene held various directorships, including with National Mutual Life Association, Hazelton Air Services Holdings Ltd, and Santos and was chairman of Pacific Dunlop and Commonwealth Banking Corporation. Other roles included board positions with the Australian Mining Industry Council, Manufacturing Industries Advisory Council and CSIRO.

Sidney Leopold Segal, Executive Director, Chairman, Consolidated Gold Fields Australia

Sidney Segal was born in 1913 in Cape Town, South Africa and died in Sydney in 1999. Segal was educated at the University of Witwatersrand, Johannesburg, graduating with a Bachelor of Arts and a Bachelor of Laws in 1935. After completing articles, he practised as a lawyer. In 1945 Segal joined the South African bar and practised for a brief period. He worked as a stockbroker before joining New Union Goldfields, where he became joint managing director. New Union Goldfields was acquired in 1959 by The Consolidated Gold Fields of South Africa. In 1960, Segal and his family moved to Sydney where he joined the newly established Consolidated Gold Fields (Australia). He commenced as the finance executive, became an executive director and went on to

---

10   Branagan, 'Cameron, Keith Addison (1902–1967)'.

become a director and chairman, as well as director and executive director of various subsidiary companies of CGFA. Segal stepped down as chairman in 1980 but remained as a director until his retirement on 31 December 1982.

Bartholomew Carrack Ryan, Executive Director, Managing Director and Chief Executive Officer, Consolidated Gold Fields Australia

Born in Adelaide on 24 August 1926, Bart Ryan died on 18 December 2018. Ryan was educated at St Patrick's College, Goulburn and the Broken Hill School of Mines, where he graduated in mining engineering in 1949. He joined Consolidated Zinc Corporation at Broken Hill as a mining engineering cadet, and was then a mine superintendent at Rum Jungle, Northern Territory, from 1957 to 1959. He was then appointed mining engineer with Zinc Corporation. Between 1959 and 1961 he was mine superintendent at Mary Kathleen Uranium and then manager of operations, Rio Tinto Collieries, Camden, New South Wales, from 1962 to 1965. He joined Consolidated Gold Fields (Australia) in 1965 and in October of that year joined Renison as general manager. In 1967 he was appointed resident manager at Goldsworthy Mining, the operating company for Mount Goldsworthy Mining Associates at Port Hedland, Goldsworthy and then Perth. He was appointed general manager in 1969. From December 1972 to May 1976 he was technical director, Consolidated Gold Fields, London. Ryan recalled that he and his wife lived a 'stone's throw' from Hyde Park in a handsome terrace house. According to Ryan's recollection, his wife considered it to be 'the best mining town they had lived in'.[11] On 14 October 1975 he was appointed deputy chairman of Consolidated Gold Fields and deputy managing director on 1 January 1976. Ryan was in contention for the role of chief executive and managing director of Consolidated Gold Fields. It was perhaps not surprising that Rudolph Agnew, a former military man, self-educated in finance and a descendant of a line of Agnews prominent in the company, would be the favoured choice to his Antipodean contender. On 1 May 1976 he was appointed managing director of Consolidated Gold Fields Australia, succeeding Sir Brian Massy-Greene. On 31 December 1980, Ryan stepped down as managing director. He remained a director

---

11   Bart Ryan, personal communication, August 2018.

of Renison Goldfields Consolidated until 1982 and had a consultancy arrangement with Consolidated Gold Fields, London. Other directorships he held included Pioneer Concrete, Placer Development and Placer Pacific.

Maxwell John Roberts, Executive Chairman, Chairman, Renison Goldfields Consolidated

Max Roberts was born in Adelaide, South Australia, in 1920 and died in 2008. He attended Nailsworth Public School and Adelaide Technical College. He joined the State Bank of South Australia before enlisting with the RAAF and training as a pilot. In 1945, he joined Castrol Australia and became South Australian state manager. Roberts moved to Sydney in 1963 as managing director of Castrol Australia. He then went to Swindon, England, where he became chief executive officer of Burmah Castrol. He moved to the United States in 1971 and presided over Burmah's purchase of Signal Oil and Gas and later its sale, after losses in Burmah's shipping business required the sale of its 22 per cent holding in British Petroleum and most of its oil and gas assets in the North Sea, North America and Australia, including controlling shareholdings in Woodside and Santos. Returning to Australia in 1980, he stayed on as non-executive chairman of Burmah Oil Australia and, having joined the board of Consolidated Gold Fields in London, became executive chairman of Consolidated Gold Fields Australia. He stepped down as managing director and chief executive of Renison Goldfields Consolidated in 1985 and remained as chairman until his retirement in 1993.

At Roberts's funeral, Campbell Anderson delivered a eulogy, part of which included:

> My recollections of Max would not be complete without making some reference to his extraordinary capacity to remember and then, incessantly, to tell jokes. I recall a plane trip from Frankfurt (so long ago that we had to buy our own drinks on board!) when Max suggested that we swap jokes, with the proviso that if the listener couldn't interrupt and correctly finish the story, he had to buy a drink. By the time we landed in London, I hadn't been able to finish one single story that Max hadn't heard—his recall for jokes was extraordinary. You could always depend on Max to have a joke—not necessarily a new one or a good one—but

he always had a joke. He also had the less than endearing habit of forever laughing at his own jokes, but this was actually quite helpful in identifying the punch-line, which his rapt audience could otherwise often miss!'[12]

Campbell McCheyne Anderson, Managing Director and Chief Executive Officer, Renison Goldfields Consolidated

Campbell Anderson (born 1941) graduated from the University of Sydney with a Bachelor of Economics and gained qualifications in accounting. After working with Priestley and Morris, Anderson joined Boral. He then became the managing director and chief executive of Reef Oil and Basin Oil. He joined Burmah Oil Australia and Burmah Oil Corporation, holding various positions including chief financial officer and group managing director in the United Kingdom from 1982 to 1985. He was appointed managing director of Renison Goldfields Consolidated in 1985 and from 1986 was chief executive officer. Following his departure from RGC in 1993, he was managing director of North Limited. He served as president and council member of the Business Council of Australia from 1998 to 2000 and held various directorships including chairman of Laguna Resources, Ampolex and Energy Resources of Australia and co-chairman of Southern Pacific Petroleum (USA) Inc. He was an advisory council member of The Sentient Group and director of Clough, as well as CGNU Australia Holdings, IBI Bank Australia and Macquarie Direct Investment and of SPP Europe S.A. Anderson also served as president of the Minerals Council of Australia, the New South Wales Chamber of Mines, Australian Mines and Metals Association and the Australia–Japan Society of Australia.

Francis Mark Bethwaite, Managing Director and Chief Executive Officer, Renison Goldfields Consolidated

Mark Bethwaite (born 1948) completed a civil engineering degree at the University of Sydney. He joined the Commonwealth Department of Construction, moved to Mobil and completed an MBA. He represented Australia in sailing at the Olympics in 1972 and 1976, and in the

---

12 Eulogy for Max Roberts, 2 January 2009. The eulogy was provided to the author by Campbell Anderson.

1980 team that did not go to Moscow. Bethwaite joined North Broken Hill, knowing Lawrence Baillieu, the chairman, with whom he had a mutual interest in sailing. In 1983, he was invited to join the board as managing director, succeeding Baillieu. At North Broken Hill, he was responsible for the acquisition of Associated Pulp and Paper Mills and the $520 million takeover of EZ Industries. Bethwaite was appointed deputy managing director of Renison Goldfields Consolidated in 1987 and managing director and chief executive officer in 1995. He left RGC in 1998 and served as chief executive of Australian Business. He held numerous directorships, including Goldfields Kalgoorlie, Pancontinental Mining and RCR Tomlinson. He also served as chairman of the Australian National Maritime Museum.

Anthony (Tony) R Cotton, Chairman and Executive Chairman, Renison Goldfields Consolidated and RGC

Tony Cotton was educated as a chartered accountant. His career at Hanson between 1973 and 1998 included roles as financial comptroller of the construction equipment division, deputy group financial comptroller, managing director of Hanson Sykes Pumps Australia, and then chief executive of Hanson Industrial Services. He served as an associate director in 1981 and was a director on the Hanson board between 1990 and 1995. Cotton took Australian citizenship and, after leaving his directorship with RGC in January 1999, he was chairman of Snowy Hydro Trading and Snowy Hydro Limited, after its corporatisation, between 1997 and 2003. Cotton was appointed chairman of Renison Goldfields Consolidated in 1994 and served as executive chairman from 1998. He was chairman of Goldfields Limited after it was formed by RGC in 1996 to hold the RGC and Pancontinental gold assets.

APPENDIX 4.
PERFORMANCE OF CGFA AND RGC INVESTMENTS

Table 4. Performance of Consolidated Gold Fields Australia investments, 1962–1966.

	($'000)				
	1962	1963	1964	1965	1966
Bellambi Coal					
Profit pre-tax	92	142	267	410	350
Profit after tax	78	142	135	191	211
Mount Lyell					
Profit pre-tax	207	1,038	1,232	1,033	3,246
Profit after tax	207	755	841	892	2,328
Lake View & Star					
Profit pre-tax	953	938	764	541	550
Profit after tax	604	591	485	350	499
Wyong Minerals					
Profit pre-tax	83	204	287	367	696
Profit after tax	83	204	209	245	421
Commonwealth Mining Investments					
Profit pre-tax	365	375	628	986	1,008
Profit after tax	356	362	581	867	939
Associated Minerals Consolidated					
Profit pre-tax	541	835	1,213	1,463	1,059
Profit after tax	365	540	734	948	720
Zip Manufacturing					
Profit after tax	144	165	503	492	317
Profit attributable to CGFA	**383**	**545**	**913**	**2,073**	**2,901**

The figures refer to the financial performance of the investments of CGFA. They are shown on a 100 per cent basis, whereas CGFA's entitlement was lower, based on its shareholding in each. Mount Lyell held a 49.97 per cent direct interest in Renison during this period and, as such, Renison is not shown separately. The result for Zip Manufacturing in 1964 was for 15 months; Commonwealth Mining Investments (Australia) figures exclude realisation of investments taken to reserves. In the final line, the attributable profit to CGFA is shown. This refers to the profit attributable to CGFA shareholders, excluding the interest of the parent, Consolidated Gold Fields in London.

Source: Consolidated Gold Fields Australia, 'Prospectus', 1974, University of Melbourne Archives (UMA), 1974.0092.

Table 5a. Consolidated Gold Fields Australia financial performance, 1967–1973.

Group results ($m)	1967	1968	1969	1970	1971	1972	1973
Group operating profit/loss before tax	9.3	11.6	18.2	27.6	22.8	18.6	15.8
Group profit/loss attributable to CGFA	**4.1**	**5.4**	**8.6**	**12.3**	**9.6**	**8.6**	**5.4**
Return on shareholders' funds (%)	11.6	13.7	15.4	20.2	15.6	12.9	10.5
Dividends (cents per share)	6.7	11	12.5	15	17.5	17.5	15.5
Divisional contribution pre-tax							
Commonwealth Mining Investments	1.4	2.7	2.7	3.6	3.1	1.9	1.1
Associated Minerals Consolidated	1.5	2.6	2.5	3.1	3.1	3.0	2.5
Mount Lyell Mining	3.9	3.3	4.3	9.1	5.7	2.4	3.9
Renison	0.1	−0.1	1.9	3.5	2.1	3.5	2.8
Bellambi Coal	0.4	0.5	0.6	0.2	0.7	0.9	0.8
Western Titanium			1.2	1.4	1.7	1.3	1.5
Mount Goldsworthy (1/3 interest)	1.6	2.7	5.0	6.2	5.9	5.7	4.3
Lake View & Star	0.6	0.5	0.3	−0.1			
Zip Holdings	0.6	0.2	0.2	0.2	0.6	0.7	0.6
Lawrenson Holdings		0.1	0.1	0.1	0.1	0.1	0.2

Table 5b. Consolidated Gold Fields Australia financial performance, 1974–1980.

Group results ($m)	1974	1975	1976	1977	1978	1979	1980
Group operating profit/loss before tax	24.6	22.5	8.1	13.7	30.2	41.2	61.6
Group profit/loss attributable to CGFA	**7.3**	**7.5**	**2.8**	**−4.2**	**8.5**	**12.2**	**21.8**
Return on shareholders' funds (%)	9.9	9.6	3.5	−5.8	12.2	15.8	24.2
Dividends (cents per share)	14.5	1	6	6	13	17.5	23
Divisional contribution pre-tax							
Commonwealth Mining Investments	1.7	1.9	1.9	1.9			
Associated Minerals Consolidated	4.3	9.3	6.4	3.2	−4.9	−0.6	4.1
Mount Lyell Mining	12.4	2.2	−4.8	−10.7	−4.4	0.8	9.5

APPENDIX 4

Group results ($m)	1974	1975	1976	1977	1978	1979	1980
Renison	4.3	6.5	5.0	19.7	32.3	41.7	47.2
Bellambi Coal	0.7	2.3	2.1	8.9	4.4	–0.4	
Western Titanium	1.4	3.3	1.4				
Mount Goldsworthy (1/3 interest)	0.2	1.4	–2.3				
Lake View & Star							
Zip Holdings	1.4	1.0					
Lawrenson Holdings	0.3	0.2	0.2	0.2			

Tables 5a and 5b show the operating profit/loss for CGFA before and after tax. The profit/loss attributable to CGFA reflects the ownership entitlement related to the CGFA shareholding not held by its parent, Consolidated Gold Fields. The contributions from the main investments are shown on a 100 per cent basis before tax. Mount Goldsworthy is shown on the basis of the one-third attributable interest to CGFA and the amount reported as profit each year (a part of the earnings was often retained or else drawn upon as a special dividend). Zip Holdings was reported in New Zealand dollars from 1971.

Sources: CGFA annual reports, 1967 to 1980; Renison Goldfields Consolidated, *Report on the 1981 Financial Year*.

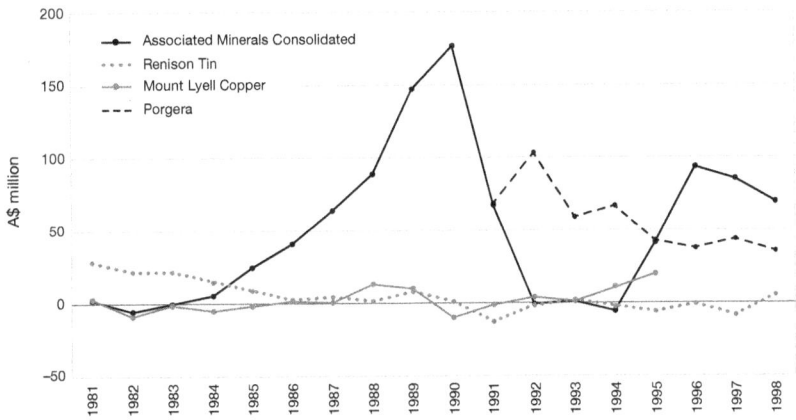

Chart 12. Divisional contribution to Renison Goldfields Consolidated results, 1981–1998, principal assets.

This chart shows the earnings contribution, before tax, of the principal RGC assets: Associated Minerals Consolidated, Renison, Mount Lyell and, from 1991, Porgera (initially owned 25 per cent and then transferred to Goldfields Limited in 1995, of which RGC held a 55.8 per cent initial interest). AMC's contribution dominated total earnings from 1985 to 1990, with the decline in the contribution from Renison evident from 1981. Between 1991 and 1994 AMC recorded accumulated losses. Mount Lyell recorded an average $2.4 million annual contribution, aided by an improvement in financial performance during its final two years of operation.

Sources: RGC annual reports, 1982 to 1997; 1998 data for period to 30 June is derived from 'Information Memorandum in Relation to a Recommended Merger by Scheme of Arrangement between RGC Limited and Westralian Sands'.

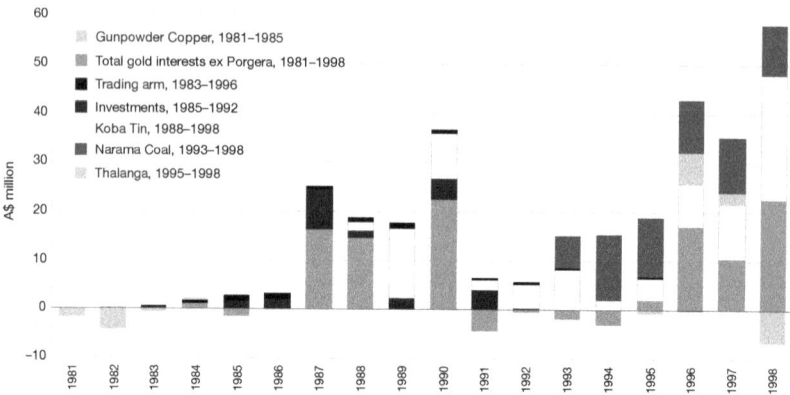

Chart 13. Asset and investment contribution to Renison Goldfields Consolidated results, 1981–1998.

This chart shows the contributions of the lesser assets of the portfolio. In 1987 and 1990, gold interests and investments made a contribution above $20 million. It was not until 1994 that Koba Tin, and Narama Coal in 1993, as well as the non-Porgera gold interests and Thalanga made a contribution, which peaked in 1998 at approximately $58 million.

Sources: RGC annual reports, 1982 to 1997; 1998 data for period to 30 June is derived from 'Information Memorandum in Relation to a Recommended Merger by Scheme of Arrangement between RGC Limited and Westralian Sands'.

Table 6. Renison Goldfields Consolidated financial performance, 1981–1989.

Group results ($m)	1981	1982	1983	1984	1985	1986	1987	1988	1989
Sales revenue	174.9	150.9	140.8	171.9	207.8	247.2	355.4	431.0	590.7
Group operating profit/loss pre-tax	35.6	–6.0	8.6	8.2	19.9	32.7	76.0	81.2	154.8
Group operating profit/loss after tax	21.0	–6.5	6.2	10.2	12.7	21.1	49.3	45.2	100.4
Extraordinary items	–0.9	–3.8	3.8		10.8	13.5			–9.9
Group operating profit/loss after tax and extraordinary items	20.1	–10.2	10.1	10.2	23.5	34.6	49.3	45.2	90.5

APPENDIX 4

Group results ($m)	1981	1982	1983	1984	1985	1986	1987	1988	1989
Divisional contribution to results pre-tax									
Associated Minerals Consolidated	2.3	−5.5	−0.3	5.3	24.6	40.8	63.6	88.5	147.1
Renison Tin	28.6	21.7	21.7	14.3	8.7	2.5	4.5	1.6	7.8
Koba Tin								1.7	14.2
Lucky Draw Gold									5.0
Pine Creek Gold						0.3	16.0	17.5	1.3
NGG Gold		0.02	0.2	1.1	−1.4	−0.3	0.4	−2.8	−6.3
Mount Lyell Copper	3.2	−9.0	−1.1	−4.9	−1.7	1.5	0.6	12.9	10.2
Gunpowder Copper	−1.6	−4.2	−0.6	0.4	0.05				
Trading			0.4	0.7	1.2	1.2	0.7	1.0	1.2
Investments					1.7	2.1	8.0	1.4	2.3
Exploration and evaluation	−7.4	−9.2	−7.2	−10.4	−14.0	−11.2	−13.3	−18.4	−24.9
Corporate & net interest	10.5	0.2	−5.1	1.9	0.9	−4.3	−4.6	−22.0	−3.0
Group return on assets (%)	11	−6	3	5	5	6	9	7	13
Return on shareholders' funds (%)	21	−9	5	7	8	11	22	18	30
Equity/debt ratio	81/19	80/20	87/13	99/1	82/18	75/25	51/49	57/43	58/42
Dividends ($m)	9.5	2.2	4.3	5.0	6.6	11.1	17.2	21.3	48.3
Dividends (cents per share)	25	5	10	10	10	15	15	15	30
Group employees	2,635	2,554	2,289	2,346	2,063	2,447	2,562	4,045	4,204

Extraordinary items influenced results in a number of years, including:
- 1983—$3.85 million profit on sale of investments
- 1985—$10.8 million Mount Lyell lease compensation payment
- 1986—$13.5 million, comprising $25.8 million profit on sale of Gold Fields House lease, partially offset by write-off of the excess of the purchase price over value ascribed for the Allied Eneabba assets
- 1989—$9.9 million, mainly related to provision for closure of the Wau gold mining operation.

Source: *RGC Annual Report 1990*, p. 57. Some figures may not add due to rounding.

Table 7. Renison Goldfields Consolidated financial performance, 1990–1998.

Group results ($m)	1990	1991	1992	1993	1994	1995	1996	1997	1998
Sales revenue	653	591	608	622	611	642	9867	970	1,011
Group operating profit/loss before tax	173.8	55.3	56.6	25.3	20.3	54.0	108.6	68.7	47.5
Group operating profit/loss after tax	116.0	36.4	8.8	11.7	1.8	32.9	76.5	35.7	−3.2
Abnormal items				−20.0	−36.1		79.6	81.0	−142.3	−67.3
Extraordinary items		−11.1							
Operating profit/loss after tax, extraordinary items	116.0	25.3	−10.1	−24.4	1.8	97.4	142.8	−78.0	−46.1
Divisional results pre-tax ($m)									
AMC	176.6	67.2	−1.0	1.3	−5.5	41.5	93.3	85.1	69.6
Renison Tin	1.2	−12.7	−1.7	1.9	−2.7	−6.0	−0.9	−8.6	5.4
Koba Tin	9.3	2.1	4.9	8.3	2.0	4.4	8.7	10.9	25.4
Porgera Gold		68.6	103.0	59.0	66.5	42.9	37.3	43.7	35.6
Lucky Draw Gold	18.2	5.9	0.7	0.5					
Pine Creek Gold	0.8	−6.7	0.1	−1.8	−3.1	1.6	2.3		
Paddington Gold						−0.5	−5.7	−1.0	14.9
NGG Gold	3.5	−3.5							
Henty Gold								−0.4	−2.5
Thalanga						−0.7	6.6	2.5	−6.5
Kundana Gold						1.0	20.4	12.0	10.2
Mount Lyell Copper	−10.1	−1.2	4.1	1.1	11.0	19.7			
Narama Coal				6.5	13.3	12.0	10.6	11.3	10.3
Trading	0.8	0.5	0.5	0.4	0.1	0.4	−0.1		
Investments	4.2	4.0	0.3						
Exploration	−25.8	−24.8	−38.0	−20.5	−21.3	−24.7	−45.7	−50.4	−52.7
Corporate & net interest	−5.1	−44.0	−34.9	−31.0	−40.1	−38.3	−36.0	−36.8	−62.2

APPENDIX 4

Group Data	1990	1991	1992	1993	1994	1995	1996	1997	1998
Group return on assets (%)	11.7	2.5	–0.9	–4.3	0.3	5.7	8.0	–5.0	–3.1
Return on shareholders' funds (%)	27.6	6.3	–1.9	–4.5	0.3	18.3	21.4	–13.6	–9.0
Equity/debt ratio	56/44	47/53	58/42	58/42	62/38	62/38	59/41	64/36	48/52
Dividends ($m)	58.0	17.9	14.9	5.0	0	20.1	31.1	21.0	0
Dividends (cents per share)	34	10	7.5	2.5	0	10	15	10	0
Group employees	4,186	3,571	3,412	3,247	2,970	3,430	3,246	3,688	3,374

Extraordinary and/or abnormal items influenced results in a number of years, including the following:
- 1991—$11.1 million loss on closure of Nelesbitan, Philippines
- 1992—$20.0 million, predominantly related to the write-down of a United States project and exploration expenditure, mainly related to Old Hickory, Virginia
- 1993—$36.1 million write-down, mainly related to Australian mineral sands assets ($33.5 million)
- 1995—$79.6 million contribution, mainly from a $104 million profit on the sale of Goldfields' shares to converting note holders, less goodwill written-off relating to the Pancontinental acquisition ($8.0 million); restructuring costs ($16.3 million); and dividend withholding tax on brought forward Papua New Guinea retained earnings ($18.4 million)
- 1996—net $81.0 million from the sale of Pancontinental non-gold assets, less tax and outside equity interests
- 1997—$142.3 million portfolio write-downs, related to Thalanga ($50.1 million), Renison ($30.0 million), Capel ($15.0 million), Paddington ($26.4 million), Kundana Gold ($11.1 million), Sierra Rutile ($25.3 million), partially offset by proceeds from the sale of tenements ($15.7 million)
- 1998—$67.3 million, asset write-downs and merger costs.

Sources: RGC annual reports, 1990 to 1997. Full details for 1998 not available. 1998 data for period to 30 June is derived from 'Information Memorandum in Relation to a Recommended Merger by Scheme of Arrangement between RGC Limited and Westralian Sands', pp. 34 and 56–57. Financial information for this year includes RGC's interest in Goldfields. Some figures may not add due to rounding.

APPENDIX 5. MINERAL SANDS PERFORMANCE, 1977–1997

Table 8a. Mineral sands performance, 1977–1983.

	1977	1978	1979	1980	1981	1982	1983
Sales revenue ($m)	38.7	38.9	44.5	56.6	66.8	58.7	44.2
Profit/loss pre-tax ($m)	3.2	–4.9	–0.6	4.1	1.1	–5.5	–0.3
Share of group assets ($m)	62.6	57.3	55.9	80.4	87.2	81.8	84.3
Return on assets (%)	5.1	–8.6	–1.0	5.1	1.3	–6.7	–0.4
Capital expenditure ($m)					6.8	8.4	7.5
Production (tonnes)							
Rutile	102,875	76,305	98,150	100,942	95,708	81,693	78,997
Synthetic rutile	18,363	42,707	43,970	49,197	57,614	52,278	31,384
Zircon	97,208	81,938	151,883	174,385	182,146	154,999	134,529
Ilmenite	95,472	198,091	299,737	393,270	400,894	266,752	107,946
Sales (tonnes)							
Rutile	107,867	95,025	102,464	109,600	98,907	82,222	68,930
Synthetic rutile	16,496	36,776	46,553	57,995	58,375	36,542	22,973
Zircon	96,794	116,542	161,436	149,300	201,749	200,474	114,571
Ilmenite	99,091	231,953	284,632	409,622	381,476	225,120	177,775
Employees	1,033	740	711	859	821	721	509

Table 8b. Mineral sands performance, 1984–1990.

	1984	1985	1986	1987	1988	1989	1990
Sales revenue ($m)	64.4	89.5	123.8	176.1	229.3	305.0	356.7
Profit/loss pre-tax ($m)	5.3	24.6	40.8	63.6	88.5	147.0	176.6
Share of group assets ($m)	71.8	74.6	136.7	180.0	196.3	222.0	369.3
Return on assets (%)	7.4	33.0	29.8	35.3	45.1	66.2	47.8
Capital expenditure ($m)	3.4	4.6	27.9	55.6	18.3	32.4	151.8
Production (tonnes)							
Rutile	62,425	82,233	90,242	115,573	106,297	97,467	113,271
Synthetic rutile	32,537	62,186	55,457	65,236	137,278	140,648	166,739
Zircon	150,993	178,573	247,556	278,101	305,572	327,054	310,552
Ilmenite	192,338	320,271	396,542	411,636	364,909	640,917	740,206
Sales (tonnes)							
Rutile	85,941	82,309	87,298	108,963	107,815	120,274	106,897
Synthetic rutile	48,434	68,534	56,691	66,103	123,775	136,625	179,475
Zircon	163,399	199,258	260,851	289,422	299,610	300,681	263,403
Ilmenite	215,335	318,010	373,998	417,292	401,774	383,614	389,842
Employees	545	414	568	683	718	751	867

Table 8c. Mineral sands performance, 1991–1997.

	1991	1992	1993	1994	1995	1996	1997
Sales revenue ($m)	236.3	173.4	201.9	208.3	286.5	374.6	462.7
Profit/loss pre-tax & abnormal items ($m)	67.2	–1.0	1.3	–5.5	41.5	93.3	85.1
Share of group assets ($m)	514.4	502.2	469.1	445.4	421.0	452.5	605.0
Return on assets (%)	13.1	–0.2	0.3	–1.2	9.9	20.6	14.1
Capital expenditure ($m)	163.8	17.0	8.3	12.3	14.6	43.2	44.4

APPENDIX 5

	1991	1992	1993	1994	1995	1996	1997
Production (tonnes)							
Rutile	95,002	58,209	81,453	93,492	93,214	108,084	173,342
Synthetic rutile	123,150	169,041	203,466	161,190	213,152	250,674	241,679
Zircon	162,607	95,433	190,107	254,093	352,313	313,103	306,020
Ilmenite	470,457	568,155	722,441	635,970	334,099	821,713	983,097
Sales (tonnes)							
Rutile	87,896	59,319	87,584	89,670	91,505	117,760	165,420
Synthetic rutile	118,895	150,855	201,205	171,175	208,281	243,036	256,758
Zircon	167,293	151,757	188,801	254,771	360,053	298,862	264,134
Ilmenite	306,201	275,689	277,310	310,505	353,992	488,972	633,327
Employees	831	776	815	754	848	899	1,020

Table 8a contains data for the years subsequent to the merger of Associated Minerals Consolidated and Western Titanium in 1976, to the last full year of Renison Goldfields Consolidated's Mineral Sands Division.

Sources: RGC annual reports, 1991 to 1997.

APPENDIX 6. RENISON PERFORMANCE, 1977–1997

Table 9a. Renison performance, 1977–1983.

	1977	1978	1979	1980	1981	1982	1983
Sales of tin concentrates ($m)	36.8	49.9	62.1	70.8	62.2	57.4	49.0
Profit/loss pre-tax ($m)	19.7	32.3	41.7	47.2	28.6	21.7	21.7
Share of group assets ($m)	38.0	50.9	63.9	73.5	47.6	43.1	46.5
Return on assets (%)	5.8	73.1	65.2	64.2	60.1	50.3	46.7
Capital expenditure ($m)					10.8	4.1	4.8
Production (tonnes)							
Ore treated	554,736	590,119	605,606	551,105	652,005	642,852	623,204
Grade tin (%)	1.33	1.32	1.29	1.27	1.2	1.16	1.12
Saleable tin concentrates	8,571	11,074	11,791	10,664	11,764	10,521	10,018
Concentrate grade (%)					47.3	49.0	51.2
Total tin in saleable concentrates	4,783	5,363	5,576	5,137	5,546	5,152	5,126
Tin sales (tonnes)							
Recovery (%)	64.7	68.8	71.2	73.6	70.8	71.6	73.8
Average tin price ($/tonne)	6,861	9,035	11,271	13,078	12,269	12,714	12,234
Employees	439	439	434	473	524	545	504

	1977	1978	1979	1980	1981	1982	1983
Ore reserves							
Proved tonnes (million)	6.0	4.57	3.27	2.63	6.74	6.42	5.1
Grade tin (%)	1.23	1.47	1.42	1.42	1.41	1.5	1.2
Probable tonnes (million)	5.9	23.13	25.57	25.76	20.08	20.5	11.6
Grade tin (%)	1.14	1.45	1.47	1.47	1.47	1.49	1.0
Total proved & probable tonnes (million)	11.9	27.7	29.3	28.4	26.8	26.9	16.7

Table 9b. Renison performance, 1984–1990.

	1984	1985	1986	1987	1988	1989	1990
Sales of tin concentrates ($m)	48.4	51.3	34.9				
Sales of tin metal ($m)				55.1	62.6	67.7	66.5
Profit/loss pre-tax ($m)	14.3	8.7	2.5	4.5	1.6	7.8	1.2
Share of group assets ($m)	44.9	37.0	41.3	53.5	46.1	46.8	45.4
Return on assets (%)	31.8	23.5	6.1	8.4	3.5	16.7	2.6
Capital expenditure ($m)	3.2	3.6	6.0	4.5	4.3	4.6	6.6
Production (tonnes)							
Ore treated	481,684	389,969	514,530	854,435	827,879	823,000	742,000
Grade tin (%)	1.04	1.01	0.98	1.08	1.03	1.11	1.34
Saleable tin concentrates	7,474	5,724	6,850	13,872	12,531	13,919	16,078
Concentrate grade (%)	51.1	50.5	53.2	49.2	49.7	49.9	48.7
Total tin in saleable concentrates	3,818	2,892	3,646	6,832	6,222	6,940	7,815
Tin sales (tonnes)	3,743	3,738	2,688	5,794	6,688	6,933	7,001
Recovery (%)	74.2	72.3	71.8	74.0	73.5	75	78.5

APPENDIX 6

	1984	1985	1986	1987	1988	1989	1990
Average tin price ($/tonne)	13,922	15,767	13,871	9,435	9,355	9,615	9,269
Employees	511	472	481	492	418	434	345
Ore reserves							
Proved tonnes (million)	5.1	6.26	5.13	4.69	4.39	4.59	4.19
Grade tin (%)	1.2	1.1	1.2	1.3	1.3	1.2	1.2
Probable tonnes (million)	11.6	12.29	13.0	9.26	9.3	5.45	5.1
Grade tin (%)	1.0	1.1	1.0	1.2	1.2	1.2	1.2
Total proved & probable tonnes (million)	16.7	18.6	18.1	13.9	13.7	10.0	9.3
Mineral resource							
Measured tonnes (million)						5.01	4.6
Grade tin (%)						1.3	1.2
Indicated tonnes (million)						7.75	7.4
Grade tin (%)						1.2	1.2

Table 9c. Renison performance, 1991–1997.

	1991	1992	1993	1994	1995	1996	1997
Sales of tin metal ($m)	46.8	36.9	62.3	48.3	55.3	65.6	65.1
Profit/loss pre-tax ($m)	−12.7	−1.7	1.9	−2.7	−6.0	−0.9	−8.6
Share of group assets ($m)	33.0	32.1	28.6	31.5	44.2	69.9	41.5
Return on assets (%)	−38.5	−5.3	6.6	−8.6	−13.6	−1.9	−20.7
Capital expenditure ($m)	5.9	2.5	5.4	7.0	14.9	30.6	11.3
Production (tonnes)							
Ore treated	548,000	534,000	565,000	624,000	650,000	706,000	692,000
Grade tin (%)	1.23	1.41	1.5	1.5	1.4	1.6	1.7
Saleable ton concentrates	10,219	11,212	12,352	13,646	14,387	16,090	16,140
Concentrate grade (%)	50.5	53.6	54.5	55.1	50.2	51.7	53.5

	1991	1992	1993	1994	1995	1996	1997
Total tin in saleable concentrates	5,120	6,007	6,732	7,525	7,287	8,319	8,637
Tin sales (tonnes)	6,217	5,114	7,407	6,842	7,164	7,953	8,165
Recovery (%)	76.2	79.6	80.1	82	78	76	73
Average tin price ($/tonne)	7,355	7,178	8,414	7,055	7,712	8,273	7,422
Employees	239	255	254	234	241	242	239
Ore reserves							
Proved tonnes (million)	2.2	1.85	2.27	2.49	1.48	2.51	2.92
Grade tin (%)	1.4	1.4	1.5	1.5	1.6	1.5	1.9
Probable tonnes (million)	3.57	3.44	2.97	6.91	5.99	3.80	2.1
Grade tin (%)	1.4	1.4	1.4	1.6	1.7	1.9	1.8
Total proved & probable tonnes (million)	5.8	5.3	5.2	9.4	7.5	6.3	5.0
Mineral resources							
Measured tonnes (million)	3.5	3.08	3.07	3.05	1.53	2.65	3.01
Grade tin (%)	1.4	1.3	1.6	1.6	1.6	1.6	2.1
Indicated tonnes (million)	7.57	7.45	6.96	9.44	7.82	5.03	3.8
Grade tin (%)	1.2	1.2	1.3	1.5	1.7	1.8	1.6

Notes: 1987 reserves adjusted to reflect an increase in cut-off grades in light of declining ore grades with depth and lower tin prices, leading to an increased grade for ore reserves (*RGC Annual Report 1987*, p. 11). As noted in the *Annual Report 1990*, the method of compiling resource and reserve statistics was changed from 1989. From 1989 ore reserves are shown as contained in mineral resources. As such, figures after 1989 are not directly comparable with those of previous years. Resource statistics are based on a cut-off grade varying from 0.6 per cent to 0.8 per cent tin (*RGC Annual Report 1990*, p. 26).

Complete data is not available for the 1998 financial year. In 1998, Renison recorded a profit after tax of $5.4 million.

Sources: Ore reserves and mineral resource figures derived from RGC annual reports, 1981 to 1997.

APPENDIX 7. MOUNT LYELL PERFORMANCE, 1977–1995

Table 10a. Mount Lyell performance, 1977–1982.

	1977	1978	1979	1980	1981	1982
Sales of copper concentrates ($m)	24.3	25.1	35.1	33.4	46.2	25.9
Profit/loss pre-tax ($m)	–10.7	–4.4	0.8	9.5	3.2	–9.0
Share of group assets ($m)	26.5	23.9	26.7	33.1	18.2	18.9
Return on assets (%)	–40.4	–18.4	3.0	28.7	17.6	–47.6
Capital expenditure ($m)					4.8	3.7
Production						
Ore treated ('000 tonnes)	1,820	1,614	1,620	1,395	1,683	1,667
Copper grade (%)	1.112	1.245	1.335	1.305	1.349	1.158
Saleable copper concentrates	70,237	70,668	77,039	64,791	80,802	68,686
Total metal in saleable concentrates						
Copper (tonnes)	17,742	17,840	19,405	16,299	20,339	17,860
Gold (kg)					467	419
Silver (kg)					3,875	2,748
Average copper price ($/tonne)	1,212	1,104	1,591	2,012	1,654	1,421
Employees	727	699	708	727	742	715

Table 10b. Mount Lyell performance, 1983–1989.

	1983	1984	1985	1986	1987	1988	1989
Sales of copper concentrates ($m)	30.9	32.3	35.3	39.0	41.3	59.1	65.2
Profit/loss pre-tax ($m)	−1.0	−4.9	−1.7	1.5	0.6	12.9	10.2
Share of group assets ($m)	19.0	20.0	21.3	17.0	18.7	18.4	24.6
Return on assets (%)	−5.3	−24.5	−8.0	8.8	3.2	70.1	41.5
Capital expenditure ($m)	2.4	3.9	0.8	3.5	1.0	4.8	8.8
Production							
Ore treated ('000 tonnes)	1,433	1,769	1,773	1,686	1,583	1,502	1,634
Copper grade (%)	1.333	1.45	1.37	1.42	1.59	1.55	1.24
Saleable copper concentrates	68,446	90,755	85,524	85,409	91,535	83,686	68,324
Total metal in saleable concentrates							
Copper (tonnes)	17,844	23,471	22,295	22,124	23,518	21,638	18,678
Gold (kg)	405	571	505	514	516	511	435
Silver (kg)	2,982	4,814	4,550	3,253	3,705	2,761	2,888
Copper sales (tonnes)		23,145	22,692	23,099	22,757	19,937	19,656
Average copper price ($/tonne)	1,811	1,631	1,870	2,031	2,036	3,271	3,518
Employees	706	689	533	525	536	556	553

Table 10c. Mount Lyell performance, 1990–1995.

	1990	1991	1992	1993	1994	1995
Sales of copper concentrates ($m)	48.8	49.8	61.9	60.1	72.0	51.4
Profit/loss pre-tax ($m)	−10.1	−1.2	4.1	1.1	11.0	19.7
Share of group assets ($m)	25.4	29.0	28.8	26.0	31.6	
Return on assets (%)	−39.8	4.1	14.2	4.2	34.8	
Capital expenditure ($m)	3,057	3,890	3,519	3,201	964	

APPENDIX 7

	1990	1991	1992	1993	1994	1995
Production						
Ore treated ('000 tonnes)	1,347	1,391	1,680	1,729	1,700	795
Copper grade (%)	1.28	1.56	1.52	1.59	1.91	1.65
Saleable copper concentrates	59,206	76,750	88,454	95,115	112,924	45,062
Total metal in saleable concentrates						
Copper (tonnes)	15,712	19,970	23,540	25,528	30,416	12,316
Gold (kg)	360	446	566	496	635	283
Silver (kg)	2,021	2,557	3,460	3,257	4,446	1,680
Copper sales (tonnes)	15,616	17,795	22,823	23,322	28,155	15,375
Average copper price ($/tonne)	3,266	2,983	2,940	2,894	2,992	3,777
Employees	475	449	454	369	240	

Sources: RGC annual reports, 1978 to 1995.

APPENDIX 8.
PERFORMANCE OF GOLD AND OTHER INTERESTS

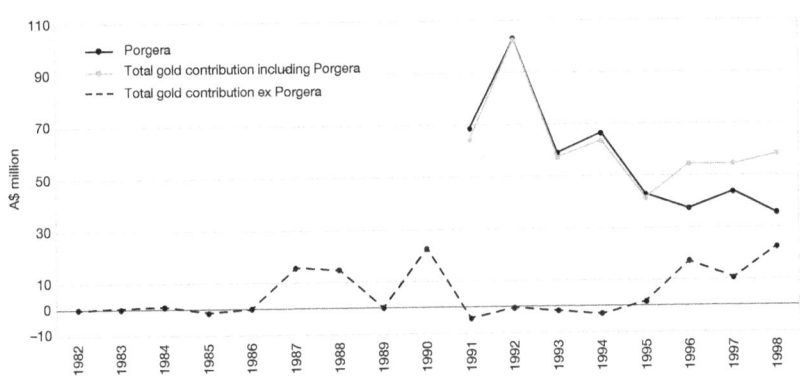

Chart 14. Gold interests and contribution to Renison Goldfields Consolidated results, 1982–1998.

Source: RGC annual reports, 1982 to 1997; 1998 data for period to 30 June is derived from 'Information Memorandum in Relation to a Recommended Merger by Scheme of Arrangement between RGC Limited and Westralian Sands'.

Table 11. Renison Goldfields Consolidated: Gold interests—Pine Creek (Northern Territory), 1986–1995.

	1986	1987	1988	1989	1990
Sales of bullion ($m)	12.5	37.9	50.5	43.5	43.3
Profit/loss pre-tax ($m)	0.3	16.0	17.5	1.3	0.8
Share of group assets ($m)	37.1	38.9	44.0	41.0	40.8
Capital expenditure ($m)	21.9	3.6	10.2	12.7	13.0
Gold production (kg)	872	1,919	2,498	2,742	2,629
Silver production (kg)	219	597	770	663	721
Gold sales (kg)	809	1,920	2,461	2,716	2,724
Gold price ($/g)	15.40	19.87	20.27	15.87	16.03
Employees	56	60	72	83	85

	1991	1992	1993	1994	1995
Sales of bullion ($m)	39.4	48.3	39.4	42.2	29.5
Profit/loss pre-tax ($m)	–6.7	0.9	–1.8	–3.1	1.6
Share of group assets ($m)	29.3	20.5	16.8	6.6	2.9
Capital expenditure ($m)	12.9	14.5	6.8	1.5	0
Gold production (kg)	2,578	3,357	2,498	2,388	1,743
Silver production (kg)	489	603	320	410	330
Gold sales (kg)	2,583	3,317	2,514	2,386	1,823
Gold price ($/g)	15.38	14.69	15.64	17.65	16.65
Employees	78	76	70	76	26

Sources: RGC annual reports, 1985 to 1995.

Table 12. Renison Goldfields Consolidated: Gold interests—Lucky Draw (New South Wales), 1988–1992.

	1988	1989	1990	1991	1992
Sales of bullion ($m)		12	37	27	3
Profit/loss pre-tax ($m)		5	18	6	1
Share of group assets ($m)		20	14	3	0
Return on assets (%)		25	128.6	200	na
Capital expenditure ($m)	1.1	19.7	3.3	0	0
Production (kg)		832	2,304	1,731	190
Silver production (kg)		16	67	65	7
Gold sales (kg)		809	2,295	1,759	190
Gold price ($/gram)		15.41	16.13	15.26	15.12
Employees		26	27	22	–

na means not applicable.

Sources: RGC annual reports, 1989 to 1992.

APPENDIX 8

Table 13. Renison Goldfields Consolidated: Gold interests—Porgera (Papua New Guinea), 1990–1994.

	1990	1991	1992	1993	1994
RGC sales of bullion ($m)		107.7	203.6	177.9	160.1
Profit/loss pre-tax ($m)		68.6	102.9	58.9	66.5
Share of group assets ($m)	160.7	276.0	300.7	302.0	276.9
Return on assets (%)		24.9	34.2	19.5	24.0
Capital expenditure ($m)	111.2	100.0	59.9	27.3	11.3
Production (kg)		23,428	46,244	38,364	36,633
Silver production (kg)		18,537	8,760	1,138	1,111
RGC gold sales (kg)		6,881	13,742	11,369	9,069
Gold price ($/gram)		15.3	14.77	15.76	17.56
Employees		1,381	1,710	1,759	1,812

Sources: RGC annual reports, 1990 to 1994.

Table 14. Renison Goldfields Consolidated: Gold interests—NGG Holdings (Papua New Guinea), 1981–1991.

	1981	1982	1983	1984	1985	1986
Sales of bullion ($m)	2.5	1.7	2.9	4.6	3.9	2.7
Profit/loss pre-tax ($m)		0.1	0.2	1.1	−1.4	−0.3
Share of group assets ($m)		0.7	0.7	2.7	6.3	21.7
Capital expenditure ($m)		0.1	1.1	0.6	4.3	13.8
Gold production (kg)	234	236	296	451	341	320
Silver production (kg)	197	204	212	328	244	367
Gold sales (kg)	na	na	na	422	248	176
Gold price ($/gram)	14.61	11.00	14.11	13.67	14.59	15.46
Employees	193	200	228	240	258	282

	1987	1988	1989	1990	1991
Sales of bullion ($m)	12.8	10.5	12.3	13.7	3.2
Profit/loss pre-tax ($m)	0.4	−2.8	−6.3	3.5	−3.5
Share of group assets ($m)	19.6	15.8	2.8	2.7	1.3
Capital expenditure ($m)	1.4	1.0	3.8	0.2	0.1
Gold production (kg)	749	571	849	884	193
Silver production (kg)	1,953	657	1,017	799	274
Gold sales (kg)	692	495	774	849	172
Gold price ($/gram)	19.23	19.87	15.40	14.66	15.60
Employees	305	291	310	277	47

na means not applicable.
Sources: RGC annual reports, 1982 to 1991.

Table 15. Koba Tin, 1988–1997.

	1988	1989	1990	1991	1992
Sales of tin concentrates ($m)	38.3	64.5	66.5	53.3	52.8
Profit/loss pre-tax ($m)	1.7	14.2	9.3	2.1	4.9
Share of group assets ($m)	78.7	84.0	75.0	71.1	65.6
Return on assets (%)	2.2	16.9	12.4	2.9	7.5
Saleable tin concentrate (tonnes)	6,799	9,122	9,884	10,054	10,018
Concentrate grade (%)	72.9	73.29	73.86	74.44	74.54
Tin sales (tonnes)	4,798	6,435	7,000	7,320	7,260
Average tin price ($/tonne)	8,420	10,093	9,298	7,281	7,277
Employees	1,681	1,877	1,724	1,606	1,484

	1993	1994	1995	1996	1997
Sales of tin concentrates ($m)	60.9	55.0	57.7	63.5	68.1
Profit/loss pre-tax ($m)	8.3	2.0	4.4	8.7	10.9
Share of group assets ($m)	65.6	70.4	78.4	73.2	76.4
Return on assets (%)	12.7	2.8	5.6	11.9	14.3
Saleable tin concentrate (tonnes)	10,091	10,821	10,155	10,829	12,684
Concentrate grade (%)	73.29	75.07	74.98	74.71	74.38
Tin sales (tonnes)	7,420	7,750	7,620	7,700	9,040
Average tin price ($/tonne)	8,372	7,115	7,611	8,305	7,130
Employees	1,447	1,438	1,429	1,444	1,433

RGC interest 75 per cent.

Complete data not available for 1998; in this year Koba Tin recorded a profit after tax of $25.4 million.

Sources: RGC annual reports, 1988 to 1997.

BIBLIOGRAPHY

Archival sources

Much use was made of archival sources in the research for this book. The primary sources used are listed here; specific references are cited fully in footnotes.

Brierley Collection

- Newspaper and broking analyst reports were made available by Sir Ron Brierley from his private collection.

Butlin Archives, The Australian National University

- AU NBAC, Box 67 and Box 80 (files related to the Lake George Mine, Captains Flat, New South Wales).

Consolidated Gold Fields Australia and Renison Goldfields Consolidated business records

- The majority of archival material related to Consolidated Gold Fields (Australia), Consolidated Gold Fields Australia, Renison Goldfields Consolidated, RGC and Westralian Sands is held by Iluka Resources in Perth, Western Australia. Iluka inherited a large store of former CGFA and RGC business records after Westralian Sands merged with RGC in 1998. The material includes minutes of meetings, annual reports, correspondence, memorandums and other business records. In footnotes this material is categorised as 'Renison Goldfields Consolidated Archives (RGCA)'.

Herbert Hoover Presidential Library, Iowa, United States

- Post Presidential Individuals File, Agnew, John A Correspondence: 1933, 1937, 1939.
- Pre-Commerce Subject File, Mining Correspondence, Agnew, John A, 1905–1914.

National Archives of Australia, Canberra (NAA)

- Files: A461, S373/1/2; A786,064/7; A1146, N6/4 Part 1; A9275 F1992/4302 Part 1 and 2; A12909, 1584, Cabinet Minute, Canberra 15 August 1977, Decision No. 3624; A12909, 1937, Cabinet Minute, Canberra 28 February 1978, Decision No. 4726.

National Archives of Australia, Tasmania (NAAT)

- Files: Mount Lyell Mining and Railway Company, NS 1711, 3244, 3357, 3924, 3988.

National Archives of Australia, Victoria

- Files: B206, C6578/19848.

National Library of Australia

- Charles Copeman, interview by John Farquarson, Session 2; G Lindesay Clark, interview by Alan Hodgart, Tape 2, Side 2, Session 4; Gold Mines of Australia and Gold Mines of Kalgoorlie, MS 10353—Western Mining Corporation Online History Collection/Series 4/Subseries 4.02/Items 4.02.038 and 4.02.039.

State Library of New South Wales

- Files: Captains Flat (Lake George) Mine Records, Accession Code 9607575.

State Library of South Australia (SLSA)

- Files: BRD65/1/1, Guinea Gold No Liability; PRG 429, Lapthorne, WPA.

State Library of Victoria

- Files: MS 10883, Historical Notes of AHP Moline (1877–1965).
- Department of Trade, 'Consolidated Gold Fields Limited, Investigation under Section 172 of the Companies Act 1948', report by Bryan James Welch and Michael Charles Anthony Osborne (inspectors appointed by the Department of Trade), Her Majesty's Stationery Office, London, 1980.

State Library of Western Australia (SLWA)

- Files: Bewick, Moreing & Co., MN 2530, 6736A.

University of Melbourne Archives

- The following collections were consulted: Australian United Corporation, 1980.0088, Box 49; Commonwealth Mining Investment (Australia) Limited Board Minute Books, 1955–1979, 2012.0202; 1974.0092; JB Were and Son, 2000.0017; Mount Lyell Mining and Railway, 1974.0067; Muddyman Collection, 1995.0041; Robinson, William Sydney, 101/70; Stock Exchange of Melbourne, 1968.0018, 1987.0138, 1990.0080, 1995.0053; Western Mining Corporation, 2012.0015.

University of Queensland

- Ian Morley Collection.

Books and journal articles

Anon, *Fifty Historical Years, 1910–1960: The Story of Lake View and Star, Limited*, Hepburn & Sons, Ltd, London.

Appleyard, RT and CB Schedvin, *Australian Financiers: Biographical Essays*, Macmillan, South Melbourne, 1988.

Bambrick, Susan, *Australian Minerals and Energy Policy*, Australian National University Press, Canberra, 1979.

Blainey, Geoffrey, *The Peaks of Lyell*, Melbourne University Press, Carlton, 1954.

Blainey, Geoffrey, *The Rush that Never Ended: A History of Australian Mining*, Melbourne University Press, Parkville, 1964.

Blainey, Geoffrey, *The Rise of Broken Hill*, Macmillan, South Melbourne, 1968.

Blainey, Geoffrey, *The Golden Mile*, Allen & Unwin, St Leonards, 1993.

Blainey, Geoffrey (ed.), *If I Remember Rightly: The Memoirs of WS Robinson 1876–1963*, FW Cheshire, Melbourne, 1967.

Bolton, Geoffrey, *A Fine Country to Starve In*, University of Western Australian Press, Nedlands, 1974.

Brummer, Alex and Roger Crowe, *Hanson: The Rise and Rise of Britain's Most Buccaneering Businessman*, Fourth Estate, London 1995.

Butler, Jeffrey, 'Cecil Rhodes', *The International Journal of African Historical Studies*, vol. X, no. 2, 1977, pp. 259–281. doi.org/10.2307/217349

Campbell, Grahame, *Clarinets, Pipelines and Unforeseen Places: The Evolution of an Engineer*, Hourigan & Co, 2016.

Cartwright, AP, *Gold Paved the Way: The Story of the Gold Fields Group of Companies*, Palgrave Macmillan, London, 1967. doi.org/10.1007/978-1-349-81679-8

Chemical Engineering and Mining Review, *Mining Handbook of Australia, 1936*, Tait Publishing, Sydney, 1936.

Chemical Engineering and Mining Review, *Mining Handbook of Australia, 1939*, 2nd edn, Taft Publishing, Melbourne, 1939.

Clark, Donald, 'Australian Mining and Metallurgy', *Australian Mining Standard*, London, 1907.

Clark, G Lindesay, *Built on Gold: Recollections of Western Mining*, Hill of Content, Melbourne, 1983.

Close, SE, *The Great Gold Renaissance: The Untold Story of the Modern Australian Gold Boom, 1982–2002*, Surbiton Associates, Kew, 2002.

Colebatch, Hal, *Claude de Bernales: The Magnificent Miner*, Hesperian Press, Victoria Park, 1996.

Consolidated Gold Fields of South Africa, *The Gold Fields 1887–1937*, The Consolidated Gold Fields of South Africa Ltd, London, 1937.

Cumming, Denis A and Richard G Hartley (compilers), *Westralian Founders of Twentieth Century Mining: Career Biographies of Mining Engineers, Mine Managers and Metallurgists who Worked in the Western Australian Mining Industry 1890–1920*, Richard G Hartley, Rossmoyne, Western Australia, 2014.

Davies, Melville, 'Claude Albo de Bernales: "Wizard" of Australia's Gold West', in Raymond Dumett (ed.), *Mining Tycoons in the Age of Empire, 1870–1945: Entrepreneurship, High Politics, Finance and Territorial Expansion*, Ashgate Publishing, Surrey, 2009.

Ellis, MH, *Metal Manufactures Limited: A Golden Jubilee History, 1916–1966*, Harbour Press, 1966.

Gibbney, HJ and Ann G Smith (eds), *A Biographical Register 1788–1939: Notes from the Name Index of the Australian Dictionary of Biography*, vol. I, Australian Dictionary of Biography, Canberra 1987.

Gibson, Rex, *Battlefields of Gold: How Gold Fields Fought for Survival and Won*, Jonathan Ball Publishers, Jeppestown, 2012.

Goodman, RH and KF O'Keefe, 'Tin ore treatment at Renison Limited, Renison, Tas', in JT Woodcock (ed.), *Mining and Metallurgical Practices in Australasia: The Sir Maurice Mawby Memorial Volume*, Australasian Institute of Mining and Metallurgy, Parkville, 1980.

Government of Western Australia, *Report of the Department of Mines for the Year 1927*, Government Printer, Perth, 1928.

Government of Western Australia, *Report of the Department of Mines for the Year 1928*, Government Printer, Perth, 1929.

Government of Western Australia, *Report of the Department of Mines for the Year Ended 1938*, Government Printer, Perth, 1939.

Government of Western Australia, *Report of the Department of Mines for the Year 1948*, Government Printer, Perth, 1950.

Greenwood, Ross, 'Renison's Rocky Revival', *Business Review Weekly*, 7–13 January 1984.

H Byron Moore, Day & Journeaux, 'Gold Mines of Australia and New Guinea. Leading Companies', H Byron Moore, Day & Journeaux, Melbourne.

Hartley, Richard, 'Bewick Moreing in Western Australian Gold Mining 1897–1904: Management Policies & Goldfields Responses', *Labour History*, no. 65, November 1993, pp. 1–18. doi.org/10.2307/27509195

Harvey, Charles and Jon Press, 'The City and International Mining, 1870–1914', *Business History*, vol. XXXII, no. 3, July 1990, pp. 98–119. doi.org/10.1080/00076799000000094

Harvie-Watt, GS, *Most of My Life*, Springwood Books, London, 1980.

Hernan, Brian, *Forgotten Flyer: The Story of Charles W Snook and Other Pioneer Aviators in Western Australia*, Tangee Publishing, Kalamunda, WA, 2007.

Heydon, PR, *Wiluna: Edge of the Desert*, Hesperian Press, Carlisle, WA, 1996.

Hore-Lacy, Ian (ed.), *Broken Hill to Mount Isa: The Mining Odyssey of WH Corbould*, Hyland House, Melbourne, 1981.

ICE Publishing, 'Obituary: Percy Frederick Tarbutt, 1848–1904', *Minutes of the Proceedings of the ICE* [Institution of Civil Engineers], vol. 157, issue 1904, 5 June 2015, pp. 380–381. doi.org/10.1680/imotp.1904.16544

Idriess, Ion L, *Gold-Dust and Ashes: The Romantic Story of the New Guinea Goldfields*, Angus and Robertson, Sydney, 1933.

Industries Assistance Commission, 'Interim Report, Copper Ores and Concentrates, 30 September 1977', no. 145, AGPS, Canberra, 1977.

Institute of Mining & Metallurgy, 'General Description of The Wiluna Mines Limited, Wiluna, Western Australia'. Prepared for members of the Australian Institute of Mining & Metallurgy, no date.

Jackson, Richard Thomas and Glenn Banks, *In Search of the Serpent's Skin: The Story of the Porgera Gold Project*, Placer Niugini Limited, Port Moresby, 2002.

Jamieson, Bill, *Goldstrike: The Oppenheimer Empire in Crisis*, Hutchinson Business Books, London, 1990.

Johnson, Paul, *Gold Fields: A Centenary Portrait*, George Weidenfeld & Nicolson Limited, London, 1987.

Katzenellenbogen, Simon, 'Southern African Mining Interests in Australia before 1939', *Business History*, vol. XXXII, no. 3, July 1990, pp. 120–132. doi.org/10.1080/00076799000000095

Kennedy, KH, *Mining Tsar: The Life and Times of Leslie Urquhart*, Allen & Unwin, Sydney, 1986.

King Island Scheelite Limited, *King Island Scheelite Mine, Grassy, King Island, Tasmania, 1937–1966*, Dominion Press, North Blackburn, Victoria, 1967.

Kynaston, David, *The City of London. Volume II: Golden Years: 1890–1914*, Chatto & Windus, London, 1995.

Lee, David, *Iron Country: Unlocking the Pilbara*, Minerals Council of Australia, Forrest, ACT, June 2015.

Lett, Lewis, *Papuan Gold: Story of the Early Gold Seekers*, Angus and Robertson, Sydney, 1943.

Macnab, Roy, *Gold Their Touchstone: Gold Fields of South Africa, 1887–1987. A Century Story*, Jonathan Ball Publishers, Johannesburg, 1987.

Mainwaring, Ross, *Riches Beneath the Flat: A History of Lake George Mine at Captains Flat*, Light Railway Research Society of Australia, Melbourne, 2011.

Mallory, Ian, 'Conduct Unbecoming: The Collapse of the International Tin Agreement', *American University International Law Review*, vol. 5, no. 3, art. 3, 1990.

Maylam, Paul, *The Cult of Rhodes: Remembering an Imperialist in Africa*, David Philp Publishers, Claremont, 2005.

Moody, Roger, *The Gulliver File: Mines, People and Land: A Global Battleground*, Minewatch, London, 1992.

Morley, IW, *Black Sands: A History of the Mineral Sand Mining Industry in Eastern Australia*, University of Queensland Press, St Lucia, 1981.

Nash, George H, *The Life of Herbert Hoover: The Engineer, 1874–1914*, WW Norton & Company, New York, 1983.

Nelson, Hank, *Black, White and Gold: Goldmining in Papua New Guinea, 1878–1930*, ANU Press, Canberra, 2016. doi.org/10.22459/BWG.07.2016

O'Brien, James J, *Hoover's Millions and How He Made Them*, Hesperian Press, Carlisle, WA, 2005.

Porter, Robert, *Below the Sands: The Companies that Formed Iluka Resources: Consolidated Gold Fields, RGC, Westralian Oil, Westralian Sands, Associated Minerals Consolidated, Western Titanium*, UWA Publishing, Crawley, 2018.

Prider, Rex T, *Mining in Western Australia*, University of Western Australian Press, Nedlands, 1979.

Pryke, Susan, Janet Van Straaten and Alan V Walker, *Boom to Bust—And Back Again: Captain's Flat From 1883*, 2nd edn, Captains Flat Residents and Ratepayers Association, 1995.

Raggatt, HC, *Mountains of Ore*, Lansdowne Press, Melbourne, 1968.

Ralph, Gilbert M, *Biographical Sketches of Some Former WMC People*, 1st edn, Western Mining Corporation, December 2004.

Reynolds, E, 'Lake George Mines', The AusIMM Centenary Conference, Adelaide, 30 March – 4 April 1993.

Rhys, Lloyd, *High Lights and Flights in New Guinea: Being in the Main an Account of the Discovery and Development of the Morobe Goldfields*, Hodder and Stoughton, London, 1942.

Roberts, Andrew, *Churchill: Walking with Destiny*, Penguin Random House, London, 2018.

Royal School of Mines, *Register of Old Students, 1851–1920 and History of the Royal School of Mines*, Royal School of Mines Old Students' Association, 1920.

Sale, AR, 'A Fortunate Life: 45 Years in Heavy Minerals', Eighth International Heavy Minerals Conference, Perth, WA, 5–6 October 2011.

Sierra Rutile Limited, *Sierra Rutile: A History*, Sierra Rutile Limited, Pionero Partners.

Snooks, GD, *Depression and Recovery in Western Australia, 1928'29–1938'39: A Study in Cyclical and Structural Change*, University of Western Australian Press, Nedlands, 1974.

Stewart, John C, *Thomas F Walsh: Progressive Businessman and Colorado Mining Tycoon*, University Press of Colorado, Boulder, 2012.

The Mines Department of WA, 'Report on the Treatment of Semi-Oxidised Ore from the Moonlight Wiluna Gold Mines, Wiluna, WA', School of Mines Kalgoorlie, 3 August 1939.

Topperwien, GH, *The History of Wiluna*, c. 1981. (Monograph held at State Library of Western Australia.)

Uren, Malcolm, *A Glint of Gold*, Robertson & Mullens, Melbourne, 1948.

Waterhouse, Michael, *Not a Poor Man's Field: The New Guinea Goldfields to 1942—An Australian Colonial History*, Halstead Press, Ultimo, 2007.

Westralia (Western Australia), *1948 Story of the Goldfields*, 1st edn, Mining World & Engineering Record, London, 1948.

White, Unk, *The Gold Fields House Story*, Sydney, c. 1965.

Whyte, Kenneth, *Hoover: An Extraordinary Life in Extraordinary Times*, Alfred A Knopf, New York, 2017.

Wilson, AJ, *The Professionals: The Institute of Mining and Metallurgy, 1892–1992*, The IM&M, London, 1992.

Yule, Peter, *Ian Potter: Financier and Philanthropist*, Ian Potter Foundation, Melbourne, c. 2003.

Yule, Peter, *William Lawrence Baillieu: Founder of Australia's Greatest Business Empire*, Hardie Grant Books, Richmond, 2012.

Internet sources

Auerbach, Geraldine, 'Albert Beit — South Africa's Financial Genius', 20 November 2017, kehilalinks.jewishgen.org/kimberley/Alfred_Beit_files.

Branagan, DF, 'Cameron, Keith Addison (1902–1967)', *Australian Dictionary of Biography*, The Australian National University, 1993, adb.anu.edu.au/biography/cameron-keith-addison-9672.

Copeman, Michael, 'Vale Charles Copeman, Hero of Robe River', Quadrant Online, 11 July 2013, quadrant.org.au/opinion/qed/2013/07/vale-charles-copeman/.

Film Australia, *Living Way Out*, 1977, wanowandthen.com/Shay-Gap.html.

Gold Fields Ltd, 'Company Profile, Information, Business Description, History, Background Information on Gold Fields Ltd', www.referenceforbusiness.com/history2/74/Gold-Fields-Ltd.html.

Healy, AM, 'Levien, Cecil John (1874–1932)', *Australian Dictionary of Biography*, The Australian National University, 1986, adb.anu.edu.au/biography/levien-cecil-john-7179/text12407.

Hopper, JR and AJ Lynch, 'Kruttschnitt, Julius (1885–1974)', *Australian Dictionary of Biography*, 1983, adb.anu.edu.au/biography/kruttschnitt-julius-7001.

Kelly, John J, 'FA Govett, Chairman and Managing Director The Zinc Corporation 1907–1926', ausimm.com/.

Kennedy, BE, 'Gepp, Sir Herbert William (Bert) (1877–1954)', *Australian Dictionary of Biography*, The Australian National University, 1981, adb.anu.edu.au/biography/gepp-sir-herbert-william-bert-6298.

Kennedy, KH, 'Corbould, William Henry (1866–1949)', *Australian Dictionary of Biography*, The Australian National University, 1981, adb.anu.edu.au/biography/corbould-william-henry-5779.

Kennett, John, 'Fraser, Sir Colin (1875–1944)', *Australian Dictionary of Biography*, The Australian National University, 1981, adb.anu.edu.au/biography/fraser-sir-colin-6236.

Koenig, Kay, 'Herbert Hoover—Australian Mining Entrepreneur', Australian Family Stories, 2012, australianfamilystories.com.au.

Langmore, Diane, 'Mustar, Ernest Andrew (1893–1971)', *Australian Dictionary of Biography*, The Australian National University, 1986, adb.anu.edu.au/biography/mustar-ernest-andrew-7719.

Laurence, John H, 'de Bernales, Claude Albo (1876–1963)', *Australian Dictionary of Biography*, The Australian National University, 1981, adb.anu.edu.au/biography/de-bernales-claude-albo-5935/text10117.

Lloyd, CJ, 'Massy-Greene, Sir Walter (1874–1952)', *Australian Dictionary of Biography*, The Australian National University, 1986, adb.anu.edu.au/biography/massy-greene-sir-walter-7512.

London Metropolitan Archives, 'Camp Bird Limited', AIM25: Archives in London and the M25 Area, aim25.com/cgi-bin/vcdf/detail?coll_id=17187&inst_id=118&nv1=browse&nv2=repos.

Marks, Shula and Stanley Trapido, 'Rhodes, Cecil John (1853–1902)', *Oxford Dictionary of National Biography*, 23 September 2004, www.oxforddnb.com.

New Zealand Government, 'The Goldfields of New Zealand: Report on Roads, Water-Races, Mining Machinery, and Other Works in Connection with Mining', *Appendix to the Journals of the House of Representatives*, 1898, atojs.natlib.govt.nz.

Ralph, Gilbert M, 'Clark, Sir Gordon Colvin Lindesay (1896–1986)', *Australian Dictionary of Biography*, The Australian National University, adb.anu.edu.au/biography/clark-sir-gordon-colvin-lindesay-12324.

Routh, SJ, 'Pinter, Joseph (1912–1981)', *Australian Dictionary of Biography*, The Australian National University, 2012, adb.anu.edu.au/biography/pinter-joseph-15465.

Stearn, Roger T, 'Rudd, Charles Dunell (1844–1916)', *Oxford Dictionary of National Biography*, 23 September 2004, www.oxforddnb.com.

INDEX

Page numbers in *italics* refer to images, references in footnotes referred to with n

Aberfoyle, 193
acid plant, Burnie, 144, 149, 159
   see also North-West Acid
Acoje Mining, 290
Adamson, J, 149, 189
Adelaide, South Australia, 35, 424–425
Adelaide Stock Exchange 40n45, 85
AGL (Australian Gas Light), 301
Agnew, John Alexander, xv, 11, 16, 23, 25–29, *26, 27,* 32–35, 37–40, 42, 44, 50, 52–55, 57–63, *59,* 71–73, 75–76, 105, 400, 419–421
   advisory committee, Western Mining Corporation, 58
   Bewick Moreing, 25, 28–29
   biographical information, 419–421
   chairmanships
      Gold Exploration and Finance Co., 58–59, 62
      GFADC, 63
      Lake View and Star, 23, 32
      Wiluna Gold Corporation, 23, 40, 48
   death, 23, 25, 27, 53–55, 420
   described as 'chief of Kalgoorlie', 32
   directorships
      Consolidated Gold Fields of South Africa,
      New Consolidated Gold Fields, 16, 25, 30, 34, 54, 59n5, 59, 420
      National Mining Corporation, 34, 72–73
      other 32–34, 40, 54, 58, 59, 59n5, 73
   health, 28–29
   and Hoover
      accompanies to China, 27
      formalises business arrangements with, 33
      joins in London, 29
      management of business interests, 29, 33
      relationship with, 27, 28, 29n14, 33
   Lake View and Star, 32, 40, 50, 52, 53, 54
   reputation, 25, 29, 54
   serves on technical committees, 32, 73
Agnew, Rudolph Ion Joseph, xvi, 105, 122n9, 214, *228,* 231–232, 234–235, 243n1, 272, 293, 295, 298, *306,* 330, 403, 417
   description of, 310
   Edwardes, Michael, view of, 311

Hanson takeover, 320, 322
Minorco takeover attempt,
  305n1, 308–311, 313, 320
Agnew, Rudolph John (Dolph), 16,
  46, 50, *59*, 65, 70
  Australian Institute of Mining and
    Metallurgy (president), 65
  biographical information, 421–422
  Chamber of Mines (vice president
    and president), 65, 422
  Consolidated Gold Fields
    (director), 422
  death, 70, 422
  GFADC (chairman, general
    manager), 46, *59*, 64–65,
    421–422
  Gold Exploration and Finance
    Company, 58
  Kalgoorlie and Boulder Mines
    Medical Fund, establishes,
    65–66
  Lake View and Star (director,
    general manager), 50, 65, 422
  Mount Ida Mine, 422
  Wiluna mine, 64
Ainge, Douglas F, 70n43, 112–113,
  227
Akenobe mine, Japan, 168
Alexander, AGL (Anthony), 330–331,
  333, 348–350, 408
Allen, Paul, 129
Allied Eneabba, 190, 211, 216, 241,
  249, 283–284, 299, 356, 433
Allied Minerals, 188–190, 212–214,
  216
alluvial gold, 10, 36, 58, 85–*88*, 90,
  260
Alumasc Holdings, 95, 102, 131–132,
  156
  see also Lawrenson Alumasc
    Holdings
AMAX, 130

AMC (Associated Minerals
  Consolidated), xiii, 95, 96, 113,
  115–118, *118*, 155, 182–183,
  186, 193n8, 208, 211–212,
  215–217, 220, 222, 229–232,
  234, 236–237, 241, 244–245,
  278–280, 282–283, 302, 318,
  348, 352, 355, 357, 401–403, 411
  acquisitions
    Allied Eneabba, 190, 216,
      241, 249, 283–284
    TAZI, 183
    Titanium Enterprises, 149, 216
  Capel, 247, 278, 280, 282
  CGFA acquires interest in, 113,
    118, 120
  chairmen, 117
  Eneabba, 190, 210–211
  environmental issues, 186, 209
  financial performance, 120, 157,
    186, 188, 210, 220, 258, 347,
    363, 379, 429–431, 433–434,
    439
  McKinsey review, 213–214, 216
  mergers
    Western Titanium, 120, 150,
      155, 190, 208, 210, 224,
      403
    Wyong Minerals, 113, 183
  Pinter, Joseph, 116–117, 182
  production, 281
  reserves, 208
  RGC Mineral Sands, renamed,
    190
  rights issue, 216, 278
American mining engineers, 25, 30,
  42, 50, 75
Amey Roadstone, 247, 287, 320
AMP, 242, 299, 404n6
Ampolex, 426

INDEX

Anderson, McCheyne Campbell, xvi, 72n4, 253, *254*, 256, 258, 267, 300–302, 330–339, 341, 343, 349, 353–355, 404, 408–409, 417–418, 425, 426
   Alexander, AGL, relationship with, 408
   biographical information, 426
   Cotton, Tony, view of, 338
   FIRB (Foreign Investment Review Board), 334–337
   Hanson, view of, 337–339, 346
   Hanson correspondence, 320–321
   mineral sands, views of, 214, 354
   Minorco defence involvement, 308, 310, 313–315, 317, 318
   Mount Goldsworthy acquisition, 298–299
   Mount Lyell, 277
   North Broken Hill, 340
   plan to succeed Roberts, 333, 335, 371
   Porgera, 293, 351
   resigns as managing director, 326, 340
   significant appointments, 241–242, 253
Anderson, McCheyne Robert, 72
Andrew, Brian W, 143, 409
Anglo American Corporation, xiii, 13, 13, 18, 62, 232, 234, 247, 305, 307–309, 312, 313n21
Annan, Robert, 11, 58–60, 62, 76
antimony sulphides, 47, 49
apartheid, 13, 323, 333
ARC Marine, 245
ARC Roadstone Division, 337
Arco Australia, Arco Coal, 250, 301
Aries Consultants, 317
Arnhem Land, 121
arsenic, 47, 160n5
arsenopyrite, 38, 47
Associated Gold Mine, 23, *51*, 52, 53, 60, 63

Associated Minerals, 188
Associated Minerals Consolidated *see* AMC
Associated Pulp and Paper Mills, 427
Associated Tailings *see* Associated Gold Mine
Austral Bronze, 103, 109n3, 423
Australian Conciliation and Arbitration Commission, 261
Australian Machinery and Investment Company, 46
Australian Stock Exchange, 18, 40n45, 109, 174, 195, 226, 237, 266, 370, 395, 404
Australian Workers' Union, 79, 82–83, 261, 265, 361
Australianisation (naturalisation, divisionalisation), 18, 109, 158, 223, 231, 233, 235, 241, 243, 251, 253, 296n20
Ayre, Mike, xvi, 261, 265–267, 275, 359–360, 405

Babilonia Gold Mines, 32
Baillieu, Clive, 63
Baillieu, Lawrence, 427
Baillieu, WL, 30, 35
Baker, FW, 34, 63n18, 77
Baker, TC, 34, 75, 79–80
Ballarat, Victoria, 58
Bangka Island, Indonesia, 267
Barrier mines, New South Wales, 30, 38
Bassett, Walter (Sir), 135–137, 139
Bathurst, New South Wales, 288
Bawdwin Syndicate, 32
Beaver Exploration, 194
Beckett, Michael, 229, 233, 243n1, 298, 308, 322, 404
Beggs, Frank Rundle, 67–69, 95, 100–101, 104, 109–110, 111n10, 116, 417
Beit, Alfred, 9
Belgium, 29, 33, 420

Bell Resources, 317
Bellambi Coal Company, 96, 109n3, 133–134, 155, 157n, 158, 176–182, 202, 207, 220, 228–229, 244, 294, 401
    CGFA acquires interest in, 96, 102, 133–134, 140
    coking facilities, 176
    Copeman, Charles, 179, 181, 197, 294
    financial performance, 134, 176, 178, 180, 429–431
    history, 133
    industrial disputes, 163, 178
    Japanese customers, 176
    Massy-Greene, Brian, 177
    sale, 150, 163, 182, 224, 244
Bemban dredge, 302, 326, 368, 384
Bendigo Mine, 59n6, 423
beneficiation of ilmenite, 120, 149–150, 185, 190, 213, 413
    see also SREP (synthetic rutile enhanced process), synthetic rutile
Berry Leads, 58
Bethwaite, Francis Mark, xvi, 242, *255*, 256, 326, 331, 333, 336, 339–340, *341*, 373–374, 382, 409, 412, 418
    appointment, managing director, 256, 340, 353n30, 408
    biographical information, 426–427
    mineral sands task force, 355–356
    Minorco defence, 313
    Mount Lyell, 359, 363
    North Broken Hill, 404
    Renison, 360
    resignation, 327, 389
Bewick, Moreing and Company, 25, *26*, *27*, 27–30, 38, 42, 419–420
BHP (Broken Hill Proprietary), 130, 153, 170, 206, 237n42, 242, 250, 252n11, 258, 297, 298–299, 302, 317, 369, 410–411

Billiton International Minerals, 307n4, 381
Bitumen and Oil Refineries (Australia) *see* Boral
Blackwater coal, 102
Blackwood ore body, 362
Blainey, Geoffrey, 37, 50, 60, 165
Blair Athol coal, 245, 250, 296, 301
Blue Metal Products, 95
Bolivia, 373, 386, 387, 389
Bolivian tin, 137, 375, 386
Bonham, DC, 334
Boral (Bitumen and Oil Refineries), 109n3, 137–141, 250, 302, 426
Borg Warner (Australia), 132
Boston Consulting Group, 373, 389–390, 392
Bougainville, Papua New Guinea, 293
Bougainville Copper, 237n42, 371
Boulder, Kalgoorlie, 50
Bow zirconia plant, New Hampshire, 241, 278, 280
Bowen Basin, Queensland, 121, 133, 202, 245, 250, 296
BP (British Petroleum), 109n3, 292, 313
BP Minerals, 310
Breen, Alan, 396n11
British Columbia, 86
British Government, 315
British Leyland, 311
British Metal Corporation (Australia), 422
British Minerals, 117
British Ministry of Supply, 79
British Petroleum *see* BP
British South Africa Company, 8
British Takeover Panel, 318
British Tin Investment, 138
Broken Bay, Hawkesbury River, 245
Broken Hill, New South Wales, 38, 67, 72, 167, 424
Broken Hill Associated Smelters, 76

Broken Hill mines, 61, 73, 75–76, 192
Broken Hill Proprietary *see* BHP
Broken Hill School of Mines, 424
Broken Hill South, 58, 110, 410
Buffer Stock Manager system, 246, 263n16, 264, 386
Bulletin ore body, 23, 38, 39, 44, 45, 48
Bulolo, Papua New Guinea, 85, 86–87, *88*, 90, 293
Bulolo Gold Dredging, 3, 86–87, *89*, 90, 290
Bungendore, New South Wales, 71, 73, 77–78
Burma Corporation, 30, 32–34, 70n43, 72–73
Burmah Castrol, 425
Burmah Oil, 235, 253, 425, 426
Burnett, JM, 152
Burnie, Tasmania, 135, 144, 149, 159
Burraga, New South Wales, 242, 288
Burrinjuck hydro-electric scheme, 78

Cameron, Keith Addison, 69, 95, 100, 110–113, 152, 409, 422–423
Camp Bird, 11, 23, 30, 32–34, 57–58, 63, 72–74, 77n25
Canberra, Australian Capital Territory, xv, 71, 172, 249, 287
Cape Keraudren, 123
Capel, 115, *184*, 187, 210, 247, 278, 280, 282, 333, 377, 387–388, 390, 395–397, 435
Capel Court, 233, 253
Captains Flat, New South Wales, 17, 23, 33, 71, 75, 78, *81*, 81, 83–84, 420
carbon-in-pulp, 242, 289, 413
Cartwright, AP, 97–98
Cassidy, Peter, 380
Castrol Australia, 425
Cavenham Forest Industries, 310

Central Mining and Investment Corporation, 61–62
Central Norseman Gold Corporation, 58
Central Yellowdine Gold Mine, 58
Cerro Corona, Peru, 250, 327, 387, 392, 406, 408–409
CGF Iron, 205
CGFA (Consolidated Gold Fields Australia), xiii–xiv, 18, 19, 68–70, 95–96, 100–105, 150–158, 194–196, 202, 226–227, 236–237, 243–244, 246, 253, 267–268, 283, 291, 294, 297, 399–402, 404, 410, 423–424
  agricultural interests, 18, 108, 149, 156, 158, 194, 207, 229
  Alumasc Holdings, 102, 131–132, 150, 156, 157n1
  AMC acquires interest in, 113, 116, 118, *see also* mineral sands
  Australianisation, naturalisation, divisionalisation, *see* Australianisation
  Bellambi Coal, 96, 102, 133–134, 150, 155, 157n1, 158, 163, 176–182, 197, 202, 207, 220, 224, 228, 244
  business model, 107–110, 146, 153, 158, 194, 217, 219–220, 223, 228, 237, 400–404, 407
  Commonwealth Mining Investments acquires interest in, 95, 109–113
  Consolidated Gold Fields, approach to and view of Australian subsidiary, 100–101, 104, 108, 110, 112, 121–122, 130, 133, 137–138, 140, 145–146, 149, 151, 153, 157–158, 162, 167, 169, 185, 197, 205–206, 214, 225–227, 229, 231–235, 241

CRA comparison with, 399
directors, 100, 107–108, 109n3, 111, 132, 152, 158, 174, 179, 181, 192, 211, 213–216, 220, 224, 226, 229, 232–235, 243, 401, 417
diversification activities, 108, 131, 137, 156, 191–194
exploration, 18, 95, 100–102, 112, 121, 124, 133, 140, 149, 156, 191, 194–195, 208
Ferro Alloys Tasmania, 149, 193
financial performance, 120, 142, 145, 152–153, 156–157, 158n3, 169–171, 174, 206, 208, 212, 219–221, 223–224, 237, 258n11, 429–431
FIRB (Foreign Investment Review Board), 232–234
Glendell Coal, 195, 236n40
Gold Fields House, 113, 151, 153, 227, 242, 251, 299, 396, 410
investments, listed companies, 107, 110, 131, 153, 156, 158, 194
iron ore, involvement, 18, 95, 102, 108–109, 121–131, *see also* MGMA
Lake View and Star, 110, 149, 156–157, 195–196
Lawrenson Holdings, 131–132, 149–150, 156, 157n1, 220, 224, 430
manufacturing interests, 18, 102, 108, 131–132, 142, 146, 153, 156–158, 219
Massy-Greene, Brian, 103, 103, 104–105, 107–108, 152, 158
steps down as managing director, chairman 105, 108, 150, 206, 226–227
minerals sands, involvement in, 18, 102, 112–113, 115–120, 146, 182–190

considers divestment, 109, 190, 208–217, 224
Mount Goldsworthy, 158, 168–175, 201–206
Mount Lyell Mining and Railway Company, 96, 104, 135–146, 158–166, 197–201
North Broken Hill, 153, 156, 192, 229, 235
OT Lempriere, 149, 193, 224
Pancontinental Mining, investment in, 150, 156, 207–208, 229, 236n40
Porgera acquires interest in, 150, 230, 236n40, 244, 291
portfolio review, 207–208, 219–225, 228–235
property investments, 18, 149, 156, 193–194, 401
public company, 3, 96, 131, 146, 153, 221, 235, 244
Renison, 101, 109, 111, 120, 135–146, 149, 156–157, 159, 161, 162–164, 166–168
Renison scheme, 229–230
Roberts, MJ (Max), 109, 150, 235–236, 241
Ryan, Bartholomew, 108, 143, 150, 201, 203, 225, 227, 234, 235, 243n1, 403, 404, 417, 424
Segal, Sidney, 108, 150, 185, 204, 235, 243n1, 417, 424
Western Titanium acquires interest in, 68, 113, 120, 149–150, 155, 185, 191
Wyong Minerals acquires interest in, 95, 118
Zip Holdings acquires interest in, 96, 102, 132, 156, 157n1
Chaffers (gold mine), Western Australia, 53–54
Chamber of Mines of Western Australia, 65, 422

Champagne Syndicate, 59n6, 63, 66n28
Chemical and Metallurgical Corporation, 34–35, 74n9
Chinese Department of Mines, 27
chloride feedstocks, 116, 120, 381
chloride pigment, 118, 182–183, 187, 355, 377
chloride process, 182, 185, 281
chloride slag, 377
Cia San Juan S A, 125
Circular Quay Holdings, 156, 193n7, 194, 207, 244, 251
City of London *see* London, City of
Clark, Lindesay, 57, 60–61, 63
Clark, William, 35
Cleveland Cliffs, 130
Cloncurry, Queensland, 34
CMI (Commonwealth Mining Investments Australia)
  arrangement with Commonwealth Treasury, 112
  Burnett, JM, 152
  Cameron, Keith, 110–113, 422
  CGFA acquires interest in, 67n32, 95–96, 101, 109, 111, 113, 116, 153
  CGFA, appointed general manager, 95
  directors, 110
  financial performance, 429–430
  history and description of, 109–111
  Kruttschnitt, Julius, 90, 110
  management committee, 113
  mineral sands investments, 113, 115
  place in CGFA portfolio, 112
  sale to National Mutual, 113, 150, 207, 403
Colinas, 149, 156, 158, 193–194, 207, 220, 224, 229, 242, 244, 299, 326, 351, 353

Collins, Christopher, 330, 335, 340, 348–349, 352–353, 393
Collins House Group, 5, 15, 30, 35, 59–60, 63, 76, 103, 110, 420, 422
Colombia, 10, 63n18, 87
Comet Gold Mine, 64
Commonwealth and Mining Finance Limited, 46, 64n19
Commonwealth Banking Corporation, 404n, 423
Commonwealth Government, 45, 49, 65–66, 79–80, 121, 123, 134, 159, 161, 163, 165, 172, 179, 197, 199, 219, 221, 241, 247, 271–272, 276, 280
Commonwealth Parliamentary Conference, New Zealand, 99
Commonwealth Treasury, 112, 139
Communist propaganda, Communists, 83–84, 305
Companies (Acquisition of Shares) Code, NSW, 316
Comstock Lode, Nevada, 34
Connor, F X, 172–173, 179
Consolidated Gold Fields Australia, *see* CGFA
Consolidated Gold Fields, London (CGF), xiii, xv, xvi, 3, 4, 18, 50, 53–55, 63n18, 97–99, 101–103, 105, 107, 110, 112, 121–122, 130–133, 137–138, 145–146, 151–153, 157, 162, 168–169, 185, 194, 205–206, 209, 214, 223–225, *228*, 229, 231–235, 236n40, 237, 241–245, 247, 250, 252–253, 260, 287, 293, 297–298, 300, 305, *306*, 313–314, 316, 320, 337 366, 401–404, 411, 424–425
  Hanson takeover, 319–322, 329, 334, 343, 407
  Minorco takeover attempt, 307–319

The Consolidated Gold Fields of
  South Africa, xiii, 3, 5, 6, 9–12,
  15–16, 18, 23, 25, 30, 33n21, 35,
  40, 54, 57n1, 59, 63n17, 71, 78,
  86–87, 95, 97, 99, 104–105, 111,
  400, 419–420
Consolidated Press Holdings, 317
Consolidated Tin Smelters, 138
Conzinc Riotinto Australia, see CRA
Cooksons, 310
Coolgardie, 17, 64
Copeman, Charles, 164, 179–181,
  195, 197–200, 207, 209, 294,
  401, 403–404, 409
copper porphyry, 34, 383n23
copper price, 143, 159–162, 164,
  193, 200–201, 220, 222, 246,
  268–273, 275–277, 363–364,
  366, 445–447
Corbould, William Henry, 65
Corrimal Coke, 176
Cotton AR (Tony), 338, 380, 389,
  393, 395–397, 408
  biographical information, 427
  mineral sands, view of 351
  RGC
    deputy chairman, chairman,
      326, 339–340, 341, 346,
      409, 418
    director, 330, 347
    executive chairman, 256, 327,
      336, 371, 390
    shareholding, view of, 351
CRA (Conzinc Riotinto Australia),
  xiii, 121, 130, 211–212, 237n42,
  258, 293, 301, 310, 317, 377,
  399
Craig, Ken, 68
CRL (Consolidated Rutile Limited),
  93, 212, 214, 249, 326, 373, 375,
  381–383, 388, 390, 394, 397,
  409, 41
CSR, 130, 237n42, 250
CSIRO (Council for Scientific and
  Industrial Research), 76, 423

CSR Minerals Division, 301
Cudgen, New South Wales, 117
Cudgen RZ, 193, 249–250, 326,
  373, 375, 381, 409, 411
Cue Shire, Western Australia, 62
Cuming Smith, 137
cyanide, 319
  leaching, 291
  process, 9, 36, 38, 42
Cyprus Mines Corporation (Cyprus
  Minerals), 95, 102, 107, 112n,
  121–122, 129, 131, 170, 202,
  365, 369

Daiwa Securities, 331
Dalgety & New Zealand Loan, 194
Dalgety Australia, 182, 194–195,
  241–242, 244, 287, 294–297n21,
  369
Darling, John, 105, 109, 243n1,
  404n6
Darwin, Northern Territory, 249,
  288, 367
De Beers Consolidated Mines, 7,
  234, 305, 307–309, 312
De Beers Mining Company, 3, 8–9,
  18
de Bernales, Claude Albo, 16, 35,
  37–38, 40–41, 46, 54, 62, 64
de Crespigny, Robert, 332
Delta Gold, 368, 380n17
Denman, Lord, 225
Department of Minerals and Energy,
  161, 172–173
Department of Munitions, 421
Department of Trade (UK), 307
Depuch Island, Western Australia,
  123
Discovery Petroleum, 288
divisionalisation, see Australianisation
Drilling Corporation of Australia,
  422
du Pont de Nemours, EI, see Dupont

INDEX

Dunlap, Al ('Chainsaw'), 311
Dupont, 116, 182, 185, 189, 212, 214–216, 249, 280, 283–284, 317, 375–376
Durham coal compensation scheme
Durham Holdings, 195, 296, 297n21

East Murchison United, 419
Eastern Titanium Corporation, 95, 113, 183n65
Eclipse Mining, 95
Edie Creek, Papua New Guinea, 36, 85, 87, *88*, 90
Edwardes, Michael (Sir), 311, 319
Elder Smith Goldsborough Mort
Elders Finance and Investments
Elders Resources, 317
Electrolytic Refining and Smelting Company, 159, 199
Electrolytic Zinc Co. of Australasia, 76
electrostatic precipitation, separation, 38, 117
Elleyou Development Corporation, 87
Elleyou Goldfields Corporation, 85
Ellis, Bryan, xvi, 343
Elmore process, 35
Elsum, David, 241, 253, 417
Email Ltd, 109n3, 137
Emu Bay Railway, 165, 200, 274
Eneabba, Western Australia, 149, 150, 155, 174, 185, 187–190, 211–214, 216–217, 247, 249, 278, 281–283, 358, 362, 377–378, 383, 388, 394, 411
  Allied Eneabba, involvement, 190, 211, 216, 241, 249, 283–284
  Allied Minerals, involvement, 189–190, 212, 214
  commissioning issues, 150, 208, 210, 246

dredge mining, 242, 374, 395
Jennings Industries, involvement, 150, 190, 211, 216–217, 249
pegging rush, 188
production issues, 210
profitability, 390
radiation, ilmenite, 247, 280–281, 356, 376
steaming coal resource, 236n40, 245, 287
synthetic rutile, 355, 374
Eneabba North, 356
Eneabba South, 356, 358
Eneabba West, 242, 249, 325, 344, 356–358, 374–375, 395, 397
The Energy Group, 391
Enterprise Gold Mines, 288, 367
Enterprise pit, 288
ERA (Energy Resources of Australia), 317, 426
Erroll, Lord, 307
exploration (Gold Fields, CGFA, RGC), 17–18, 24, 60, 61–62, 67–69, 91, 95, 100–102, 112, 121, 124, 133, 149, 156, 191, 194–195, 241, 244–245, 247, 249, 260, 287–290, 337–338, 347, 353, 368, 373, 375, 383–384, 396, 400–401, 406
EZ Industries, 144, 149–150, 153, 159, 160n5, 198, 200, 427

Faulkner, Keith, xvi, 363–364, 396n11
Federal Coke Works, 177
Federal Court of Australia, 377, 380
Ferro Alloys, Tasmania, 149, 193
Ferro Corporation, 241
Finucane Island, 123, 125, *127–128*, 297
FIRB (Foreign Investment Review Board), 232–234, 241, 244, 251, 325, 332, 334–337, 339n34, 340, 344, 352

flotation, 38, 42, 44, 50, 52, 72, 75, 77–78, 144, 167–168
49 Moorgate, London, 11, *12*, 33n21, 74, 76, 101
Frances Creek, Northern Territory, 121
Fraser Island, Queensland, 247
Fraser, Colin (Sir), 59–60
Freebairn, Anthony, 189
Fresnillo Company, 74–75
Fresnillo Mine, Mexican Corporation, 34
Fussell, Norman, 352

Gandy's Hill, 367
Gatfield, Brian, 330
Gatfield Robinson Wareing, 330
Gauci, Vince, 389, 390n36
Gencor, 307, 312–313, 381
General Mining, 13, 307
Gepp, Herbert William (Sir), 76
Getty Oil Development Company, 156, 288
GFADC (Gold Fields Australian Development Company), 3, 17, 23–24, 33n21, 41n47, 46, 48, *59*, 60, 62–67, 74n9, 91, 149
Gleeson-White, Michael, xvi, 113
Glendell Coal joint venture, 195, 236n40, 241–242, 244–245, 287, 294, 296–297, 301, 325, 351, 368, 406
Globe & Phoenix Gold Mining Company, 98
gold (price, production), 8, 18, 37, 53, 65, 157, 195, 344, 348, 445–447, 450–452
Gold Exploration and Finance Company of Australia Limited, 3, 16, 35, 57–60, 62
Gold Fields American Development Company, 3, 10, 15, 45, 57, 67, 76, 78, 86

Gold Fields Australian Development Company, *see* GFADC
Gold Fields Exploration, 241, 245, 260
Gold Fields House, 113, 151, *153*
Gold Fields Mining & Industrial, 3, 67n32, 95, 100, 128, 152
Gold Fields of South Africa (subsidiary of Consolidated Gold Fields), 100, 307, 308, 316
Gold Fields of South Africa (The), Limited, 3, 5, 8, 322, 398, 400
Gold Fields Rhodesian Development Company, 10
Gold Mines of Australia Limited, 3, 16, 57–58, 61
Gold Mines of Kalgoorlie, 59–60
Gold Mines of Tasmania, 366
Golden Age Mine, 27
Golden Horseshoe mine, 23, 53
Golden Mile of Kalgoorlie, 17, *31*, 48, 52, 427
Goldfields Limited, 368, 375, 378, 380, 383, 389, 395, 397, 409, 411, 427, 431, 435
Goldfields Philippines Corporation, 290
Goldsmith, James (Jimmy) (Sir), 310
Goldsworthy, 123, 125, 173, 194
Goldsworthy Mining, 168, 171, 173–174, 206, 207, 297–298, 424
Gove Peninsula, Northern Territory, 121
Govett, Francis Algernon, 16, 30, 32–35, 73
Govett, Sons and Co, 16, 30
Granny Smith gold prospect, 301–302
Great Boulder Main Reef, 53
Greater Boulder Perseverance Gold Mining Co., 421
Green Cove Springs, Florida, 150, 247, 278, 281, 356, 411
Griffin, Elton, 139
Grigg, Peter, 396n11

Guinea Gold No Liability, 85–87
Gunpowder Complex, Copper, 220–222, 228, 236n40, 241–242, 244, 268, 432–433

Hamersley Iron Ore, 130 172, 205
Hamilton, Frederic (Sir), 46, 54, 63
Hancock, Lang, 121
Hancock Prospecting and Wright Prospecting, (Hanwright), 149, 170
Hannan's Hill, 65
Hannan's Star Consolidated, 32, 53
Hanson, Lord, 339, 345, 408
    acquires CGF, 319–321
    Agnew meeting with, 320
    correspondence from RGC, 320, 336
    correspondence to chairman CGF, 321
    correspondence with RGC, 321, 336
    Financial Times, description of, 345
    Minorco, 319
    nominates RGC directors, 330, 340
Hanson Plc, 249–252, 256, 298–299, 337–339, 348, 351, 408–409, 411–412, 427
    approach from Westralian Sands, 19, 251, 374, 393
    budget approach, 345
    corporate dynamics, 391–392, 398, 412
    diversified business model, view of, 344, 350
    FIRB approach, 334–336, 340, 344
    reputation, xiii, 345
    and RGC
        exit shareholding, 341, 392, 395, 409
        shareholding in, 4, 19, 329–333, 343, 352
    unwinding of naturalisation status, 244, 251, 340
    takeover Consolidated Gold Fields, 18, 206, 223, 242, 247, 306, 309, 319–322, 343, 407
    view of portfolio, 250, 346, 348, 353–354, 357, 389
    view on executive chairman role, 325, 333, 407
Hanson Sykes Pumps Australia, 427
Happy Jack ore body, 23–24, 39, 44, 48–49
Harris, Arnold, 75, 78
Harvie-Watt, George Steven (Sir), 17, 95, 97–100, *99*, 102n14, 102, 104, 107, 109–111, 116, 130, 151–152, 157, 169, 322, 401, 410, 417
Hastings River, New South Wales, 193
Hawke, RJ (Bob), 276, 315
Hayes, Jerry, 189
Hemingway, AD (Tony), xvi, 243n1
Henty gold, 156, 249, 288, 325–326, 347, 353, 368, 378n, 383n22, 434
Hewitt, Lennox, 173
Hoover, Herbert C, 25, *26,* 27–35, 54, 71–72, 74, 400, 419–420
Hopkins, WE, 117
Horseshoe Wiluna Gold Mines, 24, 46, 64
Housden, Peter, 389, 396n11
Hydro Electric Commission, Tasmania, 273, 275

ICI (Imperial Chemical Industries), 137, 153, 160, 163, 165, 182
ilmenite beneficiation, upgrading, *see* synthetic rutile and SREP
ilmenite price, production, 113, 187, 280–281, 344, 356–357, 437–439
    see also mineral sands, AMC, Western Titanium

473

Iluka Resources, xv, 4, 251n10, 252n11, 268, 297, 327, 369, 397
Imperial and Foreign Group, 34
Imperial Chemical Industries, *see* ICI
Imperial Gold Mine leases, 23
Imperial Smelting Corporation, 57
Imperial Tobacco, 391
Industries Assistance Commission – Copper Producers, 165, 198
Institute of Mining and Metallurgy (UK), 55, 421
investment division, 250, 256, 260, 299–300, 351
iron ore, xiii, xvi, 7, 18, 72, 95–96, 102–*103*, 107–109, 121–131, 146, 156–157, 163, 169–171, 173– 177, 179, 201–202, 205–206, 17, 220–221, 236n40, 297–299, 316, 326, 353, 369, 401, 411
    see also MGMA
ITC (International Tin Council), 196, 246, 258–259, 261, 263–264
    Buffer Stock Manager system, 246, 386
Ivanhoe, 53
Ivanhoe Gold Corporation, 421
Ivanhoe Partners, 308, 309n8
Iwatani, 317
The Iron Ore (Mount Goldsworthy) Agreement Act, 124

Jabiluka uranium, 207
Jameson, Leander Starr, 9
Jamieson, Bill, 308, 319
Japanese steel industry, mills, 125, 130–131, 133–134, 169–177, 179, 202, 205, 208, 268, 294–295, 378
Jennings Industries, 150, 190, 211, 216–217, 249
Jerusalem Creek, New South Wales, 280
Jimblebar deposit, 170

Johannesburg Consolidated Investment Company, 61
Jones, Guy Carleton, 11

Kaiser Steel, 130
Kalgoorlie, Western Australia, 11, 28, *31*, 32, 37, 39, 44, 46, 50, 54, 58, 63–64, 195, 420–422
Kalgoorlie and Boulder Mines Medical Fund, 66
Kalgoorlie Chamber of Mines, 423
Kalgoorlie School of Mines, 421
Kaputin, John, 370
Kemerton, 149, 193
Kempsey, New South Wales, 242, 244
Kenmare, 312
Kennedy Gap, 124, 169, 173
Kerala, India, 358, 384
Kerimenge deposit, 289
Kerr-McGee, 212, 280
Kimberley district, South Africa, 5, 7
King Island Scheelite (1947), 111, 156, 192
Kinsho-Mataichi (Australia), 192
Kintore Mine, 64
Kirby, James N, 132
Koba Tin, 242, 244, 249–250, 267–268, 301–303, 326, 347, 368, 374, 384, 386, 397, 406, 412, 432–434, 452
Kober, Alfred, 298
Kohlberg Kravis Roberts, 310
Koranga Creek, Papua New Guinea, 85, *88*
Kruttschnitt, Julius, 90, 110
Kuala Lumpur Tin Market, 265
Kunanalling, Western Australia, 64
Kundana, Western Australia, 365, 434
Kutubu oil project, 371

Laguna Resources, 426
Lake George Metal Corporation, 23, 74, 76–77

Lake George mine, xv, 3, 17, 23, 33–35, 44, 66, 68, 71–80, *81, 82,* 82–84, 400, 420
  closure, 70, 84, 95
  financial performance, 79n28, 83
  history, 71–73
  lead concentrate, 76, 78–79
  strikes, 81–83
Lake George Mining Corporation, 3, 23, 76–77, 82, 84
Lake George United Mining and Smelting Company, 71
Lake Margaret power station, 135, 166, 200, 241, 275
Lake Munmorah, New South Wales, 113, 115, 183
Lake Rebecca, Western Australia, 195
Lake View Consols, 30, 32, *50*, 53
Lake View & Oroya Exploration, 32
Lake View and Star, 3, 17, 23, 27, *31*, 32, 35, 37, 42, 45, 46, 50, *50, 51*, 52–55, 60, 62–65, 66, 70, 91, 96, 99, 110, 149, 156–157, 195, 399–400, 420
  administrative control transferred to Australia, 149, 195
  Agnew, Dolph, 50, 65, 422
  Agnew, John, 23, 32, 50, 52–54
  financial performance, 46, 53–54, 67, 195, 429–431
  Poseidon NL takeover, 149
Lake View South, 423
Lake View South Extension, 24
Lancefield Gold Mine, Laverton, 27, 419
Landrigan, JP, 212
Lanz, TF, 162
Laverton, 27, 46n62
Lawrenson Alumasc Holdings, 102, 131–132, 150, 157n1, 220, 224
Lawrenson Holdings RH, 95, 131, 149, 156, 430–431
leaching, 193, 241, 268, 291, 413

lead, 5, 16, 18, 33, 35, 47, 69, 71, 73–76, 78 –80, 83–84, 116, 153, 167, 192, 378, 383n23, 387, 400, 413
Levien, Cecil John, 85
Lidcombe, New South Wales, 102, 131, 194
Liddell joint venture, 195n13, 325
Lindberg, CO, 45, 57, 61
Lion Properties, 149, 193, 220
Lionel Robinson & Clark, 35, 57
Little River Goldfields, 288, 325, 368, 383n22
Lloyd, George, xvi, 369, 393, 395, 396n11
London, Australia & General Exploration Co., 419
London, City of, 9, 11, 16, 30, 45
London & Western Australia Exploration Co., 419
London and Globe Finance Corporation, 30
London Metals Exchange, 160, 264
London Stock Exchange, 3, 5, 8, 15, 17, 23, 36–37, 40, 46, 63, 149, 322, 400
long wall mining, 134, 176, 178, 181
Loraine, Jonathan, xvi, 311
Loring, WJ, 28–29
Lucky Draw gold mine, 242, 244, 249, 288, 325, 346–347, 367, 433–434, 450

Macleay Valley, New South Wales, 193
Macpherson, Malcolm, xvi, 251, 332, 392–393, 395, 398, 409
Malaysian Smelting Corporation Board, 397
Mandated Territory of New Guinea, *see* New Guinea
Manufacturing Industries Advisory Council, 423

manufacturing interests, 13, 18, 30, 102, 108, 131–132, 142, 146, 153, 156–158, 219–220, 299, 401
Marble Bar, Western Australia, 64
Marcona, 122, 125, 172–173
marine aggregates, 245, 287
Marra Mamba ore, 169, 174
Mary Kathleen Uranium, 424
Mason, RC (Richard), 330, 404n6
Massy-Greene, John Brian (Sir), 26, 107, 113, 131–134, 140, 143, 151, 163–164, 171–172, 177, 195, 197n2, 222, 227, 409, 417, 423, 424
   appointment, general manager, 26, 104
   biographical information, 423
   chairman, 152
   description of, 104
   managing director, 26, 104, 158
   replaced as managing director, 105, 108, 150, 206, 225–226
   retires as chairman, 227
   view of CGFA, 196, 221, 224
Massy-Greene, Walter (Sir), 60, 103
McCall, Donald, 102, 111, 151, 163, 201, 227
McCamey Iron Ore Associates, joint venture, 170, 236n40, 297–298
McCamey's Monster, 149, 170
McCluskey, Sibley B, 75, 77
McGoldrick, Peter, 383
McIlwraith McEachern, 96, 109n3, 133, 134n31
McKinsey & Company, 213–214, 216
McVey, Daniel, 103, 109, 152
Meekatharra, Western Australia, 39, 40, 41, 44
Metal Manufactures, 103–104, 109n3, 137, 423
Mexican Corporation, 11, 33n, 34, 72, 74–75

MGMA (Mount Goldsworthy Mining Associates), xiii, 95–96, 123–125, 130, 150, 169–170, 424
Mill Close, Derbyshire, 421
Millennium Chemicals, 391
MIM (Mount Isa Mines), xiv, 17, 68, 70, 74, 85, 90, 110, 142, 150, 153, 156, 174, 202, 205, 250, 287, 290, 297, 299–300, 317, 320, 332, 352, 370, 390, 406, 432
Mineral and Resources Corporation, see Minorco
Mineral Deposits, 301–302
Mineral Resources Development Company, 294
mineral sands
   financial performance, 220, 222, 257, 259, 284–285, 346–348, 352, 356–357, 378–379, 437–439
   part of portfolios of CGFA, RGC, 120, 146, 155, 157, 182, 190–191, 210, 212–216, 222, 224, 228, 230, 244–245, 247, 251, 257, 260, 278, 329, 333–334, 343, 344, 346, 351–352, 358, 374–375, 383, 388–390, 399, 406–407, 412
   prices, 344, 350, 357, 379
   see also AMC, Western Titanium
Mineral Securities Australia, 193
Minerals Council of Australia, 426
Mines and Quarry Development, 95
Mining Advisors, 188
Mining Area C, 124, 131, 169–171, 173–175, 201–202, 205–206, 297, 299, 316, 326, 369, 397
Mining Corporation (Australia), 68–69, 100
Minora Resources, 241, 249, 288
Minorco (Mineral and Resources Corporation), 18, 206, 232, 234, 243n1, 247, 305, 306, 308–322
Mitchell, John, xvi, 265

INDEX

Mitsubishi Development, 192, 268, 271, 274
Mitsubishi Metal Mining (Australia), 192–194, 200
Mitsubishi Metal Mining Company, 159–160, 165, 167–168
Mobil, 426
Moline, AP, 110, 111n7
Molonglo River, 83
Monopolies and Merger Commission of UK, 305n1, 310, 312, 313n21, 314
Moonlight Wiluna Gold Mine, 3, 17, 23–24, 35, 41n47, 44, 46–49, 64–67
Moore, David, xvi, 122n9
Moreton Island, Queensland, 117, 186, 241, 247, 278, 280
Morobe district, Papua New Guinea, 85, *88*, *89*, 90
Mortimer, Gerald, 69n40, 101–102, 107, 111, 115–116, 121, 129–130, 140, 143, 209, 225, 227
Mount Charlotte (Kalgoorlie) Gold Mines, 49, 65–66
Mount Coolon Gold Mine, 58
Mount Coolon gold project, 288
Mount Elliot, 34
Mount Goldsworthy, iron ore, 69n40, 96, 101–102, *103*, 121–124, *126–129*, 128–131, 152, 155, 158, 168–175, 177, 181, 205, 228, 235, 316, 369, 399
 Area A, 124
 Area B, 124
 Area C *see* Mining Area C
 divestment, 169, 201–202, 205–207, 224, 297, 403
 financial performance, 157, 169–171, 220, 430–431
 Kennedy Gap, 124, 169, 173
 RGC offer to acquire from CGF, 242, 250, 298–299, 303

Shay Gap, 124, 169–170, 173–174, 201–202
 Sunrise Hill, 124, 173–174, 202
Mount Goldsworthy Mining Associates *see* MGMA
Mount Ida Mine, 3, 17, 24, 64–67, 70, 91
Mount Isa, Queensland, 67–68, 70, 100, 156, 192
Mount Isa Mines *see* MIM
Mount Kathleen Uranium, 111, 424
Mount Lyell Copper Division, 260, 347, 363
Mount Lyell Investments, 137
Mount Lyell Mining and Railway Company, xiii, xv, xvi, 7, 74n10, 96, 101, 104, 110–111, 120, 133, 136–140, *141*, 144, 150, 152, 155–156, 158, 181, 197, 217, 220, 222, 224, 227–228, 232, 236–237, 241–242, 243n1, 244, 246, 249, 253, 256, 265, 268, 271–273, 288, 303, 315, 325, 344, 348, 353, 359, 372, 399, 401–402, 405–407, 410–411, 422
 'A' lens ore body, 149, 165
 alternative operating strategies, *270*
 acquisition by CGFA, 141–143, 145
 Cape Horn ore body, 143, 165, 200, 246n7, 269
 closure, 326
 closure planning, 278, 351, 363–366
 cross section, *269*
 Crown Lyell ore body, 200
 Crown Three ore body, 143
 financial performance, 142–143, 157, 159–164, 166, 198–201, 230, 258–259, 270, 276, 347, 363, 365, 366, 429–431, 433–434, 445–446
 history, 135
 Horn West ore body, 143

477

Industries Assistance Commission, 165, 198
Iron Blow ore body, 135
mining series, stopes
   10 series, 149, 159, 200
   20 series, 150, 241, 269
   30 series, 150, 200, 241, 246, 269–270, 272–273
   40 series, 241, 246, 269, 271–272, 274, 277
   50 series, 241–242, 246, *269*, 270, 272, 274–277, 325, 364
   60 series, 159, 241–242, 246, 270, 272, 274, 275n46, 276–277, 363–364
   70 series, 365
Mount Lyell–Tharsis ore body, 143, 158
Prince Lyell 1995 Extension, 277
Prince Lyell Extended Plan, 150, 165–166, 200, 222, 274
Prince Lyell open cut, 137–138, 142, 143, 159
Prince Lyell ore body, 143, 158
Prince Lyell shaft, 149, 164–165, 200, 269, 275, 277
Queenstown, community, workforce, 142–143, 159, 164–166, 198, 270, 272–273, 276, 365–366
retrenchments, 164, 166n19, 200, 274–275, 365
Senate Select Committee, 165–166, 198
Twelve West ore body, 143
West Lyell open cut, 143, 149, 160
Western Tharsis ore body, 269
Mount Magnet, 58
Mount Morgan, 110, 153, 423
Mount Oxide, 192
Mount Palmer, 64
Mount Triton Gold Mine, 58
Mount Tyndall, 194
Mt Newman Iron Ore Company, 130, 172
Mukasey, Judge Michael, 318
Murchison NL, 397
Murphy, WP, 243n1, 279
Murray, HM, 135–137
Mustar, Ernest Andrew, 85

Nairn, Peter, 188
Namaliu, Rabbie, 314
Narama Coal, 244–245, 252n11, 296–297, 326, 347, 351, 368–369, 374, 388, 397, 406, 412, 432, 434
Nardell, Nardell Colliery, 296, 297n21
Narngulu, Western Australia, 242, 281–282, 325, 358, 377, 388
National Metal & Chemical Bank, 72–73
National Mining Corporation, 10–11, 30, 34–35, 72–73, 75
National Mutual Life Corporation, 113, 152n4, 207, 331, 423
naturalisation, *see* Australianisation
NCGFA (New Consolidated Gold Fields (Australasia) Pty Ltd), 3, 17, 24, 67–70, 95–96, 102, 110–112, 121
Nelesbitan gold, 289, 325, 348, 367, 435
New Broken Hill Consolidated, 153
New Consolidated Gold Fields of South Africa, 3, 10–11, 15–16, 30, 33n21, 34, 54, 57–58, 60–63, 73–74, 76–78, 100
New Guinea Goldfields Limited, 3 *see also* NGG Holdings
New Guinea, Territory, xiii, 5, 11, 16–17, 35–36, 55, 63n18, 77, 84–87, *88, 89,* 90, 91
New South Wales
   Cabinet, 186

INDEX

Chamber of Mines, 426
deputy premier, 180
Electricity Commission, 242
Government, 80, 134, 179–181, 195, 294–296, 297n21
minister for mineral resources and minister for energy, 296
Planning and Environment Commission, 186
premier, 296
Supreme Court, 316
New South Wales Clean Air Act, 179
New Union Goldfields, 105, 423
Newcastle Trades and Labour Council, 295
Newmont Mining Corporation, 308–309, 311, 316, 318
Newnham, Lindsey, 368
NGG Holdings, (New Guinea Gold Fields), 110, 150, 241–242, 244, 260, 303, 347, 433–434, 451
Niall, GM, 152, 243n1, 404n6
Nimingarra, 173, 297
NL (National Lead), 282
Normandy Poseidon, 332, 410
North Broken Hill, xiv, 58, 110–111, 153, 156, 192, 229, 235, 237n42, 250, 256, 300, 317, 340, 404, 406, 410, 427
North Broken Hill Peko, 340
North Flinders Mines, 301
North Gandy's Hill, 367
North Kalgurli tailing dumps, 23
North Limited, 426
North Stradbroke Island, Queensland, 119, 182–183, 186, 212, 241, 247, 249, 278, 375, 382
North-West Acid 149–150, 157n1, 159–160, 164, 198, 200, 207, 220
Northampton lead deposits, 47

Occidental Syndicate, 62
Office of Fair Trading, Britain, 315
Oil Syndicate, 422

Ok Tedi, 121
Old Hickory, 249, 326, 356, 358, 375–376, 388, 411, 435
1 London Wall Building, 29, 32, 33n21
Oppenheimer, Ernest (Sir), 305
Oppenheimer family, interests, 305, 307, 311, 313, 315
Oppenheimer, Harry, 234, 305
Ord & Minnett, 110, 113
Ord, Charles, 110
Oroville Dredging, 11, 30, 34, 63n18, 77, 86–87
Oroya Exploration Company, 32
OT Lempriere and Company, 149, 193, 224
Owen, Tom Mackellar, 44–45, 68, 75–77, 82–84, 95, 100, 152
oxidisation, 38, 41n47, 60, 71, 289, 325, 369, 414

Pacific Dunlop, 423
Pacific Uranium, 422
Paddington Gold mine, 347, 378n10, 380, 383n, 387n22, 389, 434–435
Pan-American Ventures, 68
Pancontinental Mining, 156, 427, 435
    acquisition by RGC, 250, 326, 347, 373, 375, 378, 379–383, 392, 409, 411
    Gauci, Vince, 389, 390n36
    investment by RGC, 299
    investments by CGFA, 150, 156, 207–208, 229, 236n40
Papua New Guinea, 150, 230, 242, 249, 258, 260, 287, 290, 290, 292–294, 308, 314, 317, 321, 325, 335, 344, 350, 367, 369–372, 378n10, 379, 435, 451
Paringa Mining and Exploration, 301, 406
Patino Mining Corporation, 138–139
Patterson, CD, xvi, 359–361
Patterson, RM, 166

479

Peabody Resources and Coal, 317
Peko-Wallsend, xiv, 179, 192, 237n42, 404n5, 410
Perella, Joe, 310
Peru projects, 250, 327–373, 375, 387, 389, 392, 408
Peruvian iron ore, 122
Phoenix Prince mine, 98
Pickens, T Boone, 308–309
pigment, 116, 118, 182–183, 187, 189–190, 212, 213, 280–284, 300n31, 320, 355, 358, 376–377, 407
Pilbara, Western Australia, xiii, 7, 18, 102, 107, 121, *129*, 130, 179, 298–299, 369
Pine Creek, Northern Territory, 241, 244, 246n5, 249, 288, 325–326, 347, 348, 353, 367, 433–434, 450
Pinter, Joseph, 116–117, 182, 186
Pioneer Concrete, 425
Pioneer International, 317
Placer Dome, 370, 380n17
Placer Pacific, 90, 287, 300, 302, 370,
Porgera, 90, 120, 150, 230, 236n40, 244, 249, 256, 258, *290*, 300, 303, 314, 317, 321, 325–326, 334, 374–375, 378n10, 383, 389, 407, 411, 432
   Anderson, Campbell, views of, 293
   description of, 260, 290–292
   development plans, 242
   equity contentions, PNG Government, 335, 344, 353, 370–372
   exploration, 287, 291
   feasibility study, 242
   financial performance, 284, 294, 344, 347, 370, 431, 434, 449, 451
   Hanson, view of, 344, 346, 350–353
   loan facilities, funding, 293, 301
   metallurgical problems, 291

pressure oxidation, 325
Robinson, Peter, 291–292
Warman Laboratory, 292
Zone VII, 291–292, 294
Porphyry (1939) Gold Mine Ltd, 3, 49, 64, 66
Port Hedland, Western Australia, 125, *126*, *127*, 424
Port Kembla, New South Wales, 78, 102, 133, 159, 180–181, 199
Port Macquarie, New South Wales, 194
Port Stephens, New South Wales, 186, 195
Poseidon, 149, 156, 196, 317, 332
Potier, Gilbert George, 95, 100–102, 104, 107, 111–112
Potter, Ian (Sir), 105, 108, 109n3, 133, 136–139, 226
Pringle, Joe, xvi, 261, 360–362
Prior, Charles, 47, 75
Privy Council, 149, 189
PT Koba Tin *see* Koba Tin

QBE Insurance Group, 380, 382
Queensland Coal Trust, 317
Queenstown Council, 275
Queenstown, Tasmania, xiii, 74n10, 135–136, 140, *141*, 142–143, 158–159, 164–166, 198, *259*, 270, 272–273, 276, 288, 335, 365–366, 410

Rand *see* Witwatersrand
Ravensworth, New South Wales, 195
RCR Tomlinson, 427
refractory ore, 39, 44, 77, 293, 414
Regan, Ronald, 318
Renison, xiii, 7, 96, 111, 136, 139 –140, 143, *144*, 149, 155, 157n1, 159, 161–162, 164, 166, 168, 196, 198–199, 202, 215, 224, 230, 232, 235, 236–237, 241, 243n1, 244–246, 249, 253, 256,

258–260, *262*, 265, 296, 303, 325, 344, 348, 359, 363, 365, 372, 384, 387–388, 399, 401–402, 405–407, 411, 424, 429
Bassett ore body, 138, 145, 167
care and maintenance, 361
CGFA shareholding in, 96, 101, 135, 138, 141–142, 145, 163, 167
cross section, *262*
Federal ore body, lode, fault, 138, 145, 149, 167
financial performance, 120, 145, 157, 168, 220, 267, 347, 360, 362–363, 385, 430–431, 433–435, 441–444
history, 137, 144, 385–386
industrial disputation, 261, 263–264, 266, 361–362
ITC (International Tin Council), 258–259, 261, 263–264
North Basset drive, 362
Rendeep, 326, 361–363, 374, 384–385
Renison scheme, 109, 146, 229–230
reserves and resources, 266–267
retrenchments, 263–264, 266
sale, 268, 374, 384, 397
survival plan, 325, 351, 361
tin concentrate, 265, 441–444
tin metal, 265, 360, 442–443
Renison Associated Tin Mines, 144
Renison Bell, 144
Renison Goldfields Consolidated (RGC), *see* RGC
Reserve Bank of Australia, 222
Reward copper, gold ore body, 327, 383n22
Reward Gold Mine (1935), 64
RGC (Renison Goldfields Consolidated), xiii, xiv, 19, 244, 373, 388–390, 399–400, 404–412, 426–427

acquisitions, 193, 241–242, 260, 299–303, 373, 375, 386–387
agricultural interests, 299, 351
Boston Consulting Group, 373, 389–390
broking analysts, views of, 257, 395
business model, 250, 344, 350, 407
coal interests, 195, 242, 245, 292–297, 326, 368–369
  see also Glendell Coal joint venture
Colinas, 242, 244, 299, 326, 351, 353
Cudgen, CRL acquisition, 381–383
delisting, 417–418
directors, 243n1, 244, 251, 278–279, 282, 296, 316, 318, 327, 329–330, 334–335, 337–340, 344, 349, 352–354, 357, 389, 395–396, 404–405, 408–410
diversification, 299
establishment, 241, 243
exploration, 249, 287–288, 383–384, 406
financial performance, 246n, 248, 256, 343–344, 347, 348, 357, 373, 387, 392, 431–435, 449, 450–452
gold interests, 244, 249, 258, 260, 288–293, 301, 325, 367–368
and Hanson
  approach to FIRB, 251, 334–341, 352
  management approach, views of portfolio, 345–353
  shareholding, 244, 247, 250–252, 298, 320–322, 329–333, 343–344, 391–392, 398, 408
investment division, 250, 299
iron ore, 297, 369

481

Koba Tin, acquisition of, 242, 250, 267–268, 301–303, 368
managing directors, 242, 253, 254, 255, 341, 373, 404, 417–418
merger Westralian Sands, 19, 251–252, 268, 327, 329, 341, 369, 374, 390–398, 409
mineral sands, 120, 190, 247, 249, 260, 278–285, 287, 343, 354–359, 374–378 see also AMC
Minorco defence activities, 247, 308–318
Mount Goldsworthy, attempt to purchase, 242, 250, 291, 297–299, 303
Mount Lyell, 143, 244, 246, 253, 268–277, 363–366
name change to RGC Ltd, 4
naturalisation, gaining and loss, 244n2, 407
oil and gas interests, 241, 288
Pancontinental Mining acquisition, 156, 250, 325–326, 373, 378–381, 411
Porgera, 369–372
portfolio, 135, 166, 244–246, 249, 373, 386, 412
Renison, 145, 246, 253, 260–267, 359–362, 384–385, 386
share price, 256–257, 331, 333, 335, 348, 352, 392–393, 407
RGC Gold Unsecured Notes, 395
Rhodes, Cecil John, xiii, 3, 5, 6, 7–10, 308–309, 322
Rhodes Room, Gold Fields House, 151
Richards Bay Minerals, 188, 211, 213–214, 307n4, 310, 312, 313n21, 354, 356, 358, 381
Rio Tinto, 376–377, 381, 410–411
Rio Tinto Collieries, 424
roasting, 38, 42, 292, 414
Robe River, 121, 130, 205

Roberts, Maxwell John (Max), 109, 150, 235, *236*, 236, 243, 253, 263–264, 335–336, 340, *341*, 403, 404, 408–409, 417–418
biographical information, 425–426
and Hanson, 320, 330, 333, 336, 350
FIRB approach, 334, 337, 339
mineral sands, 279
Minorco defence, 315
Mount Lyell, involvement with, 272–275
New South Wales Government involvement, Glendell, 294–296
retirement as chairman, 326, 339
steps down as chief executive officer, 241
Robinson Deep mine, 10
Robinson, Lionel, 15, 35
Robinson, Peter, 291–292, 396n11
Robinson, William Sydney (WS), 16, 30, 35, 57–58, 61–63, 110, 400
Rose, Hugh, 75
Rowe and Pitman, 307
RTZ (Rio Tinto Zinc Corporation), xiii, 135–137, 139, 183, 282, 308, 310, 312
Rudd, Charles Dunell, xiii, 3, 5, 6–10, 398
Rum Jungle, Northern Territory, 424
rutile, price and production, 118, 185–186, 189, 193n8, 208–211, 213, 302, 344, 356, 357, 379, 394, 437–439
see also mineral sands, AMC, Western Titanium
Ryan, Bartholomew Carrack (Bart), xvi, 108, 122n9, 143, 162, 164, 168, *203*, *228*, 234, 243n1, 403–404, 409
appointed managing director CGFA, 150, 201, 225, 227, 417

biographical information, 424–425
iron ore, views of, 205
mineral sands, 202, 211, 214–215, 216
retires as managing director, 150, 235, 403
Rye Park Scheelite, 422

Santa Gertrudis, 32, 33n, 34, 72, 74–75, 77n25
Sawyer, DPC, 162, 164
Scallan, Dick, xvi, 362
Schroder Darling, 109n3, 232
Schroders Australia, 113
SCM Chemicals, 282–283, 319n38, 320, 329n1, 358, 377
Segal, Sidney Leonard (Sid), 69–70, 105, 108, 141, 143, 151–152, 185, 187–189, 202, 204, 205–206, 210, 212, 213, 216, 226–227, 232, 234–235, 402, 409, 417
  biographical information, 423–424
  chairman, CGFA, 150, 227
  retirement, 150, 243n1
The Sentient Group, 426
Settlement Shores *see* Lion Properties
Shakesby, Roger, xvi, 287, 368
Shell, 134n31, 307n4, 381
Sierra Leone, 188, 208, 250, 281, 375, 381–382
Sierra Rutile, 250, 326, 358, 381–383, 387–388, 394, 397, 435
Signal Oil and Gas, 425
Sim Committee, 186
Simmer and Jack mines, 10
Skelton, LW, 200, 243n1
Smith, Richard Tilden, 34, 72–73
Snowy Hydro Limited, Trading 427
Societa Anonima Miniera, Cave del Predil, 421
Sons of Gwalia mine, 27, 54

The South American Copper Syndicate, 34
South Bulli Colliery, 176
South Stradbroke Island, Queensland, 182–183
Southern Cross, 58
Southern Pacific Petroleum (USA), 426
Southport, Queensland, 117, 280
Spargo's Reward Gold Mine, 64
SREP (synthetic rutile enhanced process), 281, 283, 326, 374–377, 388, 390
Sri Lanka, 384, 394, 396–397
Starlight Gold Mines, 23, 46, 64
Sub Nigel mine, 10
sulphide ores, 35–36, 38, 41n47, 44, 72–75, 291–292, 415
Sumitomo Corporation, 331–332, 352
Sumitomo Metal Mining, 331
synthetic rutile (ilmenite beneficiation, upgrading) 120, 155, 185, 187, 190, 208–210, 213, 242, 247, 278–283, 325–326, 343–344, 355–358, 374–378, 388, 392, 394, 409, 413, 437–439

Tarbutt, Percy, 9
Tasmanian
  Government, 166, 197, 200, 229, 241–242, 256, 271–277, 363, 364n63, 366
  premier, 272–275, 315, 361
TAZI (Titanium and Zirconium Industries), 183
Tennant, Sons and Company Limited, 95
Tennant Trading (Australia), 241, 243n1, 244, 250, 260, 265, 325, 351
Thalanga base metals, 326–327, 347, 383n22, 387, 397, 432, 434, 435
Thames gold fields, New Zealand, 419

Thames School of Mines, 25, 34, 419
Thatcher, Margaret, 315
Thompson, Julian Ogilvie, 305n1, 308
Thorn, Joseph Franklin, 50, 52, 54n90, 65
Timoni leases, 67
tin price, production, 220, 246, 250, 259–260, 265–267, 344, 351, 359–360, 386, 397, 441–444
see also Renison, Koba Tin
Tioxide, 213, 318
Titania dredge, *119*
Titanium Enterprises, 215–216
Trades and Labour Council (Tasmania), 360–361
Transvaal Agency, 63
Triton Gold Mine, 58, 59n6, 62
Tungsten Consolidated, 422
Tweed Heads, New South Wales, 186

Union Corporation, 34, 58, 61, 62, 211, 214
University of Cambridge, xvi, 7, 102, 423
University of Melbourne, 165
University of Sydney, 423, 426
University of Witwatersrand, 423
Uranium Corporation of Australia, 422
Urquhart, Leslie, 85–87
Utah Construction & Mining Co. (Utah), xvi, 95, 102, 107, 121–122, 124–125, 130, 133, 170, 172–173, 202, 215, 229–230, 237n42

Vail, HE (Herbert), 42, 50, 77
Victoria Gold Mining Company, 25
Vinto, EM, 387
Vinto Corporation, 387
Vivien Gold Mine, 419

Walsh, Senator Peter, 272
Warman Laboratory, 292
Wasserstein, Bruce, 310

Waterhouse, Leslie Vickery, 72
Wau, Papua New Guinea, 85, 87, 242, 260, 287, 289, 325, 367, 378n,10 433
Wauchope, BE, 243n1, 313, 329n1
Western Australian Bureau of Mines, 121
Western Titanium, 110–111, 120, 182, 184, 202, 209, 220
  Adamson syndicate, 149, 189
  Allied Minerals, overtures to, 189, 212–214
  Capel operations, 187, 210
  CGFA acquires shareholding, 68, 102, 120, 149, 182, 191, 185
  CMI sponsors listing, 113, 115
  Eneabba, 188–190, 210, 247
  financial performance, 157, 430–431, 439
  ilmenite upgrading, synthetic rutile, 155, 183, 185, 187, 222, 247
  merger with AMC, 150, 186, 190, 208, 224, 403
  Privy Council, 149, 189
  Segal appointed chairman, 402
Westralian Oil, 182
Westralian Sands, 4, 19, 156, 183, 185, 248, 251–252, 268, 282–283, 300, 318, 327, 329–330, 330–332, 368–369, 374–375, 377, 390–398, 409–410, 412
Wiles, Edward (Ted), xvi, 102, 112–113, 115
Wilkins, Herbert C, 75
Wiluna, 16, 17, 23–24, 35–36, 38, 46, 50n76, 53, 54, 60, 62, 63, 65, 75, 77–78, 399–400, 420–421
  description of early mining, 37–38, 41
  financial performance, 45, 46, 53, 66
  mining and processing, 41, 42, 43, 44–45, 47, 47–49, 52
  railway connection, 39, 40, 41

Wiluna Gold Corporation, 3, 23, 37, 40, 66
Winby, Dick, 265
Wingti, Paias, 307
Witwatersrand, 5, 8, 11, 60, 423
WMC (Western Mining Corporation), xiv, 3, 5, 16, 35, 57–59, 258, 283, 317, 332–333, 400, 406, 410, 420
Woodside Petroleum, 237n42, 425
World War I, 72
World War II, xiv, 11, 19, 36, 65, 79–80, 97, 102, 116, 312
Wright, James Whitaker, 30
Wright, Peter, 121
Wright Prospecting, 170
Wyong Alluvial, 113
Wyong Minerals, 95, 111, 113, 115–116, 118, 155, 183, 429

Yellowdine Gold Development Mine, 17, 58, 64
Yellowdine Investments, 64
Yuanami Mine, 32
Yuba gold dredging, 86

Zeehan, Tasmania, 135, 144, 167–168, 258, 362
Zinc Corporation, 30, 33, 54, 57, 63, 73
Zip Manufacturing Holdings, 96, 102, 132, 156, 157n1, 220, 224, 429–431
zircon price, production, 115, 118, 183, 186, 208–210, 212, 281, 284, 343–344, 354–357, 375, 378–379, 388, 394, 437–439
see also mineral sands, AMC, Western Titanium
Zodiac Syndicate, 95

www.ingramcontent.com/pod-product-compliance
Lightning Source LLC
Chambersburg PA
CBHW041731300426

44115CB00022B/2970